MORE OF A MAN

Diaries of a Scottish Craftsman in Mid-Nineteenth-Century North America

More of a Man presents the only known diaries of a skilled craft-worker in Victorian Canada: Andrew McIlwraith, a Scottish journeyman who migrated to North America during a tumultuous period marked by economic depression and early industrial change. McIlwraith's journals illuminate his quest to succeed financially and emotionally in challenging circumstances. The diaries trace his transformations, from an immigrant newcomer to a respected townsman, a wage worker to an entrepreneur, and a bachelor to a married man.

Carefully edited and fully annotated by historians Andrew C. Holman and Robert B. Kristofferson, *More of a Man* features an introduction providing historical context for McIlwraith's life and an epilogue detailing what happened to him after the diaries end. Historians of labour, gender, and migration in the North Atlantic world will find *More of a Man* a valuable primary document of considerable insight and depth. All readers will find it a lively story of life in the nineteenth century.

ANDREW C. HOLMAN is a professor in the Department of History and the Canadian Studies Program at Bridgewater State University.

ROBERT B. KRISTOFFERSON is an associate professor of History and Contemporary Studies at Wilfrid Laurier University.

More of a Man

Diaries of a Scottish Craftsman in Mid-Nineteenth-Century North America

EDITED BY
ANDREW C. HOLMAN AND
ROBERT B. KRISTOFFERSON

UNIVERSITY OF TORONTO PRESS
Toronto Buffalo London

© University of Toronto Press 2013
Toronto Buffalo London
www.utppublishing.com
Printed in Canada

ISBN 978-0-8020-9701-9 (cloth)
ISBN 978-1-4426-1164-1 (paper)

Library and Archives Canada Cataloguing in Publication

McIlwraith, Andrew, 1830–1891
More of a man : diaries of a Scottish craftsman in mid-nineteenth-century
North America / edited by Andrew C. Holman and Robert B. Kristofferson.

Includes bibliographical references and index.
ISBN 978-0-8020-9701-9 (bound)   ISBN 978-1-4426-1164-1 (pbk.)

1. McIlwraith, Andrew, 1830–1891 – Diaries. 2. Patternmakers – Ontario –
Diaries. 3. Patternmakers – New York (State) – New York – Diaries. 4. Drafters –
Ontario – Diaries. 5. Bookkeepers – Ontario – Diaries. 6. Immigrants – Ontario –
Diaries. 7. Scottish Canadians – Diaries. 8. Ontario – Social conditions – 19th
century. I. Holman, Andrew Carl, 1965–   II. Kristofferson, Robert, 1965–   III. Title.

HD8039.P352C3 2013   331.7'67123092   C2012-902814-2

University of Toronto Press acknowledges the financial assistance to its publishing
program of the Canada Council for the Arts and the Ontario Arts Council.

 Canada Council   Conseil des Arts
for the Arts   du Canada

University of Toronto Press acknowledges the financial support of the Government of
Canada through the Canada Book Fund for its publishing activities.

This book has been published with the help of a grant from the Canadian
Federation for the Humanities and Social Sciences, through the Awards to
Scholarly Publications Program, using funds provided by the Social Sciences and
Humanities Research Council of Canada.

Contents

Contents

Illustrations follow page 10.

Acknowledgments

The editors of this book would like to thank Professor Thomas McIlwraith (Emeritus, University of Toronto at Mississauga) for his generosity and guidance with the manuscripts of a valued ancestor of his; Tom Barclay, of the Carnegie Public Library (Ayr, Scotland) for his interest and assistance in locating documents; and the many archivists and librarians at Bridgewater State University, Baker Library (Harvard University), the Library of the Mechanics' Institute of the City of New York, Hamilton Public Library, McMaster University, Wilfrid Laurier University, University of Western Ontario, Library and Archives Canada, Ontario Archives, Listowel Public Library, and the Kitchener Public Library, who facilitated the research for this book. Thanks, too, to Len Husband and Frances Mundy at the University of Toronto Press for making the publication process advance smoothly and to Ruth Pincoe for her fine work on the index. They are grateful to the UTP's anonymous readers for their insightful and useful comments on this text.

Andy Holman wishes to acknowledge support for this research from the Center for Advancement of Research and Scholarship, the Canadian Studies Program (and Anthony Cicerone, in particular), his colleagues in the History Department and the Office of the Dean of Arts and Sciences, all at Bridgewater State University. He wishes to give special thanks to Andrea Doty, Josh Greenberg, and Bob Babcock for their careful reading of and comments on earlier draft segments of this book.

Rob Kristofferson wishes to thank Jason Philips and Neil White for their research assistance. He gratefully acknowledges book preparation and publication grants awarded by the Research Office and the Dean of the Brantford Campus at Wilfrid Laurier University. He offers profound thanks to his many colleagues at Laurier Brantford for the lively and engaging interdisciplinary atmosphere in which many of the ideas for this book were cultivated and nourished. He dedicates this book to his sons, Edwin and Henry.

A Note on the Source

Andrew McIlwraith's diaries have been transcribed from the originals with few editorial changes. Sentences in the originals frequently begin with lowercase characters and are separated with a hyphen instead of a period. We have capitalized many sentences and converted hyphens to periods to increase clarity and add to ease of reading. Similarly, we have chosen to expand many contracted words, especially in cases where we felt readers might find their meanings obscure. McIlwraith appears generally to have committed the activities of the day to his dairies each evening. However, in some cases a uniformity of ink and handwriting combined with his own editorial changes indicate to us that he sometimes waited a few days to commit pen to paper. These instances were typically in three- or four-day blocks and do not appear too different in form from more immediate, daily entries. The editors have also chosen to include the few entries that Andrew must have subsequently crossed out; we indicate these in overscored text. These entries occurred most often in references to young women, particularly Mary Goldie, suggesting the effort at self-censorship should perhaps best be viewed as a comment on mid-nineteenth-century gendered propriety. We have also provided annotations in places where we believe readers might be unfamiliar with references made to people and places in the diary entries. The original diaries are in the possession of Thomas McIlwraith, Professor Emeritus, Geography, University of Toronto at Mississauga.

Dramatis Personae

In the six years covered by these diaries, Andrew McIlwraith travelled to many places and met many people. To be specific, 488 individuals appear in his account, though not all of them, of course, played important roles in his life. What follows is a brief reference source for readers of the diary. Excluded are those names that merited only passing or fleeting references. Many of those who played the most important roles in his life in these years appear also in the lengthier, biographical footnotes provided in the annotated diary.

ANDERSON, Thomas – Dumbarton, Scotland. One of a small handful of former workmates with whom Andrew McIlwraith kept in touch after he departed for America. McIlwraith was employed at the Dumbarton 'work' not long before he departed Scotland. It may be where he apprenticed as a draftsman and patternmaker.

BARRY (or BARRIE), William – New York City. Brother to Mrs Guthrie and uncle to Sandy Guthrie, Barry was within the network of Scottish friends and acquaintances that eased Andrew's search for work and society in New York. A worker at Duncan and Crampton's machine shop, Barry helped Andrew locate work at that place.

BERTRAM, John – Dundas, Canada West. Born in Peeblesshire, Scotland, in 1829, Bertram apprenticed as a machinist in Scotland before migrating to Dundas in the mid-1850s. He was employed by Gartshore's Foundry in Dundas by 1856, not long before he became a friend and workmate of Andrew's at that shop in 1858 (both of them were laid off by Gartshore's in that same year). In Dundas, McIlwraith and Ber-

tram took singing classes together and were co-members of the local
Mechanics' Institute Debating Club. Still unemployed in 1862, Bertram
visited Andrew to ask for a job at Goldie and McCulloch's. Success
returned to Bertram when, in 1863, he formed a partnership with Robert McKechnie Jr called the Canada Tool Works (renamed John Bertram
and Sons in 1886), a highly successful company. Bertram died in 1906.

BILL (also Billie, Brother Bill) – Ayr, Scotland. William McIlwraith was
youngest brother to Andrew. Born in 1833, Bill remained in Scotland,
making his life as a newspaper reporter in Ayr. He married Margaret
McIlwrath in Newton-on-Ayr, Scotland on December 25, 1862. Bill was
a regular correspondent with Andrew throughout this period and an
important conduit for information from 'home.'

CAVEN, Mrs – St Mary's, Canada West. Margaret Caven (née Goldie)
was older sister to Mary Goldie, and Andrew's future sister-in-law.
Margaret Goldie migrated to Ayr, Canada West, with her parents and
siblings in 1844. In 1856, she was married to Rev. William Caven, a Scot
emigrant also raised in Ayr, and a United Presbyterian clergyman who
pastored in St Mary's until 1866, when he was appointed Professor of
Exegetical Theology at the University of Toronto. Close friend to her
sister, Mrs Caven also became a close friend to Andrew. Rev. Caven
assisted Rev. Dr McRuar in the marriage ceremony of Andrew McIlwraith and Mary Goldie in 1861.

CHRISTINA (née McIlwraith, also Mrs Brewster, 'Missie') – Newton-
on-Ayr, Scotland. Born in 1828, Christina was Andrew's older sister. In
1851, she was living and working as a housekeeper in the household of
her sister Jean Smith (sometimes 'Jane') Stewart (b. 1812) and her husband, Thomas Stewart, in Ayr. In June 1860, Christina married James
Brewster, a widower and photographer, in Ayr. As with his brother Bill,
Christina corresponded regularly with Andrew and kept him abreast of
family and country news from 'home.'

CONNEL, A. – Dundas, Canada West. Connel was an iron turner who
worked with Andrew at Gartshore's Foundry in Dundas in 1858. But
their acquaintance there was only a renewal; they had met and perhaps
worked together in Dumbarton, Scotland, prior to the opening of the
diaries. In Dundas, they were co-members of the Mechanics' Debating
Society. Connel followed Andrew to New York City in search of work

in 1859. They spent leisure hours together, especially on walks, and by 1860 were roommates in a New York boarding house until September of that year, when Connel married Miss Margaret McLellan, sister to New York lithographer James McLellan. When Andrew returned to Canada West in 1860, Connel stayed in New York, but the two maintained their friendship via letters.

DICKIE, Hugh – Ayr, Scotland. Good friend and occasional correspondent with Andrew McIlwraith. When Andrew returned to Scotland to visit in 1857, the two spent a good deal of time together.

GOLDIE, David (sometimes David, Davy) – Ayr, Canada West. Born in 1832, in Kirkoswold, Ayrshire, Scotland, David was the youngest son of John and Margaret (Smith) Goldie, Mary Goldie's older brother, and Andrew's brother-in-law. He came to Canada West with his family in 1844, and was married in December 1869 at Greenfield, in Ayr, CW. He became proprietor of a successful rolling mill in Ayr, owner of 'The Gore,' a country estate, and father to ten children. A familiar visitor, he seems to have seen in Andrew a good friend.

GOLDIE, James – Utica, New York, and Guelph, Canada West. Older brother to Andrew's wife, Mary Goldie, James Goldie (1824–1912) was born in Ayrshire, Scotland, and moved to America in 1842, landing work first as a gardener in Paterson, New Jersey, but later establishing his own lumber and grist mills in Utica, New York. James moved to Guelph in 1860, where he built and operated the 'Speedvale Mill' (often called 'Pipes Mill') until 1868. He became a leading citizen of Guelph, a staunch member of the local Congregational Church, an avid horticulturalist, and a prominent member of the Canadian Millers' Association and advocate for the protective tariff. Andrew met James while he still resided in Utica; once in Galt, Andrew helped keep an eye on the Guelph business, even 'posting' the mill's books for James on one occasion.

GOLDIE, Mr (also John, John G.) – Galt, Canada West. John Goldie (Jr) was the second son of John (Sr) and Margaret Goldie. Born in Ayrshire, Scotland, in 1823, he learned the trade of millwright as a youth. He moved, with his parents and siblings, to 'Greenfield,' near Ayr, Canada West in 1844. Along with a partner, fellow Ayrshireman Hugh McCulloch, Goldie purchased the Dumfries Mill in 1859, and the two trans-

formed it into 'Goldie and McCulloch and Company,' by the late 1860s
one of Canada's largest producers of boilers, engines, mill and woodworking machinery, safes and vaults. Goldie hired Andrew to become
bookkeeper for the foundry in 1861; in 1862 he became his brother-
in-law, when Andrew married John's younger sister Mary. John and
Andrew shared friendship and a common interest in Scottish culture
and self-improvement. John Goldie died in 1896.

GOLDIE, Mary (also Miss Goldie, Mary, M., M.G.) – Ayr and Galt,
Canada West. Born in 1834 in Ayrshire, she moved with her parents
and siblings to 'Greenfield,' near Ayr, Canada West, in 1844. Devoutly
Presbyterian and fond of Scottish songs and literature, she married
Andrew McIlwraith in April 1862. They lived in Galt, Canada West, and
later Listowel, Ontario. Andrew and Mary had eight children, three of
whom died in infancy. She died in Berlin (Kitchener), Ontario, in April
1911 and is buried alongside Andrew in Galt.

GOLDIE, Old Mr – 'Greenfield,' Ayr, Canada West. John Goldie, Sr,
was a world-renowned botanist and Andrew's father-in-law. Born in
1793 in Kirkoswold, Ayrshire, Scotland, he was educated at the Glasgow Botanic Gardens and the University of Glasgow and earned posi-
tions as botanist on excursions to Russia, the Congo, and Canada. In
1844, he moved his family to 'Greenfield,' near Ayr, Canada West. He
and his wife Margaret had eight children – four sons and four daughters. He died at Ayr in June 1886, in his ninety-fourth year.

GOLDIE, William (also 'Willie,' Billy or W.G.) – Guelph, Canada West.
Born in Ayrshire, Scotland, in 1835, William Goldie was the son of David
Goudie, brother of John (Old Mr) Goldie, cousin to Mary Goldie and,
therefore, cousin-in-law to Andrew McIlwraith. William migrated with
his family to Montreal 1844, where his father ran a last-making business
until he died (drowned in the St Lawrence River) in 1846. After a brief
return to Scotland, the family resettled in Montreal, where they lived
until 1853. William, his mother, and siblings moved to Ayr, Canada
West, joining their extended family, in 1858. In the years covered by the
diaries, William seems to have been apprenticing with or working for
his cousin James Goldie at his 'Speed (or Speedvale) Mill' in Guelph.
William married Nancy Malone of Ayr, CW, in 1862. In 1864, he moved
his family to Fenton, Michigan, where he engaged in a stave and coop-
erage business. In the post-Civil War years, he made, lost, and remade
a fortune in America as an inventor of a variety of industrial products.

GUTHRIE, Alexander (also Sandy) – New York City. A friend and Scottish acquaintance of Andrew's in New York, Sandy Guthrie worked in the printing office of the *New York Ledger* newspaper, in Fulton Street. Andrew visited Sandy and his mother at their residence in Laight Street on several occasions. Mrs Guthrie seems to have been an Ayrshire native and was likely a family friend.

HOSIE, Alexander (also Sandie, Sandy) – New York City. The Hosies were an Ayrshire family on whom Andrew leaned for guidance and assistance, part of the Scottish network of work and social contacts. Peter Hosie was an agent with Cunard Steamship Line in Liverpool and helped accommodate Andrew on his 1857 trip 'home.' 'Mr' Hosie was an employee at a Detroit Locomotive Works in 1857, whom Andrew visited, perhaps looking for work. Sandy Hosie was closest to Andrew – friend and workmate in New York City, with whom he spent a good many leisure hours in 1859–60.

HUNTER, Mrs – Newton-on-Ayr, Scotland. Helen Hunter (née McIlwraith) (1810–93) was Andrew's oldest sister. She was a regular correspondent with Andrew and lived in Scotland during the years covered by the diaries. A seamstress, she married Daniel Hunter in 1840 but had been widowed and was living with her mother by 1861. Helen Hunter later moved to Canada and was living in Andrew's household in 1881. She died in Galt in November 1893 and is buried in the same cemetery plot as her brother and sister-in-law.

JAMESON, A. – Sarnia and Hamilton, Canada West. Friend and workmate on the Great Western Railway, Jameson was one of the first friends Andrew made after he arrived in Sarnia. The two spent a good deal of leisure time together; Jameson taught Andrew how to play chess. When Andrew's work in Sarnia ended, Jameson stayed on and by 1858 was promoted to a position in the Engineer's Office of the GWR in the Hamilton shops. Whenever Andrew passed through Hamilton, Jameson was among those he first sought out. And Jameson returned the favour, visiting Andrew in New York City and in Galt.

LOGAN, Mrs (also Margaret, Mrs L.) – New York City and Galt, Canada West. Born in 1814, Margaret was Andrew's younger sister. She married James Logan in Newton-on-Ayr Scotland in October 1839, but seems to have been a widow by the time the diaries open in 1857, when she was living in Brooklyn, New York, and working as a housekeeper for

merchant Robert Renfrew and his family. In 1860, she followed Andrew
back to Canada West from New York, and by 1861 she was making
ends meet as a landlady in Galt. Her home seemed in some months a
regular stopping place for Presbyterian clergymen travelling through
the region. Andrew and Margaret were close friends; the two siblings
housed together for the few months before Andrew was married and
remained connected by letter when they lived in distant cities.

MACKENZIE (family) – Sarnia, Canada West. Seven brothers from
Scotland, who moved to Sarnia in 1840s and became one of Canada's
most politically prominent families and leading Liberal Party lights.
The brothers included (future Canadian prime minister) Alexander,
Charles, Hope, James, John, Robert (also Bob), and Adam. Andrew
worked with Charles in Sarnia on the Great Western Railway, and the
two renewed friendship when Charles visited Andrew in New York
City and again in Galt. The diaries record visits also from Hope and
from 'Alick,' John, and James.

MACKENZIE (or McKenzie), **Hector** – Dundas, Canada West. Like
Connel, Hector Mackenzie was an iron turner who worked with
Andrew at Gartshore's Foundry in Dundas in 1858. Like Connel,
Andrew had also known Mackenzie from Dumbarton, Scotland, where
the three must have worked together for a spell. Mackenzie also shared
time and ideas with Andrew and Connel as members of the Dundas
Mechanics' Institute Debating Society.

MARSHALL, Miss (also Mrs Abel) – New York City. Sister to Andrew's
foundry shopmate, Jesse Marshall, and a friend of McGarva's. Andrew
was attracted to her and paid several visits to her at her home to con-
verse and to hear her sing. Andrew was noticeably affected when he
learned of her unannounced marriage, to a Mr Abel, in 1860.

McCULLOCH, Hugh – Galt, Canada West. Born in Sorn, Ayrshire,
Scotland, in 1826, McCulloch moved to Canada West in 1850 and came
to Galt in 1851. With his partner John Goldie (Jr), McCulloch purchased
the Dumfries Foundry in 1859 and together turned it into 'Goldie and
McCulloch and Company,' by the late 1860s one of Canada's largest
producers of boilers, engines, mill and woodworking machinery, safes
and vaults. McCulloch became Andrew's employer in 1860 and a friend
– he acted as one of two 'bondsmen' at Andrew McIlwraith's wedding.
He retired from active work in 1906 and died in 1910.

McGARVA – Dundas, Canada West. Another member of the close-knit circle of friends and workmates at Gartshore's Foundry in Dundas and in the Dundas Mechanic's Institute Debating Society. McGarva was a frequent walking partner of Andrew's in Dundas, and the two kept in touch as correspondents after Andrew's departure. McGarva, it seems, left Dundas not long after Andrew did. One 1859 letter places him in Clinton, Huron County, Canada West.

McILWRAITH, Mary (also Mrs McI) – Hamilton, Canada West. Née Mary Park, Mary McIlwraith was Andrew's sister-in-law, wife to his closest brother, Thomas. Married to Thomas in Newton-on-Ayr, Scotland, in 1853, the two emigrated to Hamilton, Canada West, later the same year. Andrew must have come to join them not long thereafter. Mary and Thomas had four daughters and four sons, nieces and nephews to Andrew. Their Hamilton home was a comfort to Andrew, a home away from 'home.' Mary was a regular correspondent with Andrew and kept him updated with family news when he was on the tramp.

McKECHNIE, Robert (also Bob) – Dundas, Canada West. Co-worker with Andrew at Gartshore's Foundry in Dundas, McKechnie was also a co-walker. McKechnie was among the small circle of friends and self-improvers who formed and fed the Dundas Mechanics' Institute Debating Society in the late 1850s. In 1863, McKechnie used the skills he practised at Gartshore's to open his own foundry, the Canada Tool Works, in partnership with John Bertram.

McLELLAN, James and David – New York City. James McLellan, Jr (1828–60) and his brother David (b. 1825) came from a family of Scottish lithographers. James and David arrived in New York as early as 1847 and soon thereafter formed the partnership 'D and J McLellan.' By the 1850s, they had established a fine business reputation. Andrew toyed with the idea of learning the trade of lithography from James just before he accepted the offer of a job from John Goldie in Galt in 1860. Andrew visited the McLellans severally, both at their shop and at their Brooklyn home. James McLellan Jr died unexpectedly and young, in spring 1860.

McWHIRTER (family) – Paris, Canada West. The McWhirters were a family of Scottish immigrants from Ayrshire, friends and family acquaintances of Andrew and Thomas, and of the Goldies in Ayr, CW.

MOTHER (Jean Adair Forsyth McIlwraith) – Newton-on-Ayr, Scotland. Andrew's mother Jean McIlwraith was born in 1789 or 1790. A handsewer by trade, she married Thomas McIlwraith (Sr) (d. 1856) and with him had ten children; her son Andrew was the ninth among them. A regular correspondent with Andrew, she kept him abreast of news from 'home.' She died in Ayr in June 1875.

MUIR (family) – Hamilton, Canada West. The family of William (Sr) and Margaret (Howie) Muir was from Kilmarnock, in Ayrshire, Scotland, but moved to Hamilton, Canada West, in 1855. Two of the Muir children became important figures in the railway history of Ontario and Michigan. William Ker Muir (1829–92) became a superintendent of the Great Western Railway in Canada West in 1852, a position he held until 1857, when he was sent to Detroit to become manager of the Detroit and Milwaukee Railway, a GWR affiliate. His brother, James H. Muir (b. 1835), worked as a clerk for the Glasgow and South Western Railway until he followed his brother to Hamilton in 1855. He was then appointed to a management position with the GWR until 1859, when he was transferred in March 1859 to a GWR affiliate, the Detroit, Grand Haven and Milwaukee Railroad. Andrew and Thomas visited often with the Muir children – James, John, Thomas, and Alexander (Sandy) – most often when they collected in Hamilton to visit their parents.

RAPHAEL, Mr – Hamilton, Canada West. One of the many important work contacts that Andrew had in North America among his fellow Scots and tradesmen. Andrew consulted Raphael for advice just before leaving for New York City in 1859. Their relationship was more than just functional, however; Raphael must have been a family friend. He shared the traditional 'Hogmanay' meal with Andrew and Thomas on one New Year's Eve, and in another year, Christmas dinner at Thomas's Hamilton home.

RENFREW, Mr – New York City. Robert Renfrew was a Brooklyn merchant in the 1850s and '60s who imported shawls and other British dry goods for sale in the New York market. In 1859, his shop was on Pine Street, his home on Quincy Street. In 1860, he moved his family to a farm on Staten Island. Renfrew employed Andrew's sister Margaret ('Mrs Logan') as a housekeeper in these years. He was a fellow Scot abroad and seems also to have been a family friend. Andrew visited

and spent weekends at Renfrew's Brooklyn and Staten Island households on several occasions and even loaned him money.

ROBB, Mr (also Charles) – Hamilton, Canada West. Charles Robb was
a civil engineer, draughtsman, and architect who contracted his services to the City of Hamilton but also did work for the Great Western
Railway. He worked from his house on Park Street between Mulberry
and Cannon Streets, just around the corner from Thomas McIlwraith's
residence. On occasion, Robb hired Andrew to help complete drawings
he could not or did not have time to do.

ROBERTSHAW, John – New York City. Robertshaw was a fellow patternmaker with whom Andrew worked and associated in New York.
It was at his invitation, in 1859, that Andrew joined a Patternmakers' Association, an early protective organization among New York's
skilled metalworkers.

SIMM (also Syme), William – New York City. One of many friends,
workmates, and fellow Scots with whom Andrew associated during his
stint in New York City. Andrew may have known him in Dundas as
well.

SMITH, Miss – Ayr, Canada West. Born in 1852, Anne Marion Smith
was the only daughter of Elizabeth Goldie (ca 1820–54), Mary Goldie's
eldest sister, and Sydney Smith (1812–78). After Elizabeth's death, the
Goldie family in Ayr remained very close to Anne and Sydney; when
Anne was sick, it was the Goldies who nursed her to health. Andrew
seems to have delighted in his visits with his niece-in-law, and his
brother-in-law Sydney was so highly esteemed that Andrew asked him
to be his 'bondsman' at his and Mary's wedding ceremony.

SPITTAL, Mr – One of many workmates whom Andrew encountered during his travels, Spittal was a metalworker in Anderson and
McLaren's New York City shop. Andrew was a visitor at Spittal's home
in 13th Street, and the two explored together what New York City had
to offer.

STEWART, Christina – Newton-on-Ayr, Scotland. Andrew's niece
Christina was the daughter of Andrew's older sister Jean Smith (McIlwraith) Stewart (b. 1812) and her husband, Thomas Stewart. About fif-

teen years younger than Andrew, Christina was a favourite niece and a regular correspondent with her uncle. Her older brother was John 'Jack' Stewart.

STEWART, J. (also John, Jack) – Hamilton, Canada West. Born in about 1841, Jack Stewart was Andrew's nephew, son to older sister Jean Smith (McIlwraith) Stewart and her husband Thomas Stewart. By the time the diaries open, Jack had yet to emigrate to Canada (which he did in October 1857); once there, he was cared for by his other Canadian uncle, Thomas McIlwraith. By 1858, Thomas had found Jack work as a clerk in the Hamilton Gas Works. Despite their differences in age, Jack, Andrew, and Thomas were close friends, often walking and hunting together.

THOMAS (also Thos, Brother Thomas, Tom) – Hamilton, Canada West. Thomas McIlwraith was older brother to Andrew, his closest friend and an inspirational influence in his life. Born in Newton-on-Ayr, Scotland, in 1824, Thomas, an engineer, studied the new art of gaslight illumination and became manager of the Newton Gas Works. In 1853, he married and moved to Hamilton, Canada West, where he had secured a position as the Director of the Hamilton Gas Works. A respected engineer, in 1871 he started his own coal and industrial product import business. However, he made his biggest mark as a pioneering ornithologist in Canada, publishing the landmark volume *Birds of Ontario* in 1886. His home in Hamilton became a sort of bird 'museum' to which students flocked for a look at his many and various stuffed specimens. Thomas and his wife Mary had eight children, of whom seven survived. Thomas died in 1904.

TOMMIE (also Tommy, Little Tom, 'Fernig') – Hamilton, Canada West. Andrew's nephew Tommie McIlwraith was the oldest of eight children born to Andrew's brother, Thomas, and his wife, Mary. Andrew had a special fondness for Tommie.

TURNBULL, R. – Dundas, Canada West. Though a foreman, Turnbull was within the circle of Scots workmates and friends to whom Andrew clung during and after his short stay as an employee of Gartshore's Foundry in Dundas. Turnbull shared their interest in self-improvement and maintained their ties. Out of work, he showed up in New York City in 1860 seeking information from Andrew about available work.

Abbreviations

CW	Canada West (Ontario)
DCB	*Dictionary of Canadian Biography*
DR	*Dumfries Reformer*
GTR	Grand Trunk Railway
GWR	Great Western Railway
HS	*Hamilton Spectator*
LB	*Listowel Banner*
MI	Mechanics' Institute
NYT	*New York Times*
SO	*Sarnia Observer*
YMCA	Young Men's Christian Association

In an essay, remarkable at once for the originality of its views and the practical good sense it contains, John Foster recommends the propriety of every man writing memoirs of himself, not as an exercise of ingenuity – not as a means of drawing the world's regard – but to fix in a man's own mind, a sense of the progress he has made in moral and intellectual ideas to mark the change in his sensations which a prolonged experience of life produces and to excite a feeling of gratitude for those many providential interpositions which the most careful observer can scarcely fail to recognize as exercised in his behalf.

Andrew McIlwraith, Diary for 1858

Introduction:
Andrew McIlwraith and His World

This book is about identity and how one man struggled to craft a sense of himself during an era of economic and social change. It follows the intellectual, occupational, and emotional pursuits of a mid-nineteenth-century craftsworker, Andrew McIlwraith (1831–91), draughtsman, patternmaker, bookkeeper, and foundry owner in Canada West (now Ontario) and, for a spell, in New York City. McIlwraith was, in many ways, a rather ordinary mid-Victorian craftsman, perhaps even a typical one, but extraordinary in the fact that he documented an important segment of his life. We know about him because of one particularly rich source: his diaries, 1857–62.[1] They provide an illuminating account of the constraints, ambitions, and strategies of one young man attempting to achieve his goals. Since the 'revival of the narrative' among social historians in Canada and elsewhere in the past thirty years, the natural appeal of biography and its ability to tell meaningful stories about ordinary people in the past has augmented traditional interest in collectivities and anonymous North Americans.[2] Diaries like McIlwraith's are valuable to social historians of Victorian Canada who wish to take a biographical approach. Such documents are extremely rare; indeed, these may be the only known diaries of a craftsman in Canada in the mid-nineteenth century. They show us, in his words, who he thought he was and who he wanted to become. And they reflect a common trajectory for similar young men 'on the make' in the Victorian North Atlantic world.

McIlwraith's diaries remind us that his world – a mental map that wove together 'known' places in Scotland, Canada West, New York City, and their people – was smaller and more connected than those places could ever seem today. Andrew McIlwraith was not a Victorian Forrest

Gump, but in the short span of six years, he managed to traverse and make his home in places that stretched across thousands of miles and in his journeys crossed paths with some of the leading luminaries of the day: Canadian divine and educational reformer Rev. Egerton Ryerson, future Canadian prime minister Alexander Mackenzie, Canadian statesman-journalist George Brown, New York City mayor and scoundrel Fernando Wood, Britain's Prince of Wales, American evangelical icon Henry Ward Beecher, and many others. McIlwraith's story is one worth telling, both because it is inherently entertaining and because it reflects well so many of the main currents of thought, sentiment, and behaviour in the Victorian Anglo-American world. This book aims to convey the shape and feeling of that world.

Andrew McIlwraith was born in Newton-on-Ayr, Scotland, on February 14, 1830,[3] the ninth of ten children belonging to Thomas (1788–1856) and Jean Adair Forsyth McIlwraith (see Appendix 1). The son of a weaver, Andrew McIlwraith appears to have grown up in a family with middling economic comfort.[4] His older brother Thomas apprenticed and worked as a cabinetmaker before becoming manager of the Newton Gas Works near his home by the time of the 1851 census. Two years later Thomas had made the trek overseas to become manager of the newly formed Hamilton Gas Light Company in Hamilton, Canada West. From this new home Thomas also soon emerged as a notable amateur ornithologist.[5] Andrew's adolescence was almost certainly occupied with the completion of a patternmakers' apprenticeship at an engineering shop in Ayr.[6] He appears to have followed his older brother to Canada West sometime in the mid-1850s, having parlayed the intricate drawing skills acquired as a patternmaker into a temporary job as a draughtsman at the Great Western Railway in Sarnia by the time the diaries commence in 1857.

If the younger McIlwraith had aspirations to make his way as a draughtsman and patternmaker in Canada West, his arrival was well timed. Canada West was undergoing industrialization and a railway 'revolution' in the mid-1850s, and the services he could offer were in high, if sporadic, demand.[7] Andrew joined his brother in Hamilton for some months, but he stayed in no one place for very long, following work wherever it was available. From 1857 until 1861, Andrew McIlwraith worked mainly as a patternmaker in several locations in Canada West and, for a short time, in New York City while also seeking (with much more marginal results) related employment as a draughtsman and even lithographer. He returned to Canada West in late 1861 to take up a permanent, more secure position as a bookkeeper for a large foundry in Galt, continuing his employment there until 1872. He tried his hand at his own business, as a foundry owner in tiny Listowel, Ontario, but returned to Galt in 1881 to work as an accountant for the Gore Mutual Insurance Company until his death, reportedly of complications from Bright's disease, in 1891.

From the mid-1850s until the early 1860s, Andrew McIlwraith was a liminal man. He was (to borrow the *Oxford English Dictionary*'s wording) quite demonstrably 'on the threshold,' in a number of different respects. A journeyman craftsworker, he was a man in between his apprenticeship and the hope of an independent future. But connected to his workplace status were other factors. Like other young men seeking employment in the sharp economic downturn of the late 1850s, McIlwraith had difficulty nailing down steady work in one location and, as a result, was rootless for much of this time. He was propelled by a need to cultivate a polished demeanour, to become *respectable* in appearance and behaviour. A single man who desired above all else to marry the woman he loved, he could not accomplish this goal until his other challenges had been met. McIlwraith's liminality pushed him to seek refuge in several cognitive harbours – at work (when he had it), in self-improvement activities, and in his diary keeping.

McIlwraith's diaries provide a glimpse of the ways in which young male craftsworkers in this era made themselves; that is, how they crafted identities and sought to make them reality. Diaries were more than just quotidian records of one man's activities, but tools of social mobility that young men such as McIlwraith used to reflect on their lives and resolve to become something better. They were used to enable the creation of a free, independent person, a self-possessed participant in the construction of a larger emergent liberal social order.[8] They were a narrative project undertaken to negotiate the way through his young journeyman's life toward manhood. Self-improvement activities pervaded all areas of McIlwraith's life. He used these to deepen and diversify his learned skills and to better his chances for secure employment and, ultimately, independence. Andrew McIlwraith engaged in a truly impressive array of self-improving activities, but he was by no means alone. His diaries relate the fact that many of his friends and fellow travellers did these things together and shared common goals.

Why Keep a Diary?

Social historians have paid increasing attention in recent years to life writing as a source for understanding workers, including those in the crafts. However, this research agenda has been more firmly focused on working-class autobiography than on diaries.[9] Investigations of working-class autobiography have added important dimensions to our understanding of crafts- and other workers, but as John Burnett and Martin Hewitt have each suggested, the less premeditated daily-entry form of the diary may provide an even more immediate, more candid, and less constructed window on workers' identities in the past.[10] McIlwraith's diaries have this sort of candour. They reflect a particular moment in the life cycle of a journeyman patternmaker as he cycled through employment in several shops and locations in Canada West and New York City. This highly geographic and insecure period of moving from one paid position to another was perhaps prolonged by the general economic downturn, but it was a common feature of the lives of journeymen craftsworkers. Commonly termed 'the tramp,' it offered wage earning (for both subsistence and capital-accrual), skill development, and diversification using a network of (sometimes far-flung) personal and craft contacts. The tramp was a means of social mobility for many young craftsworkers.[11] McIlwraith's diaries describe and articulate the experience of one man's life on the tramp.

The diaries are essentially prescriptive as well; this sort of literary iteration was purposeful. McIlwraith's occupational journey was not unlike the geographic journeys of nineteenth-century travellers who committed their thoughts and concerns to paper in shipboard diaries. Andrew Hassam shows how emigrants journeying from Britain to Australia dealt with the uncertainty of a life transition into which many had been forced by necessity by using their diaries as tools to 'frame and control the meaning of the voyage out.' Diaries assuaged their marginal status, allowing emigrants the literary space to fit the uncertainties of their voyages into a more comfortable 'narrative of equilibrium.'[12] As a stage of craft mobility, journeywork is a process of becoming, of achieving independence as defined by developing craft custom. This stage was expanding in the mid-nineteenth century, and many young, male craftsworkers' journeys were increasingly transatlantic. For them, diaries could function as tools of masculine self-actualization.[13] In his analysis of the diaries of nineteenth-century clerks in the northeastern United States, Thomas Augst finds that young men used diaries as forms of accounting for their moral and spiritual development: 'independence became a matter of quotidian accounting.'[14]

Even a cursory reading of McIlwraith's diaries shows the thick and regular reportage of their author's self-improvement activities. His diaries are documents of his attempts to become 'more of a man,' narratives of a sort of manhood that he was willing to happen and a 'stock taking' of his progress towards that greater goal. Augst has identified New Year as the day in which most young diarists engaged in such self-examination.[15] It is no surprise, perhaps, that we find McIlwraith's views on the function of his diaries most strongly expressed in the Preface to his 1858 diary (and reprinted as a preface to our book): 'to fix in a man's own mind, a sense of the progress he has made in moral and intellectual ideas.'[16] His preoccupation with this goal was clearly expressed just a week later when he reflected: 'spent the evening in the house thinking about what I am to do to earn a living or in other words, achieve independence.'[17] Andrew's diaries functioned as moral account books, providing a running tally of his progress.

Context: Situating the Craftsworker in the Mid-Victorian Era

This description of Andrew McIlwraith – self-improving craftsworker, diarist on the tramp – may strike a discordant note with some students of nineteenth-century working-class industrial Canada. These activities do not fit into received understandings of craftsworkers and their culture in this period. Most accounts of craftsworkers over the past forty years have emphasized their emergence as wage earners and members of a working class increasingly at odds with their capitalist employers. Scholars in the late 1970s and '80s argued that industrialization in large eastern Canadian cities such as Toronto and Hamilton had reached the 'Modern Industry' stage by the early 1870s, spurring skilled workers to build lively, vibrant, and oppositional working-class identities and cultures.[18] Recently, scholars have begun to question whether craftsworkers were so universally dispossessed of their access to the means of production through this period.[19] Robert Kristofferson's recent studies of Hamilton, for example, challenge the view of the *proletarianized* craftsworker, showing instead that a structural arrangement, 'craft capitalism,' opened up to local craftsworkers a more or less hopeful experience of industrial capitalism. This optimism was rooted in industrial change that, while appreciable, was still craft-based[20] and allowed for the fundamental preservation of traditional patterns of craft mobility and the maintenance of a still-vibrant, traditional culture of the craft workplace.[21] Their class position straddled capitalist and non-capitalist worlds in a way that allowed craftsworkers to construct identities based on a generally hopeful outlook on capitalism.

One product of this view was a belief among craftsworkers in the importance of self-improvement. In Hamilton, craftsworkers demonstrated a burgeoning enthusiasm for science, technology, and other modern forms of mental education by becoming active participants in local Mechanics' Institutes, debating societies, and a host of other self-educational institutions. Kristofferson's study shows us how a culture of self-improvement was manifested in these institutions.[22] McIlwraith's diaries add to our understanding of this culture, showing us how self-improvement could become an intensely *personal* part of a craftsworker's life.

In all of this identity formation, gender played a central role. Craftsworkers developed new ways of demonstrating and asserting their masculinity in a time of uncertain economic fortunes. A handful of scholars have begun to study this phenomenon, focusing in particular on how workers in the Anglo-American world used shop-floor control, the family wage ideology, strong unions, and the labour market as arenas where their version(s) of mid-Victorian 'manliness' were articulated and acted out.[23] Arguably, craftsworkers drew their masculine identities from other wellsprings, too. For craftsworkers, manliness also derived from their expectations to rise through the craft ranks to a *respectable* position. Manliness could be pursued in other, cognitive ways. Material success was to be augmented and confirmed by the cultivation of their minds. Indeed, in an era of expanding possibilities for advancement and rapid technological change, self-improvement – particularly self-education – would vastly increase their chances of achieving upward movement through the craft ranks.[24]

Work

Andrew McIlwraith trained as a patternmaker for foundry work and was employed in that capacity through much of the period when he kept these diaries. He worked as a patternmaker at the well-known Gartshore Foundry in Dundas for seven months in 1858, and during the nineteen months he spent in New York City two metalworking factories engaged him in that capacity: Badger and Company Architectural Iron Works and Dunkin's Machine Shop.[25] To fill in the gaps he sometimes sought to transfer his patternmaker's drawing skills to brief stints of work as a draughtsman, most notably for the Great Western Railway in Sarnia for a few months after his diaries commence and on a number of quite small paid and unpaid contracts during periods of unemployment from patternmaking. Patternmaking involved highly skilled work. It was 'the most skilled,' Diane Drummond has noted, 'of all occupations concerned with foundry work.'

It was the pattern makers, a relatively small occupational group, who constructed the often intricate and complex patterns from which the moulds were formed. This work ... [required] a great deal of discretion in the planning, as well as manual dexterity and ability in constructing the wooden pattern itself. Numeracy, a good general education and the capacity for abstract thought were all necessary in translating rough diagrams and dimensions ... into the three-dimensional pattern. Accuracy was essential, while allowances had to be made for the shrinkage and cooling of the metal in the general calculations before the pattern could be constructed. Finally, the making of the pattern itself required much manual skill. The period 1843–1914 saw few changes in the actual procedure ... [but] the increasing complexity of the patterns greatly enhanced the pattern maker's skill as the period went on. With some patterns taking as long as nine days to construct both the pattern maker's skill and his product were highly valued.[26]

Work – respectable brainwork – was clearly an important source of identity for Andrew McIlwraith. In all of his weekday diary entries, the description of his work regimen took pride of place, an indication that he defined his life very much according to what occupied him during the day.

For McIlwraith, the work of patternmaking (and draughting) involved a mixture of painstaking calculation and minutely specific drawing and pattern building. While work in some mid-nineteenth-century metal shops in North America was becoming increasingly systematized, driven by steam power, and characterized by growing divisions of labour, this had only very rarely advanced to the point where craftsworkers in this industry were effectively deskilled. The Novelty Iron Works, where McIlwraith's friend Connel (his roommate for much of the time in New York City and former workmate at Gartshore's) was employed, represented one of the largest and most advanced of such workplaces in the industrialized world, employing close to one thousand workers, utilizing a highly systematized labour process organized into eighteen different departments headed by intricate webs of supervisory personnel. In such advanced workplaces the skills of some moulders or machinists might have been narrowing

somewhat, but, as Richard Stott has concluded in his study of mid-nineteenth-century New York City, by the early 1860s 'the factory had done
little to dilute workers' skills in the city's metalworking industry.'[27] In
a letter published in the *Ayrshire Times* in August 1860 and addressed
to the working men of his 'ain auld toun,' McIlwraith mused on his
eighteen months' work experience in New York City, noting that while
'appliances or the shortening of labour are much in vogue here' and
the advanced division of labour evident in such establishments as sash,
blind, door, and kindling wood factories, in the metal trades at least,
the advantage still lay squarely with the man with well-developed craft
skills. Writing on the question 'Is the working man better off in America
than in Britain?' he concluded, 'I have only to remark that a man who
has learnt his trade well at home can find himself at no loss here.'[28]

In Hamilton, Canada West, the metal industry remained even more
craft-based in this time period, with, for example, the supplementation
of moulders' skills with the employment of such less-skilled workers
as coremakers, stovemounters, and fitters still a very marginal feature
of the workplace.[29] While divisions of labour and technical innovation
appear to have been more advanced in New York City than in Hamilton, in neither place had the deep and diverse skills of the patternmaker
yet come under attack. Throughout the North American metal industry during this period the patternmaker remained firmly atop the craft
hierarchy in the metal trades, skills intact.

Work was done by task, and periods of accelerated work pace were
punctuated by periods of slow demand and even idleness. The call for
drawing, planning, and patternmaking came in fits and starts, and, as
a result, job security was less than ideal. McIlwraith's diary reveals the
intermittent pace and wide variety of work involved in mid-century
draughting and patternmaking. In the first half of 1857, his time as a
draughtsman was consumed in planning the Great Western Railway's
infrastructure at its Sarnia terminus. 'Calculating the weight of bridge
iron,' 'at plan of wood[en] platform,' 'tracing engine house plan,'
'[a]t new plan of brick tank house,' and 'drawing plan of Sarnia depot
grounds' were the jobs he described in his entries. He described similar tasks concerning his brief stint with the City of Hamilton and his
work at the Gartshore Foundry in Dundas in late 1857 and early 1858.
'[W]orked all day at Plan of Hamilton,' 'all day at Hamilton pumping engine,' and 'Worked all day at the valve patterns,' were repeated
descriptions. In New York City, McIlwraith engaged in an even greater
variety of work, such as 'patching up old patterns,' 'repairing and alter-

Andrew McIlwraith (Courtesy of Thomas McIlwraith, Mississauga ON).

June,   FRIDAY, 18.   1858.

All day at Beam Pattern — In the evening attended Mechanics debating club, the chief business of the evening being to hear an essay on "Goldsmith" from R. Mc Kicknie sent but which he changed for a discourse upon proverbs of all nations; for which thanks were voted. Some severe comments however were made on his conduct in changing his subject.

SATURDAY, 19.

Very warm weather — Mr. Inglis informed me in the afternoon that my services would be no more wanted as the work was getting scarce — Took train down to Hamilton in the evening.

SUNDAY, 20.

Heard Dr. Skinner from Waterdown preach in St. Andrews Church in the forenoon — At the dinner table Thos. proposed to his Mistress that she should take a trip home with the children — Had a walk to the cemetry with Jamieson and spent the evening in the house — very hot.

June,   MONDAY, 21.   18

Still very hot — Walk'd up town in hopes to enquire after passages to the old Country — Heard from Mr. Levegan, who mentioned Mr. Renfrews being going home. Had a very toilsome ramble along the mountain in the afternoon with the gun. Had a stroll with Jamieson in the evening.

TUESDAY, 22.

Miss Muir married this morning — henceforth be Mrs. Cowie — Met Mr. Robb in the forenoon & promised to assist him with some drawings. Did for him a design for a seal for Hamilton scientific association — Walk'd up town with Thos. and took two books, treatise on building and Rhetorical reader. Mr. Muir called in the evening and gave me some hopes of a job in Detroit.

WEDNESDAY, 23.

Work'd part of the day for Mr. Robb running about town, sketching waggon trucks &c for application to an invention for ploughing by steam — Weather awful. Took train to Dundas in the evening and ended singing practice.

Photograph of a page of diary entries, July 1858. Diaries of Andrew McIlwraith (Courtesy of Thomas McIlwraith, Mississauga, Ontario).

Thomas McIlwraith, brother to Andrew McIlwraith
(© Hamilton Public Library).

Lithographs of Great Western Railway shops, Hamilton, Canada West (*Canadian Illustrated News*, 14 February 1863).

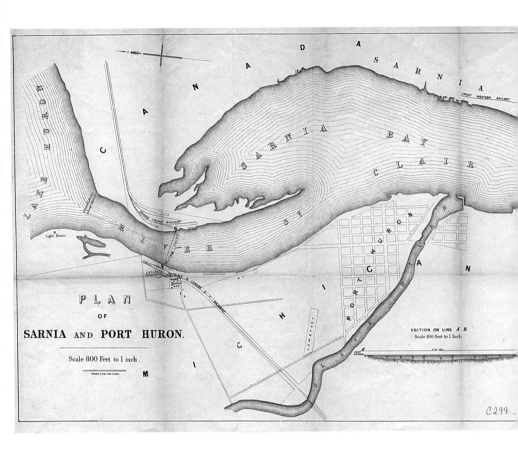

Plan of Sarnia, Ontario, and Port Huron, Michigan (London: Waterlow &
Sons, Lith., 1860) Courtesy Archives and Research Collections Centre,
D.B. Weldon Library, University of Western Ontario.

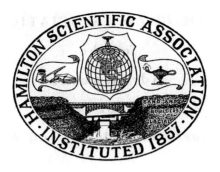

Seal of the Hamilton Scientific Association, likely drawn by Andrew McIlwraith (R. Kristofferson's collection).

Mitchell's Plan of New York &c., 1860
(Collection of The New-York Historical Society, Negative #82139T).

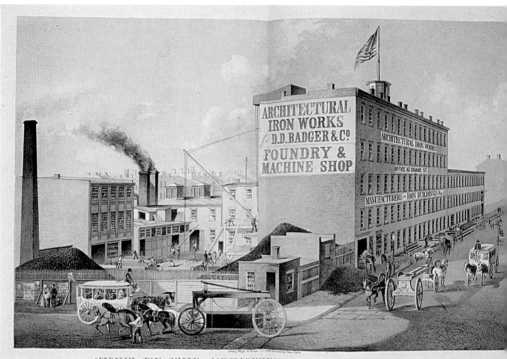

Architectural Iron Works, D.D. Badger & Company, New York
(Library of Congress).

JOHN GOLDIE, ESQ.

John Goldie, Jr (in M. Gowdy, *A Family History* … [Lewiston, ME 1919]). Courtesy Boston Public Library.

Hugh McCulloch (City of Cambridge Archives).

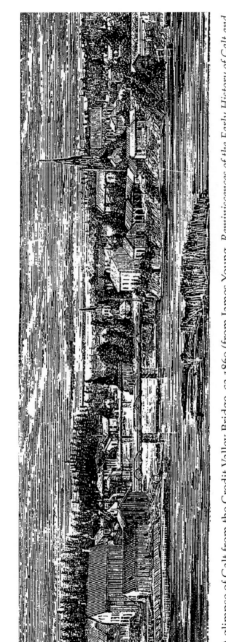

A glimpse of Galt from the Credit Valley Bridge, ca 1860 (from James Young, *Reminiscences of the Early History of Galt and the Settlement of Dumfries* [Toronto, 1880]).

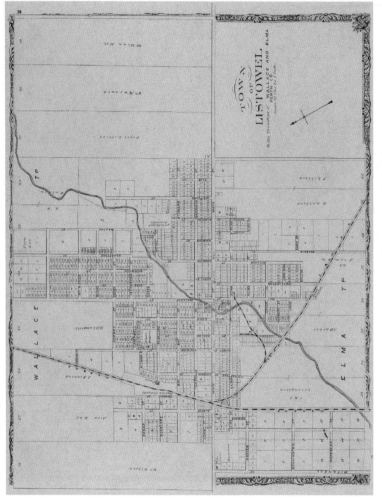

Map of Listowel, Ontario, ca 1878 (Belden & Co., *Atlas of the County of Perth* [Toronto, 1879]). Library and Archives of Canada, reproduction copy number A068014.

Andrew McIlwraith's burial plot and headstone, Mountview Cemetery,
Cambridge, Ontario (R. Kristofferson).

ing old columns ... for a shop front in Memphis, Tennessee,' and work on valve 'casing pattern,' '2 [inch] pipe patterns,' 'slide valve pattern,' 'Cross head patt'n,' 'large Pillow block for Beam engine,' 'air pump guards,' 'Piston patterns,' 'steam chest pattern,' 'crank,' and 'draw[ing] of cylinder.' Versatility was an important part of McIlwraith's craft.[30]

McIlwraith's pace of employment was notable as well. Fortunately for him, 'Full time at work,' or 'full time in the shop' were common entries throughout his diary. Occasionally, as in June 1860, a spurt in foundry business meant overtime work and wages for him. 'Made 11-1/4 hrs. at work to-day,' he reported on June 11 and June 13, and on the following day, impressively, 'Made 13-1/2 Hrs.' The downside to these bursts in foundry work were occasional slack weeks which, if they continued for long, meant the laying off of foundry workers, including even the most highly skilled. Even after a very steady summer of full employment in New York in 1859, the first signs of slackening business were interpreted ominously. 'One of our pattern-makers [was] discharged this morning,' McIlwraith noted on August 15 while employed at Badger's Architectural Iron Works, 'so am thinking my time is soon coming.'[31] Reflecting on the highly variable nature of employment in the New York City metal trades to the *Ayrshire Times*, McIlwraith claimed his fellow British immigrants to be of 'unanimous' opinion that, compared to the old country, work in New York City was typified by 'greater fluctuations in trade and diminished chance for constant employment.'[32]

Even in this uncertain environment, McIlwraith and his fellow patternmakers seemed to have retained a good deal of control over the daily work process and, in particular, the location and timing of assignments when employed. Though he spent most workdays in the shop where he kept his drawing instruments and tools, occasionally McIlwraith worked at home. On February 24, 1860, he reported spending 'All day in the house finishing the cylinder drawing' that he had undertaken for the New York firm Duncan and Crampton the previous day. In other instances, McIlwraith felt free to leave the workplace early once he had completed his current assignment. 'Left the office early and walked into the woods,' he reported in Sarnia, in March 1857. 'My job being done, went off for a stroll a round town and spent the day mostly among book stores,' he wrote in September 1859. 'Took a quarter to-day and went down to the City Hall,' he wrote on June 26, 1860, and on the next day 'Spent from 11 till 3 down town,' all of this taking place while in the employ of Badger's Architectural Iron Works in New York City.[33]

It is unclear exactly where McIlwraith received formal training for his work as a patternmaker. He was obviously an able hand; his competence was never reportedly called into question. The editor of the *Ayrshire Times* reported McIlwraith to have served a (likely lengthy) apprenticeship at a local engineering shop in Ayr before gaining 'several years' experience in 'engineering work on the Clyde.' One diary entry suggests that some of McIlwraith's journey experience may have been gained in Dumbarton, though no firm conclusions can be drawn.[34] What is clear, however, is that the job market for patternmakers in North America became increasingly competitive in the latter half of the 1850s as a severe economic downturn coupled with the continued arrival of British, Scottish, German, and Irish metal trade workers flooded the job market. Staying viable in the job market meant keeping his skills honed. McIlwraith's diary is shot through with entries describing the efforts he undertook to improve his professional skills during his non-work hours. Becoming more practised and polished at his craft and related skills was a dominant theme in his life in these years.

For all his diligence, off the job and on, McIlwraith was rewarded in pay only moderately well. Balancing the regular costs of lodging, meals, entertainment, and savings with irregular and sometimes unpredictable income was often a precarious act. For his work with the Great Western, McIlwraith was paid $65.00 each month from January until mid-July 1857, a pay rate which, given regular employment, would have placed him toward the upper end of the contemporary craftsworker and even white-collar range.[35] Indeed, during these few months of employment he was able to set aside $82 in wages to send to his brother Thomas to invest in the Savings Bank in Hamilton.[36] He was, however, without regular employment again until January 1858.[37] While he was employed as a patternmaker at Gartshore's Foundry in Dundas in 1858 and early 1859, McIlwraith's remuneration varied. His accounts show that during his first stint with Gartshore between early March and the middle of June 1858 he appears to have accepted partial wages of $6 on a biweekly basis with a balance amounting to $59.75 paid to him once he was laid off, for a total of $113.75 over those sixteen weeks. This pattern was repeated for his second period of employment at Gartshore's between early September 1858 and mid-February 1859. McIlwraith's account book entries reveal a total of $129 in wages paid to him over this period. On a daily basis this works out to somewhere in the range of $1.17 to $1.30 a day.[38] This rate was quite low for a highly skilled patternmaker and is perhaps a reflection of the declining state of the economy in the period.

Also uncertain was his remuneration in New York City, where he was most often paid on a daily rate, and sometimes by piecework. The uneven pace of mid-century metalwork business pushed foundries to expand and contract their workforces quickly to meet demands for specific jobs. In many cases, a skeleton crew of 'permanent' employees was augmented when necessary by short-term workers who hoped to catch on with the firm. McIlwraith confirmed this widespread New York City custom to the *Ayrshire Times*, commenting that in smaller metal shops it was 'especially the practice, whenever a job comes in, to advertise for hands, have as many as possible on it, to be discharged immediately on its being finished.'[39] Newcomers like McIlwraith made up the lion's share of this auxiliary workforce. Mid-nineteenth-century New York, Iver Bernstein notes, was 'host to what was no doubt the nation's most fluid labor market.' Payment methods reflected this impermanence. '[I] presume my pay is fixed at $1.50 [per day],' he wrote of his first job in New York in April 1859. From there things improved, somewhat: 'Got paid at an advanced rate as near as I can make out $1.90 per day,' reads an entry in June 1860. This rate is consistent with the wages received by local moulders and machinists in that period.[40] McIlwraith's reportage of New York foundry workers' wages in 1860 peg the typical range at between 40s and 50s a week, or $1.60 to $2.00 a day.[41] Given the elusiveness of full-time and consistent work, however, the yearly income earned by such skilled craftsworkers and the standard of living it afforded remained out of reach to McIlwraith throughout his stay in New York City. He told readers of the *Ayrshire Times* that, in contrast to the lower rate of pay that more constant employment offered in British shops, the somewhat higher pay but more variable employment in New York City 'bring the rate of wages at year's end less than if we were to take the common rate paid as an average.'[42] But even such reduced financial circumstances allowed McIlwraith shelter, food, and a fairly wide discretionary spending on self-improvement activities.

In the labour market of the depression years of the late 1850s and early 1860s, the advantage lay clearly with employers, who had their pick of employees, skilled and unskilled. Even so, labour was hardly silent in the face of the increasing power of industrial capitalists over workers. The 1850s were years of ferment, protest, and, occasionally, rebellion among some workers in mid-nineteenth-century New York.[43] Among a male workforce that was increasingly youthful and composed of recent European immigrants bent on improving their material condition, workplace conflict most often revolved around improvements

in wages. It was quite common, however, for employers to accede to
the wage requests of their men; strikes did occur but were not a defin-
ing feature of labour relations in this period. Many young men working in the factories of 1850s New York City were interested in working
hard, getting paid as much as possible, and then moving on – often
leaving the city – to better secure their economic futures. Those committing themselves to unions for the long haul were still few and far
between and, especially in the boom and bust cycles of that decade,
unions tended not to be enduring organizations, often forming and re-
forming on an annual basis. Among unions of highly skilled workers
in this decade, patternmakers remained peripheral to the most visible
of struggles, perhaps able to resolve their wage needs with employers without recourse to the strike.[44] Patternmakers were not averse to
some of the workers' tactics, however, and seemed well aware of the
potential gains from organizing to control the entry of newcomers into
the trade and, perhaps, to set a standard pay scale. McIlwraith apparently supported these aims. He 'became a member of a Patternmakers'
Association' in June 1860 at the suggestion of a fellow worker and was
elected the 'club's' vice-president in the following September. The diary
is disappointingly silent, however, on his assessment of the association's aims and purposes and the likelihood that it could be an effective
instrument to mitigate the worst effects of an unstable job market.[45] In
his letter to the *Ayrshire Times* McIlwraith reveals that for many workers
in the New York City metal crafts, including patternmakers, the possession of skill and enlightenment in the mysteries of the craft were still
enough to assure their position: 'There being no organized protection
for the employment of illegitimate hands, the only test is efficiency in
the working and such as are found wanting are summarily dealt with.'
Based on this he could optimistically conclude that, if willing to put up
with the vagaries and vicissitudes of employment in the New York City
metal trades 'a man who is anxious to do well … can do better here than
at home.'[46]

   Beyond the strike, unions helped to moderate the fluctuations of the
uncertain labour market by acting as conduits through which labour
market information could be channelled. During this period a number
of unions made it common practice to marshal and direct information
about labour market opportunities to their members. Unions such as
the Iron Molders International Union – beside whose members McIlwraith would have laboured – attempted to coordinate and control
their members' place in the North American labour market by pub-

lishing in their monthly journal accounts of job opportunities in cities and towns across North America, submitted as reports by their various union locals. A member of the union would thus be able to ascertain what cities were likely to offer work and from which ones they were best to steer clear. In cities with overstocked labour markets or where a strike was on, it was also common practice among many unions to encourage new arrivals in search of work to move on and often to aid them with union-financed train tickets to the next town.[47]

Moving On

Transiency, as Michael Katz has written, was one of the central themes of life in mid-Victorian North America. Editorials in newspapers across Canada West regularly lamented the exodus of young men in search of opportunity.[48] Transiency marked the lives of Andrew McIlwraith and many of his contemporaries in the 1850s and early '60s. In the span of five years, McIlwraith lived in five different towns and cities, boarded in at least eight different homes, and worked for eight different employers.[49] His environments changed abruptly from quaint but bustling, 'go-ahead' towns like Sarnia and Dundas, to the larger and more anonymous industrial centres of Hamilton and New York. He domiciled in places diverse in comfort and appearance. One might imagine that a rather stark contrast existed between his brother's middle-class Hamilton household and his other 'homes': rented rooms in multi-family dwellings and large rooming houses. His living situation in Sarnia, Hamilton, and Dundas occasioned little commentary in the diary; more notable were his quarters in New York City, which seem to have provided the least amount of comfort and a certain degree of anxiety. 'Tormented with the Paddys kicking up rows thro' the night in the house,' he noted ruefully after moving into Logue's Hotel in April 1859. 'Bed bugs most abominably numerous in our room this season,' he wrote in August of the next year, 'breeding among our books and crawling over them.' More often than not, McIlwraith was forced to share accommodations with one or two roommates, a situation not unacceptable when it involved someone like Connel, a friend and iron turner from Dundas, but less comfortable when it was with strangers.[50]

Andrew McIlwraith's employers ranged from those who were paternalistic or those who were seemingly indifferent to the plight of their transient workforce. In general his relations with employers in Canada West seem to have been closer and more personal than those with the men for whom he worked in New York City. The Great Western Railway, for which McIlwraith worked at the start of his diaries, was a large company, but it still fostered a strong culture of paternalism.[51] McIlwraith met Dundas founder John Gartshore, his next employer, in an arranged meeting at the Hamilton home of his friend and draughting companion Charles Robb.[52] Once employed at the Gartshore Foundry he seems to have developed a fairly personal relationship with John Inglis, his foreman. Both were active in the tightly knit Dundas Mechanics' Debating Club, with Inglis serving as vice-president at the same time that McIlwraith served as secretary.[53] After slack times necessitated McIlwraith leaving Gartshore's, he maintained enough of a relationship to meet Inglis in Hamilton to discuss employment opportunities.[54] Altogether, McIlwraith rated Inglis a 'decent quiet-looking Scotsman.' On the other hand, his New York employers appear as distant figures; not once does McIlwraith's diary record him making the acquaintance of his employers; nor does he ever recall even seeing them in person. This is perhaps a reflection of the more advanced and impersonal state of industrialization in New York City. McIlwraith's contact, rather, was with the workshop foremen who had the power to determine who could be hired and when. When he was out of work, or when it was slow, he spent many hours making and renewing connections with foundry foremen with the hope of securing employment. The diaries chronicle a rather circular pattern of activity: finding work, working steadily, being dismissed when slack times emerged, and finding work again. '[I called] round thro' a number of shops but unsuccessful in getting a job,' he noted in mid-November 1859, one week before he gained steady employment at Duncan's. However, by February 1860, a shortage of work there put McIlwraith back on the street. 'Made a tour round calling at a number of shops asking for a job but unsuccessfully,' he noted before catching on with another employer. Two weeks later, he managed to get engaged again at Badger's.[55]

In choosing to move, McIlwraith followed the path of previous transient workers, paths that were becoming increasingly well-worn in the 1850s and 60s. He seems to have spent little time puzzling over the decision to go. Having finished his plan of the Sarnia GWR Depot and his contract on the morning of July 18, 1857, McIlwraith wasted little time and emotion in departing. 'In the afternoon packed up … Got certificate and pass from Mr Gregory and bade good-bye.' Even the decision to move away to New York City seems to have involved very little consternation. On April 8, 1859, McIlwraith recorded a visit by a Mr

Raphael. 'Had a consultation about my taking a tour to look for work. Think of starting for New York.' Five days later, rather unceremoniously, McIlwraith was on a train for New York.[56]

His destinations do not seem to have been selected haphazardly. Mr Raphael was one person in a loose network of contacts that McIlwraith used to find work in these years. Brother Thomas was McIlwraith's most active advocate and ultimately his most valuable asset in finding permanent work. Notable in the diaries is that a host of lesser connections, friends, relations, and former co-workers from Scotland, Hamilton, and Dundas, provided Andrew with extra eyes and ears to find employment opportunities and also with occasions for socializing. The Renfrew family of New York was one of these connections, and a group of people with whom he felt familiar enough to spend holidays and a brief summer vacation at their Staten Island farm. Listed also in the diaries are a dozen or so metalworkers who had been working in New York's foundries before Andrew's arrival or who had followed him there. '[I] saw Murray, a fitter from Dundas, who has now started work in the Novelty Works,' he recorded in July 1859.[57]

Throughout this period, brother Thomas's house in Hamilton was Andrew's sentimental home base. Letters from both Thomas and his wife Mary brought news about Andrew's family and friends. At all times, he kept one eye on the job market in Canada West, regularly requesting and receiving updates on the availability of work. '[G]ot letters from Mrs. McIlwraith and from Jameson, Hamilton,' he wrote on March 3, 1860. 'Very dull times there yet.' Thomas informed his brother of a potential job opening for a draughtsman with the Buffalo and Lake Huron Railway in Brantford in May 1860. Andrew hastened to reply, sending a formal application the next day, but was deeply disappointed when the prospect fell through. McIlwraith was on the move, but he was not a drifter, and he looked forward to the day when circumstances would allow of his return to family and friends in Canada.[58]

Transiency for Andrew McIlwraith was a necessity. Pushed to 'tour around' to find sustainable employment, he could not practically accumulate much in the way of consumer goods, nor could he set down roots. His tool chest, his books, and a trunk of clothes seem to have been the only worldly goods that he owned. He invested little in the communities in which he lived. In Sarnia, Hamilton, Dundas, and New York, he was *in* society, but not *of* it. This sense of rootlessness weighed heavily on McIlwraith. To become established, to make it, to be wholly respectable, one had to become sedentary.

Still, for McIlwraith and thousands of journeyman craftsworkers, the tramp was the route to opportunity. Once on the tramp, he seemed invested in the network. Labour historians have often understood the tramp as a social process by gazing through the lens of such published sources as census materials or union journals and have tended to focus on the efforts of organizations such as fledgling unions in communicating geographically dispersed labour market opportunities to their members.[59] McIlwraith's diaries suggest that for some mid-nineteenth-century young craftsworkers it was the more informal networks of family, friends, and co-workers that facilitated their geographic (and social) mobility. This is indeed what Françoise Noel finds in her study of family life in central Canada in the century after 1780: intricate social networks of families and friends used correspondence and frequent visiting to cultivate economically useful support networks.[60] Andrew McIlwraith's breaks seemed to come from the help of an informal grapevine of family, friends, and co-workers, and it seems he felt compelled to pay it forward, advising his Ayrshire brethren in published form in August 1860: 'In these days of cheap locomotion, the Atlantic voyage is not a matter of great moment; and for a young man in the way of gathering information and experience, whether or not he should make up his mind to reside permanently in the States, a visit to this country is not by any means a preposterous undertaking, and cannot but be beneficial.'[61]

Transplanting Scottish Self-Improvement

In the meantime, Andrew McIlwraith sought to 'make it' in other, more immediately achievable, ways. Professionally, he was striving to become accomplished. Personally, his diary betrays a quest to become respectable or, in the words of contemporaries, *cultivated*. Perhaps above all else, McIlwraith understood his efforts towards self-improvement as his ticket to success. They were his lever to the creation of a self-possessed, liberal individual.[62]

For Andrew and other mid-century craftsworkers, self-education activities took a wide array of forms, ranging from the formalized classes of the many Mechanics' Institutes that had opened across the country by the 1850s to the informality of solitary reading. Craftsworkers explored topics that contributed directly to building knowledge in their craft, but many also launched deep explorations of literature, natural history, and other forms of scientific knowledge. For example, 'artisan naturalists' were engaged in serious study of botany, geology,

or many other features of the natural world. They built communal networks of knowledge exchange, some of which were interfaced with
corresponding networks established by the more elite 'gentlemanly'
practitioners of so-called 'high' science.[63]

Scotland was an epicentre of this craftsworker culture of self-
improvement, where it was encouraged in part by a relatively open
and accessible educational system. It obtained particular potency in
the Lowlands, in such places as Ayrshire, where McIlwraith was born
and raised.[64] His personal penchant for self-improvement was likely
nurtured in the bosom of his family. His father, a master weaver, had
the financial wherewithal to list his seventeen-year-old son William,
his youngest, as a 'scholar' in the 1851 census. Weavers in Lowland
Scotland boasted especially high literacy rates and had a particular
reputation for an active autodidacticism organized around generally
short working hours and financed with relatively good pay.[65] Andrew's
older brother Thomas (1824–1903) received an education in Newton-
on-Ayr and became in Canada a well-known amateur ornithologist
who authored *Birds in Ontario*, a study of international renown and the
standard in the field for decades. He was a founding member of the
American Ornithologists' Union and active in the management of the
Hamilton and Gore Mechanics' Institute and the Hamilton Association
for the Advancement of Literature, Science and Art for many years. The
diaries reveal his house in Hamilton, where Andrew stayed on numerous occasions, to have been something of a centre of self-improving
activity; days out collecting birds for Thomas's personal 'museum'
were frequently followed by nights of processing and identifying specimens or carrying out other investigations into natural history or engaging in a variety of literary pursuits. In later years, local working boys
attended free evening classes offered by his daughter in the basement
of the house.[66]

The area around the McIlwraiths' Ayrshire home was a community
rich with opportunity for self-improvement. As David Vincent has
noted, the semi-rural nature of places like Ayrshire offered the young
artisan-naturalist a 'huge, free laboratory.'[67] Perhaps this was the
ground in which Thomas's ornithological interests were germinated.
Perhaps too his move from the cabinetmaker trade to management of
the Newton Gas Works was inspired by the example of Ayrshire native
and local hero William Murdock, millwright and inventor of gas lighting and many other inventions.[68]

The diaries expose Andrew McIlwraith's interest in and affection for some of the central figures in the artisanal culture of self-improvement in both Ayrshire and Scotland in general. Hugh Miller, stonemason and renowned geologist, was the subject of a number of his investigations. Andrew borrowed Miller's *Schools and Schoolmasters*[69] from a friend in April 1857, finding it to be 'a most entertaining and truthful book' and purchased a copy of Miller's *Testimony on the Rocks* shortly after it was published that same year.[70] Andrew rounded out this knowledge by attending lectures on the 'stonemason of Cromarty' on both sides of the Atlantic.[71] Perhaps inspired by his brother's birding hobbies, he also spent over a month in the autumn of 1858 preparing an essay delivered to his local debating club on the well-known weaver-ornithologist Alexander Wilson, who had grown up in Paisley, Scotland, before leaving for the United States in the late eighteenth century.[72]

Ayrshire bard Robert Burns provided McIlwraith – and so many other self-improving Scottish artisans – with particular inspiration. He augmented his study of the poet's verse by reading essays on Burns by Wilson and Carlyle and attending an 'animated discussion' on the 'Morality of Burns' at the Hamilton YMCA in 1859.[73] He spent the better part of a day in 1859 reading aloud speeches from a volume commemorating the hundredth anniversary of Burns's birth in an effort to woo Mary Goldie, his future wife.[74]

Andrew McIlwraith's connection to the Goldie family speaks strongly to the rooting of his self-improvement activities in the particularly rich intellectual soil of Ayrshire. He appears to have been well acquainted with the Goldie family before coming to Canada and spent many hours engaged in a wide array of self-improvement activities with various members of that family in both Canada and Scotland over the course of his diaries. That family's patriarch (Andrew's future father-in-law) was gardener, miller, and renowned Scottish botanist John Goldie, one of the key figures of Scottish self-improvement.[75]

McIlwraith's embeddedness in this culture was vividly illustrated in his diary entries from his trip 'home' between August and November 1857. His stay in Ayr was marked almost daily by long and frequent rambles through the countryside with family and friends birdwatching and gathering shells, flowers, and other specimens of nature. These sojourns often had as their destinations such local landmarks as Crossaguel Abbey. His interest in the bard of Scotland was confirmed by two visits to the Burns monument. One particularly long day outside was broken by a noontime visit to view Rev. Grant's new aquarium. Evenings were passed in activity ranging from a visit to the theatre or local

Philharmonic to attendance at a lecture on Hugh Miller's *Testimony on the Rocks* at the local young men's association. McIlwraith's appetite for self-improvement was particularly well satiated during a three-week side trip to Edinburgh hosted by close relatives of the Goldies. There he visited a truly impressive array of museums, the botanical gardens, the zoological gardens, painting and sculpture galleries, Short's Observatory, the Library of the Society of Writers to her Majesty's Signet (where he 'got inspecting a volume of plates of Audubon's American Birds'), and more. Around these activities, he fit in long walks through the town and countryside, a course of drawing lessons with a Mr Dale, and frequent visits to the theatre. McIlwraith's easy and frequent movement from one self-improvement activity to the next signified his deep roots in this aspect of the Scottish culture of his youth. And this pace did not slow once he returned to the other side of the Atlantic.

Andrew McIlwraith spent his time in Canada West working and living in a variety of communities, including Sarnia, Dundas, Galt, and Ayr. These towns were all part of the broad social and economic hinterland of Hamilton, particularly, as John Weaver has shown, among members of the metal crafts community.[76] Indeed Hamilton – specifically, his brother Thomas's house – served as Andrew's spiritual and sometimes physical home, especially during one of the frequent bouts of unemployment that were a feature of the journeymen's life through these years. From Sarnia it would have been a cheap and easy ride down the track of the Hamilton-based GWR, his employer, to visit his brother for seasonal celebrations in late December 1856. While working as a patternmaker in Gartshore's Foundry in Dundas in 1858 and 1859, Andrew regularly set out by foot from his boardinghouse to lodge with brother Thomas for the weekend and partake in the many self-improvement activities available in that larger centre. The craft communities of Dundas and Hamilton were tightly integrated due to their close physical proximity.

This social environment provided a particularly strong footing for the interest in self-improvement that McIlwraith imported with him from Ayrshire. By mid-century, artisans in many industrial workplaces in Scotland had experienced quite pronounced effects of industrialization. Robert Gray has shown that by this time in industrializing Edinburgh, for example, 'the artisan's class position had become quite unambiguously that of a wage labourer.'[77] While some skilled workers responded by reformulating their identities around this new reality, others simply left. Such artisans commonly used emigration as a means to escape

deskilling and other negative features of the capitalist workplace and
to return to forms of production more consistent with craft traditions.
In many instances, the decision to emigrate was not made in an attempt
to turn back from industrial capitalism, but to go to places where they
perceived their experience of it would be more positive.[78] The Scottish
Highland clearances have often figured large in works on nineteenth-
century Scottish immigration to North America and elsewhere. In fact,
by mid-century, most emigrants were Lowlanders, many farmers, but
also a large contingent of artisans. Workers in such distressed trades as
weaving formed emigration societies and appealed to the government
for assistance in leaving. In many cases, however, leaving artisans had
the means to finance their own passage – and it appears Andrew McIlwraith did. Marjory Harper has characterized such emigrants 'adventurers,' young men 'rich in skills and enterprise' who 'simply saw the
potential for profitable investment of their labour, talents or capital
in the vast virgin territories or burgeoning cities of the New World.'[79]
In other words, they saw overseas an increased ability to achieve an
independence, not only in obtaining a small traditional shop of their
own (though that remained the ambition of many), but in an expanded
ability to move up through the ranks within a capitalist economy that
offered them more opportunity than back home.

In addition to these Lowlanders' traditional manual craft skills and
general determination to work hard, self-improvement would vastly
increase their chances for success.[80] As the diaries make evident, McIlwraith maintained his strong Scottish cultural roots once on this side
of the Atlantic, continuing to partake in the Scottish culture of self-
improvement and relying on networks of kin and friends from 'home'
to navigate the rapids of the new world. The sources are less revealing of how this interfaced with, or was challenged by, his identity as a
Briton within the larger empire. His decision to observe 'a general fast
on account of Indian Revolt' in October 1857 could point to the development of a more 'British' identity.[81] However, his seeming lack of hesi-
tation to leave the formal bounds of empire to work in New York City
suggests that this emergent identity had limits. Historians of empire
have warned against understanding national and imperial identities as
an 'either/or' possession. Linda Colley, for example, has argued that
a 'growing sense of Britishness' did not necessarily mean other loyal-
ties were 'supplanted and obliterated.' McIlwraith and other emigrants
possessed multiple identities, in his case both Scot and Briton.[82] In this
light, McIlwraith's work foray to New York City should be seen as

movement within an orbit still dominated by British cultural and intellectual values and identities.[83] Also, while McIlwraith and others took
with them some pre-formed British and/or Scottish identities to the
colonies, these were undoubtedly adjusted to the particularities of time
and place once they arrived. Philip Buckner and R. Douglas Francis
explain that individuals transporting national and imperial identities
to new places lived those identities 'on their own terms and in their
own way.'[84]

Strategies for Personal Self-Improvement

By leaving Ayrshire for Canada, Andrew McIlwraith significantly
improved his opportunity for rising in the world. The diaries reveal
how he eagerly inserted himself into this world. To position himself for
success, McIlwraith followed the advice of a number of contemporary
commentators, increasing the variety and deepening mastery of his
craft skills.[85] Following craft custom, Andrew maintained and honed
traditional manual skills associated with his craft.

Upon the termination of his position as a GWR draughtsman in the
summer of 1857, for example, he returned home for a few months to
visit and scout out work opportunities, which were not plentiful there.
He returned to Hamilton in December and by early the following year
was looking in earnest for work as a patternmaker. His job search was
complemented with an effort to reinvigorate his manual skills by 'purchasing a plank of cherry to make patterns' in early February 1858.
Through that month he worked busily fashioning the plank into a pattern for gearing in a shed at the gasworks managed by his brother. This
helped to limber up dormant craft skills by the time he commenced a
new job as patternmaker in the Gartshore Foundry in Dundas early the
next month.[86]

However, craftsworkers like McIlwraith understood that traditional
manual skills needed to be balanced with mental knowledge in an age
when scientific and technological advance increasingly drove industrial
development.[87] Before his first cut into the cherrywood block, hours
were spent studying the principles of gearing, performing minute calculations from gearing tables, composing detailed drawings, and preparing an odontograph for marking the outlines of gearing teeth. The
mathematical dimensions of patternmaking and draughtsman's work
were similarly exercised in one evening spent practising 'Logarithm
Calculations' in late March 1857.[88]

McIlwraith also read widely and frequently on subjects calculated to expand his 'mental culture' as it related to his crafts and doing business in general. His studies sometimes focused quite directly on his interests as a member of the metal crafts: the *Cyclopedia of Machinery* and treatises on steam engines and locomotives, for example.[89] His engagement with works on building and stonecutting in the cold evenings of January 1857 coincided suggestively with some bridge work he was assisting with as a GWR draughtsman during the day.[90] A more general reading could sometimes inform craft, such as in January 1858 when he spent part of a period of unemployment reading 'How to Do Business.' He also found solace in that mid-nineteenth-century chronicler of self-improvement Samuel Smiles, reading both *Self-Help* and, sometime later, *Brief Biographies*, which he found to be 'an interesting volume.'[91] McIlwraith was also a frequent visitor to local workshops wherever he lived or travelled. These visits were often undertaken in an effort to find work, but they also enabled him to keep abreast of the technical improvements of the day, such as in autumn 1858 when he visited the GWR shops to marvel at the new stationary engine and steam hammer.[92]

As Andrew's employment as a draughtsman suggests, he also sought to leverage his patternmaker's skills – particularly its requirement for advanced skills in technical drawing and scientific and mathematical calculation – into new, potentially rewarding areas of employment. Drawing, a skill common to both draughting and patternmaking, was a primary focus of these efforts. His purchase of a T-square during his course of drawing lessons in Edinburgh indicates this focus. Much of his non-work time was also spent drawing, detailing a variety of subjects – from nuthatches and warblers to technical things, such as cylinders – probably on the draughting board that he set up in his lodgings.[93]

McIlwraith's friendship with Hamilton mechanical engineer and architect Charles Robb helped to develop his draughting skills. During periods when McIlwraith was unemployed and living at his brother's house in Hamilton, Robb sought his drawing assistance on a variety of projects: a map of Hamilton and surrounding areas, the design of a Seal for the Hamilton Scientific Association, technical drawings of wagon trucks and a steam plough, and the tracing of plans for a hotel and the local waterworks.[94] Andrew hoped, perhaps, that the work for Robb would ultimately recommend him for paid work as a draughtsman. Alas, such a position remained elusive.[95]

Andrew McIlwraith knew he could not put all his eggs in so few baskets. He also directed his studies toward lithography and investigated the transferability of his patternmaker's skills. Early in his diaries, he toured the operations of well-known Scottish lithographers Schenk and McFarlane while on his visit to Edinburgh, marvelling at the 'great variety of maps and pictures.'[96] His interest in this field picked up more seriously in 1859 when, while working in the day as a patternmaker at the Architectural Iron Works in New York City, he began to investigate the possibilities of this trade. At church one Sunday in early October, McIlwraith was introduced to James McLellan, who treated him to a tour of his lithography establishment a short time later. The excitement of 'getting a view of the presses and having the process explained' spurred McIlwraith to further action. Evenings through the next week and beyond were occupied with 'puzzling my head with the lithographic business' and 'studying and scheming the lithographic machine.' Early efforts to 'draw some on the lithographic press,' McIlwraith complained, 'found difficulties at every step.' McLellan made his shop and presses available to the aspiring craftsman on several evenings in winter, 1859–60. Sketches for the press were also worked up at McIlwraith's boardinghouse. On McLellan's advice, he also signed up for a course of drawing lessons with 'Monsieur Calyo,' working up, among other things, 'a large view of the "Ruins of Canterbury."' This developing relationship with McLellan included talk of 'scheming a lithographic press,' but any hope McIlwraith had of getting into this business was dashed when McLellan died unexpectedly after a short illness in late May 1860.[97] Meantime, Andrew continued to pursue employment opportunities in patternmaking and draughting. He enrolled in drawing classes at the newly opened Cooper Union for the Advancement of Science and Art, one of New York City's' most shining examples of craftsworker self-improvement, in October 1860.[98]

Not all of Andrew's improving activities were aimed so directly towards employment or economic success.[99] Young craftsworkers also actively cultivated what some commentators called a 'many-sided culture' to prepare them to better exercise the new rights and responsibilities that had become theirs in an age of general social elevation.[100] At the centre of the formalized culture of craftsworker self-improvement were the numbers of Mechanics' Institutes (forerunners of public libraries) that spread widely through Britain, British North America, and the United States in the mid-nineteenth century. Making citizens out of men was a critical part of their mission. Historians of the emerging liberal social order in Upper Canada/Canada West identify Mechanics' Institutes as part of a constellation of voluntary associations used by craftsworkers and others as 'experiments in democratic sociability,' key sites in the mass making of free, liberal individuals.[101]

Mechanics' Institutes (MI) were an important part of Andrew McIlwraith's life wherever he went. The records of the local MI in Ayr, Scotland, reveal that he was a subscribing member of his hometown's institute from 1846 until 1852, that is, from age fifteen to age twenty-one (see Appendix 2). He was a prodigious reader and borrower of books; in those six years he made 292 book loans from the MI library, including volumes that reached across the full breadth of philosophical, mechanical, and literary tomes available at the time. McIlwraith's reading for fall 1849 was perhaps typical of his tastes: alongside Buchanan's *Treatise on Mill Work*, he selected volumes of *Don Quixote*, Wilson's *Isle of Palms and Other Poems*, *Accum's Treatise on Gas*, Knickerbocker's *History of New York*, and Grier's *Mechanic's Calculator* among others. The Ayr MI library, it seems, was a familiar haunt for young McIlwraith.[102]

The diaries reveal that McIlwraith joined Mechanics' Institutes in Dundas and New York City as well as Galt. He also made frequent use of the Hamilton and Gore Mechanics' Institute and the Sarnia Mechanics' Institute while in those towns. His frequent geographic movement was likely aided by the common practice between institutes to honour membership in other institutes by offering reciprocal privileges. McIlwraith spent many evenings perusing journals in institute reading rooms, making withdrawals from their circulating libraries, and attending the numerous lectures held in their halls.[103] He also attended meetings, lectures, essay readings, and other events at the Young Men's Christian Association in both Dundas and Hamilton.[104] In addition to drawing classes, he attended lectures and political meetings in the reading rooms of the Cooper Union while living in New York City.[105]

Andrew lightened his self-improvement pursuits by attending theatre performances and concerts and visiting seemingly all museums and galleries within his reach. Some off-work time in New York City, for example, was spent visiting the National Academy of Design, the Dusseldorf Gallery, and other cultural institutions.[106] He particularly enjoyed the theatre and seems to have spent almost as much of his non-work hours watching stage performances as he did with books in his hands. In mid-century New York, as John Kasson argues, the performing arts underwent astonishing growth and specialization out of which emerged a hierarchical conception of artistic performance. 'On the one side stood "high" or "refined" art (opera, particularly Wagner; symphonies, particularly Beethoven; the legitimate theater, particularly Shakespeare). On the other side lay "popular," "light," or more pejoratively and lower in the scale, "cheap," and "vulgar" amusement – no longer to be accorded the dignity of Art.'[107] Given his concern for respectability, one might expect Andrew to have attended only the former sort of entertainment. Not so. He took in both 'highbrow' and 'lowbrow.' 'Went to the Metropolitan Theatre at night and saw "Romeo and Juliet,"' he reported in April 1859; in the same month, he saw 'Antony and Cleopatra.' Other performances of this calibre that he reported seeing included such classics as Scott's *Rob Roy* and Bulwer-Lytton's *Money*. He reported seeing *Othello*, acted by the great American Shakespearean Edwin Forrest. To see these productions, he entered some of the respectable public institutions in New York in this era: Niblo's Garden Theater, Laura Keene's, Winter Garden Theater, Wallack's, and even the New York Stadt Theater, 'to hear a performance in German.'[108]

Contrasting sharply with his highbrow ventures were other performances and places that he attended. In New York, McIlwraith reported visits to see Barnum's Museum, Wood's Minstrels, Christie's Minstrels, Drayton's Parlor Opera, 'Old Grizzly Adams' California Menagerie,' 'Anderson, the Wizard of the North,' and a venture to 'the 'Melodian,' an indifferent place of amusement on Broadway.' After one such outing to the Bowery Theater for a variety show of pantomimes, feats of strength, animals acts, and the like in summer 1859, McIlwraith remarked: 'Thought the entertainment passable but audience not at all select.'[109] Getting to these performances took McIlwraith through some of mid-nineteenth-century New York's seedier parts, like the Five Points district. These neighbourhoods seem to have fazed him little, occasioning only an odd remark about their peculiar nature. 'Spent a short time in a singing tavern in Chatham St[reet],' he wrote of one evening in July 1859, 'a pretty rough sort of place.' McIlwraith's travels in New York included all parts, 'rough' and 'respectable'; both those (to borrow mid-century writer Matthew Hale Smith's terms) in 'sunshine' and in 'shadow.'[110] In all of this, his sampling of intellectual culture and popular entertainment in the metropolis mirrored the liminality he experienced in other aspects of his life. If he felt marginalized participating in high culture, he also felt out of place in the plebian haunts of the city.

His patronage of these many institutions allowed him to pursue a range of interests remarkable in their breadth. During a fairly typical month while working in Dundas, for example, McIlwraith checked out *Hogg's Instructor* and other books and attended the reading rooms of the local Mechanics' Institute; drew up the constitution and bylaws for his debating club and was an eager participant in its weekly debates; attended lectures on poetry, astronomy, and 'The Days of John Knox' at this debating club, the Dundas Town Hall, and the Hamilton YMCA; and imbibed a variety of sermons.[111]

McIlwraith pursued respectable cultivation in other ways too. He attended church services nearly every week, and often twice on Sundays. A Free Church Presbyterian, he was primarily attracted to that denomination, but he also attended services in a variety of other churches: Established and Associated Presbyterian, Episcopal, Methodist, and Universalist churches.[112] He also enjoyed singing, both as a listener and as a participant. He reported taking formal singing classes in these years to learn how to 'sight sing' and strengthen his voice. This was sometimes done in private or with a few friends. In May 1858, for example, he recorded hosting his Gartshore workmate McGarva in his boardinghouse room to sing 'Scotch songs with might and main.'[113] The more public face of this activity was evident in his participation in a number of different choirs and 'singing associations.' His efforts to improve in this art were aided by his enrolment in Mr Steves's singing class while in Dundas and in classes in singing and sight-reading at the National Musical Institute in New York City.[114]

Andrew McIlwraith's involvement in the Dundas Mechanics' Debating Club (DMDC) illustrates perhaps most clearly his commitment to the culture of self-improvement. He first received an invitation to attend 'a debating club composed of Foundry workmen' a short time after starting work at Gartshore's in March 1858. He made his 'maiden speech' on the question 'whether had war or intemperance caused the greatest misery to the human race' in mid-April.[115] Inside the old Dundas engine house members of the DMDC weekly considered such wide-ranging topics as 'Should Military Spirit Be Encouraged among Young Canadian Men?' 'Whether Geology or Astronomy Furnished the Best Evidence of Supreme Being,' and 'Whether Is Physiognomy or Phrenology the Surest Means of Testing Character.' In addition to frequent debates on contemporary questions, club members presented essays to the membership, followed by critical discussions. Essays delivered included such diverse titles as 'Daniel Webster,' 'Commerce,' 'Imagination,' and 'On Goldsmith.' Political economy was addressed in two long-running debates – 'Would Federal Union Be Advantageous to the British Provinces in America' and 'Whether an Increase of Duties in Imported Manufactures Would Benefit Canada' – during

McIlwraith's first four-month stint with the club. McIlwraith's entries about the DMDC provide a rare glimpse into the associational world of self-improvement of the nineteenth-century craftsworker.[116] And they show us how societies fostered liberal deliberative democracy through public discourse that was often beyond the control (if not the gaze) of local political elites.[117]

Less formal but equally fervent were Andrew's private improvement activities. He spent hours, feet on the fender, free reading in the comfort of his lodgings. McIlwraith was a voracious reader, but not an undiscriminating one. He supplemented his work-related reading with explorations of a wide range of treatises on history, natural history, literature, poetry, political economy, and a variety of other subjects, from the practical to the inspirational. He shared his brother Thomas's interest in ornithology, for example, and he read widely in biography, religious works, and novels of the higher order. Among the books he purchased or borrowed were Irving's *Life of Washington*, *Astoria*, and *Sketch Book*, Bunyan's *Pilgrim's Progress*, Cummings's *Evidences of Christianity*, and Hogg's *Instructions*, along with Southey's *The Doctor*, Stowe's *Sunny Memories*, and Bulwer's *Lady of Lyons*.[118] To this he added local and international newspapers and journals, often including mailed-in copies of the Ayrshire papers.[119]

In these years, Andrew McIlwraith cultivated himself, on the outside and on the inside. Although his work placed him in or near dirty workshops, he seems to have taken care to attire himself respectably. 'Had a stroll down to Grand St. and bought a pair of gaiters in the evening,' he noted in August 1860. 'I went and bought me a coat and pantaloons,' he noted two months later. The self-improved craftsworker provided an exterior view; cultivated performance encompassed personal appearance, dress, carriage, speech and demeanour.

McIlwraith's cultivation of his masculine self also included spending time in the company of male friends, sometimes in the various activities outlined above, sometimes with drink. An evening in Girvan with his friend Hugh Dickie was spent partly having a 'horn' with a Mr Drynan and, some time later, a 'pie and glass of toddy' with a 'club of Girvan young men.'[120] Similarly, on a trip from Hamilton to Greenfield, Andrew, brother Thomas, and Peter Auld ('a teamster, wanting of one foot') spent 'a little time in the village, horning in the tavern.' Lunch on a hunting ramble with his brother Thomas included bread, cheese, and beer. After a day spent hunting in April 1859 around Dundas, McIlwraith nonchalantly reported calling at the foundry at which he was recently employed and proceeded to 'ha[ve] some beers with Turnbull.'

Male sociability for Andrew often orbited around game-playing: back-gammon,[121] draughts,[122] and euchre.[123] Chess, however, appears to have occupied his attention most. His Sarnia workmate Jameson appears to have been his first chess partner. 'Played chess in the evening and got quite interested in it,' he noted in early January 1857. Jameson carefully tutored him through that winter, first playing without his Queen, and, as McIlwraith improved, without his Castle and then with a full set. Using his diary as an account book, McIlwraith faithfully recorded the result of each match, happily recording his first victory over Jameson in early February 1857. He practised against Jameson and the Mackenzie brothers through the rest of that winter. When unemployment pushed him back to Hamilton later that year he applied the experience thus gained to train up Jack Stewart, forgoing the use of his own Queen until Stewart could compete on more equal footing.[124]

Andrew exercised regularly, apparently sharing the Victorian middle-class view that true health relied on a judicious balance of mental *and* physical exertion. He was an enthusiastic walker. While in Hamilton and Dundas, he engaged in regular weekend perambulations around the Dundas Valley, between Hamilton, the Half-Way House (near Copetown), Webster's Falls, and Dundas, a total distance of about fifteen miles.[125] In New York, though the sights and sounds of his walking environment were strangely different from those in Dundas and Hamilton, McIlwraith continued a rigorous regimen of walking. He ventured out walking four days of the week on average, in all seasons, often over long distances. Most often, his walks included tours up Broadway, down the Bowery, and sometimes to the Battery district, a route that would have taken him through the most vibrant parts of mid-nineteenth-century New York City. On occasion, he took his pedestrian routine farther afield, as on September 16, 1860: 'Started early and took the Peekskill m[o]rning boat. Landed at Haverstraw and had a fine ramble and scramble to the top of the "High Turn," a high rocky peak, the culmination of a serrated range of hills overlooking the village and the Hudson River and surrounding country.'[126]

Explorations of the natural environment occupied many of these perambulations, and his interests there were wide-ranging. Like his brother, birding was a common objective of many of Andrew's excursions. He frequently joined Thomas 'with guns a-piece' in search of new specimens.[127] McIlwraith faithfully recorded the spoils of these gunning expeditions to his diary – robins, bluebirds, scarlet tanagers, red-winged starlings, and many more. Hours after the hunt were spent preparing these specimens for display in his brother's collection or applying his drawing skills to creating a sketch record of his prey.[128] At other times gathering botanical specimens was the point of his wanderings. He was especially pleased with his harvest of 'two fine plants of Twin-cap lilies about 2 miles out the 4th line by Sarnia.[129] Lengthy and sometimes arduous walks through the countryside, often with gun in hand, helped McIlwraith add a dimension of vigour to his masculine self.[130]

Perhaps in an effort to claim a field of naturalist enquiry distinct from his brother, Andrew developed an interest in lepidoptery. During the summer, much of his energy was directed towards butterflies. He made frequent expeditions for new specimens, carefully recording his noteworthy catches in his diary. When the time was available, whole days were devoted to this activity. During the work week he took advantage of the late summer sun to wander, butterfly net in hand, into the woods by his workplace once the workday was over. After the sun had gone down he spent hours fashioning wood and glass display cases in which to display his growing collection in a fashion similar to his brothers' bird museum. Put together, Andrew McIlwraith's self-educational activities aimed to expand his mental culture, to construct a well-rounded man capable of meeting the responsibilities of modern masculine citizenship and liberal individualism.

More of a Man

For Andrew McIlwraith, self-improvement was purposed to resolve his own personal crisis of masculinity. This was an ultimately resolvable crisis, rooted as it was in the traditional liminality of the journeyman, that typically insecure period between apprenticeship and independence. At work, what qualified as independence was undergoing considerable redefinition in this period. Traditionally, a male craftsworker understood himself (and was recognized by others) to have 'made it' once he was able to set himself up in his own small shop, perhaps with the aid of his saved journeyman's wages. But the endpoint that McIlwraith and many other British and North American craftsworkers were working toward had become considerably more open-ended by the 1850s. Early industrialization opened up to craftsworkers a range of possibilities for independence. Small mastership remained many young craftsworkers' goal and hope, but one might now also find a similar level of security and manhood as a junior partner in a manufacturing concern or even in a more or less permanent and elevated position as a superintendent or foreman in a medium or large manufactory. As McIlwraith's flirtation with lithography illustrates the melting of rigid lines of division between crafts during this period (especially in North America), it was also becoming more common for craftsworkers to try to leverage their apprenticed skills into independence in related trades. However, for some tradesmen, clear-cut independence at work was never achieved. Among them, 'manliness' had to be redefined around their work identities as permanent wage earners within the workforce of larger industrial operations. This crisis was more commonly felt at the core of the Western industrial world – in large urban centres – rather than on its periphery. McIlwraith's stay in New York could well have impressed upon him the spectre of life as a permanent wage labourer; that prospect may have motivated him to leave. In New York City (and in no other location), Andrew McIlwraith joined a Patternmakers' Association and had seemingly impersonal relationships with employers and foremen. That contrasted with things in Hamilton and Dundas, where he gathered with foremen and supervisors in a variety of other social situations. His solicitations for work, too, appear more personal and mutual, as with his obtainment of employment directly through a personal meeting with Gartshore, orchestrated by a friend. On the industrial periphery of Canada West,[131] McIlwraith appears to have interacted more with his various foremen, supervisors, and employers as 'craftsworkers' than as 'boss' and 'worker.'

A number of historians have identified the increasingly common prospect of lifetime wage earning as precipitating a more fundamental 'crisis of masculinity' among British and North American craftsworkers in the mid-Victorian period, causing such craftsworkers to re-centre understandings of craftsworker manhood to their involvements in unions, participation in heavily masculine shop-floor cultures of control, and through a variety of other avenues.[132] But one must also remember that while early industrialization ate away at some crafts, making traditional markers of craftsworker manhood harder to achieve, it simultaneously expanded traditional work regimes in others and even created some new crafts, thereby expanding opportunity for many. As McIlwraith's transatlantic search for work as a patternmaker clearly demonstrates, early industrialization also expanded the geographic distance craftsworkers had to travel from the homes of their youth and apprenticeship to the locations where they might finally 'make it' as a man. Compounding these changing avenues to craftsworker manhood were the periodic ups and downs of the developing capitalist economy. As McIlwraith looked longingly towards achieving his manly independence, the economic morass of the later 1850s undoubtedly weighed heavily on both mind and heart.

Beyond work, mid-Victorian craftsworkers like McIlwraith also defined the achievement of masculine independence as the fulfilment of personal goals. To be 'manly' meant also to be mature, and in these years, the most apparent sign of maturity was the status that came with being a household head. For most 'middling' men, this required marriage. Manliness, in short, was not consummated for men until they had gained a place in society as lords of their own manors, complete with wife, property, and, expectedly, progeny.

For McIlwraith and his contemporaries, marriage was a natural condition. Family life could not proceed without it. Conjugal love could not begin without the prospect of marriage. The self-improving craftsworker clearly understood that marriage was the linchpin, in many respects, to private morality and a symbol of achieving adulthood and the new status that it conveyed. The sanctity of marriage was an assumed value; it became a topic of public debate only when it was called into question by the actions of some local transgressor: when men sought the fruits of conjugal bliss before marriage or after marriage with women who were not their wives. Cases of elopement, for example, achieved considerable notoriety in the Victorian era, and newspapers provided titillating details of the couples' illicit liaisons and flight. Such accounts were tinged with moral outrage. 'Our readers in Galt and vicinity will regret to learn that Dr. Carrier, formerly resident here, has ... eloped with one of his patients,' the Galt-based *Dumfries Reformer* reported in December 1859. The elopement seemed exceptionally despicable given its particular circumstances: '[T]he Doctor [had] a wife and four children, whom he was supposed to be devoted to, as men should be.'[133] A symbol of achievement, marriage was not something considered lightly. But the importance accorded to marriage also had meaning for those who had yet to accomplish it. Across industrializing North America, most journeymen craftsworkers were single and had yet to establish their own households and, therefore, had yet to carve themselves a place in society as mature, adult men.[134]

Journeymen craftsworkers' 'crisis of masculinity' was exacerbated for many by the changes wrought by early industrialization, but was a traditional feature of the liminal space between apprenticeship and masterly independence. The ultimate resolution of this crisis, of course, was some form of success at work. Without reliable work, the acquisition of real property was unlikely. Furthermore, without reliable work, marriage and children must be delayed, often indefinitely.

For Andrew McIlwraith, this type of masculinity crisis was real. The years 1857–61 constituted a period of 'in betweenness' that were marked by his desire to become established emotionally, if only he could find work steady enough to allow him to do so. Andrew's diaries reveal some efforts to engage the attentions of young women. Mary Young appears in his diary while he lived in Sarnia. In spring 1857, he and friend James Mackenzie paid a number of visits to the garden at Springbank where she resided. Of a chance meeting at the circus in early June he comments, 'saw Miss Young looking charming.' After losing his position at the Sarnia GWR office he paid one last visit to Springbank, were she presented him with a moss rose. His last night of sleep in Sarnia was troubled: 'Dreamed of being singing "Will ye no come back again" to Mary Young and was wakened in the middle of it.'[135] Later on, attendance at Mr Mair's church singing group while living and working in Dundas also facilitated interaction with other young women. This most commonly involved escorting a young woman home after singing practice, but notably after one practice McIlwraith recorded having 'trysted Miss Geary' to accompany him to his debating club's soirée at the end of 1858.[136] In New York City, Andrew developed affection for a Miss Marshall, the sister of a shopmate. Not long after he met her, she was married to another man. Andrew seems to have been disappointed by this, and only with seeming difficulty did he record her new name (Mrs Abel) in his diary.[137]

Most of all, however, it is apparent throughout that he was in love with Mary Goldie, a young woman from Ayr, Canada West, a town in Waterloo County ten miles from Galt. It is uncertain, but the two were likely introduced by mutual friends or parishioners in Hamilton while each of them were in town visiting, though the diaries also suggest an association between their two families rooted back in Scotland. It took very little time, apparently, for them to realize their mutual affection. As early as August 1857, McIlwraith felt '[s]trongly in the belief that Mary Goldie will make the best wife for me of anybody I know.' In the few reports given about their visits, it was clear that she felt the same way. Soon, the frequency of·their visits increased and included respectable activities like churchgoing and country walks. They exchanged affections through love letters and in other ways: '[I] put some rhymes together about my Mary,' McIlwraith wrote of one evening's activity in May 1858. Still, his want of independent and secure employment kept them separated and held their relationship to a formal and preliminary courtship. After one of their visits in Hamilton in May 1858, McIlwraith confessed that he would 'like well to pop the question but feel that I have not confidence enough to open my mind freely yet,' a feeling that lingered for some time. Days later the same subject was still on his mind: 'Feeling kind of cripitty crappity on the subject of Mary[. I] blame myself for not being more of a man.'[138]

McIlwraith's move to New York separated them further. Undaunted, Andrew and Mary wrote to one another regularly (about once per month) during the year and a half during which he was away, and in this time no other really serious love interest altered his feelings towards her. Greater distance did, however, make letter writing more difficult for Andrew. '[W]rote some to Mary Goldie but [it] did not please me,' he noted in early October, 1860.[139] McIlwraith's feelings for Mary made his stay in New York City seem frustratingly long, and no doubt had much to do with his desire to return to Canada West. These feelings were central to his personal sense of crisis as he passed from one stage of the life cycle to the next and an important element in his broader sense of liminality.

Andrew McIlwraith's journey had a happy ending. In November 1860, he accepted an offer from John Goldie Jr (Mary's brother) to be bookkeeper at the Dumfries Mills (later Goldie and McCulloch Foundry) in Galt, a position he held until 1872.[140] Thomas heard of the opening and likely lobbied for his brother. Though bookkeeping was outside of Andrew's training and background, the job supplied him with a steady, salaried, and unexpectedly permanent position with a reputable employer in an industry about which he knew a great deal. McIlwraith did not report his new salary level to his diary, but it was apparently sizeable enough to afford him some comfort and stability. From the time of his return until the end of his diary in early 1862, no suggestion is made of dissatisfaction with his work; no consideration is mentioned of any further travel.[141]

Moreover, stable, remunerative employment enabled McIlwraith to address other goals in his life. Of course, he continued his pursuit of respectability once in Galt. There, he joined the local Mechanics' Institute and became a regular book borrower and debater in the association's debating club. His diary entries in these months betray a confident and purposeful man, content with his potential for a place in society. More significantly, perhaps, McIlwraith established his own household. He began to look at houses with a view towards purchasing in September 1861, and by February 1862 he had succeeded in becoming a household head, occupying a rented 'house on the hill.' Property, yet another fundamental pillar of liberal individualism, was thus closer at hand. McIlwraith made the move to formal home ownership in a few years time. But for now, as Catherine Wilson has shown, tenancy served as a 'workable temporary relationship' on the road to the creation of a free and independent person.'[142] In the following weeks, Andrew was preoccupied with furnishing his new domicile respectably and could report proudly in early April: 'Parlour looking very neat.' On 19 January 1862, he noted: 'M[ary] consented to come with me to Galt as my wife in March.'[143] At last, he resolved his own youthful crisis of masculinity in a way consistent with legions of craftsworkers before him. And he avoided the prospect of lifetime wage earning, which was throwing many of his craft colleagues in more central parts of the industrial world into a more profound crisis of masculinity.

By 1862, Andrew McIlwraith had crossed the divide between youth and independence – at work, as a married man, in his sense of 'self' and in his place as a recognized, if not leading, citizen of a busy city in Ontario's industrial belt. Along the way, he used his diaries as a pacifier and a tool. The McIlwraith diaries offer a new view into the life of the young male craftsworker in mid-nineteenth-century Canada West. Above all, they expose the centrality of self-improvement as an established and recognized route towards manhood. For Andrew McIlwraith, diaries helped him create a new man, a self-possessed liberal individual. Entry by entry, they were his running score card, a record that the right steps were being taken and a source of daily comfort that, during an extended period of uncertainty, a better future was slowly being willed into existence.

NOTES

1 The Diary of Andrew McIlwraith 1857–1862, Grace Schmidt Room, Kitchener Public Library, Kitchener, Ontario [typescript]. Originals are in the possession of Thomas McIlwraith, Professor Emeritus, Department of Geography, University of Toronto at Mississauga.
2 Lawrence Stone, 'The Revival of the Narrative: Reflections on a New Old History,' Past and Present 85, no. 1 (1979): 3–24.

3 Andrew's gravestone in Galt dates his birth as February 18, 1831 and his diary entry for February 14, 1858 claims that day as his twenty-eighth birthday. Apparently even Andrew was uncertain. Family records show that he was baptized on March 6, 1831. Thanks to Tom McIlwraith, Mississauga, for pointing this out.

4 The fact that Andrew's older brother Thomas received some education in Newton-on-Ayr and that his younger brother William was listed as a 'scholar' on the 1851 census at the age of seventeen while living with his parents suggests a level of affluence uncharacteristic of 'working-class' families in this time period. HS, February 2, 1903; General Record Office (Britain), 1851 Census, St Quivox District, Newton, Ayr, Scotland, 612/00002/00-021.

5 Thomas McIlwraith (1824–1903) was a pioneer in Canadian ornithology and author of the landmark 1886 treatise Birds of Ontario and several other important articles on the subject. He was a key figure in the development of avian biology as a scientific subject in Victorian Canada. See Henry James Morgan, ed., The Canadian Men and Women of the Time (Toronto: William Briggs, 1898), 741; Dictionary of Hamilton Biography I (Hamilton: Dictionary of Hamilton Biography, 1981), 132; Dictionary of Canadian Biography (hereafter DCB) (Toronto: University of Toronto Press, 1994), 12:646–7. See also Christopher Irmscher, 'Writing by Victorian Naturalists,' in Coral Ann Howells and Eva-Marie Kroller, eds., The Cambridge History of Canadian Literature (Cambridge: Cambridge University Press, 2009), 162–5.

6 'American Letter,' Ayrshire Times, August 29, 1860; 1851 Census, St Quivox District.

7 See Craig Heron, 'Factory Workers,' in Paul Craven, ed., Labouring Lives: Work and Workers in Nineteenth Century Ontario (Toronto: University of Toronto Press, 1995), 479–594; Douglas McCalla, 'Railways and the Development of Canada West, 1850–1870,' in Allan Greer and Ian Radforth, eds., Colonial Leviathan: State Formation in Mid-Nineteenth-Century Canada (Toronto: University of Toronto Press, 1992), 192–229; Peter Baskerville, 'Americans in Britain's Backyard: The Railway Era in Upper Canada, 1850–1880,' Business History Review 55, no. 3 (Autumn 1981): 314–36.

8 The call for historians to consider the liberal social order as fundamental to Canadian history was first significantly elaborated in Ian McKay, 'The Liberal Order Framework: A Prospectus for a Reconnaissance of Canadian History,' Canadian Historical Review 81, no. 4 (December 2000): 617–45. Major works in this genre include Jeffrey McNairn, A Capacity to Judge: Public Opinion and Deliberative Democracy in Upper Canada, 1791–1854 (Toronto: University of Toronto Press, 2000); Catherine Anne Wilson, Tenants in Time: Family Strategies, Land and Liberalism in Upper Canada, 1799–

1871 (Montreal and Kingston: McGill-Queen's University Press, 2008);
Daniel Samson, *The Spirit of Industry and Improvement: Liberal Government
and Rural-Industrial Society, Nova Scotia, 1790–1862* (Montreal and Kingston:
McGill-Queen's University Press, 2008); and Darren Ferry, *Uniting in Meas-
ures of Common Good: The Construction of Liberal Identities in Central Canada*
(Montreal and Kingston: McGill-Queen's University Press, 2008).

 9 Major works include John Burnett, *Useful Toil: Autobiographies of Work-
ing People from the 1820s to the 1920s* (London: Allen Lane, 1974); *Destiny
Obscure: Autobiographies of Childhood, Education and Family from the 1820s
to the 1920s* (London: Allen Lane, 1982); Mary Jo Maynes, *Taking the Hard
Road: Life Course in French and German Workers' Autobiographies in the Era
of Industrialization* (Chapel Hill: University of North Carolina Press, 1995);
Erin McLaughlin-Jenkins, 'Common Knowledge: The Victorian Working
Class and the Low Road to Science, 1870–1900' (PhD dissertation, York
University, 2001); David Vincent, *Bread, Knowledge and Freedom: A Study of
Nineteenth-Century Working Class Autobiography* (London: Europa Publica-
tions, 1981); Mark Traugott, *The French Worker: Autobiographies from the
Early Industrial Era* (Berkeley: University of California Press, 1993).

10 Burnett, *Useful Toil*; Martin Hewitt, 'Diary, Autobiography and the Practice
of Life History,' in David Amigoni, ed., *Life Writing and Victorian Culture*
(Aldershot: Ashgate, 2006). Burnett suggests that the more spontaneous
daily-entry diary format is less self-selective than autobiographical writing. Hewitt warns, however, that while diaries might be more spontaneous, they are still 'a potentially complex form of life writing that need to
be approached on its own terms' and considered in its own right for its
author's purposes. Other forms of spontaneous writing have also received
scrutiny. For example, the use of personal letters in nineteenth-century
Canada is considered in E. Jane Errington, 'Webs of Affection and Obligation: Glimpse into Families and Nineteenth Century TransAtlantic Communities,' *Journal of the Canadian Historical Association* 19, no. 1 (2008): 1–26.

11 Robert B. Kristofferson, *Craft Capitalism: Craftsworkers and Industrializa-
tion in Hamilton, Ontario, 1840–1872* (Toronto: University of Toronto Press,
2007), 89–90. See also E.J. Hobsbawm, 'The Tramping Artisan,' *Economic
History Review* 3 (1951): 299–320; Patricia Cooper, *Once a Cigarmaker*
(Urbana: University of Illinois Press, 1987); R.A. Leeson, *Travelling Brothers*
(London: Granada, 1980); Eric H. Monkkonen, *Walking to Work: Tramps in
America* (Lincoln: University of Nebraska Press, 1984); David Bensman, *The
Practice of Solidarity: American Hat Finishers* (Chicago: University of Illinois
Press, 1985); H.R. Southall, 'The Tramping Artisan Revisited: Labour

Mobility and Economic Distress in Early Victorian England,' *Economic History Review* 44 (1991): 272–96; Peter Bischoff, 'Another Perspective on Labour Migrations: The International Iron Molder's Union's Influence on Mobility as Seen through Their Journals, 1860s to 1930s' (unpublished paper), and Bischoff, 'D'un atelier de moulage a un autre: les migrations des mouldeurs originaires des Forges du Saint-Maurice et segmentation du marche du travail nord-americain, 1851–1884,' *Labour/ Le Travail* 40 (Fall 1997): 21–74.

12 Andrew Hassam, *Sailing to Australia: Shipboard Diaries by Nineteenth-Century British Emigrants* (Manchester: Manchester University Press, 1994), 4, 77. As Peter Bishop writes of travel narratives, 'the route is known beforehand. It is already mythic, already a narrative *before* the journey is undertaken. The journey merely activates and actualizes the route and the map.' Peter Bishop, *The Myth of Shangri-La: Tibet, Travel-Writing and the Western Creation of Sacred Landscape* (London: Athlone, 1989).

13 Hewitt, 'Diary, Autobiography and the Practice of Life History,' 26; Kristofferson, *Craft Capitalism*, ch. 6.

14 Thomas Augst, *The Clerk's Tale: Young Men and Moral Life in Nineteenth-Century America* (Chicago: University of Chicago Press, 2003), 22–3.

15 Ibid., 44.

16 Diary for 1858, Preface. Very likely from John Foster, *Essays: in a series of letters, on the following subjects: I. On a man's writing memoirs of himself. II. On decision of character. III. On the application of the epithet romantic. IV. On some of the causes by which evangelical religion has been rendered less acceptable to persons of cultivated taste* (London: Longman, 1805).

17 Diary for 1858, January 7.

18 See Gregory S. Kealey, *Toronto Workers Respond to Industrial Capitalism, 1867–1892* (Toronto: University of Toronto Press, 1980); Bryan D. Palmer, *A Culture in Conflict: Skilled Workers and Industrial Capitalism in Hamilton, Ontario, 1860–1914* (Montreal: McGill-Queen's University Press, 1979) and *Working Class Experience: Rethinking the History of Canadian Labour, 1800–1991* (Toronto: McClelland and Stewart, 1992). See Christina Burr, *Spreading the Light: Work and Labour Reform in Late Nineteenth Century Toronto* (Toronto: University of Toronto Press, 1999), for a recent account built upon this view.

19 See for example Gary J. Kornblith, 'The Artisanal Response to Capitalist Transformation,' *Journal of the Early Republic* 10 (Fall 1990): 315–21; Richard Stott, 'Artisans and Capitalist Development,' in Paul A. Gilje, ed., *Capitalism in the Early American Republic* (Madison, WI: Madison House, 1997).

20 Kristofferson, 'Craftsworkers and Canada's First Industrial Revolution: Reassessing the Context,' *Journal of the Canadian Historical Association* (2005): 101–38.

21 Kristofferson, 'A Culture in Continuity: Master-Man Mutuality in Hamilton, Ontario during Early Industrialization,' *Histoire Sociale / Social History* 39, no. 78 (November 2006): 425–50.

22 Kristofferson, *Craft Capitalism*, esp. ch. 6.

23 For examples, see Cynthia Cockburn, *Brothers: Male Dominance and Technical Change* (London: Pluto Press, 1983); Cooper, *Once A Cigar Maker*; Ava Baron, 'Questions of Gender: Deskilling and Demasculinization in the U.S. Printing industry, 1830–1915,' *Gender and History* 1, no. 1 (Summer 1989): 178–99; and 'An "Other" Side to Gender Antagonism at Work: Men, Boys and the Remasculinization of Printer's Work, 1830–1920,' in Ava Baron, ed., *Work Engendered* (Ithaca, NY: Cornell University Press, 1991). For a Canadian example see Burr, *Spreading the Light*.

24 Kristofferson, *Craft Capitalism*, 78, 112, 138, and ch. 6.

25 The dates of McIlwraith's employment were: Badger and Company Architectural Iron Works (April 19–November 7, 1859): Dunkin's Machine Shop [under William Barry] (November 15, 1859–February 11, 1860), and Badger's [again] (February 27–October 31, 1860). On the GWR, see Paul Craven, 'Labour and Management on the Great Western Railway,' in Craven, ed. *Labouring Lives*, 335–411.

26 Diane Drummond, 'Building a Locomotive: Skill and the Work Force in Crewe Locomotive Works, 1843–1914,' *Journal of Transport History* (1987): 6–7. Thanks to Ken Cruikshank, Department of History, McMaster University, for this reference.

27 Richard B. Stott, *Workers in the Metropolis: Class, Ethnicity, and Youth in Antebellum New York City* (Ithaca, NY: Cornell University Press, 1990), 46.

28 'America Letter,' *Ayrshire Times*, August 29, 1860.

29 Kristofferson, *Craft Capitalism*, 48–52. See also Kealey, *Toronto Workers*, 28–9, 64–82; W. Craig Heron, 'Working Class Hamilton, 1895–1930' (PhD diss., Dalhousie University, 1981), 127 and 'Factory Workers,' 502-3.

30 Diary for 1857, February 28, February 20, March 18, May 22, July 16 ; Diary for 1858, January 25, March 9, April 22; Diary for 1859, April 23, April 27, November 21, 22, 29, December 1, 6, 19; Diary for 1860, January 5, 21, February 6, 23.

31 Diary for 1860, June 13, 14; Diary for 1859, August 15.

32 'America Letter,' *Ayrshire Times*, 29 August 1860.

33 Diary for 1860, February 24; Diary for 1857, March 7; Diary for 1859, September 5; Diary for 1860, June 26, 27.

34 'America Letter,' *Ayrshire Times*, August 29, 1860; 1851 Census, St Quivox
   District, Newton, Ayr, Scotland, and Diary for 1858, March 14.
35 For the very limited information available on craftsworker wage rates in
   mid-nineteenth-century Canada West see Kristofferson, *Craft Capitalism*,
   83, especially Table 3.4 and fn18.
36 See McIlwraith Accounts, 1857: April 13 ($30), May 11 ($40), and June 15
   ($12), Appendix 3.
37 See 'Memoranda,' December 1857; 'Accounts,' December 1858. Appendix
   3. In late January 1858, McIlwraith agreed to do some draughting work
   for his brother Thomas, who was, at that time, director of the Hamilton
   Gas Works. Andrew did the work with the promise to himself that 'I won't
   take pay for it' but later relented, taking $10.00 for the work, presumably
   because he really needed it. Diary for 1858, January 18.
38 This figure was compiled from the McIlwraith Accounts by adding all
   income reported from Gartshore during these two periods and dividing by
   the number of weeks employed and based on a six-day week. Appendix 3.
39 'America Letter,' *Ayrshire Times*, August 29, 1860.
40 Iver Bernstein, *The New York City Draft Riots: Their Significance for American
   Society and Politics in the Age of the Civil War* (New York: Oxford University
   Press, 1991), 168. Richard Stott has determined that moulders and machinists in New York City shops took in $10–12 a week in New York metal
   shops in the 1850s. Working a six-day week, then, these workers' daily
   wages would have ranged between $1.66 and $2.00 a day. Stott, *Workers in
   the Metropolis*, 46.
41 'America Letter,' *Ayrshire Times*, August 29, 1860.
42 Ibid.
43 Bernstein, *Draft Riots*, ch. 3, and Sean Wilentz, *Chants Democratic: New
   York City and the Rise of the American Working Class, 1788–1850* (New York:
   Oxford University Press, 1984), ch. 10 and Epilogue.
44 Stott, *Workers in the Metropolis*, 155–61.
45 Diary for 1860, June 21, September 6. McIlwraith's attitude toward the
   election of pro-labour Democrat Fernando Wood in December 1859 is
   revealing: 'Think it is a pity the atrocious rascal has gained the day.' Diary
   for 1859, December 7.
46 'America Letter,' *Ayrshire Times*, August 29, 1860.
47 Peter Bischoff, 'Another Perspective'; Kristofferson, *Craft Capitalism*, 64.
48 Michael B. Katz, *The People of Hamilton, Canada West: Family and Class in a
   Mid-Nineteenth-Century City* (Cambridge, MA: Harvard University Press,
   1975), ch. 3.
49 Sarnia, Hamilton, Dundas, New York City, and Galt. McIlwraith boarded

at a private home in Sarnia, his brother's house in Hamilton, and at
boarding houses in Dundas and in New York City. In the latter location,
he lived at various places: Franklin Hotel, Brooklyn (April 16–24, 1859);
Paddy Logue's Hotel (April 24–30, 1859); Mrs Smith's (April 30–November
25, 1859); Mrs Furey's (November 25–December 1, 1859); Mrs Skinner's
(December 1, 1859–February 25, 1860); [returned to] Mrs Smith's (February
25–November 2, 1860).

50 Diary for 1859, April 24; Diary for 1860, August 17. 'Woke up this morn-
ing and found two Irishmen occupying beds in the same room with me,'
McIlwraith entered on November 27, 1859. Three days later he moved out.
Diary for 1859, November 27, December 1.

51 Craven, 'Labour and Management on the Great Western Railway,' in
Craven, ed., *Labouring Lives*, 335–411; Kristofferson, *Craft Capitalism*, esp.
105–8.

52 Diary for 1858, January 7, March 1.

53 Diary for 1858, June 4.

54 Diary for 1859, March 12.

55 Diary for 1859, November 10; Diary for 1860, February 14, 25. For examples of his contact making with foundry foremen see Diary for 1859,
November 12, 14; Diary for 1860, February 13, 22.

56 Diary for 1857, July 18; Diary for 1859, April 8, 13.

57 Diary for 1859, July 16. Other Dundas acquaintances included Hector
Mackenzie, Connel, A. Glen, Gowry, Thomas McDonald, the 'two young
McNeils,' Murdock, Murray, and William Simm. See Diary for 1859, April
29, May 13, July 8, 22, October 17, November 15; Diary for 1860, June 5,
July 18.

58 Diary for 1860, March 3, May 4, 5, 14, June 13, 20, July 16.

59 See above, note 9.

60 Françoise Noel, *Family Life and Sociability in Upper and Lower Canada, 1780–
1870* (Montreal and Kingston: McGill-Queen's University Press, 2003), 192,
255, 259, 272–5.

61 'America Letter,' *Ayrshire Times*, August 29, 1860.

62 The literature on the burgeoning culture of craftsworker self-improvement
in mid-Victorian Great Britain includes Richard Daniel Altick, *The English
Common Reader: A Social History of the Mass Reading Public, 1800–1900*, 2nd
ed. (Columbus: Ohio State University Press, 1998); Burnett, *Useful Toil*;
Burnett, *Destiny Obscure*; McLaughlin-Jenkins, 'Common Knowledge';
Vincent, *Bread, Knowledge and Freedom*.

63 McLaughlin-Jenkins, 'Common Knowledge,' esp. ch. 2; Anne Secord,
'Corresponding Interests: Artisans and Gentlemen in Nineteenth Century

Natural History,' *British Journal for the History of Science* 27 (1994): 383–408, 'Science in the Pub: Artisan Botanists in Early Nineteenth Century Lancashire,' *History of Science* 32 (1994): 269–315. On Mechanics' Institutes, see John Laurent, 'Science, Society and Politics in Late Nineteenth Century England: A Further Look at Mechanics' Institutes,' *Social Studies of Science* 14, no. 4 (1984): 585–619; Steven Shapin and Barry Barnes, 'Science, Nature and Control: Interpreting Mechanics' Institutes,' *Social Studies of Science* 7, no. 1 (1977): 31–74.

64 Jonathan Rose, *The Intellectual Life of the British Working Classes* (New Haven, CT: Yale University Press, 2001), 16, 59; Michael Shortland, ed., *Hugh Miller's Memoir: From Stonemason to Geologist* (Edinburgh: Edinburgh University Press, 1995), 9–11.

65 Rose, *Intellectual Life*, 9. Anne Secord has argued that, even in branches of weaving that had experienced deskilling, autodidactic pursuits were still actively pursued 'to restore a sense of status and respectability.' Secord, 'Science in the Pub,' 292. Weaver naturalists Joseph Gutteridge and William Heaton are discussed in Vincent, *Bread, Knowledge and Freedom*, 169–74.

66 Thomas F. McIlwraith, 'Thomas McIlwraith,' *DCB* (Toronto: University of Toronto Press, 1994), 13:646–7; 'Miss Jane Newton McIlwraith' in Henry J. Morgan, *The Canadian Men and Women of Their Time: A Handbook of Canadian Biography* (Toronto: W. Briggs, 1898), 740–1; and Thomas McIlwraith, *The Birds of Ontario: Being a List of Birds Observed in the Province* (Hamilton: A. Lawson and Company, 1886).

67 Vincent, *Bread, Knowledge and Freedom*, 169.

68 John C. Griffiths, 'William Murdock' in *Oxford Dictionary of National Biography* (Oxford: Oxford University Press, 2004), http://www.oxforddnb.com (accessed May 14, 2007).

69 Miller, *My Schools and Schoolmaster; or, the Story of My Education. An Autobiography* [1854] (Boston: Gould and Lincoln, 1857). See Diary for 1857, April 8, 11.

70 Hugh Miller, *The Testimony of the Rocks; or, Geology in Its Bearings on the Two Theologies, Natural and Revealed* (Edinburgh: T. Constable and Co., 1857); Diary for 1857, May 16.

71 Diary for 1857, November 2; Diary for 1858, December 6.

72 Diary for 1858, June 8, September 18, 21, October 7, 22.

73 Diary for 1858, January 20, August 29; Diary for 1859, March 14.

74 Diary for 1859, February 19, 25.

75 'John Goldie, Gardener and Botanist,' *Botanical Gazette* 11, no. 10 (October 1886): 272–4. See also Secord, 'Science in the Pub.'

76 John C. Weaver, 'The Location of Manufacturing Enterprises: The Case of Hamilton's Attraction of Foundries, 1830–1890,' in Richard A. Jarrell and Arnold E. Roos, eds., *Critical Issues in the History of Canadian Science, Technology and Medicine.* (Thornhill, ON: HSTC, 1983), 197–217.

77 Robert Gray, *The Labour Aristocracy in Victorian Edinburgh* (London: Oxford, 1976), 91.

78 Dirk Hoerder, 'Labour Migrants Views of "America,"' *Renaissance and Modern Studies* 35 (1992); Horst Rossler, 'The Dream of Independence: The "America" of England's North Staffordshire Potters,' in Hoerder and Rossler, eds., *Distant Magnets: Expectations and Realities in the Immigrant Experience, 1840–1930* (New York: Holmes and Meir, 1993); Hoerder, 'German Immigrant Workers' View of "America" in the 1880s,' in Marianne Debouzy, ed., *The Shadow of the Statue of Liberty: Immigrants, Workers and Citizens in the American Republic, 1880–1920* (Urbana: University of Illinois Press, 1992), 17–33; Charlotte Erickson, *Invisible Immigrants: The Adaptation of English and Scottish Immigrants in Nineteenth Century America* (London: Adam and Charles Black, 1976); and *Leaving England: Essays on British Emigration in the Nineteenth Century* (Ithaca, NY: Cornell University Press, 1994). For a more detailed discussion of this point see Kristofferson, *Craft Capitalism*, 65–8.

79 Marjory Harper, *Adventurers and Exiles: The Great Scottish Exodus* (London: Profile, 2004), 71 and ch. 3; Lucille H. Campey, *An Unstoppable Force: The Scottish Exodus to Canada* (Toronto: Natural Heritage Books, 2008), esp. chs. 1–3 and 6; Allan MacInnes, Harper and Linda Fryer, *Scotland and the Americas, c. 1650–1939: A Documentary Source Book* (Edinburgh: Lothian, 2002), Introduction; J.M. Bumsted, *The People's Clearance: Highland Immigration to British North America* (Winnipeg: University of Manitoba Press, 1982); and Malcolm Gray, 'Scottish Immigration: The Social Impact of Agrarian Change in the Rural Lowlands, 1775–1875,' *Perspectives in American History* 7 (1973): 95–174.

80 See Kristofferson, *Craft Capitalism*, esp. chs. 2, 6.

81 Diary for 1857, October 7.

82 Linda Colley, *Britons: Forging the Nation, 1707–1837* (New Haven, CT: Yale University Press, 1992), 6.

83 Sir Charles W. Dilkes, *The British Empire* (London, 1899), 9, cited in Philip Buckner and R. Douglas Francis, 'Introduction,' in Buckner and Francis, eds., *Rediscovering the British World* (Calgary: University of Calgary Press, 2005), 13.

84 Buckner and Francis, 'Introduction,' 15.

85 Kristofferson, *Craft Capitalism*, 166–7.

86 Diary for 1858, February 10, 15, 16, 19, 20, 22, 23, March 1, 2.

87 Kristofferson, *Craft Capitalism*, 160, 165–6.

88 Diary for 1857, March 27.

89 Diary for 1858, February 2, August 27, October 27.

90 Diary for 1857, January 13, 14.

91 Diary for 1858, January 6; Diary for 1861, February 23, September 11.

92 Diary for 1858, September 4.

93 Diary for 1857, October 12; Diary for 1858, January 4, 6, October 2; Diary for 1859, March 17; Diary for 1860, July 6.

94 Diary for 1857, December 14; Diary for 1858, January 7; June 22, 23; Diary for 1859, April 8.

95 Diary for 1857, December 15; Diary for 1858, April 3, August 16; Diary for 1860, May 5, 14.

96 Diary for 1857, October 13. David H.J. Schenck, *Directory of the Lithographic Printers of Scotland: 1820–1870: Their Locations, Periods, and a Guide to Artistic Lithographic Printers* (Edinburgh: Edinburgh Bibliographical Society; New Castle, DE: Oak Knoll Press, 1999); National Library of Scotland, Scottish Book Trade Index, http://www.nls.uk/catalogues/resources/sbti/index.html.

97 Diary for 1859, October 25, 28, November 1, 9, December 23; Diary for 1860, January 15, 20, 26, April 28, May 31.

98 Diary for 1859, October 28, November 1, 9, December 23; Diary for 1860, January 10, October 15.

99 He was, to borrow Charles Rosenberg's taxonomy of Victorian manliness, both 'Masculine Achiever' and 'Christian Gentleman.' A man of action in dogged pursuit of economic success, he was also one whose manliness derived from elevated self-control, compassion, sympathy for others, and benevolence. He sought to be a master of both his external environment and his inner world. See Charles Rosenberg, 'Sexuality, Class and Role in Nineteenth-Century America,' *American Quarterly* 25, no. 2 (May 1973): 131–53; Patricia Dirks, 'Reinventing Christian Masculinity and Fatherhood: The Canadian Protestant Experience, 1900–1920,' in Nancy Christie, ed., *Households of Faith: Family, Gender and Community in Canada, 1760–1969* (Montreal and Kingston: McGill-Queen's University Press, 2002), 290–316.

100 Kristofferson, *Craft Capitalism*, 168–9.

101 See NcNairn, *Capacity to Judge,* ch. 2; Ferry, *Uniting in Measures of Common Good*, esp. chs. 1 and 2; and Albert Schrauwers, *'Union Is Strength': W.L. Mackenzie, The Children of Peace, and the Emergence of Joint Stock Democracy in Upper Canada* (Toronto: University of Toronto Press, 2009).

102 Mechanic's Institute Issue Book and Members 1836–1852, Catalogue of
     the Ayr Mechanic's Library, Mechanics Institute Records, Scottish and
     Local History Library, Carnegie Library, Ayr, Scotland.
103 A selection of examples includes Diary for 1857, April 3; Diary for 1858,
     March 2, November 30; Diary for 1859, June 2.
104 A selection of examples includes Diary for 1858, May 31, October 4,
     November 22; Diary for 1859, January 24, March 14, 21. See Kristofferson,
     Craft Capitalism, 190–3.
105 A selection of examples includes Diary for 1859, May 26, December 3;
     Diary for 1860, May 28, June 30.
106 A selection of examples includes Diary for 1859, April 18, 19, 26, May 2,
     13, 16, 18, 23, July 29, August 19, September 21.
107 John F. Kasson, *Rudeness and Civility: Manners in Nineteenth-Century Urban
     America* (New York: Hill and Wang, 1990), 216.
108 Diary for 1859, April 26, 29, May 16, October 15; Diary for 1860, October
     29; Diary for 1859, November 22; Diary for 1859, September 21, Septem-
     ber 10.
109 Diary for 1859, August 19. See also Diary for 1859, April 18, May 20, May
     23, August 26, December 15; Diary for 1860, July 7, September 8.
110 Matthew Hale Smith, *Sunshine and Shadow in New York* (Hartford: J. Burr
     and Company, 1869). He was not uncritical, however. Virtually always,
     low theatre received a poor review. See, for example, Diary for 1859,
     May 23: 'Accompanied Chas [Mackenzie] in the evening to the perform-
     ances by Christie's Minstrals [*sic*]. House overcrowded and had to stand
     all the time. Entertainment but mediocre.' On the social geography of
     nineteenth-century New York City, see George C. Foster, *New York by Gas-
     Light: With Here and There a Streak of Sunshine* (New York: DeWitt and Dav-
     enport, 1850); David Scobey, 'Anatomy of the Promenade: The Politics of
     Bourgeois Sociability in Nineteenth-Century New York,' *Social History* 17,
     no. 2 (May 1992): 203–28.
111 See Diary for 1859, January entries.
112 See Diary for 1858, January 3; Diary for 1859, May 6, 15, 22, June 5, July
     17, August 14, September 4, October 23, December 25; Diary for 1860,
     January 1, 29, February 5, September 2. He must have been familiar with
     the doctrinal differences that separated the various Protestant churches at
     which he worshipped. At the time his diaries were penned, Presbyterians
     themselves were broken into multiple sects, held together only by the
     even more significant theological differences that separated them from
     other Christian churches. It is curious, then, that Andrew's diaries are
     virtually silent on religious doctrine. McIlwraith must have been a man

of some considerable religious faith, but he did not confide such thoughts
to his diary: there is not a lot of God in them. For Andrew, church was,
foremost, a source of intellectual nourishment. On the landscape of nineteenth-century Protestant churches in North America, see John Webster
Grant, *A Profusion of Spires: Religion in Nineteenth-Century Ontario* (Toronto: University of Toronto Press, 1988); Martin Marty, *Righteous Empire: The
Protestant Experience in America* (New York: Harper and Row, 1977).

113 Diary for 1858, May 4.

114 Examples include Diary for 1858, March 9, July 3, November 17, 18, 24,
December 1; Diary for 1859, January 30, July 28, August 2.

115 Diary for 1858, March 18, April 1.

116 Diary for 1858, April 12, May 7, 21, 28, June 18, November 26, December
3, 17. See also Kristofferson, *Craft Capitalism*, 197–9.

117 Who really controlled MI discourse is a matter of debate among historians. Ferry allows for working-class agency within a process of cultural
negotiation, but he ultimately sees the 'middle-class' directors of Mechanics' Institutes as attempting to 'engineer consent to a "liberal" social
order' in an effort of social control aimed at producing a 'commonsense
worldview' among its working-class elements. McNairn too argues
that Mechanics' Institutes and other voluntary associations were 'often
fostered by the locally prominent, who were eager to bolster their claims
to enlightened, benevolent leadership.' See Ferry, *United in Measures of
Common Good*, 6, and McNairn, *Capacity to Judge*, 92.

118 He reported reading Jaeger's *American Insects* in May 1859 and Wilson's
American Ornithology in November 1859. Other books listed in the diary
are *Zaidee*; *Alton Locke*; Herbert's *The Wager of Battle*; *The Club Book*; poems
of Crabbe, Heber, and Pollock; Crabbe, *Tales of the Hall*; Aiton's *Lays of the
Scottish Cavaliers*; Bremer's *Tales*; *The Virginians*; *A Life for a Life*.

119 See Diary for 1857, February 15, May 5.

120 Diary for 1857, September 9, 18; Diary for 1858, July 15; Diary for 1959,
April 9.

121 Diary for 1859, March 19, 24, 31.

122 Diary for 1857, April 25; Diary for 1858, March 27, April 5.

123 Diary for 1860, August 15.

124 See Diary for 1857, January 6, 10, 19, February 2, March 18, 25, April
27; Diary for 1858, January 5, February 1, September 20. These informal
moments afford us a fleeting glimpse of Andrew's personality, which,
despite six years of daily diary entries, is hard to capture. Formal and
governed by a sense of propriety, he also had a round sense of humour.
He seems to have been slow to anger, was very sociable, and was fond of

visiting, especially with old acquaintances. He is perhaps best described
by things he was not: spontaneous, hilarious, gregarious, or effusive. His
demeanour was calm and steady, neither dour nor excitable.

125 See Diary for 1858, January 2, March 14. See James C. Whorton, *Crusaders
     for Fitness: The History of American Health Reformers* (Princeton, NJ: Prin-
     ceton University Press, 1982). McIlwraith's diary refers to his diet only
     rarely.

126 Diary for 1860, September 16. See also Diary for 1859, May 12, 22, July 16.

127 Diary for 1857, May 9; Diary for 1858, January 15.

128 Diary for 1857, April 13, 15, 16, 17, 24, May 22, June 1, 6, December 25;
     Diary for 1858, January 1, 2, 13, February 6, November 8; Diary for 1859,
     March 16; Diary for 1860, November 6.

129 Diary for 1857, July 13.

130 For a discussion of outdoor physicality and masculine identity in late-
     nineteenth-century Ontario see Mark Moss, *Manliness and Militarism:
     Educating Young Boys in Ontario for War* (Toronto: University of Toronto
     Press, 2001), 15–17.

131 Kristofferson, *Craft Capitalism*, 244–6.

132 See note 23.

133 'Dr Carrier Elopes!' [Galt] *Dumfries Reformer*, December 21, 1859. See
     Peter Ward, *Courtship, Love, and Marriage in Nineteenth-Century English
     Canada* (Montreal and Kingston: McGill-Queen's University Press, 1990).

134 Andrew C. Holman, *A Sense of Their Duty: Middle-Class Formation in Vic-
     torian Ontario Towns* (Kingston and Montreal: McGill-Queen's University
     Press, 2000), ch. 6.

135 Diary for 1857, April 19, June 12, 27, July 10, 14, 18, 20.

136 Diary for 1858, December 30, 9, 15; Diary for 1859, February 4, 11, 13.

137 Diary for 1859, August 18, September 6, December 1, 8; Diary for 1860,
     January 2, February 20, April 23, May 3, 18, 21.

138 Diary for 1857, August 4; Diary for 1858, May 4, 2, 3. See also Diary for
     1858, March 15; Diary for 1859, May 30, June 22, July 11, September 8,
     October 24, November 23; Diary for 1860, February 25, May 7, October 16,
     29.

139 Diary for 1860, October 6.

140 Once McIlwraith commenced this position, he appears to have split his
     time between bookkeeping, patternmaking, and various other foundry
     activities.

141 Diary for 1860, October 17, 24. Census of Canada 1871, Galt, Ontario,
     31-d. Goldie and McCulloch (now Babcock and Wilcox) was the largest
     factory in Galt and among the most productive foundries in Canada.

Although Mary was the brother of John Goldie Jr, the foundry's co-owner, McIlwraith likely had more than his romantic involvement with her to recommend him. His former Dundas employer, Gartshore, had long-standing business ties with James Crombie, previous owner of the Dumfries Mills. On the founder and the company, see Theresa Falkner, 'The Goldie Mill' [typescript], Doris Lewis Rare Book Room, University of Waterloo; Falkner, 'The Goldie Saga,' Local History Collection, Ayr Public Library (Ont.); 'John Goldie Jr,' *Waterloo Historical Society* 15 (1927): 387; Katherine Hebblewaite, *Babcock and Wilcox: A History, 1844–1977* (Cambridge, ON: Babcock and Wilcox Canada, 1987), chs. 1, 2.

142 Wilson, *Tenants in Time*, 220; Diary for 1861, September 2; Diary for 1862, February 7.

143 Diary for 1862, April 12, January 19; 'Galt,' *Lovell's Province of Ontario Directory* (Montreal: John Lovell, 1871), 382.

'Is the Working Man Better Off in America than in Britain?' Andrew McIlwraith's Letter to the *Ayrshire Times*, August 29, 1860

September 22, 1860 was a fairly typical New York City day for Andrew McIlwraith: full time in the shop followed by an evening at the theatre. But a short line in that day's diary entry also opens a window to a better understanding of the mid-nineteenth-century world of McIlwraith the craftsman: 'Had Ayrshire Times from home with my letter published.' McIlwraith's very modest reference was to his 'American Letter' published in the *Ayrshire Times* on August 29, 1860. The letter provides copious details on wage rates, working conditions, living standards, industrial development, and a variety of other subjects. It also exposes the obvious epistolary abilities of a man whose surviving corpus of writing is otherwise in the form of short, often terse, daily diary entries. Though more expository than the diary entries, perhaps, the letter is no less candid. The letter encapsulates a good many of the themes we wish to emphasize in our analysis; it is a good place to start for anyone wishing to make sense of Andrew McIlwraith's mid-century world. Our thanks go to Tom Barclay at the Carnegie Library in Ayr, Scotland for locating this letter.

American Letter. British Workmen in the United States.
(To the Editor of the Ayrshire Times).

New York, August 1860.

Dear 'Times,' – Having had by a recent mail the pleasure of welcoming your advent into the ranks of cheap journalism, it has occurred to me that a few lines addressed to the working men of your 'ain auld toun,' from one who has erst been of them, as to how times go with their representatives in the Empire City of America, might

not be unacceptable. The writer, it may be premised, speaks with the
authority of some eighteen months' experience in knocking out life
as a mechanic here; and the aim of the letter is, by plain statement of
fact, to contribute a little to the solution of the question, 'Is the working man better off in America than in Britain?' – that question so often
asked in vague uncertainty by the would-be wanderer, living all wea-
rily at home; and, let us add here, not unfrequently discussed among
those who have been and put it to the test of trial.

It need scarcely be said that the great money panic of '57 bore hard
upon the mechanic in New York, and all over America. It is yet told in
this city that worthy men, willing to work, were seen going from door
to door begging for bread. Such stern fact must qualify the romance of
the 'New and happy land;' and that such hard times can possibly come
must be put in the balance in weighing the comparative merits of the
old country and the new. The country is young and strong, however,
and rallies bravely from the dire tribulation, and now for two seasons
work moves along more merrily. While winter lasts comparative scarcity of employment is always to be expected. In the spring and summer
months – beginning perhaps as early as April, – whatever building or
other work is to do is pushed on diligently, with as many hands as can
be set advantageously to it. Among employers the practice of keeping about an average number of men in constant employment is less
looked to than in the old country. The great facilities for advertising
here lets a master, if in want of hands, have his want known the length
and breadth of the city any morning, through the cheap daily newspaper; while the workman in want of a job has the same opportunity
of gaining information, and looks to the paper and its advertisements
as a sort of trade thermometer, indicating how things stand. In small
establishments it is more especially the practice, whenever a job comes
in, to advertise for hands, have as many as possible on it, to be discharged immediately on its being finished. On this point the voice of
the old country men in America, we will venture to say, is unanimous,
that the greater fluctuations in trade and diminished chance of constant
employment bring the rate of wages at the year's end less than if we
were to take the common rate, paid as an average.

And now, to come to that very important consideration, the wages.
Our rate here is always so many shillings per day, the shilling York
being equal to sixpence farthing sterling, one eighth of a dollar, American coinage. For convenience, any sums requiring mention here shall
be translated into equivalent English.

Among foundry workers, with which department the writer is most familiar, about the highest wage paid to a good man is two dollars per day, equal to 50s per week. In individual cases a higher rate may be earned, but only by such as possess superior ability and experience in some particular department, thus making their services proportionally the more valuable. A lower rate, graduating according to merit, as low as 40s per week, or lower, is common. In the height of the busy season it has lately not been uncommon for first-class moulders, having a run of work on a uniform description of article, to make what counts as one and a-half days' work each day, thus earning a wage amounting to £3 5s per week, which is a fair wage, and may compensate in a few weeks for a good many days' idleness; but such work is very hard and killing in the hot weather. For turners and fitters (machinists is the term in use here) the ordinary wage with which to start new beginners in some of the best shops is, for a good turner, 37s 6d per week, and for fitters a fraction less. There being no organized protection among the workmen from the employment of illegitimate hands, the only test is efficiency in the work, and such as are found wanting are very summarily dealt with.

In the different branches of the building trade wages I may state as rating about the same as I have now mentioned. Carpenters, masons, bricklayers, painters, plumbers, &c., whose work is especially subject to the fluctuations of the season, can get the 50s easily while the season lasts. In large well-conducted establishments the wages are paid, punctually, weekly.

Among the contingencies to which workmen may be subjected, however, one of not very rare occurrence is to find employers on a small scale, in the eagerness of competition and speculation, contracting to do work at too low a rate, and unable to pay wages for it. Carpenter work seems to be subject to this evil in particular. All round in the suburbs of the city wooden frame houses, got up with more or less taste and finish according to the circumstances of the proprietor, are the ordinary description of building, and give employment to a large force of house carpenters. Such a circumstance as one of these being all finished, and then taking fire and being burnt to the ground, is not by any means rare; nor is it uncommon to hear it stated among knowing folks that this is done by the workmen in revenge for not being paid their wages.

In regard to the manner in which work is carried on here I may speak, having heard aforetime of how hard the Americans worked. I have only to remark that a man who has learnt his trade well at home can find himself at no loss here. In thorough excellence of finished work – such as requires long experience, and an observant mind, to know and produce – it is not uncommon to hear our Glasgow men, for instance, jeer at the Americans' shortcomings, and trace their want of success in ocean steamer competition, in great measure, to imperfect workmanship. It is already well known in the old country that appliances for the shortening of human labour are much in vogue here. Familiar to the eye in the city and all over the country are factory signs, such as – 'Sash, Blind, and Door Factory,' 'Moulding and Planing Mill,' 'Scroll Sawing,' 'Chair Factory,' &c., – all these operations and descriptions of work being done with very little hand labour. And let me mention among the factories one which amused me not a little on first noticing it, 'Kindling Wood Factory' – as instancing the peculiar genius of the people for invention in little conveniences, is that that inventive genius has declared that the time-honoured work of necessity (splitting sticks to kindle the fire) need no longer be the work of paterfamilias in his shirt on a cold morning, or his assistants making much ado about their inevitable fate; and so the operation is now in New York a flourishing trade, with various designs of machines going through it wholesale – yea! even the binding up and tieing of split wood into bundles, to be retailed at two cents each, is, it is said, now accomplished by machinery.

As a matter of interest to foundry men and builders, mention may here be made of the importance which the manufacture of iron-work for buildings has attained to in this city. Springing up as it has done in the course of a few years, it is now a most prosperous, if not the leading, branch of the iron founding – several large establishments being exclusively engaged in it, and the work being recognized as a distinct department for pattern-maker, moulder, and fitter. Independent of the very extensive application of cast-iron in combination with the ordinary building materials, in the form of heavy columns, posts, girders, lintels, &c., for basement story, the erecting of entire stove fronts in cast-iron is now quite a success, and in great favour. On Broadway, where elegance and attractiveness in street architecture may be supposed to make its grandest efforts, the cast-iron front competes, and seems to be in equal request with, the stone and marble – the cost, it is said, being also about equal. The style of architecture for which it is most eminently suited is entirely in accordance with popular taste in America – lightness and profusion of ornament. Imitations of all styles of ornamental masonry will be seen repeated in the cast-iron: fluted and carved columns, and curved window arches, giving abundant light to the front, are the prevailing types. The city trade is now receiving an active impulse from the widening of a number of streets in the old business part of the city, and erecting of new and improved buildings in the room of those torn down. Extensive orders are also executed in New York for other parts of the Union, principally South and West, beyond to Cuba and South America, and, can you believe it, even into British territory. Halifax, Nova Scotia, has this season been a customer to Brother Jonathan for this one of his 'notions,' to the extent of a very considerable pile of almighty dollars. These buildings are generally fitted with shutters formed of a combination of iron rods and sheet-iron, rolling up like a blind. On the sidewalks a very successful patent has been introduced called the 'Patent Vault Lights,' where cast-iron plates are cast full of round holes, about two inches diameter, into which little bull's eye-glasses are fitted. The illumination of these in the evenings is one of the best features of Broadway lighted up.

While writing on the condition of the mechanic here, the competition to which he is subjected in his work by an overflowing population of Germans should not be overlooked. Accustomed to poverty in their own country, the lower walks and offices of society are largely monopolised by the needy German emigrant, and are to them comparative prosperity; so low even as the begging department – for the days which we have read about when there were no beggars in America have now, to all appearance, passed away. If we may believe some accounts, however, the profits of this business may not be so contemptible as the name, that is, when followed out in the proper systematic way. Respectable authorities here have assured me that it is the practice of some of these German beggars to keep boarding-houses, feeding their boarders on the fruits of their begging excursions! Be this as it may, it is true that large districts of the city and suburbs are peopled with Germans; that in the mechanical trades the perseverance and ingenuity of the German workman is acceptable in the labour market is also true; and in it their numbers and necessities tend to keep down the profits. The cordiality of feeling of the Anglo-Saxon towards the Dutchman, as he is contemptuously styled, is consequently not of the heartiest kind. In all trades it is common to hear the Dutchman complained of for working for whatever wage he can get, and being often only half taught or less, in the business he

professes to work at. Light, neat work, such as watchmaking, fancy
cabinetmaking, pianoforte-making, manufacture of sewing machines,
&c., seem best to suit his capabilities, and are the branches of trade
which suffer most. After all, however, let him have his due. He is a
quiet, inoffensive member of society generally, barring his taste for
music, and dancing, and drinking *lager beer* on Sunday, which may not
suit everybody's notions. Of his ingenuity in mechanical inventions,
instances might be multiplied did space only admit.

But the wages question is not finished in the mere mention of the
rates going – the expenses of living coming, of necessity, into the calculation before it is possible to strike a balance. As a convenient index
by which to form an idea on this subject, the rate of boarding may
be mentioned. In mechanics' boarding houses the common rates are
from three (12s 6d) to four (16s 8d) dollars per week. For a sum running between these two a man can be tolerably comfortable. Boarding
houses of this class, to be profitable to their proprietors, must have
perhaps a dozen or so of boarders who take meals at a common table,
and have their separate sleeping-rooms. For single young men a ready
calculation can thus be made. For married folk, keeping house, the
prospects are, we believe, not quite so favourable, in so far as it seems
to be the general impression that their expenses are higher in comparison with the rates of boarding than they are at home. Of the items
forming the principal cause of this, house rent must be considered the
chief – apartments for a single family in the ranks of artizans not being
had under 33s 4d to 50s sterling per month. Fuel and light are also
high-priced. These items got over, the general rate of provisions will
be in most items somewhat less than home prices.

American cookery and its effects upon health is a subject of which
much has been written by competent hands, and may not be entered
on here; but in dismissing this matter we may only repeat what has
already been granted for this country, that the labouring man of all
degrees has it in his power, and as a rule enjoys a higher style of living
than he does in Britain.

A few words on the health of the city. In tables of comparative mor-
tality I am not just now 'posted up,' as we say here, but they are so
easy of access as not to require repetition by me, my aim in writing not
being to compile book information, but to give a few notes on New
York, taken from a stand-point not usually occupied by book writers,
but which may be the more interesting to most of your readers. New
York, I believe, has been called the dirtiest city in the world, but I can

hardly think that 'the great commercial capital' of the 'model republic' can stand quite so low in sanitary matters. According to newspaper accounts, it is not for lack of disbursing public money enough that the city is not clean. After all, though, a visitor seeing only Broadway and the leading business and fashionable localities may not be struck with any shameful degree of filth. Passing beyond these, however, into regions inhabited by the poorer classes, in among interminable streets and avenues of dingy brick houses, where Mynheer and the 'bhoys of ould Ireland' prevail and flourish in all their glory – the muck, – and nearer the rivers and wharves on both sides of the island city, the lower seems to descend the sanitary condition. Here possibly the connoisseur in stinks may find variety and power, entitling New York to challenge comparison with Cologne, on the Rhine, and its thousand smells, or any of the most renowned emporiums. All along by the side walks of these alleys huge ungainly boxes are provided for the reception of ashes and sweepings from the houses. The consequences are that vegetable and animal matter in a state of putridity form a large proportion of their contents, and dainty scent bottles it may be presumed they make, more especially in the present broiling hot weather, when the thermometer is 98 in the shade. That the public health must suffer from such a state of affairs is palpable, and yet we don't hear of a great deal of epidemic sickness. If the evil could only be remedied – and time will, no doubt, bring about a better state of affairs – the city would be eminently salubrious. Even in spite of it, all people living here will tell you it is healthy. The breeze from the ocean, of which we have a little mostly all the time, makes the summer heat not quite so oppressive as it is more inland. The fever-and-ague of the western country is not much known.

And now our somewhat lengthy epistle must be brought to a conclusion. From personal observation I have spoken only of the city of New York. From all accounts that I can gather, the large Atlantic cities, New York in particular, as the largest, afford the best encouragement to the skilled workman. Going west money becomes scarce, and when you get employment, of which the chances are less than in the large city, most probably you have to be out of your money for lengthened periods, or receive orders for goods in part payment of wages. This seems to be the experience of many, who have tried it of late. That better times are in store for both East and West let us hope.

In these days of cheap locomotion, the Atlantic voyage is not a matter of great moment; and for a young man in the way of gathering information and experience, whether or not he should make up his mind to reside permanently in the States, a visit to this country is not by any means a preposterous undertaking, and cannot but be beneficial. To advise or encourage people having families to come here is a more delicate matter. It has already been remarked that advocates for both sides of the question can be met with here. That a man who is anxious to do well, however, can do better here than at home appears to be the verdict of those whose opinions are to be looked upon as most weighty. The dissatisfied are, in general, those who have been but a short time here, and have been disappointed in not finding matters quite as they expected, while those who have resolutely set themselves to make the best of things as they found them have invariably come out triumphant.

[The writer of the above served his apprenticeship in an engineering shop in Ayr, and had several years' experience of engineering work on the Clyde, which circumstances should enable him to make a pretty correct comparison of the position and advantages working men possess at home and in the United States. Most of his remarks apply to engineers, those connected with engineering, and out-door workmen, but he may in future communications be able to tell us how shoemakers, weavers, saddlers, tailors, bonnet-makers, &c., are situated. We will be glad to hear from him monthly. By folding his letter like a newspaper, open at the ends, and writing 'Press Copy' on the wrapper, the postage will be cheaper than if forwarded in the usual way. – Ed. *A.T.*]

Diary for 1857

Thursday, January 1, 1857.
At Hamilton on a visit. Made calls in company with Brother Thomas on Messrs Muir, Park St., Mr Sommerville and Mr Gordon. In the afternoon drove to Dundas in company with Mr Henry, the Messrs Muir, Jr etc. In the evening had a headache and went to bed at 7 o'clock.

Fri. Jan. 2.
Visited the station grounds in company with Mr Cant. Walked about town during the day. Drank tea in Mr Muir's residence in the evening. Received a letter from Mrs Logan. The after part of the night spent at the fireside with Thomas. Received from Mr Kerr, a pass for one trip west to London.

Sat. Jan. 3.
Took the night mail west at 1.30 in the morning, reached London about 6. Had breakfast in Robinson Hall.[1] Left London with stage at 9 a.m. Stage full. Weather snowing and blowing. Made acquaintance with Mr Pottinger in the coach after leaving Warwick. Reached Sarnia about 8 p.m. Night beautiful and clear. Received letter from Hugh Dickie date Dec. 11, 1856.

---

1 Robinson Hall Hotel was London's major stage terminus in the years before 1845. Though it burned in the 'Great Fire' of that year, the hotel was rebuilt and reopened in 1849 and soon came to be regarded as the town's most prominent hotel, even offering its customers, by 1857, the newest convenience: baths. See Michael Baker, ed., *Downtown London: Layers of Time* (London Regional Art and Historical Museums and London Regional Advisory Committee on Heritage, 1998), 94.

Sun. Jan. 4.
At church morning and evening and at Bible Class in the afternoon.
Had a walk in the woods with Hope Mackenzie and Jameson. Dined
and drank tea in Mackenzie's. Wrote to Thomas (brother) inclosing
views of Dunkeld from Robt Mackenzie.

Mon. Jan. 5.
Finished specifications of Smithy. Checking Bill of Timber for S.B. Way
Stations.[2] Day of election of councillors in Sarnia and great excitement.
Spent the evening writing to Mrs Logan.

Tues. Jan. 6.
Checking bill of timber for S.B. way stations. Had letter from Mrs
Hunter and Mr Bell, date Dec. 18. Election excitement at its height and
Clarke Curtis declared the victor over John Mackenzie by 1. Keen frost.
Despatched to-day's home letters to Mrs Logan. Took first lesson in
chess from Jameson.

Wed. Jan. 7.
Drawing plan of Platform Extension for S.B. Way Stations. The casting
vote which put Curtis in as councillor declared illegal and John Mackenzie declared victor.[3] Weather very cold and blowy. Visited A. Mac-

---

2 S.B. denotes the Sarnia Branch of the Great Western Railway. Chartered in 1845,
   the GWR connected much of the heartland of southern Ontario, running from the
   U.S. border at Niagara Falls to Toronto and westward to London and Windsor. Its
   engineering offices and shops were located in Hamilton. Operation of the line began
   in 1853, and for several decades it proved a rival to the Grand Trunk Railway in
   southern Ontario. The GWR and GTR amalgamated in 1882. C. Pelham Mulvany,
   'The Railways of the Past and Present,' *Toronto: Past and Present* (Toronto: W.E.
   Caiger, 1884), 59. The Sarnia Branch was completed in December 1858. Russell Riddell, 'Community Leadership in Sarnia: The Evolution of an Elite, 1830 to 1865' (MA
   thesis, University of Western Ontario, 1991); 'The Great Western Railway Open to
   Sarnia,' *HS*, December 30, 1858.
3 This, Sarnia's first municipal election as an incorporated town, was filled with controversy. Curtis and John Mackenzie vied for seats on the Town Council. They also
   represented rival political factions within the local Reform party, Curtis's led by Malcolm Cameron, one of the town's early elite, and the second composed of the Mackenzie family, seven brothers (Alexander, Robert, Hope, Charles, John, James, and
   Adam), who moved to Sarnia in the late 1840s and quickly challenged local politicos
   for supremacy in local and extra-local politics. The most accomplished brother
   was Alexander (1822–92), a veritable model for Samuel Smiles, who left Scotland
   in 1842 with nothing but his stonemason's tools and rose in Canada to become the
   Dominion's second Prime Minister (1873–8). See Riddell, 'Community Leadership';
   'Municipal Elections,' *SO*, January 8, 1857; *SO*, January 22, 1857.

kenzie in the evening and heard some election gossip. Hope Mackenzie and Cameron accusing each other of 'treating the electors.'[4]

Thurs. Jan. 8.

Thermometer 1 deg. above zero in the bedroom in the morning. Shaving with cold water rather a hard job. Finished plan and bill of timber for Platform extension. Spent the evening arranging and burning old letters. Subscribed for 6 months of Sarnia Observer.[5]

Fri. Jan. 9.

Ther. 14 deg. above zero. Drawing general plan of passenger platform. Had an evening walk and ½-hr skating down by the Indian Reserve.[6] Moon about full and a most lovely night. Spent evening amongst old letters.

4　Treating meant plying them with drink (or food), a not uncommon practice in colonial elections, but increasingly frowned upon by mid-century. Hope Mackenzie (1821–66), a carpenter by trade who came to Canada West from Scotland in 1843, operated a successful cabinetmaking business with three of his brothers. When all of the Centre Ward councillors were dismissed from office by a Crown inquiry into the Sarnia election in September, 1857, Hope was quickly elected mayor. He was elected to the United Canadas Legislature in 1860 and 1863. Malcolm Cameron (1808–76) was elected to the legislative assemblies of Upper Canada and the United Canadas (1836–42; 1857–63) and appointed to several cabinet posts (1842–57). The Queen's Printer for six years (1863–9), he was returned to an elected post as Member of Parliament in 1873. Born in Trois-Rivières, Lower Canada, Cameron died in office in Ottawa. See *The Macmillan Dictionary of Canadian Biography*, 3rd ed. (hereafter *Macmillan*) (Toronto: Macmillan, 1963), 106; Margaret Coleman, 'Cameron, Malcolm,' *Dictionary of Canadian Biography* (hereafter *DCB*) (Toronto: University of Toronto Press, 1972), 10:124–9; *Canadian Biographical Dictionary and Portrait Gallery of Eminent and Self-Made Men*, Ontario Volume (Chicago: American Biographical Publishing Company, 1880), 634.

5　The *Sarnia Observer* was the sole local newspaper in 1857. It was founded in 1853 by publisher John Raeside Gemmill (1808–91), a Reformer from Lanark recruited by Cameron to advance his cause. Gemmill was rewarded for his efforts with provincial appointments as Deputy Clerk of the Crown, Clerk of the County Court, and Registrar of the Surrogate Court. Riddell, 'Community Leadership,' 57, 78–80.

6　The Objibwa (or Chippewa) Reserve at Sarnia was established in 1826 when eighteen 'principal men' of the Chippewa Nation surrendered 2,200,000 acres in the Western District of Upper Canada to the British Crown, keeping four parcels of land as Reserves. Initially 10,280 acres, the Sarnia Reserve was reduced in July and August 1852, when 269 acres were ceded to the Town of Sarnia, and in 1854, when 24.5 acres were ceded to the GTR for a right of way. See Canada, *Indian Treaties and Surrenders from 1680 to 1902* (Ottawa: Brown Chamberlin, 1891) 1:65, 71, 176, 177, 193; Peter S. Schmalz, *The Ojibwa of Southern Ontario* (Toronto: University of Toronto Press, 1991), chs. 6, 7; Nicholas Plain, *The History of the Chippewas of Sarnia and the Sarnia Reserve* (Sarnia: Author, 1950).

Sat. Jan. 10.
Day snowing and not very cold. Finished drawing and made tracing
and bill of timber for passenger platform. Received letter from Thomas enclosing one from Mrs Hunter, date Dec. 18th. Played chess in the
evening and got quite interested in it.

Sun. Jan. 11.
At church in the morning. I heard Mr Walker preach from 1st Cor. 10th
and 31st.[7] Felt drowsy and lost most of it. Snow has been falling during
last night and now averages nearly a foot deep. In the afternoon walked
with Robt Mackenzie as far as the Perch Creek Bridge on the London
Road. Walked in from there in 1-¼ hrs. Very hard work.

Mon. Jan. 12.
Thermometer ½ deg. above zero in bedroom. Commenced on general
Plan of Tank House. Spent the evening writing to brother Bill.

Tues. Jan. 13.
Thermometer 14 deg. above zero. Drawing general Plan of Tank House.
In the evening, read treatise on building. Weather comparatively mild
and pleasant.

Wed. Jan. 14.
Thermometer 18 deg. above zero. Spent forenoon upon general plan
of Tank House. Afternoon upon plan of Bridge and Culvert over road
at Stn 76. In the evening finished letter to Bro. Bill. Wrote also to Bro.
Thomas. Received atlas of plates to treatise on 'Stonecutting.'

Thurs. Jan. 15.
Drawing plan of bridge at Stn 1177. Heard Geo. Brown, M.P.P. lecturing
in the Court House.[8] In the evening read treatise on Building.

---

7 Rev. David Walker came from the Presbytery of Orkney, Scotland, to take up a call
   from the Free Church Presbyterian church in Sarnia in 1855. He served there until his
   death in 1863. *The Home and Foreign Record of the Free Church of Scotland in 1855* (London: J. Nicol, 1855), 246; *The Home and Foreign Record of Canada Presbyterian Church*
   v.3–4 (Toronto: W.C. Chewett, 1864), 63.
8 George Brown (1818–80) was one of Victorian Canada's foremost journalists and
   statesmen. Born near Edinburgh, Scotland, he migrated to Toronto in 1843 and
   founded *The Banner*, a Toronto weekly, which became *The Globe* one year later. The
   most prominent voice of Reform in the Legislative Assembly of the United Canadas,
   he was elected as the member for Kent (1851), Lambton (1854), Toronto and North
   Oxford (1857), and South Oxford (1863). Though defeated in his Toronto riding in
   the election of 1861, Brown led Reformers in Canada West in support of the Confed-

Fri. Jan. 16.

Therm. 12 deg. above zero. Drawing plan of bridge and culvert at Stn 1177. In the evening played chess with John Mackenzie. Had a smart walk out the London Road by way of exercise in company with Messrs Jameson and Bellaris. Got myself weighed – weight 143 lbs.

Sat. Jan. 17.

Ther. 25 deg. above zero. At plan and bill of timber for bridge and culvert at Stn 1177. Spent the evening in the house of Mr Peffer's in company with Bellaris and Jameson.

Sun. Jan. 18.

Therm. 1 deg. below zero. Went to church in the morning in company with Jameson but found we were too late so had a walk through the woods to the shore of Lake Huron. Talked with a farmer who supposed that the ice might extend 20 miles out in the lake. Attended evening service. Mr Walker preached from Isaiah 55 and 1. Geo. Brown present.

Mon. Jan. 19.

Drawing plan of bridge and culvert Stn 1177. Read treatise on Building in the evening till 9 o'clock then played 2 games of chess which lasted till past 12. Last game stalemate, Jameson playing without his queen.

Tues. Jan. 20.

Therm. 12 above zero. At drawing and bill of iron for bridge at Stn 1177. Flocks of ducks frequent the river opposite Sarnia about this time. In the evening rather drowsy but tried to read some.

Wed. Jan. 21.

Therm. 15 deg. above zero. Making tracing of bridge, etc at Stn 1177. Mr Robb arrived from Hamilton. In the evening read till 9 o'clock and then played one game of chess with Jameson, he playing without his queen in which I checkmated him.

---

eration scheme, becoming a member of the 'Great Coalition' ministry led by John A. Macdonald, 1864–5. In Brown's last attempt at elected office (the federal election of 1873), he was defeated in the riding of South Ontario. He was appointed to the Senate in 1873. He died in Toronto from a bullet wound inflicted by a disgruntled ex-*Globe* employee. See J.M.S. Careless, *Brown of the Globe*, 2 vols. (Toronto: Macmillan, 1959); Careless, 'Brown, George,' *DCB* (Toronto: University of Toronto Press, 1972) 10:91–103; W. Stewart Wallace, 'Brown, George,' *Macmillan*, 85. For an account of Brown's speech, see *SO*, January 22, 1857.

Thurs. Jan. 22.
½ day at tracing of bridge and culvert at Stn 1177, ½ day at miscellaneous jobs. In the evening called on A. Mackenzie. Trial of the elections (validity of) in centre ward to-day at which Davis, the lawyer, accused the Mackenzies of conspiracy and A. Mc. called him a scoundrel.[9]

Fri. Jan. 23.
Extremely cold. At drawing of protection frame for piers of Brown Creek Bridge. In the evening attended a lecture in the Methodist Church on the Pleasures and Advantages of Scientific Research by T.C. Gregory which appeared to be well received.[10]

Sat. Jan. 24.
Made tracing and Bill of material for protecting branch piers B.C. Bridge. Commenced drawing of over-road bridge. Had Creighton from Plympton at tea. Played chess till near 12. Lost 2 games but won 1 from Jameson, he playing without his castle.

Sun. Jan. 25.
Heard Mr Walker preach in the morning. In the afternoon crossed over to Port Huron in company with Mr Robb and Jameson. Visited the spot where the railroad cutting was begun.[11] Heard Mr Shanks preach in the evening. Weather delightfully clear but keen cold.

Mon. Jan. 26.
At drawing of over-road bridge at Stn (Watford). In the evening cal-

---

9 In this first municipal election in Sarnia the results for Centre Ward were contested in an application to the court of Queen's Bench. While awaiting a ruling, however, the two opposing factions coalesced, each claiming the right to office and each with its own mayor, reeve, and councillors. See *SO*, January 8, 15, 22, 1857.

10 Thomas C. Gregory, Esq. was a resident engineer on the GWR at Sarnia and Windsor, and a man of science. He was a member of the Canadian Institute (1849–1914), a Toronto-based learned society for the advancement of science and industry and a donor to its natural history collections. See *The Canadian Journal: A Repertory of Industry, Science and Art* (Toronto: Maclear and Company, 1854), 2:147; *Canadian Journal of Industry, Science and Art* (Toronto: Lovell and Gibson, 1856), 1:407. His talk was promoted in the *Sarnia Observer* as 'The pleasure and benefits accruing from Scientific Research,' *SO*, January 22, 1857.

11 The cutting was the start of the GTR's standard gauge railroad line connecting Port Huron with Detroit, which was completed in 1859. With this line GTR intended to operate car ferries across the Detroit River, rivalling, perhaps, the GWR's car ferries at Detroit. George W. Hilton, *Great Lakes Car Ferries* (Davenport, IA: Montevallo Historical Press, 2003), 20.

culating tables for weights of iron. A change of weather today. In the evening, rain.

Tues. Jan. 27.
At drawing of bridge over road at Watford. In the evening engaged upon tables of the weight of Iron. Weather continues mild although slightly frosty in the evening. Troubled with a cough at present. Going to get oatmeal tea from Mrs Kent to cure it tonight.

Wed. Jan. 28.
At drawing and bill of material for Watford over-road bridge. In the evening employed upon tables of the weight of iron. Weather again frosty but very pleasant.

Thurs. Jan. 29.
Made tracing of drawing of Watford Bridge and bill of iron for it. Drank tea with Robt Mackenzie. Sarnia Observer of to-day contains a severe letter directed against that family.[12]

Fri. Jan. 30.
Made a second tracing of Watford Bridge. Weather continues very beautiful. Still troubled with cough.

Sat. Jan. 31.
At a third tracing of Watford Bridge. Likewise made some detail drawings of iron. Being still with bad cough was advised by Mr Kent not to study hard so spent the evening reading newspapers. Jameson and I practising the reading of speeches.

Sun. Feb. 1.
A cold stormy day. Kept within doors all day and took 3 pills which I found a sufficient dose. Slept part of the day. In the evening read a good sermon, Jameson joining me therein. Had a letter from Bro. Thomas speaking about beginning birdstuffing operations.

Mon. Feb. 2.
Mr Gregory left for Strathroy. At tracing No. 3 of Watford Bridge and some other little jobs but did not work hard and I found the stooping injured the chest and set the cough a-going. Left the office early and

---

12 This lengthy letter addresses the municipal election debacle earlier in the month and calls for local electors to remove the community from the 'thralldom of a junto who are determined to sacrifice the welfare and peace of a neighborhood upon the altar of personal ill-will and hissing malignancy.' See *SO*, January 29, 1857.

had a lovely evening walk out the Indian Road and back through the woods. Achieved my first victory over Jameson at chess playing with full pieces.

Tues. Feb. 3.
At drawing of general plan of Tank House. In the evening wrote to Mrs Logan. Weather appears to incline towards thaw in the evening.

Wed. Feb. 4.
At drawing of General plan of Tank and bills of timber for culverts at 1177. In the evening worked at the tables of the weight of iron. Thermometer this morning at 40 deg above zero.

Thurs. Feb. 5.
At drawing of general plan of Tank House. In the evening read treatise on Building. Weather very mild raining and thawing all day.

Fri. Feb. 6.
At drawing and Bill of material for Tank House. Got paid for January. In the evening calculated contents of tank. Weather still vary mild and thawing. Horrid soft walking. Played three games of chess, Jameson victor in two and A.M. in one.

Sat. Feb. 7.
Wet weather. Completed bill of tank. In the evening, went to the reading room which was this night open for the first time in Durand's Block.[13]

Sun. Feb. 8.
During the night the weather underwent a complete change. Saturday night the thermometer 54 deg above zero, Sunday morning 24°. At church in the forenoon and heard a stranger preach. Went to the Methodist in the afternoon. Drank tea and spent the evening at Mackenzie's.

Mon. Feb. 9.
At detailed drawing of watering apparatus. Spent the evening playing

---

13 The Mechanics' Institute had purchased for $2,000 a 'suitable site' on which to build a 'handsome building.' The Sarnia Mechanics' Institute was opened in 1853 to provide intellectual pursuits – reading, debating, instruction – for local young men with spare time. 'The Mechanics' Institute,' *SO*, February 19, 1857. See Oisin P. Rafferty, 'Apprenticeship's Legacy: The Social and Educational Goals of Technical Education in Ontario, 1860–1911' (PhD dissertation, McMaster University, 1995); Andrew C. Holman, *A Sense of Their Duty: Middle-Class Formation in Victorian Ontario Towns* (Montreal and Kingston: McGill-Queen's University Press, 2000), ch. 6.

chess with John Mackenzie. Two keenly contested games, in the first of which I was victor, and in the second he was.

Tues. Feb. 10.
At detailed drawing of watering apparatus. Bellairs, Jameson and I walked across the ice of the Bay round the point on to the shore of Lake Huron. Saw the Indians watching to spear fish through the ice. Very cold. In the evening wrote to Bro. Thomas.

Wed. Feb. 11.
At detailed plan of watering apparatus. Fine frosty weather. Had an hour's walk through the woods in the evening. Saw Mrs Robb. Wrote two sheets of note paper to Mrs Stewart.

Thurs. Feb. 12.
At detail plan of watering apparatus. In the evening wrote to Mrs Hunter and posted it with Mrs Stewart's. Called upon A. Mackenzie. Weather seems inclined to come thaw again. No sleighing since the thaw last week.

Fri. Feb. 13.
A most beautiful day. Clear and mild like a Spring day in the Old Country. Employed at detail of tank apparatus and tracing of Tank House. Called on Mr and Mrs Robb at Alexander's Boarding House in the evening.

Sat. Feb. 14.
Weather rainy and blustering. Commenced a new plan of Tank House to adapt it to pumping engines. Played chess in the evening with Jameson but got beaten.

Sun. Feb. 15.
Raining wet all day. Heard Mr Walker preach in the morning from Isaiah 55, 10 and 11. Spent the interval in Mackenzies. In evening heard Mr Walker preach from Psalm 73, v. 28. Read a sermon by Ryle upon Zeal.[14]

Mon. Feb. 16.
Still a dull wet day. At drawing of Tank House. In the evening attended the Reading Room. Read the 'Wreck of the Golden Mary' and accounts of the murder of Dr Burdell in New York.[15]

---

14 Likely John Charles Ryle, *Be Zealous* (Ipswich: Hunt and Son, 1852).
15 Charles Dickens, 'The Wreck of the Golden Mary,' *Household Words: A Weekly Journal*

Tues. Feb. 17.
At plan of Tank House. Attended meeting Of the Bible Society with [illeg] and heard some good speaking by the Rev. Mr Walker, Rev. Mr Rupel from Port Huron, the Hon. Malcolm Cameron, etc.[16] Weather very warm, Therm. in bedroom standing about 60 deg.

Wed. Feb. 18.
Marking tracing of Tank House Plan and commencing to plan a wooding shed to connect to it. Weather still wet but gets cold and freezes while it rains towards evening. Boys skating on the sidewalk. Spent the evening writing to Thos Anderson, Dumbarton.

Thurs. Feb. 19.
This morning the trees and everything outside coated with ice ¼ inch thick. Snowing most of the day. Working at wooding platform plan. Had letters from Mother and Christina acknowledging receipt of portraits. In the evening finished and posted Anderson's letter.

Fri. Feb. 20.
At plan of wooding platform. In the evening attended a meeting of the Mechanics Institute and witnessed a fierce dispute between Robt and A. Mackenzie. Played chess with John Mackenzie, one game stalemate.

Sat. Feb. 21.
A beautiful mild day. Employed upon plan of tank apparatus. Spent the evening in the reading room of the Mechanics Institute.

Sun. Feb. 22.
Weather still between freezing and thawing. Heard Mr Walker preach in the forenoon from John 21 c., 17 v. Visited Mr Peffers and had a short walk. Had Hope Mackenzie to tea. In the evening heard Mr Shank preach from 1 Cor. 10, v. 13. During the week past mails have always been late on account of bad roads.

(London: Bradbury and Evans, 1856). The murder of Dr Harvey Burdell by Emma Augusta Cunningham and subsequent trial were widely publicized events throughout North America. See Henry L. Clinton, *Celebrated Trials* (New York: Harper and Brothers, 1897); 'The Burdell Murder!' *SO*, March 5, 1857.

16 This meeting of the Sarnia Branch of the British and Foreign Bible Society was held at the Presbyterian Church. See *SO*, February 5, 1857. Like many local organizations, it was riven by divisions between new and old arrivals. See Riddell, 'Community Leadership,' 100.

Mon. Feb. 23.
Finished detail drawing of Tank Apparatus and at tracing and bill of timber for wooding platform. A beautiful day. Left the office at 4.30 and walked to Point Edward in company with Jameson across the ice which has begun to thaw. Spent some time skimming stones on the river. In the evening worked at tables for weight of iron.

Tues. Feb. 24.
This morning received notification from Bro. Thomas that on Fri. 20th inst. Mrs. McI. gave birth to a daughter.[17] Employed upon tracing of platform plan, bill of timber, etc. In the evening, wrote to congratulate Thomas and worked at tables for weight of iron.

Wed. Feb. 25.
At bill of material for platforms and calculating weight of iron in bridges. Brought some flower seed to send home and in the evening wrote to Mother. Attended Mr Vidal's lecture on Astronomy which was very good.[18] Had a trip to Port Huron to look for seeds. Tug steamer left here this morning for Detroit, the first attempt of the season.

Thurs. Feb. 26.
Calculating weight of iron in Komoka bridges and assisting with plan of Strathroy. In the evening attended meeting in the Congregational Church for the ordination to the Ministry of the Rev. Mr Shank. Heard a good speaker, Mr Wood from Brantford.[19]

---

17 Mary Duncan McIlwraith, the second of the eight children of Andrew's brother Thomas and Mary (Park) McIlwraith. See Thomas F. McIlwraith, 'McIlwraith, Thomas,' *DCB* (Toronto: University of Toronto Press, 1994), 13:646–7; Diary for 1858, February 15.

18 Alexander Vidal (1819–1906) was a provincial land surveyor, agent of the Bank of Upper Canada in Sarnia, and holder of several local offices. Born in England, he settled in Sarnia with his parents in 1835 and rose to become a prominent member of the town's old elite. An ardent temperance and social reformer and an ally of Cameron, he was appointed to the Legislative Council of the United Canadas (1863–7) and to the Senate of Canada in 1873, where he served until his death. See *Macmillan*, 771; Charlotte Vidal Nesbit, *Life and Letters of the Hon. Alexander Vidal, Senator* (Sarnia: Author, n.d.); 'Mechanics' Institute,' *SO*, February 19, 1857.

19 Rev. John Wood was pastor of the Congregational Church, Victoria Square, Brantford, Canada West/Ontario, 1853–74. See James Sutherland, *County of Brant Gazetteer and Directory for 1869–70* (Toronto: Hunter, Rose, 1870); *History of the County of Brant* (Toronto: Warner and Beers, 1883), 544.

Fri. Feb. 27.
Pretty keen frost today. Learned that the tug steamer before mentioned, could not make out her trip. Working at calculations of weight of iron in bridges. In the evening calculated tables for ditto and played chess being sadly beaten by Jameson.

Sat. Feb. 28.
Calculating weight of bridge iron. Day rather pleasant. Walked around the 4th concession and back through the woods which was wet nearly all the way. In the evening visited the reading room then came home and worked at table for iron.

Sun. Mar. 1.
Sacrament Sunday in Mr Walker's Church. Heard sermon morning and evening. A most tempestuous day. Snowing all day with strong gales of north wind. Spent the afternoon in Mackenzies. In the evening read aloud in company with Jameson, Ryle's sermons.

Mon. Mar. 2.
Thermometer in bedroom 10 deg. above zero. Morning bright and clear and very keen. Large masses of ice floating down the river and wharfs all surrounded with drift ice frozen hard. Winter back in full force. Engaged calculating bridge iron and some other little jobs. In the evening looking through old sketches.

Tues. Mar. 3.
A most uncomfortable cold morning. Had to shave while the water froze on the blade of the razor. Thermometer in the room at 9 deg. above zero. Still engaged upon calculating iron. In the evening visited the reading room.

Wed. Mar. 4.
Weather today beautifully clear and mild. Engaged calculating iron. Work in office appears to be getting slack. In the gloaming had a pretty long walk by a road beyond the London Road. In the evening read the Yellow Mask, a ghost story in Household Words.[20]

Thurs. Mar. 5.
Drawing details of gate hinges. Drank tea for the first this season by daylight. In the evening read Household Words. Weather mild.

---

20 'The Yellow Mask,' in *Household Words: A Weekly Journal* (London: Bradbury and Evans, 1850–9).

Fri. Mar. 6.
Finished details of gate hinges and commenced to plan of engine stable showing pipes for water supply, etc. Great quantities of ice coming down the river. Received paper from I.B. Dumbarton with colored
plates of the Queen, etc. Played two games of chess in the evening with
Jameson and gained one each.

Sat. Mar. 7.
At drawing of engine House pipes. A fine day. Left the office early and
walked into the woods to the farthest extremity of Wellington which is
being cleared. Found an old patlander with an axe.[21] Jameson borrowed
axe and felled a tree and I helped to chop it up. Went to reading room in
the evening. Received letter from Thomas enclosing [illeg] bill.

Sun. Mar. 8.
A fine morning. Walked a short way into the woods and thought I
heard a Blue-bird. Heard Gauld from Moore preach in Free Church in
to forenoon.[22] In the interval had a walk with Jameson, McVicar and
McCuig. In the evening heard Mr Shank.

Mon. Mar. 9.
Several inches of snow have fallen during the night. Most part of the
day, a furious snow storm blowing from the north. Working at engine
house plan. In the evening studied building and played one game at
chess with Jameson at which I came off victor.

Tues. Mar. 10.
At plan of engine house. In the evening went to the reading room and
met with A. Mackenzie. I went home with him and played 4 games of
draughts three of which I was the victor. Afterwards played one game
of chess with John Mackenzie and got beat.

Wed. Mar. 11.
At plan of engine house. Snowing heavily most part of day. Mr Gregory
went off to London. Spent the evening at chess with Jameson, three
games, he being the victor of 2 and I, 1.

---

21 An Irishman (slang).
22 Rev. John Gauld, AM (b. 1822), was pastor of the Free Church of Scotland in Moore
    Township from at least 1856 until 1861 and local school trustee. *Annual Report of the
    Normal, Model, Grammar and Common Schools in Upper Canada for the Year 1859* (Que-
    bec: Thompson and Company, 1860), 189.

Thurs. Mar. 12.
At plan of engine house. Borrowed a chopping axe and went off and in company with Jameson, chopped down a tree about 12' dia. before dark. Weather very fine. Spent evening reading treatise on building.

Fri. Mar. 13.
At plan of engine house. Weather beautiful and mild. Chopped wood for an hour in the gloaming. Read building treatise in the evening.

Sat. Mar. 14.
About 11 o'clock forenoon, Smith, a contractor arrived here from Hamilton with news of breaking of bridge at Hamilton on the 13th and death of Messrs Zimmerman, Henderson and many others.[23] Gregory and Robb left for Hamilton. At tracing of engine house plan.

Sun. Mar. 15.
Had extra of Hamilton Spectator confirming yesterday's news. Heard Mr Walker preach in the forenoon, in his sermon making allusion to the accident. Beautiful weather. Walked to the Perch Bridge on the Sarnia Branch. In the evening wrote to Bro. Thos.

Mon. Mar. 16.
Weather still very fine. Jameson, Peffers and I the only occupants of the offices here. Altering Eng. Ho. plan. In the evening studied Davies Surveying. Bradley, the contractor arrived from Hamilton with news of the death of Mr Farr, contractor, at the swing bridge.[24]

---

23 The Desjardins Railway disaster occurred on March 12, 1857 shortly before 6 p.m., when a broken axle caused a GWR passenger train to crash through the railway's Burlington Heights swing bridge just outside of Hamilton. The train plummeted into the icy water of the Desjardin Canal below. Of approximately one hundred passengers, fifty-nine were killed and eighteen injured. Samuel Zimmerman (1815–57) was a canal and railway contractor whose undertakings included the Welland Canal, the Great Western Railway, and the Niagara Suspension Bridge. A Pennsylvanian by birth, at the time of the accident he was likely the richest man in the Canadas. John C. Henderson was the brother-in-law of C.J. Brydges, managing director of the GWR. A new bridge was constructed later in the year. *Macmillan*, 822; J.K. Johnson, 'Zimmerman, Samuel' *DCB* (Toronto: University of Toronto Press, 1985), 8:963–7; Johnson, '"One Bold Operator": Samuel Zimmerman, Niagara Entrepreneur, 1843–1857,' *Ontario History* 74 (1982): 26–44; Marjorie Freeman Campbell, *A Mountain and a City: The Story of Hamilton* (Toronto: McClelland and Stewart, 1966), 113–15. McIlwraith would likely have read the extensive account of the accident provided in the *Observer*. 'Frightful Accident on the Great Western Railway!' *SO*, March 19, 1857.

24 Marshall H. Farr (b. 1817) was an American, from Chesterfield, Massachusetts, and a

Tues. Mar. 17.
Altering Eng. Ho. plan. Beautiful weather. The little steamer Mohawk went down the river from Port Huron. Had a long walk through the woods to the N.E. of Sarnia in the evening. Spent the forenight writing to Mrs Logan.

Wed. Mar. 18.
Tracing Eng. Ho. plan. In the evening read treatise on stone-cutting and played two games of chess with Jameson, gaining a game each.

Thurs. Mar. 19.
Tracing Eng. Ho. plan. Mr Robb arrived from Hamilton and brought 2 vols. Scottish Songs and Ballads.[25] Wrote to Br. Thos sending draft for £34 to invest for me.

Fri. Mar. 20.
Tracing Eng. Ho. plan. In the evening attended a lecture of the Mechanics Institute by Mr Salter upon the civilization of the ancient Romans.[26] Played one game of chess with Jameson and got beaten.

Sat. Mar. 21.
Commenced plan of details of Eng. Ho. Started for a walk about 4 in the afternoon and had a lovely walk around Point Edward and a good way up the lake banks. Saw a puddock, the first of the season, likewise heard him in the woods.[27] River full of drift ice in small pieces. A warm south wind blowing.

Sun. Mar. 22.
Heard Mr Walker preach in the morning, text 'Remember Lot's Wife.' In the afternoon had a walk with John Mackenzie and Jameson and had J. Mc. to tea. Weather inclined to be sultry and after dark, a great deal of lightning flashing zigzagedly across the Southern horizon.

---

leading contractor in the construction of the GTR. He initially survived the accident, but the *Observer* reported a few days later that 'no hopes were entertained of his recovery.' SO, March 19, 1857. See William Richard Cutter, *Encyclopedia of Massachusetts, Biographical – Genealogical* (np: American Historical Society, 1916), 338.

25 Perhaps Robert Chambers, *Scottish Songs and Ballads*, 3 vols. (Edinburgh: William Tait, 1829).

26 This lecture, entitled 'Civilization of Ancient Rome,' was delivered as part of the Sarnia Mechanics' Institute's annual course of lectures by Rev. George J.R. Salter at the Methodist Church. SO, March 19, 1857; 'Mechanics' Institute,' SO, March 26, 1857.

27 Likely 'paddock,' a frog or a toad.

Mon. Mar. 23.
At detail drawing of plan of Eng. Ho. Morning stormy. A small sail boat getting capsized in the river. Two small boats and ferry steamer 'Union' went to the rescue. Had another charming evening walk down by the river bank. In the evening read Scottish Songs and got beat at chess by Jameson.

Tues. Mar. 24.
At detail plan of Eng. Ho. Received Ayr paper enclosing lithograph view of scene of the accident at Hamilton.[28] In the evening read treatise on 'Stone-cutting.' Beautiful weather. Walked out the London Road and saw Robins and bluebirds.

Wed. Mar. 25.
At details of Eng. Ho. Gregory left here to attend his sale of lots at Strathroy. At evening walk found out a farm road through the woods behind the Court House. Had a visit of Chas Mackenzie to play chess. Jameson beat him and I and then I beat Jameson one game. While playing a steamer whistled on the river, the first up.

Thurs. Mar. 26.
At detail plan of Eng. Ho. Last night's steamer proved to be the 'Sam Ward' from Detroit. 'Forest Queen' came up tonight. Had a walk of three miles down the river bank in the evening. Fishing (spearing) extensively pursued in the upper bay this few nights, mostly by Yankees. Spent forenight at Stone-cutting treatise.

Fri. Mar. 27.
At detail plan of Eng. Ho. Weather very fine. Walked out the fourth line and back thru the woods. In the evening practiced the 'Logarithm Calculations.' Paid to Donald Mackenzie $2. for one quarter's subscription to church.

Sat. Mar. 28.
At details of Eng. Ho. Had our walk out by the fourth line again. Visited

---

28 The lithograph was very likely the one produced by a Mr Rise and first published by the *Hamilton Spectator* on March 20 or 21, 1857. See '"Just Published!" A Beautifully Tinted Engraving of the Shattered Bridge! Over the Desjardins Canal taken from the Bridge.' *HS*, March 21, 1857, cited in Joan M. Schwartz, 'Documenting Disaster: Photography at the Desjardins Canal, 1857,' *Archivaria* 25 (Winter 1987–8), 153fn3. A different, more popular lithograph of the disaster appeared in both the *Illustrated London News* and *Frank Leslie's Illustrated Newspaper* (New York), but not until April 4, 1857.

reading room in the evening then came home and played chess but got completely beaten by Jameson. This last two or three weeks there have been a great many wooden dwelling houses going up around town; Joe Ducotah building close to Kent's.

Sun. Mar. 29.
This morning had a long letter from Bro. Thos. telling me of having bought 11 shares in the Building Society for me.[29] Went to Church in the forenoon. Mr Walker rebuked his congregation for sleeping. Had along ramble to Lake Waywanash with C. Mackenzie and Jameson. Saw two bald eagles.

Mon. Mar. 30.
At Eng. Ho. details. Still lovely weather but still north wind and chilly. Saw the first swallow of the season today also the first butterfly. Visited the reading room in the evening and had James Mackenzie down practicing chess.

Tues. Mar. 31.
At Eng. Ho. details. Today wind changed to South and temperature got much milder. Had a walk around Point Edward in the evening, and saw Red-winged Starlings, etc. and heard frogs in full chorus. In the evening wrote to Bro. Thos.

Wed. April 1.
Making tracings of Eng. Ho. detail plan. Auction of town lots came off today, property of Malcolm Cameron. The lot next to the Post Office bought by McAvoy at $155 per foot front.[30] Weather completely

---

29 Before Confederation, building societies in Canada were limited ventures in which a fixed number of members purchased shares. As a society's capital grew, it purchased land and materials to build houses which, when completed, would be rented to generate more revenue. Ideally, revenue from shares, fines for late subscription payments, and rent would be accumulated until houses could be built or purchased for all members of the society. Though originated as a device for enforced savings, by the 1850s building societies were increasingly looked upon as investment mechanisms. Though the name of McIlwraith's society is not indicated, two societies operating in Hamilton at that time were the Gore District Building Society and the Western Permanent Building Society. *Gore District Building Society* (Hamilton: The Society, 1848); *The Western Permanent Building Society* (Hamilton: The Spectator, 1851). See Michael Doucet and John C. Weaver, *Housing the North American City* (Montreal and Kingston: McGill-Queen's University Press, 1991), 253–5, 259–60.

30 The editor of the *Observer* feared speculation and urged those who purchased land in town to develop their land quickly or sell to others at reasonable prices. 'Land Speculation,' *SO*, April 16, 1857; 'The Land Sale in Town,' *SO*, April 23, 1857.

changed today. Strong northerly gales with frost and snow. Walked down through the woods and viewed the lake.

Thurs. April 2.
Tracing Eng. Ho. detail plan. Weather more settled but cold and keen. Had old country papers No. 1 of Ayrshire Express.[31] Had a fine walk thru the woods in the evening. Spent the evening at arranging my cash affairs.

Fri. Apr. 3.
At tracing No. 2 of Eng. Ho. detail. In the evening walked out Cart. St. which is being cleared and in attempting to take another road home, got into a dismal swamp and had an hour's hard work to get out. Heard Mr Shank lecture on Volcanoes, rather dry.[32]

Sat. Apr. 4.
Tracing Eng. Ho. detail plan. Weather quite warm, almost sultry. Had a long walk down the river banks, frogs in the woods piping loud, snow almost disappeared. Had letter from Br. Thos including do. from Mrs Hunter of congratulations to him on his daughter's birth.

Sun. Apr. 5.
Attended church in the morning and heard Mr Walker. Rain commenced as Church came out and began to mix with snow gradually increasing to a snow storm all the remaining day. Kept the house and read Household Words and Ryle's Sermons.

Mon. Apr. 6.
At bill of material for Eng. Ho. Snow lying six inches deep. Squalls

---

31 The first issue of the *Ayrshire Express* was dated March 7, 1857. A weekly that espoused 'radical' views, it was edited by Robert Howie Smith, a former apprentice at the *Ayr Advertiser* who had been dismissed for his part in a political lampoon aimed at well-known members of that community. It continued as the *Express* until 1871, when it was published as the *Argus and Express*. It was incorporated with the more popular (and more conservative) *Ayr Observer* in April 1889. See British Museum, *Catalogue of Printed Books ... Newspapers Published in Great Britain and Ireland, 1801–1900* (London: William Clowes and Sons, 1905), 443; John Strawhorn, *The History of Ayr: Royal Burgh and County Town* (Edinburgh: John Donald Publishers, 1989), 171; Rob Close, 'Two Hundred Years of the *Ayr Advertiser*,' *Ayrshire Notes* 26 (2003): 1–41.

32 Congregationalist minister Rev. Philip Shank's lecture was delivered under the auspices of the Sarnia Mechanics' Institute at the Methodist Church. Stationed in Port Sarnia in 1857–8, he had been moved to Lanark, CW, by 1861. He died in 1873 in Queensland, Australia. *SO*, April 2, 1857; *The Congregational Quarterly* (Boston: American Congregational Union, 1874), 16:493.

with snow all day. Read Ballads and played chess in the evening, being beaten by Jameson.

Tues. Apr. 7.
At bill of Eng. Ho. and checking passenger house bill. Keen frost in the morning but evening mild. Frogs piping amid the snow in the afternoon. Spent the evening in Mackenzies playing chess. Charlie and I about matched.

Wed. Apr. 8.
Checking Pass. Ho. bill. Borrowed from Mackenzie, Hugh Miller's 'Schools and School-Masters.'[33] Had letter from P. McIntyre, Dumbarton. Spent the evening writing home.

Thurs. Apr. 9.
Checking Pass. Ho. bill. Had letter from Br. Thos enclosing do. from Mrs Hunter to him and I with congratulations to him on the birth of daughter. In the evening continued my home letters to Mrs Hunter and Br. Bill.

Fri. Apr. 10.
Good Friday and a holiday in the office. A most beautiful clear day with gentle breeze from the north. Crossed to Port Huron in company with Jameson and visited the Fort and lighthouse.[34] Had a fine view from the lighthouse. Had a long walk along the beach and collected some minerals. Came back across the river in a sail boat. In the evening played chess.

Sat. Apr. 11.
Measuring up plaster work, etc. in Freight and Passenger House. Spent the evening reading Hugh Miller's 'Schools and Schoolmasters,' a most entertaining and evidently truthful book.

---

33 Hugh Miller, *My Schools and Schoolmasters; or, The Story of My Education* (Edinburgh: T. Constable, 1857).

34 Originally the site of a French installation called Fort St Joseph, Fort Gratiot was rebuilt in 1814 and subsequently renamed after its builder and supervisor, Colonel (later U.S. Chief Army Engineer General) Charles Gratiot (1786–1855). The fort was located near Port Huron, at the point where Lake Huron empties into the St Clair River. William Jenks, 'Fort Gratiot and Its Builder, Gen. Charles Gratiot,' *Michigan History Magazine* 4 (1920): 141–55. The lighthouse was built just north of the fort in 1829. In its original form it was a 74-foot white painted-brick tower. Charles K. Hyde, *Northern Lights: Lighthouses of the Upper Great Lakes* (Detroit: Wayne State University Press, 1995), 80–1.

Sun. Apr. 12.
Heard Mr Walker preach morning and evening. Some fellow snored so loud in church that Mr W. had to notice it. Had an afternoon walk with R. Mackenzie.

Mon. Apr. 13.
Calculating quantities of Pass. and Freight house. Weather delightful, Walked towards Point Edward in company with Messrs Robb and Bellairs with their guns. Found no game but tried shooting at marks a little. In the evening, attended meeting of the Dialectic Society.[35]

Tues. Apr. 14.
Calculating and measuring quantities. In the evening wrote to Br. Thos, sending $30 to put in the bank. Snow fell thick this forenoon but evening mild.

Wed. April 15.
Weather very stormy and snowy. Still arranging and revising Bills also cleaned an old gun in company with Mr Peffers. Spent the evening writing to Mrs Logan. Had a letter from her in the morning. Mr Gregory arrived in the afternoon boat from being at Strathroy.

Thurs. Apr. 16.
Tracing Eng. Ho. plan with arrangement of pipes. Weather still squally and snowy. Made a new Ramrod. In the evening read Cockburn's 'Memorials.'[36]

Fri. Apr. 17.
Finished Eng. Ho. tracing and commenced tracing of Desjardin Bridge. Walked around by Point Edward with the gun and shot a red-winged Starling. Heard the frogs crying 'peep-peep.'

Sat. Apr. 18.
At tracing of Desjardin Bridge. Weather snowy and disagreeable. Spent the evening writing to Br. Thos.

---

35 This meeting took the form of debate around the question 'Can the giving of rewards be so conducted as to be of advantage to scholars, and to the prosperity of the schools?' The *Observer* encouraged the attendance at the meeting of 'any person interested in week day or Sabbath Schools.' McIlwraith's interest in this subject reappeared later in his life when he served as a school trustee in Galt (see Epilogue). 'Dialectic Society,' *SO*, April 16, 1857.

36 Henry (Lord) Cockburn, *Memorials of His Time* (Edinburgh: A. and C. Black, 1856).

Sun. Apr. 19.
Heard Mr Walker preach in the morning. Walked out to the Perch Bridge in company with Jameson. Day pleasant and frogs vocal but few other signs of animal or vegetable life. In the evening went to Episcopal Church. Spoke to Mary Young when church came out.

Mon. Apr. 20.
Finished Desjardin Bridge and commenced detail of Tank Iron work and pipes for Eng. Ho. Had a walk out 4th cons. before tea. In the evening went to the reading room.

Tues. Apr. 21.
At details of pipes. Went to the raffle of Howard's gun in the evening. Chas Mackenzie the winner. Weather cold and unsettled.

Wed. Apr. 22.
At details of pipes. Attended Court House for a short time in the evening.[37] Played chess all night after tea, I being beaten.

Thurs. Apr. 23.
At details of pipes. Weather bright and clear but still chilly with north wind. Spent 2 hours of the forenoon in the Court House while a case of manslaughter was being tried. Judge Richards – for the defendent, Mr Beecher. Defendent discharged.[38]

Fri. Apr. 24.
At details of pipes. Had a walk before tea with H.F. Mackenzie and Jameson. Took the gun and shot a Robin and a Bluebird. Met with Mr Hitchcock, fisherman, who had caught 4 loons in his lines. Got the two

---

37 Attending court was a common pastime among Victorian Canadians. It provided a sort of theatrical though instructive entertainment, particularly in smaller towns where leisure pursuits were few. See Paul Craven, 'Law and Ideology: The Toronto Police Court, 1850–1880,' in David Flaherty, ed., *Essays in the History of Canadian Law* (Toronto: University of Toronto Press for the Osgoode Society, 1982), 2:249–307; John C. Weaver, *Crimes, Constables, and Courts: Order and Transgression in a Canadian City, 1816–1970* (Montreal and Kingston: McGill-Queen's University Press, 1995), ch. 2.

38 In this case, Daniel May, shoemaker, was charged with the murder of a man named Shepherd, which allegedly had taken place on January 13 in Euphemia Township, Lambton County. The victim died from wounds sustained in a drunken quarrel. According to testimony, the deceased seemed to have been struck on the back of the head with the round end of a shoemaker's hammer. Though, to some witnesses, he seemed alert and able after the fight, Shepherd later died. After a short deliberation, the jury in the case returned a verdict of 'not guilty.' *SO*, April 30, 1857.

best and spent the evening skinning one, a very tough and dirty job, which I did very badly.

Sat. Apr. 25.
Rose early and dispatched 2 loons per the steamer 'Clifton' to Windsor and so on to Hamilton. At detail of pipes. Visited A. Mackenzie in the evening and played games at draughts. Weather beautiful but still chilly Flocks of wild geese to be seen flying north frequently this few days back.

Sun. Apr. 26.
A miserable, wet day. Snowing wet snow all day. I heard a Mr McLean preach morning and evening in Mr Walker's Church. A highland man and pretty dry.[39]

Mon. Apr. 27.
Cold rainy weather. At tracing of details of pipes. Spent the evening with John Mackenzie playing chess.

Tues. Apr. 28.
Drawing pipes. In the evening attended a meeting of Sarnia ratepayers in Council on the subject of removing Front St. Bridge. Speakers Messrs Davis, Archibald Young sr Alex and Hope Mackenzie, Forsyth the mayor in the chair, Alexander and Wm Vidal also spoke. The whole affair disorderly and unsatisfactory.[40]

Wed. Apr. 29.
Tracing pipes, etc. Mr Gregory left for Hamilton. Weather clear but with cold north wind. Had a long walk before tea out the Errol Road. In the

---

39 Very likely Rev. Alexander McLean (1827–64), a Free Church Presbyterian and pastor of a congregation in East Puslinch, Canada West, 1856–64. He was born and raised on the island of North Uist, in Highland Scotland. See 'McLean, Alexander' in Joseph M. Wilson, ed., *The Presbyterian Historical Almanac and Annual Remembrancer of the Church for 1866* (Philadelphia: Joseph M. Wilson, 1866), 8:372.

40 This meeting was called by Town Council as a public consultation over whether to relocate the GWR Bridge on Front Street. One large group of citizens claimed that the present bridge was awkwardly oriented to road traffic, its approaches too narrow, and was poorly constructed. Another group, which included A. Young, A. Mackenzie, and Alex. Vidal complained that relocation closer to the St Clair river was unfeasible and costly. The *Observer* reported that '[v]arious motions, amendments and reamendments were submitted to the meeting, and from the interest and excitement manifested by the audience, it was a somewhat difficult matter to arrive at a satisfactory conclusion as to the feeling on the subject.' In the end, a motion passed requiring Town Council to confer with the GWR Company about the expediency of moving the bridge closer to the river.' *SO*, April 30, 1857.

evening heard Mr Ward from Kansas lecture on the capabilities and productions of that country – rather an amusing character.

Thurs. Apr. 30.
Putting titles etc. various drawings. Spent the evening in the reading room. Wind from the south and warm, being the first day of such weather for a long time.

Fri. May 1.
Pouring rain all day. Made alterations on drawing engine and some other small jobs. Had letter from Br. Thos telling of safe arrival of 'Loons' I sent him, also speaking of his visiting me here soon. Drank tea with Alex Mackenzie, also wrote answer to Thos' letter.

Sat. May 2.
Made enlargement of drawing of Eng. Ho. pits. Weather dull and cloudy. Played chess and got beaten by Jameson in the evening.

Sun. May 3.
Rose early and had a cold bath in a tub in the room, consequently felt drowsy in Church. Day fine and church thronged. Walked through the woods to Lake Huron shore in company with Jameson, Bob Mackenzie and Mr Scott, Land agent. Saw some black butterflies and two small snakes. Took another walk in the evening as Church was crowded.

Mon. May 4.
Miserable wet day and awful wet night. At tracing of Eng. Ho. pits. Finished pump plans etc. Wrote to the Sec. of the G.W.R. stating how long I have been employed on the line. Spent the evening practicing working of Logarithms. Got pay for April.

Tues. May 5.
Tracing hydrants and Eng. Ho. floor plan. Still very wet weather. Read Chambers on Education in the evening.[41]

Wed. May 6.
Tracing Eng. Ho. floor. Heard from Br Thos of his intention of coming here in the end of the week. Of Mrs Caven having given birth to a daughter and of Catharine Drynan's marriage, she being now Mrs Ballingall. Attended a concert in the Court House in the evening.

---

41 Likely 'On Education,' a disbound volume of William and Robert Chambers, eds., *Chambers' Information for the People* (London: Chambers, 1849), 86.

Thurs. May 7.
Tracing Eng. Ho. floor plan. Weather again clear and fine. Poll of the Sarnians being taken today as to whether R.R. bridge should be moved to Christina St. which has been negatived largely.[42] Wrote to Christina in the evening.

Fri. May 8.
Commenced to drawing of Sarnia Depot Grounds. Day most beautiful and clear. Bro. Thos arrived with the 'Clifton' by moonlight between 8 and 9 at night, bringing with him a live specimen of a small owl. Had a most happy meeting with him. Called on R. Mackenzie and talked late.

Sat. May 9.
Day very sultry and lowering with gusts of wind from the south. Got the day to myself and Tom and I with guns a-piece, went a-shooting. Went out the London Road beyond the Perch Bridge. Shot Jays, Woodpeckers, etc. and came home very tired but having some nice specimens and enjoying ourselves well. Had R. Mackenzie down in the evening and spent it pleasantly.

Sun. May 10.
North wind and cold weather again. Had letters from home. Went ½ hr in Indian Church in the morning then went to Mr Walker's.[43] Dined in Mackenzie's and had a walk through the woods to the lake and home round the point. Strong N.W. breeze and vessels running down the rapids. Tom and I drank tea with Mr and Mrs Robb. Spent the evening at home and in Mackenzies. Keen frost, sidewalks frozen.

---

42 This vote resulted in the 13 yeas for moving the bridge being outweighed by the 53 nays in favour of its present location. A committee of Council was then charged with further consulting with the GWR and seeking legal counsel and the opinion of an engineer on the matter. 'The Railway Bridge,' SO, April 30, 1857; SO, May 14, 1857.

43 The British Wesleyan Methodist Society offered ecumenical services in a mission church on the Sarnia Reserve beginning in 1832. Interestingly, when the Rev Edward F. Wilson arrived at Sarnia to establish a Church of England mission in 1868 he too temporarily boarded with a 'Mrs Walker' whose 'frame, white-painted' house was located 'a little way back' from Sarnia's main street about 'a quarter hours walk' from the Reserve which 'almost adjoined the town.' See Riddell, 'Community Leadership,' 29; Edward F. Wilson, *Missionary Work among the Ojebway Indians* (New York and London: Society for Promoting Christian Knowledge; E. and J.B. Young, 1886); John Carroll, *Case and His Cotemporaries, or, The Canadian Itinerants' Memorial Constituting a Biographical History of Methodism in Canada* (Toronto: Wesleyan Conference Office, 1874), 467-8.

Mon. May 11.
Ground almost white with snow. Rose early Tom going off with the 'Clifton' at 7 o'clock. Drawing plan of Sarnia Depot grounds. Mr Gregory left for Hamilton in the afternoon. Consigned $40 to Br. Thos to be deposited in Hamilton Savings Bank. In the evening played chess and beat Jameson 2 games.

Tues. May 12.
At plan of Depot ground. In the afternoon had a drive down to Broomfield with Jameson. Day fine but chilly. Observed a pretty-species of black-headed gull. In the evening wrote to Mrs Logan also visited Port Huron before tea.

Wed. May 13.
At plan of depot. Spent the evening writing to John Stewart. Despatched the letter for him to Hamilton with $5 enclosed for transmission from there. Money to be divided between him and Bill. Mr Gregory came back from Hamilton.

Thurs. May 14.
At plan of Depot Grounds. Weather cold and raw with some little rain. Heard from Br. Thos of his safe arrival home. Spent the evening writing to Hugh Dickie.

Fri. May 15.
At plan of wing wall of Front St. bridge to be rebuilt. Still wet weather. Some Potlanders kicked up rows in the afternoon and gave the constables bloody noses and afterwards made themselves scarce.[44] In the evening visited reading room.

Sat. May 16.
At plan of Bridge wing wall. Made purchase of Hugh Miller's 'Testimony of the Rocks.'[45] Spent the evening chatting in Mackenzies.

Sun. May 17.
At church in the morning and heard Mr Walker. Had a walk to the Cull drain on the Errol Road, 8 miles distant. Day very pleasant and cool. Viewed the waves dashing into Plympton Bay. Had Chas Mackenzie at tea.

---

44 Patlanders; Irishmen (slang). See 'Police Court – Before the Mayor' *SO*, May 21, 1857.
45 Hugh Miller, *The Testimony of the Rocks; or, Geology in Its Bearings on the Two Theologies, Natural and Revealed* (Edinburgh: T. Constable and Co., 1857).

Mon. May 18.
Rose early and went shooting but shot naught but a hell-diver on the water beyond reach. At plan and tracing of Bridge wing wall. Still north wind and chilly. Walked out with the gun in the evening but birds very scarce.

Tues. May 19.
Measuring up painting of Freight and Passenger Houses. Reading 'Testimony of the Rocks.'

Wed. May 20.
Plan of Stn Yd Sarnia. Had a walk around by the 4th line. Weather still cold and but few signs of birds or vegetation to be seen. Spent the evening reading 'Songs and Ballads.'

Thur. May 21.
At plan of Stn Yd Sarnia. Mr Reid Chief Engineer, in town today.[46] Part of new R.R. wharf bulged out during the night with pressure of clay upon sheet piling. Made plan and tracing of wooden drain. In the evening wrote to Br. Thos.

Fri. May 22.
Rose between 3 and 4 and went round the Bay to try duck shooting along with C. Mackenzie (unsuccessful). At new plan of brick tank house for Sarnia yard. Spent the evening skinning a small Hawk and am under the impression that I have not much natural turn for that job.

Sat. May 23.
Weather getting warm now. At plan of brick tank house. Attempts being made under Mr Gregory's orders to pull back the wharf to its place with long 1-½ inch iron rods through piles driven into firm ground,

---

46 George Lowe Reid (1829–1907) was born at Dunfermline, Scotland. After he completed his schooling, he apprenticed to a Glasgow railway engineer, Neil Robson. In 1852 he was appointed Divisional Resident Engineer on the Great Western Railway of Canada, and later Associate Chief Engineer at the GWR's Hamilton headquarters. He became Chief Engineer in 1854, a position that he held until 1872, when he returned to Britain due to illness in his family. He was widely respected and left Canada in 1872 to several tributes. 'George Lowe Reid,' *Minutes of the Proceedings of the Institute of Civil Engineers* (London: The Institute, 1908), 173:332; Paul Craven, 'Labour and Management on the Great Western Railway' in Craven, ed. *Labouring Lives: Work and Workers in Nineteenth-Century Ontario* (Toronto: University of Toronto Press, 1995), 344.

rods having screws and nuts on ends. In the evening visited reading room.

Sun. May 24.
Heard Mr Walker preach in the morning and also admonish the congregation regarding Sabbath breaking. Day very hot. Sat all day in Mackenzie's and heard Mr Walker again in the evening. Large flocks of pigeons flying.

Mon. May 25.
The Queen's Birthday, General holiday. Attended muster of militia under Capt. Forsyth.[47] After dinner went out with Jameson in a buggy and C. Mackenzie on horse-back. Had his horse for a mile or two. Drank tea in Mackenzie's and loafed about in town afterwards, drinking popp and smoking. Day very hot.

Tues. May 26.
Making out approximate Bill of Material for Brick Tank House. In the evening played chess. Day sultry and in the evening thunder and lightning and heavy rain.

Wed. May 27.
At plan of Brick Tank House. In the evening went to concert in the Court House by Goodall, Father and Son, violinists. Performance good but pieces rather incomprehensible. Much amusement caused by a bat flying about the room. Heard the Whip-poor-will for the first time this season Nights hawks also flying plenty.

Thurs. May 28.
At plan of Brick Tank House. Weather mild and showery, Trees have all burst into leaf and blossom within this 8 days. Apples, plums, peaches, etc, in the gardens and wild cherries in the woods. Pigeons still flying

---

47 The *Observer* commented that those involved in this military drill exhibited 'an awkwardness in their movements not very pleasing to the spectators.' The newspaper also bemoaned 'a large amount of drunkenness in Town during the day, as well as several fights.' 'The Queen's Birth-Day,' *SO*, May 28, 1857. The birthday of Queen Victoria (May 24) was celebrated annually in British North America, normally in festive, public ceremonies including parades, militia mustering, and fireworks. The day was declared a legal holiday in Canada West in 1845, and a Canadian national holiday in 1901 (called 'Victoria Day') after the Queen's death. The holiday fell (and falls) on the Monday before May 25. See John Robert Colombo, 'Victoria Day,' *The Canadian Encyclopedia* (Edmonton: Hurtig, 1985), 3:1908.

but most plentiful on the American side of the river. Visited reading
room in the evening.

Fri. May 29.
At plan of Brick Tank House. Weather unsettled and chilly. People
complaining of ague. A Scarlet Tanager fell down and died in the garden. Met Mr Hannah on the wharf as purser of the 'George Moffat.'
This evening at Goodal's concert, a young lady of the audience closely
veiled, whistled a tune and won a bet of $40.

Sat. May 30.
A fine warm day. At tracing of Tank House plan. Went out with the gun
in the evening and shot 4 pigeons on the road to Seward's house. Sat
with Hope Mackenzie in the evening who had been with Tom in Hamilton on Wednesday.

Sun. May 31.
Heard Mr Walker preach in the morning. A Methodist in the afternoon
and Mr Shank at night. Had a short walk and had C. Mackenzie at tea.
Weather sultry with thunder and lightning and heavy rain at night. Got
wet coming from Church. Had a letter from Tom enclosing do. from
Mrs Stewart and Christina and from D. Andrew, Greenock. Therm. 68
deg. above zero.

Mon. June 1.
At tracing of Tank House plan No. 2. Spent the evening with Mr Robb
tracing his Hotel plan previous to his departure for Hamilton in the
morning. Walked to Seward's Farm on the Lake Shore with the gun
before tea. I shot a Scarlet Tanager but did not get any pigeons.

Tues. June 2.
At tracing of Tank Ho. Weather showery. Walked down the Lake Shore
Road in the afternoon and shot 2 pigeons. Mr and Mrs Robb left in the
morning for Hamilton. Learned that D.W. Howard was about to leave
the G.W.R. S.B. Saw a sturgeon at a shop door in town weighing 110 lbs.

Wed. June 3.
Checking Bills of Materials for Komoka bridges. Jameson and I drank
tea in A. Mackenzie's and met there a Mr Burns, saw miller.

Thurs. June 4.
Started with C. Mackenzie at 4 o'clock to pigeon shooting but morning
quite cold and flocks all flying high. Walked by Seward's road to the

Lake Shore and round Point Edward home. Wild strawberry flowers plenty. Checked Komoka bridge bills. Election for Councelor in Sarnia today in place of M. Cameron, resigned. Clarke Curtis, the old fool, 19 ahead of Archibald Young Sr.[48]

Fri. June 5.
Looked out the window about 5.30 in the morning and saw the ground white with frost. Made out Bill of Materials for Well and Curbs at Strathroy and worked at plan of Signals. Had a nice walk in the woods with C. Mackenzie in the evening and shot one pigeon. Weather cold.

Sat. June 6.
At drawing of Signals. Day fine. Afternoon rather sultry. Went down Seward's Road with Jameson and shot two pigeons. Spent evening writing to Br. Thos. Boys fishing and spearing herrings from the R.W. wharf.

Sun. June 7.
Heard Mr Walker preach morning and evening. Had a walk in the woods with Jameson in the interval. Caught a thunder plump in the evening and witnessed some intensely brilliant lightning. Posted letters to Bro. Thos and to Mr Wilson, Dundas, inquiring for Strachan's address.

Mon. June 8.
At drawing of Signals. N.E. wing wall of bridge giving way and attempts being made to pull it up with screwed rods. Day very sultry. Therm. in my bedroom at 79 deg, in the afternoon. Took a walk out by the Court House in the evening with James Mackenzie. Went into Springbank garden and viewed the greenhouse by candle-light and got a swing on a tree and a bunch of flowers from Ellen Young.

Tues. June 9.
Rose early and saw the 'Clifton' going off on a pleasure trip to Detroit. Weather turned out to be very foggy. Assisted Mr Walker in laying out a new Wing Wall of Bridge. At plan of Signals. Awaited the arrival of the 'Clifton' which took place between 11 and 12. Received pay for May.

Wed. June 10.
At plans of Signals. Spent the evening writing to Mother. Fireflies begin to appear this week.

---

48 The *Observer* recorded the vote at 34 to 14, remarking with disgust that the election of Curtis marks 'the infusion of the plebian element to Council.' *SO*, June 11, 1857.

Thurs. June 11.
At plan of Signals. Mr Robb arrived from Hamilton with letter from Br. Thos, Bill and J.W. Strachan. Finished letter to Mother and posted it away.

Fri. June 12.
At plan of Signals. Mr Howard left Sarnia finally this morning. Walked out with Jas Mackenzie in the evening and called at Springbank. Ordered a pair slippers of the Ladies Society for the benefit of the Manse Fund. News came that the favorite steamer 'Clifton' makes her last trip tomorrow.

Sat. June 13.
At plan of Signals. Weather fine. Drank tea with Mr Peffers and spent some time in his garden planting potatoes. Got a new grey coat and cap from Mr Lees.

Sun. June 14.
Mr Walker from home but heard Mr Alex. Vidal read an excellent sermon in the morning. Walked down Seward's Road to the Lake and back with R. and C. Mackenzie and Jameson. Drank tea in Mackenzies and had another walk after. Saw chipmunks in the woods, the first of the season.

Mon. June 15.
Rose early and saw Jameson off for Hamilton etc. with the Forester. At Plan of Signals, etc. Day warm with heavy rain at night. Commenced making an attempt at flower-drawing in the evening. Sent off $20 per Jameson for Br. Thos to buy me a concertina.

Tues. June 16.
Rose about 4 and spent the time till breakfast sketching Columbine flower. Office time at plan of Signals. Walked into the woods in the evening and caught a thunder shower. Watched the Night Hawks making darts perpendicularly into the woods, so quick as to sound like the snort of a stm bt engine.

Wed. June 17.
At plan of Signals. Worked an hour in the evening in Mackenzie's shop fixing a net apparatus for catching insects.

Thurs. June 18.
At plan of Signals, and calculating quantities of Delaware St. Bridge, Komoka. Weather showery. Walked out the London Road in the

evening with James Mackenzie. Visited the reading room. Called in at Springbank garden and got a bunch of flowers.

Fri. June 19.

At plan of Signals. Had an evening walk with James Mackenzie and John Stevenson, student of law from Toronto. Gathered some wild Columbine flowers which are now about past. The woods still enriched with blue Lupins which begin to form into pods.

Sat. June 20.

Rose about 5 and sketched Columbine flowers. At plan of lever switch. Weather still showery. Spent the evening between Mr Peffers and the reading room. Had a walk and a cigar with Chas Mackenzie.

Sun. June 21.

Heard Mr Walker preach in the forenoon and Mr Down of the Methodists, in the afternoon. Had Jas Mackenzie to tea. Raining nearly all day. Have been reading 'Personal Recollections of Charlotte Elizabeth.' Think she is inclined to be bigoted.[49]

Mon. June 22.

At plan of Lever Switch. Visited Springbank in the evening and got my slippers. A very rainy day.

Tues. June 23.

At plan of Lever Switch. Mr John Bailly arrived from Strathroy to join the Engineer party here and took up his quarters in Kent's with us. Had a walk with him in the evening. Also inspected an Indian dress with buckskin, the property of J.B.

Wed. June 24.

At plan of Switch. Mr Jameson arrived home from his jaunt bringing a concertina. Spent the evening strolling about. Heard from Br. Thos of his office having been broken into.

---

49 A native of southwestern England, Rev. Samuel Down was a Wesleyan Methodist preacher who served charges in Millbrook (1855), Sarnia (1856), and Chatham (1857) before he became a student at Victoria College, Cobourg (1858). He returned to the ministry in 1859, serving a series of congregations in northern and eastern Canada West. John Carroll, *Case and His Cotemporaries; or, the Canadian Itinerant's Memorial* (Toronto: S. Rose, 1877), 200; John Prince and R. Alan Douglas, *John Prince: A Collection of Documents* (Toronto: Champlain Society, 1980) 201. Charlotte Elizabeth *pseud.* [Charlotte Elizabeth (Browne) Tonna], *Personal Recollections* (New York: J.S. Taylor and Co., 1842).

Thurs. June 25.
A beautiful day. At plan of Lever Switch. Jameson and Peffers gone to
Plympton. Spent the whole evening in the house chatting with Baillie.
A number of young men of the upper ten-dom of Sarnia gave a ball in
the Court House tonight. Despatched a German newspaper to my Br.
John.[50]

Fri. June 26.
Real summer weather. At plan of Lever Switch. Stretched some maps
upon cloth. Wrote to Bro. Thos in the evening and had a stroll round
with Jameson, Baillie and Bellairs.

Sat. June 27.
Still warm, sunny weather. Van Amburgh's Circus and Animals arrived
across the river. The elephant got into the water opposite our office and
drank and splashed himself. At Lever Switch plan. Attended the Circus
in the evening and saw Miss Young looking charming. Performance
mediocre, good specimen of lions and tigers.[51]

Sun. June 28.
Heard Mr Walker preach in the morning. Weather sultry with heavy
rain in the afternoon. Wrote to Br. Thos and Mrs Logan. Heard Mr
Shank preach in the evening.

Mon. June 29.
A beautiful day but kind of cool especially as I wear white pants without drawers. At plan of Lever Switch. Made purchase of a Mink skin
ornamented with Indian work from John Ford price $ 2-½. Strolled
around town and sat in Mackenzies in the evening.

---

50 Perhaps *Der Canadische Bauernfreud* (1851–1918), a Preston weekly published by
   Abraham Erb and edited by Martin Rudolf, *Der Deutsche Canadier und Neuigkeitsbote*
   (1841–65), a Berlin (now Kitchener) weekly published by Heinrich Eby and edited
   by Christian Enslin, or *Der Neu-Hamburger Neutrale* (1855–9), a weekly published
   by W.H. Boullee and edited by Robert Storch. These Waterloo County newspapers
   would have been most accessible to McIlwraith's friends in Ayr and Galt.
51 By the 1850s Isaac A. Van Amburgh (1808–65) was a well-known American circus
   performer who rose to national prominence by innovating feline acts which included
   stepping into a cage with a lion, tiger, or other large cat and putting them through
   a series of crowd-pleasing tricks. See H. Frost, *A Brief Biographical Sketch of I.A. Van
   Amburgh* (New York: Samuel Booth, 1860). Of the circus's earlier Sarnia performance,
   the *Observer* editor was even less impressed, noting that it was 'not by any means
   calculated to advance the moral welfare of the community ... [or] to convey any
   information which will tend to make those who patronize them either wiser or better members of society.' 'The Circus!' *SO*, June 25, 1857.

Tues. June 30.
At plan of Lever Switch. Weather cold and rainy. Visited reading room in the evening and got a number of Canadian Naturalist with interesting account of butterflies and animals. Reading accounts of burning of steamer 'Montreal' with dreadful loss of life.[52]

Wed. July 1.
At plan of Lever Switch, taking as long time as possible as there is little to do. Weather still miserably cold and showery. Strolled around town and visited reading room with Jas Mackenzie.

Thurs. July 2.
Finished plan of Lever Switch and received from Mr Gregory intimation that my services would be dispensed with after 1st October. Wrote to Br. Thos.

Fri. July 3.
At tracing of Lever Switch plan. Walked out the Errol Road before tea with Jameson. After tea, strolled round town with C. Mackenzie, Baillie Peffers and Bellairs. Have been to the country since Tues. Had letters from Tom with enclosures from Mrs Hunter, Christina, Bill and from A. Liddel, pattern maker, Trenton Jersey.

Sat. July 4.
Morning dull and rainy like but brightened in the afternoon. Spent forenoon measuring wharf timbers. Crossed over to Port Huron about 3 in company with Chas Mackenzie and Jameson. Visited a saw mill and strolled around town till between 5 and 6 then took passage on board Str 'Forester' up Lake Huron calling at Lake Port and Lexington. A fine brass band on board and fiddling and dancing in the cabin. Beautiful moonlight night. Home at 10.

---

52 *The Canadian Naturalist and Geologist, with the Proceedings of the Natural History Society of Montreal* vols. 1–8 (Montreal: Dawson Bros, 1856–63); 'Horrible Catastrophe!! The Steamer Montreal Burned!' *SO*, July 2, 1857; 'The Burning of the "Montreal"' *SO*, July 16, 1857. The steamer *Montreal* made regular runs between Quebec City and Montreal. As the vessel rounded Cap Rouge about fifteen miles outside Quebec at about five in the evening on June 25, 1857 a fire was discovered in the engine room. The vessel was carrying between four and five hundred passengers, 258 of whom were emigrants recently arrived from Scotland via the *Mackenzie*. Passengers were forced to jump overboard to escape the swift-moving fire. Over a hundred were picked up by the steamer *Napoleon*, while some others swam to shore. In the end, however, at least 253 passengers perished. See also *Globe* [Toronto], June 29, 30, 1857.

Sun. July 5.
Heard Mr Walker preach in the morning. Sacrament dispensed in
the afternoon. Forenoon rainy but afternoon dry and pleasant. Had
a fine walk round Point Edward in company with Chas Mackenzie,
Jameson and John Baillie. Got a few wild strawberries, woods in most
luxuriant foliage. Heard Mr Forest preach in the Scotch Church in the
evening.

Mon. July 6.
At tracing of Lever Switch. Weather sultry. Walked out in the woods
before tea and found the beautiful lily called 'Ladies Slipper' in bloom.
Caught some little blue butterflies with the net. A tremendous shower
of rain accompanied with thunder and lightning at night.

Tues. July 7.
Finished Lever Switch tracing. Weather still warm with thunder, lightning and heavy rain. Rose early and made drawing of 'Ladies Slipper.'
In the evening wrote to Mrs Logan and Alex Liddel, Jersey. Mr Gregory
went off to Komoka.

Wed. July 8.
Still beautiful weather. At Sarnia depot plan. Walked out the 4th line
before tea and caught a big Dragon Fly in the net. Went out and inspected
Forsyth's house after tea and strolled around with Jas Mackenzie.[53]

Thurs. July 9.
Party all out on line, only Mr Robb and I in the office. Took a short walk
after dinner and caught a small butterfly of a new species. Also found
tiger lilies growing wild in the woods. At Sarnia depot plan. Walked
out towards Point Edward before tea and caught 3 black moths of a
new kind. Weather most delightful.

Fri. July 10.
At Sarnia Depot plan. In the evening went out to the woods with Jas
Mackenzie and dug up some wild flowers. Coming home, met Miss
Ellen Young and Miss Gray who went with us and helped to plant them
after which we went with them to Springbank and saw Mary. Ther-
mometer as high as 94 deg.

---

53 Thomas G. Forsyth was a prominent man in mid-century Sarnia, a County Division
   Court clerk, notary public, customs officer, and merchant/speculator. He was the
   town's first mayor, serving from March until September 1857, when his election was
   overturned by a provincial court. He departed Sarnia in 1864, reportedly for Detroit.
   Dan McCaffery, 'A Look Back,' *The Sarnia Citizen* (Fall/Winter 2007): 1.

Sat. July 11.

Weather still very hot. At Sarnia Depot plan. In the afternoon Chas Mackenzie and I Walked out to Mr Neil's, an old Irvine mason about 5 miles back behind the Indian Reserve. Saw some pretty butterflies and had a fine feed of wild strawberries and cream. Slept with Chas.

Sun. July 12.

Rose and had breakfast early. Went and called on Peter Lamb, a bachelor farmer living in a house alone. Got a rattlesnake's rattle from him. Walked round through the woods, mosquitoes ferocious and innumerable. Walked home and got home about 2 o'clock. Heard Mr Shank preach in the evening.

Mon. July 13.

Still warm. At Sarnia Depot plan. Started out the 4th line at 5 o'clock in company with Jas Mackenzie and dug up two fine plants of Twin-Cap lilies about 2 miles out. In the evening had a bathe in the river. Mosquitoes rather troublesome.

Tues. July 14.

Still very sultry. At Sarnia Depot plan. In the afternoon got leave to go and see the Sarnia Rifles practicing at a target but preferred to walk out the 4th line with Jameson.[54] Caught some nice butterflies. Walked about 4 miles out and came home on the line. In the evening called at Springbank and got Jameson's watch pocket from Miss Young. Saw the old wife, a decent old woman.

Wed. July 15.

At Sarnia Depot plan. Visited Alex Mackenzie in the evening. Wrote to Mrs Logan to come along and meet me in Hamilton.

Thurs. July 16.

At Plan of Sarnia Depot grounds. Wrote home to Mother of my intention of visiting Scotland. Also to Mr Andrew and Mr Anderson. Walked out past Springbank in company with John Mackenzie, Thos, etc.

Fri. July 17.

Started from Sarnia in a spring waggon in company with Peffers and

---

54 The Sarnia Rifles were among the many local militia units that mushroomed in Canada West due to the passage of the Militia Act (1855), which permitted an active militia of five thousand men, and the military enthusiasm that swept the colonies during the Crimean War (1853–6). Desmond Morton, *A Military History of Canada*, 4th ed. (Toronto: McClelland and Stewart, 1999), 77–84.

Jameson at 7 o'clock for Lambton station, 17 miles out. Day warm. Had my net with me and caught a large yellow butterfly, a stunner, also some others. Dined at Anderson's farm and took tea at Chamber's. Made acquaintance with Mathew Lawrie, a queer old paisley fish.

Sat. July 18.
Finished Sarnia Depot plan. Took all my tools home at dinner time. In the afternoon packed up. Drank tea at A. Mackenzie's and called on Mr Walker, inspector, and on Mr Peffers. Got certificate and pass from Mr Gregory and bade good-bye. Got a present of Indian work from Mr Baillie. Visited Springbank garden and got a moss rose from Mary Young.

Sun. July 19.
Had a walk down the river with Jack Caddie, John Baillie and Mr Jameson. Heard Mr Walker preach morning and evening. Dined in Mackenzie's and had a walk out with Robt Chas Mackenzie and Jameson. Drank tea with Mr Drake. Had Jas Mackenzie down and finished packing up. Had also a visit of Mr Robb.

Mon. July 20.
Dreamed of being singing 'Will ye no come back again' to Mary Young and was wakened in the middle of it.[55] Had breakfast and shook hands with two Mrs Kents, then the two Mrs Mackenzies and on the wharf with the Clan Mackenzie and the Engineer's staff. Morning bright with delightful breeze up the river. Met with Mr Bradley and Mr Atkins on the boat. Chatted a good deal with Atkins. At Detroit between 12 and 1. Called on Mr Hose at the Locomotive Works. Got the lightning express at 3.10 from Windsor and got in to Hamilton about 9 at night. Found only Maggy McWhirter at home. Thos and wife with Mrs Logan having gone to Paris.

Tues. July 21
Had a walk up town and then called and spent an hour or so with Mrs Muir Sr and Miss M. Brother Thos got home at 1 p.m. Spent the afternoon walking about with him. Saw Mary Goldie at Mrs Muir's in the afternoon.

---

55 'Will Ye No Come Back Again?' was a traditional Scottish song that mourned the final departure of Prince Charles Edward Stuart, pretender to the throne, after the defeat of the Scottish army at Culloden in 1746. See Rev. Charles Rogers, ed., *Life and Songs of Baroness Nairne* (Edinburgh: John Grant, 1896).

Wed. July 22.
Got a new insect net made by Maggy McWhirter and went to the cemetery in the forenoon. In the afternoon had a long ramble with Thos and had a good collection of butterflies by the evening. Spent the evening setting them up. Saw a man, Fullerton, said to have lost wife and children in the 'Montreal' and whom Thos had been assisting.

Thurs. July 23.
Called on Mr Kerr and got passes for a trip to Paris. Missed the morning train and strolled round town with Thos. Called on Mr Freeman and paid $30 for passage from Quebec to Liverpool to sail Aug. 15. Took train at 1.45 for Paris. Walked out to Mrs Jackson's house and had tea and then walked to H. McWhirter's and met Mrs Logan and Mr Kay, then to Mr Drynan's and Mrs McIlwraith's. Tommie and for the first time, little Mary Duncan McI.

Fri. July 24.
Spent last night in John Jackson's. A most deplorable wet day. Started for a fishing pond and got very wet and dirty and learned when near the journey's end that the fishing canoe was pre-occupied. The company, viz Jean McWhirter, Mrs Logan, Mr Kay and I came home rather crestfallen and spent the night in Hugh McWhirter's.

Sat. July 25.
Weather rather improved. Had some butterfly hunting. Miss Muir and Miss Goldie drove over from Ayr in the afternoon. Went out with Mr Drynan and them and searched for 4-leaved clovers. Mrs Ballingal also came to tea. Drove home with her in the evening and came back and slept in Jackson's. Br. Thos arrived from Hamilton in the afternoon.

Sun. July 26.
Went to Church in Paris with Drynan's people. Day very warm. After dinner, walked over to Hugh McWhirter's and waited tea there. Thos travelling without his coat and with Tommy on his back. Slept with Mr Drynan.

Mon. July 27.
A beautiful morning. Rose between 4 and 5 to go a-fishing with Thos. Lost our way and wandered 4 hours among brush and bogs, getting very wet and dirty. At length found the pond and boat and fished successfully catching between six and eight dozen Perch, Bass and Sunfish.

Thos having caught one very large Perch. Drive over and drank tea at
Mr Ballingal's in the evening and slept in Drynan's.

Tues. July 28.
Rose early and walked into Paris with Thos who went home. Saw Miss
Muir at the station, also David Goldie who drove me round Paris in
his buggie and then went out to Dinvin. In the afternoon went out and
gathered blueberries with Mrs Logan and caught a pretty black and
white butterfly, the first of the kind.

Wed. July 29.
Walked into and out from Paris in the morning to the Post. Afterwards
got John Jackson's horse saddled and had a ride. Mrs McI, Mrs Logan
and I all drank tea in Mr Jackson's. Slept in Drynan's. Weather fine.
Made a few butterfly captures. Saw a mink in the woods.

Thurs. July 30.
Drove in to Paris with Mrs Logan in the morning intending to go to
Brantford but could get no trains to answer. Spent the forenoon with
Mrs McI. at Drynan's and went in to Paris again to see her off but found
that she had to wait on the late train and so waited and accompanied
her to Hamilton. Found letters from Mother, Mrs H., Mrs S. and Christina and Jameson.

Fri. July 31.
Got from Hamilton to Paris with 1st train and walked out to Dinvin.
Visited McWhirter's in the afternoon. Mr Kay, McWhirter and the boys
in the wheat field cradling. Took good-bye to Dinvin about 5 and drove
to Ayr in Mr. Drynan's waggon. Got a kind reception at Mr Goldie's.
Met James Goldie for the first time.

Sat. Aug. 1.
Had a sail up the Nith in a canoe with Sandy Muir. Spent the afternoon
from 1 o'clock until near 9 in the evening assisting the Haymakers. Mrs
Logan came over in Hugh McWhirter's waggon in the evening.

Sun. Aug. 2.
Beautiful weather. Attended church and heard a very long sermon in
the forenoon. Also accompanied Mrs Logan and Mary Goldie to Church
in the afternoon and had a beautiful walk home through the bush. Sat
and ate cherries and talked about 'auld lang syne' under the verandah
in the moonlight after tea.[56]

---

56 Literally, 'old times,' refering to old country, or Scottish memories.

Mon. Aug. 3.

A beautiful warm day. Went butterfly hunting in the forenoon. About mid-day got out horse and buggy and drove Mrs Logan and Mary Goldie to Galt, 11 miles away. Went by a rough road. Foundered and nearly upset in a broken embankment. Called and left Mrs L. at Mrs Campbell's in Galt and had a nice drive by moonlight home.

Tues. Aug. 4.

Strongly in the belief that Mary Goldie will make the best wife for me of anybody I know. Forenoon warm and close. Afternoon wet. Read the Ayr Observer to Mary and Jenny in the evening. Read of Agnes Mowat's death.[57]

Wed. Aug. 5.

Men all busy preparing to work at a new dam. Packed up my butterflies in the forenoon and spent it loafing round chatting to one another. Had horse and buggy at the gate after dinner and took good-bye. Got to Paris station in good time. Sandy Muir taking home the horse. Found all well in Hamilton and drank tea in Robert Young's and afterwards called at Muir's jun. and Sr.

Thurs. Aug. 6.

Had a walk to the cemetery and caught butterflies and gathered rasps, with Mrs Logan. Got some good Camberwell beauties.[58] Had a walk along the mountain in the afternoon and met a young lady who catched an insect for me. Had James and Thos Muir and Mr Baxter calling in the evening.

Fri. Aug. 7.

Mrs Logan packed up in the forenoon and departed with the train at 1.40. In the afternoon, Thos and I walked round the Bay to Oaklands[59] and came back by the ferry steamer. Worked late in repairing my chest in the evening.

Sat. Aug. 8.

Busy all day strengthening my chest and preparing for travelling. Got two cases of insects arranged and secured in the evening. Purchased a new valise $5, also white inexpressibles $2. Sat up chatting and packing, etc. till between 1 and 2 Sunday morning.

---

57 This was the Canadian version of the *Ayr Observer*. The issue containing Agnes Mowat's obituary no longer exists.

58 Deep-purple butterflies, with yellow-bordered wings (*Nymphalis antiopa*).

59 A popular outdoor recreation area on the north shore of Hamilton Harbour / Burlington Bay.

Sun. Aug. 9.
Attended St Andrew's new Church and heard Professor Weir of Kingston.[60] On coming out, called on Mr Meikle and received parcel from
him to take home. Afterwards called on Mr Muir Sr and had a Walk
down to the hollows with Mr and Mrs Muir Jr, Miss M. and Jas and
John.[61] Drank tea with them. Spent the evening at home.

Mon. Aug. 10.
Rose early and got ready for the road. Sailed on board the 'Passport' at
9 a.m. Spent from 12 to 3 in Toronto. Met with Miss Fairgreve on board
the boat and her brother as purser. Day close but a good breeze on the
lake. Boat pitched and caused some sicknsss leaving Toronto. Met Bellairs in Toronto. His Aunt and Sister going with the 'Indian' to England.

Tues. Aug. 11.
Rose and had an hour's rambling through the streets of Kingston from
5 to 6 a.m. Met Messrs Jas Muir, Harvey and Thomson there and had

---

60 On St Andrew's Church, Hamilton, see below, fn 114. Rev. George Weir (1830–91)
was born in Aberlour, Scotland, and worked as a schoolmaster in Turriff and rector
of Banff Academy until 1853, when he moved to Canada to become professor of classics at Queen's University, where he lectured until 1864. Dismissed from Queen's, he
moved to Morrin College, Quebec, in that year and taught classics and Hebrew there
until his death. John Malcolm Bulloch, ed., *Scottish Notes and Queries* (Aberdeen: A.
Brown and Company, 1900), 1:186.

61 The family of William (Sr) and Margaret (Howie) Muir was from Kilmarnock, in
Ayrshire, Scotland, but moved to Hamilton, Canada West, in 1855. Two of the Muir
children became important figures in the railway history of Ontario and Michigan.
William Ker Muir (1829–92) began his railway career as a young man with the Glasgow and South Western Railway, where he gained knowledge of 'every form of railway work' and made a name for himself. He was recruited by C.J. Brydges to become
a superintendent of the GWR in Canada West in 1852, a position he held until 1857,
when he was sent to Detroit to become manager of the Detroit and Milwaukee Railway, a GWR affiliate. In 1865, he accepted the position of assistant general superintendent of the Michigan Central Railroad, and subsequently general superintendent
of the GWR and later general manager, Canada Southern Railways. Like his brother,
James H. Muir (b. 1835) worked as a clerk for the Glasgow and South Western Railway until he followed his brother to Hamilton in 1855. He was then appointed to a
management position with the GWR until 1859, when he was transferred in March
1859 to a GWR affiliate, the Detroit, Grand Haven and Milwaukee Railroad, to work
first as auditor, then secretary-treasurer, a position he held until his death. William
Stocking and Gordon K. Miller, *The City of Detroit, Michigan, 1701–1922* (Detroit:
S.J. Clarke Publishing, 1922), 5:260–4; Paul Leake, *History of Detroit, Chronicle of Its
Progress, Its Industries, Its Institutions, and the People of the Fair City of the Straits* (Chicago and New York: the Lewis Publishing Company, 1912), 2:527–8.

their company the remainder of the voyage. Weather kept fine and had a delightful sail to Montreal which we reached about 7 p.m. Hotels full. Got quarters with difficulty in the Montreal House and slept 4 in 3 beds. Attended theatre at night and saw Mr Bennet in 'New Way to Pay old Debts.'[62]

Wed. Aug. 12.

Had a walk through the market before breakfast. Provisions and fruit cheaper than at Hamilton. Visited large French Catholic Church and ascended tower of do. Also visited Barracks and saw 39th Regt. at drill. Our party of 4 hired a small row boat and visited Victoria Bridge in progress building. Called at Mr Fleck's shop but he not in. Walked up the mountain to the water reservoir. Left Montreal with steamer 'Quebec' at 6 p.m.[63]

Thurs. Aug. 13.

Rose early and viewed river banks approaching Quebec. Landed about

---

62 This 1625 play, a domestic comedy, was the work of English dramatist Philip Massinger (1583–1640). Bennet is likely James Bennet[t] (d. 1885), an English actor from Birmingham who worked stages in Britain, New York, and other North American locales in the 1840s and '50s; 'hardly' one contemporary noted, 'a tragedian of the first flight.' R.J. Broadbent, *Annals of the Liverpool Stage* (Liverpool: Edward Howell, 1908), 310–11; quote from George Morley, 'Victorian Shakespeare Commemorations,' *Poet Lore: A Magazine of Letters* 3, no. 4 (1891): 204.

63 The 39th Regiment was formed in Britain in 1702 but reformed as the 39th (Foot) in 1807. It served in the Plattsburgh Campaign in 1814 but removed to Europe thereafter. The 39th was stationed in Montreal in 1856 after its active duty in the Crimean War, having fought at Balaclava. It remained in Montreal until 1859. *Government of Canada Canadian Military History Gateway: Canadian Military Heritage*, vol. 2: *1755–1871*, Appendix D, Regiments and Units Serving in Canada 1755–1871. www.phmc.gc.ca/cmh/en/page_219.asp. The longest bridge in the world when it was completed in 1859, the Victoria Bridge allowed train and carriage crossing over the St Lawrence River at Montreal. Work on it began in 1854, and it was officially opened by the Prince of Wales in 1860. See A.R.M. Lower, *Colony to Nation* (Toronto: Longmans Canada, 1964), 302. Alexander Fleck was the proprietor of the Vulcan Iron Works in Montreal, a producer of prize-winning ploughs and other agricultural implements, including the 'Wilkie Scotch Plow' and a 'Light Plough' that was displayed at both the London International Exhibition (1851) and the Paris Universal Exhibition (1855). See New York State Agricultural Society, *The Cultivator*, n.s., 7 (Albany, NY: Luther Tucker, 1850), 241; *Official Catalogue of the Great Exhibition of the Works of All Nations* (London: W. Clowes and Sons, 1851), np; 1855 Committee for the Paris Exhibition, *Canada at the Universal Exhibition* (Montreal: J. Lovell, 1856), 21; H. McEvoy, ed., *Province of Ontario Gazetteer and Directory* (Toronto: Robertson and Cook, 1869), 611.

6 a.m. Put up at Russell's Hotel. Strolled round town all day visiting Citadel and forts, Plains of Abraham, etc. Tore my coat and made acquaintance of Mrs Reid and family in getting it mended. Descended Cape Diamond and walked along by the docks.

Fri. Aug. 14.

Met Thomson in Mrs Reid's in the morning and spent forenoon walking round town with him. In the afternoon hired a caleche and drove to Montmorency Falls also visited the natural steps there. Haymaking going on and wheat quite green. Met Bellairs and had a walk with him and Mr Barker in the evening.

Sat. Aug. 15.

Went off with the 'Topsy' tender to the 'Indian' steamer about 9.30 a.m. and set sail immediately. Morning beautiful, wind right astern, freshening as we went along. About 1.50, passed the wreck of the 'Canadian' miles below Quebec. River widens and shores look dim as night comes on.

Sun. Aug. 16.

Slept last night rather better than I expected. First sight in the morning a fine large ship seemingly iron, in full sail crossing our stern. High land on the North for some time and for a while nearly out of sight of land. About 2, got abreast the lighthouse on the Island of Anticosti. Fired a gun and continued sailing its coast. Land all low. Hills clothed with woods, coast precipitous in some places.

Mon. Aug. 17.

Fine weather but chilly. Sailed close along the Labrador coast in the morning. Rocky and barren with numerous small rocky islands. Saw many seabirds resembling the paties and Ailsa cocks of the Firth of Clyde.[64] Kept moving out from land and nearly lost sight of it when we began to see the headlands of Newfoundland on the right. Land at a distance on both sides in the evening as we entered the Straights of Belleisle.

---

64 Ailsa Cocks is a nineteenth-century Scots term for puffins, which were plentiful on the island of Ailsa Craig until they were decimated by brown rats in the twentieth century. John Ayto and Ian Crofton, *Brewer's Britain and Ireland: The History, Culture, Folklore and Etymology of 7500 Places in These Islands* (London: Weidenfeld and Nicolson, 2005), 13. The Firth of Clyde is a large area of coastal waters surrounded by the Kintyre Peninsula and Ayrshire on Scotland's west coast.

Tues. Aug. 18.
Out of sight of land. Weather cold, rainy and miserable. Passengers all below. Air foul. Children squalling. Vomited breakfast, took no dinner. Saw a great big iceberg. Found John Henderson on board as engineer. Drank tea with him and had to run and peuk three times in the course of it. Had Mr Ross, chief engineer also the purser, and in the engineer's room at night. Had some singing and amusement.

Wed. Aug. 19.
Forenoon sunny and more pleasant than yesterday. Still vomiting everything I eat. Found Mr Porteous, one of the engineers on board, to be a nephew of old Gilbert at Burns' Monument. Had some chat with him. Reading Sam Slick's Yankee Stories.[65]

Thurs. Aug. 20.
Weather fine with gentle breeze from S.E. Sickness quite gone. Made a hearty dinner of pea soup, fresh beef and potatoes. Played quoits with rings made of rope. Evening chilly. Stove kindled in steerage and passengers singing round it. Ships officers mostly Scotch and very civil and obliging and apparently agreeable among themselves.

Fri. Aug. 21.
Forenoon calm but fine breeze of fair wind in the afternoon, freshening up as evening advanced. Passed a large ship about mid-day hailing from Christiana, Sweden, bound for Quebec.

Sat. Aug. 22.
As yesterday, calm in the morning but breezing up in the afternoon, and still fair wind. Spent an hour in the engine room with John Henderson also drank tea with him spending most of the afternoon and evening in his room on deck. Passengers and crew all in good spirits singing 'Annie Laurie,' etc. etc.[66]

---

65 Designed by Scottish architect Thomas Hamilton, the Grecian-style monument in memory of Scottish poet Robert Burns (1759–96) was erected in Alloway, near Ayr, Scotland, 1820–3. See Miles Glendinning et al., A *History of Scottish Architecture* (Edinburgh: Edinburgh University Press), 202. Old Gilbert Porteous was groundskeeper. His gravestone at Alloway Old Kirk (the 'Kirk Alloway' of Burns's poem 'Tam O'Shanter') reads: 'To the memory of Gilbert Porteous, died 20 April 1872 aged 88 who was gardener at Burns Monument for the long period of 40 years.' Communication with Tom Barclay, Carnegie Library, Ayr, Scotland. Thomas Chandler Haliburton, *Yankee Stories* (Philadelphia: Lindsey and Blakiston, 1836).
66 'Annie Laurie,' a widely known Scottish love song, was written in the late seven-

Sun. Aug. 23.
A good steady breeze of fair wind all day. Dr Ryerson from Toronto had
service in the morning and another Rev. gentleman in the evening.[67]
Time hanging on our hands rather, heavily, but hopes of seeing land
tomorrow. Tracts distributed amongst the ship's company by a gentleman cabin passenger.

Mon. Aug. 24.
Forenoon wet and wind came round tight ahead. Saw some vessels.
Afternoon fine but hazy on the horizon. Land expected by some by
mid-day and about 6 p.m. a faint streak of high land appeared through
the haze. Shortly afterwards Torrie Lightho. and island. Drank tea with
Henderson who told me of a report being cur't in the ship that I was
going home as a prisoner for embezzling £900. Storm of thunder and
lightning in the evening tremendously loud and close at hand.

Tues. Aug. 25.
Slept none all night. The air below so close and hot. Rose at 3.30 a.m.
Ship approaching to Rattlin Lightho. Sailed past within a few miles of
Fairhead. Saw the sun rise from behind the Scotch hills. Wind blew very
strong crossing the channel, especially between the Maiden's on the
Irish Coast and the Calf of 'Man.' Weathered the 'Calf' about 4 p.m.
Dark before we neared Liverpool and spent some time waiting for a
pilot. Firing guns and burning blue lights. Clock struck 2 as we got into
harbor. Had no sleep all night.

---

teenth century by William Douglas of Fingland to honour the youngest daughter of
Sir Robert Laurie of Maxwellton, Dumfries, Scotland. See *The Annie Laurie Melodist;
Containing 84 Popular Songs and Ballads* (New York: R.M. De Witt, [ca 1860]); Ira W.
Ford, comp., *Traditional Music of America* (New York: E.P. Dutton, 1940).

67 Rev. Egerton Ryerson (1803–82) was among the most influential Canadian thinkers
and statesmen in the mid-nineteenth century. A Methodist minister, he was also a
prolific author, newspaper editor, and political critic. Perhaps his greatest public
contribution came through his work as an educational administrator, the architect of
Upper Canada's public school system and long-serving superintendent of schools,
1844–76. When McIlwraith encountered him in 1857, Ryerson was at the beginning
of a 'comprehensive educational tour' to the 'principal seats of art in Holland, Germany, Italy and France.' There, he procured copies of paintings by the old masters,
which were placed in the Educational Museum in the Toronto Normal School, where
they would educate 'the public taste' and diffuse 'a knowledge of art among the
people.' John Charles Dent, 'The Rev. Egerton Ryerson, DD, LLD,' *The Canadian Portrait Gallery* (Toronto: John B. Magurn, 1880), 1:200. See also R.D. Gidney, 'Ryerson,
Egerton,' *DCB*, XI (Toronto: University of Toronto Press, 1982), 11:783–95.

Wed. Aug. 26.

Landed shortly after daylight and spent morning rambling round streets untill the Banks opened at 10 a.m. Found the bankers would not cash my draft which was upon London. Called Peter Hosie at Cunard's Engine Works and borrowed £3 from him. Got my luggage through the Customs Ho. Officers very civil. Spent the afternoon rambling around with Mr Hosie. Visited St George's Hall, the Market, etc. and attended Gordon Cummin's Exhibition at night.[68] Slept at the Angel Hotel.

Thurs. Aug. 27.

Visited the steamer 'Indian' and dined with the engineers. Got on board the 'Princess Royal' for Glasgow which sailed at 3.p.m. Made the acquaintance of Mr Taylor, 2nd Engineer, The steamer a fine new one. Weather fine with a good view of harbor, etc. Close to Isle of Man about 10. Sea smooth. Ship very full with both passengers and luggage.

Fri. Aug. 28.

Got on deck at 6 a.m. Steamer then close to Holy Isle Arran. A delightful clear fresh morning and the sail up Clyde most glorious. Landed in Greenock at 8.30 and took the first train home. Arrived in Ayr at 12.30. Found Jane and Christina Stewart waiting. Mother and Mr H. at home. Called on Mr Park in the evening. Met John Goldie at Mrs Stewart's.

Sat. Aug. 29.

Called on Mr McIlwraith in the morning. Went to Burns Monument with John Goldie and Mrs and Miss Gray. Called on Mr Cowan and Mr Meikle in the evening. Had John Goldie at tea.

Sun. Aug. 30.

At the Newton Kirk and heard Mr Wallace, a candidate for the Church

---

68 Designed by Harvey Lonsdale Elmes and built in 1854, St George's Hall, Liverpool, was among Britain's grandest municipal concert halls. See Michael Forsyth, *Buildings for Music: The Architect, the Musician and the Listener from the Seventeenth Century to the Present Day* (Cambridge: Cambridge University Press, 1985), 140–1; Scottish hunter and traveller Roualeyn George Gordon-Cumming (1820–66) was nicknamed 'the Lion Hunter' for his exploits among big game in southern Africa. Schooled at Eton, he was a solider in India and the Cape Colony in the late 1830s and 1840s, but returned to Britain in 1848. He published an account of his hunting exploits in 1850 and created an exhibition of his hunting trophies and an illustrated lecture (billed as the 'South Africa Museum') that travelled throughout the British Isles in the 1850s. The *Encyclopaedia Britannica*, 11th ed. (New York: The Encyclopaedia Britannica Company, 1910), 12:254.

from Edinburgh. A clever preacher. Had tea all together in Mrs Stewart's. Had Nupie over and had a crack in the evening.[69]

Mon. Aug. 31.
Wrote to Mr Hosie, Liverpool. Left Mrs Campbell's parcel at Mrs Dr Craig's. Called upon and had a long talk with Mr Cavan, clothier. After dinner had a long walk with Mother round by Content along the Railway bridge over the river out the race course road and home by the shore.

Tues. Sept. 1.
Waited at the Girvan steamer for Aunt Dickie and Maggie Hogg who arrived at 11 o'clock. Spent the day with Aunt – Mrs Hunter. Her and I visited Mr Casilis' garden and got fine bunches of flowers. Had Mrs Park calling in the evening.

Wed. Sept. 2.
Called on Mr McCrae and had a walk along the Newton shore with him. Had a visit from him after dinner. Called and had a chat with Mrs Parks, also with Mrs John McIlwraith. Mr Hunter, Mother and I had tea with Mrs Andrew, Main St. Newton. Sat late at home writing to Thomas.

Thurs. Sept. 3.
Met Hugh Dickie at the Railway Station who arrived with the forenoon train. Went to the races with him and saw one or two races. Rain then came on and we made the best of our way home, being completely drenched. Came home and got changed and in the evening went to the theatre and saw two comedies pretty well acted.

Fri. Sept. 4.
Weather looking better. Mr John, Hugh Dickie, J. Stewart and I went to the races. Saw three races then Hugh and I started for the Monument. Had a chat with Gilbert Porteous there and strolled all around. Got

---

69 The Newton Kirk was the McIlwraith family's home church. Built in 1777, it was torn down in the late 1960s. Reverend Robert Wallace (1831–99) served as minister of the Newton Kirk from 1857 to 1860, his first ecclesiastical appointment after being licensed to preach by the Presbytery of Edinburgh. He achieved considerable fame in his time – as minister of Old Greyfriars, professor of church history at the University of Edinburgh, editor of *The Scotsman* newspaper, and MP for East Edinburgh – but only after he left Ayr. Communication with Tom Barclay, Carnegie Library, Ayr, Scotland; John Campbell Smith and William Wallace, *Robert Wallace, Life and Last Leaves* (London: Sands, 1903). He was warmly welcomed at Newton-on-Ayr and accepted the call as pastor there in late October. See 'Newton Parish Church,' *Ayr Observer*, September 15, 1857; 'The Newton Church,' *Ayr Observer*, October 27, 1857; 'Newton Parish Church,' *Ayr Advertiser*, October 29, 1857. A crack, or *craic*, meant a good time.

home between 6 and 7. H.D. had his likeness and mine taken on one plate. Spent the evening strolling round town, Br. Bill, H.D., and Mr Dugald Kelly.

Sat. Sept. 5.
Weather in forenoon cool and fine. Saw Hugh Dickie and Aunt off with the steamer and strolled down the quay. Some flashes of lightning appearing in the distance which increased to a thunder storm with heavy rain in the afternoon. Wm Taylor, a fisherman from Newton, Ayr, killed by lightning in his boat at the Lady Isle.[70] Called and had some chat with Maggie McIlwraith in the afternoon and again after tea.

Sun. Sept. 6.
At church and heard an elderly stranger preach. Met with Mrs Kay and her son from Mossend Farm in Mrs Stewart's between sermons. After church time in company with Christina, Mother and John, had a walk out Whitlets Road and to the waterside at over mill.

Mon. Sept. 7.
Called on Mr Cowan and ordered 1 pr pants and 2 vests. Spent the forenoon in Mrs Stewart's and strolled down the quay. In the afternoon walked out with Mrs Hunter and called at Murphy's, Archie Smith's, Vass's, and Wylie's. Spent the evening in Mrs Park's with Miss Park, Miss Sarah P. and the Mrs.

Tues. Sept. 8.
Went in to town and saw Sanger's procession of equestrian performers and bushmen.[71] Afternoon very wet. Visited McIlwraith's, and had a chat with Maggy. Drank tea in Mrs Stewart's and accompanied Christina, the two Misses Stewarts and Miss Hogg and Jack Stewart to the circus which pleased well.

Wed. Sept. 9.
Took steamer 'Scotia' at l p.m. in company with Mother for Girvan. Met James and Alex King from Glasgow on board. Had to go on shore in a

---

70 Taylor's death was the cause of great local concern because he left behind a widow and three young children. A donations campaign was quickly undertaken to benefit the family. [Letter to the Editor], *Ayr Observer*, September 8, 1857; 'The Accident at Lady Isle,' *Ayr Observer*, September 15, 1857; 'Death by Lightning at the Lady Isle,' *Ayr Advertiser*, September 10, 1857.

71 'Lord' George Sanger (1827–1911) was a circus impresario whose shows played throughout North America and Europe in the Victorian era. See George Sanger, *Seventy Years a Showman* (Toronto: J.M. Dent and Sons, 1926).

small boat and got some rocking. Walked out to Bridgmill and found all well. Went in to town with Hugh Dickie in the eve. Met Mr Drynan and had a horn with him. Got introduced to a club of Girvan young men and had a pie and glass of toddy.

Thurs. Sept. 10.
Walked with H.D. out to Curagh Farm and had a chat with Hugh Jameson and from that to Bog Head where Mother and Aunt had gone. Saw all the family and a Miss Miller from Edinburgh. Walked from there to Barows Mill and called on 'Potts' family. Met Murchie of Woodhead there and got invited to his 'Kirn.'[72] In the evening called on Mr Goldie, Dr Crawford and John Dickie and Mrs Kelly. I saw a bible in Mrs Kelly's dated 1599.

Fri. Sept. 11.
Had a walk on the North shore of Girvan with Hugh Dickie and my Mother and gathered shells. Went into town with Hugh in the afternoon and had a fine ramble along the South shore. Called on Mr McKenna, stationer, and after tea, walked out to Boghead and spent an hour there then went on to Woodhead, arriving there about 8 p.m. Danced all night in the barn Company large and respectable. Met Misses McGarvan of Girvan.

Sat. Sept. 12.
Got home from the spree at 5 a.m. Did not go to bed but took a short walk and then had breakfast. Mother and I took coach at 8 a.m. Morning most beautiful. Went by the Dailly road up by the south bank of Girvan water through Dailly and so on to Maybole amid enchanting scenery. Took train at Maybole and got home about 11. Went to bed for 2 hours and kept house all day after.

Sun. Sept. 13.
Heard Mr Wallace preach in the Newton Church as candidate for it in the forenoon. Went with John to the Burgher in the afternoon and heard Mr McInnes.[73] Had Miss Ferris company at tea and afterwards walked

---

72 Feast held on the completion of a harvest; a harvest home (Scottish and northern English dialect).
73 The 'Burgher Church' in Ayr was the Darlington Place United Presbyterian Church, built in 1799. 'Burgher,' an antiquated term, referenced a 1747 split in the Church of Scotland over the Burgess Oath, which required public office holders to affirm their belief in the religion of the Kingdom, a push that many (the anti-Burghers) loudly rejected as religious compulsion in civil affairs. The Burghers and anti-Burghers

to Kingcase Well with her, Mother, Mrs Hunter, Christina, Mrs Stewart and family and Maggy Hogg.

Mon. Sept. 14.
Walked down the quay in the forenoon and inspected the Russian gun, a 32-pounder from Sebastopol, in Fullerton's back yard.[74] About 2 p.m. started for a ramble in company with Bill and Jack Stewart on the town shore. Walked by the road to Brakeny Bay and back down the shore. Day very fine. Saw 2 seals swimming and gathered some shells. Called at McIlwraith's and had a waltz with the girls in the evening.

Tues. Sept. 15.
Christina, Maggy Hogg and myself started with the train for Maybole at 9.20 a.m. Saw Maggy off from Maybole with the coach for Girvan then Missie and I walked out to Crossaguel Abbey and had a walk through it, then back through Maybole and home by the old road over Carrick Hill, arriving about 4 p.m. in time to see an interesting spectacle of a man ascending and detaching the vane of Ayr steeple. Had Mr Cassilis calling in the evening.

Wed. Sept. 16.
Walked down the quay and loafed about untill dinner. Had a visit of Miss Maggy McIlwraith after dinner. Mother and I returned the visit to their house and then walked out to meet Mrs Stewart returning from blackberry gathering but missed her and walked round over mill and back. Saw men on the top of the steeple again.[75] In the evening had a lottery of six views of Quebec which John won.

---

reunited in 1820, but the term remained in use. Rev. Robert M. McInnes, a Glaswegian, was newly ordained as Darlington Place minister in August 1857. See William MacKelvie, *Annals and Statistics of the United Presbyterian Church* (Edinburgh: Oliphant and Company and Andrew Elliott), 407; William Stephen, *History of the Scottish Church* (Edinburgh: David Douglas, 1896), 2:521.

74 The British and French siege of Sebastopol (1854–5) was the final battle of the Crimean War. All sorts of Crimean War souvenirs – but cannons, especially – whether captured from the Russians or retired by the British, were used throughout the British Empire by the 1860s as war monuments, memorializing the war and its veterans. See Trevor Royle, *Crimea: The Great Crimean War, 1854–1856* (London: Palgrave Macmillan, 2004).

75 The Ayr town spire was being repaired and the vane replaced and equipped with a lightning rod. It had been blown down in a storm three and a half years earlier. 'The Steeple,' *Ayr Advertiser*, September 17, 1857; 'The Vane on the Spire,' *Ayr Observer*, October 20, 1857.

Thurs. Sept. 17.
Forenoon wet. Spent the forenoon mostly in Mrs Stewart's with Mr and Mrs Laughlin from Glasgow and Miss Vass. Called on Mr Cowan in the afternoon and on Mrs Park. Went to a supper party in Mrs Vass's at 8 p.m. Christina, Bill, the three Stewart's and I.

Fri Sept. 18.
Spent the forenoon writing to Br. Thomas, Mrs Logan and A. Jameson, Sarnia. After dinner, started for Moss-end. Christina, Bill and I, and got a kind reception from Mrs Kay and sons. Had a glass of toddy and some singing in the evening. The Messrs Kay, most outrageous singers. Weather most delightful.

Sat. Sept. 19.
A splendid sunny morning. Rose early and had a short walk to the Martynham Loch, also viewed Loch Snipe and Loch Fergus. Had breakfast and took the road before 9 o'clock. A delightful walk. Saw peesweeps, Larks, Yoits Robins, etc. and ate blackberries. Home about 10.

Sun. Sept. 20.
Heard Mr Dykes preach in the Newton Church. Mrs Stewart's family and our own met and got dinner with Mother after Church time. After dinner, John and I walked out the Whitlet's Road down Brocklehill Ave and across the 'Ayr' at Tarholm Brig and home by the Cumnock Road. Saw a pheasant and lots of rabbits. Walked home with Mr McCohn, sometime shop boy with Dr Tinnion.[76]

Mon. Sept. 21.
Bill and I rose early and started by 6 a.m. for Carrick Hill. Morning hazy but fine. Went up past Newark and right along the top of the hill which we reached by 8 a.m. View very fine. The white mist lying in the valleys and the hill tops appearing black. Arran, Ailsa, etc. Got home by 1 p.m. Went to Mr Cowan's and drank tea and spent the evening. Met with Mr Alex Grant.

Tues. Sept. 22.
Spent the forenoon superintending and arranging about shirt mak-

---

76 Rev. Thomas Dykes, DD, was rector of the Church of Scotland, Ayr, from 1854 to 1909. See Strawhorn, *The History of Ayr*, 194; John Tinnion, MD, was a physician in mid-century Ayr and author of an unorthodox (and poorly received) medical treatise, *A New Theory and Treatment of Disease, Founded upon Natural Principles* (Edinburgh: MacLachan, Stewart and Company, 1843). See the review by John Forbes MD, FRS, FGS in *British and Foreign Medical Review* 15 (January-April 1843): 540.

ing etc. Spent most of the afternoon and evening drinking tea at McIl-wraith's. Had a note from John Goldie with invitation to Edinburgh.

Wed. Sept. 23.

In the forenoon took a walk up the Newton Shore and met accidentally with Wm Gibb who is now staying at Prestwick Toll in delicate health. Dined in Mrs Stewart's and had a walk with Mother after dinner along the town shore to the Doonfoot and home by the race-course road. Called on Mrs Park in the evening.

Thurs. Sept. 24.

Christina and I went to attend 'Aimers' trial for embezzlement in the County buildings but found doors closed so went and had a walk thro' Imrie's Nursery and got some flowers. Had a tea party in Mother's with Miss Vass, Miss Andrew and Mr Hugh Allan.[77]

Fri. Sept. 25.

Took train at 7.15 to Kilmarnock. Rambled round the streets an hour or so and then called at the Railway work shops upon Messrs Sum-merville and Underwood. Had a walk around the works and met Thos Hart, R. Boyd and several old hands. Stopped at Irvine coming home and delivered Mr Neil's parcel to Mr Armour. Got home at 6 p.m. and in company with Bill, visited Mr Cassels, the gardener.[78]

Sat. Sept. 26.

Had an appointment with Christina and the two young Misses Stewart to have a walk but morning turned out stormy. Christina Stewart and I started at 12, took shelter from a shower in a cottage at Laigh Brig of Doon and saw a man, Wilson and family about starting for Illinois. Went down to the shore beyond Greenan Castle and gathered shells homeward. Called at McIlwraith's in the evening.

Sun. Sept. 27.

Heard a stranger preach at the Newton Church. Had Mr Service, gar-

---

77 This was a celebrated case that received a good deal of ink in the popular press. See 'Ayr Autumn Circuit,' *Ayr Advertiser*, September 24, 1857.

78 Kilmarnock was a burgeoning railway hub, and the 'extensive' railway workshops in Kilmarnock employed about four hundred hands by 1858. Hard by the work-shops near Bonnington Square was housing built for the families of artisans and others employed; in 1858, 23 houses were occupied by 92 working families. See Archibald M'Kay, *The History of Kilmarnock* (Kilmarnock: Archibald M'Kay, 1858), 257-8. McIlwraith's acquaintance with several workshop hands here may indicate that he served an apprenticeship as a patternmaker in Kilmarnock.

dener from Doonholm calling between sermons. Our folk all met to tea in Mrs Stewart's after service. Christina in the sulks, the rest all happy.

Mon. Sept. 28.
Had a letter from Thos in the morning with news of dull trade and enclosing a letter from John Armstrong from Albany. Called on Mrs Park and after dinner went to the 'Court House' and heard Lord 'Ivry' sentence a man 'Aimers' to 4 years servitude for theft. Drank tea in Mrs Park's in the evening, present my Mother, Mrs Park and her daughter from Garden St. and all Park's people.

Tues. Sept. 29.
Took the train for Glasgow at 7.15 in company with Miss Stewart. When there, visited the 'Edinburgh' steamer and thence to Gowan to deliver Mr Robb's parcel then back to Glasgow. Called upon and had tea in Mr Lachlin's. Took the Afternoon Dumbarton boat to Bowling and thence by train to Ballock. Walked to Arden and called upon Mr Begg, the gardener, who kindly kept us all night.

Wed. Sept. 30.
Rose early and had a walk around the grounds and into the house and saw the original portrait of 'Rob Roy' and also Mr and Mrs Buchanan.[79] Walked across the hills to Helensburgh and had convoy from Miss Begg most of the way. Parted from Mrs Stewart at Greenock and called and had tea at Mr Andrew's and then called on Mrs Campbell (late E. Andrews). Took steamer to Bowling and walked into Dumbarton. Stayed at Anderson's and had a visit from P. McIntyre and G. Grey. Wet.

Thurs. Oct. 1.
Rose and went to the work with Mr Anderson, also visited Dennyston Forge and Foundry. After breakfast had a walk round in company with Jas Wardropper and P. McIntyre and called on Mrs Brock and Janet. Drank tea with them in the afternoon and missed the train. Walked to Bowling and thence by boat and horse van to Paisley. Walked out to Halkid Mills and spent the night with Wm Dickie. Weather wet.

---

79 This could have been a widely published engraving done by H.H. Worthington (ca 1795–ca 1839) 'from an original drawing.' See http://www.walterscott.lib.ed.ac.uk/ portraits/engravers/images/rob_roy.html (accessed February 21, 2011).

Fri. Oct. 2.

Took the first train home. Went and viewed Noel Paton's picture of 'The Return from the Crimea' in the Assembly Rooms.[80] Brought Lizzie McIlwraith and the two Misses McGarvan over to see my butterflies. Called in McIlwraith's in the afternoon. Weather very stormy. Spent the evening at home and had Missie at tea.

Sat. Oct. 3.

Took train at 7.15 a.m. to Glasgow passing right thro' and on to Edinburgh which I reached between 12 and 1. Went to Mrs Goldie's and found John out. Walked about the streets till evening when he came home in company with Messrs Boyle from 'Raith' and Ronald from 'Binnler,' near Ayr. Went all together to the theatre 'Royal' in the evening and saw 'The Lady of the Lake.'[81]

Sun. Oct. 4.

Heard Mr Wm Reid of the U.P. Church preach in the morning and Mr Thos Guthrie in the afternoon.[82] Guthrie's church very full and had to

---

80　Joseph Noel Paton (1823–1901) was a Scottish painter who rendered historical, religious, and allegorical subjects. Admitted to the Royal Scottish Academy in 1847, his 'Home! The Return from Crimea' (1856), depicts a bandaged soldier sitting in his kitchen newly returned to his wife. One of his most popular works, a copy was commissioned in 1859 by Queen Victoria for the Royal Exhibition. Its showing in the Newton Assembly Rooms (a public space on Main Street adjacent to the school and the Newton Church) in Ayr was eagerly awaited. M.F. Conolly, *Biographical Dictionary of Eminent Men of Fife* (Edinburgh: Inglis and Jack, 1866), 356; A.R. Spofford and Charles Annandale, eds., *Century Cyclopaedia and Atlas* (New York and Philadelphia: Gebbie and Co., 1901), 6:323; '"Home" by Noel Paton,' *Ayr Observer*, September 8, 1857.

81　The first Theatre Royale was built in Shakespeare Square at the east of Princes Street in Edinburgh. Built in 1769, it was demolished not long after McIlwraith visited it, in 1859. The play was Edmund John Eyre's stage version of Sir Walter Scott's classic 1810 poem. Edmund John Eyre, *The Lady of the Lake: A Melo-Dramatic Romance in Three Acts* (London: W.H. Wyatt, 1811); Bill Findlay, ed., *A History of Scottish Theatre* (Edinburgh: Polygon, 1998).

82　Rev. William Reid (1814–96) was ordained as minister to the United Presbyterian Church, Lothian Road, Edinburgh in 1843. Though he was joined by a colleague and successor in 1866, Reid was still active in 1892, when the congregation held a jubilee ceremony for him. He was among Scotland's leading temperance advocates and orators in the 1850s and '60s and a prolific author of religious texts. Rev. Thomas Guthrie, DD (1803–73), was a prominent Presbyterian minister and philanthropist, one of the most popular Scottish preachers of the mid-nineteenth century. Educated at the University of Edinburgh, he held pastorates at Arbirlot (Angus) in 1827 and in 1837, Greyfriars in Edinburgh, where the poverty and deprivation that he witnessed stand in the passage till an old lady in the front seat took sick and went out when Mr Goldie and I got in.

Mon. Oct. 5.
Morning fine. Went out walking with Messrs Boyle and Ronald. Went to the top of Nelson's Monument on the Calton Hill, also visited the 'Museum of the College of Surgeons' and the 'College Museum.' Saw the 16th Lancers at drill on the Plain outside of Hollyrood Palace. In the evening went to an entertainment of Scottish scenery, dancing and singing.[83]

Tues. Oct. 6.
Called on Mr Jas Carrick to ask advice on taking drawing lessons, who said to postpone the affair till Thursday. Called on Miss Fulton Brewer and paid an account for Mrs Stewart. Strolled about town all day. Messrs Boyle and Ronald went home in the evening.

Wed. Oct. 7.
Observed a general fast on account of Indian Revolt. Had a walk with John Goldie round the suburbs of the town by comely bank road. Found Reid's church shut and walked thro' the town across Bruntfield Links and out as far as the Braid Hills, crossed them and on to a different road leading into town. Attended St Andrew's Church in the afternoon and on leaving it had to walk to the top of Arthur's Seat, also thro' Young's Foundry.[84]

---

pushed him to set up 'ragged' schools, improve housing and work conditions, and promote temperance. During the 'Disruption' of 1843, he led most of his congregation out of the Established Church to form the Free St John's Church at Castlehill, where he ministered until his retirement, due to poor health, in 1864. See Thomas Guthrie, *Life of the Rev. Thomas Guthrie, D.D.* (Glasgow: John S. Marr and Sons, nd); Rev. William Mackelvie, DD, *Annals and Statistics of the United Presbyterian Church* (Edinburgh: Oliphant and Company, 1873), 203–4; P.T. Winskill, *The Temperance Movement and Its Workers* (London: Blackie and Son, 1892), 261.

83 These sites were popular tourist attractions for nineteenth-century visitors to Edinburgh, each reflecting the city's character as a seat of high culture and British influence. Holyrood Palace was Queen Victoria's Scottish residence. See generally Katherine Grenier, *Tourism and Identity in Scotland, 1770–1914: Creating Caledonia* (Burlington, VT: Ashgate, 2005).

84 The Indian Revolt began as a mutiny of native Indian soldiers (sepoys) against their officers in the British East India Company's army in northern India, but developed into a proto-rebellion of several Indian groups against imperial rule. The conflict lasted from May 1857 until June 1858, when the British army gained control. The Revolt resulted in the replacement of the East India Company's regime in northern India and the imposition of direct imperial rule. These events prompted an emotional response

Thurs. Oct. 8.

Not having heard of a drawing master to suit, I took a train to Musselburgh Races. Day miserably wet. Walked along the shore at Musselburgh
and gathered shells while one race took place and then came home without seeing any. Called on Mr Carrick who recommended Mr Dale, Clerk
St. as a drawing master whom I then called upon and agreed with.[85]

Fri. Oct. 9.

Commenced my drawing lessons from 10 to 1. with Mr Dale who is a very
affable cockney gent. More of an artist and ornamental designer than an
architectural draughtsman. Strolled round town in the afternoon. In the
evening called upon Mr Small and afterwards went to practise of singing
in U.P. Church. Met and went home with the Misses Menzies.

Sat. Oct. 10.

After drawing lesson, had an afternoon walk with Mr Goldie down to
the beach above Granton. In the evening went to Cook's Circus in company with Helen Walls, Mr G's little neice. Evening very wet.

Sun. Oct. 11.

Attended Mr Reid's U.P. Church in the forenoon and in the afternoon
heard the great Dr Candlish. In the evening heard sermon in the old
church of St Giles. Thought Dr Candlish a dry sort of a customer and
felt very drowsy under him.[86]

---

in Britain. See David Savage, 'The Indian Rebellion of 1857: A Crisis in British Imperial Consciousness,' in Caroline Litzenberger and Eileen Groth Lyon, eds., *The Human
Tradition in Modern Britain* (Lanham, MD: Rowman and Littlefield, 2006), 111–26.
St Andrew's Church was built in the 1780s on George Street at St Andrew's Square,
Edinburgh. This church was the site of the Disruption of 1843 when, aggravated by the
increasing control of the government over Church of Scotland business, 470 ministers
'walked out' of their commissions and formed the Free Church. Arthur's seat is the
800-foot peak of a group of hills that overlook Edinburgh's city centre. Oliphant Smea-
ton, *The Story of Edinburgh* (London: J. Dent and Co., 1905), 2, 294.

85 Held in Leith from the late eighteenth century, horse races were moved east to
Musselburgh in 1817, where they have been held since. The races drew a colourful
crowd in the nineteenth century; race watchers were solicited by vendors of all sorts
of good and services, including prostitution. James Paterson, *History of the Regality
of Musselburgh* (Musselburgh: James Gordon, 1857), 142; Richard Holt, *Sport and the
British: A Modern History* (London: Oxford University Press, 1990), 181–2. Likely R.P.
(Randall Pool) Dale, who is listed as 'artist,' 24 Clerk Street, Edinburgh, 1854–60.
Edinburgh Directory, National Library of Scotland Online Resources, http://www.
nls.uk/catalogues/resources/sbti/sbti.pdf.

86 Robert Smith Candlish (1806–73) was among Scotland's best-known theologians

Mon. Oct. 12.
Day seeming to brighten up a little so, after lessons, had a climb to the top of Arthur's Seat up the face of the hill. Had a good view of the Bass Rock, North Berwick Law, etc. Had a walk around the Grass Market and bought a T-square. In the evening strolled round town.

Tues. Oct. 13.
Visited Short's Observatory but day rather dull to see the Camera to any advantage. Furnished with a note of introduction from Mr Dale. Called at Establishment of Schenk and McFarlane, lithographers, and was kindly shown thro' the premises by Mr McF. Saw a great variety of maps and pictures in progress of printing. Sat late in the house talking and reading. Called on Mr Small in the evening.[87]

Wed. Oct. 14.
In the afternoon after drawing lessons, visited the Museum of Scottish Antiquarian Society by an order from Dr McLagan. Saw the 'Maiden' or Scottish Guillotin. John Knox's pulpit, etc.[88] Strolled about the streets in the evening.

Thurs. Oct. 15.
Had a walk to the sea-side and thro' the village of Newhaven before

---

and preachers in the mid-nineteenth century. Born in Edinburgh, he was raised in Glasgow, educated at Glasgow College, and licensed to preach in the Glasgow Presbytery in 1828. He became prominent in Edinburgh, however, accepting a call as pastor of St George's, where he served from 1839 to 1873. A talented theologian and published author, he was also an educator, rising to position of principal of New College, Edinburgh, in 1861. William Wilson, DD, *Memorials of Robert Smith Candlish, DD* (Edinburgh: Adam and Charles Black, 1880).

87 Short's Observatory was named for Thomas Short, who owned a telescope and opened a public observatory on Calton Hill in the late 1770s. In 1822, the site became the Royal Observatory, operating on government funds. H.A. Brück, *The Story of Astronomy in Edinburgh from Its Beginnings until 1975* (Edinburgh: Edinburgh University Press, 1983). On Schenk and McFarlane, Lithographers, see Paul Barnaby, 'Schenck and McFarlane,' Walter Scott Digital Archive, Edinburgh University Library, www.walterscott.lib.ed.ac.uk/portraits/engravers/schenck.html (accessed February 21, 2011).

88 Founded in 1780, the Society of Antiquaries of Scotland was located on Chambers Street in Edinburgh. The Society's Royal Museum was a central repository for Scotland's artefactual past, including the wooden pulpit used by the father of the Scottish Reformation, removed and remounted on a museum wall, and the Scottish Guillotin, the 'Maiden,' used to mete out punishment to murderers and traitors in Scotland from 1565 to 1710. Charles John Guthrie, *John Knox and John Knox's House* (Edinburgh and London: Oliphant, Anderson and Ferrier, 1898), 121; Alan S. Bell, *The Scottish Antiquarian Tradition* (Edinburgh: John Donald, 1981).

breakfast with J.G. Heard the fishermen in the oyster boats singing at their work. After drawing, went to the Botanical Gardens and saw thro the Museum there. In the evening went to see the Queen arriving from the North and saw her cavalcade but not herself as her carriage was dark.[89]

Fri. Oct. 16.
Rose with the intention of seeing the Queen but heard the guns signalling her departure as I was getting my coat on. Had a walk round the Calton Hill with Mr Goldie. Morning miserably wet. Had a long talk with Mr Small in the afternoon. In the evening went and saw 'Patchwork,' an entertainment by Mr and Mrs Howard Paul.[90] Bought a second-hand desk.

Sat. Oct. 17.
Wrote to Bill and Mrs Stewart in the morning. In the afternoon about 3.30, started with Mr Goldie to walk to Roslin and got there in time to see the Chapel and Castle before it got quite dark. Found then that the conveyances were all gone and had to walk home in darkness. Had a fine view of the city lights. Called on the Misses Menzies when we got home.

Sun. Oct. 18.
Heard sermon in the Music Hall in the forenoon and walked in Warriston Cemetery in the interval. In the afternoon heard Dr Lees in Grayfriars Church and afterwards had a long walk to Grange Cemetery and

---

89 The fifty-acre Botanic Garden in Edinburgh was established in 1820. Its Botanical Museum was operated by Edinburgh University in the nineteenth century and used for lectures, though it was open to the public. Edward P. Alexander, *Museums in Motion: An Introduction to the History and Function of Museums* (Lanham, MD: AltaMira Press, 1996), 103–4; *Guide to the Royal Botanic Garden: Edinburgh* (Edinburgh: Edmonston and Douglas, 1873).

90 'Patchwork' was described by one contemporary reviewer as 'a clatter of fun, frolic, son and impersonation carried on by performers of unfailing dash'; an early sort of vaudeville, perhaps. Born in Philadelphia, Howard Paul (1830–1905) moved to England in 1850 to write for and act in plays on the London stage, where he met his future wife. Mrs Paul (née Isabella Featherstone, 1835–79), was a widely known actress and singer whose talents, one source implies, were not best reflected in the 'light' productions in which she was cast by her American husband. See 'Paul, Howard,' in James Grant Wilson, ed., *Appleton's Cyclopedia of American Biography* (New York: D. Appleton and Company, 1888), 4:678–9; 'Paul, Mrs. Howard,' in Charles Eyre Pascoe, ed., *Our Actors and Actresses: The Dramatic List*, 2nd ed. (London: David Bogue, 1880), 414; Allan Stuart Jackson, *The Standard Theatre of Victorian England* (Madison, NJ: Fairleigh Dickinson University Press, 1993), 143.

right round the suburbs of the town, past Marchiston and in by the West end.[91]

Mon. Oct. 19.

Had a walk to the end of the chair pier at Newhaven before breakfast. In company with Mr Goldie, visited the library of the 'Writers to the Signet' and got inspecting a volume of plates of Audubon's American Birds.[92] Afterwards walked 3 miles out to Liberton to call upon Mr Greive but found him from home. In the evening strolled round town and bot 2 pictures at Rutherford's auction.

Tues. Oct. 20.

Day close but mild and not raining. Took an afternoon walk to Musselburgh by way of Duddingstone. Called on Mr Patterson in Musselburgh and had a walk and drank tea with him. Got home by 7 and had an evening stroll round the Calton Hill with John Goldie.

Wed. Oct. 21.

Had a call of Mr Greive from Liberton at Mr Dale's in the forenoon. After leaving drawing practice, called on and had a chat with Jn Patterson at the Scotsman office, then visited in succession, the Castle and Regalia, Galleries of Painting and Sculpture and Holyrood Palace. Strolled round town and read Heart of Midlothian with John Goldie in the evening.[93]

---

91 Opened in 1843, Edinburgh's opulent Music Hall was part of the city's Assembly Rooms located on George Street. Located in north Edinburgh on the Water of Leith, Warriston Cemetery was a garden cemetery designed by Edinburgh architect David Cousin (1809–78). It was opened by the Edinburgh Cemetery Company in 1843, and included a line of catacombs at the centre of the site and a mortuary chapel. John Gifford, Colin McWilliam, and David Walker, *The Buildings of Scotland: Edinburgh* (New Haven, CT: Yale University Press, 1991), 576. Dr Robert Lee (1804–68) was minister of Old Greyfriars Church in Edinburgh and professor of Biblical Criticism and Antiquaries at the University of Edinburgh. Widely respected, he stirred controversy in 1859 when he argued in favour of innovation in Presbyterian church service. William Knight, *Some Nineteenth-Century Scotsmen* (Edinburgh and London: Oliphant, Anderson and Ferrier, 1903), 63–5. The Grange Cemetery was designed by architect David Bryce (1803–76) and laid out in Edinburgh's south side in 1847. Malcolm Cant, *Edinburgh: Sciennes and the Grange* (Edinburgh: John Donald, 1990).

92 The Library of the Writers to the Signet was located at the west end of Parliament Square on the Royal Mile in Edinburgh. Ernest C. Thomas and Charles Welch, eds., *Transactions and Proceedings of the Third Annual Meeting of the Library Association of the United Kingdom* (London: Chiswick Press, 1881), 146–7; John James Audubon, *The Birds of America*, 4 vols. (London: by the author, 1827–38).

93 Founded in 1817 as a weekly and elevated to a daily in 1855, the *Scotsman* was a

Thurs. Oct. 22.

Morning fine but foggy, the sun shining bright through it. Started before breakfast with Mr Goldie and walked along the edge of Salisbury Crags and then back thru the valley behind them to St Anthony's Chapel. The day being sacramental fast, spent forenoon writing to Tom and afternoon accompanying Mr Goldie on a walk to the Pentland Hills, ascending the top of the nearest and having a fine view.

Fri. Oct. 23.

Suffering under an attack of bile on the stomach from eating cheese the night previous. Walked down to the Zoological Gardens in the forenoon but was very sick and uneasy and came home and spent the afternoon in bed. Mrs Goldie very kind and careful in attending upon me. Took two pills and got my feet bathed and felt relieved before going to bed.

Sat. Oct. 24.

Felt quite well again this morning. Called on Dale and got my drawings. Made some purchases about town, also called on Mrs Quigly and Mr Small. Took good-bye with Goldie's people and left Edinburgh at 2 o'clock. Got home safe to Ayr about 8 and found all well.

Sun. Oct. 25.

Heard Mr Wallace (Newton minister-to-be) preach in the Newton Church fore- and afternoon. Mrs Stewart and all her family at tea with Mother after church time.

Mon. Oct. 26.

Spent the forenoon writing to Mr Jn Goldie, Mr Andrew and Mr P. Hosie. In the afternoon visited Mrs Guthrie's to deliver compliments from Mr Drynan. Spent the remainder of the day between Mrs Stewart's and home.

Liberal newspaper of national importance. Its office (in the 1850s and '60s) was on Cockburn Street and occupied the Anchor Close. Edinburgh Castle is dramatically located on prominent rock at the end of High Street opposite from Holyrood Palace, 383 feet above sea level. A classic fort built in an irregular fashion, it was believed impregnable before the days of gunpowder. It could accommodate two thousand soldiers in the mid-nineteenth century, and its armouries 30,000 stands of arms. The Regalia, or insignia of Scottish Royalty, consist of a Crown, a sceptre, and a Sword of State, which were displayed in the Crown Room of the Castle. Adam and Charles Black, *Black's Picturesque Guide to Edinburgh and Its Environs* (Edinburgh: Adam and Charles Black, 1865), 3, 25–6, 38. Sir Walter Scott, Bart, *The Heart of Mid-Lothian* (Edinburgh: Cadell and Co., 1830).

Tues. Oct. 27.
Hugh Dickie came to town with first train on his way to Wolverton.
Spent the day with him and saw him off with the train at 6.50. Had
also a visit from Mr Kay jr from Mossend, telling us of his father being
coming home.

Wed. Oct. 28.
Called on Mrs Park in the forenoon. Dined with Mrs Stewart and
started at 1.30 in company with Christina for a walk to the Greenan
Castle. Day very pleasant. The two Misses Stewart followed and came
to us at the castle. Gathered shells until near dark. In the evening called
at Mr McIlwraith's and MacKay's.

Thurs. Oct. 29.
Spent the forenoon in the house talking with Mrs Hunter and Mother.
In the afternoon went with John Stewart and took out our passage in
the steamer 'New York' for New York to sail Nov. 18th. Called at McIlwraiths in the evening and had Maggy and Aggie's company with Bill
at the Philharmonic meeting.

Fri. Oct. 30.
Day stormy. Finished and posted a letter to Tom, also wrote to Jas Mackenzie. Called upon Mrs Dr Craig. Dined with Mrs Stewart and had a
walk with Bill round the town shore, Shawfield and Castle Hill. Called
on Chas Limond. Br. John at home, bad with a sore throat.

Sat. Oct. 31.
Weather still unsettled. Had a walk up the Newton shore with Bill in
the forenoon gathering seaweed. In the afternoon he and Jane and C.
Stewart went along town shore. Held Hallowe'en with them in the
evening. Went and saw Father's grave with Mother. Br. John had Dr
Craig lancing his throat. Called on Wm Gibb, sick at Prestwick Toll.[94]

---

94 Andrew's father, Thomas McIlwraith (Sr), died at his home on Russell Street,
   Newton-on-Ayr, on July 24, 1856, at age seventy. He was buried in the Newton
   Old Churchyard, near the Newton Church, in a plot that eventually included the
   remains of his wife Jean (Forsyth) McIlwraith, three of their children (Thomas [died
   in infancy], Mary and John, and John's daughter Agnes). In the 1960s, the Newton
   Church and churchyard was demolished to make way for a new road system. The
   graves were re-interred and some of the gravestones re-erected in Wallacetown
   Cemetery, two blocks east; others (including the McIlwraith headstone) have gone
   missing, though records of the inscriptions survive. This may have been Andrew's
   first visit to the gravesite. 'Deaths,' *Ayr Advertiser*, July 24, 1856. Thanks to Tom Bar-

Sun. Nov. 1.
Attended Newton Church and heard a young man, a stranger, preach. Had Christina at tea and sat talking at home and in Mrs Stewart's all afternoon and evening.

Mon. Nov. 2.
Had a walk on the Newton Shore with C. Stewart in the forenoon, gathering seaweed, etc. In the afternoon went to town with Mother and called on Mrs Affleck. Drank tea in Mrs Stewart's and attended a meeting of young men's association and heard a lecture from the Rev. Mr Grant upon H. Miller's 'Testimony of the Rocks.'[95]

Tues. Nov. 3.
Spent the forenoon fixing seaweed. Bill and I called on Mr Grant (Rev) and inspected his aquarium. Afternoon very fine. Had a walk up the Newton shore with Christina who stayed to tea with Mother. Bill and I called upon McIlwraiths in the evening.

Wed. Nov. 4.
Wrote to Thos Anderson, Dumbarton, and Mr Greive, Libberton. Called on A. Grant, printer. Walked down the quay and then came home and had hare soup to dinner. Had a short walk up the town shore. Waited with Bill in the Advertiser office till past 12 at night.

Thurs. Nov. 5.
Mrs Hunter, Christina and I took the train for Troon at 11 o'clock. Walked from there along the shore to Barassie then came back and got tea in Mrs McNeil's. Walked down the shore from Troon and gathered some pretty little scallop shells. Night came upon us among the Knowes[96] but weather kept very pleasant. Got home about 7.

Fri. Nov. 6.
Bill and I started on foot for Dunure which we reached by the road before 10 a.m. Visited the old Castle and had some pleasant rambling among the rocks. Walked right down the shore from Dunure to the

---

clay, Carnegie Library, Ayr, for his research. Gibb was likely being 'bled,' a heroic nineteenth-century practice among physicians who sought to rebalance the body's humours. See Jacalyn Duffin, *History of Medicine: A Scandalously Short Introduction* (Toronto: University of Toronto Press, 1999), 101–2.

95 Rev. William Grant was the minister of the Wallacetown Free Presbyterian Church in Ayr. Rev. William Ewing, DD, ed., *Annals of the Free Church of Scotland, 1843–1900*, 2 vols. (Edinburgh: T and T Clark, 1914).

96 The knolls, or small hills.

Diel's Dyke and took the road home from there. Day charming. Visited McIlwraiths in the evening. Met two Misses Galloway and had some dancing.

Sat. Nov. 7.
Weather still beautiful. Mother and I walked to Burns Monument calling on Mrs Mills by the way. Had a crack[97] with old Gilbert at the Monument and got a flower and bread and cheese from him. Called upon and had a chat with Mr Steele when I came home. Learned that the sailing of the 'New York' was postponed.

Sun. Nov. 8.
Attended Newton Church in the forenoon and heard a stranger preach. Went with Bill to the relief in the afternoon.[98] The family all drank tea in Mrs Stewart's and sat there pretty late in the evening. Mr Service, gardener, from Doonholm, called between sermons.

Mon. Nov. 9.
Spent the forenoon marking new shirts. Called on Mr Steele and got him to write for a passage with the 'Kangaroo' to New York. In the evening called on Robert Donald also on Mrs Park.

Tues. Nov. 10.
Mrs Hunter and I went out to make calls. Went to Mrs Park's then to Miss Wilson and Mrs Brown, then to Mr McIlwraith's. Met young Kay in town and went with him to take out his passage to America. Called on Mrs Shank. At a tea party in Mrs Stewart's with Miss Vass and most of our folk.

Wed. Nov. 11.
Great money panic and run upon the banks in Ayr and elsewhere.[99]

---

97 Or craic; good time, laugh.
98 The 'relief' was the Relief Church, one of 136 Presbyterian congregations that had quit the Church of Scotland in the eighteenth century, principally over the right of congregations to approve their ministers (though otherwise few doctrinal differences distinguished them). The movement was led Rev. Thomas Gillespie in 1761. Ayr's Relief Church was built in 1816 on Cathcart Street. In 1847 a union was formed between all congregations of the United Secession Church, and 118 out of 136 of the Relief Churches becoming the United Presbyterian Church. Though the Ayr Church participated in the Union, it seems to have gone by its antiquated name for some time afterwards. Strawhorn, *History of Ayr*, 192; William Robertson, *Ayrshire: Its History and Historical Families* (Kilmarnock: Dunlop and Drennan, 1908), 319.
99 The Great Money Panic in western Scotland began in November 1857 when two

Spent the forenoon about Mrs Stewart's and called at Mr Steele's with young Kay, taking out a passage to America for the old son. In the afternoon commenced packing my chest. Had a call from Maggy McIlwraith.

Thurs. Nov. 12.
Busy most of the day packing my chest for going off. Paid our passage in full to New York with the 'Kangaroo' from Liverpool. Drank tea in Mr McCrae's and met with Mr Wood. Went from there to the McIlwraith's and accompanied the girls to Galloway's and saw the deacon. Worked late packing up.

Fri. Nov. 13.
Rose early and got chest despatched per Earl of Garrick to Liverpool then came home and wrote to Margaret and Tom. In the afternoon, called on Mr Cowan, Mrs Craig Mrs Bone and Mr Ferguson. Took tea at home and in Mr Park's for supper.

Sat. Nov. 14.
Took the first train to Troon in company with Bill and walked down the shore gathering shells. Saw Gibb lying sick at Prestwick Toll. Called at Vass's, Wylie's and Robert Young's and Mrs Andrew's, also Mr Cassell's and got seeds. Drank tea and spent the evening in Mr McIlwraith's. Got photograph of Mrs Stewart's family group. John hurt his leg.

Sun. Nov. 15.
At Newton Church in the forenoon and afternoon at home. Family all assembled to tea with Mother. Sat pretty late chatting by the fire.

Mon. Nov. 16.
Packed up valise, etc. in the forenoon and took good-bye of Messrs Cowan, Grant, etc. Dined at home on broth. Mother, Bill and I came in to Mrs Stewart's after dinner, taking good-bye with Park's people by the way, then called at McIlwraith's. Then with Mother, Mrs H. Mrs S. and old Mrs Stewart in boat vennel, took train for Glasgow at 5, thence by Caledonian Railway to Liverpool. Jack, Bill and the wee Stewarts seeing us off and Christina accompanying.

---

banks failed – Western Bank of Scotland (with more than one hundred branches and a capital of £5,000,000) and Borough Bank of Liverpool – which precipitated a run on bank holdings and the Depression of 1857. James W. Gilbart with A.S. Michie, *The History, Principles and Practice of Banking* (London: George Bell and Sons, 1882), 2:334–78.

Tues. Nov. 17.
Had a good run to Liverpool and put up at the Bee Hotel, Queen's Square, between 5 and 6 a.m. Walked about the town and docks all day, crossing to Birkenhead and visiting the 'Kangaroo' in a hired boat, she being out into the river. Evening wet. Had Mr P. Hosie's company at the hotel.

Wed. Nov. 18.
Mr McIlwraith, plumber, knocked us up at 7, he coming from Ayr by the night train. After breakfasting all together, had our luggage conveyed to the Prince's Pierhead and got steam tender there to take us off to the 'Kangaroo.' Christina and Mr Mc. accompanying us and bidding good-bye on board.

Thurs. Nov. 19.
Weather moderate while crossing the Channel. Took breakfast and lunch but too sick for dinner or tea. John Stewart sick all day. Our neighbors in our stateroom a Yankiefied New York Irishman and an old man from Cleveland Ohio, decent men. Saw the last of the Old Sod being the Rattlin Islands and Hills near Torrie in course of the day.

Fri. Nov. 20.
Ship in to the open sea, rolling heavily. J.S. and I both quite sick and miserable, vomiting all sorts and eating nothing.

Sat. Nov. 21.
Still rough weather and still abominably sick.

Sun. Nov. 22.
Sick.

Mon. Nov. 23.
Sick.

Tues. Nov. 24.
Weather slightly improved this morning. John Stewart on deck a short time. I made a good dinner the first time at sea of sheep's head, etc. Principal acquaintance on shipboard a young Irish farmer from Illinois, Mr Harrison.

Wed. Nov. 25.
Weather rougher again. Had the ship's surgeon seeing J.S. who told him to get up. Still squeamish myself.

Thurs. Nov. 26.
Temperature rather milder. J. Stewart on deck looking very thin.

Fri. Nov. 27.
Ship pitches and rolls considerable again. Weather very cold. Ice upon deck and some little snow falling. John and I prescribed one glass brandy with hot water, etc. to each in the evening.

Sat. Nov. 28.
Still cold. Spent most of the day reading Marryat's 'Jacob Faithful.' Brandy prescription in the evening repeated. Had a drop of real Irish whiskey from our neighbor in the stateroom, Mr Cannel, who is a nice old fellow now of Cleveland but I thought originally 'Manx.'[100]

Sun. Nov. 29.
Church of England prayers read in the cabin after breakfast by the Captain (Jeffries) to a full audience of ship's crew, Cabin and Steerage passengers. Day rather a dull one at sea, wind fair and making good progress.

Mon. Nov. 30.
Good weather and fine steady breeze of fair wind. The good ship speeding free at the rate of 11 or 12 knots. Purser took our tickets. Meeting of passengers called for the purpose of expressing thanks to the Captain and Officers for politeness, etc. I took no part in it. Resolutions passed to have a spree at night which was carried out but at which I was not present.

Tues. Dec. 1.
Mr Groves, our Irish friend and room-mate, rather bad after last night's jollification. Wind has been good all night and weather still fine but at midday, headwind. Expect to be in harbour tomorrow, land plainly in sight at 4 p.m. and pilot then came on board. At 7 p.m. ship entering New York Bay.

Wed. Dec. 2.
Steam tender came off about 9 to take us on shore. German woman fell overboard and was nearly drowned. Got on shore at the barge office and was walking from there to Pine St. when John Stewart got so tired

---

100 Frederick Marryat, *Jacob Faithful* (London: Saunders and Otley, 1834). A 'manx' is a native of the Isle of Man.

that we had to call a coach. Spent most of the day looking after our luggage. Got to Brooklyn and had a happy meeting with Mrs Logan in the evening.

Thurs. Dec. 3.

Went From Brooklyn to New York with Mrs Logan and J. Stewart and had a day's rambling about, visiting the Chrystal Pallace,[101] Water Reservoir,[102] Barnum's Museum,[103] Taylor's Saloon,[104] etc. Dispatched a pile of newspapers to my friends.

Fri. Dec. 4.

Mrs Logan, Mr Syme, J. Stewart and I went to Greenwood and spent some time there. Went from there to New York and rambled about the

---

101 New York's Crystal Palace was a magnificent building made of iron and glass and crowned by a dome 100 feet in diameter. Built in 1853 for the 'Exhibition of the Industry of All Nations,' it was inspired by the Crystal Palace built in London, England, for the Great Exhibition of 1851. Located on 42nd Street, between Fifth and Sixth avenues at Reservoir Square, the building was destroyed by fire in October 1858, less than a year after McIlwraith had visited it. See Edwin G. Burrows and Mike Wallace, *Gotham: A History of New York City to 1898* (New York: Oxford University Press), 669–70.

102 Located at Fifth Avenue and 42nd Street, the Croton Reservoir was built in 1842 to distribute water to New York City residents through an aqueduct system that delivered water from the Croton River in northern Westchester County. The reservoir had the appearance of a massive brick fortress from the outside and was a tourist haunt throughout the late nineteenth century. In 1911, the Croton Reservoir was scrapped, replaced ultimately by a huge underground tunnel. See Gerard T. Koeppel, *Water for Gotham: A History* (Princeton, NJ: Princeton University Press, 2001), ch. 8.

103 Famous showman P.T. Barnum's American Museum was located at the corner of Ann Street and Broadway in Lower Manhattan, from 1841 until it burned down in 1865. The museum contained a varied mixture of attractions from higher-brow natural history displays, aquaria, menageries, and taxidermy exhibits to more sensational and gaudy 'side show' features. The admission charged to the museum was inexpensive (25 cents), cheap enough to invite visitors from all classes and backgrounds. See 'The Barnum Museum,' www.lostmuseum.cuny.edu/archives/museum.htm (accessed February 21, 2011). On Barnum more generally, see Bluford Adams, '"All Things to All People": P.T. Barnum in American Culture,' in *E Pluribus Barnum: The Great Showman and the Making of U.S. Popular Culture* (Minneapolis: University of Minnesota Press, 1997), 1–40; A.H. Saxon, *P.T. Barnum: The Legend and the Man* (New York: Columbia University Press, 1989).

104 Located at 555 Broadway, Taylor's Saloon was an upscale restaurant in mid-century New York, extravagantly decorated in mirrored walls, gilded ceiling ornaments, and furniture 'richly upholstered.' It catered to respectable tourists and wealthy shoppers. Edward K. Spann, *The New Metropolis: New York City, 1840–57* (New York: Columbia University Press, 1983), 99.

streets for some time. Met Mr Hosie in Taylor's Saloon who treated us to seeing 'Christie's Minstrels.'[105] Got home about 11.

Sat. Dec. 5.

Spent the forenoon in Mr Renfrew's playing draughts, etc. with Mr Sym. Went with him to the Navy Yard and the Lyceum there. Saw also U.S. frigate 'Niagara.'[106] Went from there to the city and in company with Mr Hosie, visited the New York Mercantile Library Institution. Saw there the plates of Audubon's Birds and Animals of America. Hogarth's Works, etc.[107] Also visited a fine photographic gallery.

Sun. Dec. 6.

A very wet day. Mrs Logan, J. Stewart and I went to Mr Buddington's Church in the morning afterwards crossed to New York, called upon and drank tea in A. Guthrie's.[108] John Stewart and Mrs L. then went

---

105 On Christy's Minstrels, see Diary for 1859, fn 42.

106 Located on 219 acres on Wallabout Bay on the East River, the Brooklyn Navy Yard was founded by the U.S. government in 1801 and became one of the city's first large-scale industrial complexes, employing about 6,000 men by 1861. The Naval Lyceum, 'one of the world's first military thinktanks,' was established at the site in 1833. The Yard closed in 1966, when it was sold to the city of New York. Thomas F. Berner, *Images of America: The Brooklyn Naval Yard* (Mount Pleasant, SC: Arcadia Publishing, 1999), 7–8. The USS *Niagara* (1857–85) was a fast, steam screw frigate built at the Brooklyn Yard and commissioned in April 1857. It had a storied career that included laying the first transatlantic cable (1857) and serving in the Union blockade of Confederate ports. See 'USS *Niagara* (1857–1885),' Department of the Navy, Naval Historical Center www.history.navy.mil/photos/sh-usn/usnsh-n/niagra2.htm (accessed February 21, 2011).

107 Located in the 1850s at Astor Place between Broadway and Lafayette, the New York Mercantile Library was a membership library founded by wealthy merchants for their clerks in 1821. It was devoted to 'useful knowledge,' like Mechanics' Institutes and other self-improvement libraries. The NYML grew to become the fourth-largest such institution in the U.S. by 1871. See Thomas Augst, *The Clerk's Tale: Young Men and Moral Life in Nineteenth-Century America* (Chicago: University of Chicago Press, 2003), ch. 4; likely John James Audubon, *Birds of America*, 7 vols. (New York: J.J. Audubon, 1840–4); [J. Hogarth and J. Nichols, comps.], *The Works of William Hogarth; in a Series of Engravings* (London: Jones and Co., 1833).

108 William Ives Buddington, DD (1815–79), was pastor of the Clinton Avenue Congregational Church in Brooklyn. A New Englander ordained in 1840, Buddington accepted the call from the Clinton Avenue Church in 1854, having served as pastor of First Church, Charlestown, Massachusetts, until that date. 'His pulpit ministrations,' one contemporary noted, were 'marked by a high style of intellectual culture, eloquence and impressiveness.' Henry R. Stiles, *A History of the City of Brooklyn* (Brooklyn, NY: Published by Subscription), 3:795.

home and I went and heard Mr Beecher preach.[109] Streets very dirty and had some trouble in finding my way home.

Mon. Dec. 7.
Spent the forenoon till between 11 and 12 in Mr Renfrew's then took good-bye and accompanied by Mrs Logan, crossed over to New York. Had a walk about Broadway and purchased a book of Etiquette, etc. from a young Scotchman, Mr Inglis, in Fetridge's Establishment.[110] Took train to Hamilton at 4.45 p.m. and a pleasant run during the night.

Tues. Dec. 8.
Day dawned on our approach to Rochester. Reached Suspension Bridge about 1 p.m. and Hamilton between 3 and 4.[111] Met Tom and Tommy coming to the station to meet us. Found all well. Had a walk up town in the evening and heard bands of music playing at the Anglo-American and Burlington hotels, discharging of fireworks, etc. by the electioneering parties for Messrs Baker and G. Buchanan.[112]

---

109 Henry Ward Beecher (1813–87) was a Congregationalist minister and one of the best-known public figures of the mid-nineteenth century. He was pastor at the Plymouth Church of Brooklyn from 1847 until his death forty years later. Beecher's geniality and high spirits were matched only by his attachment to an array of reform causes, which he advocated convincingly from his church platform: women's suffrage and free trade, but especially slavery's abolition. His sermons were widely published and read and he wrote for and edited a succession of journals. He was handsome and voluble, and by the 1850s his weekly congregation averaged about 2,500 people. An accusation of adultery in 1870 (unproved) and an ensuing public scandal tarnished his reputation only moderately. When he died, 40,000 people viewed his body at the Plymouth Church before burial. Allen Johnson, ed., 'Beecher, Henry Ward,' *Dictionary of American Biography* (New York: Charles Scribner's Sons, 1927), 1:129–35.

110 W.P. Fetridge and Company, book and journal publisher and bookseller, was located in 1857 at 281 Broadway, opposite A.T. Stewart's department store. Originally a Boston firm, the company seems also to have sold soaps, shaving lotions, and perfumes. See, for example, its advertisement in the back pages of John Hyde, *Mormonism: Its Leaders and Designs* (New York: W.P. Fetridge, 1857).

111 Designed and built by German-born American engineer John Roebling (1806–69) from 1851 to 1855, the Niagara Suspension Bridge crossed the Canada-U.S. border over the Niagara River. It was impressive to contemporaries and technologically pathbreaking for its day, the first such structure designed to support railway cars. The bridge connected the GWR in Canada with the New York Central. Anthony J. Bianculli, *Trains and Technology: The American Railroad in the Nineteenth Century* (Newark: University of Delaware Press, 2003), 4:68–70.

112 The Hamilton contenders in the 1857 election for the Legislative Assembly of the Canadas were wholesale merchant and pamphleteer Isaac Buchanan and Hugh

Wed. Dec. 9.
Day deplorably cold, close and wet. Had to go to the station and
Custom House to get our luggage clear, also went up town to see the
nomination of the candidates for M.P.P. for Hamilton – Messrs Baker
and Buchanan. Parties pelting with mud. Baker and Buchanan carried
shoulder high. Mr and Mrs Cavan from St Mary's called in the evening.

Thurs. Dec. 10.
Had a walk round town and to the mountain with Mr and Mrs Cavan
and Miss Emors. Spent most of the day in company with them. Heard
a lecture from Mr Irvine in the Mechanics Hall in the evening, subject
'The English Merchant.'[113] Met Muir's folk at the door.

Fri. Dec. 11.
Jack Stewart and I called up and spent a while in Mrs Muir's Sr in
the forenoon. Spent the evening writing home. Thos and the Mrs out
spending the evening in Mr Osborne's.

Sat. Dec. 12.
A beautiful, bright, frosty day. John Stewart, Thos and I had a walk
round town and up toward the mountain. Called at Mr Muir's in the
evening then came home and sat late writing to Mother.

Sun. Dec. 13.
Attended St Andrew's Church and heard Mr Burnett morning and

Cossart Baker, founder, president, and manager of the Canada Life Assurance Company. This evening began with a support rally for Buchanan held at the Burlington
Hotel with an estimated attendance of 900–1,000. The friends of Baker meanwhile
called together their support rally at the Anglo-American Hotel with 'the firing of
crackers to gather the boys.' Buchanan supporters soon interrupted this meeting
and all variety of 'hisses, groans, yells and every other possible disorderly sound'
ensued before some of their members stormed the stage to offer pro-Buchanan
speeches. The meeting reportedly then degenerated into a mud-throwing match.
Buchanan won the election. *HS*, December 9, 10, 1857.

113 The lecture 'The British Merchant' was delivered by the Reverend Dr Irvine as part
of the yearly lecture series of the Hamilton Mercantile Library Association. It was
delivered in the Hall of the Hamilton and Gore Mechanics' Institute, which was
two-thirds full. Irvine traced the origins of the British commercial system for the
audience, concluding that the modern era was the 'most rational of all, but yet the
most dangerous of all.' He counselled the young men in attendance of the need for
both talent and adherence to Christian principles as requisite qualities in making
the 'British Merchant as the *beau* ideal of a Christian gentleman.' *HS*, December 11,
1857.

evening.[114] Had a visit from Mr Muir in the interval and then took a long ramble beyond Desjardines Marsh. John Stewart, Thos and I.

Mon. Dec. 14.
Took first train to London and there saw Mr Gregory and Mr Jameson. Mr G. gave me a note to Mr Gunn, Hamilton.[115] Mr Jameson came down to Hamilton with me. Mr Robb called in the evening asking my assistance in drawing a plan.[116]

Tues. Dec. 15.
In company with Bro. Thos, walked to Gunn's work shop to ask a job but found times dull. Afterwards went down to the railway station and

---

114 Rev. Robert Burnet was born in 1823 at Lady Bank, Berwickshire, Scotland, and was educated at the University of Edinburgh and Aberdeen before migrating to Canada in the early 1850s. He arrived in Hamilton in 1853 and was appointed fourth minister of St Andrew's Presbyterian Church. Almost immediately upon his arrival he began supervising the construction of a new church building at an estimated cost of $60,000. Designed by the architect William Thomas, the new church opened its doors on March 8, 1857. Burnet remained pastor of St Andrew's until 1873, when 'owing to some dispute, [he] found it necessary to leave ... taking with him the records, the silver communion service, the bible used in the pulpit, the carved offertory plates' and part of the congregation, which relocated to a building at Park and Hunter streets. In 1875, the original St Andrew's was reorganized as St Paul's and the church's hardware returned, when Burnet accepted a call to pastor in London, Ontario. 'Robert Burnet,' *Dictionary of Hamilton Biography* (Hamilton: Dictionary of Hamilton Biography, 1981), 1:40; *Concerning the St Paul's Presbyterian Church and Congregation, Hamilton, Ontario 1854–1904* (Hamilton: Spectator Printing Company, 1904), 21.
115 Daniel Charles Gunn (1811–76) started his Hamilton business life in the 1840s as a wharfinger. After the GWR began operations in 1854, Gunn switched to locomotive production, operating a plant employing about 250 mechanics and labourers at its peak in the mid-1850s. The fortunes of this thriving enterprise turned quickly when a North America–wide recession took hold by 1858, forcing Gunn into bankruptcy by the following year. 'Gunn, Daniel Charles,' *Dictionary of Hamilton Biography*, 1:88–9; Robert Kristofferson, *Craft Capitalism: Craftworkers and Early Industrialization in Hamilton, Ontario 1840–1872* (Toronto: University of Toronto Press, 2007), 24, 102; Robert R. Brown, 'Canadian Locomotive Builders: Part Two: Dan C. Gunn, Hamilton, 1857–1860' (Hamilton Public Library, typescript).
116 Charles Robb was a Hamilton-based civil engineer who contracted his services to the City of Hamilton but was also 'connected with' the GWR. He advertised himself as a 'consulting mechanical engineer and architect ... prepared to furnish plans and specifications and to superintend the construction of every description of steam engines, water wheels, machinery and buildings.' He worked out of his house on Park Street between Mulberry and Cannon Streets, just around the corner from Thomas McIlwraith's residence. *HS*, January 29, 1858; *Proceedings of the Jubilee of the Hamilton Scientific Association ... 1907* (Hamilton: [The Association], 1907), np; Kristofferson, *Craft Capitalism*, 195.

called on Mr Braid and Mr Sharpe, neither of whom required a draughts-man.[117] Had a letter from Charles Mackenzie inviting me to Sarnia.

Wed. Dec. 16.
Called at Mr Gunn's house in the morning who could give me no prospect of employment. Spent most of the day with Mr Robb assisting him in drawing geological map of the country from Niagara River to Toronto. First day of the Hamilton election and great excitement of parties for Baker and Buchanan.

Thurs. Dec. 17.
A miserable day, cold, frost, fog. Spent daylight in Mr Robb's. Buchanan declared victor over Baker.

Fri. Dec. 18.
Still wet weather. Spent the day map drawing in Mr Robb's. Tom and Mary at Mr Henry's in the evening while I sat at home writing to Chas Mackenzie.

Sat. Dec. 19.
Went up town in the forenoon and heard declaration of the result of the recent election being a majority of 304 for Buchanan. Heard a short speech from Buchanan and Baker upon the occasion.[118] Worked a while at Mr Robb's plan.

---

117 An Englishman, Alexander Braid was a locomotive superintendent in the GWR's Hamilton works. His tenure there, 1856–8, was rocky; his dismissal of a popular shop foreman in 1857 prompted a strike and his own dismissal. He was killed on the GWR near Copetown in March 1859 when an embankment gave way and the train in which he was travelling derailed. Samuel Sharp, also an Englishman, was the GWR's mechanical superintendent in Hamilton, under whom the shops 'built beautiful and innovative passenger cars … freight cars' and other equipment. Sharp returned to England for family reasons in 1863. They both began careers as practical mechanics. *HS*, September 25, 1856, May 18, 1861, February 17, 1873; *Hamilton Times*, September 2, 1863, September 3, 1863, September 4, 1863; Paul Craven and Tom Traves, 'Dimensions of Paternalism: Discipline and Culture in Canadian Railway Operations in the 1850s,' in Craig Heron and Robert H. Storey, eds., *On the Job: Confronting the Labour Process in Canada* (Montreal and Kingston: McGill-Queen's University Press, 1986), 64–5; Craven, 'Labour and Management.'

118 Buchanan arrived at this event in Courthouse Square with much pomp at the head of a large procession of supporters and offered a victory speech. Baker followed this with a concession speech and proposed a vote of thanks for the returning officer. Buchanan and his supporters, numbering 'more than a thousand,' then left in a 'cavalcade' and proceeded through city streets to Clairmont Park, Buchanan's home, where they were 'regaled in the most hospitable manner.' *HS*, December 21, 1857.

Sun. Dec. 20.
Felt bilious and did not go to Church. Took a walk along by the west end of the mountain in the afternoon; a fine clear day. Saw a flock of Cedar birds.

Mon. Dec. 21.
Thos and I left Hamilton with the morning train at 9.15, he going on to London on business while I left the train at Paris and walked out to McWhirter's. During the day called on Jacksons, Kays and Ballingalls with whom I drank tea. Encountered a severe snow storm while driving from Ballingall's to McWhirter's in the evening.

Tues. Dec. 22.
Met Thos at Paris station on the arrival of the morning train from London and started for Ayr. Hugh McWhirter driving us part of the way in his waggon. Found Mr Goldie's people all well. Had a short ramble with Thos in the bush with the gun but got no game. A few inches of snow on the ground and sleighing commenced.

Wed. Dec. 23.
Got out the horse and buggy in the forenoon and drove in to the village along with my dearest Mary. Made calls upon Mrs Goldie in Ayr and at the house of a Mr Alison, a storekeeper. Thos out in the bush with the gun and shot some purple finches, etc. Left Greenfield in the afternoon and came home to Hamilton with the late train.

Thurs. Dec. 24.
Felt rather lazy inclined after our jaunt, so did not go to Mr Robb's but walked about town and out as far as the new bridge in course of construction over the Desjardin Canal.[119] In the evening walked up town to view the market and called upon the Misses McIlwraith and saw Mr and Mrs Yale.

Fri. Dec. 25.
Christmas Day. Thos and I took a long walk along by the Western side of Burlington Bay as far as the lake shore. Got in to swamps and wet our feet. Ice strong enough to carry us across the creeks and inlets. Had the gun with us but nothing to shoot. Had our Christmas dinner and spent the evening at home.

Sat. Dec. 26.
David Goldie came down from Ayr and I spent most of the day with

---

119 See fn 23 above.

him. Had home letters from Mrs Stewart and Bill. In the evening wrote to Mrs Hunter. Weather fine for the season, snow lying on the ground and more falling.

Sun. Dec. 27.
Attended Mr Burnet's Church in the forenoon and Mr Inglis' in the evening. Like Mr I's preaching and think of taking a seat there.[120] Spent the interval between sermons in the house reading Tupper's 'Proverbial Philosophy,' the day being too cold for walking.[121]

Mon. Dec. 28.
Worked at Mr Robb's map of Canada West to the S.W. of Lake Ontario. In the evening visited Mr Fenton and had a long chat with him. News came from Lampton of Hope Mackenzie's defeat by Malcolm Cameron as parliamentary candidate.[122]

Tues. Dec. 29.
A verey mild, pleasant day. Worked all day with Mr Robb. Drank tea with him and spent a couple of hours in the evening looking through some scrap books of engravings, etc. Found Mr and Mrs Robt Young calling when I came home.

Wed. Dec. 30.
Thawing with rain and cold, raw fog all day making miserable sloppy walking. Worked at Mr Robb's plan. Mrs Campbell from Galt and Mrs Yale from Toronto with children at dinner with us. In the evening our family all drank tea and spent the evening in Mr Muir's Sr house.

Thurs. Dec. 31.
Despatched a small parcel to Sandy Howat in Berlin which I brought for him from Scotland, also received a note from Mark Braidwood of

120 See fn 114 for information on Rev. Burnet. Rev. David Inglis (1824–77) was born at Greenlaw, Berwickshire, Scotland, and attended the University of Edinburgh, where his instructors included Dr John Brown and Thomas Chalmers, a well-known leader of the Free Church movement. He came to Hamilton in the mid-1850s as the first minister of Hamilton's MacNab Street Church and pastored there from 1855 to 1871. The cornerstone of this new church was laid in April 1856 by Isaac Buchanan. 'Inglis, David,' *Dictionary of Hamilton Biography*, 1:107–8.
121 Martin Farquhar Tupper, *Proverbial Philosophy: A Book of Thoughts and Arguments* (New York: Wiley and Putnam, 1845).
122 Cameron, refusing to align himself with George Brown's populist Reform Alliance, ran as an independent against Mackenzie, Lambton Reformers' nominee, winning by only a narrow margin. See Riddell, 'Community Leadership,' 82; Careless, *Brown of the Globe*, 1:246.

instructions for sending a parcel to him and dispatched it per American Express. Spent the day with Mr Robb. Weather pleasant with not much of either frost or thaw. Took a walk up town with J. Stewart and Tom in the evening. Town very quiet. Spent the evening home reading, etc. John Stewart went to bed early. Mr Raphael, Thomas and I got our Hogmanay from Mrs Mc. near 12.[123] Some gun shots and ringing of bells signalled the closing of the old year and ushering in the new.

---

123 Traditional Scottish meal or gift of cake (normally demanded by children) on New Year's eve.

Diary for 1858

Preface

In an essay, remarkable at once for the originality of its views and the practical good sense it contains, John Foster recommends the propriety of every man writing memoirs of himself, not as an exercise of ingenuity – not as a means of drawing the world's regard – but to fix in a man's own mind, a sense of the progress he has made in moral and intellectual ideas, to mark the change in his sensations which a prolonged experience of life produces, and to excite a feeling of gratitude for those many providential interpositions which the most careless observer can scarcely fail to recognise as exercised in his behalf.[1]

Fri. Jan. 1.

Snowed a little in the forenoon but day mild and pleasant. Mr Sommerville called shortly after breakfast being first foot.[2] Jack Stewart, Thos

---

1 Almost certainly John Foster, *Essays: in a Series of Letters, on the Following Subjects: I. On a Man's Writing Memoirs of Himself. II. On Decision of Character. III. On the Application of the Epithet Romantic. IV. On Some of the Causes by which Evangelical Religion Has Been Rendered Less Acceptable to Persons of Cultivated Taste* (London: Longman, 1805).

2 Probably James Sommerville (1834–1916), editor and publisher of the *Dundas True Banner*. He was born, educated, and died in Dundas. He served as mayor in 1874 and MP for Brant (1882–1900). Before establishing the *Ayr Observer* in 1854, Sommerville apprenticed at the *Dundas Warder*. He emerged as a strong regional voice for the Reform movement. In 1858 Sommerville bought the *Dundas Tribune*, renaming it the *True Banner*, in his words, because the *Hamilton Banner* had 'backslid, gone Tory,' and had changed its name to the *Hamilton Times*. Roy T. Woodhouse, *The History of the Town of Dundas* (Dundas Historical Society, 1968), 3:63; Henry J. Morgan, *Canadian Men and Women of the Time: A Handbook of Canadian Biography* (Toronto: W. Briggs, 1898), 957.

and I accompanied him to his house and saw his wife and family; then came home all three started on an excursion with the gun, making a large circuit out by the side of the Dundas marsh and back by the base of the mountain. Got home at 4 p.m. and dined on a famous goose from Ayr C.W.

Sat. Jan. 2.
Weather slightly frosty and very beautiful. Had agreed with Mr Robb to accompany him to Dundas but missed the train. John Stewart and I went out the Waterdown road with the gun, and shot a red squirel and a red bellied Nut-hatch, also saw Cedar birds (feeding on rowans), snow flakes, Titmice, Brown tree Creeper, etc. John went in to the bush with the gun, and wandered home while I searched for him an hour. Thos and I took an evening walk up town, then home where he worked at his birds.

Sun. Jan. 3.
Heard Mr Burnet preach morning and evening in St Andrews. Br. Thos, J. Stewart and I had little Tom out for a short walk but day rather cold and raw for having any pleasure out.

Mon. Jan. 4.
Spent the forepart of the day in the house making a drawing of the red bellied Nut-hatch. For a walk along the Mountain at dusk. Mr Robb and Mr Jas Hammond called in the evening to see Thomas's stuffed birds. Wind blowing quite soft and ice and snow melting away.

Tues. Jan. 5.
Accompanied Br. Thos up town in forenoon, calling at Barnes's book store where he traded some engravings for coloured prints of birds. Met David Goldie and accompanied him in a buggy to Webster's Mill at Bullocks corners beyond Dundas, where we had a view of a lofty waterfall. Some stir in the city with elections of councillors and aldermen. Spent the evening teaching John Stewart chess.

Wed. Jan. 6.
Made a drawing of a small bird of the Warbler kind now stuffed and in one of Thos's cases. A considerable quantity of snow has fallen last night and to-day. Spent the evening in the house reading treatise upon 'How to do business' etc.

Thurs. Jan. 7.
Br. Thos came home from London during the night. Mr Robb called in

the morning to ask my assistance with his geological plan, so I accordingly spent daylight with him at a drawing showing sections of different portions of country. ~~Spent the evening in the house thinking about what I am to do to earn a living or in other words, achieve independence.~~ Asked a job from Gartshore whom I met in Mr Robb's, who had no work.[3]

Fri. Jan. 8.
Frosty and a fine clear day. Worked all day and dined with Mr Robb. Mr James Goldie called at our house before 9 o'clock on his way from Utica to Ayr.

Sat. Jan. 9.
Spent the forenoon with Mr Robb and now expect to be done with his job. Got certificate of stock from Building society for 13 shares in class 7. Went up town in the evening and spent some time at a book auction, then called at the library and got a book on Natural History.

Sun. Jan. 10.
Spent the forenoon at home reading Paterson's treatise on the Shorter Chatechism.[4] In the afternoon, John Stewart, Thos and I went for a walk and went on to the ice of the bay but turned from an attempt to cross it, as the ice appeared no more than one inch thick and was yielding – a good number of skaters on it. John Stewart and I went to hear Ormiston in his new Church, found it shut and went on to St Andrews and heard him there. Learned afterwards that the new one was not finished.[5]

---

3 John Gartshore ran a successful foundry in Dundas. See fn 29 below.
4 Alexander Smith Paterson, *A Concise System of Theology: Being the Shorter Catechism Analyzed and Explained* (Edinburgh: John Johnstone, 1841).
5 Rev. William Ormiston (1821–99) was born at Lymington, Lanarkshire, Scotland, and came to Canada with his family at age thirteen. He taught at Victoria College, Cobourg, in the late 1840s after receiving his BA from that institution. He was ordained in 1849 by the United Presbyterian Church and became pastor of St James Square United Presbyterian Church, Toronto, in 1853. He came to Hamilton in 1856 as minister of the Central Presbyterian Church, where he ministered until 1870. At the time of this diary entry he was overseeing the building of a new church for his congregation at the corner of Jackson and MacNab streets. He was also an active member of the Hamilton Scientific Association (later the Hamilton Association for the Advancement of Literature, Science and Art) and Superintendent for Classical Schools in Canada West, 1853–63. 'William Ormiston,' *Dictionary of Hamilton Biography* (Hamilton: Dictionary of Hamilton Biography, 1981), 1:161; *The Annual Cyclopedia and Register of Important Events of the Year 1899* (New York: D. Appleton and Company, 1900), 627.

Mon. Jan. 11.
Woke from sleep with the sound of a small bell which I took for the
fire bell, bell in Catholic Church rang immediately after so J. St[ewart]
and I jumped up and dressed in the dark. Went out and met a gas work
fireman at the corner who informed us that the bells were the usual
6 o'clock ones. Did not go into the house again but had a walk along
the mountain getting home at 8 a.m. Made drawings of white bellied
Nuthatch during the day. Mr Robb's essay and maps to come before the
Hamilton Association to-night.[6]

Tues. Jan. 12.
A most delightful mild sunny day. John Stewart, Thos and I took a long
ramble with the gun out the Toronto line and westward along Burlington heights. Killed nine red bellied Nut-Hatch, and two Pine Linnets
(Pinus Linarius). Roads very muddy. Had paper from the old country
with news of wreck of S.S. Earl of Carrick lost 14 lives, Wm Lawson, J.
Moore, etc. among them.[7]

Wed. Jan. 13.
Spent the day in the house making drawing of Woodpecker and Nut
hatch. Mrs Mc and I called upon old Mr Muir's people in the evening
and saw Mrs Muir, Jr and Mrs Steele.

Thurs. Jan. 14.
John Stewart and I started early in the day with the gun. Went up the
mountain to the south of Laurie's hotel and had a long walk along the
mountain edge, eastward. Day clear and sunny with enough of frost
to harden the roads. The walk altogether a charming one. Shot a speci-

---

6 The Hamilton Scientific Association was formed in November 1857 with the stated
   aims of 'the formation of a Library and Museum, the cultivation of Literature and
   Science and the illustration of the History and Physical characteristics of the country.' Charles Robb's two-part essay, entitled 'On the Geology of the Region around
   the Head of Lake Ontario,' was the fifth paper read to the association. Robb was
   active in the governance of the association, serving as a member of council (1858),
   first vice-president (1859) and overseer of library and circulation (1860). *HS*, November 4, 1857, June 4, 1858; Archives, Hamilton Public Library; Anon., *50th Anniversary
   of the Hamilton Scientific Association* (1907); Robert B. Kristofferson, *Craft Capitalism:
   Craftworkers and Early Industrialization in Hamilton, Ontario 1840–1872* (Toronto: University of Toronto Press, 2007), 193, 195.
7 The wreck of this steamer occurred on December 20, 1857 at Point Dolby, near Peel,
   Isle of Man. Among the dead were William Lawson, age 50, and James Muir, age 58,
   both from Newton, Ayrshire (Andrew's hometown). *Ayrshire Death Registers* (1958).

men each of female Cross bill and female Purple finch. Pine linnets in great flocks feeding on small cones. Nut hatches, Tits, etc. plenty. In the evening heard Mr Jenkins lecture on India.[8]

Fri. Jan. 15.
Had all breakfast by 8 o'clock and started on a birding expedition. Went by the same route but farther than yesterday into the valley beyond the bend of the Port Dover line. Saw flocks of Pine linnets, some Blue Jays and got two Tree Sparrows. On the way home Thos shot a Red-bellied Woodpecker, a beautiful bird. Morning frosty but rain and sleet came on about mid-day. Got home tired and wet from a very long walk about 5 p.m.

Sat. Jan. 16.
Walked around town with Thomas in the forenoon being looking after seats for John Stewart and I in Burnet's Church. Spent part of the afternoon and sat late in the night writing home to Christina and Bill. Thomas finished stuffing his velvet Duck and red bellied Woodpecker.

Sun. Jan. 17.
Heard Mr Burnet preach morning and evening. Day cold with some snow falling so spent the interval between church services in the house rather lazily.

Mon. Jan. 18.
Commenced to plan of the City of Hamilton to show Gas pipes, etc. for Br. Thos.[9] Called with him at the City Engineer's office, and saw the

---

8 This lecture was delivered by the Reverend John Jenkins DD (1813–90), an English-man then resident in Philadephia, under the auspices of the Hamilton Mercantile Library Association. A large crowd filled the Mechanics' Institute Hall to hear this lecture on 'India,' delivered during the First War of Indian Independence (1857-1858), often called the 'Indian Mutiny' by contemporary British commentators. The Reverend, who had served 'for a long time' as a missionary in India, spoke of the history of the East India Company, the effects of British rule, and how the country's internal 'religious prejudices' had contributed to the war. *HS*, January 13, 14, 16, 1858.

9 The Hamilton Gas Light Company was organized in 1850 by wholesale merchant John Young and a number of other prominent Hamiltonians. The company manu-factured gas from coal at its Mulberry Street plant and sent it through a pipe system to various businesses, private residences, and gaslights throughout the city's central business district. By 1857 the company had 640 customers and was operating 290 gaslights. Thomas McIlwraith became manager in 1853. M.F. Campbell, *A Mountain and a City: The Story of Hamilton* (Toronto: McClelland and Stewart, 1966), 105; 'Thomas McIlwraith,' *Dictionary of Hamilton Biography*, 1:132.

city engineer, Mr Haskins, who promised to give us what information we wanted for finishing plan. Spent most of the evening making a call upon Mr Muir Junior.

Tues. Jan. 19.

Had arranged to go upon a gunning ramble with J. Stewart and Thos and started about 9 in the face of a thick snow shower which however did not last long and day turned out fine. Ascended the mountain and went westward along the verge beyond Chaddock then descended and took a circuit across the plain towards Cootes paradise. Had to cross a creek on a fallen tree from which Jack Stewart tumbled in. Had long letters from home dated about New year time from Mrs Hunter, Mrs Stewart, etc.

Wed. Jan. 20.

Worked at plan of Hamilton. Br. Thos and J. Stewart went to the shooting and got a number of Crossbills. Day fine and frosty. In the evening, Thos stuffed birds while I read memoir of 'Fox' and Wilson's essay on Burns.[10]

Thurs. Jan. 21.

Weather still fine with moderate degree of frost. Worked at Hamilton Plan. Called on Mr Haskins, City Engineer, and got plan with laying out of New Streets. Heard tell of Mr Braid being dismissed from Superintendence of Loco. Dept. G.W.R.[11]

---

10 Likely John Bernard Trotter, *Memoirs of the Latter Years of the Right Honourable Charles James Fox* (London: Samuel R. Fisher Jr, 1812). The 'Essay on Burns' likely from Professor Wilson and Robert Chambers, *The Land of Burns, a Series of Landscapes and Portraits, Illustrative of the Life and Writings of The Scottish Poet,* 2 vols. (Glasgow: Blackie and Son, 1840). The first volume contains an introductory essay on Burns written by John Wilson (1785–1854), professor of moral philosophy at the University of Edinburgh and editor of *Blackwood's Magazine.*

11 Alexander Braid was appointed superintendent of the GWR Locomotive Department in 1856 by the company's London board of directors. Shortly after taking his post, problems with his leadership style became evident when his shop workers went on strike to protest his hasty firing of a popular shop foreman. The fact that about one hundred of his shop workers honoured his departure from the company by holding a 'parting testimonial' for him complete with dinner, speeches, and the presentation of a 'massive' silver tea service as a parting gift, suggests Braid had regained favour by the time of his departure. Braid used his speech at this dinner to offer a stinging rebuke against GWR superintendent C.J. Brydges, outlining to his former workers and the local press a number of 'prejudices' that he believed had led to his unfair dismissal. *HS,* May 1, 1858. Paul Craven, 'Labour and Management

Fri. Jan. 22.

Worked all day at plan of Hamilton.

Sat. Jan. 23.

Still working at Hamilton Plan. Had a walk up town with Thos in the evening, he making purchase of a prussian made fowling piece for 9½$.

Sun. Jan. 24.

Heard Mr Burnet preach morning and evening. In the interval, Br. Thos, John Stewart and I took little Tom for a walk down to the side of the bay down from Bay Street Bay partially frozen and boys skating on some of the inlets. Saw Dr Rae, the arctic traveler in church.[12]

Mon. Jan. 25.

Frost quite gone and some rain falling. This day observed in the city as a holiday on account of the Princess Royal's marriage. News of Have-lock's death telegraphed from New York.[13] Worked all day at Plan of Hamilton. Spent the evening arranging pictures for my scrap book.

Tues. Jan. 26.

At Hamilton Map all day and in the evening pasting scraps in Scrap Book.

_____

on the Great Western Railway' in Craven, ed., *Labouring Lives: Work and Workers in Nineteenth-Century Ontario* (Toronto: University of Toronto Press, 1995), 342, 347, 373.

12 Dr John Rae (1813–93) was born in the Orkney Islands, Scotland, and educated in medicine at the University of Edinburgh. He then worked as a surgeon for the Hudson's Bay Company, mostly at Moose Factory. He is best known as an Arctic explorer, embarking on his first northern expedition in 1846, setting out to find the fate of Sir John Franklin and his men in 1848, and undertaking a number of other surveying voyages in the early 1850s. He lived in Hamilton between 1856 and 1859, becoming an extensive landholder. He was involved with the founding of the Hamilton Scientific Association in 1857, serving as its first vice-president in 1857 and president in 1858. 'Dr John Rae,' *Dictionary of Hamilton Biography*, 1:167–8; *50th Anniversary of the Hamilton Scientific Association* (1907).

13 Sir Henry Havelock (1795–1857) was a major general in the British Army, best known for his participation in the First Indian War of Independence (1857–8). In September 1857 he led a relief column to aid besieged British forces at the High Commission grounds in Lucknow. His force succeeded in penetrating to Lucknow but was not strong enough to break the siege. A larger British force soon arrived and the siege was broken on November 18. He died of dysentery a few days later. An announcement of his death appeared in the *Spectator*, January 26, 1858.

Wed. Jan. 27.
Worked all day at Hamilton map, and a while by gas light in the evening. Had a walk out to view the new bridge over Desjardins canal.

Thurs. Jan. 28.
At Hamilton Map. Weather now frosty. Evenings moonlight. To-night remarkable as having the moon higher in the heavens than has been or will be for a long time but sky too thick to see her.

Fri. Jan. 29.
At Hamilton Map. In the evening attended Hamilton Theatre. Perform-ance by amateurs from clerks, etc. of the Great Western Railway.[14] Mr Muir appeared as 'old Rusty' in the farce of Mons. Tomson and also sang 'lord Lovel' in character. Mr Manby sang two Scotch songs in Highland costume. Entertainment concluded with performance of the 'twa Bonnycastles.'[15]

Sat. Jan. 30.
Took train at 9.15 a.m. to Dundas to ask for a job from Gartshore but found him from home. Called on Mr McGarva, a Girvan chap.[16] Walked from Dundas to Ancaster and made a long divergence into the woods by the way. Had Thos's new Prussian gun with me but saw no game. Shot one little red squirrel. Got home over the mountain between 5 and 6 at night.

Sun. Jan. 31.
Heard Mr Burnet preach morning and evening. Bundle of home letters enclosing one to me from Christina came addressed to J. Stewart, also papers to Thos. Weather now something like winter, being keen frost but no snow on the ground.

---

14 The GWR 'amateurs' were assisted by Mr Nickerson's Toronto 'professionals' in staging the two theatrical pieces. The *Spectator* commented enthusiastically that the 'acting of the professionals from Toronto was, of course, good; yet that of the Ham-ilton amateurs did not suffer by the contrast.' The performance raised £100 for the poor of the city. 'Lord Lovel' is a traditional ballad reprinted as Child Ballad #75 in volume 2 of Francis James Child, Mark F Heiman, Laura Saxton Heiman, *The English and Scottish Popular Ballads* (Northfield, MN: Loomis House Press, 2001 [1882–98]).

15 John Maddison Morton, *The Two Bonnycastles a Farce in One Act* (New York: W. Tay-lor, 185?).

16 Girvan is a small town on the southwest coast of Scotland in the District of Carrick, Ayrshire, about twenty miles south of Ayr.

Mon. Feb. 1.
Spent the day in reading home newspapers and in writing to Mrs Stewart. In the evening read the papers again and played a game at chess with John Stewart. John an apt pupil though I beat him without my queen. ~~Thos offered me $5 for making Hamilton plan but I decided not to take it.~~[17] Snow commenced between 5 and 6 and snowed the whole evening.

Tues. Feb. 2.
Snow lying 4 or 5 inches deep. Work at Hamilton plan all day. In the evening read Cyclopedia of Machinery, essay on the steam engine.[18]

Wed. Feb. 3.
Worked till dinner on the Hamilton plan. After dinner, went up town and bought some gild moulding to make picture frames. Took a walk out to the new bridge over the Desjardins Canal and crossed over it for the first time. Weather frosty with good sleighing. Read about the steam engine in the evening.

Thurs. Feb. 4.
Jack Stewart and I took a walk along the mountain edge eastward, with the gun and shot a pretty snow Flake, the only one which appeared. Day bright and frosty and snow lying pretty deep. Worked afternoon and evening at picture frames.

Fri. Feb. 5.
Finished Picture framing. Mr Ormiston lectured on spiritualism which Thos and the wife attended but did not like.[19]

---

17 McIlwraith's cash accounts show receipt on February 20, 1858 of $10 'For drawing plan of Hamilton Gas Company.' Appendix 3.
18 Likely William Johnson Cory, *The Imperial Cyclopaedia of Machinery: Being a Series of Plans, Sections and Elevations of Stationary, Marine and Locomotive Engines, Spinning Machinery, Grinding Mills, Tools andc.* (Glasgow: William Mackenzie, 1853–6).
19 Ormiston delivered this as part of the 1858 lecture program of the Hamilton Mercantile Library Association. The title of the lecture was changed to 'supernaturalism' shortly before its delivery after Professor Ormiston had difficulty obtaining the 'requisite apparatus' for the scheduled talk on 'aquatic phenomena.' The *Spectator* complained that the professor spoke over the heads of most audience members, delivering a talk more suited to 'men of strong minds, who have investigated the mysteries of matter and of natural forces such as magnetism and gravity.' A number of audience members reportedly left during the course of the lecture. The newspaper commented further that such lofty and technical discussions were better left to men of science and were dangerous for 'common people' who could be misled from 'doc-

Sat. Feb. 6.
Jack Stewart and I had a ramble west along the base of the mountain
with the gun but saw nothing to shoot. Day fine and a good deal of
sleighing going on. Our old white cat whose life had become a burden
to her, died this evening of being strangulated with a clothes line.

Sun. Feb. 7.
Attended Mr Burnet's Church morning and evening. Day cold with
some snow falling so kept the house in the interval.

Mon. Feb. 8.
Snow falling constantly all day in small flakes, but very thick and fast.
Spent all day in the house reading Appleton's dictionary of Mechanics.
Writing to John Goldie in Edinburgh.

Tues. Feb. 9.
Snow falling all day so had to keep the house. Snow lying deep now.
Thos bought a fine specimen of an Eagle Owl from a country-man for
$1 today. Spent the day mostly in the house reading, etc.

Wed. Feb. 10.
Weather still cold and frosty. Studying Geering in Appleton dictionary.[20] Walked about town a good deal and made purchase of a plank
of cherry to make patterns. Called on Muirs people in the evening and
had a chat with the old wife in the evening, the family being all out.

Thurs. Feb. 11.
An excessively cold day. Spent the day finishing Hamilton Map. In the
evening read Buckthorn[21] aloud while Thomas stuffed the owl.

Fri. Feb. 12.
Thermometer at 10° above zero in the morning. A beautiful clear winter
day, not quite so cold as the last few days. Spent the day working at
making an odontograph, etc. for geering.[22] Mrs Steele, Mrs Muir Junr
and Miss Muir spent the afternoon, and drank with us. Had the pleasure of escorting them home.

---

trines of Christianity' to 'monstrous, blasphemous dogmas of modern Spiritualism.'
    HS, February 8, 1858.

20 *Appleton's Dictionary of Machines, Mechanics, Engine-Work, and Engineering* (New York:
    D. Appleton and Company, 1856).

21 Likely a play by John Baldwin Buckstone (1802–79), English theatre manager, actor
    and playwright, and author of several farces including *The Irish Lion* (1838) and *The
    Green Bushes* (1845). See 'Death of J.B. Buckstone,' *New York Times*, November 1, 1879.

22 An odontograph was an instrument for marking teeth outlines for gear wheels.

Sat. Feb. 13.
Day snowing and storming. Worked a while in the kitchen but got to be in the way and had to stop. Letters came to Thomas from Mrs Logan, inclosing home one to her from Bill and Mrs Hunter.

Sun. Feb. 14.
Heard Mr Burnet preach morning and evening. Think him improving a little lately. Church thinly attended. Snow up to the knees off the untrodden parts and snow falling slightly all day so spent the interval in the house. Thos writing home. Today, I believe is my 28th birthday.[23]

Mon. Feb. 15.
Frosty and a fine winter day. Worked at my Odontograph, etc. out in the Metre Shed of the Gas Works. Visited the reading room in the evening. Within this last 8 days little Mary Duncan McI has been accomplishing the feat of rising to her feet and standing alone for a moment.

Tues. Feb. 16.
Spent all day in the house finishing the drawing of Odontograph and scales for geering. Saw beautiful Aurora Borealis in the evening. Had a few lines from Mr Peffers, Sarnia.

Wed. Feb. 17.
Thermometer in the Portico 5° above zero. Wind a keen, frosty. Altogether this last few days has been thoroughly Canadian winter. John Stewart and I took a long ramble with the gun up the sides of the Dundas Marsh but did not keep our powder dry so shot nothing. Spent the evening looking thro' Cassins' work on American Birds.[24]

Thurs. Feb. 18.
Had another fatiguing ramble with the gun along with Jack Stewart out among the gullies beyond the Desjardins Marsh tressle work. Shot some Purple Finches etc. but saw nothing new or rare and begin to tire of the sport. Had a packet of Home letters from Mother, Mrs Hunter, Mrs Stewart and Bill. Wrote to Mr Peffers in the evening as also to Sarnia Observer and 'Globe' papers to stop sending to me.

Fri. Feb. 19.
A very stormy day all day blowing like fury and snowing. Spent a while

---

23 This is a curious entry, given the fact that his gravestone declares his birthdate as February 18, 1831.

24 Likely *Illustrations of the Birds of California, Texas, Oregon, British and Russian America … 1853 to 1855* (Philadelphia: J.B. Lippincott, 1856).

in the house reading Gazeteer of Scotland and the remainder of the day making templates, etc. for wheelwork.[25]

Sat. Feb. 20.
Studying geering for the most part of the forenoon. In the afternoon walked up town with Thos and saw thro' McInnes's new wholesale store, which was just being occupied for business.[26] Called at Barrie's where Thos purchased 'Audubon's Synopsis' and 'Cassins Birds of America.' Also he and I in co. purchased some plates in Gentry and Brown's for our Scrap Books.[27] Got $10 from Thos for drawing Hamilton Plan. Day fine.

Sun. Feb. 21.
Heard Mr Burnet preach morning and evening. A cold blustering sort of day. Little Mary walked nearly half across the dining room to-day, almost her first attempt at walking.

Mon. Feb. 22.
Weather still cold. Spent the day in the house and about the work cutting out geering templates, etc. Forepart of the day spent in writing to my Mother and Christina Stewart which together with a sheet of writing to Jeanie Stewart were posted with to-day's mail.

Tues. Feb. 23.
Had Ayr papers from home and spent the forenoon reading them. Copied some tables for geering, etc. Weather steadily cold but fine. Had portrait of Princess Royal sent to Sale of articles for benefit of Manse fund.

Wed. Feb. 24.
Jack Stewart and I took a long ramble eastward from the City on a concession line near to and parallel to the G.W.R. Walking on the snow pretty toilsome but day pleasant. Went thro' bush and fields to the lake

---

25 Likely Rev. John Marius Wilson, ed., *The Imperial Gazetteer of Scotland or Dictionary of Scottish Topography* (Edinburgh: A. Fullarton and Co., 1857).

26 The 'McInnes Block,' as it soon became known, was commissioned by major Hamilton dry goods merchant Donald McInnes in two stages. Builder George Worthington constructed a new store for McInnes in 1856. These new premises were expanded in 1858 following the designs of the architect A.H. Hills.

27 The books purchased were likely John James Audubon, *A Synopsis of the Birds of North America* (Edinburgh: A. and C. Black, 1839) and Cassin (see fn 24 above). The 1858 city directory lists Gentry and Brown's, booksellers, 6 Lister buildings, James St.

shore at Burlington beach. Fired at and missed a meadow lark. Shot 1 snow flake at the beach. Spent the evening in the house pasting plates into the scrap book. Mr Goldie from Ayr, C.W. called and left a little spaniel pup.

Thurs. Feb. 25.
Thos, John and I started on a ramble shortly after 8 a.m. Crossed the bay on the ice and across the country beyond untill close to Waterdown, then eastward from there along the heights, down the face of which we floundered thro' the very deep snow and had an arduous job getting back to the road which we then retraced as we had come. Took a slight refreshment in Aldershot on the G.W.R. Got home about 3 p.m.

Fri. Feb. 26.
Day very bright and fine. Captain Zealand lent Thos his horse and cutter, who took Mrs Mc and Tommy out driving for an hour and half across the bay, and then returned and got Jack Stewart and I with the gun to go down to the beach where we called upon Mr Snooks, shot two snow flakes, saw some meadow larks, got upset and tumbled out the cutter and had a delightful drive home over the ice.

Sat. Feb. 27.
Sun shining strong causing thaw all day. ~~Wrote an acrostic in Miss Muir's album~~.[28] Cut out some templates for wheel teeth. Thos purchased a carcase of a shore lark and stuffed it in the evening while I read a tale of the covenanters. Thos also added a specimen of a 'Bohemian Waxwing' to his museum.

Sun. Feb. 28.
Snowing fast a large part of the day, but streets very sloppy. Suffering with a doze of cold. Heard Mr Burnet preach morning and evening and spent the interval in the house.

Mon. Mar. 1.
Mr Robb called after breakfast to tell me of a job being ready for me at Dundas at pattern-making which I gladly made up my mind to take and prepare to start tomorrow. Wrote to Mrs Logan in the evening.

---

28 An acrostic is a form of writing in which the first letter, syllable, or word of each line, verse, or paragraph spells out a message. This form of writing is frequently used as a mnemonic device to help remember information. McIlwraith's fondness for this form is also evidenced by the 'Health Alphabet' recorded in his 1858 Memoranda. See Appendix 3.

Tues. Mar. 2.

Got tools and clothes packed up in the forenoon dined at 12 and started on foot to Dundas immediately after. Found Gartshore at home and settled upon commencing work tomorrow.[29] Then called on Mr McGarva at Dickie and Watson's, and by him got introduced to a boarding house in Mrs Jones's where I drank tea and now prepare for bed.[30] In the evening attended meeting of Mechanics Institute.[31]

Wed. Mar. 3.

Started work at 7 am. and spent the day fixing up a new bench to work at. Foreman's name Inglis, a decent quiet looking Scotchman.[32] Weather

---

29 John Gartshore (1810–73) was born in New Monkland, Scotland, and apprenticed as a millwright. He opened a foundry in Dundas in 1838 that had become a sizeable operation by the mid-1850s. In 1858 Gartshore won the contract to manufacture pumps and other machinery for the Hamilton Water Works, then under construction. This contract appears to have filled much of McIlwraith's time during his employment at Gartshore's. For more on Gartshore see Woodhouse, *History of the Town of Dundas*, 2:37; Dundas Historical Museum and Archives, Margaret Wade ed., *Leaves Form a Lifetime: Being a Brief History of the Gartshore Family of Scotland; of the Gartshore and Moir Families, as Pioneers in the Early Days of Ontario; and of the Life and Reminiscences to Date of William Moir Gartshore* (London, Ontario: A. Talbot and Company, 1929); T.W. Acheson, 'The Social Origins of the Canadian Industrial Elite, 1880-1885,' in D. MacMillan, ed. *Canadian Business History* (Toronto: McClelland and Stewart, 1972), 155; Kristofferson, *Craft Capitalism*, 69, 95-6, 100, 184, 192, 197.

30 The Town of Dundas 1858 Assessment Rolls list butcher John Jones, age 42, and 'Mrs. Jones' living in a brick house (no address) and boarding Robert Foster, Robert Allan, ——— McIlwraith and Jas. Orr (Roll #s 26–30).

31 The Dundas Mechanics' Institute was founded in 1841 and had a healthy membership through much of its first decade, especially among Gartshore employees. The Institute hit financial hard times by the late 1840s but was reorganized by the mid-1850s with the organizational help of Robert McKechnie Sr and James Sommerville and a £50-a-year government grant instituted in 1855. By the late 1850s the Institute had regained a large membership, was running an annual festival, and had opened a reading room in rented space in Dundas Engine House #2. See, Woodhouse, *History of the Town of Dundas*, 3:50–1.

32 The Gartshore Foundry had a reputation for training apprentices up through the crafts ranks to journeyman, foreman, and mastership. John Inglis had apprenticed at Gartshore's and by 1858, at the age of 36, was his foreman patternmaker. By 1859 Inglis had left this situation to join with Thomas Mair to start a small foundry in nearby Guelph. Inglis moved operations to Strachan Ave. in Toronto in the early 1880s, where his highly successful business ran for many years under the name John Inglis and Sons. See *Industrial Canada*, 'Centennial Issue' (1967); Kristofferson, *Craft Capitalism,* 199; Woodhouse, *A Short History of Dundas* (Town of Dundas Centennial Souvenir, 1947), 39; Assessment Rolls, Town of Dundas, 1858, Roll #560; Dundas Museum and Archives, Woodhouse Family History Collection, 'John Inglis.'

very keen frost, about as much so as we have had this season. McGarva and I attended a practice of singing in Free church vestry room. Slept with Mr Hartshorn, a musician from York State. Had a visit from Mr Jameson from London.

Thurs. Mar. 4.
Spent part of the day fixing bench and part altering valve chest. Weather still cold and frosty. In the evening read the life of Isabella of Castile in my lodgings.[33] Got a little bedroom appropriated to myself.

Fri. Mar. 5.
All day at pattern for furnace mount. Weather still intensely cold. Heard Rev. Mr Caldwell lecture in the town hall, subject popular excitements.

Sat. Mar. 6.
At Furnace mount and door for do. Weather rather milder. Got quit at 4.30 and as soon as I got cleaned a little, started to walk down to Hamilton on foot but was overtaken by Mr Fairgreive just while leaving Dundas with horse and cutter and got a ride down. Found all well in Hamilton. Wrote to Mrs Hunter in the evening.

Sun. Mar. 7.
Heard Mr Burnet preach in the morning. Called on Mr Robb after sermon. Started for Dundas about 4. J. Stewart convoyed me to Desjardins Bridge, from which I walked up to Dundas on the ice of the canal. Time between bridge and town 50 minutes. Went to church in the evening to hear Ormiston preach, but he did not come.

Mon. Mar. 8.
Worked about half-day at furnace mouth and half at job for Hamilton Pumping engines. Spent the evening with McGarva singing etc. in his room above Dickie and Watson's store. Weather fine and not so cold as last week.

Tues. Mar. 9.
All day at Hamilton pumping engine. In the evening joined the library and then went with McGarva to Mr Bertram's house where we met a lot

---

33 Perhaps Anita George, *Life of Isabel the Catholic: Queen, in Her Own Right, of Castile, 1474; and by Marriage, of Aragon, 1479.* (New York: Scribner, 1855) or William Hickling Prescott, *History of the Reign of Ferdinand and Isabella, the Catholic, of Spain* (Philadelphia: David Mackay, 1837).

of young ladies and men and practiced church tunes, after which we all got a shock from Mr B's galvanic battery.[34] Wrote to Thomas.

Wed. Mar. 10.
All day at engines. Went with McGarva to practice of singing in Free Church vestry room in the evening.

Thurs. Mar. 11.
All day at pumping engines. In the evening attended an entertainment in the Town Hall for the benefit of the poor. Performance, recitations, songs, etc. by a number of young men amateurs of Dundas. Connel an iron turner from the Foundry, with another turner gave a scene from 'Douglas.'[35]

Fri. Mar. 12.
All day at pumping engines. Had a short letter from Thos inclosing home ones from Bill. In the evening went with McGarva to our friend Mr Hartshorn's singing school and heard them singing Yankee 'toons.'

Sat. Mar. 13.
All day at pumping engines. Quit work at 4.50 and got a pass book with

---

34 John Bertram (1829–1906) was born in Eddlestone, Peebleshire, Scotland, son of a boot- and shoemaker. After attending parochial school at Eddleston he apprenticed as a machinist in Galashiels, Selkirkshire. He married Elizabeth Bennett at Stow, Edinburgh, and shortly after sailed for Montreal. He appears on the 1856 Dundas Assessment Rolls as a twenty-five-year-old turner employed by Gartshore. He became unemployed later in 1858 and moved to a small farm near Dundas. He returned to Dundas in 1863, when he formed a partnership with Robert McKechnie Jr in the Canada Tool Works. After McKechnie retired in 1886, this highly successful company was renamed John Bertram and Sons. Bertram was remembered by one of his employees as a man of encyclopedic memory who could quote the scriptures 'freely and accurately and to an amazing extent.' Bertram also pursued deep interests in Egyptology, history, geology, and astronomy. He was also well known for constructing one of the first galvanic batteries in Ontario and experimenting with electrical power. See 'Robert McKechnie' *DCB* (Toronto: University of Toronto Press, 1994), 13: 655–6; Assessment Rolls, Town of Dundas, 1858, Roll #491; Janet Bertram Brown, *The Heritage of John Bertram* (Dundas: Janet Brown Bertram, 2000), esp. ch. 2.
35 'Douglas' (ca 1756) was a tragedy written by Rev. John Home (1724–1808), a soldier and ordained Presbyterian minister whose play was performed with great success in Edinburgh but caused so much offence in the presbytery (being 'profane') that he was forced to demit his charge. 'A Scene from Douglas,' in J.E. Carpenter, ed., *Penny Readings in Prose and Verse* (London: Frederick Warne and Co., 1866) 112; Rev. John M'Kerrow, *History of the Secession Church* (Glasgow: A. Fullarton and Co., 1841), 525–6.

some unintelligible figuring and six dollars enclosed. Strolled round town and smoked a cigar with a Mr Thomson, a cabinet maker one of our singing class.

Sun. Mar. 14.
Had a short walk with McGarva who went off to Hamilton to the opening of Ormiston's Church. After 11 a.m. called upon Hector Mackenzie, and Connel, iron turners, whom I knew in Dumbarton.[36] Wrote a few lines to Mrs MacIlwraith in Hamilton and after dinner to a walk with Mackenzie and Connel to the 'Peak' of the Heights N.W. of Dundas, and along by the waterfalls beyond, which with the snow and icicles piled up looked grand. At Free Church in the evening.

Mon. Mar. 15.
All day at Pumping Engines. Weather miserably damp and foggy. Soiree on occasion on the opening of Ormiston's Church takes place in Hamilton tonight. Some of Mrs Jones' family gone there. Wonder if Miss Goldie is there.

Tues. Mar. 16.
All day at Pumping Engines. Weather so hot that we worked with the windows open. In the evening strolled round town with McGarva.

Wed. Mar. 17.
All day at Pumping Engines. Weather still warm, and great spate of water coming down the little creek past the shop. Attended singing practice in the evening.

Thurs. Mar. 18.
Great storm of wind during last night. All day at Pumping Engines. In the evening went to a debating club composed of Foundry workmen – subject discussed 'whether had the Press or Compass done most towards civilization.' Got a good laugh at Hector Mackenzie's speech.

Fri. Mar. 19.
Hoar frost in the morning and a delightful clear, cool day. Immense

---

36 McIlwraith may have worked in Dumbarton, Scotland, a town located at the confluence of the Leven and Clyde rivers, about fifteen miles downstream from Glasgow. It was a centre of shipbuilding, marine engineering, and related metal industries. See Archibald C. M'Michael, *Past and Present: A Descriptive and Historical Account of Stirling, Dumbarton, and Linlithgowshires* (Glasgow: Hay, Nisbet and Company, 1890), 133–8.

flocks of pigeons flying west in the morning and forenoon. Remarkably early in the season for them. All day at Pumping Engines. In the
evening writing home.

Sat. Mar. 20.
Slight frost in the morning and day delightful. Heard the song sparrow
sing while dressing in the morning and the Blue bird while on the way
to the shop. At Pumping Engines all day. Took train to Hamilton at 6.
Learned Jack Stewart had got in for Gas Work clerk. Saw two new cases
of birds. Thos got up within the fortnight, one to present to Manse Fund
Bazar and one with small winter birds for himself. Had a note from
Jameson promising to see me in a fortnight.

Sun. Mar. 21.
Heard Mr Burnet preach in the forenoon. Day stormy with squalls
of snow and hail and blinks of sunshine. Started to walk to Dundas
between three and four in the afternoon. Caught a hail shower in my
teeth when about a mile out of town. Roads rather muddy. Got to Dundas by five. Went to the Free Church with McGarva and heard Mr Stark
preach in the evening.

Mon. Mar. 22.
Weather fine. Still at Pumping Engines. Saw large flock of pigeons fly
past in the evening. Got my chest and clothes up from Hamilton per
teamster 'Denis.' Had a while practicing Scottish music with McGarva
in his room above Dickie and Watson's store.

Tues. Mar. 23.
Finished a sort of Beam coupling pattern for pumping engines and
commercial small beam to connect to do. In the evening went to a meeting of council in town hall and heard some of the Dundas City fathers
holding forth.

Wed. Mar. 24.
Finished small beam pattern. Went to the singing practice in the evening
with Miss Monro. Weather very fine.

Thurs. Mar. 25.
Set on to a large Beam pattern, the seat of the pumps for Hamilton
Water Works in co. with old George Bickell.[37] Size three feet deep and

---

37 'Old' George Bickell also served as the librarian for the Dundas Mechanics' Institute
in 1855. Woodhouse, *History of the Town of Dundas*, 3:51.

three wide. Had pretty hard work handling 2 inch wood of which it is to be made. In the evening writing to Anderson, Dumbarton.

Fri. Mar. 26.
All day at Pumping Engines. Weather fine. Pigeons flying more or less in the mornings and forenoons all week. Shooting of them most successful between 9 and 12 am. In the evening heard a good lecture in the town hall by Mr Stark, minister of the Free Church subject, Concentration, Promptitude and Stability, the chief elements of success in Life.

Sat. Mar. 27.
Day kind of cold and raw. All day at pumping engines. In the evening had a walk round town and smoked a cigar with Wm Willis, my benchmate, afterwards adjourned to his lodgings and played draughts at which I beat him.[38] Had some singing with McGarva afterwards, and left him about 11 p.m. at which time the ground was white with snow.

Sun Mar. 28.
Snow on the ground in the morning but melted away as the sun rose. Attended St Andrew's Church, Dundas.[39] Service by an old missionary, their being no minister for the church at present. After Dinner had a walk up the glen to Webster and Spenser's Falls with McGarva and Will. Heard Mr Stark preach in the Free Church in the evening.

Mon. Mar. 29.
A most delightful sunny day. At Pumping engines all day. In the evening had a ramble up past the railway station and then round town with McGarva, after which we went into his room and sung scotch

---

38 Draughts is a popular strategic board game also known as checkers.
39 St Andrew's Presbyterian Church, Dundas, was a Free Church congregation connected with an Ancaster pastorate from the 1820s until 1833, when it assumed a separate existence. Rev. James Herald – a native of Aberdeen, Scotland, who came to Canada in 1857 – became its pastor shortly after McIlwraith's first visit and served there from June 1858 to 1879. The larger church 'disruption' in 1844 led to the creation of a second local congregation – Knox Church – a division that lasted thirty-five years. When St Andrew's was reunited with Knox Presbyterian, Dundas, in 1879, Rev. Herald was appointed ordained missionary to Port Arthur and Fort William, Ontario. He died in Medicine Hat, NWT, in 1890 at the age of sixty-four. 'Knox Presbyterian Church (Dundas, ON) fonds, Presbyterian Church in Canada Archives, North York, Ontario; *A Historical and Statistical Report of the Presbyterian Church in Canada ... for the Year 1866* (Montreal: John Lovell, 1867), 8; John Bulloch, *Scottish Notes and Queries* 8, no. 10 (April 1907): 145.

songs. Saw the moon rising grand and red behind Hamilton city from the mountain above the station.

Tues. Mar. 30.
At pumping engines all day. Weather still delightful. Had a walk with Will in the evening.

Wed. Mar. 31.
All day at Pumping engines. Attended singing practice in the evening. Heard the frogs for the first time this season on taking a stroll down by the canal in the evening.

Thurs. April 1.
At Pumping engines all day. Still beautiful weather. In the evening went to meeting of debating society in the old engine and made my maiden speech on the question, whether had war or intemperance caused greatest misery to the human race. I trying to maintain that intemperance had.

Fri. Apr. 2.
All day at Pumping engines. Butterflies flying about to-day and boys bathing in the creek below our workshop. Took a stroll down by the side of the canal and heard the frogs coming out in great strength – not the piping frogs but the kind which cry 'peep peep.' In the evening felt a little tired and spent most of it in the house.

Sat. Apr. 3.
All day at Pumping Engines. Left Dundas at 6 p.m. and walked to Hamilton, getting in about 7. Found the people all well and that Thos had applied for a situation for me on the Southern Railroad to Mr. Street, chief engineer. Called upon old Mr Muir's people and saw Mr Manby there. James Muir gone to Detroit 2 weeks ago. Got letters from Mrs Logan and from Home.

Sun. Apr. 4.
John Muir called and went with me to Mr Ormiston's Church and heard that gentleman preach. Met Jameson there who told me of his having commenced work in Mr Kerr's old situation on the railway. Left to walk to Dundas between 3 and 4. Got a short convoy from Thos and Tommy and from Jameson beyond Desjardins bridge. John Stewart going into lodgings to-morrow. Got caught with heavy rain walking to Dundas but saw a beautiful rainbow.

Mon. Apr. 5.
All day at Pumping engines. Spent the evening in Will's lodgings, playing draughts and singing sacred music.

Tues. Apr. 6.
Weather now quite cold. All day at Pumping Engines. Evening bitterly cold. Spent the evening in the house writing to Mrs Logan.

Wed. Apr. 7.
All day at pumping engines. In the evening went to the singing.

Thurs. Apr. 8.
All day at Pumping engines. Took a pretty long stroll in the evening out the Plank road leading to Paris and in by a cross road leading into the other end of the town. Got some rain.

Fri. Apr. 9.
All day at Pumping engines. Had our debate as to whether war or intemperance caused greatest misery in the evening again but did not finish it. Mr Gibson, a little red bearded Irishman and drill sergeant of the Dundas Hussars coming out strong on the war side.

Sat. Apr. 10.
All day at pumping engines. Some little stir in town with soldiers recruiting. Took a stroll up town in the evening and fell in with George Gray a millwright and shop mate, and visited a paper mill at the far end of the town, then spent a while in Gray's house. Mr O'Conner a teacher with a mustache arrived to board in Mrs Jones's.

Sun. Apr. 11.
An exceedingly cold stormy day, rain, sleet and snow falling incessantly all day. Heard Mr Stark preach in the forenoon. Spent most of the day in the house reading Foster's essays.[40]

Mon. Apr. 12.
Weather still cold and blustering. Half melted snow and hail keeping the streets in a deplorable state. All day at Pumping Engines. Attended a public meeting in the evening in the Town Hall, called to consider the propriety of imposing duties on manufactures being brought from the states. Mayor Bigue in the chair, McGarva, secretary. Gartshore spoke.

---

40 John Foster, *Essays*. See fn 1 above.

Tues. Apr. 13.
Weather very foggy but milder than yesterday. All day at pumping engines. Commenced reducing the weight of our large beam by planing and cutting down. Spent the evening strolling round town, and reading in his room with McGarva.

Wed. Apr. 14.
Weather now warm, but heavy rain falling part of the day. All day at pumping engines. In the evening went to practice of singing. Mr Wilson began giving us some exercises on music on a blackboard. Frogs very loud down in the swamps tonight.

Thurs. Apr. 15.
All day at pumping engines. Spent the evening studying for to-morrow night's debate.

Fri. Apr. 16.
All day at pumping engines. Had another night's debating of the war or intemperance question, but prevented from finishing it by the stubbornness of the leader on the war side, a little brass moulder by name McMillan who insisted upon having longer time to sum up.

Sat. Apr. 17.
A delightful day. George Bickell and I got finished with our big beam for the Water Works and got it carried into the shed. Got tea and started on foot to Hamilton by six, arriving there a few minutes past 7. Got in company with one of our moulders by the way, who knew And. Baird in Scotland. Found all well in Hamilton. John Stewart in his boarding house, Miss Muir going to be married. ~~Mary Goldie expected down in a fortnight~~. Called at Mr. W.K. Muir's in the evening.

Sun. Apr. 18.
Heard Mr Inglis preach in Burnet's Church. Mr W.K. Muir called on Thos after sermon with a crawfish. Started for Dundas about 3 p.m. Thos and Jack Stewart convoying me about half way. Took the road by the Desjardins Bridge. Rather late for going to church in the evening, so had another walk around Dundas after tea.

Mon. Apr. 19.
Commenced to Air pump Valves for pumping engines. A nasty blustering day. Matilda Ware my landlady's daughter sick with ague. Allan, one of our boarders, also sick. Mr Bickle who was set to work at the

same job with me off work attending to his sick children at home. Spent the evening writing home to Mother.

Tues. Apr. 20.
All day at Pumping Engine valves. In the evening called with McGarva upon Miss Foulds and had some singing and playing on the melodian with her and Miss Ballantyne. Saw Miss B. home to Coleman's house and sat for a little there. Weather dull and foggy.

Wed. Apr. 21.
At Valve Patterns all day. Went to singing practice in the evening. Reading Dicken's Christmas Stories, etc.[41]

Thurs. Apr. 22.
All day at Valve Patterns. Read Dicken's in the evening. A beautiful moonlight night. Took a solitary walk down the Toronto road after 10 at night.

Fri. Apr. 23.
At Valve Patterns. Quit at 3.30 and attended the funeral of Bickle's child helping to carry it to the grave. Went to debating club in the evening. Chairman decided that previous to the 15th century war was the greatest evil but that since then intemperance was. Cold weather with some snow falling.

Sat. Apr. 24.
All day at valve Patterns. Had a walk up over the mountain in the evening. Gathered some Hypetica flowers which are now plenty. Spent some time at an auction of books, jewelry, etc. A beautiful moonlight night but still cold.

Sun. Apr. 25.
Heard Mr Herald the new minister to St Andrew's Church preach in the forenoon and in the afternoon heard a stranger preach in the H.P. Church. In the evening, Robt McKelvie called and took me to a meeting of a bible class in the house of Mr Mair. Mr Mair questioned and explained a chap. of Jeremiah, and was very interesting and instructive.[42]

---

41 Likely Christmas stories from Dickens's magazine *Household Words* (London, 1850–9). McIlwraith also consulted this magazine on May 4, 1858.

42 'McKelvie' is likely a misspelling of 'McKechnie.' Likely Thomas Mair, listed variously as a machinist, millwright, engineer, and carpenter. By 1858 he was proprietor

Mon. Apr. 26.
All day at Valve patterns. In the evening had a long walk out the Governors Road by moonlight. Weather pleasant but chilly.

Tues. Apr. 27.
All day at valve patterns. Went to the library in the evening and got Thackeray's Vanity Fair which I forthwith commenced to pore at.[43]

Wed. Apr. 28.
All day at valve patterns. Sat the whole evening in the house poring over Vanity Fair.

Thurs. Apr. 29.
All day at valve patterns. Sat late at night again reading Vanity Fair.

Fri. Apr. 30.
Still at valve patterns. David Goldie visited me in the shop in the forenoon being on business in the foundry. Took an hour to go round town with him. Learned that Mary had gone to Hamilton. Sat late and finished reading Vanity Fair.

Sat. May 1.
All day at valve patterns. Started on foot for Hamilton at 5.15 p.m. and got home between 6 and 7. Found a tea party assembled; Mr and Mrs Muir, Senr and Junr, Mrs Steele and Mary Goldie. She and I had a while's looking thro' pictures. Walked to Muir Junr's with her.

Sun. May 2.
Heard Mr Burnet preach in the forenoon and then had a walk west along the foot of the mountain with Thos. ~~Got back about 5 and found Mary in the house. Had her at church and waiting for tea afterwards. Escorted her home to Muirs. Would like well to pop the question but feel that I have not confidence enough to open my mind freely yet~~.

Mon. May 3.
Worked all day at valve patterns. ~~Feeling kind of crippity crappity on~~

---

of the Wentworth Foundry in Dundas, manufacturers of steam engines and other products. He partnered with Gartshore pattern shop foreman John Inglis in July 1959 to open a foundry in Guelph producing flour and grist mill machinery and, later, engines and boilers. *Industrial Canada* 'Centennial Issue' (1967); Town of Dundas Assessment Rolls, 1858, Roll #250; *Dundas True Banner*, February 18, 1959; Woodhouse Family History Collection.

43 William Makepeace Thackeray, *Vanity Fair: A Novel without a Hero; with illus. on steel and wood by the author* (London: Bradbury, 1848).

~~the subject of Mary – blame myself for not being more of man~~. Started from Hamilton about 5 this morning and walked to Dundas in time for breakfast and work at 7. Thos convoyed me half way.

Tues. May 4.
At valve patterns. Went to the library in the evening and got 1 volume of Household Words, then came down with McGarva to his room and sung Scotch songs with might and main.[44] ~~Tried to put some rhymes together about my Mary~~.

Wed. May 5.
~~Posted a copy of my poetical attempts to the editor of the 'True Banner'~~.[45] Worked all day at valve patterns and in the evening attended singing practice. Heard the whip-poor-will up towards the foot of the mountain.

Thurs. May 6.
Finished valve patterns and set on to pattern of winch for pumping engines. Feel kind of lazy and low-spirited now although reason always says bear up. Spent the evening idly in the house. Weather now warm and fine. Old Kyle who used to be foreman patternmaker commenced in the shop.

Fri. May 7.
At Winch Pattern all day. Had our debate in the evening – subject would Federal Union be advantageous to the British Provinces in America. I supporting Union. Attendance small.

Sat. May 8.
Weather sultry. At Winch pattern. Had a walk out the Governor's road with Will in the evening. Between 9 and 10 at night an old shanty at the far end of the town took fire and burnt and caused some stir. Had a note from Thos enclosing a fine long letter from Mrs Hunter.

Sun. May 9.
Forenoon sultry but afternoon delightfully cool and bright. Heard Mr Herald preach in the morning. In the afternoon had a walk with

---

44 Charles Dickens's weekly magazine *Household Words* was published in London from 1850 to 1859. It covered a diverse number of topics from a wide array of contributors. In addition to first-run serialized fiction, which included Dickens's *Hard Times* and Elizabeth Gaskell's *North and South*, the magazine also contained articles on science, travel, social commentary, and much else. See also April 21, 1858 entry.

45 The *Dundas True Banner* was a Reform newspaper edited by James Sommerville. See fn 2 above.

McGarva and Will to the Sulphur spring, and home by way of Flamboro' village, a most beautiful walk. Went with R. McKechnie to Mr Mair's Bible Class in the evening.

Mon. May 10.
All day at Winch pattern. Large Walking Beam casting got broken in the yard by being let drop. Got an introduction to Mr MacFarlane and his sweetheart in the evening. Wrote some to Mrs Hunter.

Tues. May 11.
A miserable wet morning. Six o'clock bell did not ring so I lay too long to go to my work. Spent the forenoon in the house writing to Hugh Dickie and Mrs Hunter and posted their letters. Worked half day at Winch pattern. Called on Hector MacKenzie in the evening whose sister in law is like to lose her eye by an accident in the house.

Wed. May 12.
All day at Winch pattern. In the evening attended practice of singing.

Thurs. May 13.
A delightfully pleasant cool day. Had an evening walk along the railway and a short way up the glen towards the falls. The grass now in its richest green, with little violets thickly sprinkled among it. Heard two whip poor wills and then came down and whipped poor Will myself at the draughts. Took a walk thro' the shop, where the turners, etc. were at work.

Fri. May 14.
At Winch pattern all day. Attended meeting of our debating club and had the Federal Union question decided in the affirmative, the side which I had advocated but didn't do much good for.

Sat. May 15.
Still fine weather. The large bed plate for pumps cast to-day. Wm Will and I walked down to Hamilton in co. after getting quit work. Had a walk up town with Thomas and John Stewart in the evening and spent a while in Barnes Book Store.

Sun. May 16.
A delightful clear cool day. Accompanied Mrs Mc to church and heard Mr Burnet. After dinner started for Dundas and took a circuit thro' the bush with Thos and John. Had a fine view of a Humming bird at a farm house, spining round a tree in blossom. After tea in Dundas, attended Mr Mayer's Bible Class.

Mon. May. 17.
Rain pouring down in torrents in the morning and nearly all day.
Worked at winch pattern all day and in the evening wrote to Mrs Logan.

Tues. May 18.
Weather clearing up a little. At Winch pattern. Had a fine evening walk
and gathered a bunch of wild flowers. Called at the library and got a
volume of Hogg's Instructor.[46]

Wed. May 19.
At Winch pattern all day. At singing practice and had a jolly good sing
in the evening.

Thurs. May 20.
At Winch Pattern. Took the train to Hamilton at 6.55 p.m. Spent a while
walking round town there with Mr. Jameson. Got 10 dollars from Thos
charged against my savings bank deposit. Sat late talking and got a
good deal of teasing about Mary.

Fri. May 21.
Weather pleasant but chilly. Had a fine smart walk from Hamilton out
to Dundas arriving in time for breakfast and work at 7. Saw pigeons flying. Debating club met in the evening and heard an essay by Connel on
imagination, myself chairman. A lively discussion followed the essay.

Sat. May 22.
Morning most beautifully propitious for my jaunt to Ayr. Did not go
to work but took first train to Paris. Got Mr Goldie's team and waggon going out and rode to the village. Walked from there to Greenfield.
~~Found Mary to be in bed, sick, how ever; she got up by and by and sat~~
~~middling late~~.

Sun. May 23.
Mrs Goldie and Mary both sick this morning. Went to Church in the
forenoon and spent about 3 hours under Mr McCruar.[47] Heavy rain

---

46 *Hogg's Instructor* was a monthly magazine published an Edinburgh by James Hogg
between 1849 and 1855.
47 Rev. Duncan McRuar (1824–87?) was pastor at Knox Presbyterian Church (a Free
Church congregation) in Ayr, Canada West/Ontario, from 1854 to 1889 and local
school superintendant for the County of Waterloo. He had previously served Blenheim and Paris, in 1849. A graduate (and member of the first class) of Knox College,
Toronto, he officiated at the marriage of Andrew McIlwraith and Mary Goldie on
April 9, 1862. *Dumfries Reformer* [Galt], April 16, 1862; Brian John Fraser, *Church, College and Clergy: A History of Theological Education at Knox College, Toronto, 1844–1894*

caught us coming home from church. ~~Mary up again most of the after-noon and evening, so had some pleasant tete-a-tete.~~

Mon. May 24.
Morning looking dull but weather improved and turned out fine as the day advanced being a holiday at the mill as at other places on account of Queen's birth-day. D. Goldie borrowed a gun and we went out and shot two squirrels and a pigeon. Saw some leaping matches in Ayr in the afternoon. Left Greenfield about 4 p.m. in the Buggy with Mr Goldie and drove to Paris.

Tues. May 25.
Slept in Hamilton after arriving from the west. Walked to Dundas in the morning in time for work. At winch pattern all day. Weather cold and dull with heavy rain in the evening.

Wed. May 26.
At Winch pattern. Attended practice of singing in the evening. Weather wet and attendance small.

Thurs. May 27.
Commenced to footstep patterns for horizontal water wheel.

Fri. May 28.
At Water Wheel patterns. In the evening attended debating club meeting and acted as chairman in the debate as to whether an increase of duties in imported manufactures would benefit Canada.

Sat. May 29.
At Water Wheel patterns. Evening wet. Called along with Wm Will upon Jas Wilson and had some music of flute and fiddle. Had a letter from Mrs McIlwraith, Hamilton, with inclosures from home. Miss Goldie no better. Letter from Christina telling of P. Hosie borrowing money from her.

Sun. May 30.
Had a walk with McGarva before church time. Attended Mr Stark's church in the forenoon. Spent most of the day in the house writing to Thos in Hamilton. At Mr Mair's bible class in the evening.

(Montreal and Kingston: McGill-Queen's University Press, 1995), 219; *Historical Sketches of the Pioneer Work and the Missionary, Educational and Benevolent Agencies of the Presbyterian Church in Canada* (Toronto: Murray Printing, 1903), 86; Hugh Scobie, *Scobie's Canadian Almanac and Repository of Useful Knowledge* (The Author, 1849), 57. Thanks to Donna Bell, Knox United Church, Ayr, Ontario.

Mon. May 31.
At water wheel patterns. In the evening went to meeting of young mens Christian association and heard Mr Chisholm reading an essay on the Red Men of British North America.[48]

Tues. June 1.
At water wheel patterns. Weather quite sultry. Fruit trees, etc, looking beautiful. Observe some hummingbirds about them. Spent the evening writing to Christina.

Wed. June 2.
Still warm weather. Half day at Water wheel and half day at beam for Welland engine. In the evening attended singing practice and had a stroll round with McGarva afterwards.

Thurs. June 3.
All day at Beam Pattern. Took a sleep and a stroll in the evening. Weather warm.

Fri. June 4.
At Beam pattern. Debating club had semi-annual meeting in the evening and elected me Secretary. President Mr Connel, and vice-president Inglis. Debate upon tariff question went on but was not finished.

Sat. June 5.
Still beautiful warm weather. All day at Beam pattern. In the evening Wm Will and I walked down to Hamilton. Found all well there and had letters from home and from Hugh Dickie, Wolverton.

Sun. June 6.
Heard Dr Jennings from Toronto preach in the forenoon in St Andrew's Church. Morning wet but afternoon fine. Walked to Dundas, and attended Mr Mair's Bible class in the evening.

Mon. June 7.
At Beam Pattern. Still hot weather. Had a walk up the mountain in the evening then wrote to Mr Hosie, New York.

---

48 The Young Men's Christian Association (YMCA) was founded in London, England, in 1844 by twenty-three-year-old draper George Williams and soon set up North American branches. A local branch of the YMCA was active in nearby Hamilton between 1856 and about 1860. The Hamilton branch was heavily patronized by craftsworkers. When the Hamilton branch reformed in 1867, Andrew's brother Thomas donated a number of items to the association's new library. *HS*, February 4, 1867; Kristofferson, *Craft Capitalism*, 190–3.

Tues. June 8.
At Beam Pattern. In the evening took a walk out the Brock Road beyond Bullocks Corners. After coming home broke ground upon a commence-ment to an essay on 'Wilson, the Ornithologist' for the Mechanic's debating club.[49]

Wed. June 9.
At Beam Pattern. Miserable wet weather. Spent the evening in the house reading and writing.

Thurs. June 10.
Very rainy and sultry. Still at Beam Pattern. In the evening explored some of the bye lanes of Dundas down around the canal Basin then home and wrote and studied a little.

Fri. June 11.
All day at Beam. In the evening had our debate upon the tariff question concluded, the decision of the chairman (myself) being that the present protection is sufficient for manufactures for home con-sumption and that it is too expensive an undertaking for Canada to turn exporter.

Sat. June 12.
At Beam Pattern all day. In the evening went out the Ancaster old road and strolled on untill I reach the village, returning by the Hamilton road. Saw the glare of a great fire away West.

Sun. June 13.
Heard Mr Herald preach in the morning. Had a walk in the afternoon out the Sydenham road and across the country back over the Peak. At Mr Mair's bible class in the evening. Got introduced to the Misses Som-merville and Mary McKechnie, sister of my friend, Bob.

---

49 Alexander Wilson (1766–1813) was born in Paisley, Scotland. He worked as a weaver after leaving school around the age of thirteen. He also developed a fond-ness for wandering the Scottish countryside and writing poetry. His literary career as a young man was marked by the writing of a scathing critique of the relations between weavers and local merchants. He served a short prison term for this and was required to burn this tract in front of local townspeople as punishment. His dis-satisfaction with his Scottish home led him to emigrate to the United States in 1794. There, Wilson continued his weavers trade and also developed an interest in birds. He was best known as the author of the nine-volume *American Ornithology* published between 1808 and 1814.

Mon. June 14.
At Beam Pattern. In the evening had a walk down the Toronto road. Weather now fine. Whip-poor-wills very numerous.

Tues. June 15.
Weather still beautiful. All day at Beam. Had a walk with Will in the evening over the tip of the mount alongside the creek near the foundry. Saw old Pumphrey, a nigger wanting an arm and blind of an eye dancing on the sidewalk.

Wed. June 16.
Very warm. Heard of a great Sheberree having taken place at the other end of the town last night.[50] All day at beam. In the evening at the singing.

Thurs. June 17.
All day at Beam. Exceedingly hot. Had a walk out the Governors Road and round by the head of the town in the evening, then home and read Hogg's Instructor.

Fri. June 18.
All day at Beam Pattern. In the evening attended Mechanics debating club, the chief business of the evening being to hear an essay on 'Goldsmith' from R. McKechnie, Senr. but which he changed for a discourse upon proverbs of all nations; for which thanks were voted. Some severe comments however were made on his conduct in changing his subject.

Sat. June 19.
Very warm weather. Mr Inglis informed me in the afternoon that my services would be no more wanted as the work was getting scarce. Took train down to Hamilton in the evening.

Sun. June 20.
Heard Dr Skinner from Waterdown preach in St Andrews Church in the forenoon.[51] At the dinner table, Thos proposed to his Mistress that she

---

50 Probably a 'charivari.'
51 A Presbyterian dissenter from Partick, Scotland, Rev. John Skinner, DD (ca 1804–64) came from thirteen years' service in Lexington, Virginia, to pastor in London, Canada West, in 1853, where he served until he became minister of Nelson and Waterdown in 1855. He pastored in that charge until he died, in his sixtieth year. Joseph M. Wilson, *The Presbyterian Historical Almanac and Annual Remembrancer of the Church for 1865* (Philadelphia: Joseph M. Wilson, 1865), 7:346.

should take a trip home with the children. Had a walk to the cemetry with Jameson and spent the evening in the house. Very hot.

Mon. June 21.
Still very hot. Walked up town with Thos to enquire after passages to the old Country. Heard from Mrs Logan who mentioned Mr Renfrew's being going home. Had a very toilsome ramble along the mountain in the afternoon with the gun. Had a stroll with Jameson in the evening.

Tues. June 22.
Miss Muir married this morning, henceforth to be Mrs Cowie.[52] Met Mr Robb in the forenoon and promised to assist him with some drawing. Sketched for him a design for a seal for Hamilton scientific association. Walked up town with Thos and bought two books, treatise on building and Rhetorical extracts. Mr Muir called in the evening and gave me some hopes of a job in Detroit.

Wed. June 23.
Worked part of the day for Mr Robb running about town, sketching waggon trucks, etc. for application to an invention for ploughing by steam. Weather awful hot. Took train to Dundas in the evening and attended singing practice.

Thurs. June 24.
Had a very hot morning walk down from Dundas. Mrs Mc secured first class berths for the voyage home in the Nova Scotian. Spent most of the day drawing with Mr Robb. Took train again at 7 for Dundas. Called upon A. Connel and Hector Mackenzie. The moon about full, and evenings just now hot but beautiful.

Fri. June 25.
Visited the Foundry in the forenoon. In the afternoon in company with Robt McKechnie took a ramble up to Webster's falls, and round the ravines to Hopkinsons falls. Had some delicious dabling in cool shady springs. Sat a while on the peak and descended down its face. Attended debating club in the evening. Resigned my secretaryship, received a vote of thanks. Debated whether Scotland or America introduced the steamboat, and then took good bye.

---

52 The wedding of William Cowie (Cowing) and Ellen Kerr Muir took place at the Park
    Street residence of her father, William Muir, and was officiated by Rev. Ormiston.
    William Cowing was the St Catharines stationmaster for the GWR. *HS*, June 24, 1858.
    Craven, 'Labour and Management,' 399fn67. On Muir, see Diary for 1857, fn 61.

Sat. June 26.
Having squared all my accounts and received a check for my wages from Gartshore, took an early breakfast with Mrs Jones by which time Dennis called with his cart and took of my luggage from house and shop. Had one bumper at parting with McGarva and rode to Hamilton with Dennis. Spent most of the day in Mr Robb's, drawing.

Sun. June 27.
Heard Mr Burnet preach morning and evening. Weather awfully hot. Had a stroll to the side of the Bay beyond Gunn's factory along with Jack Stewart in the interval.

Mon. June 28.
All day at work with Mr Robb at drawing of steam plough. Had a walk around town with Mr Jameson in the evening.

Tues. June 29.
All day at work with Mr Robb. Met with Mr Cant in his house. Mrs Mc busy packing up for starting to-morrow for the old country. Tommy very fretful with the heat, musquito bites, etc.

Wed. June 30.
Got a pass from Mr Jameson and took the first train to Toronto. Strolled about the streets from 9.30 till 12 and then went and met Thos and wife on their arrival with the steamer Passport. Dined on board of her and saw them off, wife and wean for Scotland and Thos as convoy to Quebec. Went to the Parliament house in the evening. Had no ticket of admission, but met George Brown M.P.P. at the head of the stair, who kindly ushered me into the ladies gallery. Heard old McKenzie[53] speak on the divorce question.[54]

---

53 Likely William Lyon Mackenzie (1795–1861), reform firebrand and 1837 rebel leader, who received amnesty in 1849 and returned to Canada from exile in the United States to the life of a parliamentarian (representing Haldimand riding). This would have been one of his final speeches; his health failing, he resigned his seat in August 1858. See Frederick J. Armstrong and Ronald J. Stagg, 'Mackenzie, William Lyon,' *DCB* (Toronto: University of Toronto Press), 9:496–510.

54 In 1857, the Parliament of the United Canadas adopted the British Matrimonial Causes Act, a law that allowed divorce through the law courts. Previously, parties seeking divorce had to endure the slow and expensive process of a private act of Parliament. See generally Lorene Anne Chambers, *Married Women and Property Law in Victorian Ontario* (Toronto: Osgoode Society for Canadian Legal History, 1997). On Brown, see Diary for 1857, fn 8.

Thurs. July 1.
Worked all day with Mr Robb. Weather quite cool to-day. Spent the evening reading newspapers, etc.

Fri. July 2.
A very pleasant day, sunny and with a nice cool breeze. All day at Mr Robb's drawing. Spent the evening walking with Jameson.

Sat. July 3.
At work with Mr Robb. In the evening accompanied Mr Jameson to Mr Crawford's practice of singing in the basement of St Andrews Church.

Sun. July 4.
Jameson and I attended St Andrews church in the forenoon. In the afternoon, he and I went out walking and sat so long at the side of the Bay away beyond Gunn's factory that we were too late for church. Found a nest and four eggs among the grass. Day beautifully sunny and with a nice cool breeze.

Mon. July 5.
At work all day for Mr Robb. In the evening Jack Stewart, Jameson and I got Capt. Zealand's boat and rowed across the bay and had a while's successful fishing. Evening warm and beautiful.

Tues. July 6.
Weather still very pleasant. Worked at Mr Robb's plans and went down with a tracing to Mr Northie's shop, who is making the ploughing apparatus.[55] After tea, got out Mr Raphael's horse and had a ride for an hour then came in and played chess with Jameson.

Wed. July 7.
Weather warmer again. Went down to the wharf in the forenoon to look for Thos arriving with the steamer, but was too early and strolled round the Bay by Fisher's Foundry. Missed the boat and Thos home before me. Had a walk round town with Jameson in the evening.

Thurs. July 8.
Got a ticket from Mr Raphael to go to the Railway Celebration at

---

55 George Northey's small steam engine manufactory was located on the corner of Wellington and King William streets in Hamilton. This foundry gained profile in 1862 when T. Northey's patent, a portable and self-containing expansion steam engine, won a prize and diploma at the Provincial Exhibition in Toronto. *Hamilton Times*, October 9, 1863; *Canadian Illustrated News*, November 8, 1862.

Goderich. Went with the P.M. train from Hamilton and found that the only train from Paris to Goderich had left in the morning.[56] Walk out to Hugh McWhirter's, drank tea with him and slept in Kay's at Dinvire.

Fri. July 9.
Got mounted up on Hugh McWhirter's brown horse Brownie to ride over to Ayr but the cursed beast took fright and pitched me off about a quarter of a mile from home and ran home and left me. Went there and worked hard at hay-making all day with Hugh until about dark and came home very tired.

Sat. July 10.
Was promised a horse from John Jackson but he disappointed me. Jean McWhirter washed my white pants and shirt which had been soiled with the adventures of yesterday. Took the opportunity of driving into Paris with the Kays and arrived per train in Hamilton about three p.m. J. Stewart, Thos and I went across the Bay and fished in the evening. Very hot.

Sun. July 11.
Had Jameson at church in the morning and heard Mr Burnet preach. Spent the interval in the house with Thos reading. Jameson and I went to Ormiston's in the evening and heard a stranger preach. Day cold and rainy.

Mon. July 12.
Weather still cold and damp. Wrote letters to Christina and Bill and sent a draft for 5£ sterling – 4£ to Christina for Hosie's intromission and 1£ to buy books. Called on Mr Robb and got some plans of Water Works to trace. Walked round town with Thos in the evening.

Tues. July 13.
Weather now delightful, sunny and not too hot. Traced one of the Water Works drawings for Mr Robb. At 3 p.m. Thos and I took the Ferry steamer across the bay to Oaklands, and when there determined to walk to her landing place on Burlington Beach and so home with her.

---

56 This celebration feted the completion of the Buffalo and Lake Huron Railway. Originated in 1851 and built with English capital, the line posed some competition to both the GTR and the GWR, all of them having designs on trans-border trade in the age of Reciprocity. This theme is featured prominently in an 1858 lithograph depicting the grand opening ceremony at Goderich. 'Opening of the Buffalo and Lake Huron Railway,' *The Illustrated London News*, October 30, 1858, 405, 407.

Spent too long time on the road and was late for her. Found Capt. Caddie at the Canal with a sail boat and took passage home with him. Wind ahead. Had to pull a long way. Sailed at 8 p.m. and all night on the Bay.

Wed. July 14.
Landed from our voyage at 3 a.m. this morning, very tired with pulling and very sleepy and hungry. Took a long lie and a hearty breakfast. Thos complaining of a sore back this day or two. Traced a plan for Mr Robb, and spent part of the evening in the Reading room.[57]

Thurs. July 15.
A fine warm day. Thos and I took train for Paris at 1 p.m. Found old Peter Auld, a teamster wanting one foot at the Paris station and got a ride in his waggon right to Greenfield. Spent a little time in the village horning in the tavern with him. Found Mary in the garden when we got to Greenfield. Had tea and then a short stroll in the bush. Thos shot one black Squirrel between Paris and Ayr.

Fri. July 16.
Went out shooting in the forenoon in the bush behind Mr Goldie's house and had good sport, killing five black squirels and one large hawk. After dinner got the canoe and went up the creek fishing and caught any amount of small 'shiners.' Mary away at Galt to-day but came home in the evening.

Sat. July 17.
Forenoon rather wet but had a short walk with the gun. Weather cleared up in the afternoon which we spent walking and trying the fishing unsuccessfully in the small stream running past Mr Goldie's house. In the evening, Thos and Mary and I had a delightful little sail up the creek in the canoe.

Sun. July 18.
Day sunny and with a delightful cool breeze. Heard Mr McRuar preach in the forenoon in Ayr. Walked home to Greenfield by the back road thro' the bush. After dinner went altogether, that is Mary and Davie, Sandy Muir, Thos and I and pulled rasps and sauntered thro' the woods and fields untill too late for Church in the evening. Read a while aloud under the verandah, and went and saw the little Guernsey cows milked. Sat pretty late talking about Scotland and old times.

---

57 Likely the reading room of the Hamilton and Gore Mechanics' Institute.

Mon. July 19.
Morning still beautiful. Mary wanting to go in search of a Deutch woman to work in the garden got out the Buggy and drove two miles or so up the creek. Called upon Mr Shoemaker, an old Dutchman, proprietor of a saw mill, and saw thro' his house and garden and got a tune on the Piano from his two daughters. Drove home and got dinner and then took good bye, Sandy Muir driving us in to Paris from which we had a safe run to Hamilton and found all right.

Tues. July 20.
Still warm weather. Had out Mr Raphael's horse, riding about 4 miles out Barton St. In the evening John Stewart, Mr Jameson and I got Capt. Zealand's boat and pulled across the lake and tried fishing with small success. Beautiful moonlight.

Wed. July 21.
Mary Goldie came down with first train and landed in our house. Walked with her up to Freeland's office and left her there as she was to be Mrs Freeland's visitor. Had a long walk to catch Butterflies away up the heights towards Waterdown, and had tolerable success. Called at Freeland's and got Mary to go to the flower show in the evening.[58] Thos and her and I took a walk after leaving it.

Thurs. July 22.
Mary called at our house in the morning. Her and I went up town and looked thro' the stores, then walked up the Mountain to Lawries hotel and from there back eastward for some distance, and made the descent down the face of it. Day warm and beautiful. Mary took tea, and slept in our house as Mrs Freeland's house was full of strangers.

Fri. July 23.
Got a horse and Buggy from Mathew's stables and had Mary for a drive down to Wellington square and along the beach to the canal. Tied up horse and got ferried over in an old scow and walked down and visited the lighthouse and along the beach a short way. Got home between

---

58 Likely the July exhibition of the Hamilton Horticultural Society, held in the hall of the local Mechanics' Institute that afternoon and evening. A reporter in attendance claimed that while the show was 'not quite equal to some of the former ones' it was still a well-attended and 'credible affair.' In addition to 'sweet odors,' show-goers were also treated to the sounds of the Grossman and Jennings Quadrille Band. *HS*, July 21, 22, 1858.

3 and 4 p.m. Her and I dined together, after which she went off to Freeland's.

Sat. July 24.

Did not see her all day untill the evening, when I went down to Freeland's and got her to accompany me to our St Andrew's singing practice. Crawford the precentor did not attend which was a disappointment. Had a walk by moonlight after coming out. Moon just about full, clear and beautiful. Met Mr and Mrs Cowie, James and John Muir on the street.

Sun. July 25.

Attended church in the forenoon. Mary came down about 4 p.m. Thos and her and I had a walk out York Street and round town before going into Church. Drank tea together and saw her home to Freelands.

Mon. July 26.

Passed the day the best way I could reading Dombey and son, etc.[59] Went out for a ride in the evening and when I got back found Mary had called and gone out walking with Thos. Bye and bye they came in and had a whiles looking thro books of Scottish scenery, when I had the pleasure of escorting her home.

Tues. July 27.

Spent most of the day in the house. Went to the Freeland's between 7 and 8 to ask for Mary, found she had gone to call on Muir's people, so came right back to the house and found her in. Accompanied her to the Theatre which did not scale till near 12. Mary forgot her parasol in the theatre so that we had to return for it after being near home. However it was found, and we got home all right.

Wed. July 28.

Mary determined to go off to-day, so sat in the house untill near 1 p.m. waiting untill she should call, which she at length did but had to hurry for the train with all speed. Went down and saw her off with the 1 o'clock train.

Thurs. July 29.

Spent the forenoon writing to Mrs Stewart. Thos hurrying with his quarterly accounts. Assisted him for some time in the evening. Had a long walk over the mountain in the afternoon.

---

59 Charles Dickens, *Dombey and Son* (London: Bradbury and Evans, 1848), first published in serialized form as *Dealings with the Firm Dombey and Son*, 1846–8.

Fri. July 30.
Thos looking anxiously for word from his wife. Letters from her of her arrival in Liverpool, and from home where they were in hourly expectation of her, received about 12 a.m. Spent most of the day about the office of the Gas Works. Had a visit from Hope Mackenzie from Sarnia in the evening. Saw him off with the late train in company with Mr Procter from the same town.

Sat. July 31.
Took the ferry steamer to Oaklands at 11 a.m. Saw James Inch there who had been idle 11 months. Walked thro' Oaklands grounds and inland all the way to Waterdown village, coming home by the direct road. Arrived home about 6 p.m. Went with Jameson to Crawford's singing practice in the evening, and afterwards was till past 12 in the Gas office. Weather warm.

Sun. Aug. 1.
Heard Mr Burnet preach morning and evening. Spent the interval in the house reading, etc. Weather still warm, although not excessive. Dust on the streets very annoying.

Mon. Aug. 2.
Went out Butterfly hunting. In the forenoon tried the Cemetry but found it locked. Spent a while on a fine bank of Black Rasps near the Desjardins Bridge. After dinner went east along the mountain and caught some fine Butterflies, Black with yellow spots. Had a walk up town with Thos in the evening. The town council having refused to give the price for the Gas lighting the streets, the lam[p]s, all out to-night and the town very dark and dismal. Saw a Nigger procession in the afternoon.[60]

Tues. Aug. 3.
Made purchase of wood and glass and start to making cases for Butterflies. Had a walk with Jameson in the evening. Heavy rain falling thro' the night and part of the day.

Wed. Aug. 4.
Worked most of the day at insect cases. Persia's mail arrived, bringing letters from Mrs Mc and Mrs Hunter. In the evening called on Jameson

---

60 The local black community's Emancipation Day celebrations this day included a sermon by Rev. Mr Hebden at the Church of the Ascension followed by a procession to 'Land's Bush,' where the day was completed with a dinner and soirée. *HS*, August 3, 1858.

and spent a while at a book auction. Some thunder and lightning in the afternoon.

Thurs. Aug 5.
Worked part of the day at Butterfly boxes. In the afternoon went out with the net and caught a sphinx, the first of the kind to my collection. News arrived of the successful laying of the Atlantic Telegraph, flags flying, firemen in processions, etc. in honour thereof.[61]

Fri. Aug. 6.
Weather hot. Worked most of the day at boxes. Had a walk with Jameson and John Stewart in the evening. A circus with procession of Elephants arrived in town.

Sat. Aug. 7.
Spent the forenoon painting boxes. In the afternoon had a walk out the Toronto railway and Waterdown road. Caught some good Butterflies and gathered some Huckleberries. Went to Crawford's practice of singing in the evening.

Sun. Aug. 8.
Heard Mr Burnet preach in the morning. Had a long walk with John Stewart in the interval, out King St. and round to the edge of the marsh across from the cemetery. Went to Burnet's Church in the evening again. Weather warm.

Mon. Aug. 9.
A hot, bright day. Started early on a long ramble down to the Hamilton water works and Burlington beach and from there east along the lakeshore. The walk along the shore very pleasant. Had a bathe in the lake. Struck inland and got to the Highway a mile beyond Stoney Creek, 8 miles from Hamilton. Not very successful among Butterflies. Got home between six and seven in the evening, having walked about 18 miles.

Tues. Aug. 10.
Spent all day at home papering and finishing Butterfly boxes and got Butterflies arranged into one of them.

---

61 News of the completion of the transatlantic cable appears to have led to a spontaneous and widespread celebration in Hamilton. During the afternoon local fire companies paraded through city streets with pumping machines in tow, the Hamilton Field Battery fired a *feu de joie*, and flags festooned many local businesses. Later in the evening an 'immense concourse' of people gathered in front of the 'brilliantly illuminated' local telegraph office to enjoy a fireworks display. *HS*, August 6, 1858.

Wed. Aug. 11.
Surprised to get a call early in the day from Mr Kay, Mossend, and his son, James and Jean McWhirter as Mrs James, all on their way to Scotland. Walked around town with them in the forenoon and saw them buy the wedding ring, the marriage having taken place this morning. Saw them off with the train at two o'clock. Mr Goldie called immediately after and spent the night with us untill 3 in the morning then he departed to Utica. Day cloudy and disagreeably close and warm.

Thurs. Aug. 12.
A fine, bright, warm day. Went off butterflying along the mountain edge round by Bridge's house, down the Glen and following the course of the little stream. Butterflies begin to get scarce but got a few and some dragon flies. Had a stroll with Jameson in the evening. Wrote to Brother Bill per Canadian Mail steamer.

Fri. Aug. 13.
Went off with butterfly net immediately after breakfast and came home about 6. Went a short way out the Toronto railway and rambled through the woods and fields adjoining. Got some huckleberries. Caught some pretty good black Butterflies and also some small cries of the Frittilara order and some good Dragonflies.

Sat. Aug. 14.
Spent the forenoon till dinner time arranging and fixing yesterday's specimens. Went east along the mountain and took a circuit inland from there in the afternoon. Found small Frittilara butterflies plenty.

Sun. Aug. 15.
Still warm weather. Heard stranger preachers in St Andrew's both ends of the day. In the forenoon, a clever one, in the evening, rather dull. Had a stroll to the side of the Bay with Jameson in the interval.

Mon. Aug. 16.
Mr Muir called in the morning and promised me work in November. In the forepart of the day, walked out beyond Gunn's factory and caught a variety of Dragonflies. After tea, Jameson and I went off to see what success could be had among night insects and travelled with lighted lantern through the woods along the mountain edge east to Slabtown and back by the Port Dover Road without success.

Tues. Aug. 17.
Mr Goldie called in the forenoon on his way home from Utica. Spent the afternoon rambling thro' the woods and hollows beyond the Desjar-

dins Marsh. Waited an hour or more about the tressle Work upon John Stewart who was to appear in a boat but could not get. Walked home but feeling desperately tired. Had a visit of Mr Freeland in the evening.

Wed. Aug. 18.
This by proclamation of the Mayor to be observed as a general holiday in celebration of laying Atlantic Telegraph Cable.[62] Having spent a sleepless and feverish night, and being yet afflicted with sore back and head, kept the house all day. Took a walk up town in the evening to see the illumination which although only partial looked beautiful. Having taken medicine, had some severe vomiting of bile during the night.

Thurs. Aug. 19.
Felt rather relieved to-day but not all right. Walked out and called upon the doctor and got some more medicine, which seems to have good effect in keeping away chiliness.

Fri. Aug. 20.
Health not yet quite re-established. Spent the time mostly on the sofa in the house. Heard from Mrs Logan.

Sat. Aug. 21.
Still feel seedy. Got some more pills from the Dr. Packets of letters arrived from home, some of which should have come with last mail, which accounts for none coming with it.

Sun. Aug. 22.
Getting better but weak, and have no appetite. Time passes rather listless and drearily.

Mon. Aug. 23.
Feel about all right to-day. Set about arranging insects in cases, and got my two filled with what I have.

Tues. Aug. 24.
Spent most of the day reading in the house. Called at the library in the evening and got a volume of 'Carlyle's essays.'[63] Sat late reading them and like them well. Had letters from Mrs Logan with home inclosures. Weather very pleasant, the burning summer heat being now quite abated.

---

62 See entry for August 5, 1858.
63 Thomas Carlyle, *Critical and Miscellaneous Essays* (Philadelphia: A. Hart, 1852 [1839]).

Wed. Aug. 25.
Weather fine. Had a walk after dinner as far as Ryckman's corners on the Port Dover road. Spent the evening reading 'Carlyle' etc.

Thurs. Aug. 26.
Wrote home to Mother in the forenoon and posted it away before 12 o'clock. Spent most of the day reading.

Fri. Aug. 27.
Working a while making a drawing straight-edge and fixing up T-square. Read a while on the subject of the Steam engines. Weather pleasant.

Sat. Aug. 28.
A Batch of letters and papers arrived from home. Letters posted on the day of Newton races. Letters to Thos from his wife, and to me from Mrs Hunter and Bill. Weather rainy.

Sun. Aug. 29.
Heard a stranger preach morning and evening in St Andrews. Spent the interval sleeping and reading Carlyle's essays on Burns, etc.[64]

Mon. Aug. 30.
Worked a while at model for showing working of steam engine slide valve. Spent the evening at home reading Carlyle. Weather mild and showery.

Tues. Aug. 31.
Finished steam engine model. In the afternoon walked down to the railway and along with Wm Rankine, engine keeper, in a skiff pulled across to Willow Point and gathered some wild grapes which are as yet however, scarcely ripe and rather sour. Spent the evening at home.

Wed. Sept. 1.
Spent most of the day in the house reading Carlyle and treatise on the steam engine. In the evening called on Jameson and had a walk up town and spent a while at a book auction. Books selling high.

Thurs. Sept. 2.
A delightful mild, sunny day. Walked up Strongmans road and along the mountain edge, then inland two concessions, and eastward into the

---

64 Carlyle's essay 'Burns' is reprinted in ibid. See 24 August 1858 entry. The original essay was in *Edinburgh Review* 96 (1828): 95–115.

valley beyond the Port Dover Road and home thro' Slabtown. Most of
the common kinds of insects, Butterflies, dragon flies, grasshoppers,
etc. still plenty. Thos went to Toronto in the afternoon and I sat up waiting his arrival until past 12.

Fri. Sept. 3.
Spent the forenoon reading Scottish songs. Had a visit from Mr Goldie
before dinner. Spent part of the afternoon down about the railway, and
the remainder of the day chiefly in reading Carlyle's essays which interest me the more, the more I read of them. Weather fine.

Sat. Sept. 4.
Thos had word from his wife signifying her intention of coming out per
'Indian' to sail from Liverpool 12th inst. Visited the Railway Depot in
the afternoon and saw the new Stationary engine, Steam Hammer, etc.
Spent the most of the evening with Jameson, walking and looking thro'
his books.

Sun. Sept. 5.
Had a stranger preaching in St Andrew's morning and evening, a
young man from Brantford. Spent the interval between sermons mostly
in reading 'Carlyle's miscellanies,' viz, essays on Corn Law Ryhmes
and 'Lockhart's Life of Scott.'[65]

Mon. Sept. 6.
Spent most of the day rather idly in the house looking thro' my books.
Had a visit from Thos Hammond from Sarnia and walked down to the
Depot with him. Gave John Stewart a lesson in Chess in the evening.

Tues. Sept. 7.
Bright, hot, dusty weather. Had a walk as far as Nicol's quarry in the
forenoon. In the afternoon Thos and I took the gun and visited the
peninsula in the Desjardins marsh, a very pleasant walk, being prolonged untill evening when the heat moderated. Thos shot a night
Hawk on the wing; also each of us caught a specimen of the species of
Fly which makes the loud singing noise in the trees.

Wed. Sept. 8.
Still rather disagreeably hot and dusty. Spent most of the day in the

---

65 Very likely Thomas Carlyle, 'Essay on Corn Law Rhymes,' originally published in
    Edinburgh Review CX (1832), reprinted in his *Critical and Miscellaneous Essays*, 365–74,
    and J.G. Lockhart, *Life of Sir Walter Scott, Bart,* (Edinburgh: A. and C. Black, 1853
    [1837]).

house. Read 'Life of Lord Herbert of Cherbury.'[66] Mr Robb called about 5 p.m. and told me that I could get work at Dundas to begin immediately so purpose going off tomorrow. Spent the evening at home, Thos inditing a song about 'Mary of the Greenfield Mill.'[67]

Thurs. Sept. 9.
Took the first train to Dundas. Went direct to the Foundry and got a hearty welcome back. Dined in Mrs Jones and had my traps brought up in the afternoon per teamster 'Denis.' Had a walk a game of chess and some singing with McGarva in the evening.

Fri. Sept. 10.
Started for a walk immediately after breakfast. Visited the Sulphur spring and took a circuit round the country beyond it to Copetown and from there round by Flamboro and so home at 6 p.m. Had a walk with R. McKechnie in the evening. Some heavy showers fell in the afternoon just at the time of a great pic nic of the Dundas Oddfellows. During my walk today caught and skinned a garter snake and sent it in a paper to Thos.

Sat. Sept. 11.
A Beautiful day. Walked up the Flamboro road as far as Crook's hollow, and from there north and east reentering Dundas by the Sydenham road by dinner time. Missed seeing the review of Dundas artillery which took place in the forenoon and not the afternoon as I expected. Purchased a vol. Hogg's Instructor and spent most of the afternoon on Capt. Gordon's hill reading.[68]

Sun. Sept. 12.
Heard Mr Herald preach in the forenoon in St Andrew's. Spent most of the day reading in the house. Had a walk to the Cemetry and round thro' the bush towards the marsh in the afternoon. Felt a slight chill and sickness in the evening.

Mon. Sept. 13.
Started work in Gartshores, and got a Bench fixed up then commenced to Nozzle patterns for Water Works engines. Had a return of the chill more distinctly after tea time in the evening.

---

66 Likely Edward Herbert, 1st Baron Herbert of Cherbury, *The Life of Lord Herbert of Cherbury, Written by Himself and Continued to His Death* (London: Saunders and Otley, 1826 [1764]).

67 The song was likely a ribbing from brother Thomas about Mary Goldie, whose family home was called 'Greenfield,' near Ayr, Dumfries Township, Waterloo County.

68 *Hogg's Instructor.* See fn 46 above.

Tues. Sept. 14.
All day at Nozzles. Chill came on tonight about 5, so I felt very sick before getting home. Went right to bed on going home and lay untill it went off.

Wed. Sept. 15.
Still at Nozzles patterns, the aguish chill returning again at 5, making me feel tolerably miserable.

Thurs. Sept. 16.
Worked a Nozzles till dinner time, then called on Dr McMann, and got some medecine for the ague, a vomit, some powders, and Quinine mixture.[69] Vomited a great deal of Bile in the afternoon but had chill in the evening.

Fri. Sept. 17.
Kept the house most of the day being sick with taking medicine. Chill and sickness returning as usual at 5 p.m. Had letters from Hamilton, from John Stewart and Thos with enclosures of a letter of Mrs Mc to Thos and one for me from T. Anderson, Dumbarton.

Sat. Sept. 18.
Felt fresher in the morning and took the first train to Hamilton. Commenced writing an essay on 'Wilson, the Ornithologist' the Dundas chaps being dunning me for it. Chill did not return this evening.

Sun. Sept. 19.
Spent most of the day in the house. Jack Stewart and I walked out as far as the Delta in the afternoon. Day most beautiful and sunny, the distant forests appearing enveloped in blue haze. Had Jack's company in the evening reading, etc. Saw the Comet in N.E. for the first time although it had been visible during the week.

Mon. Sept. 20.
Took the first train fr. Hamilton and commenced work at dinner time. Still at Nozzle patterns. Had a walk with McGarva and Murche in the evening. Had two tough games of chess with Murche in which he beat me. Saw the Comet.

---

69 Made from cinchona bark, quinine was used by nineteenth-century doctors to alter a patient's temperature and restore balance in the body's 'humours.' It was used particularly in suspected cases of malaria. John Harley Warner, *The Therapeutic Perspective: Medical Practice, Knowledge, and Identity in America, 1820–1885* (Cambridge, MA: Harvard University Press, 1986), 62, 63, 69.

Tues. Sept. 21.
All day at Nozzle patterns. In the evening wrote some of my essay on Wilson for the Mechanics debating society. Mrs Jones asked me to a Breakfast extraordinary to-morrow morning on the occasion of Matilda's marriage, but declined as it interfered with working hours. Heard of the 'North Briton' being telegraphed.[70]

Wed. Sept. 22.
House all in a hubbub with women, etc. gathered to the marriage of Matilda Ware to a Mr J. Christie. Saw them going off at dinner time. All day at Nozzles. In the evening played chess with McGarva.

Thurs. Sept. 23.
All day at Nozzles. In the evening took a stroll with Robt Adam. Rain came on in the evening. Men in the shop busy preparing patent smut machine, etc. to send to the Provincial exhibition at Toronto.[71]

Fri. Sept. 24.
All day at Nozzles. In the evening went to the debate; subject whether is Physiognomy or Phrenology the surest means of testing character – sided with Physiognomy; subject a pretty good one.[72] Comet large and bright a little west of the 'Peak.'

Sat. Sept. 25.
Fine, cool weather, frosty in the mornings. Quit work at 4.30 and hurried home, dressed and started for Hamilton. Walked down in an hour. Had a happy meeting with Mrs Mc and the children. Think them, especially Mary, much smarter, and improved in speaking. Rec'd ½ doz. shirt collars in a present from Mother, also consignment of books from Bill (per order). Saw most tremendous flocks of Blackbirds flying to the marsh on the way down.

Sun. Sept. 26.
Sacremental Sabbath in St Andrews Church. Mr Burnet officiating. Heard a Jew preach in the evening. Had a walk with Jameson and John

---

70 The Royal Mail steamship *North Briton* from Liverpool arrived at Quebec City on September 21, 1858. *NYT*, September 22, 1858.

71 A smut machine cleanses the grain of smut, a parasitic fungus.

72 Physiognomy and phrenology were popular fields of nineteenth-century scientific inquiry. Physiognomists studied how the features on a human face could reveal a person's character. Phrenologists studied how bumps on a human skull revealed character. See Arthur Wrobel, ed., *Pseudo-science and Society in Nineteenth-Century America* (Lexington: University Press of Kentucky, 1987).

Stewart in the interval. Sat late at night talking with Mrs Mc about home.

Mon. Sept. 27.
Got roused at four in the morning and started on foot to Dundas, before daylight, the moon shining brightly and the Comet blazing away eastwards. Morning clear, cold and frosty. Got to Dundas at six. Worked at Nozzles all day. Played chess with McGarva in the evening.

Tues. Sept. 28.
All day at Nozzles. Weather fine. Spent the evening writing essay on Wilson.

Wed. Sept. 29.
Still at Nozzles. Tomorrow, Thursday fixed as a holiday with the workmen to go to the fair at Toronto. Took the evening train to Hamilton, and had a pleasant evening talking about home with Mrs Mc.

Thurs. Sept. 30.
Thos and I took train for Toronto. Tremendous crush in the cars. Had to sit on the platform steps. Reached the Chrystal Pallace Toronto about 11 a.m. and had a good survey although the crowd was great. Ladies work, paintings and drawings and stuffed birds the most interesting part of the show to us. Met Wm Goldie on the ground.[73] Afternoon very wet. Had a long passage home.

Fri. Oct. 1.
Had a walk around town in the forenoon. Spent a while sketching 'Little Bittern.'[74] Miss Margaret McIlwraith called and took tea in the evening; saw her home to her new house. A fine, starlight night. Comet very bright.

---

73 The site of the 1858 Provincial Exhibition was Toronto's newly constructed Crystal Palace. Inspired by the glass and iron construction of the 1851 Crystal Palace in London, England, Toronto's structure was more modest, built of glass and wood and with dimensions of about 250 by 144 feet. It was situated on twenty acres of grounds which also contained a number of other booths, sheds, and structures erected for the exhibition. Andrew and Thomas attended on the rainy third day of the exhibition along with an estimated crowd of 60,000. The *Spectator* noted especially the exhibit of Mr Gartshore's Dundas iron works, which had on display an engine constructed for the Hamilton waterworks and a treble suctioned smut machine (see note for September 23, 1858). *HS*, September 28, 29, October 1, 1858; *Globe* [Toronto], September 30, 1858.

74 The 'Little Bittern' is a wading bird in the heron family.

Sat. Oct. 2.
Had a walk to the market with Thos and Tommy. Spent most of the day finishing a drawing of little Bittern. Spent the evening writing to Mother.

Sun. Oct. 3.
Stayed home from church, not having dress good enough to go. Wrote a sheet to Bill. Took the road for Dundas a little after three. Day warm and lowering but kept dry. Went to Stark's Church with McGarva in the evening.

Mon. Oct. 4.
Alarm of fire in the town about two hours after starting work. A general turn out of all hands to it, although it turned out trifling, only a small barn. All day at Nozzles. In the evening attended a meeting of Young men's Christian association and heard an essay from 'Sommerville' of the true banner, and lessons in elocution from Mr McGonegal, a Methodist minister, which were very amusing.[75]

Tues. Oct. 5.
All day at Nozzles. Spent most of the evening playing chess with McGarva.

Wed. Oct. 6.
All day at Nozzles. Begin to feel some aguish symptoms and apply to Dr McMann in the evening and am prescribed Peruvian Bark and sherry wine.

Thurs. Oct. 7.
Felt weak and pained in the back so kept the house all day reading Wilson's Ornithology and writing part of my essay on 'Wilson.' Weather cold, rainy and rather stormy.

Fri. Oct. 8.
Felt quite well in the morning and went to work but towards afternoon had a return of sickness, vomited some. Came home and went to bed at 5 o'clock, and for two or three hours was quite feverish, affecting the brain a little.

Sat. Oct. 9.
Did not go to work to-day. Took a walk in the forenoon and discovered

---

75 On Sommerville, see fn 2 above.

a fine road down the canal side and along the edge of the marsh to the
Toronto Road. Wind blowing very cold yet observed Dragonflys, and
'Camberwell Beauties' with lesser redish butterflys on the wing. Found
one large red one fluttering on the ground. Saw also White throated
sparrows. Had letter from Thos with home inclosures.

Sun. Oct. 10.
Kept the house all day. Took a little meat, but was all the sicker, shiver-
ing and vomiting in the afternoon.

Mon. Oct. 11.
Took the morning train down to Hamilton. Weather cold, damp and
altogether aguish. Thos aguish himself, and I fancied rather snappish
to me. Had chill slightly in the evening but got well secured against it
by Mrs Mc. Commenced taking Quinine powder.

Tues. Oct. 12.
Spent the day in Hamilton. Chill did not come back tonight. Weather
still dull. Read White's natural history of Selborne.[76]

Wed. Oct. 13.
Took first train to Dundas. Did not commence work but spent most of
the day at my essay on Wilson. Ague seems gone now.

Thurs. Oct. 14.
Started work in the morning. All day at Nozzles. Spent a while of the
evening writing. Was also a short time at an auction of American books.

Fri. Oct. 15.
All day at Nozzles. Attended debate in the evening; subject an expres-
sion of opinion generally without forming sides for debate as to what
constitutes the distinguishing difference between man and the lower
animals. Decision given to his adaption to all climates.

Sat. Oct. 16.
Weather cold, raw and foggy. All day at Nozzles. Wrote my essay in the
evening.

Sun. Oct. 17.
Weather quite changed into delightfully mild and sunny. Heard Mr
Herald preach in the morning. After dinner walked three miles out the

---

76 Gilbert White, *The Natural History of Selborne* (London: White, Cochrane and Co.,
   1813).

Sydenham road to a Methodist field meeting. Brother Thos called in my absence, and again shortly after I got home. After tea convoyed him half way to Hamilton. Fine moonlight.

Mon. Oct. 18.
All day at Nozzles. Weather still fine. Saw the comet very faintly in the evening. Spent a while at essay. Commenced to quit work at 5 o'clock in the evening.

Tues. Oct. 19.
All day at Nozzles. Finished writing of essay in the evening.

Wed. Oct. 20.
All day at Nozzles. In the evening went to practice of singing in Free Church vestry. Had a glass of port and a chat with H. Fairgrieve and McGarva after coming out.

Thurs. Oct. 21.
All day at Nozzles. Spent the evening reading Hogg's Instructor and Wilson's Ornithology.

Fri. Oct. 22.
All day at Nozzles. Read my essay on Wilson to the Debating Club in the evening, which was well received. Almost no faults found. Evening altogether a very harmonious one.

Sat. Oct. 23.
All day at Nozzles. Walked down to Hamilton in the evening. Little Tom sick. Got letters from home to read.

Sun. Oct. 24.
Heard Mr Burnet preach in the forenoon. Walked to Dundas in the afternoon. Mr Raphael walked out half way with me. Spent the evening in the house reading.

Mon. Oct. 25.
All day at Nozzles. Weather clear and cold. Spent the evening in the house, playing chess with McGarva.

Tues. Oct. 26.
Weather still fine. Mornings frosty. All day at nozzles. Troubled with cough. Kept the house in the evening and went early to bed.

Wed. Oct. 27.
All day at Nozzles. Spent the evening reading treatise on Locomotives.

Thurs. Oct. 28.
All day at Nozzles. After tea, saw a great glare of fire in Hamilton.
Learned at the Telegraph office that it was about James St. Walked up to
the Station and saw Stuart, Sarnia Branch inspector on the train going
west. .

Fri. Oct. 29.
All day at Nozzles. Dull, wet weather. Spent the evening writing to Mrs
Logan.

Sat. Oct. 30.
All day at Nozzles. Some little stir among the boys on account of Halloween which dates tomorrow. Made purchase of Carpenter's Zoology
and spent the evening looking thro' it.[77]

Sun. Oct. 31.
Day rather milder. Heard Mr Herald preach in the forenoon. Messrs
McClure, two brothers from Hamilton, called upon McGarva and took
dinner. Had a walk with them to Bullock's Corners and home by way
of the Peak and Flagstaff Hill. Had some talk with McClure, a carpenter, of life in Canadian bush. Went to Mr Mair's Bible Class in his new
house on the hill – subject discussed 'Babylon.'

Mon. Nov. 1.
All day at Nozzles. Commenced to quit at half past four. Weather cold
and windy. Felt aguish and took quinine at night.

Tues. Nov. 2.
A Very rainy day. All day at Nozzles. Continued taking quinine three
times dailly. Felt rather better in the evening but still tired and pained
in the back.

Wed. Nov. 3.
Arose at three in the morning and vomited Bile, and continued to be up
and down retching and vomiting untill near midday. Got rid of a great
deal of bile, but think I had taken quinine too strong.

---

77 William Benjamin Carpenter's textbook on zoology was first published as part of the
   Popular Cyclopae Symboldia of Natural Science (1844), and later enlarged and issued
   separately as William Benjamin Carpenter, *Zoology; Being a Systematic Account of the
   General Structure, Habits, Instincts, and Uses of the Principal Families of the Animal Kingdom, as Well as of the Chief Forms of Fossil Remains* (London: H.G. Bohn, 1857–8).

Thurs. Nov. 4.
Had a little sleep during the night being so pained in Back and Stomach. Kept the house all day, and felt better towards evening. Read Carpenter's Zoology and played chess with McGarva in the evening.

Fri. Nov. 5
Went to work again and got along pretty well although somewhat weak in the back. Weather still cold and dull. Read 'Carpenter's Zoology' in the evening.

Sat. Nov. 6.
An even downpour of rain all day and I believe all night. All day at Nozzles. Wrote to Thomas in the evening. Quit work at half past three.

Sun. Nov. 7.
Heard Mr Herald preach in the forenoon. Rain falls nearly incessant. Kept the house all afternoon and went to Mr Mair's class at night, subject a chapter in Romans on carnal and spiritual mindedness. Night very dark and wet.

Mon. Nov. 8.
All day at Nozzles. After Quitting work took a walk down the canal side and fell in with Connel shooting. Heard Snipes calling in the air. Spent the evening at chess with McGarva.

Tues. Nov. 9.
Day very cold but not so wet. All day at Nozzles. In the evening had a note from Thomas with home letters inclosed, from Mrs Hunter and Bill to me. Set about writing to them in the evening.

Wed. Nov. 10.
All day at Nozzles. Heard Mr Stevens a music teacher lecturing on music in the town hall. A very home spoken old Scotchman.

Thurs. Nov. 11.
All day at Nozzles. In the evening went with McGarva to Wilson's practicing of church tunes, which was this night held in McKechnie's house. Saw Maggy Brice.

Fri. Nov. 12.
All day at nozzles. Weather cold and wet. Got started with debating in the evening the question 'Should a military spirit be encouraged among Canadian young men.' Had some good spouting from R. McKechnie Senr. and Sergt Gibson, who appeared in uniform.

Sat. Nov. 13.
All day at Nozzles. Quit work at 3.30. Weather cold and wet till towards evening when it commenced and froze very keen. Took train to Hamilton in the evening and found all well. Commenced nozzles for large cylinders today.

Sun. Nov. 14.
Heard Rev. Frank Nicol preach in Burnet's in the morning. Started for Dundas between three and four. Thos and Tommie gave convoy. Keen frosty wind blowing right head. Attended Mr Mair's Class in the evening – subject Elijah's ascending to heaven.

Mon. Nov. 15.
Still keen frost. Our working day made half an hour shorter this week commencing at 7.30. All day at Nozzles. Played chess with McGarva in the evening.

Tues. Nov. 16.
All day at Nozzles. Spent the evening writing Mrs Stewart and Bill.

Wed. Nov. 17.
All day at Nozzles. Went to practice psalmody along with Mr Stevens Class in the evening. Sandy Laing cross-questioning the old man on his singing. Some talk also took place about this class superceding our association in the use of the room. Settled that we should have it as before.

Thurs. Nov. 18.
Still cold frosty weather. All day at Nozzles. Went to practice singing with Wilson's choir. Had some good singing and walked home with Katy McMillan afterwards.

Fri. Nov. 19.
All day at Nozzles. Attended Debate in the evening. The chairman, R. McKechnie Junr gave decision in favor of the negative, the side which I had taken – viz, that it was not desirable to foster military spirit among the young men of Canada by forming volunteer companies.

Sat. Nov. 20.
All day at Nozzles. Quit at 3.30 and took a pretty long walk along the mountain edge east of the Sydenham road. Weather cold and fields bare and bleak. Bot some pictorials and sat in the house reading them.

Sun. Nov. 21.

Attended St Andrews Church in the morning and joined the precentor's choir, singing tenor. Dr Skinner from Waterdown preached. After dinner, walked up to Flamboro' with McGarva and called on Mr Boyle, teacher, who accompanied us down. Learned he was a brother of Mrs R. McIlwraith whom I knew in Dumbarton. Attended church again in the evening, and had a walk by moonlight after. Snow lying on the distant heights.

Mon. Nov. 22.

Beautiful frosty weather. All day at Nozzles. Evening cold and raw and began raining. Attended meeting of Christian association and heard an essay from Ben Clement on the temporal advantages of the Sabbath. Chisholm, Orr, R. McKechnie etc spoke after.

Tues. Nov. 23.

Forenoon wet and afternoon incessant snow. All day at Nozzles. Spent the evening studying the 'Locomotive Engine.'

Wed. Nov. 24.

All day at nozzles. Attended Singing Association in the evening, Thompson leading. Attendance small. Felt quite aguish in the evening.

Thurs. Nov. 25.

All day at Nozzles. Still rather aguish. Went to Wilson's choir practice in McDonald's house. Had songs after psalmody from Miss McDonald, Miss Bryce and also from old Mrs Ironsides. Walked home with Katy McMillan.

Fri. Nov. 26.

All day at Nozzles. Attended debating club in the evening and had an essay from J. Booth on Commerce, and also lively discussion of various subjects. The chairman, myself, not being very well up to keeping order.

Sat. Nov. 27.

All day at nozzles. Health rather improved. Walked to Hamilton in the afternoon and had the company of R. Adam by the way. Got in time for tea. Had a walk up town with Thos.

Sun. Nov. 28.

Called on J. Stewart at his lodging who had been off with sore ear. Heard

Mr Burnet preach in the forenoon. Walked to Dundas in the afternoon. Fell in with little Storov a dry-goods clerk by the way. Attended Mr Mair's Bible Class in the evening – subject Joshua's dying address.

Mon. Nov. 29.
Commenced to and worked all day at large nozzle valves. Spent the evening studying music.

Tues. Nov. 30.
All day at Nozzle valves. Ball in connexion with St Andrew's Society takes place tonight. McGarva an active hand in it. Became member of Dundas Mechanics Institute. Took a vol. of Hogg's Instructor out of the library.

Wed. Dec. 1.
All day at Nozzle valves. Went to meeting of Musical association. Attendance so small that it is thought best not to meet again at present. John Booth up in the shop, speaking of starting away for Vancouver's island.

Thurs. Dec. 2.
All day at Nozzle valves. Attended meeting of Wilson's choir in the house of a Mr Geary one of our smiths. Had a good night's practicing and songs afterwards from Misses McMillan, McDonald, Bryce, Messrs Thompson, McKechnie and self. Snow lying on the ground.

Fri. Dec. 3.
All day at Nozzle valves. Snow fell heavily during the night. Attended debating club and acted as chairman on the debate as to whether geology or Astronomy furnished the best evidences of a supreme being.

Sat. Dec. 4.
A very stormy winter day. Snow lying deep, and alternations of snow, rain, sleet and hail accompanied with wind all day. Heard from Jameson of the prospect of an opening for me in the Engineers Office, Hamilton. All day till quiting time, 3.30, at Nozzle valves. Kept the house the remainder of the day reading.

Sun. Dec. 5.
Streets very sloppy with melting snow. Heard Mr Herald in the forenoon, and sang in the choir and again in the evening heard him preach in the St Andrews Society – text the psalm 'By Babel's streams, etc.' Sang the psalm to the tune of 'Naomi.'

Mon. Dec. 6.
All day at Nozzle valves. In the evening heard a good lecture from Mr Stark subject – 'Hugh Miller.'[78]

Tues. Dec. 7.
All day at Nozzle valves. Spent the evening playing chess with McGarva.

Wed. Dec. 8.
All day at Nozzle valves. Felt aguish symptoms in the evening. Weather very cold.

Thurs. Dec. 9.
All day at nozzle valves. Went to choir practice in McKechnie's. Walked home with Kate McMillan.

Fri. Dec. 10.
All day at Nozzle valves. Felt aguish again. Weather still cold. Went to debate and sat as chairman on the question 'Whether does Astronomy or Geology give strongest evidence of a supreme being.' Gave the decision to Geology.

Sat. Dec. 11.
All day at nozzle valves. Set out for Hamilton on foot at 4.25. Took tea with Thos. Called at Jameson's and found R. Mackenzie from Sarnia. Had them down to Thos and had a while's talk.

Sun. Dec. 12.
Accompanied Robt McKenzie to church and heard Mr Burnet. He and Jameson dined with Thos. J. Stewart and them gave me convoy to the half way house coming back to Dundas. Attended Mr Mair's class in the evening – subject Abraham's faith. Invited to tea there on Wednesday first.

Mon. Dec 13.
All day at nozzles. Weather wet and sloppy. In the evening called at Wilson's for some tunes, and had a walk with Mr. Blythe his partner in the tannery business.

---

78 Hugh Miller (1802–56), often referred to as the 'stonemason of Cromarty,' was a key figure of artisanal self-improvement in nineteenth-century Scotland. Miller started his career as a stonemason before becoming a well-known author of geological and autobiographical works. See Jean L. Watson, *Life of Hugh Miller* (Edinburgh: James Gemmell, 1880).

Tues. Dec. 14.
Half day at Nozzle valves and half at Fly Wheel for Wellington square.
Wrote home to Mother in the evening.

Wed. Dec. 15.
All day at Wn. Sqr Fly Wheel. In the evening went to Mr Mair's bible
class tea meeting, and spent a pleasant evening with music, sacred and
profane, etc. Miss Foulds there with her melodian. Dispersed at 12 p.m.
Walked home with Miss Perry.

Thurs. Dec. 16.
All day at fly wheel. Went to choir practice in McDonald's house, had a
good night's singing and some songs afterward.

Fri. Dec. 17.
All day at fly wheel. Attended debating society in the evening and had
a discussion of the character of James 1st of England, as to whether he
deserved praise or censure for his governing of the country. Proposal
made to get up an anniversary soiree in connexion with the club.

Sat. Dec. 18.
All day at Fly wheel. Called upon and had a chat with John Bertram in
the evening.

Sun. Dec. 19.
Heard Mr Herald preach morning and evening, also heard a stranger in
the U.P. Church. Day very sloppy.

Mon. Dec. 20.
All day at Fly wheel. Spent most of the evening with McGarva in his
room learning Bothwell banks.[79]

Tues. Dec. 21.
All day at Fly wheel. Copied some psalm tunes in the evening.

Wed. Dec. 22.
All day at Fly wheel. Heard from Thos that he had given up the idea of
going to Ayr at this time. Went to Bertram's in the evening to practice
some songs for our Club soiree. Thompson and Aiken joining with us.

---

79 Refers to the song 'O Bothwell Bank!' (a solo or duet) reprinted in John Greig, *Scots
Minstrelsie: A National Monument of Scottish Song with a Gallery of Authentic Portraits
and Illustrated after Wilkie, Duncan, Faed, Harvey, Bough and Others* (Edinburgh: T.C.
and E.C. Jack, Grange Publishing Works, 1893), 2:xv.

Thurs. Dec. 23.
All day at Fly wheel. Had singing practice at Aiken's in the evening. Weather keen, frosty.

Fri. Dec. 24.
Finished fly wheel segment pattern. Went to debate for a short time in the evening then home and copied some Duets for the great spree.

Sat. Dec. 25.
Started on foot for Hamilton after breakfast. Got in between 9 and 10. Thos. engaged upon cases of birds. He and I went for a ramble with the gun and traversed great part of Desjardins marsh. Day beautifully clear and frosty. Got a Shrike from a man who had shot it. Saw a boy spearing muskrats in their houses, also saw spiders among the snow. Mr Raphael came and took Christmas dinner with us, also J. Stewart at 4 p.m.

Sun. Dec. 26.
Attended St Andrew's Church and heard Mr Grey. Dined with Mr. Raphael in Harris' house where he is now keeping bachelor's hall. Present Messrs Lorimer, Bryan, etc. Walked to Dundas in the afternoon. Went to Bible class and convoyed home from there two Miss Ballantynes.

Mon. Dec. 27.
All day at wheel arm. Practiced singing in the evening.

Tues. Dec. 28.
All day at Fly wheel arm. At singing in Aiken's again in the evening.

Wed. Dec. 29.
All day at Wheel arm. Weather tempestuous and snowy. Sang as usual in the evening. Thompson teaching me the tenor for chorus of Auld lang syne and also of God save the Queen.

Thurs. Dec. 30.
All day at wheel arm. Weather cold and blustering. Heard from Mr McAmmond, that there was notification in the Globe, that Brother Thos had yesterday got an addition to his family, could not say whether son or daughter.[80] Quit work to-night for the new year holidays. Went to Wilson's singing and trysted Miss Geary to the Soiree tomorrow night.

Fri. Dec. 31.
Took first train to Hamilton. Drew 20$ from Savings Bank, interest .58$.

---

80 It was a daughter. *Globe* [Toronto], December 30, 1858.

Purchased a cake basket to Mrs McIlwraith. Saw her little daughter. Mrs Chapman sent staying with her. Walked back to Dundas in the afternoon. Had our Mechanics debating club soiree in the evening which came off very well. The performance after tea opening with 'Bothwell bank' from Messrs Thompson and myself, and being briskly kept up with speechifying from McKechnie, Gibson, etc. Recitation from D. McMillan, Connel, etc. and old McGechie.

Diary for 1859

Sat. Jan. 1. 1859 – Dundas.
A fine frosty morning. Got up before six in the morning and started for Hamilton to 'first foot' Thos.[1] Got there by 8 a.m. before any of the family was astir. Spent most of the day in the house. Mr and Mrs W.K. Muir called in the forenoon. Called at old Mr Muir's and had a walk up town with him. Spent the evening quietly in the house.

Sun. Jan. 2.
Attended Mr Burnet's Church in the forenoon. After dinner walked to Dundas, Thos and Tommy giving convoy. Attended Mr Herald's Church in the evening.

Mon. Jan. 3.
A beautiful, bright, frosty morning. Took train to Paris at 9.45 a.m. and started on foot from there to Ayr. Got a ride on a waggon half way. Arrived at Greenfield early in the afternoon and got a hearty reception. Took tea in the bedroom with old Mr Goldie, Mary, Mr Steele, Mrs Smith and Aunt Jennie. Mrs Goldie absent at McEwan's in Blenheim, Mrs McE. having been confined.

Tues. Jan. 4.
About an inch of snow fell during the night. Mr McEwan came down early with sleigh from Blenheim and got all the women of the family

---

1 In traditional northern English and Scottish folklore, the 'first foot' is the first person to cross a household's threshold after midnight on New Year's Day. A dark-haired male first footer was believed to bring good luck to the home for the coming year. See Amy Stewart Fraser, ed., *Dae Ye Min' Langsyne: A Pot-pourri of Games, Rhymes and Ploys of Scottish Childhood* (London: Routledge, 1975), 182.

along with myself on board to pay a visit up there. Had a nice drive
and had tea and spent a while in his house. Mrs Goldie came with us
on returning.

Wed. Jan. 5.
Drove horse and cutter into Ayr with Mrs Steele and Mary. Spent most
of the forenoon in the house reading 'Enquire Within,' etc.[2] Got Hughie
Stevenson to drive me into Paris in the afternoon and landed in Dundas
in the evening.

Thurs. Jan. 6.
Started work in the foundry and worked till four o'clock at Fly Wheel
pattern and after that at Water Works Crane pattern till 9 at night. Quite
a snow storm all day and snow now lying deep.

Fri. Jan. 7.
Worked till 6 at night at Water Works crane. Wind blowing the snow
about the streets and very cold. Attended Debating Club meeting
and had officers elected for next half-year. President Gibson, V.P. R.
McKechnie Jr. Secretary myself. Had a pleasant evening and sat till past
10.

Sat. Jan. 8.
A very cold day. All day at Fly Wheel arm. Walked to Hamilton in the
evening. Found the family all well. Had a walk up town and sat late
talking with Thos.

Sun. Jan. 9.
Had breakfast and started for Dundas between 9 and 10. An exceedingly keen, frosty morning. Attended Mr Herald's Church in the forenoon and the U.P. in the afternoon, and Mr Muir's Bible Class in the
evening. Good moonlight but very sharp frost at night.

Mon. Jan. 10.
Slept but little last night with cold and never felt cold so much as I did
in the morning. The Pattern Shop, the only one kept going, the rest all
knocked off with the cold. Thermometer over 30 deg. below zero. All
day at Fly Wheel. Came home intended to write in the evening but
could not get warmed. I went to bed at 8 o'clock.

---

2 Robert Kemp Philp, *Enquire within upon Everything* (London: Houlston and Stone-
man, 1856). This piece was a treatise on domestic economy.

Tues. Jan. 11.
Not quite so cold this morning. Some snow fell during the day. Half day at Fly wheel and half at some pipe proving apparatus for Water Works. Spent the evening writing minutes, etc. for the Debating Club. Spent a while in the library.

Wed. Jan. 12.
All day at Water Works proving apparatus. Weather getting milder. Reading Hogg's Instructor in the evening.[3]

Thurs. Jan. 13.
All day at Water Works apparatus. Went to debate in the evening. My secretary's minutes objected to and some discussion and misunderstanding on the subject. Bertram read an essay on 'Astronomy Illustrated' which was well received.

Fri. Jan. 14.
All day at Water Works apparatus. Evening very wet. Heard Mr Babington lecture upon poetry, a nervous gentleman and too weak for speaking in the Town Hall. Got 'Castles in the Air' copied and dispatched to Miss Goldie.[4]

Sat. Jan. 15.
All day at Water Works. Spent the evening writing home.

Sun. Jan. 16.
Attended Mr Herald's Church in morning and evening. Wrote to Bill in the interval.

Mon. Jan. 17.
All day at Water Works. In the evening sat late at Constitution and Bye Laws for our Debating Club.

Tues. Jan. 18.
All day at Water Works. Spent the evening at Constitution and bye laws for Debating Club. This day commenced working full time.

Wed. Jan. 19.
All day at Water Works. Went to Gibson's house in the evening where

---

3 *Hogg's Instructor* (1848–56) was a weekly (1849–53) and later monthly (1853–56) 'non-sectarian' journal published in Edinburgh by Scotsman James Hogg (1806–88).

4 'Castles in the Air' was a popular Scottish song by James Ballantine. First printed in Ballantine, *The Gaberlunzie's Wallet* (Edinburgh: J. Menzies, 1843).

Robt McKechnie, Gibson and I had to meet as Committee on Constitution and Bye Laws. Sat till past 10. Evening fine.

Thurs. Jan. 20.
All day at Water Works. Went to debate in the evening and had our Constitution and Bye Laws passed after considerable discussion. Commenced debate upon whether 'nature in its aspects of animate or inanimate disclosed greatest wonders.' I being leader on the animate side.

Fri. Jan. 21.
All day at Water Works. In the evening went to a soiree in the Free Church and heard Mr Inglis of Hamilton speak for a while, also Mr Stevens and some of his class singing church music.

Sat Jan. 22.
Began to finish Nozzle Valve patterns. Took train to Hamilton in the evening and found all well. Keen frost again.

Sun. Jan. 23.
Started and walked to Dundas in the morning and attended Mr Herald's Church, singing tenor in the choir along with Katie McMillan. Had a long walk with Robt Adam and McGarva down by the Canal and thro' part of the marsh and got wet feet, then away down east and back over the mountain by the Sydenham Road. At Bible Class in the evening.

Mon. Jan. 24.
All day at Valves. Weather cold. Heard Mr Puller of Hamilton lecture for the Young Mens Christian Association, subject 'The Days of John Knox.'[5]

Tues. Jan. 25.
All day at valves. Spent the evening making order form for order of business re. Debating Club. The Hundredth Anniversary of Burns' birthday being celebrated tonight in Dundas and all over the world.[6] Did not quite approve of the dining affair and did not go.

---

5 Debating clubs and lectures were common features among Mechanics' Institutes and YMCAs in Victorian Ontario, their subjects and outcomes often publicized in the local press. See Andrew C. Holman, *A Sense of Their Duty: Middle-Class Formation in Victorian Ontario Towns* (Montreal and Kingston: McGill-Queen's University Press, 2000), 125–6.
6 For an account of the Burns anniversary in nearby Hamilton, see 'Centennial Anniversary Dinner in Honor of the Poet Burns' *HS,* January 27, 1859.

Wed. Jan 26.
All day at valves. In the evening wrote out minutes, etc. for Debating Club.

Thurs. Jan. 27.
At Air Pump valve for engine at Wellington Sq. In the evening went to a party in McKechnie's to welcome young Robt and his wife home from their marriage jaunt to the Falls.[7]

Fri. Jan. 28.
At altering Fly Wheel pattern for Wellington Square, reducing it in weight. Worked till 10 o'clock at night.

Sat. Jan. 29.
At Fly Wheel and valve for Wellington Square all day. Spent the evening writing to Mrs Logan.

Sun. Jan. 30.
At church morning and evening singing tenor in the choir which has now got seated in the gallery. Spent the interval reading in the house.

Mon. Jan. 31.
All day at mill pinion. Spent the evening at writing for Debating Club, copying Constitution and Bye Laws, etc.

Tues. Feb. 1.
All day at Mill Pinion pattern. Spent the evening copying Bye Laws, etc. for the Debating Club. At 9 o'clock in the evening went to Committee meeting of the Mechanic's Institution and heard a violent dispute between Gibson, our club president and Sommerville, the editor of the Dundas Banner.[8]

Wed. Feb. 2.
All day at Mill Pinion. Spent the evening writing minutes, etc. for Debating Club.

Thurs. Feb. 3.
All day at Mill Pinion. In the evening went to debate and had a toler-

---

7 Likely Niagara Falls, even at this date, a 'honeymoon capital.' See Karen Dubinsky, *The Second Greatest Disappointment: Honeymooning and Tourism at Niagara Falls* (New Brunswick, NJ: Rutgers University Press, 1999), ch. 2.
8 On Sommerville, see Diary for 1858, fn 2.

ably good night but rather disgusted with our President Gibson who is considerable of a humbug being an out and out Irishman.

Fri. Feb. 4.
All day at Mill Pinion. In the evening went to singing practice in Mrs Wilson's house. Wilson, our leader, did not come but had a good attendance of girls and got along middling well under the circumstances. Walked home with Katy McMillan.

Sat. Feb. 5.
Got woke between 12 and 1 in the morning with the alarm of fire and hurried in time to work a little and witness a great blaze of two frame stores, Bastable's and Overfield's. Worked all day at Mill Pinion. Spent the evening in the house reading the Globe, etc.

Sun. Feb. 6.
A couple of inches of snow fell during the night. Morning bright and frosty. McGarva and I started after breakfast and walked to Hamilton. Accomp'd Thos to Church and heard Mr Burnet. Dined and then called with him on his friends McClure and saw a rush of flying squirrels. Walked back to Dundas in time for tea and attended Church in the evening.

Mon. Feb. 7.
All day at Mill Pinion. Spent the evening studying for debate.

Tues. Feb. 8.
All day at Mill Pinion. In the evening went to the library and spent an hour or two there talking with McKechnie Sr Turnbull, Connel, etc.

Wed. Feb. 9.
Finished Mill Pinion and commenced to small bastard Bevel Wheel. Spent the evening writing for the debate.

Thurs. Feb. 10.
All day at Small Bevel Wheel. Had our debate concluded in the evening and got the decision on the affirmative upon which I was leader 'The Animate Nature Showed Greater Wonders than the Inanimate.' Mr Gibson got started with his essay on 'Daniel Webster' and discoursed for an hour until closing time.

Fri. Feb. 11.
All day at Small Bevel Wheel. Went to our singing practice in Garrow's in the evening and had a good night's singing. Thompson, Bennet and

McGarva being there in addition to the regular hands. Walked home with Jessie McDonald. Turnbull told me in the evening that there would be no more work for me after tomorrow at this time.

Sat. Feb. 12.
Worked till 3 o'clock and got finished with small Bevel Wheel all but putting in the arms. In the evening called on young Bob McKechnie and spent the evening with him having some singing along with his wife and her two sisters Misses Ross.

Sun. Feb. 13.
Heard Mr Herald preach in the morning and sang tenor in the choir along with Katy McMillan. After dinner had a walk up the glen to Horkison's Falls along with McGarva and Hetherington and Duncan McMillan who we picked up by the way. Made a very perilous ascent out of the glen. At Bible Class in the evening and took good-bye of Mr Mair.

Mon. Feb. 14.
Started from Dundas immediately after breakfast and walked to Hamilton. Had a walk around town and read a while in the house. In the evening assisted Thos and Jack Stewart in the Gas Office for a while counting money, it being the last day of receiving payment of quarterly gas accounts minus discount.

Tues. Feb. 15.
A dull, raw sort of day. Spent most of the day in the house reading Chambers 'Journal' etc.[9] Called on Jameson in the evening who told me that Mr Reid had applied at headquarters to have me appointed as draughtsman in his office.

Wed. Feb. 16.
Had a walk out to the Cemetery. In the evening accompanied Thos to the annual festival held by the Catholics for the benefit of Catholic Orphans.[10] Heard Mr Darcy McGee, M.P.P., J. Buchanan, M.P.P. and

---

9 *Chambers's Journal of Literature Science and Art* was a weekly publication produced by the Edinburgh literary figures and brothers William and Robert Chambers from 1832 to 1863. See W. Chambers, *Story of a Long and Busy Life* (Edinburgh: W. and R. Chambers, 1882), 39.

10 This was the Seventh Annual Festival in Aid of the St Mary's Orphan Asylum and the poor held in the Hall of the Hamilton Mechanics' Institute. The hall was 'densely crowded' with 'citizens of all denominations.' The speeches were followed with a

some other speakers, also singing of the choir and some good songs from Mrs Gordon and Mr Spence.[11]

Thurs. Feb. 17.
Took the first train to Dundas. Spent the forenoon till dinner time counting up time, etc. Called at the Foundry after dinner and got paid up and all settled satisfactory. Went to the Debating Club meeting in the evening and resigned my secretaryship, D. McMillan being appointed successor and H. Mackenzie assistant. Got Mr Gibson's essay on Webster finished and criticized pretty severely.

Fri. Feb. 18.
Had all my luggage removed to Hamilton per teamster Dennis. Spent a while of the forenoon about the foundry. After dinner had a walk in search of fossil shells along west by the railway track. In the evening called on James McFarlane and got the words of the 'Wooden Cravat' song and from his house to Herold, the minister's where our singing was being held.[12] Found quite a party assembled, being most of the choir and Sunday School teachers.

Sat. Feb. 19.
A fine, frosty, misty morning. Started after breakfast to walk to Hamilton. Diverged by a side road at Binckley's Hollow, up the mountain and making circuit round thro' the country, came in by Isaac Buchanan's. Spent the afternoon and evening mostly reading. Called at the library in the evening and got Kingsley's 'Hypatia.' Had Ayr papers with the account of Burns Centenary.[13]

---

concert by the Artillery Band and the St Mary's choir and a number of songs performed by individuals or as duets. According to one reporter in attendance, the concert concluded at 11 p.m. and was followed by supper and dancing which 'kept up 'till – well, we are not quite certain.' *HS*, February 17, 1859.

11 On the careers of prominent mid-century politicians Thomas D'Arcy McGee (1825–68) and Isaac Buchanan (1810–83), see, respectively, David A. Wilson, *Thomas D'Arcy McGee*, 2 vols. (Montreal and Kingston: McGill-Queen's University Press, 2008), and Douglas McCalla, 'Buchanan, Isaac,' *DCB* (Toronto: University of Toronto Press, 1982), 11:125–31.

12 The '"Wooden Cravat" song' likely refers to a line from the popular ballad 'Bonnie Wee Window' about a young man who gets his head stuck in the window of his lover Nell's house and is chased away by Nell's grandmother wearing the window frame like a 'wooden cravat' (When Johnnie got hame, wi' a hachet did he/ Frae his wooden cravat syne himsel' free). See W.F.H. Nicholaisen, 'Humour in Traditional Ballads (Mainly Scottish),' *Folklore* 103 (1992): 27–39.

13 Charles Kingsley, *Hypatia; or New Foes with an Old Face* (London: J.W. Parker and Son,

Sun. Feb. 20.
Heard Mr Burnet preach morning and evening. Weather cold and very blowy.

Mon. Feb. 21.
Spent most of the day in the house reading Kingsley's 'Hypatia.' Hugh McWhirter called in the evening and stayed all night. Mr Fleck from Montreal also called and sat pretty late talking.[14]

Tues. Feb. 22.
Spent the forenoon reading 'Hypatia.' After dinner walked as far as the Water Works and to the side of the great lake. Saw a black and brown catterpillar alive, crawling on the road. Mr Simmons spending a while of the evening in the house after being auditing the Gas Company's books.

Wed. Feb. 23.
Sat reading all forenoon and in the afternoon walked along the Port Dover Railway track as far as the turn of the mountain and descending to Slabtown, walked home by the road. Day exceedingly cold and blowy. Reading on Geology in the evening.

Thurs. Feb. 24.
Still very inclement weather. Kept the house reading all day. At tea time had an unexpected pleasure in the arrival of Miss Goldie from being visiting friends near Oakville.

Fri. Feb. 25.
Spent most of the day in the house reading Burns' Centenary Speeches to Miss Goldie and loafing about. Mrs Cowing called.

Sat. Feb. 26.
Spent most of the day in the house reading the papers etc. to Miss Goldie. Took a walk up town with her in the evening.

Sun. Feb. 27.
Heard Mr Burnet preach in the morning. Mr and Mrs Muir Sr called in the afternoon and Miss Goldie and I accompanied them to Church and heard Mr Ormiston. In the evening Miss G. and I went to Knox's Church and heard Dr Ryerson.

1853); 'The Burns Centenary,' *Ayr Advertiser*, January 27, 1859; 'The Burns Centenary. Ayr,' *Ayrshire Express*, January 29, 1859; 'The Centenary at Ayr,' *Ayr Observer*, February 1, 1859.

14 On Fleck, the Montreal ploughmaker, see Diary for 1857, fn 63.

Mon. Feb. 28.
Miss G. and her niece Annie Maria, little Tom and I had a walk up town
in the forenoon. Spent a while of the afternoon in the City Hall at a meeting of Council. Called at the library and got Carlyle's 'Past and Present.'[15]

Tues. Mar. 1.
Miss G., Annie Maria and I had a walk to the Cemetery in the forenoon. Day fine and frosty. Spent the afternoon mostly reading and the
evening copying some patterns for sewing.

Wed. Mar. 2.
Day beautifully clear and frosty. Miss G. and I had a long walk up the
Mountain by the road leading to I. Buchanan's and back past Lawrie's
Hotel round by the east end of the town and down to James St. Wharf.
Spent the rest of the day mostly inside.

Thurs. Mar. 3.
Rain commenced in the morning and turning into a sort of sleet, froze
on the trees and sidewalks as it fell. In the house most of the day. Messrs
Leggat, Walker and Crawford down at supper in the evening.

Fri. Mar. 4.
Miss G. determined upon going off today at 1:55 p.m. Went to the train
with her but were too late and her departure postponed until the same
hour tomorrow. In the evening, her and I went and heard Chas McLach-
lan, the Canadian Poet lecture upon Modern Poetry.[16]

Sat. Mar. 5.
Read Mansie Waugh to Miss G. in the forenoon and got down to the
station with her again, this time in plenty of time.[17] After seeing her off,
visited the grain elevator and spent a short time viewing the curlers on
the ice.

Sun. Mar. 6.
Heard Mr Burnet morning and evening. Thos and I with Tommy had a
walk to the Cemetery in the interval.

---

15 Thomas Carlyle, *Past and Present* (London: Chapman and Hall, 1843).
16 Maclachlan's lecture 'On the relative merits of Woodworth, Moore and Campbell'
   was held in the Hall of the Hamilton Mechanics' Institute but was poorly attended,
   likely due to bad weather.' *HS*, March 4, 1859.
17 David Macbeth Moir, *The Life of Mansie Waugh, Tailor of Dalkeith* (Edinburgh: Blackwoods, 1828).

Mon. Mar. 7.
Sat in the house all forenoon reading Sam Slick's 'Wise Saws and Modern Instances.'[18]

Tues. Mar. 8.
Dull and rainy. Spending my time mostly in the house reading Mansie Waugh and Carlyle's 'Past and Present.'

Wed. Mar. 9.
Day clear and bright. Started immediately after breakfast on a long walk. Went along the Railway track to where it is crossed by the road leading into Dundas from the N.E. then went northward to the edge of the mountain and followed the line of it to the Waterdown Road and home by it, a most delightful mild day. Patches of snow lying in some nooks but Bluebirds singing in the fields and one Butterfly seen. At Prayer Meeting in the evening.

Thurs. Mar. 10.
Weather still fine. Spent the day mostly in the house reading. Called upon Jameson in the evening and got the loan of some books. Wrote to Mrs Logan.

Fri. Mar. 11.
Spent the forenoon reading. David Goldie called and took dinner. After dinner Thos and I had a long walk diverging from both sides of the Dundas Road. Had the gun with us but saw nothing to shoot. Think the winter has been too mild to bring the winter birds so far south.

Sat. Mar. 12.
Spent the time mostly reading in the house. Went up town in the afternoon and met my old Dundas acquaintances Inglis and Gibson. Learned from them that the work was very slack there.

Sun. Mar. 13.
Weather most delightfully mild and sunny. John Stewart took dinner with us and after dinner, Thos and he and I had a walk eastward along the mountain edge. Met with a Post Office clerk inhabiting a cottage in the mountain and talked a while with him. Got into a sad dillemma with Tommy when walking home from Church in the forenoon. His Mamma going off leaving us and I having to escort him home bawling all the way.

---

18 Thomas Chandler Haliburton, *Wise Saws; or Sam Slick in Search of a Wife* (New York: Stringer and Townsend, 1855).

Mon. Mar. 14.
Reading Carlyle's French Revolution. In the evening, Jack Stewart and I
went to a meeting of the young mens' Christian Association and heard
an essay from a Mr Allan on the Morality of Burns and some animated
discussion on the subject after it.[19] Get some rain coming home.

Tues. Mar. 15.
Sat in the house all day reading Carlyle's French Revolution but could
not make much out of it. Called upon and spent the evening with
Jameson.

Wed. Mar. 16.
Started, along with Thos, immediately after breakfast on a gunning expedition. Went along the line of Railway east and down to the Beach and
along to Snook's where we had bread and cheese and beer. Saw a fine
bald eagle on the wing. Heard frogs piping also the notes of red-wing
Starlings, Pee-wee Fly catcher, Bluebirds, etc. Attended Prayer meeting
in the evening and saw splendid Aurora Borealis when we came out of
Church.

Thurs. Mar. 17.
Weather still fine. Spent the forenoon altering a draught board. In the
afternoon went east along the mountain with Thos and shot some Bluebirds. Mr and Mrs McKendrick at tea and spending the evening in the
house.

Fri. Mar. 18.
Thos called on Mr Reid this morning and learned that Grist had been
offered and would retain his situation at the reduced salary so there
would be no chance for me. Felt very much disappointed. Spent the
day mostly in the house reading. Evening warm and very wet.

Sat. Mar. 19.
Quite a change of weather. Snow lying on the ground and wind blowing very strong. Heard there had been an accident on the railway and
went down to the station before breakfast. Learned that it had been
caused by the sliding of an embankment near Dundas and that Mr

---

19 Thomas Carlyle, *The French Revolution: A History* (London: Chapman and Hall, 1837);
   John Allen's lecture, entitled 'The Morality of the Works of Robert Burns,' was delivered as part of the YMCA's yearly course of lectures. *HS*, March 14, 1859.

Braid and three or 4 others were killed.[20] Worked some during the day at backgammon board.

Sun. Mar. 20.
Heard Mr Burnet preach morning and evening. Spent the interval reading. Mr McKendrick called and got Thos to accompany him for a drive to the scene of the accident.

Mon. Mar. 21.
Working at backgammon board. Called on Jameson in the evening and accompanied him to the Young Mens' Christian Association where we heard an essay on the Physical Geography of South America, a tolerably good essay.

Tues. Mar. 22.
Weather dull and wet. Spent the day about the house reading and fixing backgammon board. In the afternoon attended Mr Braid's funeral in Burlington Cemetery.

Wed. Mar. 23.
About the house and the work all day. Weather very fine and warm.

Thurs. Mar. 24.
A little sick in the morning. Weather bright and mild. Wrote to McGarva, Dundas. Spent the evening with Jameson getting lessons in backgammon.

Fri. Mar. 25.
Went off for a walk with the gun. Went along the Toronto line until close to Aldershot station then got a footpath inland along by the side of the glen and immerged close to Waterdown. Passed thro' part of the village and came home by the direct road. Heard sermon by Mr Barclay, Toronto, in St Andrew's Church in the evening.[21]

---

20 The accident occurred as a result of rain washing away an embankment between Flamborough and Dundas, causing the train to plunge into a 'yawning chasm.' Five persons were killed and several others seriously injured. Alexander Braid, the former locomotive works superintendent for the GWR, was killed by an iron rod forced through his coach during the accident. *HS*, March 22, 1959; *Hamilton Times*, March 21, 1859. On Braid, see Diary for 1857, fn 117.

21 A native of Ayrshire, Scotland, Rev. John Barclay, DD, was minister of St Andrew's Church, Toronto, from 1842 to 1870. See James Croil, *Genesis of Churches in the United States of America, in Newfoundland and the Dominion of Canada* (Montreal: Foster Brown and Company, 1907), 226.

Sat. Mar. 26.
Spending the time mostly about the house reading McCauly's essays and miscellanys.[22]

Sun. Mar. 27.
Communion Sabbath in St Andrew's in which I joined. Mr Ormiston preached in the evening.

Mon. Mar. 28.
Reading nearly all day. Thos got finished with a fine case of Water Fowl with a glass front 40' by 50'. Went to Church in the evening and heard Mr Campbell of Niagara.[23]

Tues. Mar. 29.
Reading McCaulay all day. Weather stormy and rather cold.

Wed. Mar. 30.
Spent the forenoon mostly reading McCauley. After dinner, Thos and I started for a ramble with the gun. Crossed the Suspension Bridge and up the side of the Desjardine Marsh. Shot a number of Red-wing Starlings. Saw one pigeon and Thos fired at it but missed. Caught a snowstorm before getting home which we did not do until seven o'clock.

Thurs. Mar. 31.
Morning stormy and snowing. Took first train to Toronto. On landing there, called on Mr Will Sr at the Grand Trunk Railway work shops and from that to St Lawrence Foundry and another foundry asking work but found it not. Spent the evening with Jameson playing Backgammon having got home by tea time.

Fri. Apr. 1.
Thos and I went out gunning in the forenoon. Went west along the foot of the mountain. He had to leave me early to attend the Grand Jury. Got in among a flock of Gold Crested Kinglets and shot eight of them, also some Bluebirds.

Sat. Apr. 2.
Weather cold. Spent the day mostly about the house reading. Bought a large Snowy Owl in the market for a York shilling.

---

22 Likely Thomas Babington Macaulay, *Essays, Critical and Miscellaneous* (Philadelphia: Carey and Hart, 1846).

23 Rev. Charles Campbell was pastor at St Andrew's Presbyterian Church in Niagara-on-the-Lake for twenty years beginning in 1858. Janet Carnochan, *History of Niagara* (Toronto: William Briggs, 1914), 91–2.

Sun. Apr. 3.
Started for Dundas in the morning. Day clear but very blowy and right
in the teeth walking up. Found McGarva in his room above the store.
Went to St Andrew's Church with him. Spoke to Wilson, Blyth, etc.
when we came out. Dined in Jones's. Had a walk with McGarva and
Innes. Had tea with Bob McKeachnie in the afternoon and called on
Connel and Hector Mackenzie.

Mon. Apr. 4.
Spent most of the day writing to Bill and Christina. Weather very cold
and blowy. Posted my letters for home.

Tues. Apr. 5.
Spent all the forenoon in the Assize Court, a case of disputed boundary
being in hand all the time. Went out with the gun in the afternoon but
met with but small success as I ran short of powder. Shot a robin and a
red squirrel.

Wed. Apr. 6.
Commenced reading 'Zaidee,' a romance.[24] Weather dull and cold.

Thurs. Apr. 7.
Mr Drynan called in the forenoon. Went out walking with him till dinner time. After dinner accomp'd him down to McClellan's farm. Had
the gun and took a circuit on the way home. Shot a Cow Bunting. Mr D.
stayed at McClellan's. Mrs Muir and Mrs Cowing at tea. Walked home
with Mrs C. and spent a short time in her house.

Fri. Apr. 8.
Read 'Zaidee' in the forenoon. In the after-noon assisted Mr Robb in
transplanting some fruit trees and bushes. Took tea with him. Mr Raphael called in the evening. Had a consultation about my taking a tour to
look for work. Think of starting for New York.

Sat. Apr. 9.
Started out with the gun after breakfast. Took the Dundas Road until
near the Half-way House then made toward the Mountain and kept
along by it for some miles, finally taking a cut across the country to
Dundas. Called at the foundry. Had some horns of beer with Turnbull.
Got a convoy from McGarva. Shot 2 bluebirds.

---

24 Margaret Oliphant, *Zaidee: A Romance*, 3 vols. (Edinburgh and London: William
Blackwood and Sons, 1856). The story originally appeared in serialized version in
Blackwood's Magazine.

Sun. Apr. 10.
Heard Mr Burnet preach morning and evening. Spent the interval reading in the house.

Mon. Apr. 11.
Last night wet. Sharpening saws in the forenoon preparatory to going off to New York. In the afternoon took a ramble with the gun up by the Desjardine Marsh. Shot 3 blackbirds and a gold crested Kinglet. Got caught in a thunder storm and got somewhat wet. Copied Kate Dalrymple for Jameson in the evening.[25]

Tues. Apr. 12.
Day beautiful and mild. Set out with the gun after breakfast and had a walk up the Strongman Road and straight back south some miles. Shot two winter wrens, two woodpeckers, a yellow-bellied and a Hairy, and a Bay-winged Bunting. Called on Jameson in the evening.

Wed. Apr. 13.
Spent the forenoon packing up clothes and preparing to start for New York. Sold Gas shares $60 to J. Stewart. Took train for New York at 3.25. Jameson furnishing me with a pass to the Falls.

Thurs. Apr. 14.
At Albany about 4 in the morning and had a fine run down on the Hudson River Ry. Rain commenced when about half way to New York. Reached there about 10 a.m. Called at Mr Renfrew's store and went from there to the house and spent the remainder of the day with Mrs Logan. Slept in the Fulten Ave. Club House, Mr Renfrew having a stranger staying with him.[26] Awfully wet all day in N.Y.

---

25 'Kate Dalrymple' is a traditional Scottish reel whose words were written by Scottish poet William Watt (1792–1859). Alexander G. Murdoch, *The Scottish Poets Recent and Living* (Glasgow: Thomas D. Morison, 1883), 144. It was published as *Kate Dalrymple, and the Flowers of the Forest; To Which Is Added, Loud Roared the Dreadful Thunder, The Bonny Blue Bonnet, This Is No My Plaid, Ye Banks and Braes* (Glasgow, 18–).

26 Robert Renfrew was a Brooklyn merchant in the 1850s and '60s, who imported shawls and other British dry goods for sale in the New York market. His shop was on Pine, his home on Quincy Street. John Doggett, *Doggett's New-York City Directory for 1850* (New York: J. Doggett, Jr, 1850), np; *Trow's New York City Directory for 1855–56* (New York: J.F. Trow, 1855), np. A member of the St Andrew's Society of New York, he seems to have been a Scot, one of the many nodes in McIlwraith's network of Scottish contacts in North America. See Secretary to the Society, comp., *The Saint Andrew's Society of the State of New York Record Book* (New York: Douglas Taylor and Company, 1895), 168. Mrs Logan was Andrew's sister, Margaret (née McIlwraith) (b. 1814), who married a James Logan in Newton-on-Ayr on October 3, 1839. It is unclear if she was a widow,

Fri. Apr. 15.
Drove to the ferry with Mr Renfrew in the morning and called on Mrs Guthrie, Laight St. and from there to her brother Wm Barry at Dunkin's Machine Shop away up the North River.[27] Got some information from him about the shops. Strolled about town a while then out and had tea in Mr Renfrew's and had to come down town again to sleep.

Sat. Apr. 16.
Fine weather. Spent the day visiting different foundries asking work. Called on Jones, foreman pattern maker at the Novelty Works who held out some hopes for me getting a job either with him or some of his acquaintances.[28] Spent the evening with Guthrie's people in New York and slept at the Franklin Hotel, Brooklyn.

Sun. Apr. 17.
In the morning walked over to Laight St. and breakfasted with Guthrie's. In company with Mr G. visited the 'Adriatic' Str now lying up and had

---

but throughout the diary she appears to be alone. Mrs Logan seems to have worked as a housekeeper in Renfrew's house 1857–60; she moved to Canada with Andrew in November 1860, settling first in brother Thomas's Hamilton household, but moved again to Galt in June 1861, where she made ends meet as a landlady. Public Record Office, Scotland, Old Parish Registers Marriages 612/002/0020 0415 Newton on Ayr, p. 447, Scotland's People, www.scotlandspeople.gov.uk (accessed 26 May 2009). See Diary for 1860, November 1, 2; Diary for 1861, June 6.

27 John T. Dunkin's machine shop worked on steam engines and 'general' jobs. The shop changed addresses in the 1850s and '60s, but remained on West 27th Street, at no. 350 in 1856, no. 410 in 1867, and no. 556 in 1874. *Trow's New York City Directory 1856–57* (New York: J.F. Trow, 1856), np; *Trow's New York City Directory 1867–68* (New York: J.F. Trow, 1867), np.; Thomas Dunlap, comp., *Wiley's American Iron Trade Manual of the Leading Iron Industries of the United States* (New York: John Wiley and Son, 1874), 95. See Diary for 1860, fn 29.

28 The Novelty Iron Works was the largest of New York City's factories that produced steamship engines, boilers, castings, machinery, agricultural implements, and other heavy items. Founded in 1830 at the East River and the foot of 12th Street by T.B. Stillman and Horatio Allen, it was a 'five-acre maze' of buildings and a remarkably modern business structure that had as many as 1,200 workers organized into eighteen separate departments by the early 1850s. By the late 1850s, it was considered a centre of innovation in the development of machine tools, yet by 1870 it had become so 'old and out of date' that it closed its doors. Edwin G. Burrows and Mike Wallace, *Gotham: A History of New York City to 1898* (New York: Oxford University Press, 2000), 659–60; John Leander Bishop, *A History of American Manufactures from 1608 to 1860*, 3rd ed. (Philadelphia: Edward Young and Company, 1868), 3:125–7; Iver Bernstein, *The New York City Draft Riots: Their Significance for American Society and Politics in the Age of the Civil War* (New York: Oxford University Press, 1990), 109–204.

a view of the engines. Saw Mrs Logan in Brooklyn in the afternoon then came back and took up my quarters in Guthrie's.

Mon. Apr. 18
Visited Mr Guthrie at his place of work. Spent some hours of the forenoon in Barnum's museum.[29] After dinner, went out and saw Mrs Logan then had a tour thro' Williamsburgh and across to N.Y. at the Houston St. ferry. Called on J. Robertshaw at the 9th St. and walked home to Guthrie's by way of Grand St.

Tues. Apr. 19.
Left the house early and spent some time in Washington Market, then from that to National Academy of Design exhibition of paintings, from there to the Novelty Works and saw Mr Jones who recommended me to try the 'Architectural Iron Works' for a job, which I did and got engaged there.[30] Got my chest moved over in the afternoon and then went out and saw Mrs Logan who seems recovering her health.

Wed. Apr. 20.
Started work at 7 a.m. in Badger's Architectural Iron Works, foreman pattern-maker Mr Fairfield. Worked all day repairing a couple of old column patterns. Like the shop pretty well. Had a walk in the evening with Mr Barry who came down to Guthrie's.

Thurs. Apr. 21.
Weather fine. Still working at altering columns. Have a long walk between Laight and 14th St. and felt pretty tired when I get home. Wrote to Thos in the evening.

---

29 On Barnum's American Museum, see Diary for 1857, fn 103.
30 Located at the East River shore and Avenue C between 13th and 14th Streets, Daniel D. Badger's Architectural Iron Works was a pioneer in architectural iron construction, creating the first full cast-iron buildings and building facades on lower Broadway in the 1850s. The Works opened in 1846 and grew quickly. In 1855, Badger (1806–84) employed 125 men full-time at his Works at the wage of $44 a month and 25 boys at $16 a month. The firm became incorporated as the Architectural Iron Works in 1856. In 1865, the company began to produce a beautiful large-format sales book of its designs for buildings and building fronts, warehouses factories, and bridges. Badger retired in 1873, and without his direction, the company's fortunes declined quickly; the Works closed in 1876. See Margot Gayle and Carol Gayle, *Cast-Iron Architecture in America: The Significance of James Bogardus* (New York: W.W. Norton, 1998), 157–8; J. Leander Bishop, *A History of American Manufactures from 1608 to 1860* (Philadelphia: Edward Young and Co., 1868), 3:205; Adolf K. Placzek, *Macmillan Encyclopedia of Architects* (New York: Free Press, 1982), 1:124.

Fri. Apr. 22.
At columns and some other small jobs all day. Weather most deplorably wet. Getting along pretty agreeably in the shop. Looking out for lodgings but not yet succeeding in finding good ones.

Sat. Apr. 23.
Working away patching up old patterns. Quit work at 5 p.m. Called on McGarva's friend, Miss Marshall at Gideon Pott's, 23rd St. Had tea there and made enquiry about boardings. Was recommended by the waiting man to 'Logue's' Hotel and determined to go there.

Sun. Apr. 24.
Accompanied Mr Barry to Grand St. Church and heard Dr Thompson.[31] Dined with Mr Renfrew in Brooklyn. Moved my traps up to Paddy Logue's Hotel in the evening. Tormented with the Paddys kicking up rows thro' the night in the house.

Mon. Apr. 25.
Working away at patching up. Received $6.00 from the foreman so presume that my pay is fixed at $1.50. Called on Guthrie's in the evening.

---

31 The Grand Street Presbyterian Church was a large, elegant white marble construction, located at the corner of Grand and Crosby streets. Until 1853, it had been occupied by a congregation of old Scotch Presbyterians pastored by Dr Joseph McElroy (see Diary for 1860, fn 7). In that year, a congregation of Associate Presbyterians purchased the church for $55,000. From 1851 to 1861, the Grand Street congregation was pastored by a Scotsman, Rev. John J. Thomson, DD, previously of St David's Church in St John, New Brunswick. In 1861, Dr Thomson departed his New York pastorate to accept a call at Knox's Presbyterian in Galt, Canada West, where he remained until 1863. In the following year, he returned to his former charge in New York when his successor at Grand Street, Rev. Samuel Ramsay Wilson (1818–86), was forced to resign when he lost his voice. Thomson's second pastorate at Grand Street lasted from 1864 to 1875, when ill health forced him to retire to Scotland. The Grand Street congregation of Associate Presbyterians moved to a newly constructed edifice on 34th Street in July 1866 and became known as the Fourth Presbyterian Church. *Centennial Services of the Fourth Presbyterian Church of the City of New-York* (New York: Fourth Presbyterian Church, 1885); *National Cyclopaedia of American Biography* (New York: James T. White and Company, 1904), 12:95; Moses King, *King's Hand-Book of New York City*, 2nd ed. (New York: M. King, 1893), 365; C. Van Renssalaer, ed., *The Presbyterian Magazine* (Philadelphia: The Presbyterian Office, 1853), 3:202; *The Home and Foreign Record of the Presbyterian Church in the United States* (Philadelphia: Publication House, 1853), 4:159; *Home and Foreign Record of the Canada Presbyterian Church* (Toronto: Canada Observer Office, 1863), 3:155; 'The Fourth Presbyterian Church, New York,' in Joseph T. Cooper and W.W. Barr, eds., *The Evangelical Repository and United Presbyterian Review*, n.s., 5 (Philadelphia: William S. Young, 1866), 306–12.

Tues. Apr. 26.
Fine warm weather with some showers. Full time patching up old patterns. Went to the Metropolitan Theatre at night and saw 'Romeo and Juliet.'[32]

Wed. Apr. 27.
Still at work all day repairing and altering old columns, etc. In the evening had an exploring stroll away down the Bowery and Chatham Sts and up Broadway. Saw a fire in a store in Broadway and the great rumpus of the firemen and engines running to it.[33] Got word of a boarding house a Mrs Smith, on 10th St. and called and engaged a room.

Thurs. Apr. 28.
Still all day at the same kind of jobs. Had a walk away up town in the evening as far as 27th St. and down 6th Avenue.

Fri. Apr. 29.
Full time. Learned today that our foreman, Mr Fairfield, was leaving and a new one coming. Found A. Connel at the gate at 6 p.m., he having left Dundas. Got him to accompany me to my Hotel. Had tea and then went down to 'Niblo's Garden' theatre and saw 'Anthony and Cleopatra' acted with good scenery altho' but poor acting.[34]

---

32 Located on Broadway, opposite Bond Street, the New York Theater and Metropolitan Opera House was built in September 1854 on the site of the conflagrated Tripler Hall. From 1856 until 1859, the Metropolitan (formally renamed the New Theater, but never fully shaking its old name in the popular mind) was operated by English actor and impresario William Evans Burton (1804–60). After Burton's departure, the theatre was refitted in September 1859 and renamed the Winter Garden Theatre. See Diary for 1859, fn 66 ; H.P. Phelps, *Players of a Century* (Albany, NY: Joseph McDonough, 1880), 299.

33 The fire occurred at 536 Broadway, home to William Raymond and Company, metallic burial case manufacturers, and Henry Storey, cabinet manufacturer, causing $2,800 worth of damage. 'Fire in Broadway,' *NYT*, April 28, 1859.

34 Niblo's Garden and Theater was 'an attractive and popular little theater' that opened in 1828 in the summer garden of William Niblo on Broadway, near Prince Street. The original theatre burned down in 1848, but it was rebuilt in 1849–50 and enlarged in 1854. It was demolished in 1895 to make room for an office building. Like other concert saloons of the time, Niblo's featured every kind of entertainment from serious drama to minstrel shows. Popular actress Julia Dean Hayne starred as Cleopatra in the production that McIlwraith saw. James Grant Wilson, ed., *The Memorial History of the City of New York* (New York: New York History Company, 1893), 4:482; Mary C. Henderson, *The City and the Theatre: The History of New York Playhouses, a 250-Year Journey from Bowling Green to Times Square* (New York: Watson–Guptill, 2004), 64–5; Stephen Jenkins, *The World's Greatest Street: The Story of Broadway, Old and New, from the Bowling Green to Albany* (New York: G.P. Putnam's Sons,

Sat. Apr. 30.
A most beautiful day. Connel engaged to commence work in the Novelty. Shifted my lodgings in the evening to Mr Smith's No. 357 Tenth St. Ave. B. Connel and I called on Guthrie's people in the evening. Mr Fairfield, our foreman, finishes his engagement in the establishment today.

Sun. May 1.
Still most beautiful weather. Called for Connel at Logue's Hotel and had a walk with him up town right away up 5th Ave. to 123rd St. Saw boys out bird catching with trap cages. Saw a small flock of Cedar birds in an orchard. Dined in my lodgings and then crossed to Green Point and had a long tour to Quincy St. Brooklyn, to see Mrs Logan. Wrote to Thos for my clothes.

Mon. May 2.
Full time at the usual kind of jobs. Connel and I walked down the Bowery in the evening and I bought a fluid lamp for my room, $.87-½. Connel started work in the Novelty today. Bustle in the streets today with people moving their houses. Had a view of the Planet Saturn thro' a telescope in Broadway.

Tues. May 3.
Still delightful weather. All day patching and altering. Had a walk down town in the evening. Took my watch to the watchmaker to get a new main spring and made a purchase of Jae[g]er's book on 'American Insects.'[35]

Wed. May 4.
Full time at alterations of columns, etc. for a shop front for Memphis Tennessee. Had a walk about town with Connel in the evening. Got my watch back with new main spring for $1.00. Beautiful sunny weather.

Thurs. May 5.
Still full time at the same job. Rec'd my chest per Express Co. from Hamilton with letters from Thos and Bill enclosed. Connel came down in the evening and gave me a hand up with it to my rooms. Walked over to West 26th St. to call on Wm Barry but he was not at home.

1911), 204; T. Allston Brown, *A History of the New York Stage: From the First Performance in 1732 to 1901* (New York: Dodd, Mead and Company, 1903), 1:188.

35 Benedict Jaeger, assisted by H.C. Preston, MD, *The Life of North American Insects* (Providence, RI: Sayles, Miller and Simons, 1854).

Fri. May 6.
Still delightful weather. All day at Memphis job. In the evening accompanied Mr Davis to the Eleventh Presbyterian Church to a Prayer Meeting in the basement. People burning the old straw of the beds in the streets all over the town at present.[36]

Sat. May 7.
Still warm weather. Still working at Memphis job mostly. Connel and I walked down town and called on Guthrie's. Saw Mr Barrie there.

Sun. May 8.
Sat in the house all forenoon writing to Mother. After dinner, Connel and I walked down town and caught the 3 o'clock str to Staten Island. Had a very refreshing sail over there and a walk down to near the new Battery at the Narrows. Saw Mrs Logan in the evening and got home late.

Mon. May 9.
Full time at job for Memphis. Spent the evening in the house writing to Thos. Still very hot weather.

Tues. May 10.
Weather quite changed being cold and blustery and threatening rain. Full time in the shop. Had a visit from Connel in the evening.

Wed. May 11.
Very wet and cold all day. Full time in the shop. Had a walk with Connel in the evening down the Bowery, round the City Hall and up Broadway.

---

36 The Eleventh Presbyterian Church was at the corner of Fourth Street and Avenue C from 1842 to 1863; the pastor was Rev. J. Parsons Hovey. 'The Churches of New York,' *Frank Leslie's Sunday Magazine* 12, no. 4 (October 1882): 388–9. 'May Day' (May 1) was a traditional moving day for the working class in antebellum New York City, when annual leases expired and families sought better or more affordable accommodation. Though it was dreaded by many, it was also host to ritual street celebrations, dancing, and bonfires – the 'burning of the straw' – that would have seemed disorderly, even chaotic, to outsiders. It was a 'bold assertion of working-class dominion of the streets.' The *Times* reminded its readers that May 1 also symbolized for some New Yorkers the start of summer homelessness. Kenneth A. Scherzer, *The Unbounded Community: Neighborhood Life and Social Structure in New York City, 1830–1875* (Durham, NC: Duke University Press, 1992), 23–25; 'Moving Day,' *NYT*, May 3, 1859.

Thurs. May 12.
Full time in the shop. Had a long walk down the Bowery in the evening perusing the shop windows.

Fri. May 13.
Weather improving again. Full time in the shop. Had a visit of Chas Mackenzie in the evening from Sarnia and spent the evening with him in Laura Keene's Theatre and walking around.[37]

Sat. May 14.
A delightful day. Full time in the shop. In the evening Connel, C. Mackenzie and I had a tour down the Bowery, round the City Hall and up Broadway.

Sun. May 15.
Still fine, bright weather. Called for C. Mackenzie in the morning at No. 144 Fourth St. and walked with him down Broadway and Wall St. and crossed to Brooklyn. Heard Mr Beecher preach and dined afterwards in a restaurant then went to Mr Renfrew's.[38] Mr and Mrs R. from home. Had a walk to the Evergreen Cemetery.

Mon. May 16.
Full time in the shop. In the evening accompanied C. Mackenzie to the Niblos Garden Theatre and saw 'Rob Roy' acted in a kind of middling style.[39]

---

37 Opened in November 1856, Laura Keene's Theater was located on the east side of Broadway, at no. 624. Laura Keene (1830–73) was a talented actor and a remarkably adept theatre manager. From 1856 to 1863, she ran a wide variety of shows from Shakespearean drama to burlesque and instituted in New York the British custom of long-running productions. She became the first woman to successfully manage her own theatre in America, trained her own actors, adapted most of her scripts, designed costumes, and did publicity. She also acted roles in many stage productions at her own theatre and others, including one in 'Our American Cousin' at Ford's Theater in Washington, DC, during which Abraham Lincoln was assassinated. Brown, *History of the New York Stage*, 2:123–46; John Creahan, *The Life of Laura Keene; Actress, Artist, Manager and Scholar* (Philadelphia: The Rodgers Publishing Company, 1897).

38 On Beecher, see Diary for 1857, fn 109.

39 *Rob Roy* was produced by Edward Eddy's drama company, with the American-born Eddy (1821–75) as the title character. Brown, *History of the New York Stage*, 1:188.

Tues. May 17.
Full time in the shop. Called on Charles at his lodgings and along with him, went and visited Miss Marshall at Gideon Potts, No 48 Fourteenth St. Had a walk down Broadway afterwards.

Wed. May 18.
Full time in the shop. Went along with C. MacK. to hear Piccollomini sing in the Academy of Music, 14th St. The piece performed being the opera of Don Giovanni. Singing scarcely came up to our expectations.[40] A very wet night came on.

Thurs. May 19.
Full time in the shop. In the evening Charlie and I walked down town and visited the 'Tribune' office and saw the operation of folding and putting up the papers going on.[41]

Fri. May 20.
Full time in the shop. Still dull, wet weather Charles and I spent the

---

40 Located at 14th Street and Irving Place, the 4,600-seat Academy of Music opened in October 1854 and was home to musical performances and instruction for thirty years. New York's first 'democratic' opera house, it sought to rescue opera from the classes and offer it to the respectable masses, including their children. Here, as one contemporary noted, 'the public are to be regarded as pupils' not just consumers. Karen Ahlquist, *Democracy at the Opera: Music, Theater and Culture in New York City, 1815–1860* (Champaign-Urbana: University of Illinois Press, 1997) 147–9. The *Times* theatre critic was a little more complimentary than McIlwraith on the quality of singing: Piccolomini sang 'excellently'; Amodio 'not quite so remarkable'; Mme Strakosch 'carefully and well'; Brignoli 'good'; and Junca 'better than many of his predecessors.' 'Academy of Music,' *NYT*, May 19, 1859.

41 The *New York Tribune* was a daily newspaper founded in 1841 and edited by Horace Greeley (1811–72) until his death. Its office was on Nassau Street near Spruce. In the years leading up to the Civil War, the *Tribune* was avowedly Republican, distinctive for its inflammatory and impassioned editorials. The *Tribune* merged with a former rival in 1924 to make the *New York Herald Tribune*. In its production process, the *Tribune* would have been typical of a mid-century American daily. For a good description of the *Tribune*'s daily production regimen, see James Parton, 'Day and Night in the Tribune Office,' in *The Life of Horace Greeley, Editor of the New York Tribune* (Boston: Houghton, Mifflin and Company, 1889), 391–411; Stephen L. Vaughn, *Encyclopedia of American Journalism* (Boca Raton, FL: CRC Press, 2007), 343–45; George G. Foster, *New York by Gas-Light and Other Urban Sketches* [1850] (rep. Berkeley: University of California Press, 1991), 34.

evening hearing Wood's Minstrels perform.[42] Saw a pretty good pantomime there.

Sat. May 21.
Full time in the shop. In the evening Chas Mackenzie, Connel and I
walked down the Bowery and Chatham St., round the City Hall and
up Broadway.

Sun. May 22.
Weather sultry and lowering with gleams of sunshine. Called for
Charles at his lodgings, both of us lame-footed with walking so much.
Rode down to the City Hall and walked from there to the Staten Island
Ferry. Steamed over there but caught heavy rain and did not travel far.
Had tea in Mr Renfrew's and Messrs Kerr, Syme MacKenzie and I went
and heard Beacher.

Mon. May 23.
Full time in the shop. Weather brightening up again. Accompanied Chas
in the evening to the performance by Christie's Minstrals. House over-
crowded and had to stand all the time. Entertainment but mediocre.

Tues. May 24.
Full time in the shop. Chas' last night in New York. Had a walk round
town with him and bade good-bye. Came home late and very tired.

Wed. May 25.
Full time in the shop. Went to bed immediately after tea and made up

---

42 Wood's Minstrels was a popular blackface troupe owned and managed by Henry
   Wood (d. 1883?), brother of the city's Democratic mayor, Fernanado Wood (see
   fn 91 below). From 1857 to 1859, they played at Henry Woods' Marble Hall at 561
   Broadway near Prince Street. Wood's Minstrels was advertised boldly as the oldest
   and largest minstrel company in the world, offering 'Select Negro Minstrelsy in Old
   Virginny style.' 'Amusements,' *NYT*, May 20, 1859. The production that McIlwraith
   saw was 'Genii of the Lake,' which the *Times* described as 'an irresistible attraction
   ... [a] splendid programme of Ethiopean [*sic*] minstrelsy.' 'Wood's Minstrels,' *NYT*,
   May 23, 1859. In 1850s New York, several blackface troupes vied for popular favour,
   among them Christy's Minstrels, a group owned and managed by George Christy
   (1827–68) and R.M. Hooley that performed regularly at George Christy's Opera
   House, 444 Broadway. McIlwraith saw this group on the House's opening night.
   Edward Le Roy Rice, *Monarchs of Minstrelsy, from Daddy Rice to Date* (New York:
   Kenny Publishing Company, 1911), 19–22, 74–5; Mary C. Henderson, *The City and
   Theatre: The History of New York Playhouses* (New York: Watson-Guptill, 2004), 93–4;
   'George Christy's Opera House,' *NYT*, May 23, 1859.

some lost sleep. Mr Barry called after a while and I walked out a short way with him.

Thurs. May 26.
Full time in the shop. Weather again hot. In the evening went to a meeting of American Institute in Cooper's buildings but felt most confounded sleepy.[43]

Fri. May 27.
Full time in the shop. Spent the evening in my room cogitating and trying to keep cool, also writing up this, my diary.

Sat. May 28.
Full time in the shop. Visited Guthrie's in the evening in co. with Connel. Made purchase of some planes in the Bowery.

Sun. May 29.
Still fine weather. Started away to Brooklyn immediately after breakfast and spent most of the day with Mrs Logan. Wm Sym gone to Canada. Met and had a talk with an old French Entomologist on the road out a-hunting. Had a walk with Connel in the evening.

Mon. May 30.
Full time in the shop. In the evening wrote to Miss Goldie.

Tues. May 31.
Full time in the shop. After tea had a walk over in Green Point and saw some of the fast trotters coming home from the great race between Flora Temple and Ethan Allen.[44] Wrote to Jack Stewart.

---

43 The Cooper Institute (or Cooper Union) was an educational establishment built (1854–7) at the junction of Third and Fourth avenues largely with funds from New York philanthropist Peter Cooper. Motivated by the mid-Victorian mission of self-improvement, it was 'devoted forever to the union of art and science in their application to the useful purposes of life.' The Institute offered adults lectures and courses in 'mechanical arts,' especially architectural, form and free-hand drawing, painting, and engraving. Courses were also offered in music, English literature, physics, astronomy, and chemistry. It housed a museum, Free Library, and Reading Room. See Clara Erskine Clement Waters and Laurence Hutton, *Artists of the Nineteenth Century and Their Works* (Boston: Houghton, Osgood, 1879), 1:lxxx; 'Cooper Union, or Institute,' *The Encyclopedia Americana: A Library of Useful Knowledge* (New York: The Encyclopedia Americana Corporation, 1918), 638.

44 Greenpoint was a working-class neighbourhood in Brooklyn. Flora Temple, a smallish bay mare, and Ethan Allan, a 'great' Morgan horse and the 'pride of New England,' began a lengthy rivalry in 1856, when they trotted their first race against one

Wed. June 1.
Full time in the shop. Had a walk round town with Connel in the evening.

Thurs. June 2.
Full time in the shop. In the evening visited and joined the Mechanics' Institute. Took Aiton's 'Lays of the Scottish Cavaliers' out of the library.[45]

Fri. June 3.
Full time in the shop. In the evening started for Brooklyn to see Mrs Logan and caught a storm of thunder, lightning and heavy rain by the way. Was persuaded to stay all night.

Sat. June 4.
Left Mr Renfrew's by five and got over in time for work. Full time in the shop. Called on Guthrie's and gave Mrs G. a shawl in a present.

Sun. June 5.
Beautiful bright and cool weather. Heard Mr Thompson in Grand St. Church in the forenoon. In the afternoon had a sail up the Hudson to Fort Lee in co. with Connel.

Mon. June 6.
Full time in the shop. Fell asleep after tea and slept till bed-time. Had a letter from Mrs Mac. at Ayr C.W. enclosing one from Thos written on board the steamer going down the St Lawrence on his way home.

Tues. June 7.
Full time in the shop. Spent the evening writing to Bell and walking up to the post with it.

Wed. June 8.
Full time in the shop. Attended Debating Club in the Mech. Ins. in the

---

another. In the race McIlwraith references, the first of the season, Flora Temple beat Ethan Allan by a length and a half, in 2 minutes, 25 seconds for a purse of $2,000 at the Fashion Race Course at Flushing, Long Island. The horses were driven 'to wagon'; that is, harness racing. 'The Turf and the Trotting Horse in America,' *The Atlantic Monthly*, May 1868, 521–2; Hiram Washington Woodruff, *The Trotting Horse in America: How to Train and Drive Him with Reminiscences of the Trotting Turf* (New York: J.B. Ford and Company, 1869), 295–6; 'The Turf,' *NYT*, June 1, 1859.

45 William Edmonstone Aytoun, *Lays of the Scottish Cavaliers, and Other Poems* (Edinburgh and London: W. Blackwood and Sons, 1849). The book was composed of a series of Jacobite ballads.

evening and heard a discussion as to whether slave labour was beneficial to the United States which was decided in the affirmative.

Thurs. June 9.
Full time in the shop. Connel called on me in the evening and we had
a walk down Broadway. Wrote and posted a letter to Mrs Mac. at Ayr
C.W.

Fri. June 10.
Full time in the shop. In the evening had a walk as far as the Bellevue
Hospital. On the way home heard the fire bell and saw the great glare
on the sky so went away down following it and found it in Rivington
St. below Houston. A great crowd around it.

Sat. June 11.
Full time at work. Connel and I had a walk in the evening as far up
town as the Reservoir of the Water Works. Fine moonlight.

Sun. June 12.
Beautiful cool weather. Had a walk before Church time through the five
points and all around that district then went and heard Mr Thompson
in Grand St. Church. After dinner took boat from 10th St. to Calvary
Cemetery and walked from there to Mr Renfrew's. 12 at night when I
got home.

Mon. June 13.
Full time at work. Spent the eve'g writing to Mr Jameson in Hamilton.

Tues. June 14.
Full time in the shop. Had a walk with Connel in the evening.

Wed. June 15.
Full time in the shop. In the evening called at the Mech. Ins. and got
'Alton Locke.'[46] Walked down town and called on Guthrie's in Laight
St.

Thurs. June 16.
Full time in the shop.

Fri. June 17.
Full time in the shop. Reading Alton Locke in the evening.

---

46 Charles Kingsley, *Alton Locke, Tailor and Poet: An Autobiography* (New York: Harper
and Brothers, 1850).

Sat. June 18.
Full time in the shop. Walked out to Brooklyn and saw Mrs Logan.

Sun. June 19.
Fine, bright weather. Thought of going to Church in the morning but was asked by a fellow boarder to go and take a walk so Connel, he and I went down town and got the boat to Coney Island. Spent some hours there and had a long walk along the shore.

Mon. June 20.
Full time in the shop. In the evening finish reading 'Alton Locke.' Had a letter from McGarva.

Tues. June 21.
Full time in the shop. In the evening wrote to Thos and Christina and posted it away.

Wed. June 22.
Full time in the shop. Called at the Mech. Ins. in the evening and got 'The Wager of Battle' by Herbert.[47] Afterwards had a walk with Connel. Had a letter from Mary Goldie.

Thurs. June 23.
Full time in the shop. In the eve'g walked out to Brooklyn and saw Mrs Logan who was purposing going to the country on Saturday.

Fri. June 24.
Full time in the shop. Connel and I went walking in the evening as far as Bellevue Hospital. Finished reading 'The Wager of Battle.' Bought Cumming's 'Evidences of Christianity,' 38-½¢.[48]

---

47 Henry William Herbert, *Wager of Battle: a Tale of Saxon Slavery in Sherwood Forest* (New York: Mason Brothers, 1855).

48 The Bellevue Hospital was a complex of three four-storey bluestone buildings located on twenty acres of 'finely cultivated' land on Twenty-Sixth Street at the East River. Originally housing an almshouse (1816) and prison (1816), and later a public hospital (1826), after 1848 the site became dedicated wholly to the latter function. An institution for the sick poor, Bellevue had become by the 1850s a place of medical progress in America, home to one of the country's earliest maternity wards (1799) and a teaching clinic established by medical faculty at New York University. Rev. J.F. Richmond, *New York and Its Institutions, 1609–1873* (New York: E.B. Treat, 1872), 385–8. The book was likely John Cumming, DD, *Is Christianity from God? Or, A Manual of Christian Evidence: For Scripture Readers, City Missionaries, Sunday School Teachers and c.* (London: Arthur Hall and Co. and J.F. Shaw, 1847).

Sat. June 25.
At a job in a hurry and worked on till 7 o'clock at night. Had a walk down the Bowery with Connel afterwards.

Sun. June 26.
Warm weather. Heard Dr Thompson preach in Grand St. Church in the morning. After dinner, Connel and I had a walk over in Jersey City.

Mon. June 27.
Full time in the shop. Had a letter from Mrs Mc. of Thos' safe arrival and from Jameson.

Tues. June 28.
Full time in the shop. Very hot weather. Connel and I walked down to Laight St. and called on Guthrie's in the evening.

Wed. June 29.
Full time in the shop. The hottest day this season as yet. Thermometer 98 deg. in the shade, some say 110. Called at the Mech. Ins. in the evening and got a vol. of stories entitled The Club Book.[49] Caught a storm of thunder and lightning on the way home.

Thurs. June 30.
Full time in the shop. Weather much cooler today. Reading stories in The Club Book in the evening.

Fri. July 1.
Full time at work. In the evening Connel, Burrhaus, a fellow boarder, and I had a walk up Broadway beyond Union Park.

Sat. July 2.
Full time in the shop. Got paid before quitting work, Monday being a holiday. In the evening walked out to Brooklyn and saw Messrs Renfrew and Syme. Mrs Logan not yet returned from Mr Dale's where she has gone on a visit.

Sun. July 3.
Hot, lowering weather. Our boarders all except myself and other two all out of the City. Had a ramble round town in the forenoon. In the afternoon crossed the ferry at Hunter's Point and had a tour round the country back to Green Point but caught a thunder storm and got wet.

---

49 Andrew Picken, ed., *The Club-Book; Being Original Tales and c. by Various Authors* (New York: J. and J. Harper, 1831).

Came home and slept till tea time was all past. Great firing of crackers on the streets.

Mon. July 4.
A fine, bright, cool morning for the Great Holiday. Left the house early and saw the parading of the soldiers at Union Park, thence down the Bowery and got my likeness taken. Then called on Guthrie's then round the Battery and over to Brooklyn. At 12.50 got on board the Harlam boat. Went up as far as High Bridge per str and then walked out past King's Bridge and along the farther side of the Spyten Dugvil Creek to the line of the Hudson R.R. and down the the track to Fort Washington, thence per rail into the city. Had a stroll round thro' the Five Points and down to the City Hall and saw the fireworks.

Tues. July 5.
Full time at work, although getting little to do in the shop. In the evening wrote to Mrs Hunter.

Wed. July 6.
Still fine, cool weather. Full time at work. Had a walk down Broadway with Connel in the evening who had been away in Connecticut spending his 'Fourth.'

Thurs. July 7.
Full time in the shop. Had a letter from Mrs Hunter detailing Thomas's arrival at home. In the evening went out to Mr Renfrew's to see Mrs Logan but found she had not arrived from the country.

Fri. July 8.
Full time at work. Was asleep after tea in the evening when Connel called with two young men from Dundas, Gowry and Murdock. Murdock an old Kilmarnock railway hand.[50] Went out and had a walk down town with them.

Sat. July 9.
Weather getting warm again. Spent the eve'g strolling round with Connel and the strangers. Visited a Dutch 'Garten.'[51] Full time at work.

---

50 See Diary for 1857, fn 78.
51 A Dutch garden was a formal rectangular garden, full of dense, symmetrical plantings and brightly coloured flowers, and edged with a firm structure, usually trimmed shrubs or a low wall. New York's old Dutch gardens seem to have been a remnant of the city's Dutch colonial past. The garden's presentation, one nineteenth-

Sun. July 10.
A very hot day. Wrote to Mrs Mac. in Hamilton in the forenoon. Spent some time with Connel and the other two gents and in the afternoon went to Mr Renfrew's but found that Mrs Logan had not yet come home. Spent part of the afternoon and all the evening with Mr Sym who was keeping house alone.

Mon. July 11.
Full time at work. Awfully hot weather now. Wrote to Miss Goldie in the evening.

Tues. July 12.
Full time in the shop. Weather getting still hotter. This day, I think, the hottest we have had. Spent the evening sleeping and wandering down about Tenth St. Pier to try and get cooled. Fine moonlight.

Wed. July 13.
Fore part of the day still bright and awfully hot. Full time in the shop. Afternoon darkened down and from four till six had a most tremendous storm. Wind and dust all was dark in the first place and then thunder, lightning and deluging rain. Heard a report like a gun which one of our men said was from a meteor exploding in the yard. Evening fair. Had a walk with Connel.

Thurs. July 14.
Temperature considerably moderated although still close and sultry. Full time at work. Fell asleep in my room immediately after taking tea and did not wake until 12 o'clock at night. Fisher, one of our pattern-makers, came to board in our boarding house.

Fri. July 15.
Weather quite pleasant. Full time at work. Sat about the stoop in front of the house most of the evening with Messrs Davis, Burrhaus, etc.

Sat. July 16.
A very wet drizzling day. Full time at work. Called on Connel in the eve'g and saw Murray, a fitter from Dundas, who has now started work in the Novelty Works. Had a walk round town down Broadway and across to Chatham St. past the five points. Got wet coming home.

---

century writer noted, was 'formal, with its trees and shrubs clipped into fantastic shapes, and its puerile, toy-like ornamentation.' Charles Sprague Sargent, 'Formal Gardening: Where It Can Be Used to Advantage,' *Garden and Forest* 6 (January–December 1893): 129.

Sun. July 17.
A fine bright morning. Attended Grand St. Church in the forenoon. In the afternoon Murray, Connel and I went walking to Calvary Cemetery. Accomp'd Mr Davis to 11th Presbyterian Church Ave. C. in the evening.[52]

Mon. July 18.
Full time at work. In the evening accomp'd Connel down to Guthrie's, he being in the thought of going to keep an engine along with A. Guthrie.

Tues. July 19.
Full time at work. In the evening wrote to Jack Stewart.

Wed. July 20.
Full time at work. Heard from Mrs Logan now staying with Mr Dale at Syosset, Long Island. Connel, Murray and I went and visited Jones' Wood where a mammoth festival is being held all week. Heard some good instrumental music and saw some good fireworks.[53]

Thurs. July 21.
Full time at work. Heard from Mrs Mac. that Thos would return to Hamilton by way of Montreal. Spent the evening writing to Thos Anderson, Dumbarton.

Fri. July 22.
Full time in the shop. In the evening Connel, Murray and I visited Robertshaw on Ninth St. and spent a while in his house.

---

52 Built in 1839, the Eleventh Presbyterian Church was located on the corner of Fourth Street and Avenue C in Manhattan. Rev. J. Parsons Hovey, DD (d. 1863), served as pastor of the congregation, 1850–63. During the Civil War, the Eleventh Church moved to a new building on West 55th Street. J. Alexander Patten, 'Our Sunday-School Superintendents,' *Frank Leslie's Sunday Magazine* 16 (July–December 1884): 359.

53 The Mammoth Music Festival was held at Jones's Wood throughout the second week of July 1859. For an admission fee of 25 cents, New Yorkers could enjoy an orchestra, fireworks, Tournoure's Circus, magic shows, balloon ascensions, and dancing. The festival featured a German chorus production as well, and the city's recently arrived German population was largest among its patrons. Jones's Wood was located between Third Avenue and the East River and between 68th and 77th streets. Roy Rosenzweig and Elizabeth Blackmar, *The Park and the People: A History of Central Park* (Ithaca, NY: Cornell University Press, 1992), 235; Edward K. Spann, *The New Metropolis: New York City, 1840–1857* (New York: Columbia University Press, 1983), 165.

Sat. July 23.
Full time in the shop. Connel, Murray and I had a walk down town. Spent a short time in a singing tavern in Chatham St., a pretty rough sort of place.

Sun. July 24.
Fine, cool weather. Took a trip per str 'Geo Law' up the Sound to Glencove. Met Connel there and came home together. Our str upset a boat on the East River, one woman had a narrow escape from drowning.

Mon. July 25.
Full time in the shop. Visited Mechanic's Institute and walked down Broadway in the evening.

Tues. July 26.
Full time at work. Had a walk with Connel down the Bowery in the evening. Weather still mild and pleasant.

Wed. July 27.
Full time at work. Spent the evening smoking and loafing about the stoop in front of the house.

Thurs. July 28.
Full time at work. Went and joined the 'National Musical Institute,' 554 Broadway, in the evening where I expect to learn sight singing.[54]

Fri. July 29.
Full time at work. In the evening Connel, Murray and I went to Niblo's Garden Theatre and saw Mr Burton, a good comic actor, in the 'Serious Family' as 'Toodles.'[55]

---

54 The National Musical Institute opened its doors on Broadway in 1859. A formal school of music, co-directed by Thomas D. Sullivan (ca 1826–63) and Carl Anschütz (1813 or 1815–70). Students could take direction on a variety of instruments or singing and they occasionally offered public concerts. See Vera Brodsky Lawrence, ed., *Strong on Music: The New York Music Scene in the Days of George Templeton Strong* (Chicago: University of Chicago Press, 1999), 3:297; *Prospectus of the National Musical Institute of the City of New York* (New York: The Institute, 1859). On Anschütz, see Diary for 1860, fn 4.

55 'The Serious Family' was a three-act comedy written by Morris Barnett (1800–56), an English music conductor, journalist, and playwright. Barnett's most successful play, it was first performed in 1849. William Evans Burton (1804–60) was an English-born actor who came to the United States in 1834, first to Philadelphia, then New York, where he managed and acted in theatre companies. He was, a biographer noted, 'one of the funniest creatures that ever lived.' James Grant Wilson and John Fiske,

Sat. July 30.
Full time at work. In the evening Connel and I walked down town and
called at Guthrie's.

Sun. July 31.
Went to Grand St. Church but found it closed. After dinner, Connel and
I had a ride per cars up to the 'Central Park' and from there to Manhat-
tanville and into town again per stage along the Bloomingdale Road.

Mon. Aug. 1.
Full time at work. Called on and had a walk with Connel. Met Murray
who got discharged from the Novelty and is now at work over in Jersey
City. Weather fine and cool.

Tues. Aug. 2.
Weather getting warm again. Full time at work. In the evening Fisher
and I went to the singing school and heard some pretty good practicing.

Wed. Aug. 3.
Full time at work. A pretty hot day. In the evening Fisher and I went to
singing class and got started with our lessons.

Thurs. Aug. 4.
Full time at work. Had letters from Mrs Hunter of Thos having left
home on his return here. Called on and had a walk with Connel. Made
purchase of the poems of Crabbe, Heber & Pollock. 50¢.[56]

Fri. Aug. 5.
Full time at work. Some very heavy rain fell to-day. Called at Mr Ren-
frew's in the evening and found him returned from Scotland. Mrs
Logan not yet returned from the country but expected tomorrow.

Sat. Aug. 6.
Full time at work. Had a walk up Broadway in the evening.

Sun. Aug. 7.
A bright warm morning. Started early and walked to Mr Renfrew's but
found the people all at church and Mrs Logan not yet home so came
back and dined in my lodgings. In the afternoon Connel and I crossed to
Guttenburg and had a fine country walk round and in to Hoboken City.

---

eds., *Appleton's Cyclopaedia of American Biography* I (New York: D. Appleton and
Company, 1888), 472–3.

56 *The Poetical Works of Crabbe, Heber, and Pollok* (Philadelphia: Grigg and Elliott, 1839).

Mon. Aug. 8.
Full time at work. Spent the eve'g writing to Bill.

Tues. Aug. 9.
Full time at work. Attended singing class and had a walk round town along with Fisher.

Wed. Aug. 10.
Full time at work and at singing class in the evening.

Thurs. Aug. 11.
Full time at work. Connel called in the eve'g and engaged to come and board in Mrs Smith's, he and I to occupy one large room.

Fri. Aug. 12.
Full time at work. Talk in the shop of work being slack and expect a payoff soon. Called at Mech. Ins. in the eve'g and got 'The Doctor' by Southey.[57]

Sat. Aug. 13.
Full time at work. Heard from Thos in Hamilton. Report of jobs getting scarce in our shop and Harrison the carver, discharged. Called for Connel at Logue's Hotel after tea and found Mrs Murray there seeking her husband. Connel and I went off to Jersey and found him. Saw the arrival of the Richmond Greys a military parade.[58]

Sun. Aug. 14.
Connel and I took steamer to Newark in the forenoon. Very hot day. Had a fine sail and like the appearance of Newark very much. Walked home and attended divine service in Cooper Institute. Connel bad with headache came home with the boat.

---

57 Robert Southey, *The Doctor and c.* 7 vols. (London: Longman, Rees, Orme, Brown, Green and Longmans, 1834–47).

58 Founded in 1844, the Richmond Grays were a militia company in the 1st Regiment, Virginia Volunteers. Along with the 'Blues' and the 'Howitzers,' the Grays were the pride of the citizens of Richmond, ambassadors who marched at civic functions. They helped suppress John Brown's Raid in October 1859; John Wilkes Booth – President Lincoln's assassin – was among the company's members. Their five-day goodwill tour of New York included public marching and inspection, visits to the city's institutions and West Point, receptions, and a banquet hosted by the mayor. 'Visit of the Richmond Grays,' *NYT*, August 15, 16, 1859; 'Civic Banquet to the Richmond Grays,' *NYT*, August 17, 1859; [Jeffrey D. Wert], 'Richmond Blues,' in Patricia L. Faust, ed., *Historical Times Illustrated Encyclopedia of the Civil War* (New York: Harper and Row, 1986), 632.

Mon. Aug. 15.
Full time at work. Had some smart showers of rain. Fisher and I attended singing class in the evening. One of our pattern-makers discharged this morning so am thinking my time is soon coming.

Tues. Aug. 16.
Full time at work. Weather very cool. Connel boarding here to-day. Wrote to Thos in the evening.

Wed. Aug. 17.
Full time at work. Attended singing class in the evening.

Thurs. Aug. 18.
Full time in the shop. In the evening Connel and I went and called on Miss Marshall in 14th st. Weather very fine.

Fri. Aug. 19.
Full time at work. In the evening Connel and I went to the Bowery Theatre and spent the night seeing 'Charles XII of Sweden,' scenes in India, scene from 'Othello,' pantomime, etc. Thought the entertainment passable but audience not at all select.[59]

Sat. Aug. 20.
Full time in the shop. Connel and I called at Guthrie's in the eve.

Sun. Aug. 21.
A beautiful, bright morning. Fisher and I got up and away before breakfast. Had some coffee in a restaurant. Took steamer from Spring Street for Keyport going inside Staten Island. Had a walk around Keyport, gathered some Huckleberries and had a bathe in the sea. Got home alright and heard sermon in the Cooper Institute.

Mon. Aug. 22.
Full time at work. Had a note from Mrs Logan of her having arrived in

---

59 Built in 1826, the [Old] Bowery Theater was originally intended for an upper-class audience but by the end of the 1830s had developed a more plebeian clientele. It was located at 46 Bowery, near Canal Street. Minstrel shows and melodramas were regularly played by travelling troupes, but Bowery audiences reserved their favour for American plays and players, especially Edwin Forrest (see Diary for 1860, fn 90). The Old Bowery burned down four times in the nineteenth century, and was rebuilt every time. After the arrival of New Bowery Theatre (two blocks north) in 1859, its hold on theatrical productions in the city began to slip. Brown, *History of the New York Stage*, 2:189; Sean Wilentz, *Chants Democratic: New York City and the Rise of the American Working Class* (New York: Oxford University Press, 2000), 257–9.

Brooklyn again and started off to see her after tea. Found her well. Mr and Mrs Renfrew insisted on me staying all night which I did.

Tues. Aug. 23.
Had an early walk and ride from Brooklyn back here. Full time in the shop. Report in the shop that our foreman Johnson is left which I rather regret.

Wed. Aug. 24.
Full time at work. In the eve. Fisher and I went to singing class and had a while do, re, mi, fol, fa-ing.

Thurs. Aug. 25.
Full time at work. Work getting slack. Jackson, a Dane, working in the shop, had a quarrel with an Irish boy, an apprentice, and both got discharged. Connel and I had a walk up Broadway to see the new Broadway hotel now open in Madison Square.[60]

Fri. Aug. 26.
Full time in the shop. Mr Cheyne, one of the partners in the firm of Badger & Co. taking charge in our shop now. Expecting to get discharged to-day but did not. Connel and I spent the evening in the 'Melodian' an indifferent place of amusement on Broadway.[61]

Sat. Aug. 27.
Full time at work. In the evening Connel and I called on the Guthrie's and saw Barry there. Bought a writing case to give to Mrs Logan. 3-½$

---

60 Likely the Fifth Avenue Hotel, which opened at the junction of Broadway, Fifth Avenue, and 23rd Street opposite Madison Square Garden, to a good deal of notice in 1859. The hotel was six storeys high with room enough for one thousand guests and the first hotel passenger elevator in the city. George Ripley and Charles Anderson Dana, eds., 'New York (City),' *The American Cyclopedia* (New York: D. Appleton and Company, 1883), 12:383; Thomas Bender, *The Unfinished City: New York and the Metropolitan Idea* (New York: New York University Press, 2007), 39.

61 Founded as Buckley's Music Hall in 1853, the Melodeon Concert Hall (1858–61) was managed by George Lea and was counted among what one scholar has called New York's 'alcohol-dispensing concert saloons.' Located at 539 Broadway, in New York's 'tenderloin' district, it was host to comparatively 'low' cultural entertainment, including blackface minstrel shows, dancing performances, and comic singing. See Lawrence, ed. *Strong on Music*, 3:466; Ruth Crosby Dimmick, *Our Theatres To-Day and Yesterday* (New York: The H.K. Fly Company, 1913), 38; Stephen Jenkins, *The Greatest Street in the World: The Story of Broadway* (New York: G.P. Putnam's Sons, 1911), 211.

Sun. Aug. 28.
Spent the forenoon in the house and after dinner went to Mr Renfrew's and spent the remainder of day there. Having a walk with Marg't. Saw a most splendid Aurora Borealis in the sky between 9 and 10 as I was coming away from home in the evening. Weather too got wondrous cold.

Mon. Aug. 29.
Full time in the shop. Weather almost cold. Connel and I moved in to a larger room on the top flat and think our circumstances improved thereby.

Tues. Aug. 30.
Beautiful cool weather. Full time at work. Spent all the evening reading, etc. in our new room which I am going to like well. Only a little, or should I say, considerable with musquitoes, bedbugs cockroaches, etc.

Wed. Aug. 31.
Full time at work. Fisher and I attending singing class in the evening.

Thurs. Sept. 1.
Full time at work. In the evening Connel and I called and spent a while in John Robertshaw's.

Fri. Sept. 2.
Still beautiful bright clear weather. Full time in the shop although jobs are getting pretty well through. My friend Fisher discharged to-day. Had a letter from Thos but no prospect of work in Canada as yet.

Sat. Sept. 3.
Full time at work. Mrs Logan called for me at Smith's about six. Walked down Broadway with her and spent a while in Guthrie's where she was to stay for the night.

Sun. Sept. 4.
Went to Guthrie's immediately after breakfast. Weather fine. Mrs L. and I took the ferry boat to Hoboken and from there had a fine walk back and along the heights to Wuhawken. Took ferry from there to 42nd St. And down to Guthrie's per cars. After seeing her off, attended Universalist Church in Broadway.[62]

---

62 In 1859, the Fourth Universalist Church was located on Broadway near Spring
   Street. The pastor of the church was Rev. Edwin Hubbell Chapin, DD (1814–89),

Mon. Sept. 5.

Went to work in the morning and worked quarter day. When my job being done, went off for a stroll round town and spent the day mostly among book stores about Fulton St. Bought 'Byron' and Pilgrim's Progress. Mosquitoes awfully troublesome in the evening.[63]

Tues. Sept. 6.

Full time in the shop. In the evening Connel and I called on Miss Marshall in 14th St.

Wed. Sept. 7.

Full time at work. Attended singing class in the evening. Walked down town and saw two pair of live humming birds in glass cages in the window of Taylor's Saloon, prices respectively 25$ and 20$.

Thurs. Sept. 8.

Full time at work. Patching up old patterns all the time just now. Little else being done in the shop. Weather beautiful and cool. Attended singing class in the eve. Had a letter from Miss Goldie.

Fri. Sept. 9.

Full time in the shop. In the evening went to Brooklyn and saw Mrs Logan, getting home by way of Green Point cars and ferry past 11 o'clock.

Sat. Sept. 10.

Full time in the shop. Had letters from home in the evening. Connel and I had a walk down the Bowery and spent a short time in the 'New York Stadt' theatre hearing performance in German.[64]

---

who rose to considerable fame as a speaker, theologian, editor, and religious writer in Victorian New York. After pastorates in Richmond, Virginia, and Charlestown, Massachusetts, Chapin accepted a call to the New York's Fourth Universalist Society in 1848, a position that he held for the remainder of his life. In part because of Dr Chapin's growing following, Fourth Universalist was forced to move to a new site at Fifth Avenue and 45th Street in 1866. As a preacher, Chapin was 'ripe, scholarly and elegant.' Rossiter Johnson, ed., *The Twentieth Century Biographical Dictionary of Notable Americans* (Boston: The Biographical Society, 1904), 2:np; 'The Late Dr. Chapin,' *The Sunday Magazine* 9, January–June 1881 (New York: Frank Leslie's Publishing House, 1881), 368–71.

63 McIlwraith purchased one of the countless editions of Bunyan's classic Christian allegorical tale, first published in 1678 – perhaps John Bunyan, *The Pilgrim's Progress, from This World to That Which Is to Come* (New York: H. Dayton, 1859); likely Thomas Moore, *Life of Lord Byron, with His Letters and Journals* (London: John Murray, 1851).

64 The (old) Stadt Theater Company was created in 1854 by Otto Hoym at the site of the old Amphitheater, 37–39 Bowery. The Stadt produced a repertory of German

Sun. Sept. 11.
Spent the forenoon reading and loafing in the house and after dinner, sailed up the East River to Harlam, walking part of the way home. Attended church in the Cooper Institute in the evening.

Mon. Sept. 12.
Full time at work. Spent the evening mostly writing to Mother.

Tues. Sept. 13.
Full time in the shop. Spent the evening writing home.

Wed. Sept. 14.
Full time at work. Attended singing class in the evening which gets along pretty well. Mr Sullivan, our teacher, promises a prize of 2$ to the pupil who gives in the best thesis of the month's lessons at the end of the month.

Thurs. Sept. 15.
Full time at work. Caledonian Club festival takes place at Jones' Wood to-day. Connel off there. Weather very cold. Pity the Kilties there. Saw them walk down Broadway in the evening. Connel and I went to Laura Keene's Theatre and saw Laura in a play of Tom Taylor's, 'The World and the Stage.'[65]

Fri. Sept. 16.
Cold, foggy weather. Full time in the shop. A new foreman, the brother of Mr Cherry, partner in the firm of Badger & Co. entered into office to-day. Connel is off work with machinery being stopped in the Novelty. Purchased a large gun at an auction down town.

---

operas, comedies, and classics. The company moved to the New Stadt Theater (43–47 Bowery) in 1864 but went bankrupt in 1872. Don B. Wilmeth, ed., *The Cambridge Guide to American Theatre*, 2nd ed. (New York: Cambridge University Press, 2007), 616; Frederick Herman Adolph Leuchs, *Early German Theatre in New York, 1840–1872* (New York: Columbia University Press, 1928), 74.

65 'The World and the Stage' was a three-act comedy written, actually, by prolific English dramatist and novelist John Palgrave Simpson (1807–87) and first produced in England in March 1859. Over his thirty-three years of playwriting, he produced sixty dramatic pieces. Tom Taylor (1817–80) was also an English dramatist and littérateur whose many plays ran on Broadway stages in the 1850s. 'Simpson, John Palgrave' in Sidney Lee, ed., *Dictionary of National Biography* (New York: Macmillan Company, 1897), 52:274–5; Thompson Cooper, 'Tom Taylor, Dramatist and Critic,' in *Men of Mark: A Gallery of Contemporary Portraits*, 5th series (London: Sampson Low, Marston, Searle and Rivington, 1881), 23.

Sat. Sept. 17.
Full time in the shop. Murdoch from Newburgh came home with Connel to tea, he having engaged to go to Cuba with engine and sugar mill which he had been at work upon. Evening very wet so did not go up town.

Sun. Sept. 18.
Weather brightening up a little again. Walked down to the docks on the East River along with Murdock to see the vessel and machinery that he was going away with. In the afternoon visited Mrs Logan and went to hear Beecher preach his evening sermon.

Mon. Sept. 19.
Full time at work. Jobs going on rather brisker with the new foreman. Went to singing class in the evening.

Tues. Sept. 20.
Full time at work. Spent the evening in the house with Murdoch and Connel.

Wed. Sept. 21
Full time in the shop. Weather miserably wet. In the evening Murdoch, Connel and I went to the 'Winter Garden' Theatre and saw the play of 'Dot' being Dicken's tale of the 'Cricket on the Hearth' dramatized and were much pleased with it.[66]

Thurs. Sept. 22.
Full time at work. Weather still awfully wet. Wrote to McGarva in the evening.

Fri. Sept. 23.
Full time at work. Kept to the house in the evening with Murdoch and Connel.

---

66 Known until September 1859 as the Metropolitan Theatre, it was refitted and renamed the Winter Garden in that year when playwright Dion Boucicault and William Stuart leased the building. The theatre stood on the west side of Broadway opposite the end of Bond Street. One contemporary called 'Dot' (Boucicault's adaptation) 'clever and successful.' The *Times* called it 'an admirable version of ... "Cricket on the Hearth," acted by a company of the first class.' Laurence Hutton, *Plays and Players* (New York: Hurd and Houghton, 1875), 191–3; 'Amusements,' *NYT*, September 19, 1859; Charles Dickens, *The Cricket on the Hearth: A Fairy Tale of Home* (New York: Harper and Brothers, 1846).

Sat. Sept. 24.
Full time in the shop. In the evening Murdoch, Connel and I attended Niblo's Garden Theatre and saw a pantomime, tight rope, dancing, etc.

Sun. Sept. 25.
Still showery although not so constantly wet. Attended Grand St. Church in the afternoon and heard Dr Dill from Ireland on the subject of the recent Irish revivals.[67] Spent the evening with Mrs Logan in Brooklyn.

Mon. Sept. 26.
Full time in the shop. At singing class in the evening and had a pretty good practice in sol-fa-ing from Mr Sulivan, the conductor. Commenced the winter arrangement of time to-day taking ½ hr to dinner and quitting at 5.30 p.m.

Tues. Sept. 27.
Took good-bye of Murdoch in the morning who expects to sail during the night. Full time in the shop.

Wed. Sept. 28.
Full time at work. In the evening spent a while writing to Jameson when Murdoch came in. His vessel the schooner 'Sarah Sears' not yet having set sail. Slept with me for the night and went off in the morning.

Thurs. Sept. 29.
Full time in the shop. Attended singing class in the evening.

Fri. Sept. 30.
Full time in the shop. In the evening travelled out to Bedford Ave and accompanied Mrs Logan to church. Heard Mr West preaching.[68]

---

67 Rev. Samuel Marcus Dill, DD (1811–70) was, from 1853, pastor at Ballymena Presbyterian Church in the west of Ireland and, after 1866, professor of theology at Magee College, Derry. Along with Rev. John Edgar of Belfast and Rev. David Wilson of Limerick, Dill was part of a delegation to North America in 1859 to report on the ongoing evangelical revivals in Ireland and to raise funds for the Presbyterian Home Mission. 'The Revival in Ireland … Sermons by the Rev. Dr. Dill,' *NYT*, September 26, 1859; W.T. Latimer, 'The Twelve Dills,' *The Witness* (Belfast), June 20 and July 4, 1902; transcribed at http://freepages.genealogy.rootsweb.ancestry.com/~dill/TheTwelve-Dills.pdf (accessed February 9, 2009).

68 The East Reformed Dutch Church was founded at Bedford Avenue near Jefferson Street in Brooklyn in 1853. Rev. Jacob West (1818–90) became the pastor in 1856 and served in that capacity until 1868. Henry Reed Stiles, *A History of the City of Brooklyn* (Brooklyn: By subscription, 1870), 645; na, *A History of the Classis of Paramus of the Reformed Church* (New York: The Board of Publication R.C.A., 1902), 421–2.

Sat. Oct. 1.
Full time in the shop. Connel and I visited Guthrie's in the evening.
Walked home by way of the Bowery.

Sun. Oct. 2.
Spent the forenoon in the house reading, etc. After dinner Connel and I
crossed the ferry to Green Point and walked right away up to Astoria.
Had a view of Hellgate. Crossed the river to New York and walked
down home. Sat in the house and read one of Spurgeon's sermons in
the evening.[69]

Mon. Oct. 3.
Full time at work. At singing class in the evening and had a good night's
practicing. Carter there. He and I walked home together.

Tues. Oct. 4.
Full time in the shop. Weather bright and warm. Thermometer as high
as 87 deg. Gowery from Newburgh called in the evening. Accompanied
him to the theatre and saw the 'Sea of Ice' in Laura Keenes.[70]

Wed. Oct. 5.
Full time at work. Kept the house in the evening reading Crabbes 'Tales
of the Hall,' etc.[71]

Thurs. Oct. 6.
Full time in the shop. Attended singing class in the evening.

Fri. Oct. 7.
Full time at work. In the evening proceeded to Brooklyn and saw
Marg't. Had a letter from Thos which I took out and left with her. Met
with Mr Ambrose Dale and Mr Alex Hosie in Mr Renfrew's. Left 100$
as a loan to Mr Renfrew for which he promises interest 8 per cent.

Sat. Oct. 8.
Full time in the shop. Spent the whole evening in the Palace Garden,

---

69 Charles Haddon Spurgeon, *Sermons* (New York: Funk, 1857).

70 Adolphe Philippe D'Ennery and Ferdinand Dugué, *The Sea of Ice: Or, A Search for
    Gold, and the Wild Flower of Mexico* (New York: S. French, nd). The play was an Eng-
    lish version of a five-act French melodrama, *La Prière des Naufragés*. The play was
    introduced to New York theatre by Laura Keeene's company in 1858; it became
    popular quickly and was repeated. Creahan, *Life of Laura Keene*, 21; Laurence Hutton,
    Plays and Players (Charleston, SC: BiblioBazar, 2008), 102.

71 Rev. George Crabbe, *Tales of the Hall* (Boston: Wells and Lilly, 1819).

14th St. where the Fair of the American Institute is now being held.[72] Was well pleased with it. Got wet on the way home.

Sun. Oct. 9.
Attended Grand St. Church. Got a seat there from Mr McLellan, a friend of Connel's. A lady who I knew in the Kangaroo Str sat in the same pew. Weather wet in the afternoon. Kept the house all the day.

Mon. Oct. 10.
Full time at work. Weather wet and cold. Went down to Grand St. Church and took a sitting in the evening and afterwards went to singing class.

Thurs. Oct. 11.
Full time at work. Spent the evening writing home to Mr Stewart. Between 10 and 11, went up to post my letter in Station 'D' post office and saw an immense procession of the Society of the Sons of Malta, members all dressed alternately in black and white robes, officers cap-a-pie.[73]

---

72 Organized in 1829, the American Institute was a voluntary organization of manufacturers, artisans, and others convened for the purpose of encouraging scientific and philosophical study, invention, and the promotion of domestic industry. In New York, the Institute held annual fairs at which were demonstrated the products of American manufacturers and other scientific, agricultural, and horticultural exhibits. The Palace Garden was located on 14th Street near Sixth Avenue, a site that was first used for the fair in 1859, to the disappointment of Institute officers. The 1859 fair was a bust and sustained 'heavy losses' financially in part because the venue did not suit the fair's size. The Board of Managers' report in 1860 indicates that it, unlike McIlwraith, was not 'well pleased.' Wilson, *Memorial History*, 4:435; 'Report of the Board of Managers of the Thirty-Second Annual Fair of the American Institute,' in *Transactions of the American Institute of the City of New York for the Years 1860–61* (Albany: C. VanBenthuysen, 1861), 25; 'American Institute Exhibition,' *NYT*, October 10, 1859; 'The American Institute Fair,' *NYT*, October 14, 1859.

73 The Sons of Malta was a short-lived, national (but largely urban) antebellum secret society organized in 1856 by A.G. Barnett and Morton Taylor. The group was characterized by elaborate ceremony and dress and a simple, two-part purpose: fun and charity. Their beneficence was checked by their ridiculous rites of initiation, which were exposed by New York publisher Frank Leslie in 1860. Embarrassed, the association collapsed by the onset of the Civil War. The New York State lodge was incorporated on July 1, 1859, with 12,680 members. The procession that McIlwraith saw was the 'Festival of the Seven Cardinals,' in which about 500 Sons, 'clad in armor, with vari-colored robes and plumage,' paraded from their lodge on 814 Broadway to Union Square before retiring to the Malta Saloon for a private dinner. A large crowd assembled along the route greeting them with 'cheers, jeers and shouts.' Cap-a-pie

Wed. Oct. 12.
Full time in the shop. Spent the evening visiting Mrs Logan at Brooklyn. I walked both away and back and felt very tired. Connel informs me my Kangaroo acquaintance sails today per str for England.

Thurs. Oct. 13.
Full time in the shop. Went to singing class in the evening but found it closed, the gas being off.

Fri. Oct. 14.
Full time in the shop. Spent the evening in the house being rather tired with so much evening travelling during the week. Mosquitoes quite troublesome in the room yet.

Sat. Oct. 15.
Full time at work. In the evening Connel and I went down to Wallack's Theatre and saw Bulwer Lytton's play of 'Money' pretty well done.[74]

Sun. Oct. 16.
A fine bright morning. Left the house before breakfast and got the morning boat up the Hudson to Peakskill. Landed there and decided to walk along the river bank to Cold Spring, 12 miles. Enjoyed the walk very much. Got in to Cold Spring about 5 p.m. and took up our quarters in the 'Alhambra' tavern, a very clean tidy place and a little black-eyed girl, daughter to the landlord.

---

means 'from head to foot.' Albert Clark Stevens, *The Cyclopedia of Fraternities*, 2nd ed. (New York: E.B. Treat and Company, 1907), 284; *Historical and Statistical Gazetteer of New York State*, 7th ed. (Syracuse: R.P. Smith, 1860), 148; *Notes and Queries* (Manchester, NH: S.C. Gould, 1905), 23:96; [Frank Leslie], *The Sons of Malta Exposed ... By One Who Was 'Sold'* (New York: Published by the Author, 1860); 'Masquerade of the Sons of Malta,' *NYT*, October 12, 1859.

74 Edward George Earle Lytton Bulwer-Lytton, *Money: A Comedy in Five Acts* (London: Saunders and Otley, 1840). The theatre was formally called Wallack's Lyceum. Built in 1850 on Broadway at Broome Street (and originally called Brougham's Lyceum), it was managed by J.W. Wallack (1795–1864) from 1852 until 1861, when a new Wallack's Theatre was constructed on Broadway at 13th Street. Throughout the 1850s, Wallack's was among the New York theatres most popular among the middle class, offering a succession of largely English 'manners and romantic comedies' that aimed (in Wallack's words) 'to delight with laughter, not move to tears.' Don B. Wilmeth and Christopher Bigsby, eds., *The Cambridge History of American Theatre* (New York: Cambridge University Press, 1998), 1:202; Martin Banham, *The Cambridge Guide to Theatre* (New York: Cambridge University Press, 1995), 1183; 'Wallack, James William,' in Rossiter Johnson, ed., *The Twentieth Century Biographical Dictionary of Notable Americans* (Boston: The Biographical Society, 1904), 10:np.

Mon. Oct. 17.
Still fine, bright, frosty weather. Had breakfast early along with the landlord, his wife and daughter. Visited West Point foundry and saw a young man, Glen, at one time in Gartshore's. Then made the ascent of 'Bull's Hill' and had a fine high broad prospect. Was disappointed in getting a forenoon train home so walked on to Newburgh, 6 miles, and saw Gourie. Took passage home per barge leaving at 9 at night.

Tues. Oct. 18.
Got up on deck about 5 a.m. and found our barge passing the upper part of the city. Got home in time for breakfast and work. Had full time. Day come on very wet. Yesterday had been pretty much a holliday on acct of the great triennial procession of all the fire companies.[75]

Wed. Oct. 19.
Full time at work. Spending the evening rather idly and lazily.

Thurs. Oct. 20.
Full time in the shop. Attended singing class in the evening and had a good nights on practicing on seconds and thirds.

Fri. Oct. 21.
Weather quite cold and wintry. Full time at work. Spent the evening idling in the house which begins to feel rather cold and comfortless and in want of a fire.

Sat. Oct. 22.
Full time in the shop. Called at Guthrie's in the evening.

Sun. Oct. 23.
Attended Grand St. Church in the forenoon taking possession of my new sitting in the gallery. After dinner went out to Mr Renfrew's and spent the afternoon there. Mr Syme and I went to Beecher's Church but could not get in.

---

75 Lined up by companies, six thousand firemen marchers were led by a magnificent blue silk banner and were greeted, one contemporary noted, 'with shouts of recognition … and waving of handkerchiefs from the ladies and children.' The parade was a singular public spectacle. One hook and ladder company had a frightened black bear chained to the roof of its truck; another had a fox similarly 'attached.' New steam fire engines were paraded as well, harnessed to horses for mobility. J. Frank Kernan, *Reminiscences of the Old Fire Laddies and Volunteer Fire Departments of New York and Brooklyn* (New York: M. Crane, 1885), 291; 'The Firemen's Parade,' *NYT*, October 17, 18, 1859.

Mon. Oct. 24.
Felt a little sick in the morning and did not go to work until 9.30. Spent the evening writing to Mary Goldie.

Tues. Oct. 25.
Full time in the shop. In the evening Connel and I called upon and spent the evening in Mr McLellan's, Lithographer, in North Moore St. talking of scheming a steam lithograph press.[76] Quite a snow storm in the evening. Some inch or so lying on the street on our way home.

Wed. Oct. 26.
Still cold blustering weather with snow. Full time in the shop. In the evening went over to Brooklyn and saw Mr Syme and Mr Hosie from Detroit. Visited the Brooklyn Reading Room.[77]

Thurs. Oct. 27.
Full time in the shop. Attended singing class in the evening and had a good night's practicing.

Fri. Oct. 28.
Full time at work. Spent the evening visiting Mr McLellan's litho-

---

76 James McLellan, Jr (1828–60) came from a family of Scottish lithographers. He was younger brother (by three years) of the more widely known lithographer David McLellan (b. 1825) and son to James McLellan, Sr, a lithographer who must have taught his sons the trade. All three were working in New York City by the 1850s, James and David having immigrated as early as 1847, soon after forming the partnership 'D and J McLellan.' They established 'an enviable reputation for business energy and integrity.' James McLellan, Jr died suddenly in spring 1860; see Diary for 1860, May 31. Steam power lithography was first employed in lithography in Philadelphia in 1850, but not widely outside of that city until the 1870s. George Cuthbert Groce and David H. Wallace, eds., *Dictionary of Artists in America, 1564–1860* (New Haven, CT: Yale University Press, 1957), 417; William Young, *A Dictionary of American Artists, Sculptors and Engravers* (np: W. Young, 1968), 311; Peter Ross, *The Book of Scotia Lodge* (New York: Raeburn Book Company, 1895), 53; John William Reps, *Views and Viewmakers of Urban America: Lithographs of Towns and Cities in the United States and Canada ... 1825–1925* (Columbia: University of Missouri Press, 1984), 33.

77 Located at the corner of Atlantic and Clinton streets, the Brooklyn Athenaeum and Reading Room was incorporated in January 1852, and opened its newly constructed building to the public in April 1853. The Athenaeum was a three-storey building that housed both the reading room and a hall for lectures, concerts, debates, and classes. The Athenaeum's collections were merged with those of the Mercantile Library Association of Brooklyn in 1858, and by 1859 patrons of the reading room could select from among 11,400 volumes. Henry R. Stiles, *A History of the City of Brooklyn* (Brooklyn: by Subscription, 1870), 3:899–901; William Jones Rhees, *Manual of Public Libraries, Institutions and Societies in the United States and British Provinces of North America* (Philadelphia: J.B. Lippincott and Co., 1859), 238–9; 'Brooklyn City,' *NYT*, April 21, 1853.

graphic establishment getting a view of the presses and having the process explained.

Sat. Oct. 29.
Full time at work. Spent the evening in the Palace Garden, viewing the Fair of the American Institute, this being the closing night. Got a fire set a-going in our room in the evening after much ado.

Sun. Oct. 30.
Went to Grand St. Church in the morning. Spent the afternoon in Brooklyn with Mrs Logan.

Mon. Oct. 31.
Full time at work. In the evening attended singing class. Had some Hickory nuts because it was Hallowe'en.[78]

Tues. Nov. 1.
Full time in the shop. In the evening began to draw some on the Lithographic press but found difficulties at every step.

Wed. Nov. 2.
Full time in the shop. Sat puzzling my head with the lithographic business for a while then wrote to Thos, it being a long time since I have done it. Connel's sister from Holioake came to visit him to-day.

Thurs. Nov. 3.
Beautiful bright, cool weather. Full time at work. Had a short note from Thos to know what was up with my not writing. Attended singing in the evening.

Fri. Nov. 4.
Full time in the shop. Spent the evening in the house studying and scheming the lithographic machine.

Sat. Nov. 5.
Full time at work. In the evening walked down to Laight Street and called on Guthrie's people. Found that Mrs G. had given birth to a son on the Sunday previous.

---

78 In Britain, Hallowe'en was called in many places Nutcracker (or Nut-Crack) Night, where nuts were used to foretell the future before they were eaten. Hickory nuts were put in a fire and watched; if they burned quietly, their owner could expect a happy courtship and marriage; if they flew apart, trouble was ahead. Alvin Boyd Kuhn, *Halloween: A Festival of Lost Meanings* (Pasadena, CA: Theosophical Press, 1966), 19–20; Robert Haven Schauffler, *Hallowe'en: Its Origin, Spirit, Celebration and Significance as Related in Prose and Verse* (New York: Dodd, Mead, 1961), 95.

Sun. Nov. 6.

Get late for the Grand St. Church and so went in to Dr Bellow's on Fourth Avenue and heard that gent.[79] After dinner went to Brooklyn and spent the afternoon with Marg't. Met Mr Hosie. Mrs L, he and I attended Beecher's Church Mr H. providing us with a seat. Heard a good discourse from Mr B.

Mon. Nov. 7.

Full time in the shop. When getting paid in the evening, Mr Cherry told me I would have to lie off for a time as the work was getting slack. Felt kind of sick and aguish.

Tues. Nov. 8.

Called and asked a job in the Novelty Works. Had a ramble down town. Election of State officers, etc. takes place to-day but City unusually quiet. Spent an hour or two in the afternoon in the Astor Library[80] looking thro' Wilson's American Ornithology[81] – original edition with colored plates. Took an emetic in the evening to try and clear off bile.[82]

Wed. Nov. 9

Kept the house mostly during the day and made some sketches for lith-

---

79 Dr Bellows's church was the Unitarian Church of All Souls located on Fourth Avenue at the corner of 20th Street. The church was built in an eccentric style, with alternating brick and cream-coloured stone, which caused contemporaries to nickname it 'Church of the Holy Zebra.' Henry Whitney Bellows (1814–82) served as pastor for forty-three years beginning in 1839. He was editor of the *Christian Inquirer* newspaper and an originator of the United States Sanitary Commission: an intellectual and social leader in his time. Benson J. Lossing, *History of New York City* (New York: Perine Engraving and Publishing Company, 1884), 2:729; *Memorial Biographies of the New England Historic Genealogical Society*, vol. 8: *1880–1889* (Boston: The Society, 1907), 88–9.

80 The Astor Library was created in 1849 due to the generosity of the late New York merchant John Jacob Astor (1763–1848), who willed $400,000 for the establishment of a free public library in the city. The library was constructed at Lafayette Place and opened its doors in 1854 with shelving sufficient for 100,000 volumes. It was merged with two other bodies in 1895 to form the modern New York Public Library. Wilson, *Memorial History*, 3:436; Edward Edwards, *Memoirs of Libraries* (London: Trubner and Company, 1859), 700, 702.

81 Alexander Wilson, *American Ornithology; or, the Natural History of Birds of the United States*, 9 vols. (Philadelphia: Bradford and Inskeep, 1807–14).

82 Commonly used emetics (to induce vomiting) in the mid-nineteenth century included tartar emetic (antimony potassium tartrate – a poisonous crystalline salt with a sweet, metallic taste) and ipecacuanha (a syrup made from the root of a South American shrub). John Harley Warner, *The Therapeutic Perspective: Medical Practice, Knowledge and Identity in America, 1820–1885* (Cambridge, MA: Harvard University Press, 1986), 92.

ograph press. Connel and I called at James McLellan's, North Moore St. in the eve'g. Met Miss Connel and Miss McLellan there.

Thurs. Nov. 10.
Called on Mr Jones at the Novelty Works and learned that there would be no opening with him at present. From there to call on Barry in 29th St. and round thro' a number of shops but unsuccessful in getting a job. Made acquaintance with Messrs McFarlane and Spittal in Anderson and McLaren's shop.[83]

Fri. Nov. 11.
Walked down Broadway and made the ascent of Trinity steeple in the highest viewing station inside.[84] In the afternoon went to Brooklyn to Mr Renfrew's but found the door locked. Came down town and tried some shops. Spent the evening with Messrs Hosie and Syme learning to play whist.

Sat. Nov. 12.
Walked down the Bowery and round town generally. Called for a Mr Diack, an acquaintance of Mr Hosie's at Hoe's Foundry. Connel and I visited the printing office of the New York Ledger where A. Guthrie is now engineer.[85]

---

83 James Anderson and John McLaren operated a metal shop in mid-century New York, where they invented, improved, and produced machines for industrial production. They are listed as 'machinists' in the 1862 *Trow's New York City Directory 1862* (New York: J.F. Trow, 1862). As early as 1857, they (along with John Bryant) published one of their patented innovations in Philadelphia's *Journal of the Franklin Institute*, an 'Improved Lathe for Cutting Fluted Mouldings,' *Journal of the Franklin Institute*, series 3, vol. 33 (Philadelphia: Pergamon Press, 1857): 33.

84 Located on Broadway at Wall Street, Trinity Episcopal Church is among New York's oldest congregations. The original structure (built in 1698) was consumed by fire in 1776; a second church built on this site in 1790 was damaged beyond repair by heavy snow in 1839. Opened in 1846, the third Trinity was designed by architect Richard Upjohn (1802–78) in a classic Gothic design marked by its slender front and impressive 281-foot spire, the highest built point in the city until 1890. One contemporary advised tourists to climb the heights and see this 'really beautiful prospect ... the view stretches for miles, a wilderness of roofs and steeples.' 'A Glimpse from Trinity Steeple,' *Appleton's Journal of Literature, Science and Art* (New York: D. Appleton and Company, 1872), 7:659; Burrows and Wallace, *Gotham*, 104, 937; Morgan Dix, ed. and comp., *A History of the Parish of Trinity Church in the City of New York*, 2 vols. (New York: G.P. Putnam's Sons, 1898).

85 R. Hoe and Company was one of New York's largest and best-known mid-century industrial establishments, a manufacturer of saws and, especially, printing presses that supplied newspaper publishers across the country. Founded in 1819 by Robert Hoe, Sr (1784–1833), by the 1850s that company had grown to a large campus of

Sun. Nov. 13.
Attended Grand St. Church in the forenoon. Got wet coming home. Called at Guthrie's in the afternoon and heard that there was prospect of a job with Barry. Had tea in Guthrie's.

Mon. Nov. 14.
Fine bright, cool weather. Walked down Broadway and saw a [illeg] with a fire and engines all turned. Called out at Quincy St. and had dinner with Mrs Renfrew and Mrs Logan. Met with Mrs Dale there. In the afternoon Mr Hosie and I started to visit an acquaintance of his at the Globe Foundry, 33rd St. a Mr Patterson, and had tea with him.[86]

Tues. Nov. 15.
Learned that Barry had been calling for me the night previous so went over to his place and got fixed up to start work there tomorrow. Had a visit from Thos McDonald and A. Glenn, old Dundas men, in the evening. Had my tool chest moved over to 27th St.

Wed. Nov. 16.
Walked over to 27th St. and started work at 7 am. Very tired with walking so far in the evening. My mate at patterns in the shop an Englishman named RobJohn. An old Scotchman named Harper also at work.

Thurs. Nov. 17.
Full time in the shop. At singing class in the evening.

Fri. Nov. 18.
Full time in the shop. At casing pattern. In the evening wrote to Thos.

---

workshops and warehouses on Broome, Sheriff, and Columbia streets, where four hundred operatives were employed in fifteen separate departments. The founder's sons, Richard M. Hoe (1812–86) and Robert Hoe, Jr (1815–84), ran the company in the 1850s and kept it competitive by inventing, introducing, and patenting new machines, including the rotary press. The company passed from Hoe family hands in 1924. 'Manufacturing. R. Hoe and Co.'s Establishment,' *NYT*, October 19, 1855; Frank E. Comparato, *R. Hoe and Company and the Printing Press as a Service to Democracy* (Culver City, CA: Labyrinthos, ca 1979).

86 The Globe Iron Works was among New York's largest and earliest metal works in mid-century. Located on 33rd Street near Eleventh Avenue, the Globe produced railcar wheels and castings, frogs and switches, and 'other Iron Work for Railroad Superstructure.' The company was founded by Amos Cheney White (ca 1777–1852); by 1860 it was owned by Moores M. White. By the end of the century, the foundry had moved to 556 West 34th Street and operated under the name White Manufacturing Company. Henry V. Poor, *History of the Railroads and Canals of the United States* (New York: John H. Schultz and Co., 1860), 1:629; *Directory to the Iron and Steel Works of the United States* (Philadelphia: American Iron and Steel Association, 1894), 254.

Sat. Nov. 19.
Full time at work. Got quit at half past four. Spent the evening in the house reading Miss Bremer's Tales.[87]

Sun. Nov. 20.
Spent the forenoon in the house reading. After dinner went off to Brooklyn. At Mr Renfrew's, met and drank tea with Mr Cochrane from Hamilton. Had a walk with Wm Syme.

Mon. Nov. 21.
Full time in the shop. Still at casing pattern. Spent the evening writing home to Christina. A very wet night.

Tues. Nov. 22.
Full time at work. At 2 in pipe patterns. Connel and I went to the theatre in the eve'g and saw a 'Wife's Secret,' Miss Laura Keane taking the leading lady character.[88]

Wed. Nov. 23.
Full time at pipe patterns. Robjohn and I called at one or two boarding houses but did not find any to please us. Went out to Brooklyn in the evening. Had a long letter from Thos enclosing one from Mary Goldie.

Thurs. Nov. 24.
Thanksgiving Day in New York, and a general holiday but went to work as usual, our work being in a hurry. Still at pipes. Connel off shooting up the East River. Very tired and went to bed early.

Fri. Nov. 25.
Full time at pipes. Had a regular tour in search of a boarding house and at last engaged quarters at 189 Tenth Ave. with one Mrs Fury.

Sat. Nov. 26.
Full time at pipes. Had chest packed up and despatched to Tenth Ave. Had aguish symptoms in the evening. Had a long letter from Bill, also a paper.

---

87 Fredrika Bremer, *Tales of Every-day Life in Sweden* (Boston: J. Munroe and Co., 1843).

88 His most famous play, British playwright George W. Lovell's five-act Spanish romance *The Wife's Secret* first ran at the Park Theatre in New York in 1846 and was revived at Laura Keene's Theater for a run beginning November 9, 1859. 'Lovell, George William' *Dictionary of National Biography* (New York: The Macmillan Company, 1909), 12:17; William G.B. Carson, ed., *Letters of Mr and Mrs Charles Kean – Relating to Their American Tours* (np: Leffmann Press, 2007), 76.

Sun. Nov. 27.

I woke up this morning and found two Irishmen occupying beds in the same room with me and at breakfast that the co. were all do. Spent the forenoon reading and in the afternoon visited Mrs Logan. Mr Robt Hosie there.

Mon. Nov. 28.

All day at pipes. Walked down to 13th St. and called on Mr Spittal and spent an hour or so with him and thence to the singing class but was late for it.

Tues. Nov. 29.

At slide valve pattern. Went down to Guthrie's in Laight St. in the evening.

Wed. Nov. 30.

Full time at work on cross head. Met Messrs Robt and Alex'r Hosie at Mr Patterson's, 316 35th St. and spent the evening there.

Thurs. Dec. 1.

Full time at Cross head patt'n. Went to singing in the evening. Mr Rob-John and I went and engaged boarding with Mrs Skinner, 341 Eighth Ave. Called upon Miss Marshall in Gideon Pott's, 14th St.

Fri. Dec. 2.

Full time at work on Cross head. Attended a lecture by Bayard Taylor on 'Humboldt' in the large hall of the Cooper Institute in the evening and afterward spent a while in the free reading room in the same building.[89]

Sat. Dec. 3.

Full time in the shop at Cross head pattern. Drove down town immediately on quitting work to try and see Mr Hutchison in Beaver St. but was late. Came round by Tenth St. and brought away some clothes and then got my valise brought away from Mrs Furey's in the Tenth Ave. to

---

89 Bayard Taylor (1825–78) was a celebrated American journalist, critic, novelist, poet, translator, and travel writer. Among his many publications was an introduction to a biography of Alexander von Humboldt, which appeared in print in 1860, not long after McIlwraith saw Taylor hold forth on his subject at the Cooper Institute. Inez N. McFee, 'Bayard Taylor, 1825–1878,' in *Studies in American and British Literature* (Chicago: A. Flanagan Company, 1905), 323–28; Richard Henry Stoddard, *The Life, Travels and Books of Alexander von Humboldt, with an Introduction by Bayard Taylor* (New York: Rudd and Carleton, 1859).

Mrs Skinner's in the Eighth. Spent a short time in a political meeting in the Cooper Institute.

Sun. Dec. 4.
Weather wet and stormy with occasional hail showers. Streets awfully sloppy with stayhail. Spent the forenoon reading in Mrs Skinner's sitting room. RobJohn and I went to Grand St. Church in the afternoon and in the evening heard a lecture on the history of the English Bible in a Presbyterian Church in 9th Ave.[90]

Mon. Dec. 5.
All day at Cross head. Went to singing class in the evening, also made a trip to Brooklyn and got my watch from the watchmaker.

Tues. Dec. 6.
All day at large Pillow block for Beam engine. Went over to my old boarding house in the evening and brought away my books, Connel having got a mate in to the room which he and I used to occupy. Spent a while with Mr Blocktone and got inspecting his bed, a very ingenious piece of mechanism.

Wed. Dec. 7.
All day on Block. Weather dismally wet. Yesterday being election day, it is this morning made public that Fernando Wood is elected Mayor of the City. Think it is a pity the atrocious rascal has gained the day.[91] In the evening went and made purchases of a lot of things I required. Wrote to Thomas.

---

90 Likely North Presbyterian Church, 374 Ninth Avenue at 31st Street, host to a 'serious revival' in 1857–8. The pastor there from 1856 to 1863 was Rev. Dr Edwin Francis Hatfield (1807–83), a powerful speaker. *The National Cyclopaedia of American Biography* (New York: James T. White and Company, 1909), 10:70; William C. Conant, *Narratives of Remarkable Conversions and Revival Incidents* (New York: Derby and Jackson, 1858), 417.

91 Fernando Wood (1812–81) was elected mayor of New York City three times, serving 1855–8 and 1860–2. A central figure in the radical wing of the Democratic Party, a Locofoco, he publicly championed equal opportunity and gained the trust of New York's labouring and immigrant – chiefly Irish – classes. Castigated by patrician New Yorkers and political enemies as an untrustworthy scoundrel, he built a powerful political network based on patronage that rivalled the reach of Tammany Hall. Personally, he was driven by the quest for money, power, and respectability. See Jerome Mushkat, *Fernando Wood: A Political Biography* (Kent, OH: Kent State University Press, 1990); Leonard Chalmers, 'Tammany Hall, Fernando Wood, and the Struggle to Control New York City, 1857–1859,' *New-York Historical Society Quarterly* 53, no. 1 (1969): 6–33.

Thurs. Dec. 8.
Morning cold and blustering. A fall of snow having come down during the night. Full time at Pillow block. Evening exceedingly sharp cold, the streets and side walks all ice and moon at the full. Called upon Miss Marshall in 14th St.

Fri. Dec. 9.
Full time at work on Block. Called upon Connel at my old quarters in 10th St. and from there along with him to the reading room of the Cooper Institute where we spent some time.

Sat. Dec. 10.
Walked down to Guthrie's and met Connel there and in co. with him, took the road thro' the Bowery coming home. Evening cold and frosty. Full time at work on Block in the shop.

Sun. Dec. 11.
Kept the house in the forenoon and started for Brooklyn immediately after dinner. Spent a pleasant afternoon and evening there. Was late for the boat from Greene Point to 23rd St. and had to walk from 10th St. Ferry home. Spent a while in Peasnell's house on my way over.

Mon. Dec. 12.
Full time at work on Pillow block for Beam. Called at my old lodgings in the eve'g and found a letter and paper from McGarva from Clinton C.W. where he has now settled. Went from there to the singing.

Tues. Dec. 13.
Full time at work on different little jobs. Called for Mr Spittal in the eve'g and had his company to our monthly concert night of singing class.

Wed. Dec. 14.
Full time in the shop at valve connections. Spent the eve'g writing to Robt McKech[nie] in Dundas.

Thurs. Dec. 15.
Full time at valve fixings. Expected Mrs Logan over to go to the theatre in the evening but she did not come so went alone to Drayton's Parlour Opera in Hope Chapel, Broadway. Thought the entertainment but mediocre.[92]

---

92 Drayton's Parlour Opera was a new sort of entertainment introduced in New York

Fri. Dec. 16.
Full time at work on valve connections. Met Connel in the Cooper Institute reading room in the eve'g and spent a while in the reading room.

Sat. Dec. 17.
Full time in the shop at a variety of jobs. The evening remarkably wet and boisterous. Helped my friend Robjohn with his box over to 26th St. where he has moved, being dissatisfied with Mrs Skinner's. Myself well satisfied to be shet of him as I think him a grumbling John Bull. Spent a while with Connel in the Cooper Institute.

Sun. Dec. 18.
Kept the house reading all day. Only for a short time in the evening that I walked up 8th Ave. as far as the commencement of the Central Park.

Mon. Dec. 19.
Full time in the shop at air pump guards. Walked down town in the evening to try and get a Bill of Exchange for home but was unsuccessful. Was also ill pleased to find that there was no singing class.

Tues. Dec. 20.
Deplorable wet weather. All day at Air Pump valves. Took 1-½ hrs and went down town and got a draft for 3£ for home.[93] Wrote in the evening.

Wed. Dec. 21.
Full time in the shop. In the eve'g met and spent a while with Connel reading in the Free Reading Room of the Cooper Institute.

Thurs. Dec. 22.
Full time in the shop. Attended singing class in the evening and had a tolerably fair practice.

---

in 1859, a 'miniature English opera with a French flavor' invented by American-born actor Henri (né Henry) Drayton (1822–72). Educated and trained in France, Drayton was a celebrated singer, actor, and playwright who moved to New York in 1859 to manage the Drayton Parlour Opera Company. He returned to Europe for good in 1861 and finished his career in England. Lawrence, *Strong on Music*, 3:313. Situated on the east side of Broadway, below 8th Street, Hope Chapel was a former church that by the 1850s had been transformed into a venue for lectures, panoramas, minstrel shows, concerts, and literary soirées. On Sunday nights, it was 'occupied' by a meeting of Spiritualists. See Brown, *History of the New York Stage*, 1:288.

93 'Home' was, for McIlwraith, Scotland. It is not clear to whom he was sending this money.

Fri. Dec. 23.
Full time at work. In the evening Connel and I called and spent the evening in Mr McLellan's, North Moore St. Had a long letter from Mrs Hunter.

Sat. Dec. 24.
Full time in the shop. Met Connel in the eve'g and he and I went down town and saw Sandy Guthrie in his place of work in the printing office, 115 Fulton St. Had a tour of the establishment and saw the operation of printing, type setting, etc. going on. Came home late.

Sun. Dec. 25.
Walked down to Grand St. Church and heard Dr Thompson in the fore-noon. After dinner started off to Brooklyn and spent the day until 8 at night with my friends.

Mon. Dec. 26.
Observed as Christmas Holiday throughout the City but our work con-tinued to go on as usual. Went to Singing class as usual in the eve'g. Very small attendance.

Tues. Dec. 27.
Full time at Casing pattern (alterations). Met Connel in the evening at the Cooper Institute and spent a while reading there.

Wed. Dec. 28.
Exceedingly bitter cold weather. Full time in the shop partly on Casing and partly on Piston pattern. Went and bought a pair of boots, 3$ in the evening and spent the remainder of the evening in the Cooper Institute reading room.

Thurs. Dec. 29.
Full time at work. Went to singing class in the evening and found that a great schism had taken place between teacher and directors of the Insti-tute. Mr Sullivan being dismissed, threatens to prosecute the directors. Snow falling heavily all evening.

Fri. Dec. 30.
Snow lying pretty deep to-day. Barry and I worked untill 7 o'clock at a job for the 'Alice Prince' steamer. Spent the evening in Mr Patterson's 33rd. St.

Sat. Dec. 31.
Full time in the shop. Met with Connel in the eve'g and called along

with him on Gourie who is now living in Tenth St. and working in Newark. Called upon and spent a while in Guthrie's. Tried to find a Nigger church open to see the ceremony of watching the coming in of the New Year but did not find any.[94] New Year's morning before I got home. Weather cold and frosty. Had a letter from Thos.

---

94 Customarily held on December 31, Watch Night services in antebellum Black churches involved prayers, songs, and testimonies – sometimes spectacular events that started in the mid-evening and lasting until a church watchman rang in the New Year. Adapted from early English Wesleyan Methodist custom, after 1862 Watch Night was used to commemorate the arrival of Lincoln's Emancipation Proclamation, which took effect on January 1, 1863. Henrietta Buckmaster, *Let My People Go: The Story of the Underground Railroad and the Growth of the Abolition Movement* (New York: Harper and Brothers, 1969), 303; William H. Wiggins, Jr, '"Lift Every Voice": A Study of Afro-American Emancipation Celebrations,' in Roger D. Abrahams and John F. Szwed, eds., *Discovering Afro-America* (Leiden: E.J. Brill Archive, 1975), 50.

Diary for 1860

We suffer and we strive
Not less nor more as men and boys
With grizzled beards at forty-five
As cut at twelve in corduroys,
And if in time of sacred youth
We learned at home to love and pray
Pray Heaven that early love and truth
May never wholly pass away.

Come wealth or want, come good or ill,
Let young and old accept their part,
And bow before the awful will
And bear it with an honest heart.
Who misses or who wins the prize?
Go, lose or conquer as you can
But if you fall or if you rise
Be each, pray god, a gentleman.

THACKERAY.[1]

Sun. Jan. 1. 1860.
NEW YORK. Attended Dr Thompson's Church[2] in the morning. After

---

1 William Makepeace Thackeray, 'The End of the Play,' in *Ballads* (Boston: Ticknor and Fields, 1856), 224–48.
2 Rev. Joseph Parrish Thompson's Church was the Broadway Tabernacle, which opened in 1836 at Broadway between Worth Street and Catherine Lane. The church's

dinner had a walk up to the Central Park over the skating pond there and in by way of the Bloomingdale road. In the eve'g went and heard Dr Cheever preach in his church in Union Sqr.[3]

Mon. Jan. 2.
Holiday all over in New York. Called for Connel at Smith's in the morning then went and had a likeness taken for posting home. Then made calls upon Messrs Patterson, Robertson, Spittal, McLellan Gourie, Guthrie and Miss Marshall. By four o'clock got sickened with eating drinking smoking, etc. and staid over the evening in Guthrie's thereby breaking my promise of visiting Mr Renfrew's.

Tues. Jan. 3.
Sharp frosty weather. Started for Brooklyn early, after getting leave of absence for the day. Found Marg't much disappointed at not seeing me yesterday. Spent all day with her and had her down town in Brooklyn in the eve'g making some purchases.

Wed. Jan. 4.
Got set to work again. All day at Piston Patterns. Spent the evening writing to Jameson in Hamilton.

Thurs. Jan. 5.
Full time in the shop at 20 in. Piston Patterns. In the eve'g went to sing-

---

interior was physically beautiful – an amphitheatre with curvilinear seating surrounding the stage – and ideologically progressive; by mid-century, 'the crucible of the antislavery crusade.' A widely published moralist and leading American Congregationalist minister, the Philadelphia-born Thompson, DD (1819–79) was pastor of the Broadway Tabernacle from 1845 to 1872. On the church, see Jeanne Harden Kilde, *When Church Became Theatre: The Transformation of Evangelical Architecture and Worship in Nineteenth-Century America* (New York: Oxford University Press, 2005); Edwin G. Burrows and Mike Wallace, *Gotham: A History of New York City to 1898* (New York: Oxford University Press, 1999), 859. On Thompson, see George Ripley and Charles Anderson Dana, eds., *The American Cyclopaedia: A Popular Dictionary of General Knowledge* (New York: D. Appleton and Company, 1876), 15:717.
3 Dr George Barrell Cheever's church was the Congregational Church of the Puritans in Union Square, New York. Built in 1846 and razed in 1868, the church was a hotbed of abolitionist discourse, and its pastor (1818–90) a leader (in voice and print) in the mid-century campaign against slavery; he 'hurled his denunciations' from the pulpit. See 'Cheever, George Barrell,' *The National Cyclopaedia of American Biography* (New York: James T. White and Company, 1897), 7:82–3; David W. Dunlap, *From Abyssinian to Zion: A Guide to Manhattan's Houses of Worship* (New York: Columbia University Press, 2004), 177.

ing class and had a very good lesson. Mr Carl Anschutz being present and assisting the young man who is now acting as teacher.[4]

Fri. Jan. 6.
Full time at piston. Weather still fine and frosty. Had a walk down Broadway in the evening, visiting the Apprentices Library.[5]

Sat. Jan. 7.
Got finished with the Piston Patterns and did some little jobs about fixing drilling lathe. Streets in a deplorable state with water in the eve'g Connel and I attended Laura Keenes Theatre and saw the 'Green Birches.'[6]

Sun. Jan. 8.
Got a seat from Mr Spittal in Dr McElroy's Church, 14th St.[7] Spent the

---

4   Carl Anschütz (1813 or 1815–70) was a renowned musician, composer, and orchestra leader in mid-century New York. He made a permanent move to New York in 1857 and quickly established his German opera company there as a mark of musical 'progress.' He also taught music at the Academy of Music (East 14th Street) and the National Musical Institute (365 Broadway). Edwin M. Good, 'William Steinway and Music in New York, 1861–71,' in Michael Saffle, ed. *Music and Culture in America, 1861–1918* (London: Taylor and Francis, 1998), 13; *American Musical Directory, 1861* (New York: Thomas Hutchinson, 1861), 100; J.P. Wearing, *American and British Theatrical Biography: A Directory* (Metuchen, NJ: Scarecrow Press, 1979), 36.

5   Established in 1820 by the General Society of Mechanics and Tradesmen, the Apprentice's Library was located at Mechanics' Hall, 472 Broadway near Grand Street. Access to the lending library holdings was free for apprentices and $1 annually for journeymen. *Gazetteer of the State of New York ... 1860* (New York: R.P. Smith, 1860), 435; George Riplay and Charles A. Dana, eds., *The American Cyclopaedia* (New York: D. Appleton and Company, 1875), 10:405. On the Society's history, see 'General Society of Mechanics and Tradesmen,' http://www.generalsociety.org/about_us/history.asp (accessed February 2, 2009).

6   A play written by English actor and playwright John Baldwin Buckstone (1802–79) and first performed in England in 1845, 'The Green Bushes; Or, A Hundred Years Ago' was a three-act melodrama, the story of a refugee from the Irish Rebellion who escapes to Mississippi and falls in love with a native huntress, only to be found by his abandoned Irish wife. The play ran in Laura Keene's Theatre from December 30, 1858 to January 9, 1859. Tracy C. David and Ellen Donkin, eds., *Women and Playwriting in Nineteenth-Century Britain* (New York: Cambridge University Press, 1999), 114; T. Allston Brown, *A History of the New York Stage, from the First Performance in 1732 to 1901* (New York: Dodd, Mead and Company, 1903), 2:137. On the theatre, see Diary for 1859, fn 37.

7   Rev. Dr Joseph McElroy (1792–1876) was pastor of the old Scotch Presbyterian Church on Fourteenth Street, 1853–71; Emeritus pastor, 1871–76. See Prof. George Macloskie, 'Honors to Scotch-Irishmen' in *The Scotch-Irish in America* (Nashville, TN:

afternoon and evening with Mrs Logan in Brooklyn. Mr Renfrew gone
home with last Cunard Str.

Mon. Jan. 9.
Full time at Lathe fixings. Attended singing class in the eve'g and had
lessons under the superintendance of Mr Anschutz. Met A. Hosie at the
Mercantile reading room and joined that institution.[8] Took the 'Virginians' at the library.[9]

Tues. Jan. 10.
Set to work on Valve casing patterns, 3/4 day and the rem'dr, jobbing.
Visited the Cooper Institute in the eve'g to enquire about drawing class,
but unsuccessful in being rec'd as a student.[10] Called and spent a while
in Guthrie's afterwards.

Wed. Jan. 11.
Full time at casing. Waited in the shop and made a drawing board after
work hours. Spent the rem'dr of the eve'g writing home to Mrs Hunter.

Thurs. Jan. 12.
Full time at valve casing. At singing in the eve'g. Not much pleased
with the progress of the class.

Fri. Jan. 13.
Full time at Valve casing. Sat late reading the 'Virginians.'

Sat. Jan. 14.
Full time in the shop. Called upon and spent a while in Patterson's,
34th St. in the eve'g then home and read the 'Virginians.' A fine book
that.

Sun. Jan. 15.
Attended church in the forenoon and on coming out was asked by Mr
McLellan to dine with him. Left his house for Brooklyn about two and

---

Scotch-Irish Society of America, 1901), 190–1; 'McElroy, Joseph' in John M'Clintock
and James Strong, eds., *Cyclopaedia of Biblical, Theological and Ecclesiatical Literature*
(New York: Harper and Brothers, 1889), 2:709.

8 The Mercantile Library was established in 1820 by the city's Chamber of Commerce.
   Housed in the old Astor Opera House, by mid-century it had a collection of 37,000
   volumes and over 4,000 members. See Burrows and Wallace, *Gotham*, 498, 733, 782.

9 William Makepeace Thackeray, *The Virginians: A Tale of the Last Century* (London:
   Bradbury and Evans, 1858).

10 On the Cooper Institute, see Diary for 1859, fn 43.

spent the rest of the day with Mrs Logan. Met Messrs Kerr and Boyd there.

Mon. Jan. 16.
All day at Valve Casing. Went to singing class in the eve'g but no teacher appeared. Finished and posted letter for home containing portrait.

Tues. Jan. 17.
Half day at casing and half jobbing. Reading the 'Virginians' in the eve'g.

Wed. Jan. 18.
Full time at Casing. Went down town and spent a while in the Cooper Institute and then home and pored over the 'Virginians.'

Thurs. Jan. 19.
Full time at Steam Chest. Called for Connel in the eve'g and he and I attended Shakesperian readings (viz Bulwer's 'Money') by Mr and Mrs Vandenhof in a place on Broadway. Only about half pleased with them.[11]

Fri. Jan. 20.
Part day at Casing and part jobbing. In the evening Connel and I visited McLellan but did not find the gentleman in.

Sat. Jan. 21.
Made a final finish of steam chest pattern and worked on some other jobbing besides. Had a walk with Connel in the eve'g and visited the Cooper institute and Mercantile Library.

Sun. Jan. 22.
A most charming, mild sunny day. At Dr McElroy's Church in the forenoon and in the afternoon in Brooklyn, where I had Marg't most of the time by herself. Near 12 when I got home.

Mon. Jan. 23.
All day at Crosshead pattern. Had letter from Mrs Hunter[12] direct to

---

11 The Vandenhoffs performed their dramatic readings in Hope Chapel, Broadway. George Vandenhoff (1820–84) and Mary E. Vandenhoff (née Makeah) (d. 1883) were trained actors who earned their living from teaching elocution and from public dramatic readings in mid-century New York. William C. Young, *Famous Actors and Actresses on the American Stage*, vol. 2 (New York: R.R. Bowker, 1975); 'Amusements This Evening,' *NYT*, January 30, 1860.
12 Mrs Hunter was Andrew's sister Helen Hunter (née McIlwraith, 1810–93), a seam-

my present lodgings, also Punch's Almanac[13] and Ayrshire Express.[14] Attended singing and had a good practice under Mr Anschutz in the eve'g, Mrs H. making mention of the probability of Christina's being married soon to Mr Brewster.[15]

Tues. Jan. 24.
Full time at work on cross head.

Wed. Jan. 25.
All day at cross head pattern. Called at McLellan's in the eve'g but found Mr James out. Spent most of the eve'g in the Mercantile reading room.

Thurs. Jan. 26.
Full time at work on Cross head patterns. Called on Mr McLellan in the eve'g and on the subject of drawing lessons was advised by him to apply to Mr Calyo, fresco and scene artist – a Frenchman.[16] Attended singing class afterwards.

Fri. Jan. 27.
Full time in the shop, part time cross head and part on slide valve.

---

stress and widow who was living with her mother in the 1850s. She later moved to Canada and was living in Andrew's household in 1881. She died in Galt in November 1893 and was buried in the same cemetery plot as her brother (Mountwood Cemetery, Cambridge, Ontario). General Record Office of Scotland record 578/00 0046, 'Scotland's People,' www.scotlandspeople.gov.uk (accessed February 19, 2009).

13 *Punch; or, the London Charivari* was published from 1841. From 1842 on, an annual issue included 'Punch's almanack' (London: The Proprietors, 1841–).

14 The *Ayrshire Express* was one of three weeklies published in Ayr, Scotland, in the 1860s. The others were the *Ayr Advertiser* and the *Ayr Observer*. See *Catalogue of Printed Books in the British Library Museum. Newspapers Published in Great Britain and Ireland, 1801–1900* (London: William Clowes and Sons Limited, 1905), 443.

15 Christina McIlwraith (b. 1828) was Andrew McIlwraith's sister. A 'spinster,' she was living and working as a housekeeper in the household of her sister Jean Smith (sometimes 'Jane') Stewart (b. 1812) and her husband, Thomas Stewart, in Ayr in the 1851 census. Christina married James Brewster, a widower and photographer, in Ayr on 6 June 1860. Jane Stewart and Will McIlwraith were witnesses. Register of Statutory Marriages 1860, p. 23, General Record Office of Scotland record 578/00 0046, 'Scotland's People,' www.scotlandspeople.gov.uk (accessed August 1, 2008).

16 Nicolino Calyo (1799–1884) was an accomplished New York painter (in watercolours and oils), whose landscapes, miniatures, and portraits were acclaimed by contemporaries. He also designed sets and painted scenes for the theatre. He was, in fact, Italian; born in Naples he left for political reasons. See 'Nicolino Calyo' in San Antonio Museum of Art, Lisa B. Reitzes et al., *A National Image* (Austin: University of Texas Press, 2003), 79–80; Mantle Fielding and James F. Carr, *Dictionary of American Painters, Sculptors, and Engravers* (New York: J.F. Carr, 1965), 54.

Called upon Mr Calyo, 21st street and engaged him to give me lessons in drawing.

Sat. Jan. 28.
Still fine, mild weather. All day at Colwell's pipes. Called down at Guthrie's in the eve'g. Sandy speaking of his place of work being recently on fire.[17]

Sun. Jan. 29.
Went to Mr Brach's church in Jane Street in the forenoon and found a pretty homely looking Scotch congregation assembled. After dinner, proceeded to Brooklyn as usual and spent the afternoon. In the eve'g Mrs Logan and I went to a Methodist Church and saw and heard the 'Praying band' of that body at their devotions.[18] Saw Guthrie's shop all burnt up on the way home.

Mon. Jan. 30.
Full time in the shop, part on pipes and part on slide valve. Went down town with Robjohn and spent a while in the Mercantile library, then called upon and spent a while with Connel. Had a letter from Thos from Canada.

Tues. Jan. 31.
Weather most beautiful and mild. Full time at work. All day on slide valve pattern. In the eve'g went to start operations with Mr Calyo but found the old gent gone out and so, went down to Laura Keene's

---

17 The *Times* reported that fire destroyed the connected buildings at 46–50 Ann Street and 111–115 Fulton Street. These buildings housed several businesses including the printers for the New York newspapers *The Ledger, Mercury, Atlas,* and *Spirit of the Times,* as well as a druggist shop, a retail shop specializing in ink, optical instruments, and art materials, and an insurance company. Guthrie was employed in the printing office at 115 Fulton Street (see Diary for 1859, entry for 24 December 1859). See 'Destructive Fires,' *NYT,* January 28, 1860.

18 Rev. John Brash's Church was the Jane Street United Presbyterian Church, a small congregation that formed in the mid-1830s and disbanded in 1885. A Glaswegian, Rev. Brash, A.M. (1824–81) was ordained in 1851 and left Scotland to become pastor of the Jane Street Church in 1855. He was released from it in 1867. One of the oldest churches in the Ninth Ward, its congregation was described by one source as 'largely of old Scotch families.' See *Evangelical Repository and United Presbyterian Review,* n.s., 6 (Philadelphia: William S. Young, 1867), 265; Charles Force Deems, 'Religious Notes and News,' *Frank Leslie's Sunday Magazine* 17 (January-June 1885): 473.

theatre and saw 'Jeanie Deans' acted.[19] Very good. A fierce snow storm in my teeth walking home.

Wed. Feb. 1.
All day at Valve Pattern. In the evening went again to Monsieur Calyo and spent the evening in his studio getting lessons, his son, Nicolini being also present. Think I will like them pretty well.

Thurs. Feb. 2.
Full time in the shop at Valve and Pillow Block for main shaft of Beam Engine. In the evening called on Connel and walked down the Bowery with him, he being looking out for a case of drawing instruments which he procured at 12$. Great fire burning in Elm Street, a tenement house in which great loss of life has occurred.[20]

Fri. Feb. 3.
All day at Pillow Block. Had drawing lessons from Mr Calyo in the evening.

Sat. Feb. 4.
All day at Pillow Block. Went down and spent a while in Guthries in the evening. Sandy out keeping watch over the ruins of his old place of employment.

Sun. Feb. 5.
Weather cold and raw. At Grand St. Church in the forenoon. Dined down town and walked out from Fulton ferry to Mrs Renfrew's. Saw Messrs Syme and Hosie there, and in co. with Mrs Renfrew and Mrs Logan, and A. Hosie went to Beecher's church and heard an eloquent discourse from him and also the result of the forenoon collection from

---

19 'Jeanie Deans' was Dion Bourcicault's theatrical adaptation of Walter Scott's *Heart of Mid-Lothian*. The *Times* reviewer echoed Andrew's comments: 'It is splendidly acted and faultlessly produced.' *NYT*, January 30, 1860. The Dublin-born Bourcicault (1820–90) had changed the spelling of his name to Boucicault by this time.
20 Though originally thirty people were presumed killed in the Elm Street Tenement House Fire of February 1860, only nine actually perished. Still, the episode became both a curiosity to gawking New Yorkers and, in the long term, a cause for reform. The *Times* devoted a great deal of ink to the fire and the subsequent coroner's inquest. See 'Calamitous Fire,' *NYT*, February 3, 1860; 'Tenement Traps,' *NYT*, February 4, 1860; 'The Elm-Street Fire,' *NYT*, February 4, 1860; 'The Late Catastrophes,' *NYT*, February 7, 1860.

the congregation to free a young slave girl. Over 1,000$ being over 100$ more than her price.[21]

Mon. Feb. 6.
Miserable wet foggy weather. At work all day partly on Pillow Block and partly on alteration of crank. Had a visit of Sandy Hosie in the evening and he and I spent a while in Paterson's.

Tues. Feb. 7.
At work on Crank all day. At Mr Calyo's at drawing in the evening.

Wed. Feb. 8.
Full time in the shop. Spent the evening practising landscape sketching.

Thurs. Feb. 9.
Full time in the shop at a variety of jobs, there being rather a scarcity of them now. At drawing lesson in the evening, and got along pretty well.

Fri. Feb. 10.
Weather quite stormy and cold. Worked 1-½ hours when a number of bricks fell in the shop and several of us thought it expedient to quit untill the storm blew over. Strolled all round town and visited the Dusseldorf gallery of paintings.[22]

Sat. Feb. 11.
Cold weather. Altering Valve guard all day. Got discharged at paying time.

---

21 On Grand Street Church, see Diary for 1859, fn 31. The subject of a well-circulated pen-and-ink sketch, the slave purchase episode became very famous as antislavery rhetoric peaked in the months before Abraham Lincoln's election. The slave girl, 'Pink,' was about nine years old, 'having in her veins only one-sixteenth part African blood (although that was more than enough to make her a slave),' the *Times* reported. Her mother sold to a southern slave trader, Pink had been living with her grandmother when her Washington City owner decided to put her on the market for $800. With her owner's permission, she was taken to New York by an Episcopal minister seeking benefactors to rescue the slave via purchase. 'Many persons crowded around ... to congratulate the little girl on her new-found freedom, which she is now too young fully to appreciate.' *NYT*, February 6, 1860.

22 Located on Broadway, the Dusseldorf Gallery of Fine Arts was established in 1849 by Johann Gottfried Böker, a promoter of modern European art and especially the works of artists at the Dusseldorf Academy in Germany. See R.H. Stehle, 'The Düsseldorf Gallery of New York,' *New York Historical Society Quarterly* 58, no. 4 (1974): 305–17.

Sun. Feb. 12.
At Thompson's Church in the morning, and in the evening at W.P. meeting in Lamartine Hall, Eighth Avenue which I mistook for a spiritualist meeting held on the flat above.[23]

Mon. Feb. 13.
Visited Badgers shop and the Novelty Works, but both slack.[24] Called upon and spent a while with Barry at his lodgings in the evening.

Tues. Feb. 14.
Made a tour round town calling at a number of shops asking a job, but unsuccessfully. Wrote to Thos in the afternoon. Had drawing lesson in the evening.

Wed. Feb. 15.
~~Spent the forenoon making a tour round town calling at a~~. Kept the house nearly all day studying Perspective. Snowing outside.

Thurs. Feb. 16.
Started for Brooklyn after breakfast and waited to dinner in Mr Renfrew's, with Mrs R. and Mrs L. Snow lying deep, got boots soaked and felt sick in the afternoon. Went to drawing in the eve'g. Mr Calyo took me down to the Academy of Music to see the Opera of 'Der Freyschutz,'[25] with a new scene painted by his son.[26]

---

23 Lamartine Hall was on the corner of Eighth Avenue and 29th Street. Regular spiritualist meetings (with 'trance speakers') took place at Lamartine Hall on Sunday evenings throughout the 1850s and '60s. See Emma Hardinge Britten, *Modern American Spiritualism* 3rd ed. (New York: Author, 1870), 509; Bret E. Carroll, *Spiritualism in Antebellum America* (Bloomington: Indiana University Press, 1997). The meeting that McIlwraith attended was likely a Presbyterian Church service held for a small congregation that had been supplied pastoral service by the New York Presbytery only in 1859. See W.S. Young, ed., *The Evangelical Repository* (1859), 18:361.

24 On Badger's Architectural Iron Works, see Diary for 1859, fn 30; for the Novelty Iron Works, see Diary for 1859, fn 28.

25 'Der Freischutz' was a romantic three-act grand opera written by German composer Carl Maria von Weber (1786–1826) and first performed in New York in 1825. On the Academy of Music, see Diary for 1859, fn 40.

26 Hannibal Calyo (1835–83), Nicolino's son (not the reverse, as Andrew had it in a February 1 entry), was a talented New York theatre scene painter who learned the art from his father but gained renown on his own merits. See Robin Thurlow Lacy, *A Biographical Dictionary of Scenographers, 500 BC to 1900 AD* (Westport, CT: Greenwood Press, 1990), 103. Hannibal Calyo's stage set was noticed by the New York *Evening Post* as well: 'snow covered peaks ... gleaming in the moonlight.' Quoted in Vera

Fri. Feb. 17.
Day clear and frosty. Spent nearly all day in the house sketching. Called upon and spent the evening with Connel.

Sat. Feb. 18.
A furious snow storm all day. In the house in the forenoon and in the afternoon went off to Brooklyn and had a pleasant evening, singing, etc. with Mrs R. Mrs L and Wm Sym. Slept all night here.

Sun. Feb. 19.
Cold frosty weather, about the coldest of the season. Marg't and I kept house in the forenoon. In the afternoon I went to church with Wm Simme. Evening spent in the house.

Mon. Feb. 20.
Had Marg't over in the city and spent the day rambling round visiting the Astor library, calling on Miss Marshall, Mrs Skinner, and Mrs Guthrie.[27] Had tea in Guthrie's. Saw her off at Fulton ferry and then called upon and spent a while in Spittals in 13th Street.

Tues. Feb. 21.
Spent the day mostly in the house. In the evening had a drawing lesson from Mr Calyo Jun'r, the old gent being absent.

Wed Feb. 22.
Very wet, thick, disagreeable weather. Kept the house most part of the day. Called at Badger's and was requested to call again on Saturday. Procession, etc. in town in celebration of Washington's birthday.[28] Met with Connel in the evening and walked down to Guthrie's.

Thurs. Feb. 23.
Called at Dunkin & Cramptons and walked round a little in the fore-

---

Brodsky Lawrence, ed., *Strong on Music: The New York Music Scene in the Days of George Templeton Strong* (Chicago: University of Chicago Press, 1999), 3:323.

27 See Diary for 1859, fn 80.
28 'Happily our population is amphibious,' the *Times* editor quipped, 'and neither the opening of the flood-gates of the heavens nor the closing of the flood-gates of the sewers could prevent the street demonstrations in honor of the day … The military, the firemen, the civic societies, the national organizations and the religious assemblages all vied with each other in doing honor to the occasion.' 'Washington's Birthday. The Celebration in This City,' *NYT*, February 23, 1860.

noon, and staid in making drawn of cylinder, etc. most of the remainder of the day.[29] Copied the cane bottomed chair for home in the eve'g.

Fri. Feb. 24.
All day in the house finishing the cylinder drawing. After tea called on Robt Patterson and had him up in my lodgings a while.

Sat. Feb. 25.
Called at Badger's in the morning and got engaged to set to work on Monday morning, then at the Novelty Works a short time and at Mrs Smith's and secured my old quarters in the room along with Connel. Had a letter from Miss Goldie which had been lying here. Got tools and clothes moved over in the afternoon and took drawing lesson in the evening.

Sun. Feb. 26.
Heard Mr Thompson preach in the forenoon, and after dinner in Mrs Smith's, started and walked to Brooklyn, spending afternoon and evening with our friends there.

Mon. Feb. 27.
Sketched for a while in the evening and then wrote home to Bill. Full time at work in Badgers.

Tues. Feb. 28.
Full time in the shop. Principal job going on, a number of store fronts for Bennet in Halifax, Nova Scotia. Had my drawing lesson from Mr Calyo in the evening.

---

29 John T. Dunkin and Joseph Crampton were machinists and metalworkers on West 27th Street in 1850s New York. McIlwraith visited Dunkin's Machine Shop on April 15, 1859, shortly after he arrived in New York, to seek employment. Whether or not Dunkin and Crampton had become partners in the same location by 1860, or were the sites of two separate visits on McIlwraith's walk, is not clear. See Diary for 1859, fn 27. Joseph Crampton appears as a 'machinist' working at 860 West 27th Street (home at 825 West 27th Street) in 1855. *Trow's New York City Directory 1855–56* (New York: J.F. Trow, 1855). He must have been successful. By 1864, Crampton was listed among the officers on the 'Machinery Committee' of the New York Metropolitan Fair alongside some of the city's largest and wealthiest metal founders and shipbuilders, including Cornelius H. Delameter (of the Delameter Iron Works) and Horatio Allen (of the Novelty Iron Works). *A Record of the Metropolitan Fair in Aid of United States Sanitary Commission, Held at New York in April 1864* (New York: Hurd and Houghton, 1867), 252.

Wed. Feb. 29.
Full time at work, and in the evening fully occupied copying a Forest scene, from a drawing of Mr Calyo Junr.

Thurs. Mar. 1.
Weather miserably dull and foggy. All day at work and at Mon. Calyo in the evening.

Fri. Mar. 2.
Full time in the shop. Working close at my drawing in the evening.

Sat. Mar. 3.
All day at work. Walked up to Mrs Skinner's in the evening and got letters from Mrs McIlwraith and from Jameson, Hamilton. Very dull times there yet.

Sun. Mar. 4.
Spent daylight entirely in the house reading the Pilgrim's progress, great part of it. In the evening went and heard the rev. Mr Guiness from Ireland preach in the Cooper institute, but was rather disappointed with him after the accounts I had previously heard of him.[30]

Mon. Mar. 5.
Full time in the shop. Received pay at the same rate as before (1.75 per day). Spent the evening copying Grand Vesper Chorus music for Mrs Renfrew.[31]

Tues. Mar. 6.
Full time in the shop. At Mr Calyo in the evening. Weather delightfully fine and mild. Mr Fairfield sometime foreman in Badgers commenced working journeyman at patterns with us today.

Wed. Mar. 7.
Full time at work. Sat till past 11 at night drawing, while Connel read aloud 'Massinger's Virgin Martyr.'[32]

---

30 A renowned evangelist, Rev. Henry Grattan Guinness arrived in New York to great acclaim (the *Times* published a two-column biography) and recollection of the 'remarkable stir' that he created on previous visits. On this visit, he stayed for eight days and preached ten times in eight different churches. See 'Rev. Henry G. Guinness,' *NYT*, February 25, 1860; 'Religious Notices,' *NYT*, February 25, 1860.

31 McIlwraith was copying sheet music, viz. August Browne, creator, 'Grand Vesper Chorus – Sabbath – Begin, my soul, rejoicing – He sees, and He believes' [1846]. See *Music for a Nation: American Sheet Music, 1820–1860*, Library of Congress Digitized Historical Collections, http://memory.loc.gov/ammem/smhtml/ (accessed February 21, 2011).

32 'The Virgin Martyr' was a post-Reformation, Catholic 'saint's play' about the perse-

Thurs. Mar. 8.
Full time in the shop. Spent the evening drawing.

Fri. Mar. 9.
Full time at work. In the evening ~~Connel and I called upon and spent the~~. Had a visit from Chas McKenzie from Sarnia who leaves per steamer Glasgow for the old country tomorrow.

Sat. Mar. 10.
Full time at work. At drawing lesson in the evening.

Sun. Mar. 11.
At Mr Thompsons church in the morning and heard a young man a stranger preach. After dinner proceeded to Mrs Skinner's and got home and Canada letters, and then to Brooklyn and spent the afternoon and eve'g there. Met Mr Charles, a reporter to the 'Herald' and Miss Becky Johnson in Mr Renfrew's.

Mon. Mar. 12.
Full time at work. In the evening at Mr Calyo, and got started on a large view of ruins at Canterbury.[33]

Tues. Mar. 13.
Full time in the shop. Spent the evening in the house sketching. Had a visit from R. Turnbull from Dundas in the evening who is now out of a job.

Wed. Mar. 14.
A cold blustering March day. Full time at work. Had a note from Mr Calyo desiring my lesson postponed untill Saturday. Connel and R. Turnbull off taking a tour round town.

Thurs. Mar. 15.
Full time in the shop. Had a visit from Turnbull in the evening to tea again. Spent the night in the house drawing.

---

cution of Christians under the Roman emperor Diocletian, written by Philip Mass-inger and Thomas Dekker in 1622. The version McIlwraith and Connel were reading from was likely much more recent, perhaps Philip Massinger, *The Virgin Martyr* (London: R. Clay, 1844).

33 Likely a print of C.F. Wicksteed, *Ruins at Canterbury*, a painting he completed in 1814 and exhibited in the Royal Academy of Arts, London. Algernon Graves, *The Royal Academy of Arts: A Complete Dictionary of Works and Their Contributors from Its Foundation in 1769 to 1904* (London: Henry Graves and Co. Ltd., 1904), 8:263.

Fri. Mar. 16.
Full time in the shop and in the evening Connel and I called upon and spent a while in Mr James MacClellands.

Sat. Mar. 17.
Full time at work and in the eve'g had my lesson from Mr Calyo.

Sun. Mar. 18.
At Mr Thompson's church in the forenoon and in the afternoon at Brooklyn with Marg't.

Mon. Mar. 19.
Full time in the shop. In the evening at Mr Calyo.

Tues. Mar. 20.
All day at work. Spent the eve'g in the house drawing.

Wed. Mar. 21.
Full time at work. At Mr Calyo in the evening.

Thurs. Mar. 22.
Full time at work. In the house all evening drawing.

Fri. Mar. 23.
Full time at work. In the house drawing all the eve'g.

Sat. Mar. 24.
All day at work. Spent the evening drawing. Wm Syme called and spent a while with me, he being now boarding in Tenth Street.

Sun. Mar. 25.
Wm Syme and I went to McElroy's church in the forenoon and heard Dr Ferries, principal of Columbia College, preach.[34] Mrs Logan came over in the afternoon and accomp'd me to Grand St. church. Her and I had tea in Guthries.

Mon. Mar. 26.
Full time in the shop. At Mr Calyo in the evening. Called at Mrs Skin-

34 Most likely Rev. Isaac Ferris, DD, LLD (1798–1873), who, though a graduate of Columbia College (1816), was never an officer there. He was, rather, chancellor of New York University (1853–70) and an ordained minister in the Dutch Reformed Church. See 'University Necrology,' in *Proceedings of the Tenth Anniversary of the University of the State of New York … 1873* (Albany: The Argus Company, 1874), 235–8; 'Ferris, Isaac,' in James Grant Wilson and John Fiske, eds., *Appleton's Cyclopaedia of American Biography*, rev. ed. (New York: D. Appleton and Company, 1900), 2: 442.

ner's in the eve'g and got a short note from Mrs Hunter brought out by R. Hogg who had called there but could get no clue to my present residence.

Tues. Mar. 27.
All day at work. Spent the evening drawing, finishing the small landscape with view of a cross.

Wed. Mar. 28.
All day at work. Went to drawing lesson but was dissapointed. Mr C. being particularly engaged for the eve'g. Spent some time in the Mercantile reading room.

Thurs. Mar. 29.
Full time in the shop. Spent the evening writing home to Mother.

Fri. Mar. 30.
Full time in the shop. Had drawing lesson from Mr Calyo in the evening.

Sat. Mar. 31.
Warm weather. Mr Gordon an acquaintance of J. Stewart called with letters from Hamilton, He having brought the parcel with my pants, vest, etc which were left last night. Full time at work. Had long letters and paper from Bill. Spent the evening drawing.

Sun. Apr. 1.
Weather quite close and sultry. Called for J. Stewart's friend Gordon at his lodgings in the Bowery and had a walk with him in the forenoon down to the Battery, etc. Then after dinner out to Brooklyn. Heard a short letter from Christina to ask our approval of her marriage with Mr Brewster.

Mon. Apr. 2.
Weather cold and clear again. Full time in the shop. At Mr Calyo drawing in the evening.

Tues. Apr. 3.
All day at work. In the evening drawing in the house.

Wed. Apr. 4.
Full time at work. At drawing of wayside shrine in the house in the evening.

Thurs. Apr. 5.
Full time in the shop. At drawing in the evening.

Fri. Apr. 6.

Full time in the shop. In the evening draw in the house. Took a run up to Broadway and saw a painting of the first preaching among the Pilgrim fathers on their landing in America by a German artist Scwarz.[35]

Sat. Apr. 7.

Worked all day on a door sill plate for Ball, Black and Co., Broadway, and had to wait untill dark to finish it.[36] Sat drawing in the house untill twelve.

Sun. Apr. 8.

A rainy day. Sat in the house all forenoon. After dinner, Connel and I walked up to 33rd St. and called on Robt Patterson whom we found had left the Globe foundry and was working at Yonkers. Went to Grand St. Church in the eve'g, it being Sacrament Sabbath there.

Mon. Apr. 9.

All day at work. Went to Mr Calyo in the evening and instead of waiting on a lesson, got a ticket from him for the opera and went and heard Miss Patti in the Opera of the 'Barber of Seville.'[37]

Tues. Apr. 10.

Full time and half day over time, having to work till ten at night along with Bill Papps and Peasell at girder pattern till ten at night.

---

35 Dutch painter Johan Georg Schwartze (1814–74) was a member of the Dusseldorf School and a producer of historical scenes, including *Waiting, First Divine Service of the Puritans in America* (1858). John Denison Champlin and Charles Callahan Perkins, eds., *Cyclopedia of Painters and Paintings* (New York: Charles Scribner's Sons, 1887), 4:155.

36 Ball, Black and Company was the leading American retail jewellery house in the nineteenth century. Located at the 'Sign of the Golden Eagle,' 247 Broadway, opposite City Hall, it advertised itself as 'Manufacturers and Importers of Silver and Plated Ware.' See Mid-Manhattan Picture Collection, Picture Collection of the New York Public Library, NYPL Digital Gallery, http://digitalgallery.nypl.org/nypldigital (accessed February 21, 2011).

37 Born to Italian parents in Madrid, Spain, Adelina Patti (1843–1919) moved with her family to New York as a child. She was the youngest and most gifted member of a family of eight opera singers; she first performed professionally at age seven. Her most famous part was as Rosina in Rossini's *Barber of Seville*. In this performance in New York's Academy of Music, Patti reprised her role, executing it, the *Times* noted, with her 'usual neatness.' 'Amusements,' *NYT*, April 10, 1860. William Lines Hubbard, *The American History and Encyclopedia of Music* (New York: Irving Squire, 1910), 138; Henry T. Finck, 'The Reign of Patti,' *The Bookman* 52 (September–February, 1920–1): 166–8.

Wed. Apr. 11.
Cold, dull weather. Full time in the shop. In the evening finished drawing of Wayside shrine.

Thurs. Apr. 12.
Full time in the shop. With Mr Calyo in the evening, the old gentleman
going out early and leaving me with Joseph.

Fri. Apr. 13.
Fine weather. Full time and a quarter day extra in the shop. Wrote to
Christina to congratulate her on her prospect of matrimony.

Sat. Apr. 14.
Full time at work. Spent the evening in the house at drawing landscape
with old mill.

Sun. Apr. 15.
Connel and I got up early and had a walk round by Guthrie's before
church time. At Mr Thompson's Church in the forenoon, and in the
afternoon at Brooklyn, spending it with Mrs Logan. Mr Renfrew's folk
about moving to Staten Island, and her thinking about coming to the
city with me.

Mon. Apr. 16.
Full time in the shop. In the evening drawing.

Tues. Apr. 17.
Full time at work. At Mr Calyo in the evening.

Wed. Apr. 18.
Full time in the shop. In the house drawing in the evening.

Thurs. Apr. 19.
Full time at work. Spent the evening partly reading Mrs Stowe's Sunny
Memories and in part writing to Jack Stewart.[38]

Fri. Apr. 20.
Full time in the shop. Had a Hamilton paper recording the birth of Thomas's fourth child, and third daughter on the 18th of the month.[39] Had
old Blockson in talking a long time in our room in the evening. Had a
little while drawing.

---

38 Harriet Elizabeth (Beecher) Stowe, *Sunny Memories of Foreign Lands* (Boston: Phillips,
     Sampson, 1854).
39 See 'Birth. At Mulberry Street,' *HS*, April 19, 1860.

Sat. Apr. 21.
Full time at work. At Mr Calyo in the evening. Had a walk down Broadway after coming out.

Sun. Apr. 22.
At Mr Thompson's church in the morning. Went out and saw Marg't in the afternoon. The whole family to be moved to Staten Island in a day or two.

Mon. Apr. 23.
Full time in the shop. Went to call on Miss Marshall in the evening, and was told that she had got married on Saturday last. Came down town and spent a while in the annual exhibition of the National Academy of Design.[40]

Tues. Apr. 24.
Full time at work. At Mr Calyo in the evening and told him I would not be back to continue my lessons beyond the current quarter.

Wed. Apr. 25.
Full time in the shop. In the evening drawing in the house. Had a letter from Thos to see if Marg't[41] would not go up to him and spend a while. Also speaking of his having been at Quebec on parliamentary business.[42]

Thurs. Apr. 26.
Frosty morning and fine cool day. Full time at work. Work seeming to be now very busy. At Mr Calyo in the eve'g.

---

40 The National Academy of Design was a New York–based national organization of artists spawned from the New York Drawing Association in 1826. It had a large exhibition room at Broadway and Leonard Street, where its annual shows were staged at mid-century. The *Times* was not very enthusiastic, calling the 1860 exhibition a 'general glitter of gilt frames and a kaleidoscopic glow of colors' on a 'goodly number of canvasses' but politely avoiding commentary on quality. Winifred E. Howe, *A History of the Metropolitan Museum of Art* (New York: Metropolitan Museum of Art, 1913), 65–7; 'The Academy Exhibition of 1860,' *NYT*, April 12, 1859.

41 'Margaret' was Andrew's and Thomas's sister, Margaret Logan (née McIlwraith), who had been living and working as a housekeeper Robert Renfrew's Brooklyn household. See Diary for 1859, fn 26.

42 From 1849 to 1865, the Parliament of the United Canadas met alternately at Toronto and Quebec City. Parliament assembled in Quebec City on February 28 and adjourned on May 19, 1860. Thomas's business is unclear. S.J.R. Noel, *Patrons, Clients, Brokers: Ontario Society and Politics 1791–1896* (Toronto: University of Toronto Press, 1990), 174; William H. Withrow, *A Popular History of the Dominion of Canada* (Boston: B.B. Russell, 1878), 444, 445.

Fri. Apr. 27.
All day at work and in the evening occupied with my landscape sketching.

Sat. Apr. 28.
Full time in the shop. Connel and I paid a visit to Mr Jas McLellan in the eve'g and saw his little daughter, born a week or two ago. Met a Mr Campbell, Stewart, in the str Africa.

Sun. Apr. 29.
At Mr Thomson's church in the morning, then came home and had a hearty dinner and a very refreshing siesta after. Had a visit of Wm Simm in the evening.

Mon. Apr. 30.
Full time in the shop. Spent the evening sketching in the house.

Tues. May 1.
Called upon Mr Calyo and wound up my drawing lessons with him. Got one or two originals to keep and brought away drawing of a ruin at Canterbury which has been occupying me all this term. Parted good friends with the old gentleman and am to call again.

Wed. May 2.
Full time at work. Wet weather. In the evening made a journey to the Eighth Avenue and called upon Mrs Skinner, then from there to Spittals and spent a while.

Thurs. May 3.
Full time at work. In the eve'g crossed over to Green Point and attended a temperance meeting and heard Miss Marshall, a sister of Jesse Marshall a shopmate of mine sing the 'drunkard's Wife.'[43] A lovely evening on the river.

Fri. May 4.
All day at work. Alex Hosie called at the shop in the forenoon with a

---

43 There were several mid-nineteenth-century temperance songs that went by the title 'The Drunkard's Wife.' Perhaps the most popular was one by Edwin Paxton Hood, which began 'Softly the drunkard's wife breatheth her prayer' and ended with a husband reformed. See Paxton Hood, *The Book of Temperance Melody, Adapted and Arranged to Popular Airs*, 2nd ed. (London: Charles Gilpin, 1850), 10. On the mid-century temperance movement in New York City, see Paul O. Weinbaum, 'Temperance, Politics, and the New York City Riots of 1857,' *New York Historical Society Quarterly* 43 (July 1975): 246–70.

letter from Thos to tell me that there was the prospect of a job for me
on the Buffalo and Lake Huron Railway. Connel and I went to Laura
Keenes theatre in the eve'g and saw the 'Coleen Bawn,' a piece of Mr
Boucicault's composition.[44]

Sat. May 5.
Warm weather. Dispatched an application for a job as draughtsman to
Mr Park, Brantford.[45] Full time in the shop. Walked down to Fulton's in
the evening but found the door locked.

Sun. May 6.
The hottest day of the season so far. Wm Simm called for me in the
morning and we together took the 10 o'clock boat to Staten Island and
on landing there sought out our way to Mr Renfrew's farm, where the
family are all now. Had a beautiful walk and country fare, and came
home by the 6 o'clock boat from Factoryville.

Mon. May 7.
Full time in the shop. Spent the evening writing to Thos and to Mary
Goldie.

Tues. May 8.
Full time at work. Walked down town to Guthries and spent a while
there in the eve'g. Also passed some time in Coupils print store.[46]

Wed. May 9.
Full time in the shop. Had a visit of Wm Simm in the evening.

---

44 Dion Boucicault, *The Colleen Bawn; or, The Brides of Garryowen. A Domestic Drama, in
   Three Acts* (New York: T.H. French, 1860). Set in Ireland, this melodrama told the
   story of the forbidden love between a poor but virtuous girl and an impoverished
   aristocrat torn between true love and his family's reputation.
45 Likely John Carter Park (1822–96), a native of Aberdeen who was appointed locomotive superintendent of the Buffalo and Lake Huron Railway in 1859. He returned to
   Britain in 1866 when the B. and L.H.R. was absorbed by the Grand Trunk Railway.
   'John Carter Park,' in J.H.T. Tudsbery, ed., *Minutes of Proceedings of the Institute of
   Civil Engineers* (London: The Institution, 1897), 127:383–4.
46 Goupil and Company was a French art business that acquired original artworks, reproduced them in many forms, and sold both the originals and the prints in their own art
   galleries. Though the business was rooted in Paris, branches were opened in several
   European cities and, by 1846, in New York, at 772 Broadway. Michael Knoedler (1823–
   1878) managed the New York branch from 1852 and bought it in 1857. John Hannavy,
   Encyclopedia of Nineteenth-Century Photography (London: CRC Press, 2008), 1:601–3.

Thurs. May 10.
All day at work. In the eve'g visited the International gallery of paint-ings, and spent an hour or two.[47]

Fri. May 11.
Full time in the shop. Had a letter from Hamilton from Mrs T. Mc. Had a visit of Stephen McKechnie from Dundas in the eve'g.

Sat. May 12.
All day at work. Heard from Mrs Hunter. Connel and I went to the new Bowery theatre in the evening, and saw 'O'Neil,' the great, an Irish melo-drama, etc.[48]

Sun. May 13.
Kept the house all forenoon, and at Thompson's church in the after-noon. In the evening heard Mrs Corra B. Hatch.[49]

Mon. May 14.
Full time in the shop. Had a note from J. Park, Brantford, saying that he would likely require my services as draughtsman soon. Visited the Mercantile Library in the eve'g.

Tues. May 15.
Full time in the shop. In the evening Connel and I had a tour away down the Bowery and Chatham St. Purchased a coat and pants in Dun-ham and Brockaws, 3rd Ave.[50]

---

47 A rival to the Dusseldorf Gallery (see fn 22), The International Gallery was opened in New York in 1859 by Wilhelm Aufermann and served as an American house for the German art academies of Dusseldorf, Dresden, and Berlin. The gallery seems not to have operated longer than one year. Robert Ernst, *Immigrant Life in New York City, 1825–1863* (Port Washington, NY: I.J. Friedman, 1965), 146.

48 Opened on September 5, 1859, the New Bowery Theatre was located between New Canal and Hester streets, two blocks north of the Old Bowery Theatre, to which it became a formidable rival. The New Bowery had a seating capacity of 2,500 and ran a wide range of productions from high drama to low comedy. It was destroyed by fire in 1866. Brown, *History of the New York Stage*, 2:189–221.

49 Cora L.V. Hatch was a colourful lay preacher in 1860s New York. In 1860, she preached every Sunday afternoon and evening at Hope Chapel, Broadway. Known for her discursive agility, she sometimes allowed a 'committee of the audience' to choose her subject of discourse. See for example 'Religious Notices,' *NYT*, January 28, 1860; 'Religious Notices,' *NYT*, May 12, 1860.

50 Dunham and Brokaw was one of New York's largest retail and wholesale clothing businesses in the mid-nineteenth century, specializing in men's and boy's fine cloth-

Wed. May 16.
Full time in the shop. In the eve'g wrote to Mrs McI, Hamilton.

Thurs. May 17.
Full time at work. Worked an hour over time. Had a visit of Wm Simm in the eve'g.

Fri. May 18.
Weather continuing dull and chilly. Full time in the shop. Work very busy. Called on Miss Marshall that was, now Mrs Abel in the eve'g and got introduced to Mr A. who showed me new invented gas nippers, which himself and a partner have patented.

Sat. May 19.
Full time at work. In the eve'g Connel and I walked down to Guthries but got the door locked.

Sun. May 20.
Started for North Richmond immediately after breakfast but was late for the boat so went to Quarantine landing and thence to Mr Renfrew's. A fine warm day. Had the co. of a young German, 2nd carver in Sweeney's Hotel, on the road. Heard the Boblink singing beautifully. Had a pleasant visit to Springfield farm and got home by 7 o'clock.

Mon. May 21.
Full time in the shop. Visited Wm Simm at his lodgings in the eve'g and from him to Mrs Abel's in 17th St.

Tues. May 22.
Full time in the shop. Spent the evening writin home.

Wed. May 23.
Full time at work. In the eve'g Connel and I went to Wallack's Theatre and saw the 'Overland route' with which we were highly entertained. Mrs Hoey as Mrs Seabright first rate.[51]

---

ing. See 'Brokaw Brothers,' in *Illustrated New York: The Metropolis of To-Day* (New York: International Publishing Company, 1888), 146.

51 On Wallack's, see Diary for 1859, fn 74. First staged in London, Tom Taylor's *The Overland Route* was one of the first stage dramas set on the western frontier. A professor of English at University College, London, and a later bureaucrat with the London Board of Health, Taylor (1817–80) wrote three books, wrote for and edited *Punch*, and somehow produced over one hundred dramatic pieces during his career. The *Times* reviewed the play at length and agreed with McIlwraith's assessment: an 'ingenious and creditable piece of work.' David Patrick, ed., *Chambers's Cyclopaedia*

Thurs. May 24.
Full time at work. Wm Simm called in the evening and spent a while.

Fri. May 25.
Full time in the shop. In the eve Connel and I called down upon Mr Jas McLellan. Met his brother David there and got an invitation to their house in Grove St. Weather warm.

Sat. May 26.
Full time at work. Weather close and lowering in the morning and in the afternoon torrents of rain with thunder and lightning. Evening still wet and stormy. Connel and I sat all night in the house smoking and reading Shakespeare's Tempest.[52]

Sun. May 27.
At church in the afternoon. Went out in the evening intending to go to someone and got wet. Had a walk around Green Point in the forenoon.

Mon. May 28.
Full time in the shop. In the evening went to Mr Milburn's lecture in the Cooper institute, 'What a blind man saw in England.'[53] Liked him very well as a speaker. House full. Peale's great picture the Court of Death exhibited after the lecture.[54]

Tues. May 29.
Full time in the shop. Kept the house in the evening reading a 'Life for a Life.' Think it a very well written book showing good insight into human nature and with a pure moral tone all through.[55]

---

of English Literature, new ed. (London and Edinburgh: W. and R. Chambers, Limited, 1903), 3:463; 'Wallack's Theatre,' NYT, May 15, 1860.

52 William Shakespeare, The Tempest (London: Printed by Isaac Iaggard and Ed. Blount, 1623).

53 A blind man and Methodist minister, Reverend William H. Milburn (1823–1903) was a well-known mid-century writer and lecturer, and later became chaplain of the United States Senate (1893–1902). The event was a repeat performance and a benefit, the proceeds of which went to Rev. Milburn. See 'City Intelligence,' NYT, February 11, 1860.

54 Rembrandt Peale's travelling Court of Death (1819–20) was a massive moral allegory, featuring several representative figures including Death, War, Conflagration, Pleasure, Suicide, Despair, and Hypochondria, among others. Oil on canvas, 11 ft. 6 in. '23 ft. 5 in.; it is now in the Detroit Institute of Arts. Entry to hear Milburn and see Peale was a 'two for one' deal at the Cooper Institute: 25 cents. 'A Blind Man Saw,' NYT, May 28, 1860; Russell Lynes, The Art-Makers (New York: Atheneum, 1970), 22–4.

55 Dinah Maria (Mulock) Craik, A Life for a Life (New York: Harper and Brothers, 1859).

Wed. May 30.
All day at work. Evening wet. Sat in the house reading a 'Life for a Life.'

Thurs. May 31.
Full time at work. Had a visit of Wm Simm who spent some time with me. Connel came in late and told me that Mr Jas McLellan was dead, having been ill only since last night. Sad affair. His wife with a baby two months old.

Fri. June 1.
Full time in the shop. Spent some time in the Mercantile reading room in the eve'g. Called on Wm Simm.

Sat. June 2.
Weather quite hot. Connel and I knocked off work after working ¼ day and hired a carriage for Jas McLellan's funeral. Spent the afternoon from one till about six, in attendance on it, driving to Greenwood Cemetry. Called at Guthries in the evening and learned that Sandy had just left with the Str Adriatic for Europe.

Sun. June 3.
Weather bright and warm. At church in the morning. Spent the remainder of the day sleeping and reading.

Mon. June 4.
Fine, warm weather. Full time in the shop. Mr Fairfield left the shop today to be foreman in the new shop in 19th St. Visited Mr Simm in the eve'g.

Tues. June 5.
Still hot weather. Full time. Spent a while in Robertshaw's house, 9th St. in the evening and saw there, two young McNeils from Dundas. Stephen McKechnie called at our place in the evening.

Wed. June 6.
Hot! hot! Full time. Smoked one cigar and wrote one half sheet to Thos in the evening. Reading Hogg's Instructor of which I bought two vols. on my way home on Saturday night.[56]

Thurs. June 7.
Full time at work. After tea, W. Simm and I started to visit Hosie in Brooklyn. Walked down the Bowery and crossed at Catherine St. Ferry. Sat with Hosie and Arthur playing whist until past ten.

---

56 See Diary for 1859, fn 3.

Fri. June 8.
Full time at work. Had letters from home of Christina's marriage to Mr Brewster being fixed for June 6th (two days ago).

Sat. June 9.
Full time at work. Hurried down to Cortland Street North river as soon as I got quit and caught the Staten Island boat. Wm Simm in waiting there. Some amusement in getting a small donkey shipped. Had a strong breeze going down, and a fine walk out to Mr Renfrew's where we arrived about dark.

Sun. June 10.
Beautiful warm weather. Rose early and strolled around the farm. W. Simm and I walked inland to church in the village of Richmond. The red-eyed Cicada, commonly known as the Seventeen year Locust in great numbers. Came home again in the evening and had quite a breeze.

Mon. June 11.
Made 11-¼ ho. at work to-day, working till 7 at night. Spent the eve'g in the house.

Tues. June 12.
Worked to 7 at night. Weather very fine and warm. Spent the eve'g at home.

Wed. June 13.
Made 11-¼ ho. at work to-day. Heard from Thomas but no word of the Brantford situation.

Thurs. June 14.
Made 13-½ hours at work to-day. Harriet Smith married in the eve'g to Modena. Joined the party about 10 o'clock and spent till after twelve. Kind of dull affair.

Fri. June 15.
Full time at work. Called on Wm Simm at his lodgings in the eve'g. Employed him to get a $25 draft for me to send home.

Sat. June 16.
Started work at six o'clock and worked right on till three so as to get off to see the Japanese Embassy. Said Embassy with escort, etc. passed up the Bowery about 4.30 where I had a good view of them and again going down Broadway, where there was a grand turnout of Millitary.[57]

---

57 The first Japanese legation to the U.S. numbered an unwieldy seventy-six officials.

Sun. June 17.
Weather very hot. Had W. Simm at Mr Thompson's Church in the fore-
noon. Lay down and slept most of the afternoon and then Connel and
I crossed over and had a pleasant evening walk around Greenpoint.

Mon. June 18.
Full time in the shop. Got paid at an advanced rate as near as I can
make out, $1.90 per day. Worked in the shop until 7.30. After tea, called
upon and spent a while with W. Simm.

Tues. June 19.
Full time. Commenced writing home. W. Simm called to tell me of Mr
Renfrew having very carelessly neglected procuring a money order for
me which he had taken in hand to do.

Wed. June 20.
Full time at work. Heard from Mr Park, Brantford that the Railway
directors had not passed the order for building their elevator yet and
that consequently he could not send for me yet. Spent the eve'g writing
home.

Thurs. June 21.
Full time at work. Attended a meeting and became a member of a patternmakers' association, John Robertshaw being my proposer.[58]

First arriving in San Francisco in March 1860, it crossed the continent at Panama,
then visited Hampton Roads, Washington, and Philadelphia before appearing in
New York, its final destination, on June 16. The Japanese stayed in New York for
almost two weeks, where they enjoyed a military escort, a march up Broadway, and
several banquets. Though June 16 was declared a civic holiday in honour of the visitors, McIlwraith seems still to have gone to work. See 'Reception of the Japanese,'
NYT, June 16, 1860; 'The Japanese Embassy,' *NYT*, June 18, 1860; 'The Japanese in
New York,' *NYT*, June 18, 29, 1860. Masao Miyoshi, *As We Saw Them: The First Japanese Embassy to the United States* (Philadelphia: Paul Dry Books, 2005).

58 This organization is notable for its early date. Patternmakers (and other metalworkers) in 1850s New York City were remarkable for a lack of unity due largely
to worker itinerancy, employer opposition to unions, and jealously guarded craft
distinctions between draughtsmen, patternmakers, machinists, and others. Until the
end of the Civil War, trade union organizations in the city's foundries and machine
shops were short-lived and 'notoriously unsuccessful.' Conditions changed, however, in the postwar years. In May 1872, the *Times* reported a meeting of patternmakers in Germania Assembly Rooms 'to organize a strike.' See Iver Bernstein, *The New
York City Draft Riots; Their Significance for American Society and Politics in the Age of the
Civil War* (New York: Oxford University Press, 1990), 108, 185; 'Meeting of the Pattern Makers,' *NYT*, May 23, 1872.

Fri. June 22.
Full time at work. Received a parcel of law papers from Thos for my signature, being the purchasing of some property with Building Society stock.[59] Wm Simm called with my money order to send home ($25) and I finished my letter and got it despatched.

Sat. June 23.
Full time in the shop. Wm Simm called in the eve'g. Walked up town with him and then down and visited Mrs Guthrie.

Sun. June 24.
Started from the house early and got a boat at 9.30 from Park M.R. to Port Richmond. Found Marg't Housekeeping in Mr Renfrew's, the family being at Church. Had a very pleasant day. Met a Mr Jameson on a visit.

Mon. June 25.
Full time at work. Didn't do anything particular in the evening.

Tues. June 26.
Took a quarter day to-day and went down to the City Hall on Thos' business but the Mayor not at home.[60] Saw some of the Japanese on Broadway coming home. At work the remainder of the day.

Wed. June 27.
Weather very warm. Spent from 11 till 3 down town on Thos' business but did not yet get it finished. The Mayor at home but could not be seen. At work the remainder of the work hours. In the eve'g Wm Simm, Sandy Hosie, another young gent and I crossed to Green Point, hired a boat and had a fine moonlight pull away up the Newton Creek.

Thurs. June 28.
Full time at work. W. Simm called in the evening with Thomas' papers which he had succeeded in getting the Mayor's seal and signature to. He and I walked across town to the foot of Hammond Street and saw the Great Eastern,[61] there newly moved to her dock.

59 On pre-Confederation building societies in Canada, see Diary for 1857, fn 29.
60 At this time, the mayor of New York was Fernando Wood (1812–81), a Tammany Hall Democrat and Civil War era (Confederate-sympathizing) 'Copperhead,' who served two terms in office (1855–7, 1860–2). See 'Wood, Fernando,' *Dictionary of American Biography* (New York: Charles Scribner's Sons, 1936), 10:456–7. It is unclear what Thomas's business was, but it may have involved Gas Works.
61 Built in 1857 and originally named *Leviathan*, this British steamship became the *Great*

Fri. June 29.
Full time at work. Got parcel of papers despatched to Thos per express.

Sat. June 30.
Weather still bright and warm. Full time at work. In the eve'g visited exhibition of drawing of Cooper Institute pupils, then called on Guthries in Laight St. Sandy home from his voyage with the Adriatic, but not in the house.

Sun. July 1.
Weather pleasantly warm. At Grand St. Church in the morning and heard an old man a stranger preach, our pastor being gone to Scotland. After dinner started for a walk. Called at Bob Patterson's old house at 35th St. but he moved to Yonkers. To Ferry from 42nd St. to Weehawken, and so walked down the river side to Hoboken, getting a good view of the Great Eastern.

Mon. July 2.
Not so oppressively hot to-day. Full time at work. In the eve'g deposited 77$ in the Mariner's Savings bank, No. 1, 3rd Ave.[62] Spent an hour or so in the Cooper Institute reading room.

Tues. July 3.
Full time. Got down town in time to catch the Port Richmond boat. Getting gloamed as I got out to Mr Renfrew's. W. Simm met me about half way. Mr R. promising us a hard days work tomorrow at repairing a road.

Wed. July 4.
Roused early with the alarm of the Cattle being into the garden. Had an early breakfast preparatory to roadmaking but got through with that business very easily. Alex Hosie came out before dinner, while I was mak-

---

Eastern in 1859. It reached New York in June 1860, where it was exhibited to the public with great fanfare. Its huge length and 700-ton capacity made it a sight to be seen. Thousands of people 'swarmed' about it as soon as it arrived. See 'The Great Eastern,' NYT, June 29, 1860; U.S. Department of the Navy, Naval Historical Center webpage, www.history.navy.mil/photos/sh–civil/civsh–g/gt–eastn.htm (accessed December 7, 2011).

62 Incorporated in 1852, the New York's Mariners' Savings Bank, corner of 3rd Avenue and 9th Street, was an independent institution whose president was former city mayor Jacob Westervelt. An independent institution, it offered its clients 6 per cent interest on balances of $500 or less, and 5 per cent on sums greater than that amount. See 'Bank Notices,' NYT, April 9, 1855. General Index of the Laws of the State of New York (Albany, NY: Weed, Parsons and Company, 1859), 103.

ing a sketch of the house. After dinner, Simm and he and I went down to Pt Richmond, hired a boat and had a pull down to Elizabethport. Put in to Jersey shore by stress of a shower of rain and were treated to cigars and a sherry by a party of three young men in like circumstances.

Thurs. July 5.
All day at work. Spent some time in the Cooper institute reading room in the evening.

Fri. July 6.
Full time in the shop. Visited the Mercantile library and got out a book on drawing.

Sat. July 7.
Full time in the shop. Spent the evening on a visit to Old Grizzly 'Adam's' California menagerie. A very large Grizzly bear, Samson in the collection.[63]

Sun. July 8.
Weather very pleasant. Took a trip per Str to Flushing and with 'Hoggs Instructor' as a companion spent most of the day rambling from there to Whiteston and back to College Point. At no church to-day.

Mon. July 9.
Weather getting warm again. Had an hour extra time hurrying up work for Mobile. In the Mercantile reading room in the eve'g.

Tues. July 10.
Full time in the shop. Had a walk down and visited Guthrie's in the evening.

Wed. July 11.
Full time at work. In the evening commenced copying my sketch of Mr Renfrew's house for Mrs R. to send home.

Thurs. July 12.
Full time at work. In the evening going on with drawing of house.

---

63 'Mountain man' J.C. Adams's (d. ca 1861) California Menagerie was located in a tent at the corner of 15th Street and Fourth Avenue. The emporium was managed by P.T. Barnum and billed as the 'greatest novelty in America,' featuring a sea lion, dancing grizzly bears, lions, tigers, ostriches, and buffalo, all 'wild animals from the Pacific … Animals fed at 4 PM.' They were all reputedly captured by the mysterious Adams. 'J.C. Adams' California Menagerie,' *NYT*, June 22, 1860; Brown, *History of the New York Stage*, 2:244.

Fri. July 13.
Full time at work. Hurrying up work for shipping off to Mobile. Sketching in the evening.   .

Sat. July 14.
Full time in the shop. Kept the house in the eve'g and finished drawing of Mr Renfrew's house.

Sun. July 15.
Day warm and beautiful. Took Staten Island Ferry boat to Vanderbilt landing about ten in the forenoon, and had a fine walk from there out to Mrs Renfrew's. Met her boy France there. Delivered my sketch of the house which gave great satisfaction. Got drive in in the waggon in the evening.

Mon. July 16.
Full time at work. Heard from Thos. Expects me to be sent for in a week or two. Inclosed a lettergraph portrait group of himself and two children, Tommy and Mary, for Mrs Logan. Had a walk down town to the old watchmaker Frierlinck with my watch in the eve'g. Webber leaving our room to-night.

Tues. July 17.
Full time at work. In the eve'g wrote to Mrs T. McI. now at Greenfield, Ayr, Canada West.

Wed. July 18.
Full time. Wm Simm called in the evening, he having now moved his boarding house from Tenth St. to Franklin St. but don't like his new house.

Thurs. July 19.
Full time. Weather being pretty warm, staid in the house and smoked a cigar at the open window.

Fri. July 20.
Full time at work. In the evening doing nothing.

Sat. July 21.
Full time. On quitting work at 5 p.m. went right across town to the Great Eastern, went on board, and inspected her internals, etc. Afterwards had a ramble round town.

Sun. July 22.
At Grand St. church in the morning and felt exceedingly drowsy so

much so that Connel averred that I slept all the time of the sermon. After dinner, slept in bed untill near tea time, then after tea read a sermon of Mr Beecher's in the 'Independent.'[64]

Mon. July 23.
Full time at work. Wm Simm called in the evening and I had a stroll round with him.

Tues. July 24.
Full time. Hurried up town in the eve'g and spent a short time viewing Church's picture 'Twilight in the Wilderness.'[65] Admired it very much. Then down town to Guthries and saw Mrs Logan there. A. Guthrie drunk.

Wed. July 25.
Full time. Weather quite cool. News to-day of the Prince of Wales having landed in Newfoundland.[66] Mrs Logan called for me in the evening, also Wm Simm and we all three had a walk down Broadway and an ice cream in Taylor's Saloon.

Thurs. July 26.
Full time and an hour over. Wrote a piece to Hugh Dickie in the evening.

Fri. July 27.
Full time. Fine cool clear moonlight night. Spent a while down on Tenth St. Pier.

Sat. July 28.
Full time at work. Marg't called during the day and borrowed 20$ for

---

64 'Sermons by Henry Ward Beecher' was a regular feature in New York's *The Independent*, a weekly published by S.W. Benedict and in circulation from 1848 to 1928. Beecher's sermon sprang from a central theme in nineteenth-century social discourse: 'the love of money is the root of all evil ... the treasures of the world are in the human heart.' 'Sermons by Henry Ward Beecher,' *The Independent*, July 19, 1860.

65 Frederick Edwin Church, *Twilight in the Wilderness* (1860). Oil on canvas, 40' 60 in. The painting was shown at Goupil's Gallery, 772 Broadway. 'Amusements This Evening,' *NYT*, July 18, 1860. See fn 46 above. It is now at the Cleveland Museum of Art.

66 The arrival of Edward Albert, the eighteen-year-old Prince of Wales at St John's was a celebrated event and the first stop in a five-month tour of Canada and the United States. News of his arrival on the continent made the front page of the *Times*. 'The Prince of Wales. His Arrival and Reception at St John's,' *NYT*, May 25, 1860. On the pageantry and meanings of the visit, see Ian Radforth, *Royal Spectacle: The 1860 Visit of the Prince of Wales to Canada and the United States* (Toronto: University of Toronto Press, 2005).

Mr Renfrew. Connel and I had a walk down Broadway as far as Grand
St. and up the Bowery in the eve'g. Visited London Stereoscopic Ware-
house on Broadway.[67]

Sun. July 29.
Day lowering but did not rain untill eve'g. Took 9.15 boat to Port Richmond and started to walk to Mr Renfrew's but lost the way and found
myself at 'Old Place' opposite Elizabeth Port. Must have walked 12
miles before I got Mr Renfrews. Got drove in to Vanderbilt landing and
home with the late boat. Evening quite wet.

Mon. July 30.
Full time. Called upon and spent a while with Miss Marshall in the
evening (Mrs Abel I should now call her).

Tues. July 31.
Full time. Weather warm. Came home and lay down in bed after tea
and slept all evening.

Wed. Aug. 1.
Mrs Logan and I had set to go on an excursion and after viewing
the arrival of the Great Eastern from Cape May from Robinson St. Pier,
left with the Alice Price for Keyport. Had delightful weather and a fine
sail.

Thurs. Aug. 2.
Full time. Attended Patternmakers club meeting in the evening and
walked home with Jackson and the two Robertshaws.

Fri. Aug. 3.
Full time. Spent the eve'g finishing a letter to Hugh Dickie.

Sat. Aug. 4.
Full time. Work still keeps very busy, one of the principal jobs in hand
being a large building for Milwaukie. Visited Guthries and the watch-
makers in the evening.

---

67 The London Stereoscopic Company was a showroom at 594 Broadway where stere-
oscopes of American and European scenes were demonstrated and sold. The company was founded in London, England, in 1854 and opened its short-lived operation
in New York in 1860. Peter E. Palmquist and Thomas R. Kailbourn, *Pioneer Photog-
raphers of the Far West: A Biographical Dictionary, 1840–1865* (Palo Alto, CA: Stanford
University Press, 2000), 374. See advertisement in *The Independent*, October 11, 1860.

Sun. Aug. 5.
At Grand St. church in the morning and in the afternoon sailed up to Harlem and walked into the country as far as the village of West Farms. Warm, warm weather.

Mon. Aug. 6.
Still hot. Connel absent to-day and yesterday. He and I seeming to get cold towards one another. Full time in the shop.

Tues. Aug. 7.
Full time. Awfully hot weather. Lie down and sleep on getting home in the evening.

Wed. Aug. 8.
Full time at work. Writing to Bill in the evening.

Thurs. Aug. 9.
Full time. Writing in the evening goes on slowly. I feel so tired when getting home.

Fri. Aug. 10.
Full time in the shop. Very warm weather. Writing in the evening.

Sat. Aug. 11.
Full time. Weather cloudy and somewhat cooler to-day. Wm Simm call and spent a while in the eve'g. Walked with him down the Bowery and Catherine St. to Catherine Ferry.

Sun. Aug. 12.
Fine warm weather. Went to Staten Island in the morning and walked out to Mr Renfrew's from Vanderbilt landing. Met Mrs Wyckoff and Mrs Jameson there. Got late for the Factoryvill boat coming home and had to walk round to Vanderbilt landing. Caught a butterfly of a kind I did not possess before.

Mon. Aug. 13.
Weather changed to-day being quite cool. Full time. At letter to Bill in the evening. Mr Cheney our Foreman off work sick.

Tues. Aug. 14.
Raining nearly all day. Full time at work. In the evening finished and posted letter to Bill.

Wed. Aug. 15.
Full time at work. In the eve'g made a trip to Brooklyn and visited Wm
Simm in his new lodgings 73 Fulton Av. Took some lessons in euchre
and had some singing of hymn tunes.

Thurs. Aug. 16.
Full time. Visited the Library in the evening and got Irving's
Astoria.[68] Wrote to Thos in Hamilton. Str Great Eastern sailed for
Europe to-day.

Fri. Aug. 17
Full time. In the evening commenced writing to Jameson. Bed bugs
most abominably numerous in our room this season, breeding among
our books and crawling over them.

Sat. Aug. 18.
Full time. Walked down and visited Guthrie's in the evening. Sandy
sober now. Work continues busy in the shop, I being kept going at John
McIntyre's jobs most all the time.

Sun. Aug. 19.
Left the house early and got the 8 o'clock boat for Long Branch. Very
warm bright weather. Had a pleasant sail around Navesink Highlands,
along to Branch Port and from there walked across to the sea shore and
had a stroll along. Saw the folks bathing in the surf opposite the hotels
in long lines, all holding on by a rope. Arrived in the city about 8.

Mon. Aug. 20.
Full time in the shop. Finished letter to Jameson in the evening.

Tues. Aug. 21.
Full time. Weather close and dull and evening very wet. Called at the
library for the second vol. of Astoria which I have been reading but
found it closed for a fortnight.

Wed. Aug. 22.
Full time. Came home and slept all evening. Great Camp meeting at
Sing-Sing this week. Boice the foreman moulder gone to it.[69]

---

68 Washington Irving, *Astoria; or, Enterprise beyond the Rocky Mountains*, 3 vols. (Philadelphia: Carey, Lea and Blanchard, 1836).
69 The Methodist Camp Meeting at Sing-Sing Heights-on-the-Hudson, New York, was
   an annual ten-day event that began in the 1830s. Originally, it was purely a revival

Thurs. Aug. 23.
Full time. Spent the evening reading and loafing.

Fri. Aug. 24.
Full time. Very lazy inclined at present, lying down and sleeping after tea.

Sat. Aug. 25.
Full time. Connel and I had a stroll down town in the evening.

Sun. Aug. 26.
Beautiful bright weather. At Staten Island to-day. Took a new route from Vanderbilt landing, having a fine view of all the lower bay. Mr Jameson at Mr Renfrew's. Came home with the Flora.

Mon. Aug. 27.
Weather warm but breezy and pleasant. Dispatched newspapers to Mary Goldie. Full time at work. Spent the evening reading. Have got cold and cough a little.

Tues. Aug. 28.
Full time. Had a stroll down to Grand Street and bought a pair of gaiters in the evening.

Wed. Aug. 29.
Full time and a quarter over. Kept the house in the evening.

Thurs. Aug. 30.
Fine weather. Full time. Musquitos begginning to come in upon us now, so I made two frames for the window and have netting over them. Spent the evening about this job.

Fri. Aug. 31.
Full time. Got through with working two or three weeks for John McIntyre and am now on a job for Rio Janeiro. Spent the evening in the

---

meeting with conversion of souls its principal goal. By mid-century, it had become a sort of religious summer vacation destination – 'good beds' for 50 cents a night; 'excellent board' $1.00–$1.50 per day – with a tight schedule of prayer meetings and singing services. Cindy S. Aron, *Working at Play: A History of Vacations in the United States* (New York: Oxford University Press, 2001), 102–3; 'Sing Sing Camp Meetings,' Alfred Emanuel Smith, *New Outlook*, August 27, 1898, p. 1034.

house. Old Blockston from next room came in and talked a while about the Presidential election,[70] Prince of Wales, etc.[71]

Sat. Sept. 1.
Full time at work. Walked down town and called on Guthries folks in the evening.

Sun. Sept. 2.
Went down to Grand St. church in the morning but found it closed. Came home and had a nap before dinner, and then a long snooze after ditto. Mr Blockson and I attended service in the Episcopal Chapel in the eve'g.

Mon. Sept. 3.
Full time. Wrote to Mrs Brewster and posted it off in the eve'g.

Tues. Sept. 4.
Full time. Weather very delightful. Had an Ayrshire Express, which had lain over at the P.O. on account of being wrong addressed. Sat reading of the volunteers grand review at Edinburgh, etc. in the eve'g.[72]

---

70 By late August 1860, the four-candidate U.S. presidential race had already proved heated and controversial. Disagreement over northern Democrats' (and Stephen Douglas's) 'popular sovereignty' policy split the Democratic Party at its April convention in Charleston, South Carolina, and when it reconvened in Baltimore in June, southern Democrats split for good, nominating their own presidential candidate, John C. Breckinridge. In May, the remnants of the American ('Know-Nothing') Party shed their anti-immigrant plank and formed the new Constitutional Union Party, with John Bell as nominee. Also in May, the Republican Party held its nomination convention in Chicago, where its frontrunner, W.H. Seward, was defeated on the third ballot by Illinois lawyer and slavery opponent Abraham Lincoln. Well before the November election, the political atmosphere was highly charged and the future of slavery was at its centre. James M. McPherson, *Ordeal by Fire: The Civil War and Reconstruction* (New York: Alfred A. Knopf, 1982), 117–26.

71 The Prince of Wales had been in North America for a little more than a month. See Diary entry for 25 July 1860.

72 On 7 August 1860, Queen Victoria and the Royal Family reviewed the 22,000 members of the Scottish Volunteer Rifle Corps, which assembled at Holyrood Palace in Edinburgh. It was, one commentator wrote, 'one of the grandest and most successful public spectacles ever witnessed by Old or New Edinburgh.' James Grant, *Old and New Edinburgh: Its History, Its People, and Its Places* (London, Paris, and New York: Cassell, Petter, Galpin and Company, 1882), 2:284; 'The Volunteer Review,' *Ayrshire Express*, August 11, 1860.

Wed. Sept. 5.
Full time in the shop. Spent the evening sketching Wm Simm as he appeared making roads on the Fourth of July.

Thurs. Sept. 6.
Full time. Attended meeting of Pattern makers club in the eve'g and was elected vice-president. Walked home with the Robertshaws, father and son.

Fri. Sept. 7.
Full time. Weather sultry. Lay down on bed after tea and slept till late or early with clothes on.

Sat. Sept. 8.
Full time time. Hurried down town to try and get to Staten Island but was late. Went to the Winter Garden Theatre and saw 'Anderson, the Wizard of the North.' Thought the tricks clever but was not highly amused, or edified.[73]

Sun. Sept. 9.
Morning dull and cold. Got down to Pier 2 in time to catch the 'Flora' at 9.15, and got out early to Mr Renfrew's and found Marg't keeping house, quite lame with Musquito bites. Left Factoryville at 5. Had a walk down by the wharves in Brooklyn, and then went and heard Beecher. Had a walk with Sandy Hosie afterwards.

Mon. Sept. 10.
Full time. Weather continuing quite chilly. Had letters from Mrs Hunter and Mrs Brewster and also 'Ayrshire Times.' Kept the house reading them in the evening.

Tues. Sept. 11.
Full time. Called at the library in the eve'g and got vol. 2 of Irving's 'Astoria.'

---

73 A native of Aberdeen, John Henry Anderson (1814–74) was the well-travelled 'illusionist,' or stage magician, and juggler who billed himself as 'Professor Anderson, Wizard of the North.' He came to New York in 1851 and performed often in Broadway theatres. His act, contemporaries noted, was in presenting 'many schemes of legerdomain'; a 'system of puffery little short of the marvelous.' Edward Stirling, *Old Drury Lane: Fifty Years' Recollections of Author, Actor and Manager* (London: Chatto and Windus, 1881), 328; Maurice Willson Disher, *Clowns and Pantomimes* (New York: B. Blom, 1968), 312; 'Anderson, John Henry,' in James Grant Wilson, John Fiske, eds., *Appleton's Cyclopaedia of American Biography* (New York: D. Appleton and Company, 1891), 1:69.

Wed. Sept. 12.
Full time at work. In the evening sat in. Had a visit of Sandy Hosie. Sat
late reading 'Astoria.'

Thurs. Sept. 13.
Full time. In the evening finished the perusal of Irving's 'Astoria' hav-
ing been much entertained with it. Afterwards read Bulwer's 'Lady of
Lyons.'[74]

Fri. Sept. 14.
Full time, being employed on large building for Milwaukie this last two
weeks. Had Ayrshire Express[75] per Str 'Asia.' Sat reading it and New
York Herald in the evening.[76]

Sat. Sept. 15.
Full time at work. Called on Guthrie's in the eve'g. Sandy still purposing going out to Cuba.

Sun. Sept. 16.
Started early and took the Peekskill morning boat. Landed at Haverstraw and had a fine ramble and scramble to the top of the 'High Turn'
a high rocky peak, the culmination of a serrated range of hills overlooking the village and Hudson river and surrounding country.

Mon. Sept. 17.
Full time. Wrote to Hamilton to Mrs Thos in the eve'g. Great demonstration of Democrats around the Cooper Institute when I went up to
post my letter.[77]

---

74 Edward George Earle Lyton Bulwer-Lytton, *The Lady of Lyons, or, Love and Pride. A
    Play, in Five Acts* (New York: Harper and Brothers, 1838).
75 On the *Ayrshire Express*, see Diary for 1857, fn 31.
76 The *New York Herald* was a daily city newspaper founded in 1835 by an immigrant
    Scot, James Gordon Bennett (1795–1872). In its early years a Whig voice, it had
    become more centrist in tone by the late 1850s. It claimed a circulation of 84,000 by
    1861. In 1924, the paper merged with a former rival to form the *New York Herald
    Tribune*. On the *Herald*'s important place among mid-century newspapers, see Carl
    Sandburg, *Storm over the Land: A Profile of the Civil War* (New York: Harcourt Brace,
    1942), 86–9.
77 Organized by followers of John C. Bell's Constitutional Union Party, it was attended
    largely by Breckinridge southern Democrats. Nationally prominent politicians spoke
    inside the Union and outside, where a firing cannon could be heard and a long pro-
    cession seen down Broadway. The meeting called for a union of Democrats of all
    stripes to stop Abraham Lincoln in the coming (November) election. The call was
    repeated several weeks later in a torchlight procession of anti-Republicans. 'Presi-

Tues. Sept. 18.
Full time. In the evening called at the library and then on Mr Spittal, 13th Street, and spent an hour or two chatting there.

Wed. Sept. 19.
Weather kinder dull. Full time. Sat in the house reading the Herald and 'Irving's Sketch Book'[78] in the evening. Connel speaking of going away to Cuba. Herald reports the Prince of Wales being at Hamilton yesterday.[79]

Thurs. Sept. 20.
Full time. Scottish games to come off at Jones Wood to-day but weather deplorably wet.[80] Spent the evening rather lazily reading the news of the Prince of Wales, etc.

Fri. Sept. 21.
Full time at work. Kept the house in the evening.

Sat. Sept. 22.
Full time. Had 'Ayrshire Times' from home with my letter published.[81] Went to the theatre in the eve'g and saw Mr and Mrs Barney Williams, the Irish boy and Yankee girl. Kind of second rate entertainment.[82]

---

dential. Anti-Republican Mass Meeting,' *NYT*, September 18, 1860. See Diary entry for October 23, 1860.

78 Washington Irving, *The Sketch-Book of Geoffrey Crayon, gent.* (New York: C.S. Van Win-kle, 1819–20).

79 'The Visit of the Prince of Wales,' *New York Herald*, September 19, 1860.

80 New York's Caledonian Club (organized in 1856) held Scottish Games annually at Jones's Wood on the East River between 65th and 70th beginning in 1858. Normally the games included throwing the hammer, tossing the caber, and a series of foot races. Indeed, wet weather forced the club to postpone the Games until the following Monday, when they were attended by 'six or seven thousand spectators.' New York Common Council, *Valentine's Manual of Old New York* (New York: Valentine's Manual, 1917), 147; George B. Kirsch, ed., *Sports in North America: A Documentary History* (Academic International Press, 1992), 3:312; 'Scottish Games. Fourth Annual Exhibition,' *NYT*, September 25, 1860.

81 His letter was a long, detailed outline of work conditions and prospects for Scottish tradesmen in New York City. 'America Letter,' *Ayrshire Times*, August 29, 1860. It is reproduced in full in the Prologue of this book. Thanks to Tom Barclay, Carnegie Library, Ayr, Scotland, for locating it.

82 Born Bernard O'Flaherty in Cork, Ireland, Barney Williams (1824–76) was a comedian, theatrical writer, and actor in New York, and, for a time, manager of the Broadway Theatre. In 1850, he married Maria Pray (b. 1828), who thereafter appeared with him as 'Mrs Williams' in his comedic sketches. The Williamses were financially

Sun. Sept. 23.
Started out early and caught the Keyport boat. Landed from her at Chelsea landing in the Kills and walked from there to Mr Renfrew's. Found the folks all well. Marg't talking about coming to the city to stay.

Mon. Sept. 24.
Full time. Spent the evening reading 'Irving's life of Washington.'[83]

Tues. Sept. 25.
Full time and a quarter over. Found Marg't in my boarding house when I got home. Had come of from Mr Renfrew in the pet. Mrs Smith agrees to take her in for the time. Had a visit of Messrs Spittal and McIntyre.

Wed. Sept. 26.
Full time although I slept in and had to go without breakfast in the morning. Sat in my room with Marg't in the eve'g.

Thurs. Sept. 27.
Full time. Mrs Logan not staying here to-night. Called at Cooper institute and spent a while.

Fri. Sept. 28.
Full time at work. Connel asked me in the morning to go over to McLellans with him in the evening so went over after tea to some sort of a party. After being there some short time, the Rev. Dr Morrison arrived and my friend Connel was then and there married [to] Miss Marg't MacLellan. Kept up the spree singing, etc. to four o'clock.

Sat. Sept. 29.
Full time. Had a parcel from Canada containing Christina's Photograph and a piece of bride's cake but no letter from Tom. Had a stroll round by Broadway and the Bowery in the evening, and slept very long and sound after last nights exhertions.

Sun. Sept. 30.
At church in the forenoon and saw Mr and Mrs Connel kirkit.[84] Spent all the remainder of the day reading 'Life of Washington.'

---

successful as actors; their comedy, one biographer noted, was 'broad but effective.' The 'Irish Boy and Yankee Girl' was a series of comedic duets in a style that was later known as vaudeville. *The National Cyclopedia of American Biography* (J.T. White, 1894), 5:440.
83　Washington Irving, *Life of George Washington* (New York: G.P. Putnam and Co., 1855).
84　At church (old Scots dialect).

Mon. Oct. 1.
Dull rainy weather. Full time. Connel packing up and moving in the evening. Mrs Logan not returned here yet.

Tues. Oct. 2.
Full time at work. Kept the house reading, etc. in the evening.

Wed. Oct. 3.
Full time. Grand torch light procession of the republican Wide Awakes to-night.[85] Walked down town and called on Guthries then saw the procession on the way home. From Grace Church to the park one blaze of light.

Thurs. Oct. 4.
Full time. In the evening at pattern makers meeting which got along pretty well adding several new members to the society.

Fri. Oct. 5.
Full time. Marg't and I at a concert in City Assembly rooms, mostly all Scottish songs by Miss Sutherland, Messrs Cummings, Anderson, etc. Highly pleased with the entertainment.[86]

Sat. Oct. 6.
Full time. Read Washington in the evening, also wrote some to Mary Goldie but did not please me. Had a long letter from Thos.

Sun. Oct. 7.
Fine weather. At Thompson's Church in the afternoon. Finished vol. 3 of Irving's life of Washington.

Mon. Oct. 8.
Full time. Marg't at work in my room in the evening.

---

85 A paramilitary organization made up largely of young working–class men, the Wide Awakes were the ground troops of the Republican party. They had distinctive uniforms (oilcloth capes with caps or helmets), zigzag marching patterns, songs, war chants, and cheers. Their assemblies were impressive and intimidating. This torchlight procession included Wide Awake clubs from across the American north and west. The *Times* estimated their numbers to have been 12,000; the *Tribune* hazarded 20,000. 'The Presidential Campaign. Grand Wide-Awake Demonstration,' *NYT*, October 4, 1860; Edward K. Spann, *Gotham at War: New York City, 1860–1865* (Wilmington, DE: SR Books, 2002), 3–4.

86 New York's City Assembly Rooms were on the east side of Broadway just above Grand Street. Though she was from England, Agnes Sutherland was known as the 'Scottish Nightingale.' She moved to the U.S. in 1857 and sang in concert halls across the country. Lawrence, *Strong on Music*, 3:310. On Anderson, see fn 73 above.

Tues. Oct. 9.
Weather dry and cool. Finished fixing up Frieze pattern for Snooks. Marg't and I writing in our room in the evening. Wrote to John Park to return my certificates.

Wed. Oct. 10.
Full time. Called at the reading room and got vol. 4 of Washington. Banked $60 in 3rd Ave. Savings bank.

Thurs. Oct. 11.
Knocked off work at half time to see the reception of the Prince of Wales. Went down the Bowery on the cars to the Park and spent a while in Barnum's Museum. Saw that worthy himself. Museum much crowded, so came out and got a position nearly opposite Trinity Church, where I saw the Prince passing up.[87]

Fri. Oct. 12.
Full time. Called on Mr Connel now living with his wife at her father's in Grove St. in the eve'g.

Sat. Oct. 13.
Full time. Marg't stayed in the City to-night to see the grand torch light procession of firemen. Her and I went up round Madison Square, stood a while opposite the 5th Ave. Hotel and saw the Prince making his bow when the last Fire Co. went past.

Sun. Oct. 14.
At church in the forenoon and heard Mr Thomson. Weather very cold and blustering so kept the house with Marg't all the day after that. Had

---

87 The Prince of Wales's five-day visit to New York City (October 12–16) was received warmly and enthusiastically by New Yorkers, who clambered to get a glimpse of royalty. The *Times* covered the prince's every public move, and he made many, filling his days with tours of the city's libraries and academies, official receptions, processions and military reviews, church attendance at Trinity, and browsing in mercantile establishments on Broadway. He was championed as the 'young hope of Britain' whose presence in the metropolis symbolized a new era of friendship between his nation and the United States. See 'The Prince in the Metropolis,' *NYT*, October 11, 1860; 'The Prince of Wales in New-York,' *NYT*, October 11, 1860; 'Welcome to the Prince,' *NYT*, October 12, 1860; 'The Reception of the Prince of Wales,' *NYT*, October 12, 1860; 'The Prince in the Metropolis,' *NYT*, October 13, 1860; 'Movements of the Prince,' *NYT*, October 15, 1860. 'An immense throng of people eager to see the Prince took possession of Broadway long before the appointed hour; admission to the church was by ticket only, and perfect order was preserved by a strong force of police.' Morgan Dix, ed. and comp., *A History of the Parish of Trinity Church in the City of New York* (New York: G.P. Putnam's Sons, 1906), 4:469. See also Radforth, *Royal Spectacle*, 336–63.

a good view of the Prince of Wales coming home from church, he having been attending service in Trinity Church.

Mon. Oct. 15.
Full time. In the evening Webber and I went to Cooper Institute class. Being the first night was spent in organizing the class. Had my certificates returned from Mr Park.

Tues. Oct. 16.
Full time. Marg't in the room sewing at her skirt in the evening. Cold weather. Sat late and wrote to Mary Goldie.

Wed. Oct. 17.
Full time. Posted letter to Ayr in the morning and at noon had one from Thos inclosing one from John Goldie in Galt, proposing that I should come and be bookeeper in the Foundry with him.

Thurs. Oct. 18.
Full time. Worked on along with Magee the Carver who works overtime just now, at fixing up my chest. Had another note from Thos advising me to go to Galt. Wrote answer to him accepting.

Fri. Oct. 19.
Full time. Worked till near ten at my chest.

Sat. Oct. 20.
Full time. Worked on at my box for a while.

Sun. Oct. 21.
Too tired to go to church to-day. Sat in the house and read in the forenoon, and in the afternoon had a walk down town, and round by the docks on East River.

Mon. Oct. 22.
Full time in the shop. At Cooper Institute school in the evening and like it pretty well.

Tues. Oct. 23.
Full time at work. Great Torchlight demonstration of Democrats and Union men to-night.[88] Walked down to Guthrie's and met Mrs

---

88 Two weeks before the election, anticipating defeat if they did not unite, supporters of the northern and southern Democratic presidential nominees (Stephen Douglas and John C. Breckinridge, respectively) and those of the Constitutional Union Party (John Bell) paraded in New York to promote the 'combination all of the elements opposed … to Lincoln.' Albert Shaw, *Abraham Lincoln: The Year of His Election* (New York:

Logan there. Her and Mrs Guthrie and I went and viewed the parade on Broadway opposite Taylor's Saloon. 12 o'clock before we got home.

Wed. Oct. 24.
Full time. Worked at my chest till between 7 and 8. Had a visit of Wm Simm, and walked with him down as far as Grand St; he being now boarding in East B'way. Heard from Thos that he had written to John Goldie my acceptance of the job as bookkeeper.

Thurs. Oct. 25.
At work all day and had overtime on girder pattern along with Wolfe and the two Peasells till Ten o'clock.

Fri. Oct. 26.
Full time in the shop. Worked on at my chest till about 8. Visited the Mercantile reading room a short time and strolled down Broadway and up the Bowery. Mrs Logan gone to spend the eve'g with Mrs Lyle.

Sat. Oct. 27.
Full time. Hurried down town in the evening and in company with Wm Simm, took passage in the Flora for Staten Island. Got a hearty reception from Mrs Renfrew.

Sun. Oct. 28.
Rose early and Wm Simm and I walked in to church in Port Richmond and heard Mr Brownlee.[89] Came home with the Flora in the evening. Called on A. Hosie and accompanied him to Mr. Beecher's preaching.

Mon. Oct. 29.
Full time at work. Wm Simm called in the eve'g and Mrs Logan, he and I all went and saw 'Othello' acted by Edwin Forest in Niblos

---

Review of Reviews Corp., 1929), 104. The *Times* called it the 'Union Demonstration ... decidedly magnificent and imposing.' 'The Presidential Campaign. Great Fusion Demonstration,' *NYT*, October 24, 1860; 'The Demonstration Last Night,' *NYT*, October 24, 1860.

89 Rev. James Brownlee, DD (1808–95), was the long-serving pastor (1835–95) of the Port Richmond (Dutch) Reformed Church on Staten Island. 'In his preaching he dwelt much upon the great doctrines of the Gospel ... His hearers were always edified.' Edward Tanjore Corwin, *A Manual of the Reformed Church in America, 1628–1902*, 4th ed. (New York: Board of Publication of the Reformed Church in America, 1902), 348.

Theatre.[90] Had final letter from Thomas about going off and also from M.G.

Tues. Oct. 30.
Full time in the shop. In the evening went to see Barry and also Mrs Abel but was disappointed in finding either.

Wed. Oct. 31.
Mrs Logan and I had an overhawling and cleaning of my chest. Called on Mrs Abel, 134 E. 25th St. Wm Simm called in the evening and him and I went and bought me a coat and pantaloons. Mrs Logan hurried down town to see Mr Renfrew on the subject of going with me but he had left.

Thurs. Nov. 1.
Mrs L. assisted me to pack my clothes chest in the morning. At noon bade good bye to my shopmates and had my chests shipped off as freight. Called at Mr Renfrew's store and got agreed with Mr R. to have Mrs Logan with me, and then her and I went and took out tickets and she went down to Staten Island. Wrote home in the eve'g and packed my valise which kept me up late.

Fri. Nov. 2.
Had breakfast and bade good bye to Mrs Smith by 6 a.m. and got on board the 'Armenia' for Albany by 7. Had a pleasant sail up the river and found Mrs Logan at the R.R. Station having come by rail. Had from 5 till 11 to spend in Albany and had a walk round. Read Adam Bede awhile.[91]

Sat. Nov. 3.
At Rochester shortly after daylight after a tolerably comfortable night

---

90 Philadelphia-born Edwin Forrest (1806–72) was America's first great actor, a hand-some, athletic man whose sonorous voice and appetite for classic leading roles won him broad critical praise in the U.S. and Europe and financial success in the 1830s and '40s. By 1860, Forrest's star had fallen somewhat, his reputation stained by his alleged role in the Astor Place Opera House riot (1849) in which twenty-two people were killed, and his messy, public, and prolonged divorce trial (1851). Even after these unsavoury events, he was still able to consistently pack theatre houses until his death in 1872. The *Times* described this performance as 'one of his best Shakespear-ian characters' who played to a 'crowded' house. 'Niblo's Garden,' *NYT*, October 30, 1860; 'Forrest, Edwin,' in Allen Johnson and Dumas Malone, eds., *Dictionary of American Biography* (New York: Charles Scribner's Sons, 1931), 6:529–31.
91 George Eliot, pseud., *Adam Bede* (New York: Harper and Brothers, 1859).

in the sleeping car. Crossed the Niagara in the forenoon and landed in Hamilton soon after 12. Met Thomas with Mary and Tommy on the platform. Mrs Mac absent at Detroit, came home in the afternoon.

Sun. Nov. 4.
At Mr Burnet's church forenoon and evening.[92] The interval spent in the house.

Mon. Nov. 5.
Mrs Mac and I visited old Mr Muir's in their new house, Park Street. Also I called on Jameson at the Railway Engineer's Office.[93]

Tues. Nov. 6.
Thos and I started early in the forenoon and borrowed Capt. Zealand's buggy and horse, and had a drive down to the Beach visiting the Water Works where I saw Jas McFarlane. Found good sport along the beach Thomas obtaining specimens of Shore Lark, Golden Plover and Arctic Longspur. Kept the house in the eve'g.

Wed. Nov. 7.
Took the 8.30 train to Galt and walked from the station right to the Foundry. Had to wait a little before Mr Goldie appeared. Met with Sidney Smith for the first time. Got notice of my chests having arrived at the station and had them brought down to Mr Goldie's he having agreed to take me in as a lodger.

Thurs. Nov. 8.
Thick hoar frost on the ground in the morning. Commenced making entries in the Day Book and Cash book today. David Goldie came in in the afternoon and Sydney Smith went off with him. Spent the evening in the house talking over things in general with J.G.

Fri. Nov. 9.
Weather fine and mild. Nights dark and cold. Keeping the house in the evening.

Sat. Nov. 10.
On duty all day. Had the paying of the hands to do in the evening. Mary Goldie came in to town with Sidney Smith and I met her at the

---

92 Rev. Robert Burnet's church was St Andrew's Presbyterian in Hamilton, Canada West. On Burnet, see Diary for 1857 fn 114.
93 The Great Western Railway Engineer's Office was in Hamilton, Canada West. One of McIlwraith's first visits was paid to his old friend Jameson.

house at dinner time. Wm also came down from Guelph and altogether stayed all night.

Sun. Nov. 11.
Mary and William went off early in the morning with the buggie. J.G. and I went and heard my old pastor Mr Thompson preach in the Free Church. Spent the evening in the house of our neighbour Mr Strickland of Billing & Strickland.

Mon. Nov. 12.
About the Foundry all day. Willie Goldie returned from Ayr and went off with the late train for Guelph.

Tues. Nov. 13.
All day on duty. Spent the evening writing home.

Wed. Nov. 14.
About the work all day. Keeping house in the evening reading, etc.

Thurs. Nov. 15.
Drawing mill and working around all day. John Goldie and I visited the Galt reading room in the evening.

Fri. Nov. 16.
About the work drawing, etc. all day.

Sat. Nov. 17.
Drawing at Mill most part of the day. Had a walk round town in the evening.

Sun. Nov. 18.
Heard Rev. Mr James preach morning and afternoon. Liked his discourse pretty well only tho't 3 ho. rather long a spell. John Goldie and I had a walk down the river bank in the interval.

Mon. Nov. 19.
Weather blustering. Barn burnt in our neighbourhood today. Spent most the day making sketches of Bark Mill from one that came down from Guelph. James Goldie came down from Guelph in the evening and stayed over night. Had note from Thomas along with parcel of shirts per express.

Tues. Nov. 20.
Ground white with a thin sprinkling of snow in the morning. Snowing fast considerable part of the day.

Wed. Nov. 21.
At mill drawing to-day but feeling rather at fault with it for want of information, McCulloch being mostly from home. Keeping house in the evening. Had a visit from David Goldie.

Thurs. Nov. 22.
Stuck pretty close to drawing to-day. Weather very cold.

Fri. Nov. 23.
An exceeding wet, blustering day. At drawing most of to-day at small mill for John Stewart, Carluke, near Ancaster.

Sat. Nov. 24.
Great change in the weather again, being frosty with snow and very cold.

Sun. Nov. 25.
Grand river frozen nearly across opposite the house, and all day blowing a breeze of wind bitterly cold. Had Mr and Mrs Strickland and family in at dinner. J.G. and I at Mr James church both ends of the day.[94]

Mon. Nov. 26.
Still frosty but calmer. Snowing great part of the day. Our family making preparation to move into their new house, the one lately occupied by Mr Crombie, opposite the work.[95] Mrs J. Goldie's sister arrived from the country to assist her with moving, etc. Wrote to Mrs Logan.

Tues. Nov. 27.
Making out accounts most part of the day. Had tea in the new house and slept there in the evening.

Wed. Nov. 28.
Fine frosty weather. At drawing part of the day and part day at books. Kept the house all the evening. The moon about full the prospect of the Grand river rather pleasing in the moonlight from the back of the river.

---

94 Rev. John James's church was the Galt United Presbyterian Church, a new institution established in April 1857. Rev. James pastored there from May 1857 until he resigned in May 1861. A Scotsman, he was educated in Glasgow and Edinburgh and following his stint in Galt served pastorates in Paris, Canada West, Wolverhampton, England, Albany, New York, Hamilton, and Walkerton, Ontario, from 1861 to 1894. See James A.R. Dickson, *Ebenezer: A History of the Central Presbyterian Church, Galt, Ontario* (Toronto: William Briggs, 1904), 29, 33–50.

95 The house of James Crombie, Gentleman, was on Hawthorn Street in Galt's Ward Three. The property was assessed at $500 in the 1860 town assessment rolls. Assessment Roll for the Town of Galt … 1860, p. 25.

Thurs. Nov. 29.
Finished drawing and copy of Stewart's mill. Have to go at posting soon now which will keep me busy for a time.

Fri. Nov. 30.
Had a visit of David Goldie on his way to Guelph. Things moving along about the usual way about the Foundry.

Sat. Dec. 1.
David Goldie along with Hugh Stevenson arrived in the forenoon, so them and I got off in the buggy in the afternoon. Keen frost and roads very bad for the horse, his feet not being sharpened. Arrived at Greenfield[96] somewhere about 3 or 4 o'clock and got a kind reception.

Sun. Dec. 2.
At church in the morning and heard the Rev. Mr McRuar. Walked out and in with M.G. Had a long walk out the road with David and A. McEwen.

Mon. Dec. 3.
Mary G. decided on accompanying me in the buggy to Galt and so on to Guelph to fetch aunt Betsy. Detained a little untill the horse Bob got his feet sharpened for the ice. Had a pleasant drive in. In the afternoon, John and her went off in the buggy to Guelp. Had the servant boy from Greenfield sleeping with me as he had come in to take home the horse.

Tues. Dec. 4.
J.G. and Mary drove down from Guelp, arriving about midday, Aunt Betsy being greatly better.

Wed. Dec. 5.
Busy journalizing November transactions. Find the cash pretty troublesome.

Thurs. Dec. 6.
Observed as a thanksgiving day by proclamation of the govnor.[97] Took

---

96 Greenfield was a small settlement near Ayr, Canada West, where John Goldie, Sr (1793–1886), the famous botanist, moved his family from Scotland in 1844. Family seat to both his employer (John Goldie Jr [1823–96]) and his future bride (Mary Goldie [1834–1911]) – children of John Goldie, Sr – Greenfield was a second home for Andrew McIlwraith. Mahlon M. Gowdy, *A Family History Comprising the Surnames of Gade-Gadie-Gaudie … and the Variant Forms from* AD 800 *to* AD 1919 (Lewiston, ME: Journal Press, 1919), 245–56.

97 Sir Edmund Walker Head (1805–68), Governor of the United Canadas from 1854

a trip per rail up to Guelp and visited Jas Goldie and the rest of the folks about the new mill. Snowing fast nearly all day.

Fri. Dec. 7.
Nearly all day engaged on journalizing. Sat till 10 o'clock in the office. Weather quite mild and thawing.

Sat. Dec. 8.
Spent most of the day making out accounts and preparing for paying hands.

Sun. Dec. 9.
Heard Mr James in the U.P. Church morning and eve'g. Spent the interval and remaining part of the day rather dully in the house.

Mon. Dec. 10.
Had parcel with shirts from Hamilton, and letters from Thos and Marg't. Keeping late hours in the office.

Tues. Dec. 11.
Cold blustering weather. Kept in the office for some time after quitting time, assisting John to make drawing of portable Grist mill.

Wed. Dec. 12.
Still busy journalizing. Had some singing in the house in the eve'g. Miss Alexander and I. Hugh McCulloch and a force of Millwrights went off to Carluke near Ancaster with material for a small Grist Mill.

Thurs. Dec. 13.
Cold weather. Busy with my books and got my cash to come out right in the journalizing. Wrote letters in the eve'g to Thos and to Jesse Marshall New York.

Fri. Dec. 14.
The coldest day of the season so far. Vapor rising from the river and covering all the town. Posting into the Ledger to-day. Had Hugh McCulloch in the house in the eve'g a while. Had a visit of David Goldie.

Sat. Dec. 15.
The portable engine out in the yard with steam up, set agoing to-day.

---

to 1861, declared the Day of Thanksgiving 'for the bountiful harvest.' The public schools were closed as well. 'Head, Sir Edmund Walker,' *DCB* (Toronto: University of Toronto Press, 1976), 9:381–86; Adolphus Egerton Ryerson, ed., 'Educational Intelligence,' *The Journal of Education for Upper Canada* (Toronto: Lovell and Gibson, 1860), 13:188.

Visited the reading room in the evening and got a book out the library. Cold weather.

Sun. Dec. 16.
Heard Mr James in the morning and in the afternoon attended St Andrew's Church and heard an old Missionary preach a short dis-course.[98] On leaving the church, had a walk of a mile or two out the 11th concession toward Ayr.

Mon. Dec. 17.
Weather not so very cold now. Portable engine for I.M. Williams sent off to-day per rail to Wyoming Station, Sarnia Branch.

Tues. Dec. 18.
Fine mild weather neither frost nor thaw. Wm Goldie arrived from Guelph in the eve'g and stayed and slept with me. Had Mr Strickland in a while in the fore night.

Wed. Dec. 19.
Slight frost in the morning but started raining early in the forenoon and continued deplorably wet all day. Willie Goldie went off walking to Ayr and soon after he left his father came in with the cutter all drenched with rain. Wrote to my old landlady Mrs Smith in the eve'g.

Thurs. Dec. 20.
Miserable sloppy walking now. Miss Smith came down from Guelph with the morning train and Willie Goldie from Greenfield with the cut-ter so; Miss S. went off with it and Will'm waited on all day about the Foundry and went off with the train in the eve'g to Guelph.

Fri. Dec. 21.
Making up mens books and other such like little jobs about the office but not much bookkeeping doing at present. Hugh McCulloch came home from the country and brought a new horse with him which he had bought up the country.

---

98 St Andrew's was Galt's oldest Presbyterian Church, one that remained affiliated with the Established Church of Scotland (Kirk) after the 'Disruption' of 1843. In late 1860, the church had no settled pastor, Rev. Hamilton Gibson (pastor from 1850 to 1860) having demitted his charge. Rev. John Hogg of Guelph was moderator pro tem until Rev. Robert Campbell accepted a call from St Andrew's in 1862 and pastored there until 1866. St Andrew's united with the Union Presbyterian congregation in Galt to form the Central Presbyterian Church in 1880. Dickson, *Ebenezer*, 102–28.

Sat. Dec. 22.

Lots of frost and snow again. Kept pretty busy to-day preparing to pay hands, etc. Kept house in the evening while the gudeman and gudewife were up town to see the Christmas market.[99]

Sun. Dec. 23.

Plenty of snow for good sleighing again. At St Andrew's Church in the morning and heard a young man a stranger preach a pretty good sermon. Heard Mr James in the afternoon.

Mon. Dec. 24.

Fine frosty weather. A sister of Mr Goldie in from the country to-day. In the Office till nine o'clock or so and then sat late in the house, singing and carrying on nonsense.

Tues. Dec. 25.

Very little office work doing at present. Worked a little fixing up a picture for to give to my landlady. Hugh McCulloch came home with his cutter all broken, his new horse having turned out a kicker.

Wed. Dec. 26.

Mr A. McEwen, Mrs McEwen, and the children, and Mary Goldie all in to-day in McEwen's sleigh. McCulloch went off with them, also Mrs Goldie's youngest sister.

Thurs. Dec. 27.

Still cold weather. Things in general about the foundry just moving along in the ordinary style to-day.

Fri. Dec. 28.

Following after our ordinary business without anything remarkable happening to-day.

Sat. Dec. 29.

Busy preparing for posting Dec. affairs. Had a visit of old Mr Goldie from Ayr.

Sun. Dec. 30.

At Mr James church morning and evening. Had a walk of a mile or two out towards the N.E. in the interval between sermons.

---

99 Goodman and goodwife. Master (male) and female heads of a household (Scottish dialect, archaic); Mr and Mrs Goldie.

Mon. Dec. 31.

Foundry boys off to-day and a number of the other hands. Kept on about the shop untill close on train time and had a hard run over. Found the folks of Thos family all assembled waiting my arrival with the Hogmanay dinner.[100] Had a merry time with the children. John Jackson, his wife and children called and sat unreasonably long.

---

100 Andrew travelled to Hamilton to have New Year's Hogmanay with his brother's family. See Diary for 1857 fn 123.

Diary for 1861

Tues. Jan. 1. 1861.
Having sat out the old year, Thos and his wife Mrs Logan and I wished each other a good New Year before retiring to bed. Had a number of visitors during the day and Thos and I made calls on Mr Hutchinson, Crawford, Muir and Miss McIlwraith. Met Mr Campbell from Galt in Miss Mc's. Thos showing me several eagle skins added to his collection.

Wed. Jan. 2.
Walked up town and got through with some little business then in the afternoon took train to Galt again. Sat late in my room and wrote to Mary G.

Thurs. Jan. 3.
Close at work now writing up the books for December. Sat in the office till 10 o'clock.

Fri. Jan. 4.
Messrs Goldie and McCulloch taking stock and I in the office at the books. Sat till half past 9. Still very cold weather.

Sat. Jan. 5.
Still cold. Sidewalks all ice. One or two hands only at work. In the office till between 8 and 9 and got through with writing in the journal, the cash book, day book and B.Bk transactions for December.

Sun. Jan. 6.
At church both ends of the day. In the interval had a walk out the Preston Road. Keen bright frosty weather.

Mon. Jan. 7.
Posting in the ledger today. Kept in the office till 12 o'clock.

Tues. Jan. 8.
Still cold weather. Mr McCulloch got home from Carluke this evening bringing with him a new brown mare purchased for a hundred dollars.

Wed. Jan. 9.
Busy with account writing. James Goldie came down from Guelph and shortly after him, Mr Goldie Sr from Ayr came in.

Thurs. Jan. 10.
All day writing accounts. Had Mr Billing in for a short time looking over my book operations. Mary in town to-day. Saw her only a few minutes.

Fri. Jan. 11.
Quite busy with the books writing out Mr Crombie's a/c.

Sat. Jan. 12.
Busy at the books, keeping in the office untill ten o'clock. Exceedingly cold weather. Wm Goldie down with a specimen of flour from the mill at Guelph.

Sun. Jan. 13.
About the coldest morning in the season. Rose early and slipped out of the house before the folk were astir and walked out to Ayr which I reached after wandering several miles off the road. Went to church and sat two hours or so, the Sacrament being administered. Then out to Greenfield. Sitting late with M.

Mon. Jan. 14.
Not so cold but snowing fast all forenoon. Had the boy drive me in to Galt with Bob in the cutter. Did some bank business for Mr Goldie. In the office till 11.

Tues. Jan. 15.
Busy at books and sitting late in the office in the evening.

Wed. Jan. 16.
Miserable sloppy weather, raining and thawing. Still busy at the ledger in the eve'g.

Thurs. Jan. 17.
Slight frost again. Mr Goldie in to-day.

Fri. Jan. 18.
Busy with books, sitting late. Wrote to M. at night.

Sat. Jan. 19.
Still busy with office work. Pay night to-night.

Sun. Jan. 20.
At St Andrew's Church in the morning and the Free Church in the eve'g,
spending the interval reading in the house.

Mon. Jan. 21.
Still fine cold winter weather and still hard at work in the office. Made
a blunder in the rate of John Little's pay and had John in to see about it.

Tues. Jan. 22.
Still cold weather. Visited an auction of crockery, etc. going on in town
under Mr Strickland's supervision.

Wed. Jan. 23.
Had a letter from Connel from New York.

Thurs. Jan. 24.
Quite a fall of snow during the night. Busy with a/cs being in the office
till 11 o'clock. David Goldie in to-day. Excitement among the bosses
about the clearing out of a Mr McNaughton, a heavy creditor.[1]

Fri. Jan. 25.
Cold frosty weather. Busy with account making out. Attended a concert
in the town hall in the eve'g and heard the Galt Band and some singing.[2]

Sat. Jan. 26.
Busy a/c writing. Kept in the office untill about 10.

Sun. Jan. 27.
Rose early and kindled the stove, having an idea of walking out to Ayr
but could not get away. St James Church in the forenoon. In the afternoon, got a chance of a sleigh ride with Mrs Alexander, John Goldie's
mother-in-law, and right drove out to beyond Greenfield with them.
Came in to Greenfield at dusk.

Mon. Jan. 28.
Fine winter morning. Some signs of snow. Had Bob harnessed up by 9

---

1 Likely Alexander McNaughton, a local notable in early Galt and Dumfries Township. In an 1864 town directory, he is listed as a 'gentleman,' resident on Ainslie
   Street. James Sutherland, *County of Waterloo Gazetteer and General Business Directory*
   (Toronto: Mitchell and Co., 1864), 141.
2 Founded in 1855, the Galt Band was one of many voluntary organizations in mid-century Galt that aimed to provide entertainment for the townspeople and raise funds for
   charity. See Andrew Holman, *A Sense of Their Duty: Middle-Class Formation in Victorian
   Ontario Towns* (Montreal and Kingston: McGill-Queen's University Press 2000), ch. 4.

o'clock or so and got Mary and Anne Maria in the cutter and had a fine ride in to Galt. Sat late writing in the office. Willie Goldie, down from Guelph, drove the ladies out.

Tues. Jan. 29.
Still cold wintry weather. Busy writing out accounts. Sat in the office till near 12.

Wed. Jan. 30.
A most tempestuous snowy day. John Goldie gone to Guelph to-day driving. Got home about six at night after being overturned in the snow and having to walk, pushing the cutter, thro' the snow wreaths quite a distance. Kept in the office till 10 o'clock writing a/c's.

Thurs. Jan. 31.
Very close at work. Finishing up and arranging accounts, etc.

Fri. Feb. 1.
Snowing fast nearly all day. James Goldie here from Guelph. Got about finished up with Account writing.

Sat. Feb. 2.
Pay day in the work. James Goldie staid all night and slept with me. Trains making very bad time just now on account of the snow being so deep and drifting with the wind.

Sun. Feb. 3.
At Mr James' Church morning and evening. Had Mr Strickland in most of the eve'g.

Mon. Feb. 4.
Spent the forenoon at office work and immediately after dinner started out thro' the town delivering accounts which took me till past 5.

Tues. Feb. 5.
Mrs Goldie sick. Jas Harriet's daughter assisting with the housework. Sat late and finished writing home to Christina, despatching it with Canadian Mail.[3]

---

3 The Canadian Mail Service originated in 1853, when the Allan Line, a Scottish transatlantic family shipping business (and its Montreal agent, Hugh Allan) won a contract from the Government of Canada to run regular mails between Britain and Canada. By the end of the decade, the company had built four new screw steamships for the purpose. The service began as a fortnightly trip in summer (Liverpool-Quebec) and monthly in winter (Liverpool-Portland, Maine); by 1859, Canadian mail

Wed. Feb. 6.

Air cold and raw with not much of either frost or snow. Mrs Goldie sick and her mother in from the country to attend her. Old Mr G. in from Greenfield. Made a very short stay.

Thurs. Feb. 7.

A most tempestuous morning, the snow having fallen fast thro' the night and drifting about with the wind. Wm Goldie down from Guelph and got Hugh McCulloch away with him and both came back after waiting some hours as the train cars got in some time in the afternoon and W.G. sat up all night expecting to get to Guelph with them but was disappointed. Walked up town in the afternoon and thought it the coldest I had ever experienced facing the North wind.

Fri. Feb. 8.

Weather rather moderated to-day but no mails, the railways and roads being blocked up. Willie Goldie went off in the afternoon. Mr McCulloch at home assisting me some in checking the books.

Sat. Feb. 9.

Quite a fine winter day. Trains running to-day. Up town in the afternoon and paid some accounts then started for Hamilton per train about 5.50. Found on arriving at Harrisburg that we were late for the train it should have connected with. A large squad of Irishmen travelling down from being clearing off the track.[4] Had a regular concert with them in the waiting room, they having set to the singing to pass the time. A most

---

steamers ran weekly all year round. 'Allan, Andrew,' in George Maclean Rose, ed.,
A Cyclopaedia of Canadian Biography (Toronto: Rose Publishing Compnay, 1886), 317;
'James Allan,' in James MacLehose, *Memoirs and Portraits of One Hundred Glasgow
Men* (Glasgow: James MacLehose and Sons, 1886).

4 The Irish made up a significant portion of the 'navvy' or public works construction workforce in the 1840s, '50s and '60s Canada. While in Canada West most Irish immigrants became rural dwellers and farmers fairly quickly upon arrival. Nevertheless, for others, wage work on public construction projects bridged the gap between an uncertain arrival and a degree of self-sufficiency. See Ruth Bleasdale, 'Class Conflict on the Canals of Upper Canada in the 1840s,' *Labour/ Le Travailleur* 7 (Spring 1981): 9–39. Important correctives to the impression of the Irish as predominantly and permanently urban and wage earning can be found in Donald H. Akenson, *The Irish in Ontario: A Study in Rural History* (Montreal and Kingston: McGill-Queen's University Press, 1984); Gordon Darroch and Michael Ornstein, 'Ethnicity and Class: Transitions over a Decade,' *Canadian Historical Association Historical Papers* (1984), 111–37.

wearisome time to wait to about two in the morning that the train got along. Got in to Hamilton about 4.

Sun. Feb. 10.
Found M.G. had got down the night previous. At Burnett's Church all together in the forenoon and at Ormiston in the afternoon, keeping the house in the evening.[5] Day extraordinary warm for a winter day.

Mon. Feb. 11.
Took the first train up and got up in good time. Mrs Goldie's mother still in the house, not having got home. Keeping late hours in the office. The settling of a/c with Mr Crombie taking up considerable time and attention. Raining and thawing to-day making miserable sloppy walking.

Tues. Feb. 12.
Still thawing, fast. John Goldie went off with Mrs Alexander in the cutter in the afternoon. Still bothering with Mr Crombie's a/c but got it all straightened I believe in the end.

Wed. Feb. 13.
J.G. got in in the forenoon and brought Jennie with him. In the office late to-night. Weather again changed to frost.

Thurs. Feb. 14.
Mr McCulloch and I started after breakfast in the cutter for Fisher's Mills about 6 or 8 miles out on the Guelph Road to sketch a cleaning machine which we accomplished. Enjoyed the ride well although it was blowing strong and drifting the snow, making pretty hard travelling. In the office till 11 o'clock.

Fri. Feb. 15.
More snow during the night. Have the cold a little and felt a little tired at night so did not wait past 7 to night to which time the hands in the Finishing Shop are now working.[6]

---

5 On Burnet and St Andrew's Presbyterian Church, see Diary for 1857, fn 114. On Ormiston and Central Presbyterian Church, see Diary for 1858, fn 5; 'Ormiston, William,' *Appleton's Annual Cyclopedia and Register of Important Events of the Year 1899* (New York: D. Appleton and Company, 1900), 627; and 'Rev. William Ormiston, DD,' *NYT*, June 22, 1874.
6 It was not unusual for early industrial workers to work between ten and twelve hours per day. See Robert B. Kristofferson, *Craft Capitalism: Craftsworkers and Industrialization in Hamilton, Ontario, 1840–1872* (Toronto: University of Toronto Press, 2007),

Sat. Feb. 16.
Pay day with the hands. David Goldie called in the evening on his way to Guelph driving.

Sun. Feb. 17.
Felt rather sick with cold and thought of keeping house all day but at breakfast was asked to drive out to Ayr with Miss Alexander. George Strickland being going in one cutter while I should take the Foundry one. Started about 10 o'clock and had rough work meeting all the teams coming in to church. George and his wife got capsized. Dine in Dr McGeorge's in Ayr and afterwards called at Greenfield and spent an hour or two. Found M. had got home from Hamilton.

Mon. Feb. 18.
Cold pretty well out of my chest but in to the head badly. Old Jennie sick with it too, and in the evening quite bad. In the office until near 10 making out a new Balance Sheet. Mr McCulloch gone off to the States on a tour this morning.

Tues. Feb. 19.
Cold and raw. Most remarkably afflicted with cold in the head. Old Jenny up and rather better again but Mrs Goldie a-bed and John still bad with it too. Started reading the History of Kilmarnock by snatches now.[7]

Wed. Feb. 20.
James Goldie down from Guelph to-day. To-night had an invitation to tea in Mr Campbell's so went there and spent a rather pleasant evening.

Thurs. Feb. 21.
Busy journalizing for January now. Mr McCulloch got back from the States to-night.

Fri. Feb. 22.
Mr Goldie Sr in to-day. Quite a snow storm.

Sat. Feb. 23.
Raining and thawing fast to-day making most awfully sloppy roads.

---

ch. 7; Bryan D. Palmer, *A Culture in Conflict: Skilled Workers and Industrial Capitalism in Hamilton, Ontario, 1860–1914* (Montreal and Kingston: McGill-Queen's University Press, 1979), ch. 5.

7 Likely Archibald M'Kay, *The History of Kilmarnock*, 1st ed. ([Kilmarnock]: Mathew Wilson, 1848), or 2nd enlarged and revised ed. (Kilmarnock: Archibald McKay, 1858).

Called at the library in the evening and got 'Self Help' by S. Smiles.[8]
Frost setting in again in the evening.

Sun. Feb. 24.
Sharp frost again. At church in the forenoon and heard an Irish clergyman preach. Kept the house reading all day after. Rough sleighing and
very slippery walking.

Mon. Feb. 25.
Busy with January's journalizing.

Tues. Feb. 26.
A most delightfully mild and beautiful morning. Posting January into
the Ledger to-day.

Wed. Feb. 27.
Things moving along about the usual way in the shop.

Thurs. Feb. 28.
[No entry].

Fri. Mar. 1.
Dull warm weather.

Sat. Mar. 2.
Thaw still continuing and water rising fast in the river. Streets miserably
sloppy. Visited the Reading Room and got a volume of essays from the
London Times.[9] Pay night in the shop.

Sun. Mar. 3.
Morning dark and wet but took the road to Ayr notwithstanding. Miserable roads. Got in to the village just in time for church and made up on
the Greenfield folks at the door. Heard Dr Thompson from N.Y.[10] Got a
ride out from Mrs Anderson. Road awfully rough outside Ayr. Water
very high in the creek.

---

8 Samuel Smiles, *Self-Help; with Illustrations of Character and Conduct* (New York:
   Harper, 1859). The library to which he refers was the Mechanics' Institute
   Library.

9 Likely Samuel Phillips, *Essays from the London Times: A Collection of Personal and Historical Sketches* (New York: D. Appleton and Company, 1852).

10 Rev. John J. Thomson, DD, was visiting Galt from New York City, where he was
   pastor at the Grand Street Presbyterian Church. Thomson's appearance in Galt fore-
   shadowed his move there, later in 1861. He was pastor of Knox's Free Presbyterian
   Church, Galt, from 1861 to 1863. See Diary for 1859, fn 31.

Mon. Mar. 4.
Morning quite bright and frosty. David for Galt so him and I drove in in the buggy. Roads very rough. Came near capsizing several times.

Tues. Mar. 5.
Busy drawing. The man quite lame just now and Mr McCulloch at home most of the time.

Wed. Mar. 6.
Keep at drawing most of the time at present. Preparing drawings to send with mach's to Cuba.

Thurs. Mar. 7.
Engaged at drawing of cleaning machine principally. M. in to-day. Fine bright weather. During the night Mrs Goldie presented her husband with a son.[11]

Fri. Mar. 8.
Finishing drawing of cleaning machine. John Goldie gone to Guelph to-night and I had to write to Greenfield to notify the folks of the birth of the boy. Mr Halm in and settled on going on with his new mill.

Sat. Mar. 9.
Considerable snow during the night, but melting off with the sun during the day. Engine and saw mill stuff being packed up for Cuba to-day.

Sun. Mar. 10.
Fine frosty weather. At the Free Church in the forenoon, James being closed. Heard a stranger preach. After dinner had a walk out through Preston and round by Carlyle.

Mon. Mar. 11.
Outside a good part of the day marking Cuba boxes of mach'y.

Tues. Mar. 12.
Cuba stuff all shipped off to-day.

Wed. Mar. 13.
Make a start on posting up February's affairs.

---

11 The child was John Goldie (the third, 1861–73), born to Andrew's employer (and future) brother-in-law John Goldie (1823–96) and his first wife, Elizabeth Alexander (d. ca 1869?), who died young. The child died at the age of twelve years. Mahlon M. Gowdy, *A Family History Comprising the Surnames of Gade-Gadie-Gaudie-Gawdy … and the Variant Forms … From AD 800 to AD 1919* (Lewiston, ME: Journal Press, 1919), 249.

Thurs. Mar. 14.
Fine weather. Get working pretty steady at books now. In the office till eleven.

Fri. Mar. 15.
Beautiful weather. Slight frost. New cupola put up to-day. Finished posting February.

Sat. Mar. 16.
Pay day. Had Feb. all posted up and gave out the men their books. Visited the Reading Room for a short time in the eve'g. Wrote to Wm Barry, New York, after coming home, also to M.G. and to Mrs Logan.

Sun. Mar. 17.
Keen frosty weather again. At James['s] Church morning and evening. Reading lectures to young men in the evening.

Mon. Mar. 18.
Still bitter cold. M.G. in to-day and drove out to Preston.

Tues. Mar. 19.
Weather still frosty. Busy preparing for getting new pattern book for the Dumfries Foundry.

Wed. Mar. 20.
The part of the Foundry roof raised up to the height to-day for accomodation of new crane. Still cold frosty weather.

Thurs. Mar. 21.
Considerable snow fallen during the night. Finished drawing of buildings for in Mr Halm's mill. G[oldie &] McC[ulloch] gone to Guelph.

Fri. Mar. 22
[No entry].

Sat. Mar. 23.
Forenoon mild and showery but afternoon deplorably wet.

Sun. Mar. 24.
A favorable change in the weather taken place during the night, the ground being frozen with a high wind and frequent snow storms. Had breakfast early and started for Ayr. Took the way of the 10th Con. thro' the Alps.[12] Got to the church in Ayr a little late. After sermon walked out

---

12 The 10th Concession in North Dumfries was called the 'The Alps' because of its steep hills and valleys, which made passage difficult. It is called Alps Road today. See Andrew Taylor, *Our Todays and Yesterdays* (Ontario: North Dumfries Township, 1967), 163.

to Greenfield along with M. and the rest and spent the day about the house.

Mon. Mar. 25.
Slight frost in the morning. Bob and the buggy being lent out, David had Charlie saddled and him and I undertook to take a ride about into Galt. I got on when a mile or two out but the brute shied at crossing of cedar creek and wheeled about so I had to give up for a time but got along better afterwards. At lecture on Palestine by Lachlin Taylor in the eve'g and saw a number of interesting relics of the east.[13]

Tues. Mar. 26.
Heavy rain nearly all day. Did a little at drawing of Whitehead's building but had a lot of letter-writing to do and did not progress much with it. At Lachlin Taylor's lecture the evening and saw a lot more of his collection of curiosities.

Wed. Mar. 27.
Weather frosty. Visited Mr Campbell in the evening and met a young man, a Mr McDonald from Toronto there.

Thurs. Mar. 28.
Preparing for starting on compilation of new pattern list. Heard Lachlin Taylor in the evening and had a view of his Egyptian Mummy, etc.

Fri. Mar. 29.
Heard Lachlin Taylor deliver a concluding lecture in the evening on Jerusalem. Mr Sidney Smith staying all night in the house.

---

13 The Rev. Lachlin Taylor, DD (1815 or 1816–1881) ,was a well-known Wesleyan Methodist clergyman in Canada. Born in Scotland, he was educated in Glasgow and moved to Canada with his family while a teenager. He was ordained a minister in 1843, and served congregations in Ottawa, Kingston, Hamilton, and Montreal. He was an agent for the Upper Canada Bible Society, 1851–63, and travelled widely in Canada West as a speaker and evangelist. In 1858–9, he travelled to Egypt and Palestine in the company of Montreal mayor James Ferrier, returning with an array of artefacts that became the subject of a popular lecture series he delivered throughout Canada West. In Galt, he delivered four lectures and displayed such exotic items as a 'mummied Cat' and a 'perfect Mummy.' W.J. Rattray, *The Scot in British North America* (Toronto: Maclear and Company, 1880), vol. 3, part 4: 899–900; Gayle Gibson and Caroline Rocheleau, *Society for the Study of Egyptian Antiquities Newsletter* (Winter 2007): 8; [John Carroll], *Past and Present, or a Description of Persons and Events Connected with Canadian Methodism for the Last Forty Years* (Toronto: Alfred Dredge, 1860), 284–6; 'The Holy Land,' *DR*, March 27, 1861.

Sat. Mar. 30.
Pay day in the shop. Visited the reading room for a while in the evening. A large quantity of ice coming down the river today from the dam.

Sun. Mar. 31.
Heard a young man, a stranger, preach in James' Church in the morning. Had a short walk with John Goldie and in the evening read them all asleep in the house.

Mon. Apr. 1.
Bank Holiday. Assisting Mr McCulloch with drawing for Whitehead's Mill, etc.

Tues. Apr. 2.
Enough snow falling for sleighing. Mr Smith, David Goldie and M. all in today. Sidney stayed night. In the office late at pattern book.

Wed. Apr. 3.
Thawing and very sloppy. Close at pattern list. In the office till past ten. James Gunney about the work a good deal and got away drawing of new mill for Whitehead.

Thurs. Apr. 4.
Fine moderate weather. Hard at work at pattern list and marking of patterns. In the office till ten o'clock. Contract concluded between Winger of Berlin[14] and G. McC. Co.[15] for engine.

Fri. Apr. 5.
Trying to push on with pattern book but little jobs at drawing, etc. interfering with it. In the office until late at night.

Sat. Apr. 6.
Wet weather and awfully bad roads. Our team away at Guelph today and had like to get stuck.

Sun. Apr. 7.
At James['s] Church morning and afternoon, and heard a stranger preach and read a letter from Mr James, now in Scotland for the benefit of his health.

---

14 In the 1860s, John Winger [Sr] was a manufacturer of pumps and broom handles in South Ontario Street in Berlin. *The Province of Ontario Gazetteer and Directory*, ed. and comp. H. McEvoy (Toronto: Robertson and Cook, Publishers, 1869), 55; W.V. (Ben) Uttley, *A History of Kitchener, Ontario* [1937] (rep. Waterloo: Wilfrid Laurier University Press, 1975), 69, 169.

15 G. McC is a short form for Goldie and McCulloch.

Mon. Apr. 8.
Mr McCulloch gone off on a country tour. Close at work in Pattern book all day.

Tues. Apr. 9.
Still close at work on pattern list. Rather bothered about getting the advertising part of it in good shape. Mr McIntosh here from Shakespeare and agreed on giving mill contract to the Dumfries Foundry. Heard from Thos of his intention of visiting Greenfield this week.

Wed. Apr. 10.
A most charming, mild, bright day. Finishing up pattern list which is now just about ready for the printer.

Thurs. Apr. 11.
Still beautiful weather. Had all the pattern book sheets taken up to Jeffrey, the printer, David Goldie in and went to Guelph. While he was away I got Bob and the buggy out and drove Mr John out to call on Bechtel at Carlyle. Spent a while in the reading room in the eve'g.

Fri. Apr. 12.
Weather beginning to break into rain. Mr McCulloch came home from the country. Got started to posting March.

Sat. Apr. 13.
Mild but moist weather. Pay day in the shop. Globe of today contains notice of the first commencement of war in the United States at Charleston.[16]

Sun. Apr. 14.
Started for Ayr early. Roads in good condition for walking. Walked by the Ayr Road. Got into the village early for church and walked out the road until I met Mr Goldie. Thos and Tommy drove in with David in the buggy afterwards. Heard Mr McRuar. Had a walk along the road in the afternoon.

---

16 On April 12, 1861 the American Civil War commenced with the firing of Confederate troops on the U.S. federal installation, Fort Sumter, in Charleston Harbor, South Carolina. The war lasted four years, ending on April 9, 1865, with the surrender of Confederate General Robert E. Lee's Army of Northern Virginia to Union General Ulysses S. Grant's Army of the Potomac at Appomattox Court House, Virginia. The war fascinated foreign observers, especially Canadians, for whom the threat of being dragged into the hostilities was daunting. See Robin Winks, *Canada and the United States: The Civil War Years* [1960] (rep. Montreal and Kingston: McGill-Queen's University Press, 1998); 'War Commenced! Fort Sumpter Attacked!' *Globe* [Toronto], April 13, 1861.

Mon. Apr. 15.
Thos, Tommy and I got the buggy to drive to Galt. Came by way of the 9th Concession.

Tues. Apr. 16.
Drawing most of the day at new plan for Whitehead's Mill buildings. Mr McCulloch at home drawing too. A house on fire across the river. Had a run over and a spell at the machine.[17]

Wed. Apr. 17.
Frosty but bright and sunny. Mr Goldie came in with Anne Maria and M. Saw them off with the train to Guelph. Working at new tracing of Whitehead's Mill.

Thurs. Apr. 18.
Dr Thompson's Induction to the charge of the Free Church takes place today.[18] Got finished Whitehead's Mill plan and sent it off with Tunny again. Quite a fall of snow in the morning. A small engine in course of being built in the shop sold tonight to go to Rockton.

Fri. Apr. 19.
Still beautiful, bright weather. Mr McCulloch gone to Baden. Getting along steadily with Journal. D. Goldie and Rob Fulton called in the afternoon on their way to Dundee.

Sat. Apr. 20.
Kind of cold and raw. Worked pretty steady at journalizing and got through with writing.

Sun. Apr. 21.
At Mr James' church in the morning. After dinner John Goldie and I had quite a long walk down the river side west bank. Mr Thompson enters on his duties in Knox's Church today.

---

17 The fire broke out in the chimney of Adam Hood's house, South Water Street; 'strenuous exertions' of townspeople and firemen saved the main portion of the building. 'Fire in Galt,' *DR*, April 17, 1861. McIlwraith was likely referring to a 'hand engine' (a cart-mounted device that sprayed water pressurized from hand-pumping), which was used in Galt until 1873. See James Young, *Reminiscences of the Early History of Galt, and the Settlement of Dumfries* (Toronto: Hunter, Rose and Company, 1880), 189.

18 The local newspaper called him 'a very impressive and interesting character.' See 'Induction of Dr Thompson,' *DR*, April 17, 1861. On Thomson, see fn 10 above, and Diary for 1859, fn 31.

Mon. Apr. 22.
Fine weather. Billie Bank in from Ayr with word of something the matter with the water wheel at Greenfield. John and Hugh both went out and staid all night.

Tues. Apr. 23
Finishing posting for the month of March. St George's dinner comes off in the Queen's Hotel to-night.[19] John Goldie gone. Spent the evening mostly in the reading room. The Whip-poor-will heard by J.G. on the road last night.

Wed. Apr. 24.
Fine warm spring weather. Got finished writing up men's books, etc. McIntosh, a boilermaker, started work today at 2.50 per day having been engaged in Buffalo as a first class hand.

Thurs. Apr. 25.
Kind of cold and raw. Heard from Mrs Logan. John Goldie making a start digging his garden.

Fri. Apr. 26.
A beautiful day. Mr Goldie Sr in today reporting old Mrs G. and Miss Smith as being sick and scolding about Mary not being home from Guelph. Did a little at drawing of Whitehead's Mill. Mr McCulloch got home from Plattsville having got the new double acting pump to work well which had been a failure at first.

Sat. Apr. 27.
Pay night in the work. A solid horizontal engine frame cast in the foundry tonight, the first cast in that style about the place. M. came down with the train at 6 p.m. Had a walk up town with her. Heavy rain when we were out.

Sun. Apr. 28.
Delightful spring day. M. and I hearing Dr Thompson morning and evening and spending most of the interval walking round along with Annie Maria down by the river side and up to the cemetery above the town on the south side. Found the buggy waiting for her when we came

---

19 Named for the patron saint of England, St George's Day (April 23) was celebrated fairly regularly in mid-nineteenth-century Galt. The day's festivities, normally a picnic followed by a banquet, were organized by the Galt St George's Society (1852–77) (and later by the local Sons of England Benevolent Society, 1883–?) and received coverage in the local newspapers. See Holman, *Sense of Their Duty*, ch. 4.

home from church so she had to start off about 9 at night, her mother being very sick.

Mon. Apr. 29.
Still fine weather. Preparing for posting April. Mr McCulloch away at Baden, coming home in the eve'g.

Tues. Apr. 30.
A Fair in Galt today and quite a stir with horses and cattle and farmer's waggons. Visited the reading room a while in the evening. Mr McC. away to Hamilton tonight. Dr McGeorge and his lady dining in John Goldie's today, the old Dr with symptoms of having been horning.[20]

Wed. May 1.
Ground white with snow in the morning and cold holding on till the evening. At work on April's writing up of the books. Mr McC. got home, having been unsuccessful in making the large force pump work at the Oil Works.

Thurs. May 2.
[No entry].

Fri. May 3.
Had letters from Mrs Brewster and Mrs Hunter.

Sat. May 4.
Got letters posted for home. James Goldie and his little boy here on their way home from Ayr.

Sun. May 5.
A fine bright day but cold wind. Heard a stranger in Mr James's church, in the forenoon and in the afternoon heard an old negro in Aitchison's church and afterwards had a walk down by the river bank on the south side.[21]

---

20 Imbibing strong drink.
21 Rev. John James's church was the United Presbyterian Church, where he served as pastor 1857–61 until he departed due to ill health. Located at the corner of Metcalfe Street and the Blair Road, the UP Church underwent a series of name changes after Rev. James's departure, becoming the Second Presbyterian Church in 1861 and the Melville Church in 1866. It merged with the Bayne Presbyterian Church in 1870 to form the Union Church, which itself merged with St Andrew's (in 1880) to form Central Presbyterian. Rev. Robert Acheson served as pastor of First Associated Presbyterian Church in Galt, 1858–73. The 'old negro' was, as the local newspaper noted, 'Rev. Mr Basfield, a colored clergyman of London, C.W.,' who was seeking donations for

Mon. May 6.
Day rather milder but showery. Busy posting Ap'l. Mr Sidney Smith came in the evening to stay all night.

Tues. May 7.
Cold with heavy showers. Finished posting April. Sidney went off driving a new horse he bought from Oliver in an old buggy.

Wed. May 8.
Still cold blustering weather. An American gentleman here with drawings for oil stills to be made for Williams & Co. in Hamilton. Took dinner and tea with us and gave some notes about life in Kentucky.

Thurs. May 9.
Sun shiny but still chilly. Mr McCulloch off on a tour in search of a horse, came home with a large brown one from near Preston. Jameson called on me in the afternoon and he and I had a walk around town together.

Fri. May 10.
Still cold disagreeable weather. Took a spell at drawing of Whitehead's Mill. In the office late making up men's books.

Sat. May 11.
Day rather warmer. Shooting and shining. Men's books given out with pay today. Started for Ayr after six o'clock and had a fine walk out by the 10th Conn, thro' the Alps, and got to Greenfield about 9 o'clock.

Sun. May 12.
A most lovely morning. Rose early and had a walk up thro' the bush. At church in the forenoon and witnessed the ordination of elders. After dinner had a long walk with M. thro' the upper bush to the end of a loaming.

Mon. May 13.
David and I started early driving in to Galt, with Bob in the buggy. M. accompanying us to the end of the 9th con. James Goldie down from Guelph with morning train and David and he returned with the up one.

---

the construction of an 'establishment … for the care and protection of Negro orphan children.' See J.A.R. Dickson, *Ebenezer, A History of the Central Presbyterian Church, Galt, Ontario; with Brief Sketches of Some of Its Members Who Have Passed On to the Other Side* (Toronto: William Briggs, 1904), 30–50; Andrew C. Holman, 'Aspects of Middle-Class Formation' (PhD diss., York University, 1995), 492–3; *DR*, May 8, 1861.

Tues. May 14.
David down from Guelph this morning. Goes home to send his miller, Albert, up to Guelph to take the place of Hugh Stevenson for a short time who has left just now. Employed on drawing mach. of Whitehead's Mill at present.

Wed. May 15.
Fine weather. Busy with Whitehead's Mill drawing. Hugh Stevenson in at tea in the evening who has been kind of crazy this sometime and done considerable damage to the business of the Mill at Guelph by carelessness and bad management of the working.

Thurs. May 16.
Still at work on Whitehead's drawing.

Fri. May 17.
Still at Whitehead's drawing.

Sat. May 18.
Still drawing some. The first loam casting of the establishment made tonight but turned out bad vis. a large open boiler for Patrick and Paton's Woolen Factory.[22]

Sun. May 19.
Twice at St Andrew's Church hearing a Mr Smith from Illinois and in the evening at Mr James'. In the interval had a walk thro' the woods west of St Andrew's Church between the 11th and 12th con.

Mon. May 20.
James Goldie came down from Guelph today again. The Mill being not yet in proper trim. Has got Hitchcock to go up with him. Mr Sam Smith spending the evening and night in John Goldie's. Strickland in, talking politics until 12 o'clock. Had a stroll thro' the pine woods on the far side of the river.

Tues. May 21.
Still sticking close to drawing. A new tubular boiler being tried today

---

22 Likely the cloth factory operated by Andrew Paton and 'another man' in Galt from 1855 to 1861. A Scotsman from Stirling, Paton (1833–92) moved to Waterloo in 1861 and then to Sherbrooke, Canada East, in 1866, where he founded the large and prosperous Paton Manufacturing Company, the first textile company to produce Scotch tweeds in Canada. George Maclean Rose, 'Paton, Andrew,' *A Cyclopaedia of Canadian Biography* (Toronto: Rose Publishing Company, 1888), 448; R.E. Rudin, 'Paton, Andrew,' *DCB* (Toronto: University of Toronto Press, 1990), 12:827–28.

and turning out bad in the rivetting. McIntosh, the new boiler-maker discharged tonight as not being suitable for the work.

Wed. May 22.
Busy with mill drawing for Whitehead. Spent a while in Mr McCulloch's in the evening, being the first time of meeting Mrs McC.

Thurs. May 23.
Day fair. Afternoon rather sultry. Busy on Whitehead's Mill plan now just about finished. Heard from John Stewart that he would not get up to visit Galt so I went down with the evening train. Found all well. Got a little book of McKay's poems from Bill per mail.[23]

Fri. May 24.
A suffocatingly hot dusty day. Thomas engaged all forenoon about preparing for the great baloon ascension. Saw John Stewart in the Firemen's parade but did not speak to him. Mrs Logan proposing coming to Galt to go into housekeeping. Came home per evening train in time to see torchlight procession of firemen in Galt.[24]

Sat. May 25.
Quite a fine day after having a thunderstorm during the night. Have the roofers putting asphalt roof upon new room built for accommodation of blowing cylinders, etc. Mr Goldie from Greenfield in city being hurrying back to hear Dr Thompson preach.

Sun. May 26.
Heard Mr James preach and give notice of his intention of giving up his charge. Day rather lowering with light thundery showers in the afternoon. Watching the hummingbirds for a while in the garden. Had a walk out by the mill creek and then to Thompson's church and heard a young man from Toronto.

Mon. May 27.
A cold blowy day. Close at work all day tracing Whitehead's plan. Mr McCulloch away at Waterloo.

Tues. May 28.
Day bright but still chilly. At tracing of Whitehead's plan. David Goldie

---

23 Likely Charles Mackay, *Poems* (London: Wm. S. Orr and Co., 1848).
24 The torchlight procession of firemen, 'the best display of the kind ever witnessed among us,' capped off a day of celebration in Galt in honour of the Queen's birthday. 'Queen's Birthday in Galt,' *DR*, May 29, 1861.

in and gone to Guelph per morning train. M. in with him. Her and I out driving in the afternoon with John Goldie's baby.

Wed. May 29.
Still bright and cool. Loam casting of pan turned out bad again tonight. Finished with tracing Whitehead's plan.

Thurs. May 30.
Still fine weather but cold.

Fri. May 31.
Preparing for the month's postings.

Sat. June 1.
Finished journalizing the cash and some other preparation for posting. A number of hands working late connecting the engine to the new blowing cylinders.

Sun. June 2.
Heard Mr Herald preach in St Andrew's Church in the forenoon and at James's in the evening. John Goldie had his boy christened in church, John Charles.

Mon. June 3.
Still cold blustering weather. Connexion completed between engine and machinery in new building for fans, blowing cylinders, etc.

Tues. June 4.
Working steady at books. So cold today that I got a fire on.

Wed. June 5.
About finished with the posting. The new blast cylinders started today and did past expectation, melting the iron quickly. John Stewart to leave Hamilton for Scotland today.

Thurs. June 6.
David Goldie in this morning and Mrs Logan arrived from Hamilton to look after settling in Galt. Went over to town with her in the evening and inspected a large house belonging to old Mr Smith.

Fri. June 7.
Weather getting warmer. Mrs Logan going round house hunting and settled on taking old George Biggar's for a short time if agreeable to the

present inmates who propose leaving soon.[25] Her and I called at Barbour's and priced some furniture.

Sat. June 8.
Quite warm today. John G. and the Mrs gone to Ayr in the afternoon. Heard from St Mary's from M.G. asking me to postpone my visit there for another week. I had already written to the same end. Pay day in the shop and a pretty heavy one, $340.00. Posting all finished and books given out tonight.

Sun. June 9.
Summer in full blast now. Heard Mr James preach in the forenoon and in the afternoon had a stroll thro' the English Church cemetery and the woods beyond.[26] John and the wife home before dark.

Mon. June 10.
Still scorching hot. Got a sheet stretched for a drawing of Halm's Mill. Heard from St Mary's from M. not to go up till next Saturday, Mrs Cavan having had an addition to her family of a son.

Tues. June 11.
Still very hot. Started on Halm's Mill drawing but did not do much. Men in the Foundry digging a pit for loam casting.

Wed. June 12.
Beautitul weather, not so warm. Mr McCulloch in Hamilton. At work on Halm's Mill drawing. John G. out at Dryden's in the afternoon and I walked out the road and met him.

Thurs. June 13.
Quite cool now. At Halm's Mill plan. David Goldie in and reported the Greenfield mill dam broke. James came down with the afternoon train and John and he drove out after tea.

Fri. June 14.
Still cool. At work on Halm's Mill drawing. Got a £4 draft to send home.

Sat. June 15.
Quite a thunder storm early in the morning but day fine. Took train for

---

25 George Biggar was a moulder who had moved to Elora when the assessment of 1861 was taken. His Galt house was on Church Street in Ward 5. His total value was $48. Assessment Roll for the Town of Galt, 1861, p. 30.

26 The English Church cemetery was located beside Trinity Anglican Church (on Blair Road just west of the Grand River), then under the rectorship of Rev. Dr Michael Boomer, who served in that capacity from 1840 to 1872.

Guelph and St Mary's at 10.50 and had a pleasant run up there, getting a view of Berlin, Stratford, etc. Got a kindly reception at St Mary's. Miss Cavan being there on a visit besides M. Two stranger ministers at tea. Had a walk down the river after tea with the girls and children.

Sun. June 16.
At church morning and evening hearing Mr Cavan. Kept the house all of the interval, the children preventing much reading. Met an old acquaintance, Mr Flaws, on the way home from church. Evening exceedingly chilly for the season.

Mon. June 17.
Still fine weather. Spent the forenoon walking round the village and along the Sarnia Bridge of the Grand Trunk Ry. Called on Mitchell, the old clerk of the Dumfries Foundry. Took train with M. about mid-day and had a delightful run down. In the evening Mrs G., M and I went and viewed new monument erected to Dr Bayne.[27] Afterwards we had a moonlight walk.

Tues. June 18.
Mr Goldie Sr came in and took M. home with him. Electioneering excitement beginning in the country now. Jacob Hespeler out as ministerial candidate for this county.[28] At work on Halm's Mill drawing. Mr

---

27 A native of Greenock, Scotland, Dr John Bayne (1806–59) was a central figure in the history of the Presbyterian Church in Canada. Educated at the universities of Glasgow and Edinburgh, he came to Canada as a missionary in 1834 and accepted a call to St Andrew's, Galt, in 1835. A powerful preacher, he was a Canadian leader of the Disruption, the separatist movement within the Kirk among those who opposed state interference in church affairs. He helped found the Presbyterian Church of Canada (Free Church) in 1844, but it cost him his pastorate. Bayne led most of his congregation out of St Andrew's in 1844, forming Knox Presbyterian in Galt, a congregation he led until his death in 1859. 'Bayne, John,' *DCB* (Toronto: University of Toronto Press, 1985), 8:67–8.

28 The Conservative party candidate, Jacob Hespeler (1811–81). was one of the most influential men in mid-century Waterloo County. Born in Germany and educated in France, he migrated to Canada as a young man and in 1835 settled in Preston, where he became a prominent miller and distiller. In the late 1840s and '50s, he built a variety of new mills in New Hope (later renamed Hespeler in 1859). He served as a town councillor in both places before he ran in the provincial election. After a large fire severely damaged one of his Hespeler mills in 1869, he moved to California for a number of years. He returned to Hespeler and died there in 1881. 'Jacob Hespeler,' Hall of Fame Members, City of Cambridge Archives, Cambridge, Ontario, www.city.cambridge.on.ca/cs_pubaccess/hall_of_fame.php?cpid=33andsid=34 (accessed July 14, 2009).

McCulloch's young brother arrived from the Old Country on Saturday last.

Wed. June 19.
Close and hot. Towards evening some showers and lightning. A large oil still attempted to be cast in loam in the foundry tonight band failed, involving heavy loss.

Thurs. June 20.
Busy with Halm's Mill drawing. Mr Cowan out as Liberal candidate for the county.[29]

Fri. June 21.
Still close at work on Halm's Mill drawing. Fine growing weather to-day. Mr Goldie Sr drove in with James today. Beautiful moonlight nights just now. John and I spent a while in the reading room in the evening.

Sat. June 22.
Party feeling waxing strong on the election question. Pay night in the shop. Heard Jacob Hespeler speak in the Town Hall in the evening and also some of the Grit party overbawl him. Osborne,[30] Young[31] and Elliott[32] speaking.

---

29 Born in Peebleshire, Scotland, James Cowan (1803–1900) came to Canada in 1834 and rose to local prominence as a farmer and agricultural reformer. He purchased an interest in an agricultural implement manufactory in 1853 and turned his attention to politics in 1857, running (unsuccessfully) as a Reform candidate for Gore District in the Provincial Assembly. He ran again in 1860, winning in two successive elections. In 1867, he changed his party affiliation to John A. Macdonald's Conservatives, but lost to Liberal James Young in Canada's first federal election. 'James Cowan,' Hall of Fame Members, City of Cambridge Archives, Cambridge, Ontario, www.city.cambridge.on.ca/cs_pubaccess/hall_of_fame.php?cpid=33andsid=34 (accessed July 17, 2009).

30 William Osborne was a dry goods merchant and grocer in 1850s Galt and a Reform politician who was elected councillor for the town's Ward 4 in 1857. In business with his half-brother, David Spiers, he lived in Galt through 1865 but had moved to Hamilton by 1886. See James Young, *Reminiscences of the Early History of Galt and the Settlement of Dumfries, in the Province of Ontario* (Toronto: Hunter, Rose and Company, 1880), 231, 254.

31 James Young (1835–1913) was perhaps Galt's most prominent Liberal Reformer, making his political views known publicly as editor of the weekly newspaper *Dumfries Reformer* (1853–63), and as an elected politician: Member of Parliament for Waterloo South (1867–78) and member of the Ontario Legislature (1879–86).

32 Born in Dumfriesshire, Scotland, Andrew Elliott (b. 1809) moved to Galt in 1834, where he was a grocer and Reform-oriented politician. Elected as reeve of Galt in 1850 and 1851, he ran as a 'Baldwin Reformer' for Waterloo in the 1857 provincial election but was defeated. After his Galt business burned down in 1851, he invested

Sun. June 23.
Heard Mr James preach in the forenoon. After dinner had a long walk out the turnpike road towards Beverley and back across the country toward the Grand River, coming out below the town.

Mon. June 24.
Still working at Halm's Mill plan. Spent a short time in Mr McCulloch's in the evening.

Tues. June 25.
Quite hot. Mrs Steele in with Jane Muir today. Mr Goldie Sr driving. Mr McCulloch and I had quite a job unloading boiler tubes at the station. Still at work on Halm's Mill plan.

Wed. June 26.
Beautiful weather. Still at work on Halm's Mill plan. A Mr McLellan calling today enquiring about getting work done. Mr Leggat and a Mr Dunlop from Hamilton called at the house in the evening. Had a long stroll along with George McCulloch in the evening down the river and round by Sprague's road.

Thurs. June 27.
Weather still fine. Still at work on Halm's Mill plan. Spent some time in the reading room in the evening.

Fri. June 28.
Still working at drawing.

Sat. June 29.
Busy drawing at Halm's. Walked out to Greenfield after night and met a Mrs Muir and family there, also all the family. All well. Slept with David.

Sun. June 30.
At McRuar's church in the forenoon. Very disagreebly dusty walking. After dinner had a stroll with M. over the river on the boom and down below the cedar swamp. Get into the wrong bedroom when retiring for the night.

---

in a woollens manufactory in Preston, but found much greater success when he moved to Almonte in fall 1869 and established the Victoria Woollen Mills, a company that by 1880 employed hundreds of workers and produced $100,000–$120,000 worth of tweeds annually. 'Andrew Elliott, Almonte,' *The Canadian Biographical Dictionary and Portrait Gallery of Eminent and Self-Made Men, Ontario Volume, 1880* (Toronto: American Biographical Publishing Company, 1880); Young, *Reminiscences*, 115, 169, 217–18, 231.

Mon. July 1.
Day cool and a little lowering. After breakfast had the mare hitched up and got Billy to drive me in to the end of the 9th Conn. on Sprague's Road. Nomination of Parliamentary candidates takes place today at Preston gained by Cowan.

Tues. July 2.
Wonderfully cool for this season. Doing a little drawing. Evening clear and cold. A bright large comet very visible about from 9 till 12. Heard from Mrs Logan of her intention of being up tomorrow.

Wed. July 3.
Getting warm again. Tracing Halm's Mill plan.

Thurs. July 4.
Working at drawing a little. Weather very warm. Mrs Logan came up in the evening.

Fri. July 5.
Hot weather. Mrs Logan's furniture arrived trom Hamilton. David Goldie in today.

Sat. July 6.
Hot – hot. Electioneering excitement growing strong. Made a caricature of Hespeler riding on a whiskey barrel. News from Toronto in the evening of George Brown's having lost the election there.[33] Mrs Logan busy getting her home in order.

Sun. July 7
Regular July weather now. Mrs Logan and I at St Andrew's Church in the forenoon and J. Goldie and I in the afternoon at James's and heard it declared vacant. Mr James having gone off to the Old Country in ill health.

---

33 George Brown was the leader of the Liberal Reform faction, the 'Clear Grits.' His defeat in the Toronto East Riding by Tory John Crawford in the 1861 Province of Canada election was a great surprise, especially since the Liberals did so well collectively, winning 58 of the 128 seats in the Assembly. The loss forced him to resign as Parliamentary party leader, Sarnia's Alexander Mackenzie taking control. Brown was returned to the legislature (and the party leadership) in an 1863 by-election in South Oxford. Alexander Mackenzie, *The Life and Speeches of Hon. George Brown* (Toronto: The Globe Printing Company, 1882); J.M.S. Careless, *Brown of the Globe*, vol. 2: *Statesman of Confederation 1860–1880* (Toronto: Macmillan, 1963). On Brown, see Diary for 1857, fn 8. McIlwraith's caricature reflected Hespeler's identity as the owner of a distillery.

Mon. July 8.
Great electioneering excitement. David Goldie in in the afternoon. Geo. Strickland lost his vote by his name having been entered wrong on the roll. Cowan the Reform candidate, 90 ahead in the evening. Messrs McCulloch and Crombie gone off early in the morning.

Tues. July 9.
Cowan still keeping ahead. Mr Lothian from Inverhuron here and ordered some mill machinery. John Goldie and I uptown in the evening awaiting the poll returns. 155 majority for Cowan. Foundry boys had out the cannon and fired 21 guns.[34]

Wed. July 10.
Cool with a fine refreshing shower of rain in the afternoon. Slept in Mrs Logan's mansion Legsmaleerie.[35] Large cylinder casting in loam for Canadian Oil Co. came off tonight alright.

Thurs. July 11.
Men with the exception of one or two cleared out of the shop at quarter time to go to Preston to declaration of the poll. A very long procession of waggons from Galt out there. John Goldie and I part of the way and got part of the way in Cowan, the M.P.P. elect's waggon. Heard Cowan and Hespeler deliver their orations on the occasion.

Fri. July 12.
Men mostly at work again. Weather cool almost to coldness. Finished up tracing of Halm's Mill plan.

Sat. July 13.
Fine, bright weather. Preparing for posting June. Mr McCulloch got

---

34 The salute was evidently in celebration of the election of James Cowan as the Reform Member of Parliament for South Waterloo. The 'foundry boys' were perhaps from Lutz and Company, a Galt agricultural implement manufacturer in which Cowan held a substantial interest. 'Glorious Victory,' *DR*, July 19, 1861; *Lovell's Canadian Dominion Directory* (Montreal: Lovell, 1871).

35 Likely a derivation of *Whigmaleerie*, a lowland Scots word meaning 'a fantastical ornament in masonry' or a 'fantastic ornament, trinket or knicknack with no monetary value.' The term is used in the first sense in Walter Scott's *Rob Roy*, where Andrew Fairservice describes the Glasgow Cathedral as a 'brave kirk ... nane o' yer whigmaleeries ... about it.' An avid reader of Scott, McIlwraith may have gotten the term here. John Ogilvie, *The Imperial Dictionary of the English Language* (London: Blackie and Son, 1883), 4:626; John Jamieson, *A Dictionary of the Scottish Language* (Edinburgh: William Tait, 1856), 748; Walter Scott, *Roy Roy* (Edinburgh: James Ballantyne and Co., 1818).

home from being away all week at Clinton and round there. Mrs Muir
and family along with M. in today and called on Mrs Logan.

Sun. July 14.
At Thompson's Church in Mr Campbell's seat in the forenoon. Thought
the Doctor rather dreich.[36] Spent the afternoon with John Goldie accompanying him to church in the evening and having a walk round the N.E.
quarter of the town after church sealed.

Mon. July 15.
Busy now with posting June.

Tues. July 16.
Hard at work on books.

Wed. July 17.
Busy at books. Mr Campbell gone off to drive to Hamilton with horse
and waggon today.

Thurs. July 18.
Busy book posting. Had a visit of John Goldie and the wife for a while in
the evening.

Fri. July 19.
Fine warm day with thunder and lightning and heavy rain in the afternoon. Oil Company's big cylinder being turned off in the lathe today.
Had letters from home from Bill and Mrs Hunter. Mr McCulloch away
at Hawksville. Great storm of wind and heavy rain about 7 o'clock.

Sat. July 20.
Weather fine again. Had men's books made up and gave them out with
the pay today. Started for Greenfield after six. Heard the whip-poor-
will by the way. Moon about full. Had a stroll in the moonlight with M.
David gone to Guelph in the afternoon driving and James down with
the train at Galt.

Sun. July 21.
Beautiful weather. Heard Mr McRuar in the forenoon. Got a ride with
M. in A. McEwan's waggon along to the bridge and came back to Green-
field down the river bank. David and Aunt Betsy got home 7 p.m. from
Guelph.

---

36 'Dreich' is an Old Scottish term for dreary or bleak. It was normally used to describe
   wet weather.

Mon. July 22.
Got Billy to drive me to the school house, 9th conn. and Sprague's Road.
Got in to the office about 10. Had a busy afternoon getting things prepared for shipping with Tunney, who was here. John Goldie and the
wife over at tea in Mrs Logan's.

Tues. July 23.
Still fine, bright weather. Not at all oppressively hot. Mr Cavan and Rev.
Mr Hamilton in from Greenfield today. Had me with them round town
looking at buggies and waggons. Wrote to Thos in the evening sending
Mr Barbour's a/c.

Wed. July 24.
Commenced drawing of Inverhuron Mill.

Thurs. July 25.
Heard from Hamilton of the intention of our friends to be up here on
Saturday night. At work on Inverhuron drawing some time. Weather
quite fine.

Fri. July 26.
Busy drawing.

Sat. July 27.
Finished up and traced the Inverhuron mill drawing. Jas Goldie down
in the morning. Thomas and all the family came up with the evening
train. J.G. and the Mrs over meeting them.

Sun. July 28.
Exceedingly wet afternoon. Thos and I at Thompson's Church in the
forenoon but the Dr himself from home. Afternoon cleared up a little
and Thos and the wife, Tommy, Mary and I walked over and called on
John Goldie.

Mon. July 29.
Thos went off to Hamilton with the morning train. Weather brightening
up some and children enjoying themselves tolerably.

Tues. July 30.
Fine, warm weather again. Had a visit of Mrs Cavan and M. who took
tea in Legsmaleerie. Drove the buggy for them some 4 miles out.

Wed. July 31.
David Goldie called in the morning on his way to Guelph to assist in
raising frame of new building at the mill. Still warm weather.

Thurs. Aug. 1.
Exceedingly hot. Had a job outside checking over importation of iron newly come in from England.

Fri. Aug. 2.
The hottest day of the season so far. Regular Canadian summer weather. Thomas came up from Hamilton in the evening.

Sat. Aug. 3.
Folks all gone on a picnic excursion with Campbell's family to their farm. Started to walk to Greenfield after six and got a ride from Peter Hope from the school house 9th cons. to Ayr. Dan'l Calligan, a brother of Mike, one of our strikers, got sunstruck and died today.[37] Found Jenny sick and M. and I had to go and visit her at a house along at the bridge over the Nith.

Sun. Aug. 4.
At Mr McRuar's church in the forenoon. Had a walk thro' the back bush with M. in the afternoon. Quite a thunderstorm in the evening. James Goldie's two boys staying at Greenfield just now.

Mon. Aug. 5.
Drove in with Peter Hope and the two boys on the way home to Guelph. Had tea in John Goldie's along with all my friends and Mr and Mrs McCulloch and also a son of Sidney Smith.

Tues. Aug. 6.
Weather dull and raining now. Principal job in hand in the office figuring up the cost of the newly come in importation of iron, boiler and gas tubes.

Wed. Aug. 7.
Still dull and wet.

Thurs. Aug. 8.
Still at work on iron figuring. Mr and Mrs Campbell at tea and the children spending the afternoon in the empty rooms upstairs and making great noises.

Fri. Aug. 9.
Got thro' with iron calculations now. Sat reading McGeorge's Tales,

---

37 Daniel Callaghan reportedly became sun-struck in mid-afternoon while working outside plastering a new schoolhouse outside of Galt. 'Death by Sun-Stroke,' *DR*, August 7, 1861.

etc. in the eve'g, and then sat late and had also to rise early writing to M.[38]

Sat. Aug. 10.
Weather brightening up again. John Goldie gone off to visit his relations in the eve'g. Thomas came up with the late train.

Sun. Aug. 11.
Heard Mr Thom from Woolwich preach in the Hill Church. Ferunig and his papa with me, Mary and Mrs Logan in another quarter. Had a walk with Thos, Mr Campbell and the children in the afternoon down as far as Mr Potter's hydraulic ram.[39]

Mon. Aug. 12.
Making a start at posting up July transactions. Mr Goldie Sr in today. Day cold and wet.

Tues. Aug. 13.
A Mr McEwan came with his spring waggon today and took away the whole of our Hamilton visitors. Mr Rannie, Mrs Logan's boarder went away home to Guelph, sick, today.

Wed. Aug. 14.
Getting well thro' journalizing July. Finished and posted letters to Mother and Christina.

Thurs. Aug. 15.
Lovely morning but chilly. Busy posting July. Mrs Logan and I had quite

---

38 Rev. R.J. MacGeorge, *Tales, Sketches and Lyrics* (Toronto: A.H. Armour and Co., 1858).
39 Rev. James Thom, formerly Presbyterian minister in Three Rivers, Canada East (1844–54), was called to pastor in 1854 at Woolwich, where he served until at least 1866. *A Historical and Statistical Report of the Presbyterian Church of Canada, in Connection with the Church of Scotland for the Year 1866* (Montreal: John Lovell, 1867), 24, 105. Fernig was likely a playful nickname Andrew had for his nephew, Thomas's son. An archaic British form (sometimes *fainaigue*), it meant to shirk or evade work or responsibility, or to cheat at cards. See J. Drummond Robertson, comp., *A Glossary of Dialect and Archaic Words Used in the County of Gloucester* (London: English Dialect Society, 1890), 48. A hydraulic ram was a water pump that employed hydropower to move water to elevations higher than a river or stream. The original concept is credited to John Whitehurst in Cheshire, England, in 1772, but the invention was not patented until 1797. The principal producer of hydraulic rams in the nineteenth century was Englishman Josiah Easton's company, run by his son James (1796–1871). Hydraulic ram technology fell into disuse by the 1890s, when it was eclipsed by the electric water pump. See C.A. Crowley, 'Hydraulic Rams Furnish Water Supply to Country Homes,' *Popular Mechanics*, August 1937, 306–11, and September 1937, 437–77.

a walk in the moonlight round town toward Preston and then in and visited Goldie's.

Fri. Aug. 16.
Weather still cool. Finished up posting July today. Feel quite bilious.

Sat. Aug. 17.
Busy all day writing up men's books and preparing for the pay which was this evening.

Sun. Aug. 18.
Kept the house all day reading Douglas Jerrold's Life by his son.[40] Don't admire the book very much. Had a walk thro' the pine woods above the station in the afternoon.

Mon. Aug. 19.
Getting over aguish symptoms again. Had a game of chess with Rennie in the eve'g and beat him.

Tues. Aug. 20.
Had letter from M. also from Thos enclosing home ones from Mrs Hunter. Sat late and wrote to M.

Wed. Aug. 21
Fine day, quite warm in the evening. Had a hard contested game of chess with Rennie in the evening, but came off victor.

Thurs. Aug. 22.
Fine weather. Went out in the afternoon and made a sketch of the foundry building.

Fri. Aug. 23.
Not much pushed with work in the office now. No drawing going on. Think of starting balancing and making a general revision of the books.

Sat. Aug. 24.
Mr Goldie Sr in in the forenoon. Walked out in the evening to Greenfield. Thos got out about 10 o'clock bringing with him a case of stuffed birds, a present to Mr Goldie.

Sun. Aug. 25.
At Mr McRuar's church in the forenoon and after a short walk in the interval, went and heard a Mr Irvine, successor to Mr Ritchie, in the other church.[41]

---

40 Blanchard Jerrold, *The Life and Remains of Douglas Jerrold* (London: W. Kent, 1859).
41 Rev. Alexander Ritchie (1795–1862) was pastor of the United Secession Presbyterian

Mon. Aug. 26.

Spent a while of the forenoon sketching an old house and tree in the neighborhood of Greenfield. After dinner, Thos, Tommy and I went up the creek in the canoe and had a while's fishing. In the evening, David, Thos, Mr Mc., M. and I went all in to a concert in the village, having Peter Auld to drive us in.

Tues. Aug. 27.

Morning close and lowering. Got up by 5 o'clock and started in the buggy between 6 and 7, David and Thos being going to Guelph. Had a very pleasant ride in by the 11th cons. D. and T. went on with the train coming down with it again in the afternoon. Great thunder storm with heavy rain after night fall.

Wed. Aug. 28.

Mr McCulloch gone off on Monday morning to be away all week. Reading Russell's letters on the Crimean War in the evening.[42]

Thurs. Aug. 29.

Still fine cool weather. Getting a little time now for a general overhauling of the books. John Goldie and I visited the reading room in the evening and had a look thro' Punch on the subject of the Yankees running away at Bull Run.[43]

---

congregation of West Dumfries, about a mile east of the village of Ayr, Canada West. Because of declining health, his obituary noted, he was 'loosed from his pastoral charge by the Presbytery of Flamboro' in the summer of 1861. See 'Obituary. Rev. Alexander Ritchie, Ayr, C.W.,' *The Home and Foreign Record of the Canada Presbyterian Church* (December 1861), 39–40; Rev. George Irving (1835–65) succeeded Rev. Ritchie as pastor in 1861, changing the church's name from West Dumfries to Stanley Street Presbyterian Church, Ayr. He died of a disease 'that baffled all medical skill' in his thirty-first year. Rev. William Cochrane, DD, *Memoirs and Remains of the Reverend Walter Inglis, African Missionary and Canadian Pastor* (Toronto: C. Blackett Robinson, 1887), 116; *DR*, January 25, 1865.

42 *London Times* war correspondent William Howard Russell (1820–1907) published his Crimean dispatches in one volume as *The British Expedition to the Crimea* (London: G. Routledge and Co., 1858).

43 *Punch* was a conservative political humour magazine published in London that had a critical view of Lincoln and the Union, the predominant British angle on the U.S. Civil War. In its issue of August 17, 1861, *Punch* carried a poem about the Union Army embarrassment at the recent (First) Battle of Bull Run, set to the tune of 'Yankee Doodle': 'Yankee Doodle near Bull's Run; Met his Adversary, First he thought the fight he'd won; fact proved quite contrary.' An accompanying cartoon depicted Union soldiers in full retreat. *Punch*, 17 August 1861, 4–5, quoted in Russell Duncan, ed., *Blue-Eyed Child of Fortune: The Civil War Letters of Robert Gould Shaw* (Athens: University of Georgia Press, 1999), 143. See William S. Walsh,

Fri. Aug. 30.
Beautiful weather. Had an advertisement of Private Boarding in the Reporter paper today.

Sat. Aug. 31.
Pay day in the shop. Mr McCulloch got home after being absent all week getting S. Austin's squad started at Whitehead's Mill.

Sun. Sept. 1.
Mrs Logan and I at the Hill Church in the forenoon and heard an old man preach. Had a walk thro' the pines above Elliot's toward evening.

Mon. Sept. 2.
Had a talk with Mr Malcolm in the shop about his property now for sale. Price asked $1,300.00. Have a notion of buying it. Mr McCulloch at home most of the day. Busy in the office writing letters etc. Shop working 1 hour late.

Tues. Sept. 3.
Making a start on posting August. Toothache troublesome. Sidney Smith in from Ayr reports M. and nearly all of the others sick.

Wed. Sept. 4.
Busy with books. Mrs Logan much annoyed with boys and cows committing messing in her garden. Cow been in two nights and eaten all the Indian corn and great part of cabbages, beets, etc.

Thurs. Sept. 5.
Toothache continuing very annoying so went and got it pulled. A large double one in the lower right hand jaw.

Fri. Sept. 6.
Busy with books. Heard from Thos giving advise on the buying of property and also inclosing home letters. Begin to think I wont invest at present.

Sat. Sept. 7.
Had tea in Jno. Goldie's between 4 and 5 o'clock and set out for Ayr after. Had a smart walk out by the 9th Conn.

Sun. Sept. 8.
M. continuing rather weak and poorly. At church and heard Mr McRuar in the forenoon. Day fine but chilly.

Abraham Lincoln and the London Punch (New York: Moffat, Yard and Company, 1909), 34.

Mon. Sept. 9.
Had to walk in, the horse and buggy being both under repair. Had a very pleasant walk by way of the 10th Conn through the so-called Alps. Got in by noon. Mr Goldie in driving afterwards, their old buggy left for repair and the Foundry new one borrowed.

Tues. Sept. 10.
Busy with books again. Mr Campbell's store closed this week, he being understood to have made an assignment to Buchanan & Harris.[44]

Wed. Sept. 11.
Getting well through with month's postings now. At the reading room in the eve'g and get an interesting volume entitled 'Brief Biographies' by Mr Smiles.[45]

Thurs. Sept. 12.
Mrs Campbell and Miss McIlwraith spending the afternoon and at tea attacked me to take Mrs L. to hear the Swiss Bell Ringers so I had to consent and went with the party. Mr and Mrs C., Mrs L. and I all tho't the entertainment contemptible. Against my will to go in the first place.[46]

Fri. Sept. 13.
Beautiful mild day. Making up the men's books preparatory to paying tomorrow. Mr Rennie at Mrs Logan's in the evening packing up to leave for a length of time on a/c of his health.

Sat. Sept. 14.
Pay day in the shop. D. Goldie in in the eve'g quite lame from a knock he had got on the knee. John and the wife gone out to their friends. John Stewart came here with morning train.

Sun. Sept. 15.
At the Hill Church in the forenoon and heard Mr Herald from Dundas.

---

44 Almost certainly Alexander Campbell (b. 1817), a tailor and dry goods merchant in Galt (1854–61), described by the R.G. Dun Company's local credit reporter as 'of good character and habits ... a cannie Scotchman.' Buchanan and Harris was a Hamilton-based wholesale house established in 1840 and, by the late 1850s, one of the largest in Canada. Through credit, the company controlled dozens of local merchants like Campbell. See R.G. Dun Credit Records, vol. 23, Simcoe, Stormont, Victoria, Waterloo, 1851–76, 118h, 123, Baker Library, Harvard University. Douglas McCalla, *The Upper Canada Trade 1834–1872: A Study of the Buchanans' Business* (Toronto: University of Toronto Press, 1979).

45 Samuel Smiles, *Brief Biographies* (Boston: Ticknor and Fields, 1860).

46 One local organ offered a similar assessment: 'rather "behind the times"' and 'not very harmonious.' 'The Swiss Bell Ringers,' *DR*, September 18, 1861.

In the afternoon Jno. Stewart and I had a walk up by the riverside above the Dickson dam.

Mon. Sept. 16.
J.S. went off with the morning train. Weather cold and showery.

Tues. Sept. 17.
Begin a revising of last year's balance sheet to try and get it to come out right. In the eve'g make a start at sketching some.

Wed. Sept. 18.
Making a new balance sheet for last year. Spent the evening sketching.

Thurs. Sept. 19.
Start trying finishing of balancing books last year.

Fri. Sept. 20.
Wet weather. Still at work trying to balance December but as yet without success.

Sat. Sept. 21.
Mr McCulloch home after two days absence. New man pleasing pretty well so far. Start for Greenfield after six o'clock and found M. a good deal better than she was the last time I was out. Mrs Steele still there.

Sun. Sept. 22.
Fine bright morning. Some frost had been during the evening. Heard Mr McRuar preach in the forenoon and had a walk with M. in the afternoon as far as the new bridge in course of construction over the river. Mr Smith, a veterinary surgeon new from Ayrshire, called in the eve'g at Greenfield.

Mon. Sept. 23.
Get the buggy out and got a convoy in it from M. Left her about 5 miles out from Galt and got a ride from a deaf farmer nearly all the rest of the road.

Tues. Sept. 24.
M. and her father in today. Had her over to tea in the afternoon. Sergeant Cromach of the Canada Rifles came to board with Mrs L. today. A very decent, quiet Scotchman he seems to be His mission here to drill the Galt Rifle Corps. Wrote a dunning letter to Mr Renfrew, New York.[47]

---

47 Mr Renfrew was the Scottish acquaintance of Andrew's in New York City who employed his sister (Mrs Logan) as a housekeeper in 1859–60. See Diary for 1859. By

Wed. Sept. 25.
Fine weather. Provincial Show opened now but the fare per railway being high, there are but few people going from Galt.[48] The Sergeant getting along very agreeably.

Thurs. Sept. 26.
Weather broken again. Mr McCulloch gone to the exhibition.

Fri. Sept. 27.
Quite a wet afternoon. Rev. Mr Miller from Stratford came to sojourn for a time with Mrs Logan.[49]

Sat. Sept. 28.
Mr and Mrs Goldie in today. Weather quite cold. Pay day in the shop. Visited the reading room with the Serg't in the evening.

Sun. Sept. 29.
Heard the Rev. Mr Miller preach twice in the Hill Church and narrating anecdotes most of the time in the house. Weather cold and raw.

Mon. Sept. 30.
Mr Miller sick with cold and confined to the house for the most part.

Tues. Oct. 1.
Things moving smoothly about the Foundry. Spending the evening at present making some sketches of Foundry, etc. to send home.

Wed. Oct. 2.
[No entry].

Thurs. Oct 3.
Beautiful weather.

Fri. Oct. 4.
County Exhibition takes place in Galt today. James Goldie and S. Smith here. Half holiday in the shop. Mrs Logan and I at the show.[50] Day most unfortunately wet. Eve'g very much so.

---

this letter, Andrew may well have been trying to recover the money that he loaned Renfrew in July 1860.

48 The Provincial Exhibition took place in London, CW. 'The Provincial Show,' *DR*, September 26, 1861.

49 Rev. Mr Miller was pastor of a Presbyterian Church in Stratford from 1857 to 1863. William Johnston, *History of the County of Perth from 1825 to 1902* (Stratford: W.M. O'Beirne, 1903), 489.

50 The Annual Exhibition of the Agricultural Society of the South Riding of Waterloo attracted between four and five thousand visitors. 'South Riding Show in Galt,' *DR*, October 9, 1861.

Sat. Oct. 5.
Still deplorably wet.

Sun. Oct. 6.
A very wet day. Heard Mr Miller morning and afternoon. Dined in the
interval in Jno. Goldie's. Mr M. telling yarns all eve'g.

Mon. Oct. 7.
Mr Miller took his departure today. Mr McCulloch and I drove in the
sulky to Berlin where he took train for up the country and I drove home
alone. Wrote home in the eve'g.

Tues. Oct. 8.
Made a start on the books in the afternoon to write up Sept. Kept at it till
late.

Wed. Oct. 9.
Posted a package of sketches for home. In the office late at the books.

Thurs. Oct. 10.
Hard at work at the books and finished journalizing in the evening.

Fri. Oct. 11.
Very wet and cold. In the office till past 9 and got well thro' with posting.
Some noise going on up about the Buck Tavern about a widow getting
married, her intended however cleared off.

Sat. Oct. 12.
Still showery and miserably cold. Mr McCulloch got home today, having been put back by stress of weather when on his way per steamer
to Inverhuron. After paying the hands, started for Greenfield, arriving
about 9. David in the mill till 12.

Sun. Oct. 13.
At church in com. with all the family and heard Mr McRuar. Had two
walks to the new bridge over the creek in the afternoon. One with M.
and one with David. Billy Bank left to start learning wrightwork with
A. Malcom.

Mon. Oct. 14.
Fine, bright, frosty morning. Walked all the way in.

Tues. Oct. 15.
Weather still keeping fine. At work on trial balance for Sept.

Wed. Oct. 16.
[No entry].

Thurs. Oct. 17.
[No entry].

Fri. Oct. 18.
[No entry].

Sat. Oct. 19.
[No entry].

Sun. Oct. 20.
Heard the Rev. Mr Cameron in the Hill Church morning and afternoon and liked him very well.

Mon. Oct. 21.
Sharp frost in the morning. Took a spell at digging potatoes in the afternoon.

Tues. Oct. 22.
Dull and cold. Got my trial balance for Sept. brought out right.

Wed. Oct. 23.
Write a few lines to Mr Goldie, Ayr. In the course of the day had him in the office. Mr Cameron gone away and two young men in the railway employ come to stay a week or two.

Thurs. Oct. 24.
[No entry].

Fri. Oct. 25.
[No entry].

Sat. Oct. 26.
Pay day in the shop. Had John Goldie and the wife calling in the eve'g.

Sun. Oct. 27.
At church expecting to hear Mr Hay but he did not come and we had old Mr Thom from Warwick instead. A meeting of the congregation held after the service and a resolution formed to try and get Mr Cameron back to preach two Sabbaths.[51] Took a walk up by the Buck Tavern in the

---

51 Likely Rev. Mr Thom from Woolwich. See fn 39 above. Likely Rev. George Haigh, ordained as pastor of the Doon and Hespeler congregation in 1863. See George Simpson, ed., *Presbyterian Year Book for the Dominion of Canada and Newfoundland, 1891*

afternoon and was informed that Bob Matheson was dead. Very sudden, he being at work a short time on Saturday morning.

Mon. Oct. 28.
Very anxious for word from M. Have some singing in the eve'g now with Ker and Crawford, the two railway hands.

Tues. Oct. 29.
Work stopped at noon on a/c of Robt Matheson's funeral. Interment in the Hill Church yard.

Wed. Oct. 30.
At work on trial balance beginning at the beginning of the ledger. Finished perusing Dean Ramsey's 'Reminiscences of Scotland.'[52] Heard from M.

Thurs. Oct. 31.
Still dull, cold weather. Working at trial balance for the first term's posting. Spent the evening drowsily at home reading a lecture about Cicero.[53]

Fri. Nov. 1.
Had a letter from M. that all was satisfactory on the part of the old folks. Back in the office a while in the eve'g.

Sat. Nov. 2.
Quite a storm of wind and rain during the night, and day pouring wet out and out.

Sun. Nov. 3.
At James['s] Church and heard an old gentleman preach in the forenoon. Kept the house the most of the remainder of the day.

Mon. Nov. 4.
Only a few showers today but quite cold. Mrs Goldie and Davy in and went with the morning train to Guelph to fetch home Willie if possible. In the office till past 9 journalizing cash.

(Toronto: Presbyterian Printing and Publishing Co., 1891), 104. Likely Duncan Cameron, ordained as minister of Knox Church, Lucknow, March 3, 1854. A.F. Kemp, F.W. Farries, and J.B. Halkett, eds., *Hand-Book of the Presbyterian Church in Canada: 1883* (Ottawa: J. Durie and Sons, 1883), 179.

52 E.B. (Edward Bannerman) Ramsey, *Reminiscences of Scottish Life and Character*, 3rd ed. (Edinburgh: Edmonston and Douglas, 1859).

53 Likely C.J. Vaughan, *Passages from the Life of Cicero: A Lecture Delivered before the Young Men's Christian Association in Exeter Hall, January 24, 1854* (London: J. Nisbet and Co., 1854).

Tues. Nov. 5.
Close at work journalizing October.

Mon. Nov. 6.
Close at work on books. Wrote to Thomas, also to M.

Thurs. Nov. 7.
Busy with October posting. Had a spell at sawing wood in the evening.

Fri. Nov. 8.
Taken away from my posting to make a sketch of a circular saw mill to go to California.

Sat. Nov. 9.
Pay day in the shop. John and the Mrs off to Ayr in the eve'g and I started soon after six. Got a ride part of the way. Got a welcome as usual.

Sun. Nov. 10.
Heard Mr McRuar in the forenoon. After dinner David and John and I had a walk down by the side of the creek. About 4, David hitched up the mare and drove John and I about half way home. We walking the remainder.

Mon. Nov. 11.
Fine weather. M. in today and her mother down from Guelph, both to stay here until tomorrow. Had a stroll with M. in the eve'g and spent a while in John's.

Tues. Nov. 12.
Old Mrs Goldie and a M. over visiting Mrs Logan and went off per Bob and the buggy in the eve'g. Finished posting.

Wed. Nov. 13.
Working at trial for October. An old gentleman arrived in the evening to be a boarder with Mrs L. In the office till past ten.

Thurs. Nov. 14.
Funeral of J.K. Andrews took place today, he being one of the oldest residents of Galt. The stores closed for a short time and Free Masons took part.[54] Jacob Hespeler called in the eve'g to speak about work for his

---

54 J.K. Andrews was a well-known merchant, miller, councillor, and long-time resident of Galt. His funeral also attracted attendees from Berlin, Waterloo, and other nearby towns. 'Funeral of Mr Andrews,' *DR*, November 20, 1861; Young, *Reminiscences*, 109.

Cotton Factory. Staid late in the office and got out trial balance for October. All correct.

Fri. Nov. 15.
[No entry].

Sat. Nov. 16.
Moon about full. Started for Greenfield near 7 o'clock and got out about 9. Found all well. Mr Goldie Sr just arrived from a visit to Hamilton.

Sun. Nov. 17.
At church in the forenoon and had Davy to drive me in the afternoon with Fanny, the mare.

Mon. Nov. 18.
[No entry].

Tues. Nov. 19.
[No entry].

Wed. Nov. 20.
[No entry].

Thurs. Nov. 21.
[No entry].

Fri. Nov. 22.
[No entry].

Sat. Nov. 23.
Pay day in the shop. J.G, and the wife gone to Ayr to Dr McGeorge's wife's funeral. Rev. Mr White from Arthur came to stay with Mrs Logan and preach on Sabbath. I took the eve'g train up to Guelph and landed at the Speedvale Mill about ten o'clock.

Sun. Nov. 24.
Went with the family to the Congregationalist Church in Guelph.[55] Had a walk with M. to the cemetery in the afternoon but snow rather sloppy and nasty.

---

55 The first Congregational Church was a small stone chapel built on Quebec Street East in 1839 and dedicated in 1840. It was replaced in 1868 by a new stone building constructed at the corner of Norfolk and Liverpool streets. Church member James Goldie contributed 'large subscriptions' and stone from the quarry near his mills. Leo A. Johnson, *History of Guelph 1827–1927* (Guelph: Guelph Historical Society, 1977), 116, 229.

Mon. Nov. 25.
Had a walk in to Guelph with Jas Goldie in the forenoon and after dinner, a tour thro' the mill with Wm Goldie. Came down to Galt with the eve'g train and went to Maitland's singing after.

Tues. Nov. 26.
Assisting John G. some with drawing down the big Lathe in the shop to make additions of power to it on being moved across the shop. Mr Goldie Sr in.

Wed. Nov. 27.
Cold and raw with some snow. Two railway men left Mrs Logan today.

Thurs. Nov. 28.
M. arrived from Guelph in the evening and took up her quarters for the time with Mrs Logan.

Fri. Nov. 29.
[No entry].

Sat. Nov. 30.
Had the foundry horse and sulky out and went out as far as Holm's new mill in the afternoon. Got Bob McCulloch in with me and had a breakdown with one of the springs when just about home. John Goldie and the wife over to tea in the evening. Heard from Thomas of a little boy being added to his family last night.

Sun. Dec. 1.
At the Hill Church morning and afternoon. M. and Mrs Logan there in the afternoon. At tea in John Goldie's in the evening. Had a great job carving a W.F.D. at dinner.

Mon. Dec. 2.
Snow still on the ground and sleighing going on to some extent. Reading 'The Mysterious Stranger' to M. in the evening.[56]

Tues. Dec. 3.
A fine, cold winter morning. Had business taking me out to Greenfield

---

56 There are several pre-1861 books and short stories that carried this title, but given his literary tastes, Andrew and Mary were likely reading Geoffrey Crayon [Washington Irving], 'The Adventure of the Mysterious Stranger,' in *Tales of a Traveller* (New York: George P.Putnam, 1851), 73–82, or Amelie Anderson Opie, 'The Mysterious Stranger,' in *Tales of Real Life* (Boston: S.G. Goodrich, 1827), 201–58.

More of a Man

so got M. with me in the buggy and drove out the 12th Conn. and home by the Ayr road.

Wed. Dec. 4.
Hard at work now to try and get Nov. transactions posted before the end of the week, but a good deal interrupted by letter-writing, etc. In the office late.

Thurs. Dec. 5.
Complete thaw now but without rain. Close at work and late at posting.

Fri. Dec. 6.
Still close at work with the books and got finished with posting about 10 at night.

Sat. Dec. 7.
Got the men's books all fixed up and given out with the pay. A very wet night. Rev. Mr Dobbie came to stay over Sunday. In the evening had a whiles conversing with him.[57]

Sun. Dec. 8.
Started for Ayr in the morning and got in in time to hear Mr McRuar's sermon. M. keeping the house with a sore throat. Had a walk with Davy to the new bridge after dinner. Ker & Crawford also here to stay over Sunday.

Mon. Dec. 9.
Started for Galt on foot and got in by 10.30. Roads very heavy for driving but not so bad for walking. Made sketch of a saw mill building for a Mr Sullivan, Watertown. Mr Dobbie went off in the evening.

Tues. Dec. 10.
[No entry].

Wed. Dec. 11.
[No entry].

---

57 Likely Rev. Robert Dobie (1826–88), a prominent Canadian Presbyterian churchman in the mid-nineteenth century. A native of Stirlingshire, university-educated at St Andrew's and·Glasgow, he was ordained in 1853 and served as pastor of a congregation in Osnabruck, Glengarry, Canada West, from 1853 to 1868. Following this he served congregations in Lindsay and Milton, Ontario. 'Obituary Notices,' *The Church of Scotland Home and Foreign Mission Record* (Edinburgh: Publication Offices of the Church of Scotland, 1888), 16:500–1.

Thurs. Dec. 12.
[No entry].

Fri. Dec. 13.
[No entry].

Sat. Dec. 14.
Beautiful weather with splendid moonlight in the eve'g. Ker & Crawford came down from Hespeler to spend Sabbath.

Sun. Dec. 15.
Felt rather aguish and took physic and staid at home all day.

Mon. Dec. 16.
Busy a/c writing. Had a good practice of singing with Maitland in the eve'g and gave Dr Richardson's cow a tremendous busting when I came home. News from England rather warlike. Cause of disturbance being the taking of Mason and Slidell from a British vessel.[58]

Tues. Dec. 17.
Beautiful moonlight morning when going to work at 7 o'clock. Busy making out a/c's now. Mr McCulloch away to Guelph. Jas Goldie down.

Wed. Dec. 18.
Still fine, dry weather. Close at account writing.

Thurs. Dec. 19.
Rose and had breakfast early being down to the work before the half hour bell rang. Mr Goldie in today. Close at work on account writing. Posted letters to Mrs Hunter and to Thomas.

Fri. Dec. 20.
[No entry].

Sat. Dec. 21.
[No entry].

---

58 On November 8, 1861, Captain Charles Wilkes of the U.S. ship *San Jacinto* stopped and boarded the British merchantman *Trent*, which was carrying Confederate agents John Slidell and James Murray Mason from Havana to Europe (Slidell to Paris, Mason to London) to rally support for the Confederacy. Wilkes arrested the men and returned with them to the mainland. The *Trent* continued to England, but the event – soon called the 'Trent Affair' – sparked considerable official and popular protest in Britain and British North America, where, it was argued, neutrality had been contravened. See Robin W. Winks, *The Civil War Years: Canada and the United States*, 4th ed. (Montreal and Kingston: McGill-Queen's University Press, 1998 [1960]), ch. 6.

Sun. Dec. 22.

Still cold, frosty weather. At church with M. and the rest of the family and heard Mr McRuar. David drove half road in with me in the afternoon.

Mon. Dec. 23.

Several inches of snow lying in the morning having fallen during the night. Kept the house in the eve'g being a little bilious. Read part of Emerson's 'English Traits' and had some singing with Ker & Crawford.[59]

Tues. Dec. 24.

News of Prince Albert's death came by telegraph today.[60] Snow lying rather dry for good sleighing. Mr McCulloch got a new buggy horse bought from Todd. Mr McCulloch gone off up the country.

Wed. Dec. 25.

Town very quiet, just like Sunday. Snow too dry for sleighing and roads rough. M. and Maria came in in the evening. Mrs Logan, her and I all at tea in John's, also Strickland and the wife.

Thurs. Dec. 26.

Mild and foggy with heavy showers in the afternoon. M. went off at mid-day. Wm Bell and I out with the new mare a bit in the afternoon. A nice little animal but light for the work.

Fri. Dec. 27.

Blowing strong all night and a regular freeze up in the morning. One of Crombie's horses ran off and hurt itself badly today.

Sat. Dec. 28.

Busy getting forward with all possible work preparatory to going off for the holidays. Took a spell at cutting wood in the afternoon then left per train between 5 and 6. Met Thos half way down to the station at Hamilton and found all well in the house.

---

59 Ralph Waldo Emerson, *English Traits*, 1st ed. (Boston: Phillips, Sampson and Company, 1856).

60 Prince Albert of Saxe-Coburg and Gotha (Francis Albert Augustus Charles Emmanuel, 1819–61) was a German nobleman and the husband of Queen Victoria (and also her first cousin). Upon their marriage in 1840, he became HRH Prince Albert and in 1857 officially Prince Consort. See Stanley Weintraub, *Uncrowned King: The Life of Prince Albert* (New York: Simon and Schuster, 2000). The Canadian reaction was subdued but respectful; see 'Death of Prince Albert,' *Globe* [Toronto], December 25, 1861.

Sun. Dec. 29.
At Mr Burnett's Church in the forenoon and heard his funeral oration
on the death of Prince Albert. Church draped in black. Had a walk with
Jameson in the afternoon.

Mon. Dec. 30.
Miss McIlwraith getting married to Mr Magee today.[61] Thos and the wife
off most of the day at the marriage. Visited Fisher's old foundry to look
at a big lathe there. Also called on Rankin at the freight house G.W.R.
and had a walk through the wheat elevator building.

Tues. Dec. 31.
Rose early and went down and had a tour thro' the Railway Shops. Thos
and I went up to Dundas per stage at noon and walked round there for a
while. Came down with the train and had our Hogmenay dinner. Some
visitors in at the very time for it causing some delay and loss of temper.

---

61 Agnes McIlwraith was the daughter of John McIlwraith (1778–1853), an Ayrshire
   plumber and Convener of Trades who moved to Canada in 1845 and died in Hamilton, CW, in 1853. They were distant relatives on Andrew's side and may have
   guided Thomas and Andrew when they came to Canada West. She married David
   McGee, of New York. 'Married,' *HS*, December 31, 1861.

Diary for 1862

Wed. Jan. 1. 1862.
Walked up as far as the P.O. with Thos in the morning. Day came on very stormy with squalls of sleet and snow. Sat in the house, very dull, all day. Thos being out most of the day. No visitors at the house but Mr Walker and the Muirs. Thos, Mrs McI. and I went to the Muir's in the evening to a party given in honour of Mr. and Mrs Jas Muir on a visit from Detroit. Home somewhere about 3 o'clock.

Thurs. Jan. 2.
Clear and frosty. Thos and I walked out with the gun and visited Mr Larkin near the Delta to talk to him about supplying the Foundry with sand. Left with the eve'g train for Galt.

Fri. Jan. 3.
No work doing about the shop only repairs of machinery. Not fairly set agoing with office work either.

Sat. Jan. 4.
Started for Greenfield after quitting time. Roads pretty rough and hard with the frost, but got out in the 2-½ hours. Found all well. David made purchase yesterday of a new team of horses and all the accompanyment of waggon, sleigh, etc. for Jas at Guelph.

Sun. Jan. 5.
At church and heard Mr McRuar.[1] Heard bad reports about Mr Irvine, the U.P. minister in Ayr. Got David to drive me in a piece of the 11th Concession and got home between six and seven.

---

1 On Rev. Duncan McRuar, see Diary for 1858, fn 47.

Mon. Jan. 6.
Making a start with December posting now and working late at them.

Tues. Jan. 7.
Still close at work and late at books.

Wed. Jan. 8.
Still working close and late at books.

Thurs. Jan. 9.
Still working close and late at books.

Fri. Jan. 10.
[No entry].

Sat. Jan. 11.
Still busy with a/c's and have a lot of them mailed. Rev. Mr Hogg arrived in the eve'g to officiate in the Hill Church tomorrow.[2] Snow on heavy and promise of cheap wood now.

Sun. Jan. 12.
Snowing fast part of the day. Heard Mr Hogg preach in morning and afternoon. Spent the eve'g in Jno. Goldie's.

Mon. Jan. 13.
Still busy at a/c's. David Goldie in in the evening. Mrs Logan's boarders all gone off today. Ker and Crawford to Hamilton and Noah who took French leave to Berlin is as supposed.

Tues. Jan. 14.
James Goldie down from Guelph this morning with his driving horse which has got so fierce as to be scarcely manageable. Came down about as quick as the train. Mr McCulloch took her out in the afternoon and had a hard task with her too. The coldest day of the season. Thermometer 22 below. Still working late at a/c's.

---

2 Rev. John Hogg was pastor at St Andrew's Presbyterian (Church of Scotland), Guelph (1857–77). See C. Acton Burrows, *The Annals of the Town of Guelph, 1827–77* (Guelph: Herald Steam Printing House, 1877), 159. The 'Hill Church' must have referred to St Andrew's Presbyterian, one of several Galt Presbyterian congregations. '[T]he little brown church on the hill,' Rev. James Dickson recalled, was 'so difficult of access, and so hard to heat in winter, and so oppressive with the evil odour of ill-trimmed oil lamps.' Its congregation moved (with others) to form Central Presbyterian Church in 1880, on the bank of the Grand River. James A.R. Dickson, *'Ebenezer': A History of the Central Presbyterian Church, Galt, Ontario* (Toronto: William Briggs, 1904), 136–7.

Wed. Jan. 15.
[No entry].

Thurs. Jan. 16.
Quite heavy fall of snow thro' the night again. Still busy closing up accounts.

Fri. Jan. 17.
Weather somewhat milder but snow lying deep. Mrs Logan went off to Hamilton with eve'g train and I took up my quarters for the time being with Jno. Goldie. Had an alarm of fire during the night which turned out to be Mr Smith's Prince Albert lagar beer shop burned down.[3]

Sat. Jan. 18.
Pay night in the shop. After tea started for Greenfield. Snow deep and but poorly tracked in most part of the 9th Cons. Eve'g close, foggy and warm. Farm lights glimmering thro' the mist. Had a hard task toiling thro' the snow.

Sun. Jan. 19.
At church with all the family. More snow fallen during the night. M. consented to come with me to Galt as my wife in March.

Mon. Jan. 20.
Got a ride in to Galt with Mr Goldie who had to come in on Bank business. Snowing most of the way. In the office late at the books.

Tues. Jan. 21.
My wood contracts being filled up now, viz. 5 cords soft wood and 5 do. green hard wood. Still working late preparing for showing the balance for 1861.

Wed. Jan. 22.
Still fine winter weather. Plenty of wood coming in but so much demand for it that the price keeps up. Had a rumpus with an Irishman from

---

3 The fire was actually at 'Schmitt's Lager Beer Saloon' at the head on North Water Street in Galt. The blaze erupted about 1:30 in the morning on Friday. Fire engines dispatched to the fire were unusable in the extremely cold temperatures. As a result, both the main structure and its barn were completely consumed. Witnesses noticed Frank Schmitt, the occupant of the property, departing along the road to Preston as the fire broke out. A coroner's inquest the following day revealed that Schmitt was behind in payments on the property and had carted away the contents of the premises in the few hours before the fire. The coroner then committed Schmitt and his wife to jail to await trial. *DR*, January 22, 1862.

across the street about beating his pig out of our yard. Still working late.

Thurs. Jan. 23.
Had John Goldie and the wife over to tea tonight. Tried to play some on the flutina but could not get it done for the baby who was like to go into fits when it sounded.

Fri. Jan. 24.
Still more snow. Still working late at my balance.

Sat. Jan. 25.
In the office till past ten at night getting Canadian Oil Co's a/c straightened up preparatory to getting a settlement with them.

Sun. Jan. 26.
Quite blowy and snowing fast part of the day. Heard Mr Campbell fore and afternoon who seemed to please the folks very well.

Mon. Jan. 27.
A very keen, cold, frosty morning. Bob McCulloch gone off to visit his farm with the Foundry horse and cutter. Day turned out quite fine. M. and her father in for a short time. Went up into St Andrew's Church tower and took templates off the shape of the bell for the purpose of getting a new one made.

Tues. Jan. 28.
Quite blowy all day and a sort of thaw with rain and sleet in the evening. In the office late finishing up the balance sheet for the present year. Strickland in a while making himself a nuisance by interrupting my work. Got my balance sheet finished tonight making a favorable appearance for the business Mr Crombie got an order from Cuba for an engine, etc. from here.

Wed. Jan. 29.
Still thawing this morning. Mr McCulloch and Mr Scott away to Hamilton.

Thurs. Jan. 30.
[No entry].

Fri. Jan. 31.
[No entry].

Sat. Feb. 1.
Got all hands paid and books given out and got Wm Bell to give Mr

Dryden and I a ride out as far as his house after quitting time. Fine frosty night with the moon a few nights old. In the afternoon Mrs Logan made a purchase of ½ doz. of hair cloth bottomed chairs for me. Peter Hay to come to board with Mrs L. tonight.

Sun. Feb. 2.
At church with all the family in the morning. Found John in the house when I came home from church. Had a stroll with David along the new bridge and up the hill till past Dr Lett's in the afternoon.

Mon. Feb. 3.
Mr Goldie going to Guelph so get a ride in with him, arriving before 10 o'clock. Day pretty cold with some snow falling. Mrs Logan and I went round in the evening and called on Mrs Mathewson about taking her house. Think she will let it but has not decided on what rent to ask.[4] Had some flute playing from P. Hay in the evening.

Thurs. Feb. 4.
Still fine winter weather. Bought a clock from Mrs Logan and had quite a row with her about getting up in the morning. Adam Austin[5] called at the house in the eve'g but I did not see him, being in the office till 10.

Wed. Feb. 5.
Still fine weather and good sleighing. Contracted for another 6 cords of hard wood at $2.50 from a Mr Decker. Spent the eve'g at home.

Thurs. Feb. 6.
Raining heavy part of the day. Invited to tea in Strickland's and spent quite a merry eve'g until near 12. Mr McCulloch got home from the States having bought a lathe and a shingle machine.

Fri. Feb. 7.
Frost again. Had a visit from A. Scott in the forenoon to speak about the house on the hill and about concluded on getting it.

Sat. Feb. 8.
Still fine, wintry weather. Some snow falling during the day. Started for

---

4 Mrs Matthewson, widow of William B. Matthewson, leased a house on Hay Street to McIlwraith in 1862. See Assessment Rolls for the Town of Galt, 1862, Ward 5, p. 44.

5 McIlwraith and Austin partnered to purchase a foundry in Listowel in 1872. At this point Austin reportedly worked in the millwright department of Goldie, McCulloch and Company. *LB*, April 11, 1872. See Epilogue.

Greenfield after quitting work and walked all the way. Walking not bad at all. Found all well.

Sun. Feb. 9.
At church with the family and heard Mr McRuar. In the afternoon David hitched up Fanny and gave me a ride in most of the way. Rev. Mr McDonald from Fergus stopping over Sunday in Mrs L.'s.[6]

Mon. Feb. 10.
Posted a letter home to John. Making but slow progress with my monthly posting, having a good deal of interruption with letter-writing, etc.

Tues. Feb. 11.
Snowing most part of the day. M. and Miss Smith came in today. Miss Smith went home in the eve' and M. staid overnight. Mrs Goldie and her called on Mrs L. in the eve'g and had some flute playing from Peter Hay. Mrs Campbell and Miss McIlwraith also called.

Wed. Feb. 12.
Still fine winter weather. Mr Goldie in today. M. went home late in the afternoon with Robin Fulton and the wife. Called on Mrs Mathewson in the eve'g and arranged with her about taking her house.

Thurs. Feb. 13.
Going on some with journalizing Jan. but had too much other business to get on well with it. In the office untill about 10 in the eve'g.

Fri. Feb. 14.
Quite cold this morning yet.

Sat. Feb. 15.
Still fine, frosty weather. Met Mr Burnett at the station in the eve'g and got him home to Mrs L.'s to stop over Sabbath.

Sun. Feb. 16.
Heard Mr Burnett preach morning and afternoon. Spent a while of the eve'g in Jno. Goldie's.

Mon. Feb. 17.
Mr McCulloch went off driving on a long tour up towards Goderich. Mr Burnett went off with the down train.

---

6 Margaret Logan's house, it seems, was employed regularly by visiting Presbyterian ministers invited to preach in Galt.

Tues. Feb. 18.
Finishing up journalizing. Late at work in the office.

Wed. Feb. 19.
Busy finishing posting Jan. In the office till ten at night. Quite a stormy night. High gales of wind with snow.

Thurs. Feb. 20.
An exceedingly cold morning. Day rather fine again for the winter. At work on trial balances for Dec. and Jan. Heard from M. Spent the forenight copying some of Moore's 'Irish Melody Music.'[7]

Fri. Feb. 21.
Doing a little at trial balance. In the eve'g Peter Hay and I went to the Good Templar's soiree which was held with a variety of speechifying, music, etc. till about 11 p.m. Mr Vinten, an American Senator addressed the meeting.[8]

Sat. Feb. 22.
Weather mild and thawing. Got a new shingling machine over from the station, made in Lockport and to be sent with engine, etc. to Cuba. Preparing to start on foot to Greenfield in the evening but found the Greenfield cutter at the gate when I came over in the eve'g, and got a ride out with David G. Greenfield folk had a visit from Katy Brydon who arrived between 11 and 12 at night.

Sun. Feb. 23.
At church with all the family in the forenoon. Had a walk with David to see the ruins of Dr Lett's house which was burned to the ground on Friday morning. One of his children badly frozen, expected to lose her toes if her life is not endangered.[9]

---

7 Thomas Moore, *Irish Melodies* (Philadelphia: M. Carey, 1815).
8 The Independent Order of Good Templars, Silver Spring Lodge No. 541, was founded in Galt in 1861 and lasted until 1866 (it was revived in the mid-1880s). A temperance organization open to both men and women, IOGT sponsored lectures, soirees, and festivals designed to warn local citizens away from drink and to act as a watchdog of sorts on the local drink traffic. The Order was founded in Utica, New York, in 1851. See Andrew C. Holman, *A Sense of Their Duty: Middle-Class Formation in Victorian Ontario Towns* (Montreal and Kingston: McGill-Queen's University Press, 2000), ch. 5. The speaker was the Hon. J.E. Vinton, a popular temperance speaker from the United States. *DR*, February 26, 1862.
9 The fire completely consumed the house of Rev. Dr Lett of Blenheim, near Ayr. *DR*, March 5, 1862.

Mon. Feb. 24.
Rose about six and went round to Mr Alexander's who spoke about going into Galt today. Morning the most tempestuous one of the season. Heavy snow fallen and still falling and drifting with the storm. However the old man started and had a hard job to get thro' the drift in some places. Mr McCulloch home from up the country.

Tues. Feb. 25.
Close at work on trial balances and back late in the office. Weather still cold and frosty. Called on Barbour and ordered a sofa and purchased a bookcase.

Wed. Feb. 26.
Still wintry weather. More snow falling. Prospects of plenty of work ahead in the Foundry. Contract concluded for wheels for Haut and Elliott and some more orders in from Cuba.

Thurs. Feb. 27.
Busy on trial balances for Dec. and Jan. but find them a rather tough job.

Fri. Feb. 28.
[No entry].

Sat. Mar. 1.
Busy with pay, etc. Dr Skinner from Waterdown arrived at Mrs Logan's in the afternoon. New bell put up today and sounds very satisfactory.

Sun. Mar. 2.
At church fore and afternoon and heard Dr Skinner. Had the pleasure of his company in the eve'g which if somewhat amusing, was not particularly edifying in a religious point of view.[10]

Mon. Mar. 3.
A very cold blustering day, raining and freezing. Dr Skinner took his departure nevertheless.

Tues. Mar. 4.
Still at work on trial balances.

---

10 Rev. John Skinner, DD (1805–64), a native of Partick, Scotland, was a minister of Presbyterian congregations in Nelson and Waterdown, CW, 1855–64. He had previously pastored in Lexington, Virginia, and London, CW. Well known regionally, he was 'sound and animated in his preaching … vivacious and agreeable in conversation.' 'Died,' *The Presbyterian* [Montreal] 17, no. 5 (May 1864): 134.

Wed. Mar. 5.
Still cold stormy weather. Had a visit of Jno. Jackson in the eve'g who
had been thro' the town with a load of lumber. Spent some time in the
reading room.

Thurs. Mar. 6.
Still fine winter weather. At work on trial balances for all last year and
James Goldie down and brought his books down for me to post. Spent
the eve'g in the house at them.

Fri. Mar. 7.
A fine mild day. Thawing in the afternoon. Making sketches of the small
engine about to be sent to Cuba. Ball got up by the Foundry hands came
off tonight. Goldie and McCulloch with their wives in attendance. I also
attended and danced till near daylight in the morning.

Sat. Mar. 8.
No work going on today. Start for Ayr in the afternoon and got in before
six. Very soft, sloppy walking. Considerable part of Spreague's Road
blocked up with snow. M. got home from Hamilton after I got out.

Sun. Mar. 9.
At church with the family in the forenoon. Day stormy so kept the
house reading etc. all day after.

Mon. Mar. 10.
Morning pouring rain so could not propose starting for Galt. Read the
story of 'Wee Davie' in the house.[11] Towards three o'clock the boy Tom
got out the cutter and we started by way of the 11th Conn. Let him turn
back about a mile from the Black Horse, the road got so bad and walked
in the remainder.

Tues. Mar. 11.
Hard at work on Feb. posting now and worked late in the office.
Weather frosty again.

Wed. Mar. 12.
Still busy on Feb. books. In the office till 10 p.m. and finished journalizing.

Thurs. Mar. 13.
Finished posting today. Jas Goldie down and staid all day.

---

11 Likely the popular new Carter's Fireside Library book by Rev. Norman MacLeod,
   Wee Davie (New York: Robert Carter and Brothers, 1862).

Fri. Mar. 14.
At work on trial balance for Feb.

Sat. Mar. 15.
Raining hard again. Men's books made up and given out for Feb. today.
Ker & Crawford arrived in the eve'g to spend over Sunday.

Sun. Mar. 16.
At church in the forenoon and heard McDowal.[12] Have got a cold and
kept the house all day after.

Mon. Mar. 17.
Beautiful wintry weather. David Goldie and M. came in in the morning.
David went to Guelph and came down again with the eve'g train and
had tea all together in Mrs L's. M. went up to Guelph in the eve'g.

Tues. Mar. 18.
Keen frost during the night but sun strong during the day. Making plan
of engine and boiler to send to Cuba. M. down from Guelph in the
evening. Mr Sherde's funeral took place today.[13]

Wed. Mar. 19.
Frosty during the night but thawing thro' the day. Mrs Mathewson taking away her last load of furniture today. M. still in town. Mrs Goldie
and her spending the afternoon in Mrs Logan's at carpet making.

Thurs. Mar. 20.
[No entry].

Fri. Mar. 21.
[No entry].

---

12 Rev. James McDowall (ca 1826–64). Licensed to preach in 1856, he served a congregation in Bermuda until ill health compelled him to move to St Vincent, Sydenham,
and Euphrasia, Grey County, CW (ca 1862), where he pastored until his death in
1864. Henry J. Morgan, *Bibliotheca Canadensis; or a Manual of Canadian Literature*
(Ottawa: G.E. Desbarats, 1867), 265; *Home and Foreign Record of the Canada Presbyterian Church* (Toronto: W.C. Chewett, 1864), 3:29, 261.

13 Likely a misspelling referring to the high-profile funeral of Absalom Shade (1793–
1862), a pioneering Galtonian who had established a grist mill on the Grand River in
partnership with Hon. William Dickson and oversaw the construction of the Main
Street Bridge by the 1820s. Galt was originally known as 'Shade's Mills.' *DR*, March
19, 1862. On Shade, see Leo A. Johnson, 'Shade, Absalom,' *DCB* (Toronto: University
of Toronto Press, 1976), 9:717–18; James Young, *Reminiscences of the Early History of
Galt and the Settlement of Dumfries, in the Province of Ontario* (Toronto: Hunter, Rose,
1880), esp. chs. 2 and 3.

Sat. Mar. 22.
Day of the moderation of the call to Mr Campbell. Was in attendance and heard Mr Hogg preach and then signed the call.[14]

Sun. Mar. 23.
Heard Mr Hogg morning and afternoon and Peter and I read lectures to young men in the eve'g aloud.

Mon. Mar. 24.
Keen frost in the morning and fine bright day. Engine and shingle mach. being shipped for Cuba today. At work on Jas and Wm Goldie's books.

Tues. Mar. 25.
Still beautiful winter weather. Got the key of the house from Mrs Mathieson today. Heard from M. that she cannot be ready before 9th April. Also had a letter from Thos.

Wed. Mar. 26.
[No entry].

Thurs. Mar. 27.
[No entry].

Fri. Mar. 28.
[No entry].

Sat. Mar. 29.
Evening fine and had good roads, walking all the way by the 9th Conn. Got John to hand out the pay and so got off a little early. Found all well. Mrs Cavan expected on Monday.

Sun. Mar. 30.
At church with the folks. Spent the day reading and had a short stroll with David in the eve'g.

---

14 Rev. Hogg was in Galt to act as Moderator in a call, when congregants nominated a new pastor for St Andrews' Church, Galt. The call was sustained by the Presbytery on April 1 and Rev. Robert Campbell was inducted as pastor at St Andrew's on April 10, 1862. *DR*, March 22, 1862. Campbell (1835–1921) achieved a measure of fame in Canada as a botanist, author, educator, and minister at Montreal's St Gabriel Presbyterian Church – after he left Galt in 1866. See Dan Shute, 'Campbell, Robert,' *DCB* (Toronto: University of Toronto Press, 2005), 15:194–6. On the ordination, see also 'St Andrew's Church, Galt,' *The Presbyterian* [Montreal] 15, no. 3 (March 1862): 121.

Mon. Mar. 31.
David going to Paris drove me in thro' Ayr in the cutter and in the Ayr Road as far as the school house at the 9th Conn. Got a chance most of the remainder with a butcher's cart. Frosty and pretty tolerable roads.

Tues. Apr. 1.
Had a cook stove sent up to the house and Strickland and I went up in the evening and set it up preparatory to having a woman in to clean tomorrow. Started to finish saw mill drawing pencilled out by Mr McCulloch.

Wed. Apr. 2.
Large pipe casting in loam came off tonight for Fraser, Elora. Mr Topper called at the Foundry and a walk around, then had tea with us and had a while's music. Him and Peter H. Felt sick and went early to bed. Quite a thunderstorm in the afternoon.

Thurs. Apr. 3.
Busy with saw mill drawing for Cuba and California. Called on Mr Barbour and selected a lot more furniture. In the evening Peter and I carried up the parlour carpet, and Mrs Logan, him and I laid it down.

Fri. Apr. 4.
Day rather fair. M. and Miss Cavan in today but missed the chance of speaking to them, being detained in the office until past five with Mr Atwood, etc. Close at work on sawmill tracings. Mr McCulloch back from Hamilton and reported Mrs Mac. as being sick with ague.

Sat. Apr. 5.
Heavy rain all forenoon but brightened up about noon and Mr Barbour took up some furniture and Wm Bell some more from the house. Mrs Logan finished laying the carpets in the bedrooms. Heard from Thos of little Tom getting his thumb hurt and that Mrs Mac would not think of being up to my wedding.

Sun. Apr. 6.
No sermon at the Hill Kirk today. Got to be late for church in the forenoon so Peter Hay and I started and had a long walk along the railway track towards Brantford. Very blowy and frosty. At the Free Church in the eve'g.

Mon. Apr. 7.
Still exceedingly cold and windy. Wm Goldie down from Guelph

on his way to Ayr. Finishing up sawmill tracings for Cuba and California.

Tues. Apr. 8.
Stormy and cold as ever. Sydney Smith down today on the way to Ayr.
Him and Mr McCulloch and I went and called on Mr Sparrow and got
a licence, they being bondsmen.[15] Thos and the wife and Jno Stewart
came up with the evening train.

Wed. Apr. 9.
Had a carriage and span of horses and buggy and single horse hired
from Scott and Stevens and started a little after 8, viz Thos and his wife,
Mrs Logan, Jno. S. and I. Made up on Jno. Goldie a little way out of
town. Had tolerable dry, frozen roads, snow nearly gone but at the turn
of the road leaving the 12th Conn. a lot lying badly drifted. Got out all
safe by 10 a.m. and got married by somewhere about 12. Mr McRuar
officiating and Mr Cavan assisting. Got under way about 3 o'clock. Mr
and Mrs Mac., Mrs Logan and J.S. in the carriage, my wife and I in
the buggy, last in the cavalcade in starting but carriage horses balked
among the snow near the 12th and we got ahead and were in to Galt 1st.
However, we all got off with the cars at 5.35 and M. and I put up for the
night at the Newbigging Home, Toronto.[16]

Thurs. Apr. 10.
Went out shopping in Toronto. Also called and had photographs taken
for sending away. Delightfully bright, beautiful weather. Good view of
the Bay from the hotel.

Fri. Apr. 11.
Still beautiful weather, getting warmer. Had a trip on the street cars
and paid a visit to the University, inspecting the Library and the

---

15 Sydney Smith was Andrew's brother-in-law, widower of Elizabeth Goldie (d. 1854),
the oldest sister of Mary (Goldie) McIlwraith. Smith was an Englishman, born near
London in 1812. He died in Galt in 1878. Mahlon M. Gowdy, *A Family History Comprising the Surnames of Gade-Gadie-Gaudie ... from AD 800 to AD 1919* (Lewiston, ME:
Journal Press, 1919), 250–1. More generally, see Peter Ward, *Courtship, Love, and Mar-
riage in Nineteenth-Century English Canada* (Montreal and Kingston: McGill-Queen's
University Press, 1990). Thomas Sparrow was the Town Clerk in Galt. James Suth-
erland, *County of Waterloo Gazetteer and General Business Directory for 1864* (Toronto:
Mitchell and Co., 1864), 145.
16 The *Reformer* reported: 'Married, At the residence of the bride's father Greenfield
Farm, near Ayr, On Wednesday the 9th inst., by the Rev. D. McRuar, Mr. Andrew
McIlwraith, of Galt, to Mary, youngest daughter of Mr John Goldie, near Ayr.' *DR*,
April 16, 1862.

Museum. Saw the soldiers marching thro' the grounds. Took the evening train home to Galt. Mrs Logan and Mrs Goldie in the home to receive us.

Sat. Apr. 12.
Down at the office and made up the pay. Got boxes with books, etc. moved up in the evening. Parlour looking very neat.

Sun. Apr. 13.
At church and heard Mr Campbell preach his introductory discourse. At tea in Mrs Logan's in the evening.

Mon. Apr. 14.
Going about the work as usual again. Weather very fine now. Quite warm with frogs piping. Called on Mrs Logan and had a flitting of dishes in the eve'g.

Tues. Apr. 15.
Still sultry weather. River about the highest. Mr Goldie Sr, Maria and the girl Emily all in and paid a short visit. Seed Fair in Galt today.[17]

Wed. Apr. 16.
Still warm. Received photographs by mail from Toronto and put up one to send home to Scotland. Started making a kitchen table in the evening.

Thurs. Apr. 17.
[No entry].

Fri. Apr. 18.
[No entry].

Sat. Apr. 19.
[No entry].

Sun. Apr. 20.
At church and heard Mr Campbell fore and afternoon. Mrs Logan spent the interval with us.

Mon. Apr. 21.
At meeting of trustees of church in Pollock's Office in the evening and was kept quite late. Day wet and stormy. M. waited at Mrs Logan's until the meeting dispersed.

---

17 Refers to the Galt Spring Horse Exhibition and Seed Fair. *DR*, April 16, 1862.

Tues. Apr. 22.
All afternoon up at St Andrew's Church attaching cards of the seats.
Had a spell at my table in the eve'g.

Wed. Apr. 23.
Busy posting March. Had Mr and Mrs Goldie and Mrs Logan and P. Hay
at tea in the evening and had a rather pleasant evening singing fluting,
etc. untill 10 o'clock. Mr Goldie Sr in today and took dinner with us.

Thurs. Apr. 24.
Fine weather but cold. Finished posting March. In the eve'g worked at
the table.

Fri. Apr. 25.
Frosty morning and beautiful bright day. Matthew Craig started to
work on our garden. Settled a/c with Mr Barbour. Met Mr Raphael on
the street.

Sat. Apr. 26.
Had men's books made up and given out with the pay for March.

Sun. Apr. 27.
[No entry].

Mon. Apr. 28.
[No entry].

Tues. Apr. 29.
[No entry].

Wed. Apr. 30.
[No entry].

Thurs. May 1.
[No entry].

Fri. May 2.
[No entry].

Sat. May 3.
Mary went off with Mr. Strickland in the morning to visit Greenfield. Willie Goldie in from Ayr on his way to Guelph and to wait on
David who was to be in the afternoon. Got tired of waiting and started
off. David arrived shortly after I started in Pursuit. McCulloch with him
and brought back the buggy which I get to ride out with in the eve'g.

Sun. May 4.
At church with the rest of the folks.

Mon. May 5.
Got the buggy and the mare Fanny to ride in. David being coming from Guelph and to take her home.

Tues. May 6.
[No entry].

Wed. May 7.
[No entry].

Thurs. May 8.
[No entry].

Fri. May 9.
[No entry].

Sat. May 10.
[No entry].

Sun. May 11.
[No entry].

Mon. May 12.
Matthew Craig finished his digging today and get settled with him, $7.12-½

Tues. May 13.
At Berlin with Mr McCulloch today and brought home the buggy. Very hot and dusty. Went and came by way of Doon.

Wed. May 14.
Had Mr Toppen to tea with us in the evening. P. Hay invited but could not come, the toothache was so bad. Mr Cavan came up with Jno. Goldie and the wife in the eve'g. Mr C. staying with us all night. Had Mr Toppen performing on the violin a while.

Thurs. May 15.
Mr Cavan preaching in the U.P. Church today and slept in our house again, being Sacramental Fast Day in the Free Church.[18]

---

18 William Caven (1830–1904), future principal of Knox College, Toronto, and public intellectual. Born in Kirkcolm, Scotland, he moved with his family to North Dum-

Fri. May 16.
[No entry].

Sat. May 17.
Mr and Mrs Goldie in today and spent most of the day with Mary.

Sun. May 18.
At the Sabbath School in our Church in the morning as a teacher, also at Church fore and afternoon and heard Mr Hogg from Guelph.

Mon. May 19.
[No entry].

Tues. May 20.
[No entry].

Wed. May 21.
[No entry].

Thurs. May 22.
At tea in Mr Caldwell's in the evening and met Misses and Mr Reid and Craig, also Gavin Caldwell, an old school fellow. At Ree's sale and bought a lot of books, 2-vols Leisure Hours and 2 of Chalmer's Sermons, etc.[19]

Fri. May 23.
Went with W. Bell to the bush in the morn'g to show him the cord wood purchased from Oliver. Got men's books made up and prepared for pay in the eve'g. Mr McCulloch went off to New York in co. with Crombie in the afternoon.

Sat. May 24.
Rose before six and had Bob hitched up and went off to Greenfield, per

fries Township, near Ayr in Canada West, in 1847. Educated at Knox College, he was ordained to and served in the charge of St Mary's and Downie (1852–65). In 1865, he was appointed a temporary chair Exegetical Theology and Biblical Criticism at Knox. He rose to the position of principal and served there with distinction and prominence, 1870–1904. In 1856, Caven married Margaret Goldie, sister of McIlwraith's employer John Goldie and McIlwraith's future wife, Mary Goldie, in 1856. George Maclean Rose, ed., 'Caven, Rev. William, DD,' *A Cyclopedia of Canadian Biography* (Toronto: Rose Publishing Company, 1886), 61–2; William Stewart Wallace, 'Caven, William,' *Macmillan Dictionary of Canadian Biography*, 4th ed. (Toronto: Macmillan of Canada, 1978), 142.

19 *The Leisure Hour; A Family Journal of Instruction and Recreation. Weekly* [1852–80] (London: W. Stevens); Thomas Chalmers, *Sermons and Discourses* (New York: R. Carter, 1844).

11th Conn. My wife, Maria and I in the buggy. Spent a while of the forenoon sketching the old mill. In the afternoon drove over to Doon[?] and
visited Mr Dryden. Met Mr and Mrs Ballingal there. Queen's Birthday
Holiday kept with great spirit in Galt.[20]

Sun. May 25.
At church and heard Mr McRuar. Had a stroll with David in the back
bush after dinner. Frost has been very injurious to the garden. Its effects
were visible in the bush and thro' the fields. Rode home in the eve'g by
way of the 9th Conn.

Mon. May 26.
Weather still dry and but little growth for want of rain.

Tues. May 27.
[No entry].

Wed. May 28.
[No entry].

Thurs. May 29.
[No entry].

Fri. May 30.
Mr McCulloch got home from New York. Mr Goldie in from Greenfield.

Sat. May 31.
Still dry, scorching weather. Our cat lost for 2 days and this eve'g discovered in a tall dead tree on the brae below the house. Got a boy, Gourlay
to climb up but could not get her down. S. Nevin and I started to chop
down the tree but while we were at work, the glare of fire rose over the
town and we ran up and found Fleming and Robinson's stores all in a
blaze. Set to and worked at the trakes carrying out goods of Polson's, carrying out water etc. till 12 o'clock when I got home. 6 stores in the Stone
block.[21] At Mrs McIlwraith's funeral today who died in Campbell's.[22]

Sun. June 1.
No rain yet to cheer the thirsty ground. Slept till 10 o'clock, only up at

---

20 For an account of the Queen's Birthday in Galt see *DR*, May 28, 1862.
21 This large fire resulted in the destruction of two-thirds of the large three-storey granite buildings which lined the south side of Main Street in Galt. *DR*, June 4, 11, 1862.
22 Likely the wife of John McIlwraith (1778–1853) plumber and one time Convener of
   Trades in Ayr, Scotland, a distant relative of Andrew's who moved to Canada in 1845
   and died in Hamilton, CW, in 1853. See 'Deaths,' *Ayr Advertiser*, March 31, 1853.

five and found the cat had got home. At church fore and afternoon and heard a strange young man preach.

Mon. June 2.
Parties of rifles going round town today seizing stolen goods but no commitments made for lack of different store proprietors not being able to swear to them.

Tues. June 3.
Mr McCulloch at work on plan of mill for P. Fisher, Guelph and I at work to complete the drawing.

Wed. June 4.
Busy with Fisher's Mill plan. Mrs Cavan and Mrs Hall from St Mary's arrived with afternoon train. Jameson came up from Hamilton with eve'g train and also stopped with us over night.

Thurs. June 5.
Close at work on Fisher's Mill plan.

Fri. June 6.
Still close at work on Mill plan. Busy at summer house in the eve'g and getting pretty well up with it. Mr Goldie in today from Greenfield.

Sat. June 7.
Tracing Fisher's plan for sending away and got all thro' with it. Pay day in the shop. Our visitors departed today for Greenfield. D. Goldie gone to Guelph.

Sun. June 8.
Still hot dry weather with never a drop of rain. Over six weeks now since there has been any of any account in this quarter. Had Mary at school with me in the morn'g.[23] Mr Campbell preached in the forenoon only today.

Mon. June 9.
Jas and D. Goldie down from Guelph per cars this morning.

Tues. June 10.
Wrote home sending a sketch of our cat in the tree.

---

23 Andrew McIlwraith taught and, according to one church newspaper, took 'a warm interest' in the Sunday school at St Andrew's. See 'St Andrew's Church, Galt, Sabbath School,' *The Presbyterian* [Montreal] 23, no. 1 (January 1870): 18.

Wed. June 11.
Mary out making calls in the afternoon and Maria made tea for me.
Went for her to Mrs Bank's in the eve'g and then we all went to call
on Mrs Caven near the R. station. Got ferried over the river in coming home and thought we were going to get drowned with a clumsy
boatman.

Thurs. June 12.
Day observed by the St Andrew's Church as a fast day.

Fri. June 13.
Mr Caven and Mr Hall called and took tea with us in the eve'g and got
Jno. Goldie to drive them out to Greenfield being on their way home
from the Synod in Toronto.[24]

Sat. June 14.
At church and heard sermon from Mr Campbell's brother preparatory
to the Sacrament. Jas Goldie and his brother-in-law, Mr Owen, driving
out to Ayr tonight and took Jno. Goldie with them. Getting some cab-
bage, cauliflower and tomato plants planted today.

Sun. June 15.
Sacrament Sabbath in our church. Attended forenoon and evening.
Found Jas. Goldie and Mr Owen at the gate when we came home in the
afternoon who took tea with us.

Mon. June 16.
Mrs McEwan with two children came in with John this morning and
took up quarters with us. Mary working hard in expectation of Thomas
and all the family to arrive in the evening but they did not come. Mr
McCulloch and I drove to Paris, he going off up the country and I bringing home the horse.

Tues. June 17.
Busy preparing drawings and specifications for wheat cleaning machine
which Wm Goldie means to patent if possible.

Wed. June 18.
Jameson called in the forenoon and brought Tommie from Hamilton
with him. In the afternoon I had prepared to start with the buggy for

---

24 Ecclesiastical court of the Presbyterian Church, which lay above local presbyteries,
   but below the General Assembly. See W. Gregg, *History of the Presbyterian Church in the
   Dominion of Canada* (Toronto: Presbyterian Printing and Publishing Company, 1885).

Guelph to get Wm Goldie's signature to patent papers so Jameson rode with me as far as Hespeler. Got to Guelph in good time and went to a J.P. with Wm and got the papers and drawings all signed.[25] Sidney Smith thru in the eve'g.

Thurs. June 19.
Get down to Galt by 10 a.m. and get the patent documents and model dispatched.

Fri. June 20.
Thos and the wife and whole family arrived in the forenoon train. Mr McEwan and Mrs Goldie in and took away Mrs McEwan. Rain is heavy in the evening.

Sat. June 21.
Children still all more or less affected by the whooping cough. Janey in particular very dowie.[26]

Sun. June 22.
At church in the forenoon only. Quite cold and frosty in the morning and day fine. Thos, Tommie and I out walking down the riverside and round through the cedar swamp below Crombie's.

Mon. June 23.
Thick drizzling rain nearly all day.

Tues. June 24.
[No entry].

Wed. June 25.
At a teacher's meeting in Mr Campbell's lodgings tonight. Evening quite sultry.

Thurs. June 26.
[No entry].

Fri. June 27.
Still hot, dry weather. Jas Goldie and the Mrs down visiting Mary

---

25 William Goldie was issued a patent by the government of the United Canadas for a 'Wheat Cleaning Machine' on July 14, 1862. *List of Canadian Patents, from the Beginning of the Patent Office, June, 1824, to the 31st of August 1872* (Ottawa: Maclean, Roger and Co., 1882), 65.

26 Dreary, or dismal (Scottish or northern English dialect).

today. Mr G. spending the afternoon untill towards evening. D. Goldie to leave for Scotland from Hamilton this morning. Boat race on Dickson's dam tonight.[27] Maria and Tommie and I up and saw it.

Sat. June 28.
Got letter this morning of Mrs Stewart's death forwarded from Thomas in Hamilton. Jno. Stewart came up with Thos in the evening.[28]

Sun. June 29.
Weather showery. At church morning and evening. Jno. S. away out calling on some acquaintances part of the day.

Mon. June 30.
Thos and John went off with morning train.

Tues. July 1. to Thurs. July 17.
[no entries]

Fri. July 18.
Mrs Mac. gone to Hamilton to see her brother Wm.

Sat. July 19.
Mrs Mac. returned from Hamilton and brought some home presents of photographs, etc. brought out by her brother Wm.

Sun. July 20.
Mr Campbell from home. Mr Nessmore preached and did very well.

Mon. July 21.
Mr Goldie in this morning and took away Mrs Mc., the team also coming and taking the whole family.

Tues. July 22.
[No entry].

Wed. July 23.
[No entry].

---

27 At seven-thirty in the evening, the 'Gentle Annie' and the 'Dart' raced from the dam, up to the bend in the river and back again. The Galt Band provided musical accompaniment. The 'Gentle Annie' won. *DR*, July 2, 1862.

28 Mrs Stewart was Andrew McIlwraith's sister, Jean Smith (McIlwraith) Stewart (b. April 12, 1812 in Newton-on-Ayr), married Thomas Stewart in 1839; John 'Jack' Stewart was her son.

Thurs. July 24.
Jas Goldie at dinner with us and left to walk out to Ayr in the afternoon.

Fri. July 25.
Took the afternoon to go to our Sabbath School picknick which was a very successful affair, the children going down the river side past Crombie's and getting ferried over to Moffat's bush where swings were erected and there was quite a good time until eve'g. Mary's Aunty Jess came in with Jas Goldie to stay with us for a while. Thos and Wm Park arrived in the eve'g. Jenny went off to Guelph with James Goldie. Mrs Logan and all of us at the picnick.

Sat. July 26.
Thos and Wm Park left to walk out to Ayr in the morning, Mr P. going on to Detroit to a situation with Mr Muir.

Sun July 27.
Heard Mr Campbell morning and evening. Sunday School rather thin.

Mon. July 28.
Weather still showery. A severe thunderstorm passed over the town in the eve'g, about 7 o'clock. Busy at odd times transplanting leeks and onions. Scarlet Malope in flower now.

Tues. July 29.
Had a visit of Bill Lloyd from Dundas who took dinner. In the evening transplanted asters which we had grown from the seed.

Wed. July 30. to Sat. Aug. 2.
[No entries].

Sun. Aug. 3.
Had Mr Campbell at home at morning and evening service. My class in school but poorly attended and lessons but poorly said.

Mon. Aug. 4.
Mary and I made a call at Mr Robert Malcom's in the evening.[29] Garden work pretty well forward now. Corn coming in to ear. Spring beans a tolerable.

---

29 Robert Malcom was listed as a grocer on Main Street, Galt, in one 1864 directory. James Sutherland, *County of Waterloo Gazetteer and General Business Directory for 1864* (Toronto: Mitchell and Co., 1864), 142.

Tues. Aug. 5.
Our Hamilton friends all in from Greenfield with the team today and passed on per car for Hamilton. Aunty Jess went home with the team. Little Nelly left with Mrs Logan to stay a few days.

Wed. Aug. 6.
[No entry].

Thurs. Aug. 7.
[No entry].

Fri. Aug. 8.
The most oppressively hot day of the season so far. Forenoon quite cloudy and close. Little Nelly sick during the night and Mrs Logan thought it best to take her down to Hamilton in the eve'g and so left with the 4.40 cars.

Sat. Aug. 9.
Rain on heavy this morning between 7 and 8. Mrs Logan home per forenoon train. Greenfield team in in the afternoon bringing word of Mrs McEwan and Mrs Goldie being both sick. Mary and I went along with the team, having intended doing so. Found old Mrs G. very poorly and rather unfavorable a/c's of Mrs McE.

Sun. Aug. 10.
Tommy, the boy, dispatched to McEwan's in the morning and bringing back unfavorable word from there, Mary went away up. Went to church with Mr Goldie, Jno. Goldie out in the forenoon and he and I walked in together in the eve'g.

Mon. Aug. 11.
Mrs Jno. Goldie rode out to Ayr with Mr McCulloch today and returning in the evening, brot word of Mrs McEwan's death, having occurred about noon today. Jno. Goldie and I went up town and engaged a buggy for me to start for Guelph in the morning to let Jas and Mrs know to attend the funeral at 3 pm. tomorrow.

Tues Aug. 12.
Started for Guelph before daylight and returned with Mrs Goldie by 11 o'clock then left for Ayr along with John in the Foundry buggy, driving right through to McEwan's and returning with the funeral cortege to the burying place in Ayr. Returned to Galt in the eve'g, having travelled about 70 miles.

Wed. Aug. 13.
Started painting the floor of the dining room and kitchen while Mary
is away.

Thurs. Aug. 14.
[No entry].

Fri. Aug. 15.
Mr Sydney Smith in town today. Great cricket match came off today
between the Galt Club and the Officers from Hamilton.[30] The Misses
McWhirters up from Hamilton.

Sat. Aug. 16.
Mr Smith waited over today about Galt and he and I drove out to
Greenfield in the eve'g. Mrs Goldie continuing very poorly.

Sun. Aug. 17.
At church along with Mr Goldie. Walked home by way of the 9th Conn.
in the evening.

Mon. Aug. 18. to Thurs. Aug. 21.
[No entries].

Fri. Aug. 22.
Mrs McCulloch arrived from Scotland today.

Sat. Aug. 23.
Mary in today along with Millie Fulton. Went out with them in the
eve'g. Fulton's old mare pretty slow, being taigled[31] with her colt. Late
when we got out.

Sun. Aug. 24.
Mr Goldie and I at church together and heard Mr McRuar. Mrs Cavan
staying here and sick with cold. John and the wife out at her folks. Him
and I came in together in the Foundry buggy. Eve'g quite chilly.

Mon. Aug. 25. to Thurs. Aug. 28.
[No entries].

---

30 Billed as the 'Grand Promenade Concert and Cricket Match,' this event attracted
   over 5,000 attendees. A special train transporting the Hamilton team, their supporters, and the Band of the Queen's Own Rifle Brigade arrived mid-morning with play
   commencing at 11 a.m. The band played through the afternoon and concluded with
   the National Anthem at 5:30 p.m. *DR*, July 30; August 13, 21, 1862.
31 Hindered, or delayed. John Jamieson, DD, *Supplement to the Etymological Dictionary of
   the Scottish Language* (Edinburgh: W. and C. Tait, 1825), 2:526.

Fri. Aug. 29.
Mr Goldie Sr in today also Jas on his way to Guelph. Mary waiting now to see David who is expected tomorrow night.

Sat. Aug. 30.
Pay day in the shop. Got the books made up and given out. Spent a while with Jno. Goldie in the eve'g.

Sun. Aug. 31.
At church and Sabbath school in the forenoon and started and walked to Ayr in the afternoon. Went by the 10th Conn. thro' the Alps. Gathered a lot of hazelnuts. David Goldie not arrived but expected tomorrow. The old Mrs Goldie not so well for two days again.

Mon. Sept. 1.
Morning dull and wet like. Tommy drove me in all the way. Mrs Logan going out with him. A large train, said to have left for the Falls this morning. Jno. Goldie gone to Guelph driving, only Mr McCulloch about the work. Had a whiles working about the garden in the afternoon making a box and taking in some Capricum plants. Slept in Mrs Logan's.

Tues. Sept. 2.
Quite a cold morning. Mr McEwan came in in the forenoon with his team and brought in Mrs Logan, Maria and little Fanny McEwan.

Wed. Sept. 3.
Quite a heavy coating of hoar frost this morning. Capsicum berries seem to be the only articles touched with it yet. At work on tannery machinery drawing and about thro' with it. Mr McCulloch gone to Hawksville.

Thurs. Sept. 4.
Fine warm weather again. David Goldie in today and went on to Guelph per train. Had a letter from home thro' him.

Fri. Sept. 5th to Wed. Sept. 10th
[No entries].

Thurs. Sept. 11.
All day at work on drawings of Tannery machinery.

Fri. Sept. 12.
Busy with drawings for Tannery. Mrs McCulloch spending the afternoon with Mary.

Sat. Sept. 13.
Pay day in the shop. Mr Crombie arrived from the Old Country today.

D. Goldie in and went on to Guelph with the eve'g train. Wrote to Thos sending $100.00 to put in to the savings bank.

Sun. Sept. 14.
At school and church in the forenoon. D. Goldie came down from Guelph in the afternoon and staid overnight with us. Day beautiful and mild. Had also a visit of Mr Raphael in the afternoon.

Mon. Sept. 15.
Weather wet and warm.

Tues. Sept. 16.
[No entry].

Wed. Sept. 17.
Mrs Logan, Mary, Maria and I all went to a Soiree of U.P. Church in the Town Hall tonight. Heard a number of clerical speakers. On the way home Mrs L. got an attack from Mrs Jno. Goldie when passing the house.

Thurs. Sept. 18.
Close at work on Tannery drawing.

Fri. Sept. 19.
Got a Hamilton paper this morning from Thos with Mrs Muir's death in it. Funeral today.[32]

Sat. Sept. 20.
Mr Goldie in this morning and took Mary and Maria away out. Old Mrs Goldie said to be worse.

Sun. Sept. 21.
At Sabbath School in the morning and started for Ayr on foot immediately after its dismissal. Mrs Goldie a great deal better.

Mon. Sept. 22.
Had Tommy to drive me in, Jenny coming down in the morning from Guelph. Mr McCulloch home from a tour up the country with several orders making the work rather busy.

Tues. Sept. 23.
At work a little on Hick's mill machinery plan. Mr Goldie brought Mary

---

32 Eliza Muir died young at age 34. She was the wife of railwayman William K. Muir, whose family was of Ayrshire origin, but had transplanted to Hamilton, CW. See Diary for 1857, fn 61; and 'Died,' *HS*, September 19, 1862.

in today. Her and I at the performance of 'The Wizard of the Natto' in the Town Hall in the eve'g.[33]

Wed. Sept. 24.
At work on Hick's drawing. Mary and I left for Hamilton in the afternoon. Mrs Caldwell and Mrs Ballingal called just when we were about starting. On arriving in Hamilton found that Thos and the wife were away at the show.[34] Them and Wm Park got home about a couple of hours after we landed.

Thurs. Sept. 25.
M. and I took train at 5.35 for Toronto. Weather very fine. Tremendous crushing about the show. More toil and annoyance than pleasure about it. Left at 4 o'clock for Hamilton again.

Fri. Sept. 26.
Called on Mrs Cowing and had some walking around town in the forenoon. In the afternoon Thos and I had a ramble with the gun out beyond the cemetery marsh. Mr Muir Sr called in the evening.

Sat. Sept. 27.
Had a walk up thro' the market early in the morning then started per first train for the West. Men mostly at work and pay day in the shop.

Sun. Sept. 28.
At School and Church in the forenoon and at Mr Murdock's church in the evening. M. and I had a walk to Dickson's bush in the interval.

Mon. Sept. 29.
Busy at Hick's mill drawing. Mr Goldie in today and brought in Maria taking Mary out with him again for two days. Jno. G. speaking in excuse for his wife today that she was affected with St Vitus Dance.[35]

---

33 This appears to have been a magic show put on by Prof. Anderson, a Scotsman called 'the Wizard of the North.' *DR*, September 24, 1862. McIlwraith had seen Anderson perform in New York City. See Diary for 1860, fn 73.

34 Undoubtedly the Provincial Exhibition in Toronto. See Keith Walden, *Becoming Modern in Toronto: The Industrial Exhibition and the Shaping of a Late Victorian Culture* (Toronto: University of Toronto Press, 1997); Elsbeth A. Heaman, *The Inglorious Arts of Peace: Exhibitions in Canadian Society during the Nineteenth Century* (Toronto: University of Toronto Press, 1998).

35 Likely a reference to the September 17, 1862 entry, when Mrs Goldie 'attacked' Andrew's sister, Mrs Logan. Also called 'Sydenham's chorea,' St Vitus's dance is commonly associated with rheumatic fever and is characterized by jerky, uncontrollable movements of the arms and legs. James Tyson, *The Practice of Medicine* (London: Rebman Limited, 1907), 1091–7.

Tues. Sept. 30.
Weather getting overcast and rain on in the afternoon. Got a lot more strawberry plants from S. Cant and am planting them.

Wed. Oct. 1.
A very dull cold wet day. Show at Ayr to take place today. Wm Bell going out with his horse.

Thurs. Oct. 2.
Mary got in from Ayr today and brought word of Jane Esely having been drowned off the boom in the dam at Greenfield Mill. No prize for Willy Bell. Mr McCulloch called in the evening and had a talk about Mrs J. Goldie's state.

Fri. Oct. 3.
Busy at work on Hick's Mill plan.

Sat. Oct. 4.
Mr Goldie Sr and Mr Alexander came in today to see about Jno's wife. Finally agreed for her to go out for a time with her father and they left accordingly. Jas Goldie and the wife came down in the afternoon and were persuaded to spend the night with us.

Sun. Oct. 5.
At church both ends of the day. Jno. Goldie spending part of the day with us.

Mon. Oct. 6.
Drove to Berlin with Mr McCulloch. Got some rain coming home. Jas Goldie and the Mrs staid a while on their way away from Ayr.

Tues. Oct. 7.
Making tracing of Hick's mill plan to give to A. Austin for working by.[36]

Wed. Oct. 8.
Jas Goldie down today. Caught a pig in the garden and shut it up. Had a row with Blain about it in the evening.

Thurs. Oct. 9.
Started work at posting Sept. Fast day of all the Presb'n Churches so attended church.

---

36 Likely Adam Austin, with whom McIlwraith would partner in a Listowel Foundry a
    decade later. See Epilogue.

Fri. Oct. 10.
Hard at work posting. Mr McCulloch came home today from being away about Clinton.

Sat. Oct. 11.
Finished posting by noon and got men's books made up and pay in the afternoon. Think this is the quickest posting I have done yet.

Sun. Oct. 12.
First severe touch of frost during the night. Balsams etc. completely used up. Sacrament in church today. Rev. D[r] George assisting Campbell.[37] Had old Mrs Kay and her son at tea, they having come in from Ayr to attend sacrament.

Mon. Oct. 13.
Attended church and heard Dr George again. Willie Goldie down from Guelph today on his way to Ayr with the team.

Tues. Oct. 14.
[No entry].

Wed. Oct. 15.
[No entry].

Thurs. Oct. 16.
Mrs Mac. came up with the forenoon train today and went off to Greenfield, the buggy having come in for her. Maria went with her. Jameson from Hamilton also up on business and stayed all night with us. Having some game at backgammon.

Fri. Oct. 17.
Mr J. went off with morning train.

Sat. Oct. 18.
[No entry].

---

37 Rev. James George, DD (1801?–1870), was appointed minister to a Stratford Presbyterian congregation in 1862, where he served until his demise. Born in Perthshire, Scotland, he was ordained a Presbyterian minister in New York and served a congregation in Scarborough, CW (1834–53), until he was appointed professor of Logic and Moral Philosophy at Queen's College (Kingston, 1853–62). *A Historical and Statistical Report of the Presbyterian Church in Canada ... for the Year 1866* (Montreal: John Lovell, 1867), 35; 'The Rev. James George, D.D.,' *The Journal of Education for Ontario* 23, no. 10 (October 1870): 153.

Sun. Oct. 19.
At church morning and evening. Mary and I had a long walk to the¹ cemetery on the S. side of the river and beyond it. Read aloud the Pilgrim's Progress.

Mon. Oct. 20.
John G. and the wife came in from Ayr this morning and brot Maria with them.

Tues. Oct. 21.
[No entry].

Wed. Oct. 22.
[No entry].

Thurs. Oct. 23.
Tracing Egmondville Tannery plan and spent the evening reading stories.

Fri. Oct. 24.
Finished and sent away plan for Tanners at Egmondville. Posted J. Goldie's ledger in the evening.

Sat. Oct. 25.
Fields hoary with sleet or snow in the morning and some snow falling during the day. Assisting in finishing a drawing of a Portable Engine. Payday in the shop. Sat late and completed J. Goldie's trial balance.

Sun. Oct. 26.
At church morning and evening. Reading the Pilgrim's Progress during the day. A stranger minister from Ancaster preaching today.

Mon. Oct. 27. to Wed. Oct. 29.
[No entries].

Thurs. Oct. 30.
Fine weather. Drove to Berlin with Mr McCulloch today. Jas Goldie down. Apples not all off the trees yet on the orchards between here and Berlin. Went and came by way of Preston.

Fri. Oct. 31.
Got all little jobs pretty well forward and took evening train down getting to London by between 9 and 10. Put up at Strong's Hotel.

Sat. Nov. 1.
Started for Sarnia this morning at 7. Had a wearisome ride but weather

beautiful. Went straight to McKenzie's store on landing and got a hearty welcome from Charlie. After dinner in Jno's, Alick and I had a drive round by the Grand Trunk station and in round town. Jameson came up with evening train. Had tea all together in Alick's.[38]

Sun. Nov. 2.
At church hearing Mr Walker. Weather came on miserably wet so that we could have no walking out. Visited Jas McKenzie's and then went and spent a while and had tea in Hope's, attending church after.

Mon. Nov. 3.
Took train from Sarnia at 7 o'clock. Had two or three hours to spend in London. Got home in good time in the evening and found Mary home and all well.

Tues. Nov. 4.
[No entry].

Wed. Nov. 5.
[No entry].

Thurs. Nov. 6.
Subscriptions being taken up in the work for the destitute in England. Over $25.00 subscribed by the men and $10.00 by the bosses.[39] Wm Anderson and the wife from Ayr called and brought a crock of butter.

Fri. Nov. 7.
Mr Goldie and Aunt Betsy in today. Maria at home from school with her face swelled with the mumps.

Sat. Nov. 8.
Ground white with snow in the morning and snow falling all the fore part of the day. Pay day in the shop.

Sun. Nov. 9.
Heard Mr Campbell in the forenoon. His sermon being on the subject of the destitution in England. Mary and Maria neither of them quite well so did not go out in the evening but read the Pilgrim's Progress.

---

38 'Alick' was likely Alexander Mackenzie. On the Mackenzie family of Sarnia, see Diary for 1857, fn 3.
39 An article in the previous day's edition of the *Dumfries Reformer* pointed out that farmers had thus far contributed to this cause but solicited Galt townsfolk to also take up contributions. *DR*, November 5, 1862.

Mon. Nov 10.
A beautiful morning. Snow nearly away again.

Tues. Nov. 11th to Thurs. Nov. 27th
[No entries].

Fri. Nov. 28.
Jno. Bertram called at night after the arrival of the eve'g train and staid all night.

Sat. Nov. 29.
Bertram came down to the shop with me and asked a job and got offer of one for a short time. Then started on foot for Dundas.[40]

Sun. Nov. 30. to Wed. Dec. 3.
[No entries].

Thurs. Dec. 4.
Day of Thanksgiving observed today by proclamation of the Governor Gen.[41] Attended church, sawed wood awhile and had a practice of music for the approaching soiree. Had Day Book and Cash Book home and worked at them till late.

Fri. Dec. 5.
Started journalizing this morning and took the Journal home and finished it by 12.30 in the eve'g.

Sat. Dec. 6.
Desperate keen frost accompanied by a smart breeze of wind. M. and I up town in the evening. Had letter from Hamilton with the news of Bill being to be married on Christmas.[42] Posted up the ledger in the forenoon and made up men's books and pay for the evening.

---

40 Likely John Bertram, with whom McIlwraith worked at the Gartshore foundry in the late 1850s. See Diary for 1858, fn 34.

41 This occasion was one of many irregular days of Thanksgiving proclaimed by pre-Confederation governors to give thanks for an abundant harvest. In Toronto, ministers also used the day to sermonize on the evils of war and hope for a peaceful resolution to the U.S. Civil War. 'Thanksgiving Day,' *Globe* [Toronto], December 5, 1862.

42 Andrew's younger brother William McIlwraith (b. August 18, 1833), a newspaper reporter, married Margaret McIlwrath in Newton-on-Ayr, Scotland, on December 25, 1862. See Register of Marriages for 1862, District of Ayr, County of Ayr, Scotland, p. 65, PRO. Statutory Marriages 578/00 0129. Accessed via Scotland's People, www.scotlandspeople.gov.uk/ (accessed July 12, 2008).

Sun. Dec. 7.
Mr Hogg preached morning and evening. Mr Sydney Smith came up in the afternoon and spent the time until bedtime.

Mon. Dec. 8.
Snowing pretty much all day.

Tues. Dec. 9th to Wed. Dec. 31st
[No entries].

Epilogue: Endings and Beginnings

He was one of those noble, worthy, diffident men, of whom the noisy world hears least, but who are generally best worth hearing of.
Rev. James A.R. Dickson, 'Memorial Sketch' of Andrew McIlwraith (1895)[1]

On Monday, December 8, 1862, Andrew McIlwraith stopped recording his daily activities and accomplishments, but he hardly quit his habit cold turkey. Beginning in the summer months, he missed an occasional day but remained otherwise regular. By October and November, he missed days in a row in several instances, and even when he did make entries they became noticeably thinner than in earlier years. The subtle act of ending his diary writing without any summary or sign off in December 1862 is itself a curious piece of evidence for his biographers and for students of nineteenth-century diary keeping. We might read the ending of McIlwraith's diary – the record of his progress as a young man – as a signal (to himself or posterity) that he had outgrown his previous life; that his life on the craftsworker's tramp from Newton-on-Ayr to Dundas, Hamilton, New York, and Galt had produced a successful result; that he had made it. By the end of 1862, McIlwraith was a man married to a woman he loved, a salaried bookkeeper (and sometime draughtsman), and a recognized presence with the most successful industrial enterprise in the region. He had become, moreover, a public (if not prominent) and respected man: Sunday School teacher, church manager, Mechanics' Institute member. He was enmeshed in several thick and overlapping networks of friends, family, and local associates in Galt, a man who had seemingly integrated into a community with considerable ease. If Andrew McIlwraith's life was a Broadway romance of the sort that he frequented during his time in Gotham, December 1862 would provide a tempting juncture to draw the curtain, gather the characters onstage, and invite the applause.

Diaries such as McIlwraith's are tricky for the historian because they telescope the past. They play havoc with historical perspective. In their richness, they tempt biographers to assume too much – that is, to believe that the documents they have at hand typify the whole lives of their subjects and that they should illuminate the parts of their lives about which no rich documentation exists. Historians who use diaries must take care to avoid that temptation and to test their assumptions thoroughly. They must see their subjects' lives as a series of complex stages that may reflect change as much as they do continuity. The materials that describe Andrew McIlwraith's life from the end of his diary keeping in 1862 until his death in Galt in 1891 are largely objective sources. They do not provide anything close to the sort of subjective insight that his diary offers. This unavoidable evidentiary imbalance provides a prickly interpretive challenge.

And yet, even with this 'typicality' caveat in mind, what is most remarkable about the way in which Andrew McIlwraith lived his post-diary life is its consistency with the themes that dominate his daily entries in the years between 1857 and 1862. The craftsman's concerns for economic independence, respectability, and self-improvement were present throughout the remainder of his life. These were not goals that mid-Victorian men could ever consider done, accomplished, nailed down, or behind them. To borrow a hackneyed modern phrase, success was a life-long challenge, and rather a Sisyphean chore. After 1862, it was a challenge that McIlwraith chose to meet with different tools, a wife and new, helpful, and challenging in-laws, but without his diary, his epistolary mirror. Whatever measure of success and security he had gained by 1863 seemed to stir his appetite for more.

In truth, at the beginning of 1863, Andrew McIlwraith had by no means *made it*. Economic security was not economic independence, and still he was working for somebody else. McIlwraith's marriage into the Goldie family, despite genuine and oft-expressed love for his wife, contained a clear economic dimension. By 1862, he was a trusted lieutenant in the firm, an important manager of the books and a business confidant. Though his diary entries demonstrate a (sometimes) faux formality and distance between himself (an employee) and 'Mr McCulloch' or 'Mr Goldie,' in reality, his relationships with these Ayrshire-born men (four and seven years his senior, respectively) were much closer and interdependent, as occasional slips when he refers to Hugh or John reveal. Andrew's marriage to Mary Goldie meant much more than the realization of romantic love; it symbolized his entry into the growing entrepreneurial network that was the Goldie family. The nodes of this network were clear to see – the Dumfries Foundry in Galt its heart, David Goldie's Milling Company in Ayr, and James and William Goldie's Speedvale Mills in Guelph its extended limbs.[2] Andrew, himself, would soon extend it further.

There is not a great deal of documentary evidence that describes McIlwraith's life in 1860s Galt; the post-diary light that we can shine on his life gets much dimmer. Still, what does exist reveals a stage in his life when he began to enjoy his small degree of comfort and security economically and, we might imagine, emotionally. By 1864, the town assessment rolls reveal that Andrew and Mary had moved from a rented house on Hay Street and had become freeholders, owners of a house on lots 3, 4, and 5 on the western end of Cedar Street, where they continued to reside through 1871.[3] His occupation reported variously as 'clerk' or 'bookkeeper,' McIlwraith's real property was valued by 1869 at $800, his personal property (a suspiciously low estimate) at $24, and his taxable income at a respectable $400, a white-collar salary a little low, perhaps, for the times. It may have been a 'family discount.'[4] In 1871, McIlwraith's estate included a modest half-acre of land, a dwelling house, $1,200 worth of property and income, and one cow. In the decade since he left New York, he had hardly gained riches, but he had established himself in Galt, a man of enough bearing to warrant entries in the county's business directories and the provincial gazetteer.[5]

In the 1860s, Andrew and Mary McIlwraith began to grow a family and did so at a rather steady pace. For them, as for most Victorian respectables, children must have been considered both delight and duty, gifts from God and a symbol of full membership in local civil and religious society. Having children may also have been considered a family responsibility, a way of contributing to and memorializing their legacies. This 'kin obligation' (as Herbert Gutman has called it) is at least hinted at in the names they chose for their children.[6] On December 15, 1863, Mary gave birth to a daughter, Margaret, named, perhaps after Andrew's sister, the 'Mrs Logan' of his diary who followed him from New York to Hamilton to Galt (and who may well have been present at the child's birth). A son, born in Galt on March 9, 1867, was named William Forsyth, an echo of both Andrew's younger brother and his mother's maiden name. A second daughter, Jean Carrick McIlwraith, was born in Galt on April 10, 1870, her name, almost certainly, a tribute to Andrew's mother. In this, perhaps first, phase of family making, Andrew and Mary chose to honour his roots, the Ayrshire McIlwraiths whence he sprang.

Andrew McIlwraith invested himself in the civic life of Galt in the 1860s. Though he shared the Scotch roots of the town's oldest families, he was himself clearly a newcomer. And yet he did much to become a respected public presence – a townsman – in this time by participating in, and becoming identified with, the community's civic institutions. He gravitated toward the Galt Mechanics' Institute, a version of the self-improvement society he grew up with in Scotland, which he cherished and relied on in every place he resided in Canada. A committed user of the Institute's library holdings, he also became a leader in these years. When John Goldie resigned from the Institute's General Committee in 1868, Andrew was named in his place. In the same year, McIlwraith was appointed to the Institute's Canvassing Committee for the town's west side.[7] He was a committed member of St Andrew's Presbyterian Church who demonstrated 'a warm interest' in the church's Sabbath school, as one report in the ecclesiastical newspaper *The Presbyterian* noted in January 1870.[8] His name appears, moreover, as a member of the Galt militia (2nd class) from 1864 to 1868, during the heady days of the U.S. Civil War and the subsequent Fenian raids on Canada, when townsmen across the province formed local rifle units to defend their homes and their new country.[9] McIlwraith was becoming a Galtonian.

Still, economically speaking, McIlwraith was a *Goldie* in function if not in name, and it is difficult to see his years of work as a bookkeeper at the Dumfries Foundry in 1860s Galt as anything other than an apprenticeship, a preparatory – or prefatory – phase before he lit out to the territories to expand the company's and the Goldie family's enterprise. By 1870, Andrew McIlwraith must have seen and become familiar with (if not expert in) virtually every aspect of the foundry business – from sales to moulding, patternmaking to worker relations. All he would have required in order to expand the business was the needed capital. In 1872, he got his chance.

In 1872, Andrew McIlwraith packed up his family and moved to Listowel, in Perth County, 47 miles to the northwest of Galt, to try his own hand at the foundry business. It is not clear why, of all potential places, he chose to go to Listowel. He could have gone anywhere. Listowel, home to a little more than 2,000 people, was newly incorporated as a town in 1874. A classic Ontario agricultural service centre, it was a place of some small regional importance to the local farmers of wheat and corn, but a mere speck on the map when compared with a burgeoning industrial centre such as Galt. Physically, it was unlike Galt. It was flat, with the trickling Maitland River traversing a rather plain rectilinear street plan. But Listowel was not unlike many other developing, proto-industrial towns in Ontario in the 1870s. As John McCallum wrote in his classic work, *Unequal Beginnings*, Ontario's industrial development was broad and organic, emerging as forward linkage from a wheat-based economy. By the 1870s, growing local farm populations needed agricultural implements, textiles, and other manufactured goods, and industries arose in the countryside – in small cities and towns – to meet their needs: 'The enterprising blacksmith became a founder ... [m]arkets, capital, materials, and labour were overwhelmingly local.'[10] Industrialization was dispersed and happened all across the province, in locations large and small. In this way, the farmers in Elma and Wallace townships in Perth County looked to small-scale industrial enterprises in nearby towns like Listowel to meet their needs.

In April 1872, Andrew McIlwraith and a partner, Adam Austin, took control of the Listowel Foundry and Machine Shop, a business established in 1863 and originally operated by Messrs Turnbull and James Lockie. The foundry was located at the corner of Dodd and Bay streets, near the centre of town. It seems to have been a small affair compared with the impressive workshop that was the Dumfries Foundry, but it produced a notable variety of goods and services. In 1867, the owners advertised wares and services to local farmers in the local newspaper, the *Listowel Banner*: a 'Self-Regulating Thrashing machine,' a 'two-Wheeled Cultivator,' steel and cast plows, and, importantly, repairs.[11] The foundry business grew quickly and gained notice (locally anyway) for its innovations. One August 1872 *Banner* editorial waxed enthusiastic over 'Messrs McIlwraith & Austin['s] ... new saw Gumming machine,' which took worn circular saw blades and cut new teeth in them. 'We believe this is the first machine of its kind manufactured in the Province.'[12] By 1877, the Listowel Foundry offered area farmers mowers and reapers, ploughs, straw cutters, root cutters, field rollers, horse powers, sawing machines and drag saws, and sulkey rakes.[13] In the summer of 1877, they had succeeded well enough to employ a commercial traveller, J.B. Wright, to call upon farmers and promote the foundry's products.[14] 'Upwards of twenty regular hands' worked at the Listowel Foundry in 1876; by 1879, the number had slipped reportedly to 'about a dozen hands steadily employed.'[15] In either measure, it was a 'humming' local business.

Who was Adam Austin? Andrew McIlwraith's partner in the foundry business in Listowel was a Dumfriesshire-born Scot, a pattern-maker with whom Andrew had worked at the Dumfries Foundry in Galt as early as 1862.[16] He was reportedly a very able mechanic and a man with a taste for Reform politics. Austin appears briefly, but revealingly, in the Diary for 1862. On February 4, 1862, 'Adam Austin called at the house in the eve'g but I did not see him, being in the office till 10.' On October 7, 1862, McIlwraith recorded that he was 'making tracing of Hick's mill plan to give to A. Austin for working by.' Though he spent most of his days in the books, McIlwraith occasionally also performed draughting and patternmaking at the foundry. By the end of the decade, the two would have known each other's work, character, and habits and shared, it seems, a common ambition to try their hands at entrepreneurship. Goldie and McCulloch had brought them together and cultivated their partnership.

But Goldie and McCulloch was much more than a supportive midwife to the birth of McIlwraith and Austin; the Galt company was more like a looming parent. Though the Listowel Foundry operated under its local proprietors' names in 1870s, it is evident that Goldie and McCulloch bankrolled the enterprise. As the Galt town assessment rolls 1862–71 reveal, McIlwraith had no sufficient capital of his own to start up such a company; we cannot imagine that Austin did either. Moreover, in an era when the expansion of commercial and industrial enterprise demanded a more comprehensive and extensive knowledge of new businessmen's creditworthiness for potential investors, we might expect that McIlwraith and Austin would warrant some investigation. Yet, neither Andrew McIlwraith nor Adam Austin appear in the credit reports for the R.G. Dun Company, the largest and most far-reaching credit reporting network in nineteenth-century North America. The likelihood is that no report and no outside credit was needed; in Galt, McIlwraith and Austin had all the financial backing they could ever require. The clearest clue to this arrangement was revealed when McIlwraith closed the business in 1881. To 'facilitate the winding up of his affairs,' the *Banner* noted, he 'placed the property in the hands of Messrs Goldie & McCulloch, of Galt, for the benefit of his creditors.' One need not speculate too far to conclude that his creditors and Goldie and McCulloch were one and the same.[17]

Life in Listowel must have been both liberating and difficult for the McIlwraiths. The distance between Galt and Listowel was not so great that, in good weather, the foundry and the family would have had regular visits from the Goldies in Galt, Ayr, and Guelph – for business *and* pleasure. Andrew's 1861 and 1862 diaries note frequent travel by the Goldies between Hamilton, Galt, Guelph, and Ayr, for example. The Goldies could get around. The psychological, rather than physical, distance between Andrew and his in-laws might have been more profound. Though tethered by their capital investment, in Listowel McIlwraith was free from the daily over-the-shoulder gaze of men whose success in the foundry business was almost unmatched in the Dominion of Canada.

Personally, Andrew McIlwraith does not seem to have been lonely or felt isolated in Listowel (though it is almost impossible to gauge what Mary felt). The couple would have been kept busy by the work of child-rearing, of which they did a considerable amount in their home on Elma Street. The nuclear family of five that came to Listowel in 1872 (Andrew and Mary, Margaret, William, and little 'Jane') grew to seven by 1881. The Listowel-born McIlwraiths seem to have been named to pay tribute to Mary's side of the family. On December 27, 1874, David Goldie McIlwraith was born and on December 14, 1876, Mary Elizabeth Owen McIlwraith followed. As much joy as this growing family must have brought Andrew and Mary, there was a large measure of sadness, too. Three boys born to them in these years – John Goldie McIlwraith (March 21, 1872), Thomas Steele McIlwraith (July 27, 1873), and Andrew Caven McIlwraith (December 5, 1875) died as children. Out of eight births in the McIlwraith family only five survived.[18] To help raise the children and, perhaps, to help Andrew and Mary cope with their tragedies, Andrew's older sister, Helen Hunter, came to live with them in Listowel and must have remained connected to the household until she died in Galt in 1893.[19]

In civil life, Andrew McIlwraith continued to pursue the sort of self-improvement activities that he had wherever he had been – Scotland, Hamilton, Dundas, New York, or Galt. He joined the Listowel Mechanics' Institute soon after his arrival in town and for three years, 1876–8, rose to the organization's presidency. Under his leadership, the Institute held monthly meetings, formed a literary and debating society, augmented its Reading Room's collection of books, and lobbied the town council for funds.[20] In Listowel, however, McIlwraith and his Mechanics' Institute colleagues were in for a challenge. Societies such as this one had to be promoted and explained in ways they did not in industrial Hamilton or Galt, where workingmen's self-help was more culturally 'hard wired' among the population.[21] Listowel town had a small population, and young, male, waged workers composed only a fraction of that. Alas, the Institute seems not to have had much success in these years. In 1880, Town Council called a public meeting to consider and adopt a plan for the 'revival of the Mechanics' Institute.'[22] In addition to his work with the MI, McIlwraith was elected a school trustee by his townsmen in January 1877, a position he held for two years.[23]

McIlwraith's entry into entrepreneurship in Listowel also came to an unsuccessful end. It does not seem to have been a precipitous fall; the end came gradually. In November 1878, the *Banner* reported that McIlwraith's legal partnership with Austin had expired. We can assume that neither party desired its extension, though the record does not indicate why. What is clear is that the breakup was not caused by either party wishing to quit Listowel.[24] In October 1879, McIlwraith placed an advertisement in the *Banner* seeking a new partner for the Listowel Foundry.[25] He must have felt pressure to do so; one month earlier, Austin had announced that he planned to build a new foundry in town.[26] He did, though it took until April 1880 for the Adam Austin and Company foundry to be built near the fairground at Alma and Mill streets. The new foundry was sizeable – two stories, 75 feet long by 25 feet wide – and included a machine shop, an engine house, a blacksmith shop, and a moulding department. By June, Austin's foundry furnace was reportedly in full blast and his business accepting orders for repairs, castings, and mill furnishings and manufacturing a wide range of agricultural implements.[27]

For McIlwraith, the writing was on the wall. The prospects for Listowel and environs supporting two foundries were gloomy, and though Andrew had gained a respectable clientele and a 'large circle of friends' in the 1870s, Austin was more mercurial, more aggressive, more 'pushing,' to use the business language of the times.[28] In light of their family tragedies, moreover, Andrew and Mary may have become tired of Listowel, for them three times a place of sadness. Business slackened in 1880 and by the early months of 1881, Andrew McIlwraith began to seek an exit strategy. In February, the *Banner* reported that he had decided to retire from business and offered the foundry for sale.[29] There were no interested buyers, apparently, and by April he had suspended the manufactures and repairs parts of the business, though he continued to offer his stock of implements for sale.[30] By that point, he had decided to move his family back to Galt. In March, the *Banner* noted that

the family's 'fine brick residence' was for sale, but it remained unsold
by May.[31] In September 1881, Andrew leased, 'for a term of years,' the
old Listowel Foundry building to E.B. Sutherland, a local manufacturer
whose own factory had burned in a recent fire. Within weeks, however, the arrangement had changed and Sutherland bought the foundry building from McIlwraith (or perhaps more accurately, Goldie and
McCulloch) outright.[32]

The McIlwraiths moved to Galt not long after Andrew sold the foundry in fall 1881. It must have been heartbreaking to lose his business
and to leave their friends. Still, finding a job in Galt proved no great difficulty. Andrew arrived to a position as accountant at the Gore Mutual
Fire Insurance Company, a job he held for the rest of his life. It may
have been found for him; among the members of the company's board
of directors in these years were his former employer ('Hugh McCulloch, Esq., Galt') and his brother-in-law ('James Goldie, Esq., Guelph').[33]

Having to lean on the kindness of others would have grated on a man
who measured his worth by his independence. Moreover, Andrew and
Mary returned to Galt as tenants. In the first year after their return, they
rented a house from hardware merchant and grocer Gavin Hume on
Elliott Street in Ward Three, east of the Grand River. In 1883, the McIlwraiths moved to Bridge Street in Ward 5, west of the river, where they
rented space from Robert Broomfield, a sawmiller. They remained there
– in what must have been cramped quarters for a household of eight
people – for three years, until 1886. In that year, Andrew McIlwraith
became a householder once again, having purchased a house and lot
at no. 12 Lansdowne Road worth $1,600. The purchase was, itself, a bit
of a homecoming; Andrew's Lansdowne house was located in Ward 4,
only about three blocks west of the Dumfries foundry and about the
same distance from St Andrew's Presbyterian Church. The Lansdowne
house seems to have signalled the return of a level of comfort; by 1887,
the McIlwraiths had even acquired a family dog.[34]

Back in Galt, Andrew McIlwraith resumed his pursuit of self-
improvement among the town's familiar institutions and familiar faces
and did so with seeming vigour. Sometime in the 1880s, he became a
member of the board of managers for St Andrew's Presbyterian Church
and, for a time, the board's secretary-treasurer. 'He was trusted,' Rev.
Dickson recalled, 'one of the most respected members' of the church.[35]
In these years, McIlwraith was appointed a member of the Galt School
Board. Andrew also threw himself into the work of the Galt Mechanics'
Institute, which must have seemed like an old friend. He continued to

read 'omnivorously' (he was a 'a solid lover of books' as one memori-alist put it) from the Institute's library collections, in the same way he had as a youth in Newton-on-Ayr (see Appendix 2). He was rewarded with the presidency of the Mechanics' Institute in spring 1891 and was among those members who in the same year pushed the local MI to establish the Galt Scientific, Historical and Literary Society (GSHLS), 'for the promotion of scientific and literary culture by discussions, orig-inal essays, historical research, and the practical work done on the field and in class.' As MI president, McIlwraith also held a seat on GSHLS board. In September 1891, he addressed the Society on a favourite topic: 'The Native Flora of Galt District, their Homes and Habits, what may remain with us, and what are likely to become extinct.' His paper, the GSHLS Minutebook recorded, was a 'strong plea for the preservation of our wildflowers.'[36] It was published in the town newspapers, about three months before he died.

By the late 1880s, Andrew McIlwraith had begun to suffer from the effects of what Victorian physicians called Bright's disease, or in today's parlance, nephritis: chronic inflammation of the kidney's blood vessels and the presence of protein in the urine. It would have been painful. Headaches, loss of appetite, vomiting, fever, discoloured urine, and, on occasion, the swelling of the face and hands accompany its onset. It is likely that McIlwraith developed a chronic variety of the disease; he was reported to have experienced its effects 'for some time.' To treat it, he sought the medical services of a Galt physician, Dr James S. Ward-law, himself a Scottish-born migrant to Galt and who, perhaps not coincidentally, 'when a boy, [had] learned engineering with Goldie and McCulloch, Galt.'[37] He may have been Andrew's own apprentice. In the first week of December 1891, Andrew McIlwraith's health began to worsen. A stoic, he continued to tend to his commitments at work and in civic life. On the evening of Friday, December 4, 1891, while walk-ing home on Main Street in Galt from a school board meeting, Andrew McIlwraith was stricken by illness, fell down on the sidewalk uncon-scious, and died. By chance, his new son-in-law, Charles Turnbull (hus-band to McIlwraith's oldest daughter, Margaret) had crossed paths with the man just before his fall. Turnbull carried his father-in-law to the nearby office of another local physician, Dr Hawk, but all efforts to revive Andrew McIlwraith were unsuccessful. He was deemed to have died from heart failure.[38] He was sixty years old.[39]

The mourning of Andrew McIlwraith's passing was fitting for some-one who had become in Galt a public, if not prominent, presence. His

funeral was attended, reportedly, by 'a large number of citizens,' including the directors of the Gore Mutual, the school trustees, and many of
the 'senior pupils of the Public Schools.' In fact, Galt's schools were
closed on the Monday afternoon following McIlwraith's death, 'out of
respect to the deceased.' In addition to the lengthy notice in the *Listowel
Banner*, the *Dumfries Reformer* published a long obituary on its front
page on December 10, 1891.[40] McIlwraith was memorialized, moreover, in the civic spaces that he loved and by the people with whom he
chose to consort: his fellow self-improvers and his co-religionists. The
Galt Scientific, Literary and Historical Society mourned his loss both
privately, at its regular meeting following his death, and publicly, in
an ode to him published in the *Reformer*.[41] McIlwraith's pastors at St
Andrew's, Rev. Dr Robert Campbell and Rev. James Dickson, respectively, memorialized him with grand and sweeping descriptions of
his life and character.[42] Dickson's, perhaps, cut quickest to the heart of
McIlwraith's essence, a fitting tribute to a man whose pursuit of 'character' and self-improvement gave shape to every contour of his life.

> A man of refinement and culture, [he] was an educative force on everyone'
> he touched; extremely modest, but a thoroughly brotherly and compan-
> ionable man. He was kind and sympathetic, unobtrusive and reserved. He
> would not thrust himself upon your attention, but if you desired to enter
> into fellowship with him there was a large and liberal feast of good things
> awaiting you, one that enriched you with influences that stirred thought
> and awoke feeling, and made their impact upon the will strongly felt.[43]

Today, we can have that sort of connection only through the pages of
his diaries, the ones that helped make him 'more of a man.' In them, as
we have seen, good things indeed await historians of work, migration,
class, and gender in the Victorian Atlantic world.

NOTES

1 Rev. James A.R. Dickson, '*Ebenezer': A History of the Central Presbyterian
   Church, Galt, Ontario; with Brief Sketches of Some of Its Members Who Have
   Passed On to the Other Side* (Toronto: William Briggs, 1904), 307.
2 See 'Goldie Family,' *Historical Atlas of the County of Wellington* (Toronto:
   Historical Atlas Publishing Company, 1906).
3 The social geography of McIlwraith's house on Cedar Street is revealing.

In the 1871 Dominion manuscript census for Galt, the census taker records McIlwraith's dwelling as Household number 33; Household number 32 is Hugh McCulloch's and Household number 34 belongs to John Goldie. Andrew was sandwiched between his employers. 1871 Dominion of Canada Census [manuscript], District 3, South Waterloo [Ontario], Subdistrict d, Division 3, p. 8.

4 Historians still know very little about white-collar salaries in nineteenth-century Ontario, much less than they do about them in Britain and the United States in the same era. Some fragmentary evidence, however, is revealing. 'Clerks, and shop assistants … can always get employment, at salaries ranging from eight to twelve dollars per week' (or from $384 to $576 per annum, if work was constant). Englishman now resident in the country, *For the Million: A Sketch of Canadian Life* (Toronto, 1875), 32. In 1861, Robert Pinkerton, a clerk in the Crown Land Office in Goderich, was reported in the R.G. Dun ledger to be earning $500 per annum. An 1878 wage table constructed by the United States Commercial Agent in Goderich lists an 'Iron-foundery bookkeeper' as earning $625 per annum and millwrights, moulders, and blacksmiths in that town's iron foundry making up to $600 a year. 'Report, by Commercial Agent Abbot, on the rates of wages, cost of living, &c., in the District of Goderich, Ontario,' in *The State of Labor in Europe: 1878* (Washington, DC: Government Printing Office, 1879), 55–7. See also Andrew C. Holman, *A Sense of Their Duty: Middle-Class Formation in Victorian Ontario Towns* (Montreal and Kingston: McGill-Queen's University Press, 2000), ch. 3.

5 'Andrew McIraith [sic],' James Sutherland, comp., *County of Waterloo Gazetteer and General Business Directory for 1864* (Toronto: Mitchell and Co., 1864), 141; 'McIlwraith, Andrew,' *Gazetteer and Directory of the County of Waterloo, 1867* (Toronto: Henry Rowsell, 1867), 97; 'McIlwraith, Andrew,' *Lovell's Province of Ontario Directory for 1871* (Montreal: Lovell, 1871), 382.

6 Herbert G. Gutman, *The Black Family in Slavery and Freedom, 1750–1925* (New York: Vintage Books, 1977), chs. 5, 6.

7 Minute Book, Galt Mechanics' Institute, 1862–1877, January 10, 1868, City of Cambridge Archives, Cambridge, Ontario.

8 'St. Andrew's Church, Galt, Sabbath School,' *The Presbyterian* [Montreal] 23, no. 1 (January 1870): 18.

9 Town of Galt Assessment Rolls, 1864–8. On the Civil War, the Fenian raids, and militia see Robin W. Winks, *The Civil War Years: Canada and the United States*, 4th ed. (Montreal and Kingston: McGill-Queen's University Press, 1998 [1960]).

10 John McCallum, *Unequal Beginnings: Agriculture and Economic Development*

in Quebec and Ontario until 1870 (Toronto: University of Toronto Press, 1980), 6. See also Jacob Spelt, *Urban Development in South-Central Ontario* (Toronto: McClelland and Stewart Limited, 1972), esp. chs. 4, 5.

11 'Listowel Foundry and Machine Shop,' *LB*, May 4, 1867.

12 'Messrs McIlwraith & Austin,' *LB*, August 8, 1872. See also 'Listowel Foundry,' *LB*, April 11, 18, 1872.

13 'Implements Manufactured and for Sale at the Listowel Foundry' *LB*, June 22, 1877. See also 'New Machinery,' *LB*, September 3, 1876; and advertisement, *LB*, January 12, 1877.

14 'Notice to Farmers,' *LB*, June 1, 1877. Wright was succeeded by a Jacob Shumaker, from Blenheim, in 1878. 'Listowel Foundry Implement,' *LB*, May 10, 1878.

15 'Listowel Foundry,' *LB*, June 9, 1876; 'Listowel Foundry,' *LB*, October 24, 1879.

16 Austin's father, John Brown Austin, brought his family from Dumfriesshire to Galt, Canada West, in 1853. Austin *père* was a miller who followed his trade in Galt until 1872. In that year, he moved to Carleton Place, staying only a short time until he joined his son's household in Listowel. He died in Listowel in 1879. 'Obituary,' *LB*, August 22, 1879.

17 'Suspended,' *LB*, April 15, 1881.

18 The McIlwraith's eight children are named in Mahlon M. Gowdy, *A Family History Comprising the Surnames of Gade-Gadie-Gaudie ... from AD 800 to AD 1919* (Lewiston, ME: Journal Press, 1919), 256–7. None of the three boys appears in the McIlwraith household in either the 1881 or 1891 manuscript census returns. John Goldie McIlwraith died at two months old. See Dominion of Canada 1881 Census, North Town Of Listowel, Division 2, District 172, North Perth Co., p. 48; Dominion of Canada 1891 Census, District 123, Waterloo South, District C, Town of Galt, pp. 127–8; 'Died,' *LB*, July 25, 1872.

19 Helen Hunter was born on July 1, 1810 in Newton-on-Ayr and married Daniel Hunter there on June 2, 1840. She is buried in the same plot as Andrew and Mary (Goldie) McIlwraith, and Jean Carrick McIlwraith – sometimes called 'Jane' (d. 1960), in Mountview Cemetery, Galt (Cambridge), Section 3, 18E-32. The four of them share two sides of the same pink granite headstone.

20 *LB*, March 9, 1877, 'Listowel Mechanics' Institute,' *LB*, October 12, 1877; 'Listowel Mechanics' Institute,' *LB*, October 26, 1877; *LB*, June 11, 1880.

21 'Institute,' *LB*, June 1, 1877; 'Listowel Mechanics' Institute. The Reading Room,' *LB*, June 22, 1877.

22 'Town Council,' *LB*, December 10, 1880. An account of the May 1878

annual MI meeting recorded in attendance only 'half a dozen, more or less.' 'Institute,' *LB*, May 31, 1878.

23 'School Trustees,' *LB*, January 12, 1877; 'Trustees,' *LB*, December 27, 1878. His Scottishness followed him too. McIlwraith gathered with expatriate Scots in January 1880, giving a 'eulogistic' speech on poet Robert Burns at the St Andrew's Society of Elma Township's Burns Anniversary proceedings. 'Newry,' *LB*, January 28, 1880.

24 McIlwraith believed that small, country agricultural implement makers could not compete with large urban foundries for the 'provincial trade.' He was among the Listowel businessmen supporting the formation of a joint stock company for this purpose in December 1878. Despite lengthy discussion, nothing came of the scheme. *LB*, December 27, 1878.

25 'The Listowel Foundry,' *LB*, November 15, 1878; 'Listowel Foundry – Partnership,' *LB*, October 24, 1879.

26 'New Foundry,' *LB*, September 5, 1879; 'New Foundry,' *LB*, March 26, 1880.

27 'New Foundry,' *LB*, April 9, 1880; 'New Foundry,' *LB*, April 30, 1880; *LB*, June 11, 1880; Austin's new partners were W.D. Bell, a long-time Listowel resident and 'first-class machinist,' and Samuel Davidson, Jr, a moulder who had recently finished his apprenticeship. They may both have been former employees of McIlwraith & Austin. 'New Foundry,' *LB*, June 25, 1880.

28 Andrew and Mary were well liked, it seems. Andrew's death in 1891, fully ten years after their departure from Listowel, elicited a full obituary in the *Banner*. 'Sudden Death of Mr. Andrew McIlwraith,' *LB*, December 11, 1891. But Austin had the favour of the *Banner* editor it seems. See his endorsement in 'Austin & Co.,' *LB*, December 23, 1881. Austin had political prominence as well ('a thorough Reformer'), having served as a town councillor for the Listowel's Centre Ward, 1875–7. See 'The Town of Listowel,' *Illustrated Historical Atlas of the County of Perth Ont.* (Toronto: H. Belden and Co., 1879), xii; *LB*, January 19, 1877; 'Dissolution,' *LB*, August 22, 1879.

29 'Foundry for Sale,' *LB*, February 4, 1881. McIlwraith's decision to leave may have been made in December 1880, when he began to lease out a portion of the foundry property to 'a gentleman' who wished to operate a storehouse for pressed hay. 'New Industry,' *LB*, December 10, 1880. To add insult to injury, *Austin's and Bell's* enterprise (at Mill and Elma streets) came to be known as the Listowel Foundry by 1881, essentially erasing the name of McIlwraith's foundry. See 'Listowel Foundry,' *LB*, August 19, 1881; and advertisement for 'Listowel Foundry' in *County of Perth Gazetteer and Directory for 1882-6* (Hamilton: W.H. Irwin, 1882) 94.

30 'Sample Reaper,' *LB*, April 30, 1880.

31 *LB*, March 11, 1881; 'Sale,' *LB*, May 20, 1881.

32 'Enterprising,' *LB*, September 16, 1881; 'The Hum,' *LB*, September 30, 1881; 'Sold Out,' *LB*, January 27, 1882. The machinery had been sold much earlier, by May 1881. 'The Foundry,' *LB*, May 20, 1881.

33 Hon. James Young, *History of the Gore Fire Insurance Co. from 1839 to 1895* (Galt: Jaffray Brothers, 1895), 2.

34 See Town of Galt Assessment Rolls, 1882–91. By 1890, moreover, Andrew appears to have ventured into landlordhood himself. Though the assessment rolls are not entirely clear on this matter, a notation in the 1890 roll indicates that McIlwraith was an owner of property on Bell or Best Street in addition to his home on Lansdowne. Moreover, the total value of his real property increased from $1,800 in 1889 to $2,500 in 1890, and his taxable income from $500 to $1,000. Though he seems to have started drawing income from a non-salary, land-related source, puzzlingly, he does not appear anywhere in the 1890 roll as a landlord to another Galt household. McIlwraith was listed as 'accountant, h Bridge' in William W. Evans, comp., *Waterloo County Gazetteer and Directory for 1884–5* (Toronto: Hill and Weir, 1884), 197 and 'accountant, Lansdowne Road' in the *County of Waterloo Gazetteer and Directory for 1886–89* (Berlin: W.H. Irwin and Company, 1886), 147.

35 Dickson, *'Ebenezer,'* 306.

36 Minutebook, Galt Scientific, Historical and Literary Society, In connection with the Mechanics' Institute, 1891–1902. Entries for April 7, April 14, May 12, and September 8, 1891. City of Cambridge Archives, Cambridge, Ontario.

37 'James S. Wardlaw,' in Rev. Wm. Cochrane, DD, ed., *The Canadian Album: Men of Canada, or Success by Example* (Brantford: Bradley, Garretson and Co., 1893), 2:302.

38 'Sudden Death of Mr. Andrew McIlwraith,' *LB*, December 11, 1891.

39 He left behind his wife, Mary, and five children, two of whom, David (sixteen years old) and Mary (fourteen years old), lived at home. Andrew's oldest son, William, had at the time of his father's death secured a 'good position' in New York. His oldest daughter, Margaret, lived locally with her husband Charles Turnbull. Daughter Jane had only recently (1891) moved to Winnipeg. Mary (Goldie) McIlwraith lived in Galt for much of the remainder of her life. She died in 1911 and was buried with Andrew in Galt's Mountview Cemetery. Dominion of Canada 1891 Census, District 123 Waterloo South, District C, Town of Galt, pp. 127–8; 'Death of an Old Resident,' *The Ayr News*, April 13, 1911.

40 'Death of Mr. A. McIlwraith,' *DR*, December 10, 1891.

41 Minutebook, Galt Scientific, Historical and Literary Society, In connection with the Mechanics Institute, 1891–1905, December 8, 1891; 'Resolution of Condolence,' *DR*, December 10, 1891.

42 Dickson, *'Ebenezer,'* 306–8; Rev. Dr Robert Campbell, 'Statistical Register of St. Andrew's Church,' cited in Dickson, *'Ebenezer,'* 306.

43 Dickson, *'Ebenezer,'* 307.

ENDIX 1
McIlwraith and Goldie Family Trees

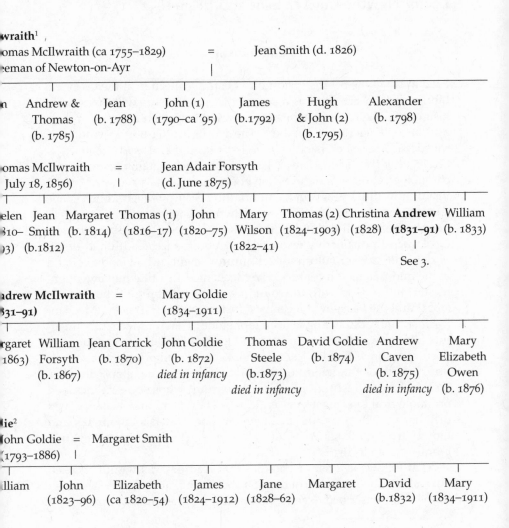

wraith[1]

omas McIlwraith (ca 1755–1829)　　　=　　　Jean Smith (d. 1826)
eman of Newton-on-Ayr　　　　　　　|

| n | Andrew & Thomas (b. 1785) | Jean (b. 1788) | John (1) (1790–ca '95) | James (b.1792) | Hugh & John (2) (b.1795) | Alexander (b. 1798) |

omas McIlwraith　　=　　Jean Adair Forsyth
July 18, 1856)　　　|　　(d. June 1875)

elen	Jean	Margaret	Thomas (1)	John	Mary	Thomas (2)	Christina	Andrew	William
10–	Smith	(b. 1814)	(1816–17)	(1820–75)	Wilson	(1824–1903)	(1828)	(1831–91)	(b. 1833)
3)	(b.1812)				(1822–41)				See 3.

drew McIlwraith　　=　　Mary Goldie
31–91)　　　　　　|　　(1834–1911)

| rgaret 1863) | William Forsyth (b. 1867) | Jean Carrick (b. 1870) | John Goldie (b. 1872) died in infancy | Thomas Steele (b.1873) died in infancy | David Goldie (b. 1874) | Andrew Caven (b. 1875) died in infancy | Mary Elizabeth Owen (b. 1876) |

ie[2]

ohn Goldie　　=　　Margaret Smith
1793–1886)　　|

| lliam | John (1823–96) | Elizabeth (ca 1820–54) | James (1824–1912) | Jane (1828–62) | Margaret | David (b.1832) | Mary (1834–1911) |

anks to Tom Barclay, Carnegie Library, Ayr, Scotland, for his invaluable assistance in compiling this chart.
ahlon M. Gowdy, *A Family History Comprising the Surnames of Gade-Gadie-Gaudie ... and the Variant Forms*
m AD 800 to AD 1919 (Lewiston, ME: Journal Press, 1919), 245–57.

APPENDIX 2
Andrew McIlwraith's Mechanics' Institute Library Loans, Newton-on-Ayr, Scotland, 1846–1852

Editors' Note

Filed away in the Scottish and Local History collection at the Carnegie Library in Ayr, Scotland, is a source that provides us with invaluable insight into the reading habits of Andrew McIlwraith and his community in early Victorian Ayrshire. The worn, leather-bound volume is called *The Mechanic's* [sic] *Institute Issue Book and Members 1836–1852. Catalogue of the Ayr Mechanic's* [sic] *Library* and contains handwritten, chronological records of all of the books and journals acquired by the Institute in these years and, importantly, each member's book loans and returns. Entries for Andrew McIlwraith begin in 1846 and appear in every year until the end of the volume, in 1852. The *Issue Book and Catalogue* is a distinctive resource that reflects the breadth and depth of the craftsworker culture of self-improvement in Lowland Scotland in the mid-nineteenth century. The Mechanics' Institute movement got its start in Scotland with the founding of the Edinburgh School of Art (1821) and the Glasgow Mechanics' Institute (1823).[1] The Ayr Mechanics' Institute could not have been far behind. The Ayr Mechanics' Institute Library was founded in 1825 and located in High Street. One 1836 document shows that tradesmen, shopkeepers, and professionals made up the bulk of the Institute Library's eighty-five members.[2] In 1840, the Mechanics' Institute housed a 'museum' whose objects included ornithological specimens, an antique metal vessel and an improved drill harrow.[3] By 1845, the membership had grown to about 145 and the library's holdings were 2,500 volumes. The Mechanics' Institute Library closed in 1870.[4]

What follows is a list of volumes that Andrew McIlwraith checked out and returned, for each of the years between 1846 and 1852. The titles have been transcribed exactly; no spelling or grammatical errors have

---

1 W. Marwick, 'Mechanics' Institutes in Scotland,' *Journal of Adult Education* 6 (1932–4): 292–309; Charles W.J. Withers, *Geography, Science and National Identity: Scotland since 1520* (Cambridge University Press, 2001), 161.
2 See Allan Leach, *Libraries in Ayr 1762–1975* (Ayr: Ayr Public Library Committee, 1975), 74.
3 *Ayr Advertiser*, July 16, 1840.
4 Leach, *Libraries in Ayr*, 74.

been corrected. The volume and range of Andrew's literary consumption in these years – from age sixteen to age twenty-two – is remarkable and presages his lifelong commitment to self-improvement.

1846   T = 53 *volumes borrowed*
Beauties of Scotland vol. 4
Davy's (Sir Humphry), *Salmonia*
Mr Wm Parker, *Beauties of the Poets*
The Prairie (3 vols.)
Waverly Novels
Garities and Gravities vol. 1 of 3
Sir Walter Scott, *Novels & Romances, from Waverley to the Chronicles
    Canongate* 1st Series.
Boswell, *Tour to the Hebrides*
Bells *Select British Theatre.*
Critical Review. New Arrangement. Vol. 8 (1793)
Dr Johnson, *Works* (12 vols.) vols. 1, 2, 3
Duncan's *British Trident* vols. 1, 2
Constabels Miscellany vols. 63–4. Sutherland's Knights of Malta
Moors Hindu Infanticide by George McCartney, Cumnock.
Col. Fullerton, *Statement Respecting the Affairs of Trinidad.*
Taits Magazine (40 vols.)
Tom Cringles Log by Michael Scott. 1 vol. 12 mo.
Monthly Review (1832–6) 15 vols.
Bracebridge Hall vol. 1
Griers Mechanic'l Calculator
Catlin's *North American Indians*, vol. 1
Grier's Mechanic's Pocket Dictionary
The Bagmans Bioscope [by] Mr. Wm. Parker
Chamelion (8 vols.)
Dick's Philosophy of Religion. [by] Mr. W. Forest.
Burns, *Works* (wi/ Life of the Author by Alan Cunninghame, vol. 1)
The Annual Register (for 1762)
[Dr David] Irvine's *Lives of the Scottish Poets* (2 vols.)
McKenzie's *Thousand Experiments*
Eulers *Letters to a German Princess*
[Capt.] Kincaid, *Adventures in the Rifle Brigade in the Peninsula from 1809
    to 1815*
Smith's *Panorama of Science and Art* vol. 2

Sketches of Ancient Biography vols. 1, 2
Constable's Miscellany vols. 66–7 (Conway's Travels in Switzerland and
  the Pyrenees)
Constable's Miscellany vols. 60–1 (History of the War of the Independ-
  ency in Greece)

1847   T = 51 *volumes borrowed*
Goldsmith's *Works* (vol. 1)
Josephus *Works* (vol. 4)
Constable's Miscellany
Bancroft on *Permanent Colours* (vol. 2)
Lardner's Encyclopedia
Waverly Novels
The Last Days of Pompeii
Constable's Miscellany vol. 28. Memorials of the War
Tytler's *Life of the Admirable Crichton*
PicNic
Cooper's *Pioneers*
Beauties of Scotland vol. 2
*Life and Correspondence of Thomas Jefferson Late President of the United
  States of America* vol. 2 of 4
(Sir N.W.) Maxwell Wraxall (Bart.) *Posthumous Memoirs of His Own
  Times* vols. 1, 2.
Hone's *Every Day Book and Table Book* vol. 3
Chambers *Collection of Scottish Ballads*
Smiths School of Arts vol. 1
Henry's *Elements of Chemistry* vol. 1
Bells *Select British Theatre* vol. 6
Library of Entertaining Knowledge, History of Vegetable Substances,
  Timber Trees and Fruits. Vol. 2.
Anacharsis the Younger's *Travels in Greece during the Middle of the
  Fourth Century befire the Christain* [sic] + *Era* by the Abbe Barthelemy
  vol. 3.
Boswel[l]'s *Life of Dr Johnson*, vol. 1
(Thomas) More, *Life and Journals of Lord Byron*, vol. 1
Nicolson's Student Instructor in the Five Orders of Architecture
Nicolson's Mechanic's Companion
Chemical Recreations
(Dean) *Swift's Letters* vol. 1
Parry's *Last Days of Lord Byron*

Mills *History of Chivalry*, vol. 1
Harris, *Wild Sports of Southern Africa*
(Professor) Wilson's *Isle of Palms and Other Poems*
The President's Daughters by Mary Howitt vol. 1, 3
Paul Periwinkle or the Pressgang vol. 1
Chronicles of the Canongate vols. 1–3
Sir Walter Scott's *Novels & Romances from Waverly to the Chronicles of Canongate* 2 vols.
Edinburgh Review vol. 59
Beckford's *Italy with Sketches of Spain & Portugal* vol. 1 Chateaubriands *Travels in America & Italy* 2 vols.
Adventures of a French Serjeant

1848 T = 34 volumes borrowed
Waverly Novels
Edinburgh Review
Curiosities of Literature vols. 4, 5
Sketches of Ancient Biography vols. 1, 2
Wilson's *City of the Plague & other Poems*
Bulwer's *Phelham*
Don Juan by Lord Byron
Burke on the Sublime & Beautiful
Bells *Select British Theatre* [1 of 14 vols.]
Ferguson's Mechanics
Ayrshire Magnet (The)
Llorente's *History of the Spanish Inquisition*
Emerson's Mechanics
Ossian's Poems 2 vols.
Johnstone's *Edinburgh Magazine* (1 vol.)
Diary of a Late Physician by Samuel Warren vol. 1 of 2
Stuart; (Wortley) *Visit to Antwerp*
Library of useful Knowledge, Natural Philosophy vol. 1
Cornwall's (Barry) *Flood of Thessaly and Other Poems* 1 vol.
Hibbert's *Philosophy of Apparitions*
St Clair, or the Heiress of Desmond
Lord Byron's *Works* [vol. 3 of 6]
Adventures of a Kings Page [vol. 1 of 3]
Rousseau's (J.J.) *Thoughts on Defferent* [sic] *Subjects*
Hume & Smollett's *History of England* [vols. 5, 6 of 13]
Goldsmith's *Essays and Poems*

Prairie (The) [vols. 2, 3 of 3]
Lardner's Encyclopedia
Cooper's Pioneers

1849   T = 62 volumes borrowed
Nicolson's Student Instructor in the Five Orders of Architecture
Nicolson's Mechanic's Companion
Cooper's *Pilor*
The Spy by Cooper [vol. 1 of 3]
Adventures of a King's Page [vol. 1]
Confessions of an English Opium Eater
The Neibours by Mary Howitt [vol. 2 of 2]
Lardner's Encyclopedia
The Miser's Daughter by Wm. H. Ainsworth vols. 1, 3
Birkbeck's *Notes of a Journey in America*. Adam Cowan.
Lord Byron's *Works* [vol. 6 of 6]
The Bagman's Bioscope. Mr. Wm. Parker
Lectures to Young Men
Literary & Scientific Men of France [vol. 1 of 2]
Delphine, by Madame DeStael [vols. 1–3 of 6]
The Lost Senses
Asiatic (The) Annual Register from 1799 to 1810–11 [vol. for 1801]
The Staff Officer [vol. 3 of 3]
Robison's Natural & Mechanical Philosophy [vol. 2 of 4]
Memoirs of a Physician by Alexr Dumas [vol. 2 of 3]
London Mechanics Magazine vol. 8
Memoirs of a Physician [vol. 2 of 3]
Taits Magazine. 1839.
Constables Miscellany vol. 73. Taylors Civil Wars of Ireland
Library [of] Entertain[in]g Knowledge vol. 23d. Faculties of Birds
Ossian's Poems vol. 1
The Black Prophet by Wm. Carleton. 1 vol.
Library of Useful Knowledge. Lives of Eminent Persons, 1 vol.
Tales of My Landlord. 1st Series. [vol. 1 of 4]
Delphine [vol. 6 of 6]
Consuelo by George Sand [vol. 2 of 2]
Paul Periwinkle or the Pressgang [vol. 2 of 3]
Count Fathom
Bells *Select British Theatre* [vol. 5 of 14]
Spark's (Jared) *Life of George Washington* [vol. 1 of 2]

Huttons Mathematics [vol. 2 of 3]
Accum's Treatise on Gas. 1 vol.
Library of Useful Knowledge, Natural Philosophy. 1st vol.
Buchanan's *Treatise on Mill Work*. 2 vols.
Don Quixote. Transláted by Ozell. 4 vols.
The Pleasures of Hope and Other Poems by T. Campbell Esq.
Wilson's (Proffesor[sic]) *Isle of Palms and Other Poems*
Grier's *Mechanic's Calculator*
Knickerbocker's *History of New York*
Hazlitts *Select Poets of Great Britain*
Johnson's (Dr) *Works* [vol. 11 of 12]
Library of Useful Knowledge, Mathematics vol. 1st
Naturalists' Library by Sir William Jardine
Chemical Recreations
Blackwoods Magazine vol. 2
Huttons Mathematics [vol. 2 of 3]
Valerius, A Roman Story [vols. 1, 2 of 3]

1850   T = 50 volumes borrowed
Parks *Chemical Essays* [vol. 1 of 5]
Allisons *Essays on Taste* [vol. 2 of 2]
Adventures of Telemachus
Valerius, A Roman Story [vol. 3 of 3]
Edinburgh Review
Cornwall's (Barry) *Flood of Thessaly and Other Poems*
Beauties of Scotland [vol. 1 of 5]
'Whales'
Lardner's Encyclopedia
Naturalists' Library
British Birds vol. 12
'Pelham'
Cunningham's (Allan) *Lives of British Painters, Sculptors, and Architects*
    vols. 1–6
Griffin's (John Joseph) *Chemical Recreations and Romance of Chemistry*
Nicolson's Students Instructor in the Five Orders of Architecture
Childe Harold. By Lord Byron.
Wraxall (Sir N.W. Bart.) *Posthumous Memoirs of His Own Times* [vol. 1 of
    3]
Thomson's (James) *Works* [vol. 1 of 2]
Don Quixote vols. 1–4

Lord Byron's Works [vols. 2, 4 of 6]
The British Essayists [vol. 12 of 45]
Library of Useful Knowledge, America & West Indies
Treadgold on the S[t]eam Engine on Steam Navigation &c [vol. 2 of 2]
Criticisms on Some of Shakespeare's Characters
Cottagers of Glenburnie
Shakespeare's *Works* [vol. 3 of 12]
The Devil on Two Sticks
The Pleasures of Hope and Other Poems by T. Campbell Esq.
Johnson's (Dr.) *Works* [vol. 1 of 12]
Wilson's (Proffesor[sic]) *Isle of Palms and Other Poems*
Edinburgh Review vol. 9th
Notable Things (Fifteen Hundred)
Grier's Mechanic's Calculator
Horace Translated by Greech
Robinson Crusoe (Life and Adventures of) by Daniel Defoe, To which is
   appended Howell's *Life of Alexander Selkirk*
Moore's [sic] (Thomas) *Life and Journals of Lord Byron* [vol. 1 of 2]
The Last Days of Pompeii, by Bulwer
The Sketch Book vol. 1st
Strutts *Sports and Pastimes of the People of England*. Edited by Wm. Hone

1851   T = 39 *volumes borrowed – Jan–August*
Crokers *Fairy Segment of the South of Ireland*
Motherwells *Minstrelsy Ancient and Modern*
Edinburgh cabinet Library. Iceland, Greenland &c.
Blackwoods Magazine 1849
Colton's *Lacon*. 1 vol.
Englishwoman in Egypt [vol. 1 of 2]
Constables Miscellany [vol. 10 of 16]
Paula Monti
New Monthly Magazine for 1823
New Monthly for 1832
'Bride of &4'
Swainson on Taxidermy 1 vol.
Buckinghams *Travels in Palestine* [vol. 1 of 2]
Library of Useful Knowledge, Natural Philosophy vol. 2
Edinburgh Review [1 vol.]
Lectures to Young Men
Pope's *Poetical Works*

Blackwood's Magazine, 1850
Waverly Novels [vols. 27, 28 of 32]
Queen of Denmark [3 vols.]
Mechanic's Own Book
Lardner's Encyclopedia
Schunderhannes, The Robber of the Rhine
Book of English Songs
Dict. of Terms. Neale [vol. 1 of 2]
'Pic H. Hours'
Steam Boilers. Armstrong
'Tarro' [or Tasso] 2 vols.
'Yeats'
Comic Offering
Irving's Tales of the Alhambra
Civil Engineering. [by] Law.
Railways [by] Stephens

1852   T = 53 volumes borrowed
Well Digging & Boring. By Swindell
'Mech. Jour.'
Warming & Ventilation [by] Tomlinson
Longfellow's Seaside & Fireside Ballads
Longfellow's Belfry of Bruges
Treadgold on the S[t]eam Engine [vol. 2 of 2]
Hone's Every Day Book and Table Book [vols. 1, 2 of 3]
Naturalists Library by William Jardine
The Robber by James
The Prairie by Cooper
Tubular Bridges &c [by] Dempsey
Constable's Miscellany vol. 80. The Book of Butterflies vol. 3rd.
Boswell's Life of Johnson
Edinburgh Review vol. 72 nos. 145–6.
Heylyn (Peter) History of the Sabbath. London. Printed by Henry Scile
    1636.
'Em. Man'
Gil Blas
The Rival Beauties [vol. 1 of 3]
Master Humphrey's Clock by Charles Dickens 2 vols.
Longfellow's Outre Mer
Heir of Wast Weyland (M. Howitt)

Humboldt's *Cosmos* [vol. 2 of 3]
Hutton's *Mathematical Recreation* [vol. 1 of 4]
Gowrie, or the King's Plot by James
Antar [4 vols.]
Harris, *Wild Sports of Southern Africa*
Spanish Literature
German Literature by Gostic
Panopticon: Postscript part 1st.

APPENDIX 3
Memoranda, Cash Accounts, and Letters Sent and Received, 1857–1862

Editors' Note

Appendix 3 presents the memoranda, cash accounts, and record of letters (sent and received) kept by Andrew McIlwraith in his diaries. They contain the sort of untidy private reminders and remarks that most of us make and discard; however, Andrew's survive. They are collected and presented here together and provide sporadic glimpses into his varied interests. Andrew's memoranda cover the first four diary years only and comprise the most eclectic collection. They contain information about potential contacts and their addresses in other cities, letters that he delivered on behalf of others, poems, and interesting and potentially useful facts (such as an 'antidote to mosquitoes'). His cash accounts, kept in detail for the years 1857, 1858, and 1859, and for two months of summer 1861, give readers a window on his monthly spending and consumption. In these, Andrew itemizes such expenditures as books and other readings, medicine, pay for a servant (room cleaning, presumably), groceries, cigars, entertainment and church collection, and rent. Finally, Andrew seems to have wanted to record his own epistolary history and has carried out a monthly detailing of letters sent and received. He must have grown tired of this; he completed only one year of it and did not continue the practice after 1857. Read alone, these entries provide little more than anecdotes of Andrew McIlwraith's life. But when read as addenda to the diaries, they help confirm our impressions of the man.

Memoranda 1857

James Hosie, Detroit Loco. works. Learned St. or 134 Fifth St. village of
  Mandaumin.
Appearance of Lake Huron and River St. Clair
Duck shooting and fish spearing.
Contents of tank 13,236.21 Imp. galls. How the water smokes with
  cold.
No. of my watch – 1882
No. of West Per. Building Society Certificate for $140.25 – No. 252
Thursday June 18 – postage for letter to Mr Robb, 17¢ paid

Saturday June 20 Mr Jameson 19cts.
Tuesday 23   do. 5c.
Friday 26   do. 9c.
Antidote to mosquitoes. Glycerine 4 oz. Oil of Peppermint 2 ½
    drachms. Oil of Turpentine 4 drachms
John Hastings, Mason, 149 Drumlinrig Street Thornhill from C.
    Hastings.
James Meikle, baker, Greenock, brother of Mrs Drake. Mr McLean,
    postmaster, Dunkeld, from Misses Mackenzie, also John Robison,
    shoemaker, Dunkeld.
Jane Fleming now Mrs Atkins.
Rev. Mr Walker Carnivath from Mr Robt Walker
To bring a yorkers worth of green kail seed also one pound of good
    carrot seed.
Hugh Jameson, Curagh, Girvan from Hugh McWhirter.
From Mr Goldie compt, to Mr Wm Goudie, Hamilton st. Girvan
    and Dr Crawford, Girvan, also Mr Paterson, 16 Market Street.
    Musselburgh.
    From Mr James Goldie to Robt Greive, florist, Kaim's Cottage,
    Liberton.
Hugh Orr, 31 John St, New York, call for Mr James Goldie.
From Mr Cant, Hamilton, ask for Hugh McLean, millwright or George
    Monroe, ask at Grahmes of Partick.
Mr Sinclair, Main St. Hamilton to Mr Peter Sinclair, baker, Colzean.
Mr John Goldie, 59 Cumberland St. Edinburgh from Mr Wm K. Muir.
Mrs Inglis, 41 St. Joseph's, suburbs, Montreal Bennings Building.
Weight of bell 11 ton, icwt, i gr.
Abutment and 7 piers about finished on Montreal side of tubular
    bridge. Peter Hosie, Mrs J. Miller, 52 New Boundry St. Liverpool.
Mrs Stewart to Fulton Brewers, Edinburgh to send per Robt Burns
Mr Hugh Andrew, Victoria P.O. Knox County Ill.
Mr James Goldie, Box 148 P.O. Utica
Height of Montreal Cathedral tower 225ft. Up here on it Aug. 12 – 10
    p.m.
At Wolfe's Monument 2 p.m. Aug 13. Inscription on one side 'Here
    died Wolfe, victorious, Sept. 13th 1759.' Opposite side 'This pillar
    was erected by the British Army in Canada A.D. 1849. His Excel-
    lency Lieut. Gen. Sir Benjamin D'Urban G.C.B. K.C.H. K.C.T.S.V.,
    Commander of the Forces to replace that erected by Gov. Lord
    Aylmer G.C.B. in 1832 which was broken and defaced and is depos-

ited beneath.' Was shown through the Citadel by D. Murphy, soldier
who had a Sebastopol medal, Regiment 17th.
James Porteous No. 90 Aughton St. near Nutherfield Road, Liverpool.
Mrs Murdock, 5 Christie St. Paisley
Mrs McCallum 259 Main St. Bridgeton Glasgow
Mr Peter Hosie, 378 Great Howard St. Liverpool
Mr John Armstrong, 108 2nd St. Aurbour Hill, Albany

> There are tones that will haunt us, though lonely
> Our path be o'er mountain or sea.
> There are looks that will part from us only
> When memory ceases to be.
> There are hopes which our burden can lighten
> Though toilsome and steep be the way.
> And dreams that like moonlight can brighten
> With a light that is clearer than day.

Hamilton 28th December 1857. Money belonging to me in Savings
Bank in Thomas's name. £17-18-9. Cy.

Memoranda 1858

THE FISHER'S LASSIE
(I)
Tall and comely, wi' wavin' hair,
    Doon by the waters o' Morantassie,
Never a kennin' or wrang or care.
    (A life o' joy for the fisher's lassie).
Lovers seekin' her ilka day
    Roon' by the waters o' Morantassie -
'My fisher-lad I will Lo'e for aye!'
    (Simmer a' year for the fisher's lassie).
Village gossips mention her name
    Doon by the waters o' Morantassie.
'A waddin' we'll hae when the men come hame.
    (Ribbons and braws for the fisher's lassie).
'Lads an' lassies frae faur an' near
    Will come by the waters o' Morantassie,
For, wow, but er Lo'e the lassie dear!
    (A ring of gowd for the fisher's lassie).

(II)
A waesome nicht when the men come hame -
 Wild the waters o' Morantassie.
Billows black wi' a crest o' foam.
 (A nicht of fool for the fisher's lassie).
Lood the thunder the breakers mak'
 Heaven' the waters o' Morantassie.
San's an' rocks a' strewn wi' wrack.
 (It's oh! and oh! for the fisher's lassie).
'Oh! say, is ma fisher lad safe an' weel -
 Safe frae the waters o' Morantassie?
Never a word they answer, I tweel.
 (A broken he'rt for the fisher's lassie)
Cauld in her room the lassie lies
 Near by the waters o' Morantassie.
Nocht is heard but the sea-bird's cries
 (Linen white for the fisher's lassie).

HEALTH ALPHABET
The Ladies' Sanitary Association of London gives the following simple
rules for keeping health which we find copied in the Sanitarian:-
A-s soon as you are up, shake blanket and sheet;
B-etter be without shoes than sit with wet feet;
C-hildren, if healthy, are active, not still;
D-amp beds and damp clothes will both make you ill;
E-at slowly and always chew your food well;
F-reshen the air in the house that you dwell;
G-arments must never be made too tight;
H-omes should be healthy, airy and light;
I-f you wish to be well, as you do I've no doubt;
J-ust open the windows before you go out;
K-eep the rooms always tidy and clean;
L-et dust on the furniture never be seen;
M-uch illness is caused by the want of pure air;
N-ow to open the windows be ever your care;
O-ld rags and old rubbish should never be kept;
P-eople should see that their floors are well swept;
Q-uick movements in children are healthy and right;
R-emember the young cannot thrive without light;
S-ee that the cistern is clean to the brim;

T-ake care that your dress is all tidy and trim;
U-se your nose to find if there be a bad drain;
V-ery sad are the fevers that come in its train;
W-alk as much as you can without feeling fatigue;
X-erxes could walk full many a league;
Y-our health is your wealth, which your wisdom must keep;
Z-eal will help a good cause and the good you will reap.

Memoranda 1859

Chas Cherry Cummins, Pittsburg Comp't for R. Turnbull Dundas.
Mr Marshall Gideon Pott, 41 East 23rd St.
New York Comp't from J. McGarva, Dundas
A. Guthrie. 60 Laight St.
252 26th St.
Allairs, Cherry St. Pease and Morphy Fulton Foundry – Morgan's
   Foundry – Neptune Foundry – Novelty Works, 12th St. Ask for Mr
   Jones.
Down East River – Bunces near the Battery.
Mr Barry, 252 West 26th St. – Mr Corbett.
Billing and Brothers Printing office Duane St.
Enoch's
Burke's Boarding House, 9th St.
Billings, brother 223 William St.
White Fish (Coregonus Albus)
Fairfield, Badger's Foundry, 14th St.
Paddy Louge – Pott's
Church of Messiah, 728 Broadway
Mr Anderson, 144 4th St. (Chas McKenzie)
Wm Spittal, 203 West 13th St.
Petricola Pholadiformis (Shell)
Petricola Dactylus, shorter and smaller kind.
Mr Alex Hutchison
Messrs Gilkinson 90 Beaver St. N.Y.

Memoranda 1860

Repairing Straw Cutter $3.50
Wm Barrie 252 W. 26th St. N.Y.
For article on English surnames Edinburgh Review Vo. C.1.

H.H. Date Temporary Planing mach. knife		75¢
Ball		28¢
Jas Kay paid		$1.20
Robson		2.20
Patrick & Co.		5.30

Cash Accounts 1857

January

2	For chess board and men	2.12-½
	Tennyson's poems	.75
	Brown, Jones and Robinson	.25
	Longfellow's poems	.50
	Diary	.50
3	Breakfast in London and coach fare to Sarnia	4.50
	Punch's Almanac	.12-½
	Dinner in Warwick	.25
	Arrears to Mrs. Kent up to this date	25.00
5	Postage stamps for U.S. Letters	.60
7	One month's pay	65.00
	Repayment of loan from Baillie	5.00
	for a thermometer	.75
8	6 months of Sarnia Observer	1.00
14	Repairing bow pen	.25
17	Pair of overshoes	1.00
25	Paid to Manse Fund	1.00
25	Ferryage to Port Huron	.25
28	Medicine for cough	.37-½
31	To Mrs. Kent for board for 4 weeks	20.00
		59.22-½

February

2	Cough medicine	.25
6	Subscribed to Bible Class	1.00
8	Collection in Methodist Church	.25
15	Collection In Free Church	.25
17	To Bible Society	.25
17	Hair pomature	.25
20	Postage stamps to England	1.00
22	Collection in Free Church	.25
24	Flower seeds	.36

24	Ferryage and postage		.17
28	Paid Mrs. Kent for 1 month		20.00
28	For kid gloves		1.25

March

8	Church collection		.12-½
13	Paper cutter		.18
15	Church collection for Ministers' Widows Fund		.25
16	Small lantern		.62-½
16	Lent to Old Kent		20.00
14	Lent to Mr. Peffers		10.00
14	Pay for February	65.00	
18	Draft for £34		.34
19	Interest on Gas stock	7.00	
19	2 vols. Scottish Songs and Ballads		6.00
19	Lent to A. Jameson		2.00
24	Received re payment from do.	2.00	
26	Subscription to Church		2.00
29	Collection in do.		.25
28	Old Kent's loan of $20.00 put to account of board to this date		
		74.00	41.77

April

8	Pay for March		65.00
10	Two letter files and two pictorial papers		.31-½
10	Ferryage and expenses in Port Huron		.83-½
11	Subscribed to Mechanics Institute		1.00
13	Posted for investment to Br. Thos.		30.00
15	Postage upon do.		.10
17	Stake for raffle of Howard's gun		1.00
17	for Stationery		.50
17	Powder flask		.37-½
24	New hat		2.00
24	Knife		1.00
25	Repairs to boots		1.00
26	Collection to Manse fund in Church		.52
27	Paid Mrs. Kent 4 weeks board up to 25th inst.		20.00
29	Postage for letters and papers rec'd		.25
	Lecture on Kansas		.25
29	Carriage of 2 loons to Hamilton		1.00

May

1	Cash in hand	4.00	
4	Pay for April	65.00	
4	Repayment of loan – Peffers	10.00	
9	Two cakes maple sugar		3.36
9	One box sardines		.54
11	Shot		.25
11	To servant girl		1.00
11	To Br. Thomas for investment in Savings Bank		40.00
14	Postage stamps		2.20
13	To Bill and J. Stewart, a present		5.00
16	'Testimony of the Rocks'		1.25
23	Paid Mrs Kent, one month		20.00
25	Dining, smoking and drinking		2.00
27	At concert		.25
31	Collection for Manse Fund		.62-½

June

1	In hand	2.52-½	
1	Bill of exchange and postage of money to Br Bill		.60
1	Powder flask No. 2		.37-½
1	Lent to Mr Robb		1.00
9	Received pay for May	65.00	
9	Cigars		.30
9	Gunpowder		.30
9	Repayment of loan, Mr Robb	1.00	
15	Sent to Hamilton per Mr. Jameson for purchase of concertina		8.00
15	Invested in Savings Bank		12.00
17	Paid Mr Lees for coat and cap		10.50
18	Insect net		.30
20	Cleaning watch		2.00
21	Church collection		.15
20	To Mrs Kent for month's board		20.00
22	To Ellen Young for 1 pr fancy slippers		2.00
22	Cigars		.25
28	Church collection		.30
29	Mink skin pouch		2.50

July

3	Postage on letters from Tom		.10

3	Cigars		.25
4	Postage on Dumbarton letters and paper		.23
4	Pleasure sail up Lake Huron		1.75
5	Church collection		.11
10	Lemonade and postage		.25
11	Cigars		.25
11	Pay for June	65.00	
11	Old C. gold ½ sov. sold	2.40	
16	Treating in Smith's		.25
17	do. in the country		.25
18	Ammunition		1.00
18	To Mrs Kent for board		20.00
18	Padlock and rope for packing		.50
19	Horning in the Western		.30
19	Church collection		.10
20	To servant girl		1.00
20	Expenses from Sarnia to Hamilton		3.00

August
Expenses of voyage home

	Valise	5.00
10	Fare from Hamilton to Montreal	9.00
	Cigars, etc.	.50
11	Montreal to Quebec	3.50
	Hotel Bill in Montreal	2.50
	Theatre and sights	1.00
	Hotel Bill in Quebec	6.25
11	Maps, guide books, etc.	4.25
	Driving to Monmorenci	2.50
	Utensils, Cigars, etc. for voyage	2.00
	Fare to Liverpool from Quebec	30.00

September
A. McI. lent to J. Stewart

Friday and Saturday, one meal	.25
Car fare to Greenwood and back	.10
Home at night	.05
From Navy Yard, down	.05
Ferryage	.06

Cars home at night			.05
Sunday, one meal			.15
Car fare down			.05
To Guthries			.05
Back			.05
Ferryage			.04
Monday, Cars down			1.05
Ferry			.02
Dinner			.25
Refreshment at Falls			.18

November

16	Borrowed from Mrs Stewart	£18 - -

Cash Accounts 1858

January

1	In Savings' Bank	71.75	
9	Drew from S. Bank	25.00	25.00
	To Building Society		3.77
	Cash in hand	15.00	
12	Drawing paper and gum		1.00
19	Carriage of coat from New York		1.25
19	Postage		.26
21	Church Seat rent		1.00
14	Jenkin's lecture on India		.25
29	Theatrical ticket for benefit of poor		1.00
30	Expenses going to Dundas		.37-½
		111.75	33.90-½
30	Board for one month		13.00
		46.90-½	46.90-½
		69.74-½	
	Amount still in Savings Bank	46.75	
	Hand	23.00	

February

1	In hand	23.00	
1	One pr. boots and repairs		3.50
1	Papers to send home		.12-½
3	Gilt picture framing		2.28

4	Glass for do.		1.12-½
8	Postage stamps		.50
8	Punch's Almanac		.12-½
10	Plank of Cherry wood		.20
17	Refreshment while shooting		.25
20	Plates for scrap book		.56
20	For drawing plan of Hamilton to Gas Co.	10.00	
27	Paid Mrs. J.W. for board		13.00
		33.00	21.66-½
		21.66-½	
		11.34-½	
	Unaccounted	2.00	
		9.34-½	

March

1	Gas Stock dividends	7.00	
1	Household Words		.12-½
1	Carried over from Feb.	9.34-½	
1	Postage		.12-½
4	Pair Overalls		.75
5	Mechanics Lecture		.25
9	Mechanics Library		.25
11	Entertainment for the Poor (pd. in o.)		.25
17	Subscription for shop clock		.25
19	Psalm Tune Book		.75
20	Three weeks board to Mrs Jones		9.00
20	Shoe brush		.25
21	Church Collection		.25
22	Carriage of chest from Hamilton		2.25
13	Part wages from Gartshore	6.00	
20	Overshoes		1.00
26	Lecture on Concentration, etc.		6.00
27	One weeks board to Mrs Jones		3.00
27	Postage stamps		.50
27	'True Banner' newspaper		.62-½
27	Rec'd from Gartshore	6.00	
		28.34-½	19.50
		19.50	
		8.84-½	

April

1	In hand	8.84-½	
3	Expenses at Hamilton		.67-½
3	One weeks board to Mrs Jones		3.00
5	Subs. to Methodist Church		.25
10	Week's board		3.00
17	do.		3.00
17	Expenses at Hamilton		.12-½
20	Entrance money to Debating Club		.12-½
10	Part wages from shop	6.00	
24	do.	6.00	
24	Black ink and blacking		.18
24	One week's board		3.00
		20.84-½	13.34-½
		13.34-½	
		7.50	
	Unaccounted for	.50	
	Balance in hand	7.00	

May

1	In hand	7.00	
1	One weeks board		3.00
	Expenses to Hamilton		.25
8	Board		3.00
8	A hone		.56
8	Sponge		.83-½
8	Postage		.25
8	From Gartshore	6.00	
11	Postage		.32-½
20	Took from Savings Bank	10.00	
	Expenses of jaunt to Ayr		2.50
15	Board		3.00
22	do.		3.00
29	do.		3.00
29	Washing		2.50
25	From Gartshore	12.00	
31	Postage		.25
31	Repairs of watch		1.25
		35.00	23.71
		23.71	
		11.29	

June

1	Brt forward	11.29	
8	From Gartshore	6.00	
5	Board one week		3.00
5	Expenses to Hamilton		.25
10	Seat rent in Church		1.00
12	Board one week		3.00
19	From Gartshore	6.00	
19	Board		3.00
19	Expense to Hamilton		.25
22	Books		.62-½
23	Expense at Dundas		.37-½
26	Board		3.00
26	Horning, etc.		.63-½
29	Incidentals		.50
29	From Gartshore	59.75	
30	At Toronto		2.77-½
		83.04	18.40
		18.40	
		64.64	

July

1	In hand	64.64	
3	Lent to Mr. Robb		10.00
	Paper, etc.		.50
	Postage		.25
12	do.		.16
12	Repayment from Mr. Robb	10.00	
12	Sent to Scotland		25.00
19	Expenses to Ayr		2.00
19	Bookbinding, etc.		.75
20	Fishing line		.25
21	Horning, etc.		.50
25	do		.25
22	Horse and buggy, etc.		2.12-½
27	Theatricals. etc.		2.25
27	J.E. Reid's Acct.		1.25
17	One month's board		13.00
31	Expenses at Waterdown		.25
24	From Mr. Robb Payment for work	10.00	
		84.64	48.53-½
		48.53-½	
		36.10-½	

August

3	Glass and lumber	1.10
4	Hinges and brads	.37-½
5	Paint	.25
7	Paint and screws	.30
9	Travelling expenses to Stoney Creek	.32-½
16	Fixtures for insect cases, etc.	.25
14	One month's board	10.00
19	Medicine, etc.	1.00
26	Post	.12-½
28	Illus. Lon. News	.20
31	Postage stamps	.04
31	Dr. Rosebrugh for pills	.75

September

9	Transporting chest		1.00
10	Traveling expenses		.50
10	3 mos. 'True Banner'		.50
11	Hogg's Instructor and Chamber's Repository		1.28
11	Incidentals		.50
16	Dr. McCann		1.00
17	Fare to Hamilton		.12-½
18	do		.12-½
20	Servant Girl		.25
18	Mrs Jones 1-½ week's board		4.50
25	do 1 do		3.00
25	Melons		.37-½
30	Expenses at Toronto		2.25
30	Postage		.50
30	Paper and ink		.25
25	Received from Gartshore	6.00	
25	One month's board to Mrs McI.		10.00

October

2	To Mrs Jones		3.00
6	Medicine		1.00
12	do.		.50
12	Travel Expenses		.37-½
20	2 weeks board to Mrs Jones		6.00
9	From Gartshore	6.00	

9	Subscription for poor		.50
10	Quinine		.25
18	Sweet Oil and Candles		.25
23	Mrs Jones		3.00
23	From Gartshore		6.00
23	Repair to Boots		1.00
25	Medicine		1.25
31	Horning at Bullock's Corners		.25
31	Mrs Jones		3.00
30	Carpenter's Zoology		3.00
30	Postage stamps		.25

November

6	From Gartshore	6.00	
6	To Mrs Jones		6.00
6	Peruvian Barks and Wine		1.10
14	Writing paper		.25
14	Mrs Jones		3.00
14	Expenses to Hamilton		.25
14	Suspenders		.32-½
14	Binding the 'Newcomer'		.62-½
20	From Gartshore	6.00	
	To Mrs Jones		3.00
	Papers		.15
27	To Mrs Jones		3.00
	Washing		2.50
	Expenses to Hamilton		.12-½
29	Brad Awls		.12-½
30	Mech. Ins. (Chd in office)		1.00

December

4	From Gartshore	6.00	
	To Mrs. Jones		3.00
5	Church Collection		.35
6	Stark's lecture		.12-½
11	Going to Hamilton and Mrs Jones		3.12-½
13	Music paper		.25
18	From Gartshore	6.00	
	To Mrs Jones		3.00
	Church collection		.15

24	[do] subscription for precentor (Chd in office)		1.00
	To Children		.50
25	To Mrs Jones		3.00
31	do		3.00
	Presents to Mrs McIlwraith		6.13
	Expenses to Hamilton		.25
	Soiree ticket		.75
	From Gartshore	6.00	

Cash Accounts 1859

January

2	Church collection		.25
5	Jaunt to Ayr C.W.		1.75
8	T. Exp. at Hamilton		.12-½
15	Paper		.12-½
22	Free Church Soiree		.25
22	T.E. at Hamilton		.25
29	5 week's board		15.00
	Church seat		1.00
	Paper		.12-½
15	From Gartshore	6.00	
29	do	6.00	

February

12	From Gartshore	6.00	
5	To Mrs. Jones		3.00
15	Boots		4.00
16	Cap		1.50
	Punch		.12-½
17	From Gartshore	63.00	
	To Mrs. Jones		2.12-½
	To washerwoman		2.87-½

March

5	Gen'l expenses		1.50
31	Expenses at Toronto		2.25

April

9	Exp at Dundas		30.00
13	Repairs to clothes		1.50

To New York   9.50

Cash Accounts 1861

July
To Mrs Logan, freight   2.04
Stove Finishing   .55
   "   "   3.17-½
26   Cash   .25
     Bucksaw   87-½
     Hooks for walls   .16
     ½ cord wood   .75
     Postage   .13
     Cash   10.00
     5 cords H.D.wood   12.50
     5 do   soft do   9.25
     2 do   12"   5.00

August
Aug. Cash   2.00
     Advertising   1.00
     Bats   2.
     Oil Can   1.
     Clock   3.

Letters Sent and Received 1857

Letters Received – January
3   From H. Dickie of date Dec. 11th
10   From Br Thos enclosing one from Mrs Hunter of date Dec. 18
2   Mrs Logan
6   Br Bill and Mrs Hunter of date Dec. 18
Letters Despatched – January
4   Br Thos
6   Mrs Logan enclosing home letters
15   Br Thos
15   Br Bill
Letters Received – February
1   Br Thos
7   do. enclosing letter from Mrs Hunter of date Jan. 16
19   Mother and Christina

24   Mrs Logan of date Feb. 15
24   Br Thomas of date Feb. 20
Letters Despatched – February
4   Mrs Logan
10   Bro. Thomas
12   Mrs Stewart and Mrs Hunter
19   T. Anderson, Dumbarton.
24   Br Thomas.
26   Mother
Letters Received – March
7   Br Thomas enclosing do. from Bill.
19   Br Thomas per Mr Robb.
29   Of date 24th from Br Thos.
Letters Despatched – March
15   Br Thos
17   Mrs Logan
19   Br Thos (money letter)
31   Br Thos
Letters Received – April
4   From Br Thos of date April 1 enclosing from Mrs Hunter of date
     March 13th
15   Mrs Logan of date April 9th.
17   Br Thos of date Apr. 14 enclosing letter to him from Bill of date
     March 24th
29   Mrs Hunter of date April 9th
8   P. McIntyre, Dumbarton date Feb. 22
Letters Despatched – April
15   Br Thos (money letter)
15   Mrs Logan
19   Br Thos
9   Mrs Hunter and Br Bill
Letters Received – May
1   Br Thos
6   Br Thos date May 4
10   Br Bill and Mrs Stewart and Christina date Apr. 24
14   Br Thos
31   Br Thos enclosing do. from D. Andrews, Greenock of date 4th
     May.
Letters Despatched – May
1   Bro. Thos

7   Sister Christina
13   Mrs Logan
13   J. Stewart (money letter)
14   Hugh Dickie
21   Br Thos
Letters Received – June
11   Br Thos per Mr Robb enclosing do. from James Strachan and letters to him from Mrs Hunter and Bill
16   Wilson, Dundas, in reply to mine.
24   Br Thos per port also per Mr Jameson.
27   Mrs Logan.
Letters Despatched – June
7   Br Thomas
7   Mr Wilson, Dundas
15   Thos also his wife, per Mr Jameson
28   Br Thos
28   Mrs Logan
Letters Received – July
3   Br Thos of date June 30 and July 1
3   A. Liddel in Trenton of date 28th June.
3   Br Bill of date 25th May and 12th June.
3   Sister Christina of date May 24th.
3   Mrs Hunter of date May 25 _
4   Thos Anderson, Dumbarton.
13   Br Thos enclosing from Mrs Hunter to him.
30   Mr Jameson, Sarnia, also from Mother, Mr Stewart, Mrs Hunter and Christina.
Letters Despatched – July
2   Br Thos
7   Mrs Logan
7   Alex Liddel, Trenton, Jersey
12   Br Thos
16   Mother and Misses Andrew and Anderson
29   Mr Jameson, Sarnia.
Letters Received – August
6   A. Jameson, Sarnia.
Letters Despatched – August
14   Br Thos
14   C. Mackenzie.

Index

Page ranges joined by a dash indicate references on consecutive pages, but not necessarily consecutive days. Page ranges followed by 'passim' indicate frequent references over an extended time, but not necessarily on every page within the range.

Hamilton and Gore Mechanics'
Institute. *See under* Mechanics'
Institutes
Hamilton Horticultural Society,
169n58
Hamilton Mercantile Library Asso-
ciation, 127, 137
Hamilton Savings Bank, 12, 83, 159,
191
Hamilton Scientific Association, 24,
135n5, 136n6, 139n12
Hamilton Spectator, 72, 74n28, 140n14,
141n19, 180n73
Hamilton Theatre, 140
Hamilton Water Works, 146n29, 150,
298
Hammond, James, 134
Hammond, Thomas, 176
Hannah, Mr (purser on George Mof-
fat), 86
Harper, Marjory, 22
Harrison, Mr (Illinois farmer), 122
Hartshorn, Mr (New York musician),
147, 148
Haskins, Mr (Hamilton City engi-
neer), 138
Hassam, Andrew, 6
Hatch, Cora L.V., 273
Havelock, Sir Henry, 139
Hawk, Dr, 395
Hawksville (CW), 332, 377
Hay, Peter (Peter H., P. Hay), 356–7,
363, 367
'Health Alphabet,' 416–17
health and illnesses: ague cases in
Dundas, 154–5; Andrew's illnesses
(cold, ague, fever, back aches,
bilious attacks), 65, 117, 130, 174,
177–8, 181–2, 183, 184–5, 187, 242,
311–12, 336, 349–50; Andrew's last

illness and death, 395; Andrew's
weight, 63; garbage and refuse
disposal, 57; of Mary Goldie,
159–60; of Mrs Goldie (Mary's
mother), 375–7; 'Health Alphabet,'
416–17; mumps, 383; rheumatic
fever, 379n35; seasickness, 101,
122–3; whooping cough, 372
Henderson, John (engineer on
'Indian'), 101–2
Henderson, John C., 72
Henry, Mr (Hamilton), 59, 129
Herald (Herold), Rev. James, 151n39,
155–200 passim, 325, 339
Herbert, Edward, 1st baron Herbert
of Cherbury, 177
Herbert, Henry William: *Wager of
Battle*, 221
Hespeler (formerly New Hope, CW),
327, 327n28, 349, 372
Hespeler, Jacob, 327–8, 330–1, 345
Hetherington (Dundas), 199
Hewitt, Martin, 6
Hitchcock, Mr (Sarnia), 79
Hoe's Foundry (New York), 243
Hogarth, William, 125
Hogg, James, 159n46, 195n3
Hogg, Rev. John, 303n98, 353, 362,
368, 385
Hogg, Maggie (Maggy), 104, 105, 107
Hogg, R., 267
Hoggs Instructor (magazine), 27, 29,
159, 163, 177, 183, 188, 195, 276
holidays and public celebrations:
Emancipation Day, 171n60; for
fire companies (New York), 239;
Halloween, 184, 241; Hogmanay,
191–2, 305, 351; for Japanese
embassy in New York, 277–8n57;
July 4 (New York), 222–4; for Prin-